EXAMPLES&EXPLANATIONS

Securities Regulation

EXAMPLES&EXPLANATIONS

Securities Regulation

Sixth Edition

Alan R. Palmiter
Howard L. Oleck Professor of Business Law
Wake Forest University

Wolters Kluwer
Law & Business

Published by Wolters Kluwer Law & Business in New York.

Wolters Kluwer Law & Business serves customers worldwide with CCH,
Aspen Publishers, and Kluwer Law International products.
(www.wolterskluwerlb.com)

To contact Customer Service, e-mail customer.service@wolterskluwer.com,
call 1-800-234-1660, fax 1-800-901-9075, or mail correspondence to:

Wolters Kluwer Law & Business
Attn: Order Department
PO Box 990
Frederick, MD 21705

Printed in the United States of America.

1 2 3 4 5 6 7 8 9 0

ISBN 978-1-4548-3392-5

Library of Congress Cataloging-in-Publication Data

Palmiter, Alan R.
  Securities regulation / Alan R. Palmiter, Howard L. Oleck Professor of
Business Law, Wake Forest University. — Sixth edition.
     pages cm. — (Examples & explanations)
  Includes bibliographical references and index.
  ISBN 978-1-4548-3392-5 (perfectbound : alk. paper)
  1. Securities–United States. I. Title.

KF1440.P25 2014
346.73'0922–dc23

2014006029

SFI Certified Chain of Custody
Product Line Contains At Least
20% Certified Forest Content
www.sfiprogram.org
SFI-00756

About Wolters Kluwer Law & Business

Wolters Kluwer Law & Business is a leading global provider of intelligent information and digital solutions for legal and business professionals in key specialty areas, and respected educational resources for professors and law students. Wolters Kluwer Law & Business connects legal and business professionals as well as those in the education market with timely, specialized authoritative content and information-enabled solutions to support success through productivity, accuracy and mobility.

Serving customers worldwide, Wolters Kluwer Law & Business products include those under the Aspen Publishers, CCH, Kluwer Law International, Loislaw, ftwilliam.com and MediRegs family of products.

CCH products have been a trusted resource since 1913, and are highly regarded resources for legal, securities, antitrust and trade regulation, government contracting, banking, pension, payroll, employment and labor, and healthcare reimbursement and compliance professionals.

Aspen Publishers products provide essential information to attorneys, business professionals and law students. Written by preeminent authorities, the product line offers analytical and practical information in a range of specialty practice areas from securities law and intellectual property to mergers and acquisitions and pension/benefits. Aspen's trusted legal education resources provide professors and students with high-quality, up-to-date and effective resources for successful instruction and study in all areas of the law.

Kluwer Law International products provide the global business community with reliable international legal information in English. Legal practitioners, corporate counsel and business executives around the world rely on Kluwer Law journals, looseleafs, books, and electronic products for comprehensive information in many areas of international legal practice.

Loislaw is a comprehensive online legal research product providing legal content to law firm practitioners of various specializations. Loislaw provides attorneys with the ability to quickly and efficiently find the necessary legal information they need, when and where they need it, by facilitating access to primary law as well as state-specific law, records, forms and treatises.

ftwilliam.com offers employee benefits professionals the highest quality plan documents (retirement, welfare and non-qualified) and government forms (5500/PBGC, 1099 and IRS) software at highly competitive prices.

MediRegs products provide integrated health care compliance content and software solutions for professionals in healthcare, higher education and life sciences, including professionals in accounting, law and consulting.

Wolters Kluwer Law & Business, a division of Wolters Kluwer, is headquartered in New York. Wolters Kluwer is a market-leading global information services company focused on professionals.

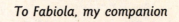
To Fabiola, my companion

Summary of Contents

Contents

Contents

Contents

Chapter 13 U.S. Regulation of Cross-Border Securities Transactions 595

Preface

Securities Regulation earns the perennial accolade of being among the toughest courses in law and business schools. This is not surprising. Its vocabulary is arcane and clubbish, its guiding principles nuanced and even contradictory, its structure convoluted and layered. Like the illusions of an M.C. Escher print, the subject flashes back and forth between two conceptual states — sometimes esoteric and sometimes mundane. The subject also builds on business and financial concepts that are new and mysterious to many students.

But for those who pass through its Byzantine gates, the study of Securities Regulation offers many rewards: solving the anagram of statutory definitions and substantive prohibitions; contemplating the majesty of the judge-made law of securities fraud; and discovering the many levels of public and private securities enforcement.

All these matters and more are within your grasp — with some practice, some trial and error. That is the idea of this "examples and explanations" book. Each chapter, after sketching the key concepts of U.S. securities regulation, offers you a chance to compare your responses to concrete examples with my explanations. You will discover it invigorating (and downright fun) to work through the securities statutes, to analyze the accompanying rules and interpretive case law, and then to arrive at the same answers as sophisticated securities practitioners.

January 2014   *Alan R. Palmiter*

Acknowledgments

I appreciate the intellectual curiosity and encouragement from my Wake Forest students, as well as students who have used the book in other schools. Their comments, questions, and insights continue to inspire this book.

I give special thanks to Sean Gannaway ('14) for his useful research and editorial help. He reviewed the content of the leading Securities Regulation casebooks and identified current topics and materials for insertion in this new edition. This was particularly challenging given the ongoing deregulatory changes put into motion by the JOBS Act of 2012.

I am also grateful to the many colleagues — in law and business schools here and abroad—who have recommended the book to their students. In fact, a business school colleague's suggestion led me to discover the book also can serve as the text for a business school course!

Special Notice

Citation form. To reduce the distraction of citations, this book departs from standard citation form:

1. *Dates.* References to statutory sources and SEC rules are usually undated. All such references are to compilations as of 2013, unless a different date is given.

2. *Federal securities statutes.* The book abbreviates the references to the major federal securities acts by giving the section number of the act, but not the U.S. Code citation:
   - Securities Act of 1933, at 15 U.S.C. §§77a et seq.
   - Securities Exchange Act of 1934, at 15 U.S.C. §§78a et seq.
   - Investment Company Act of 1940, at 15 U.S.C. §§80a-1 et seq.
   - Investment Advisers Act of 1940, at 15 U.S.C. §§80b-1 et seq.

   For example, section 15 of the Securities Exchange Act of 1934 is cited as "Exchange Act §15," without a cross-citation to 15 U.S.C. §78o. In addition, the book refers frequently to three important legislative reforms—the Private Securities Litigation Reform Act of 1995 (cited as "PSLRA"), the Sarbanes-Oxley Act of 2002 (cited as "Sarbanes-Oxley"), the Dodd-Frank Wall Street Reform and Consumer Protection Act of 2010 (cited as "Dodd-Frank"), and the Jumpstart Our Business Startups Act of 2012 (cited as "JOBS Act").

3. *SEC rules and regulations.* The book abbreviates the references to rules of the Securities and Exchange Commission by giving the rule number, but not the Code of Federal Regulations citation. Rules promulgated under the various federal securities acts can be found as follows:
   - Securities Act of 1933, at 17 C.F.R. Part 230
   - Securities Exchange Act of 1934, at 17 C.F.R. Part 240
   - Investment Company Act of 1940, at 17 C.F.R. Part 270
   - Investment Advisers Act of 1940, at 17 C.F.R. Part 275

   The rules promulgated under the Securities Act are numbered sequentially from 100 to 1001, and are divided into various regulations. For example, Regulation D contains Rules 501-508, which can be found at 17 C.F.R. §§230.501-230.508. The rules promulgated under the Exchange Act are numbered according to the section of the Act under which they are promulgated. For example, Rule 10b-5 is the fifth rule promulgated pursuant to Exchange Act §10(b), and the rule can be found at 17 C.F.R. §240.10b-5.

4. *SEC regulations.* The book also abbreviates the references to SEC regulations, which can be found as follows:
   - Regulation S-X (Qualifications and Reports of Accountants), at 17 C.F.R. Part 210
   - Regulation Crowdfunding (General Rules and Regulations), at 17 C.F.R. Part 227
   - Regulation S-B (Integrated Disclosure System for Small Business Issuers), at 17 C.F.R. Part 228
   - Regulation S-K (Standard Instructions for Filing Forms), at 17 C.F.R. Part 229
   - Regulation M-A (Mergers and Acquisitions), at 17 C.F.R. §§229.1000 et seq.
   - Regulation S-T (Rules for Electronic Filings), at 17 C.F.R. Part 232
   - Regulation M (Anti-Manipulation Rules), at 17 C.F.R. §§242.100 et seq.
   - Regulation SHO (Short Sales), at 17 C.F.R. §§242.200 et seq.
   - Regulation ATS (Alternative Trading Systems), at 17 C.F.R. §§242.300 et seq.
   - Regulation AC (Analyst Certifications), at 17 C.F.R. §§242.500 et seq. Regulation FD (Selective Disclosure), at 17 C.F.R. Part 243
   - Regulation G (Disclosure of Non-GAAP Financial Measures), at 17 C.F.R. Part 244
   - Regulation BTR (Blackout Trading Restrictions), at 17 C.F.R. Part 245

5. *SEC releases.* The book provides a basic citation (number and year) for SEC releases, which are reprinted in transfer binders of the *Federal Securities Law Reporter* (CCH), as well as on Westlaw and Lexis-Nexis.

6. *Case citations.* For state cases, the book cites only to the West regional reports. The book typically does not indicate subsequent case histories, such as *certiorari denied* or *remanded on other grounds.* For cases decided by the U.S. Supreme Court, the book cites to the "U.S." reports or, when not yet available, to "Sup. Ct" reporter.

Special Notice

> **Internet access.** Most of the primary materials referred to in this book are now available online. The federal securities laws and SEC regulations/rules, as well as links to other useful sources, may be found at Securities Lawyer's Deskbook (published by the University of Cincinnati College of Law): taft.law.uc.edu/CCL.
>
> SEC releases may be found on the SEC website: www.sec.gov/rules/final.shtml (final rules); www.sec.gov/rules/interp.shtml (interpretive releases); and www.sec.gov/rules/proposed.shtml (proposed rules).
>
> Supreme Court decisions may be found at Legal Information Institute: www.law.cornell.edu/supremecourt/text/home.

Securities Regulation

CHAPTER 1

Introduction to Securities Markets and Regulation

Securities regulation is about protecting investors—whether they buy securities from an issuer, trade on securities markets, vote their shares, or sell in a tender offer. In the United States, securities regulation is mostly a matter of federal law. Its premise is that mandatory disclosure (along with liability for fraud and regulation of securities intermediaries) will equip securities investors and their advisers with the information to evaluate the return and risk entailed in a securities investment—thus to move capital to its optimal uses, a critical aspect of a healthy economy.

This chapter covers:

- an overview of the U.S. securities markets and their participants, as well as the effect of information technologies like the Internet [§1.1]
- the hypothesis that U.S. public securities markets are "informationally" efficient and thus disclosure to some participants in the market functions as disclosure to all (the *efficient capital market hypothesis*) [§1.2]
- the basic framework and philosophy of federal securities regulation [§1.3]

§1.1 SECURITIES MARKETS AND PARTICIPANTS

§1.1.1 Primary and Secondary Markets

Securities transactions occur in two settings: sales of securities to investors by issuers seeking to raise capital for their business (issuer transactions) and buy-sale transactions among investors of already-issued securities (trading transactions). Whether buying in the *primary market* or trading in the *secondary market*, investors depend on information to value the securities: the financial rights of the securities being transacted, the issuer's financial performance, the issuer's prospects and management, competitive information, economic trends, political news, consumer trends, ad infinitum.

Primary Market (Issuer Transactions)

Issuers can raise capital by selling their securities in public markets or in negotiated, private placements. Private placements are the most prevalent and span the gamut:

- A closely held company issues ownership interests to its founding members.
- A start-up business issues preferred stock to venture capitalists who are willing to capitalize the business in exchange for a preferred financial position and a management role.
- A public corporation issues trading-restricted securities (typically debt securities) to institutional investors, such as pension funds.

Issuers that seek to raise capital from a larger pool of investors can make a public offering (primary distribution). Raising capital from the public for the first time is called an *initial public offering* (IPO). For example, in 2006, companies raised over $3.9 trillion by selling debt and equity securities in U.S. primary markets, with $3.3 trillion coming from public offerings and $562 billion from private placements. Of the public offerings, $3.2 trillion came from debt issues and $188 billion from equity issues, with $46 billion raised in IPOs. (These figures declined significantly after the financial crisis of 2008, with debt and equity offerings totaling only $1.5 trillion in 2011.)

Secondary Market (Trading Transactions)

Securities trading of already-issued securities does not raise capital for the issuer. Instead, investors get cash for their investments by selling to other investors in privately negotiated transactions or in public trading markets (such as through a stock exchange or computerized trading by securities firms). Secondary markets provide liquidity to investors, which in turn invigorates primary markets. Securities trading on secondary markets accounts for about 99 percent of all securities transactions.

There are two principal markets for public trading of securities in the United States: exchange markets and over-the-counter markets. On the *exchange markets* buy and sell orders arrive at a centralized location where "specialists" maintain a "book" of orders to match buyers and sellers — a continuous auction. The New York Stock Exchange (NYSE) is the largest and most famous stock exchange.

In the *over-the-counter* (OTC) *markets* buying and selling occurs between securities firms that have access through computer terminals and price sheets to information on bidding and selling prices offered by other securities firms. The most famous OTC market is NASDAQ, an electronic "spider's web" originally created by the nonprofit National Association of Securities Dealers (NASD) to permit its members linked by computers to quote prices and make trades with each other. (In 2001, the NASD divested NASDAQ, which is now owned and operated by a for-profit corporation.) Securities firms that use NASDAQ act as intermediaries (brokers) in matching customer orders or as principals (dealers) trading for their own account.

In addition to the exchanges and the OTC markets, computer-based trading systems allow investors (particularly large institutional investors and securities firms) to trade directly without the need for additional intermediaries. Known as *electronic communication networks* (ECNs), these alternative trading systems allow their subscribers to trade privately and at less expense.

§1.1.2 Functions of Securities Markets

Securities markets serve three basic functions:

Capital formation   Securities markets bring together capital-laden investors and capital-needy businesses, whether through the issuance of equity securities (common stock and preferred stock) or debt securities (bonds, debentures, notes, and commercial paper).

Liquidity   Securities markets bring together investors wishing to sell (or liquidate) their investment and new investors willing to buy. *Liquidity*, the ability to sell readily an investment instrument, is an important attribute of securities, and its availability often determines whether investors will invest in the first place.

Risk management   Securities markets permit investors to minimize risk by diversifying and hedging their investments. By purchasing a basket of securities with different risks, investors can create a *diversified portfolio* whose overall risk is lower than the separate risks of its components.

By purchasing *derivatives*, investors can lock in investment gains and set floors on investment losses. Derivatives are financial instruments whose price is derived from prices of underlying securities — they are essentially side bets to reduce risk. On the other side of a derivative are speculators willing to gamble that markets will behave differently than anticipated.

Securities markets offer investors a rich variety of financial products to satisfy their investment strategies. For example, investors who want a financial interest in a broad category of stocks, but with investment and voting discretion consolidated in the hands of another, can buy a mutual fund. An investor who wants to limit how much she might lose in her stock portfolio can buy a *put option*, which represents a promise by the option seller to *purchase* stock, upon the exercise of the option by the buyer, on a specified date for a specified price; with the option the investor can sell at a set price even if the market price falls below that. (A *call option* is the converse, a promise by the option seller to *sell* stock, on the exercise of the buyer's option.) Similarly, if an investor who holds a portfolio representing a whole market wants to hedge against a falling market, he can enter into a *futures contract*, a binding agreement to buy or sell a particular commodity at a fixed price on a specified date in the future, typically with standard terms set by a clearinghouse that guarantees each side's obligation.

Securities markets also produce a collateral benefit — the revelation of prices for specific companies and for the overall economy. Securities prices provide a scorecard of management performance, and they provide a valuation for tax and other purposes. Yet despite their price transparency, U.S. securities markets remain relatively opaque with respect to revealing who is setting the price. Surprisingly, there are almost no rules that require traders (or intermediaries who process the trades) to reveal their identities as they trade.

§1.1.3 Participants in Securities Markets

There are three essential categories of participants in securities markets: investors, who seek a return on their investment; issuers of securities, who make financial commitments to provide a return as dividends or interest payments, appreciation, and liquidation rights; and intermediaries, who bring issuers and investors together.

Types of Investors

Investors include individuals who own securities directly or indirectly, and *institutional investors* that own securities on behalf of others (see list below). About one-half of U.S. households are direct or indirect holders of securities, with equity securities accounting for more than 40 percent of their financial assets. The trend has been toward indirect ownership of securities by institutional investors, whose share in equity securities markets has grown dramatically from less than half to about two-thirds over the past two decades:

Types of investors (in U.S. equity holdings)	1991 $ billions (percent)	2011 $ billions (percent)
INDIVIDUAL INVESTORS – direct ownership (typically securities held in brokerage accounts)	$2,751 (56.8%)	$8,357 (37.1%)
INSTITUTIONAL INVESTORS* **(TOTAL)**	$2,096 (43.2%)	$14,165 (62.9%)
Pension funds – invest retirement savings of employees, in both public and private sector	$1,202 (24.8%)	$3,833 (17.0%)
Mutual funds – pool investments of many individuals (now largest and fastest-growing category)	$331 (6.8%)	$5,385 (23.9%)
Insurance companies – invest insurance premiums set aside to cover risks (subject to state regulation)	$230 (4.7%)	$1,667 (7.4%)
Financial institutions – invest pools of individual savings (for banks, only trust department can invest in equity securities)	$14 (0.3%)	$67 (0.3%)
Governments (federal/state/local) – invest tax revenues (includes federal government bailouts)	$6 (0.1%)	$164 (0.7%)
Securities firms – invest funds in own account (includes hedge funds)	$14 (0.3%)	$101 (0.4%)
Foreign investors – individuals and institutional investors from other countries	$299 (6.2%)	$2,948 (13.1%)

* Includes endowment funds, which invest money given for charitable and educational purposes (invested through insurance companies, securities firms, mutual funds).

Issuers

Issuers include business corporations, federal agencies, state and local governments, not-for-profit organizations, and mutual funds that pool together investments. In the last decade, *securitization* has allowed even individuals to become indirect issuers of securities through the pooling together of their many individual payment obligations, such as on houses and cars. The pooled obligations are then packaged and sold as a security that provides a blended return on the combined obligations in the pool.

Financial Intermediaries

Intermediaries offer a dizzying variety of services and financial products. They include securities firms (often known as *broker-dealers*) that buy and sell securities for customers, investment advisers that provide investment information and advice to customers, investment companies (including *mutual funds*) that pool the money from many investors to create a securities portfolio in which all investors share, and *investment banks* that advise and assist companies issuing securities and raising capital. Even *commercial banks* are intermediaries in securities markets, offering securities brokerage services through affiliates or acting as agents for the placement of high-grade commercial paper to institutional investors.

In addition, *accounting firms* that audit the financial statements contained in the SEC filings of reporting companies serve as monitors of the completeness and accuracy of disclosures made to public markets. *Credit rating agencies* are companies that assess the creditworthiness of companies that issue debt (fixed income) securities and provide specific ratings (like "AAA" or "not investment grade") for companies' debt obligations. Finally, *institutional investors* — although not formally charged with processing information for public investors — serve this role by their large and active trading in public securities markets.

§1.1.4 Interconnection Among Financial Markets

The markets in which investors seek capital returns and issuers look to meet their capital needs are interconnected, in competition with each other, and subject to different regulatory regimes.

Here is a sketch of the regulatory framework in the United States:

Public securities markets	*Public securities markets* (debt and equity) are subject to full-fledged securities regulation, which includes mandatory disclosure, heightened fraud standards, and regulation of market participants.

	This regulation is administered by the Securities and Exchange Commission (SEC).
Private securities markets	*Private securities transactions* are not subject to mandatory disclosure, but instead are subject to modified fraud standards, state regulation, and specific federal exemptive conditions.
Nonsecurities lending markets	*Nonsecurities lending* (primarily bank lending) is not subject to securities regulation, but banking regulation applies.
Derivatives markets	Regulatory authority over *derivative markets* (such as options and futures) is divided between the SEC and the Commodities Futures Trading Commission (CFTC).
Foreign capital markets	Outside the United States, securities transactions in public and private markets can become subject to U.S. securities regulation if they involve U.S. investors or flow back into the United States. Otherwise, foreign securities regulation applies.

Regulatory Competition

The interconnected securities markets compete with each other for issuers and investors. Today issuers can choose to raise capital in private and public markets in the United States, as well as abroad. In addition, investors can trade in the same securities in different markets, often 24 hours a day. Not only is there competition for issuers and investors on the basis of products, services, and price, but competition also arises among securities regulation regimes. If there is too much regulation in one market — that is, the cost of regulation outweighs its perceived benefits — issuers and investors can and do migrate to other markets. An example is the U.S. debt market, where issuers shun public markets by selling to sophisticated (often institutional) investors in private markets, thus avoiding the detailed disclosure obligations and liability risks of public markets. Or U.S. issuers issue debt on the Eurobond market to European investors who seek dollar-denominated investments in bearer form (the quintessential "Belgian dentists"), thus avoiding the higher regulatory costs of a securities offering in the United States.

Regulatory Overlap

Regulatory overlap arises when different regulators assert jurisdiction over the same financial transaction, as occurs when state and federal securities laws both regulate a securities offering (see §§4.2.6, 5.3) or when U.S. and foreign regulators assert jurisdiction over the same tender offer (see §13.3). In addition, regulatory overlap arises when new financial products combine the characteristics of instruments subject to different regulatory regimes. For example, who regulates an "index participation" (IP), a contract in which the seller promises to pay the buyer the value of a stock index? If it is a "futures contract," the CFTC has exclusive jurisdiction; if a "securities option," it is subject to SEC regulation. See *Chicago Mercantile Exchange v. SEC*, 883 F.2d 537 (7th Cir. 1989) (holding that IP has attributes of futures contract and thus is subject to exclusive CFTC jurisdiction).

The question of how to characterize an IP reveals the complex and specialized nature of modern financial instruments. Under the terms of an IP, the seller (without having to own the underlying securities) agrees to pay the buyer the value of a stock index. The IP is indefinite and freely tradeable but periodically permits the buyer to seek a cash payment directly from the seller. The contract's terms are standardized by a clearinghouse that actually issues the contract to the buyer and pays the seller, thus becoming guarantor of the seller's obligations. From the perspective of the seller, the IP has the characteristics of a *futures contract* because it is a binding agreement to sell a particular commodity (a portfolio representing stock index) at a fixed price on specified dates in the future; the seller speculates that stock prices will be below expectations. From the perspective of the buyer, the IP looks like a *stock call option* because it is a binding promise by the seller to deliver a pool of underlying securities (or their value) at a fixed price on a certain date if the buyer exercises her cash-out option. Also from the buyer's perspective, the IP looks like ownership of *securities* in the stock index that, because the IP is freely tradeable, can be cashed out at any time, and the seller is obligated to make cash payments to reflect any dividends; the buyer invests in an IP as an alternative to purchasing the index.

§1.1.5 New Technologies

Federal securities regulation is about getting information into the hands of investors and securities professionals, so that the prices in securities markets reflect all available public information. Over the last two decades, computers and communications technology have made the dissemination of information and its management dramatically easier and less expensive. Along with developments in finance theory, new technologies have facilitated the pricing and trading of securities. The technologies have also been a major factor behind the globalization of securities markets and activities.

The possibility that every computer can receive securities information, be the originating point for investment orders, and be linked to a centralized trading system has far-reaching implications for securities markets and securities regulation.

Examples

1. You want to buy General Electric stock at the prevailing market price, as published each day in the newspaper's financial section.
   a. How can you buy?
   b. Will you own stock in your own name?
   c. How would you sell the stock?

2. You come into a large inheritance and want to diversify your securities portfolio.
   a. You want to buy corporate bonds. How can you?
   b. You want to invest in start-up firms as a venture capitalist. How can you?

3. You become so good at playing the market, you take a new job as the manager of a large investment portfolio.
   a. You worry about your portfolio's holdings in multinational companies. These companies do a significant amount of business outside the United States, and if the U.S. dollar falls compared to other currencies, their dollar-pegged earnings will also fall. How can you protect your portfolio against a falling dollar?
   b. You are convinced that the Federal Reserve will raise interest rates, causing a decline in the value of equity securities. If you sell your holdings, which are significant, you will likely drive down the market price by your very selling. How do you avoid losses to your portfolio without selling your holdings?

Explanations

1. a. As an individual investor, you will rely on securities intermediaries to match your buy order with another's sell order. You will probably call a stockbroker (a salesperson at a brokerage firm, let's say Merrill Lynch) and give the broker an order for your account, such as a buy order for 100 shares of General Electric stock at the market price — a *market buy order*. (You can also place a *limit order* that specifies quantity and the price you are willing to buy, such as 2,000 shares at $17.50; if the market price is $18, your order will not be executed until the price falls to $17.50.) Merrill Lynch can fill your order in several ways:

   Exchange (auction) markets. If the stock is "listed" on a stock exchange — the NYSE in the case of GE — Merrill Lynch (acting as your agent, or "broker") can relay the order to the "floor" of the exchange, where trading occurs. Stock listed on an exchange is offered for sale and purchase by a single *specialist* in that particular stock, so there is always a seller to match every buyer. Your buy order either will be matched to another's sell order in a continuous auction or, if there is no matching order, the specialist will sell the stock himself at the then-prevailing price. Either way, you are assured that you will buy at the market price. The specialists' market-making role provides *continuity* and *liquidity*, thus preventing erratic price swings and assuring ready buyers and sellers. Along the way, Merrill Lynch and the specialist will charge commissions for bringing you and the seller together.

Over-the-counter (dealer) markets. Merrill Lynch can fill your buy order by using a computerized system that quotes available prices from other brokerage firms that sell for their own account. The principal system, known as the NASDAQ (once the acronym for the National Association of Securities Dealers Automated Quotations System), is often referred to as an *over-the-counter (OTC) market*. Most stocks available on the OTC market are not listed on exchanges, though lately there is greater overlap. It used to be that NYSE members were barred from buying or selling NYSE-listed stock off the NYSE, but the infamous NYSE rule that limited this competition was rescinded in 2000.

Merrill Lynch (acting as a buyer and seller, or "dealer") can use NASDAQ to buy stock for its account and then resell it to you at a markup. In the OTC market, some dealers (on average eight for NAS-DAQ stocks) act as *market makers*, performing much the same role as specialists on exchanges. Market makers display their current bids and offers on NASDAQ's computer system, with a spread between the bid (buying) and offer (selling) price. Orders on the OTC market are placed by telephone or computer, rather than being routed to a central exchange. Instead of receiving a commission, Merrill Lynch will earn the difference between its purchase price and its price to you. Although less common, Merrill Lynch also can act as a broker on the OTC market by purchasing stock from another NASDAQ dealer on your behalf and charge a commission for acting as your agent. Merrill Lynch must tell you in which capacity it is acting. See §11.2.3.

Sell from inventory. If Merrill Lynch owns GE stock, it can sell you the stock from its own "inventory." Whether it buys through NASDAQ or sells from its own account, however, the broker-dealer is supposed to execute at the best available price. See §11.2.4. If it sells from inventory, Merrill Lynch will make a profit or absorb a loss depending on the price at which it originally bought the stock. Selling from inventory is controversial, since it "hides" information about customer orders from the rest of the market, such as when a customer places a "limit sales order" that specifies the lowest price the customer will accept.

Lately, individual investors need not rely as much on securities intermediaries. For example, instead of calling a salesperson at your brokerage firm, you can place your order through E*Trade or other electronic brokers directly from your computer. The broker will then fill your order using one of the methods described above. You will receive an electronic confirmation when the order has been completed, typically at a much lower cost than if you had called your broker.

In addition, electronic trading systems that compete with the NYSE and NASDAQ allow securities buyers and sellers to deal directly with each other through online trading systems — known as electronic communication networks (ECNs). The ECNs eliminate the usual intermediaries by allowing investors (both individuals and institutions) to place their orders online, such as a limit order to buy 2,000 shares of General Electric at $17.50. Once placed, the ECN electronically matches the buy order with pending sell orders and executes the trade. If there are no matching sell orders, the buy order is posted until a matching sell order is received. The ECN receives a commission for its online matching service. See Exchange Act Rel. No. 40,760 (1998) (authorizing ECNs, to choose to be regulated either as stock exchanges or broker-dealers). Some ECNs, such as Archipelago, are linked to NASDAQ and display the current high bids and low offers in NASDAQ's system, thus giving traders on the ECN a sense for current prices. Some ECNs, such as Instinet, are widely used by to institutional investors and account for a significant proportion of overall trading volume — 5 percent on the NYSE and 30 percent on NASDAQ.

Notice that your "buy" takes place in the secondary market and does not involve GE. The only time you would buy directly from GE would be if the company were issuing stock in a public offering. Some companies now offer to their shareholders direct purchase programs in which shareholders can purchase shares (or reinvest dividends) without using a broker-dealer.

b. No. Like most investors, you will probably never receive certificates for your stock. After your "buy" transaction closes — which must occur within three days after the trade is executed — your account with Merrill Lynch will reflect that you own 100 General Electric shares. You will be the *beneficial owner* of these shares, but will not receive share certificates unless you ask for them. And some companies will not give you certificates even if you ask. Instead, your ownership will be reflected on the books of Merrill Lynch, which will act as your *nominee*. As nominee, Merrill Lynch owns your stock in "street name." Your beneficial ownership does not show up on General Electric's shareholder records (which are kept by a transfer agent, usually a bank) since Merrill Lynch is the record owner of your shares.

(The SEC is considering a proposal for a direct registration system in which transfer agents would electronically register securities under investors' own names.)

The "street name" system, though seemingly cumbersome, means your transaction (and thousands of others like yours) need not be recorded on General Electric's books. Proponents of the system point out that it is easier to consolidate the record of these ever-shifting investments by listing Merrill Lynch (or even a depositary company) as the record owner, rather than listing each individual owner. Investors, as beneficial owners, retain the power to sell their shares and to decide how they are voted. Under SEC rules, General Electric must ensure that proxy materials are made available through Merrill Lynch or directly to you if you consent to having General Electric informed of your beneficial ownership. You will exercise your voting rights either by filling out a proxy card (now online) or by instructing Merrill Lynch how to complete the card on your behalf.

c. The sale of stock reverses the transactions described in 1a for the purchase of securities. The one difference is that, except in the unusual circumstance of a company involved in a repurchase program or a self-tender offer, issuers do not repurchase their own equity securities. A liquid securities market will be a key factor in the pricing of the securities and your decision to invest.

2. a. Problematic. The market in debt securities is largely oriented toward larger, institutional investors. To reduce financing costs, companies sell their debt in large denominations (often $100,000 and up) only to institutional investors, thus avoiding the underwriting costs of a wide offering and the regulatory costs of a registered public offering.

Nonetheless, individual investors can own portfolios of corporate bonds by buying shares of mutual funds — that is, a portion of a diversified pool of corporate bonds. The mutual fund, set up as a corporation or a trust, invests corporate bonds of many companies and sells interests in the fund to individual investors. Mutual funds can be purchased from the brokerage arms of mutual fund "families" (such as Fidelity Investments or Vanguard Group) or through brokerage firms that offer their own mutual funds. Some mutual funds are "no-load," meaning that there is no commission for purchasing shares in the fund, though there are periodic fees assessed by the fund advisers and managers that are ultimately borne by fund owners.

b. More problematic. Venture capitalists are wealthy, sophisticated investors who invest in start-up companies, typically buying a significant minority position (20 to 49 percent) of the company's shares and receiving agreed-upon management prerogatives. The securities laws exempt such investments from mandatory disclosure and heightened antifraud liability if the investor meets sliding scale tests of sophistication and wealth. See §§5.2.2-5.2.4. An individual investor who does not meet these criteria cannot invest as a venture capitalist.

Although it would seem possible for individuals of modest means to invest in start-up companies through mutual funds that act as venture capitalists, the federal securities laws effectively prevent this. Under federal securities law, any mutual fund that says it is "diversified" cannot hold more than 10 percent of the stock of any one company, thus disabling these mutual funds from actively controlling companies in their portfolios. And under federal tax law, mutual funds that are not "diversified" are subject to a fund-level tax, rather than the more desirable flow-through tax treatment. The combination of securities and tax law effectively eliminates mutual funds as venture capitalists.

3. a. You can buy currency futures. A currency future is a contract in which the seller promises to sell a particular currency (or a basket of currencies) at a fixed price on a fixed date in the future. By buying currency futures you lock in exchange rates for foreign currencies, even if you do not actually hold these currencies. If exchange rates fall and hurt the dollar-denominated value of your multinational securities portfolio, the value of the currency futures rises to offset (wholly or partially) the loss in your securities portfolio. This illustrates the interconnectedness of the many capital markets.

   b. You can sell index futures. An index future is a contract in which the seller promises to sell in the future at a specified price a block of stocks that represents a stock index (typically the Standard & Poor's 500). If you want to hedge against a decline in stock prices represented by the portfolio, it is cheaper and quicker to sell stock index futures than the actual stocks in your portfolio. It is cheaper because the commissions are lower for futures contracts than for the sale of all the stock represented by the index. Also the futures index is deeper (more large buyers and sellers) than the market in the underlying stocks. And it is quicker because the sale of a futures contract can be consummated immediately, compared to selling and closing on the many sales orders for the stocks in your portfolio.

§1.2 EFFICIENCY OF PUBLIC STOCK MARKETS

It is often said that many U.S. public securities markets, such as the NYSE, are *efficient*. Those who make this assertion usually mean that the markets are "informationally efficient" and that prices at any time "fully reflect" all information "available" to the public. Simply stated, the efficient capital market hypothesis posits that particular information in an efficient market affects the market price of a company's stock as though everyone had the same information at the same time. New information becomes impounded in the stock price so that it is as though all investors simultaneously discovered the information and reached a consensus on a new price. In an efficient market, there are no opportunities for super-profitable trading strategies.

Do securities markets impound all information into prices?

Weak-Form Efficiency

Many kinds of information can affect stock prices. When a stock market impounds information about historic trading patterns so that investors can't draw charts of past prices to extrapolate future prices, the market is said to have *weak-form* efficiency. A French mathematician noticed at the turn of the last century that prices on the Paris stock market exhibited "weak-form" efficiency because stock price patterns were completely random, like the Brownian motion of particles suspended in a liquid. There was no way to guess the next move in the price of stock based on past patterns. Studies of prices on U.S. stock markets show the same "random walk."

Semistrong-Form Efficiency

When a stock market promptly impounds all publicly available information, the market is said to have *semistrong-form* efficiency. This means that ordinary investors can't beat the market systematically by using public information that affects stock prices — such as information on a company's earnings, competitors' products, government tax policies, changes in interest rates — because the market will already have discerned the information and reacted to it. In fact, a large body of evidence indicates public stock prices for widely followed companies in the United States change almost instantly and in an unbiased fashion (neither too much nor too little) in response to new public information. Often formal announcements of new developments, such as corporate earnings or new products, are already old news to public trading markets. Semistrong markets behave like a herd of stampeding animals that instantly change course when just a few animals in the herd change direction — as though the herd has a single mind.

What are the market mechanisms that rapidly transform new information into new prices to produce market efficiency? The answer lies not merely in the transmission of information, but rather in the activities of market professionals. A minority of sophisticated buyers and sellers who control a critical amount of trading volume move stocks from "uninformed" to "informed" price levels. These traders (many advised by professional securities analysts) collect, process, and transform information; in this way, new information is almost instantly translated into a new "consensus" on the stock price. These securities traders, each trying to make money by outguessing the market, follow the activities of larger public corporations in the hope of gaining an informational advantage. Once one of them identifies a nugget, such as confirmation of a rumor that the company will declare a larger-than-anticipated dividend, the trader will immediately initiate a profitable trade. Just a few well-placed professional traders, with others following their lead, can drive market prices. Although over time these traders will beat the market a little, they will earn just enough to recompense their effort. The paradoxical effect of many analysts and professional traders working assiduously to beat the market is that none can systematically do so. The cap on trading profits is illustrated by the fact that mutual funds (which professionally invest money for many small investors) on average only slightly outperform the market—in fact, not enough to cover their fees. Although there is much evidence to suggest that larger U.S. securities markets exhibit semistrong efficiency, there are a number of disturbing incongruities. For example, studies show systematic mispricing over time of certain investments (particularly in smaller or high-risk companies). The "irrational exuberance" exhibited by U.S. investors during the late 1990s, particularly in high-tech and telecommunications sectors, and then the failure of global investors to notice the over-valuation of sub-prime mortgages, which led to the Financial Crisis of 2008, both undermine the argument that stock markets always behave rationally.

Strong-Form Efficiency

One thing to bear in mind is that the public stock markets are not perfectly informationally efficient. That is, public stock markets do not impound all information that affects stock prices; they do not exhibit "strong-form" efficiency. Evidence of this is that corporate insiders can often use their informational advantages to reap significant trading profits by exploiting market ignorance of their inside scoops.

Even though the public stock markets exhibit weak and even semistrong efficiency for many U.S. public corporations, this does not mean that the stock markets and stock prices are necessarily efficient in allocating capital—*allocative efficiency*. That is, just because Mega Motors is trading at $58 does not mean its actual future returns will justify a society allocating capital at this price. Because financial returns do not capture all the costs and benefits of a business activity, it may not be socially desirable to pay $58 for Mega Motors shares, as opposed to paying $58 for shares of Healthy Bicycles. Although studies indicate that countries with active stock markets have more economic growth, informational efficiency does not necessarily translate into "fundamental efficiency." It just means that the public stock markets act like a herd of stampeding animals that behaves as a single organism, not a collection of individuals. But informational efficiency doesn't mean the herd isn't heading over a cliff.

Examples

1. You inherit some money from your great-aunt. You remember her pleasure in playing the stock market, and in her memory you consider some investment possibilities for your small inheritance.

   a. You have always enjoyed the child's game of connecting the dots. You get on your computer and go to *Yahoo Finance* to chart Mega Electronics' stock price over the last six months. You notice a pattern: The price falls the first week of each month and then rebounds in the next three weeks. "Buy low, sell high," you mutter. Should you buy after the first week and sell at the end of the month?

   b. Every morning you read the *Wall Street Journal*, cover to cover. One day you notice a story that Mega's board approved a $4.40 dividend the day before. You have received a number of securities firms' reports on Mega, each predicting no more than a $3 dividend. Should you call your broker immediately with a buy order?

   c. Last quarter Mega changed its accounting for merchandise sales from FIFO (first-in-first-out) to LIFO (last-in-first-out). As a result, its most recent income statement shows a 10 percent *decrease* in merchandise earnings as appliances sold from inventory have a higher LIFO cost than the prior FIFO cost. You figure the stated earnings decline, due to an accounting change, could mislead investors to sell Mega. Should you sell before Mega's stock price falls?

2. You learn about Starstruck Software, a producer of kids' educational software. The company has annual revenues of $50 million, but its stock is not yet publicly traded.

   a. Starstruck makes an IPO. First Lynch Securities, a well-known regional securities firm, acts as underwriter. The offering price is $10 per share, and within three days Starstruck is trading at $14.25. Should you buy?

   b. Starstruck's stock trades through NASDAQ. One morning you read in the *Sacramento Bee* that the California Department of Education has announced a policy encouraging public schools to buy educational software, mentioning Starstruck by name. You know that many public school systems follow California's educational technology lead. Should you buy Starstruck stock?

   c. Your brother-in-law works in the city planning office. Late last night he called to say that Starstruck had just submitted a preliminary (and confidential) rezoning proposal for a large new software-development campus. There had been some speculation whether Starstruck would be expanding aggressively. Should you buy Starstruck now?

Explanations

1. a. Don't bother. It is highly unlikely that you have identified more than a random pattern in recent stock prices. If Mega is followed by professional securities analysts, which is the case for the 1,000 or so largest U.S. companies, there is little chance that past price patterns will repeat themselves. That is, stock prices for such companies exhibit weak-form efficiency.

   Nonetheless, a growing body of studies by finance economists (bolstered by the activities of "high frequency traders" who use computer algorithms to rapidly trade securities) suggest that there are regular anomalies in stock prices, suggesting the stock markets are not perfectly weak-form efficient. For example, studies have identified a so-called January effect: prices tend to rise abnormally at the start of the year. But as each of these anomalies is identified, securities traders rush to profit from the pattern, thus affecting prices and wiping out the anomaly. For example, if there truly were a first-week-of-the-month price anomaly for Mega stock, professional traders armed with computers and statistical tools far more powerful than your pointplotting would have already undertaken the strategy of buying after the first week (thus driving prices higher) and selling at the end of the month (thus driving prices down). No profit opportunity would be left for you.

   b. You're probably too late. Even though the increase in dividends will be of great interest to the securities market, it is almost certain that professional securities analysts and traders already know and have acted on the "dividend news." That is, the news has already been impounded in the price of Mega. In fact, studies show that the market (acting on conjecture, rumors, patterns of trading by insiders, and company hints) discerns information about dividend policies long before formal announcement of the change. It is not unusual for unexpectedly higher dividends to be preceded by price increases days and even weeks before the formal announcement.

   Are all publicly traded companies followed with such exactitude? Of the approximately 5,000 operating companies in the United States whose stock is publicly traded, only 1,000 or so are regularly followed by a sufficient number of securities analysts to produce the kind of informational efficiency predicted by the efficient capital market hypothesis. Not surprisingly, securities professionals concentrate their attention more on NYSE stocks than on OTC stocks. For those segments of the market that attract little attention by institutional investors, such as the non-NASDAQ portion of the OTC market, informational efficiency is weak.

Are prices in closely followed companies set by well-informed, rational traders or by uninformed ("noise") traders? For example, studies show that there is a strong price effect on stock added to the Standard & Poor's 500 Index because of greater demand by index funds for the stock, even though fundamental performance of the company is unaffected. Other studies show that prices are often affected by similar uninformed demand, such as when stock indices reach a milestone or investors follow trendy investment strategies. That is, the market may not have enough rational traders to overcome the sentimental "noise" traders who act for reasons unrelated to investment information.

c. By and large, the securities markets see through accounting changes. You should not expect any price effects resulting from the change in earnings if the change relates only to accounting methods. Studies indicate that in companies followed by market professionals, accounting changes do not affect valuation of the companies' future prospects, namely the likely cash flow to the investor.

The confidence that developed securities markets can see through accounting gimmicks has been drawn into question by the accounting frauds at Enron that came to light in 2002 when the company (once the seventh largest in the United States) declared bankruptcy. Although touted by *Fortune* magazine as the most innovative company in the country, Enron's energy business was actually far less profitable than its financial statements showed. It accomplished this accounting deception primarily through bogus self-dealing transactions that created the appearance of revenue gains. Why wasn't this deception detected? A number of warning signs in Enron's public disclosures went unnoticed for more than five years. For example, Enron properly disclosed during this period in its publicly available tax reports that these transactions generated no gains; Enron's reported accounting data led MBA students at Cornell to publish an investment report in 1998 that the company had been manipulating earnings; and the *Wall Street Journal* ran a story in 2000 that reported Enron's reported profits were actually unrealized, noncash gains.

Despite this public information, no securities analysts, institutional investors, credit-rating agencies, or hedge fund operators (who look for aberrations in market pricing) noticed that much of Enron's reported profits were built on speculative self-dealing transactions or that two-thirds of the company's debt obligations were kept off its balance sheet. Only in 2002, when Enron's long-standing financial woes were exposed by the financial press, did the securities markets react. It seemed that the company's equity and debt investors, caught up in the euphoria of the company's and stock market's rising fortunes, preferred to disregard the gathering storm clouds.

2. a. Not necessarily. Even though Starstruck's price rose significantly and immediately after the offering, as is typical of IPOs, studies show that on average IPOs underperform the market over time. (In one study, IPOs were shown to generate returns over their first two years that were 22 percent lower than an investment in the S&P 500.) This initial underpricing of IPOs, followed by eventual overpricing, has attracted a great deal of attention. For investors, the phenomenon creates supra-normal profits for investors who buy at the IPO price and then sell immediately after the predicted early price spike. It also means that, in general, IPOs are not good investments during the early IPO years. According to academics, IPO mispricing raises doubts about the efficient capital market hypothesis and exposes a number of inefficiencies in securities markets: systematic underwriter mispricing, the "bull market" mentality surrounding IPOs, investors' gambling mentality, and analyst overoptimism.

    b. Perhaps. It is possible that you have gained an informational advantage and that news of Starstruck's likely increase in sales has not yet been impounded in its stock price. There are nearly 3,000 companies whose shares are traded through NASDAQ, not all of them followed closely by securities analysts. Whether pricing of Starstruck's stock exhibits "semistrong" pricing efficiency is a testable empirical question, which can be analyzed by observing how quickly changes in Starstruck's fortunes (earnings reports, new product announcements, personnel shake-ups) affect the stock price.

    c. You will likely profit, but may be liable for insider trading. You have a clear informational advantage, assuming news of this new campus has not otherwise seeped out or been the motivation for trading by company insiders. If pricing of Starstruck stock is not strong-form efficient, as is likely, you stand to profit from your "good news." The problem, however, is that your brother-in-law may have a duty to maintain the confidentiality of the rezoning plan. Your use of information that you knew came from a source who breached a duty when he told you may subject you to "tippee" liability for using "misappropriated" information. See §10.2.2.

§1.3 FEDERAL SECURITIES REGULATION — OVERVIEW

The federal securities laws represent one of the most enduring successes of the New Deal legislation. They grew out of the public outcry for reform of the securities markets, which had lost more than half of their value between 1929 and 1933. The effects of the financial collapse spread beyond Wall Street. As of 1933 one-fourth of the U.S. labor force was unemployed, and productivity was down half from 1929 levels. In all, the crisis and its aftermath provided emphatic evidence of how fragile and precious our capital markets are.

From 1932 to 1934 the Senate Banking Committee held hearings on securities market practices, and out of the shambles of the boundless optimism of the 1920s came disturbing stories of rampant speculation, management high-handedness, and Wall Street manipulation. President Franklin Roosevelt arrived in Washington in the spring of 1933 with a mandate to fill the gaps in state law and Wall Street's often weak self-regulation. Yet there was no clear view of what course federal regulation should take. In fact, the 1933 debate in Washington over the reasons for the financial collapse and how to prevent future failures still resonates today.

§1.3.1 Securities Act of 1933

The first securities bill that went to the new Congress, drafted by Federal Trade Commission (FTC) Commissioner Huston Thompson, proposed "merit regulation" of securities offerings to the public. That is, government agencies would decide the soundness of investments to be sold to public investors. Similar "blue sky" legislation at the state level had already implemented such a scheme but with limited success against unscrupulous promoters. State regulators lacked expertise and resolve; many exemptions, particularly for offerings through the mails and for stock listed on national exchanges, gutted the states' effectiveness. The Thompson bill received a cool reception in Congress. Many argued that the better solution to speculative investment is informed private investors, not government paternalism.

President Roosevelt, who agreed with a disclosure philosophy, asked Felix Frankfurter (then a Harvard law professor and a member of Roosevelt's "brain trust") to assemble a new drafting team to be guided by Louis Brandeis's famous aphorism: "Sunshine is said to be the best of disinfectants; the electric light the best of policemen." The team was composed of three of Frankfurter's former law students: James Landis, a Harvard administrative law professor; Thomas Corcoran, a government lawyer; and Benjamin Cohen, a securities lawyer. The three met over a weekend in April 1933 to draft a "disclosure" statute. For political reasons, they retained the structure of the Thompson bill but inserted a disclosure scheme drawn from the English Companies Act of 1929. In addition, they created far-reaching liability for participants in securities offerings, a reform that would become the central focus of congressional deliberations that led to enactment of the Securities Act of 1933. The drafters delighted in the statute's interwoven complexity and hidden traps. You will, too.

The Securities Act was understood as the first step in a comprehensive scheme of federal securities regulation. It covered the issuance of securities to public investors by requiring the filing of a registration statement with the Federal Trade Commission (later the Securities and Exchange Commission), mandating the dissemination of a disclosure document known as a "prospectus," and erecting a complex liability scheme for misinformation in the registration statement, in the prospectus, or during the distribution of new securities to public investors. Failure to register carried criminal penalties, administrative sanctions, and private civil liability.

§1.3.2 Securities Exchange Act of 1934

The second step in the federal regulation of securities practices was the Securities Exchange Act of 1934, a more politically ambitious and far-reaching legislation than the Securities Act of 1933. The 1934 Act, less idiosyncratic and easier to read than the 1933 Act, covered a number of fronts:

- creation of the Securities and Exchange Commission, with broad powers to enforce the federal securities laws (§4)
- regulation of the securities industry, namely, the stock exchanges (§6) and securities firms (§15)
- regulation of margin for the purchase of securities (§7)
- prohibitions against manipulative stock market practices (§§9, 10)
- requirement of periodic disclosure by public companies (§§12, 13)
- regulation of proxy voting by shareholders in public companies (§14)
- regulation of insider trading in public companies (§16).

Over the years, the 1934 Act has been amended on numerous occasions. Although some securities lawyers and federal courts refer to the Securities Exchange Act as the "1934 Act," it is more accurate to refer to it as the "Exchange Act" because its many amendments have significantly extended its reach and vision beyond that of 1934.

Integrated Disclosure

During the first 50 years of federal securities regulation, disclosure requirements under the Securities Act and the Exchange Act lived in separate worlds, reflecting the historical accident that while they were born a year apart, they grew up separately. In 1982, the SEC created a unified approach to disclosure under both acts. Securities Act Rel. No. 6383 (1982). The forms under each act pick and choose specific disclosure items (set out in Regulation S-K for nonfinancial disclosure and Regulation S-X for accounting information), thus standardizing and integrating the disclosure requirements under the two acts. For example, the form for companies making an IPO under the Securities Act (Form S-1) requires information on executive compensation and refers to Item 402 of Regulation S-K; likewise, the form for companies required to file a proxy statement under the Exchange Act (Schedule 14A) requires information on executive compensation by referring to the same item.

Audited Financials

The Securities Act and the Exchange Act, consistent with a philosophy of leaving the responsibility for sound securities practices to self-regulating private actors, call for financial statements to be audited by public accountants. In the United States the accounting profession, rather than a corps of government auditors, is largely responsible for setting the accounting and auditing standards for financial information filed with the SEC.

The Sarbanes-Oxley Act of 2002 (see §1.4.1 below) revised the regulatory structure for accountants that audit the financial information of publicly traded companies. Accounting firms that act as public auditors must register with the Public Company Accounting Oversight Board (PCAOB), which is responsible for creating audit standards and disciplining firms and individuals that violate the rules. The members of the Board are appointed by the SEC, and its rules and disciplinary actions are subject to SEC review. See *Free Enterprise Fund v. PCAOB*, 561 U.S. _____ (2010) (upholding Sarbanes-Oxley provisions on PCAOB appointment, but striking down and severing for-cause removal provision).

Glass-Steagall Act (and Repeal)

An important component of the New Deal securities legislation was the separation of commercial banking (the accepting of deposits and making of loans) from investment banking (the underwriting of securities for sale to the public). This separation was meant to eliminate the conflicts of interest when the same financial institution sells securities to customers while lending them money to buy the securities on credit. The separation, known as the Glass-Steagall Act, was passed within a few days of the Securities Act. Over time, permissive rulings of federal bank regulators and federal courts eroded the once high wall separating banking and securities.

In 1999, the investment-commercial wall crumbled when Congress formally repealed the Glass-Steagall prohibitions on combining financial services. Under the Gramm-Leach-Bliley Act of 1999 a financial services company's various activities are subject to separate functional regulation — its securities activities regulated by the SEC, its banking activities regulated by federal or state bank regulators, and its insurance activities regulated by state insurance agencies. But the functional units can all exist under common ownership.

After the financial collapse of 2008, many asserted that the exposure of banks to risky subprime mortgage investments was the cause of their insolvency and urged that banks not be permitted to use depositor assets to make risky investments. The Dodd-Frank Act of 2010 (see §1.4.2 below) sought to address the stability of the banking system and, among many other things, adopted the "Volcker Rule" (named after the former Fed chair) to limit the ability of banks to engage in proprietary trading, though banks may still invest up to 3 percent of their core capital in hedge funds and private equity funds. Dodd-Frank §619.

JOBS Act of 2012

The Jumpstart Our Business Startups Act of 2012 (JOBS Act) — which amends both the Securities Act and the Exchange Act — seeks to stimulate economic growth and thus create new jobs by easing the regulatory burdens on business start-ups seeking to raise capital in securities markets. Some of the JOBS Act provisions just tinker with existing rules, but some reflect a shift in the federal securities regulatory paradigm. Here are the three big changes:

(1) **Crowdfunding.** The JOBS Act allows small companies to sell securities online to many small investors (something called "crowdfunding"). Thus, non-public companies — for the first time — can raise money from public investors without registering their offerings under federal or state law. Numerous conditions apply, including that the issuer prepare a detailed offering document and that the offering be conducted through an SEC-registered intermediary. See §5.2.5.

(2) **General solicitations.** The JOBS Act makes it easier for companies to market their private placements. Companies (both private and public) that make private offerings under Regulation D can engage in broad public marketing of their securities, so long as the offered securities are eventually sold only to "accredited investors." See §5.2.4 — Prohibition on General Solicitations.

(3) **Emerging growth companies.** The JOBS Act removes some regulatory burdens for "emerging growth companies"—both in their initial public offerings and later in their periodic filings. Emerging growth companies (with revenues up to $1 billion) face fewer restrictions in registering their IPOs, such as confidential filing and the ability to "test the waters." Then, for up to five years, emerging growth companies receive dispensations from some of the disclosure and corporate governance rules otherwise applicable to public companies, such as having "say on pay" votes or having their internal controls audited. See §8.3.1—Special Rules for "Emerging Growth Companies".

§1.3.3 Specialized Securities Laws

The Securities Act and the Exchange Act formed the foundation of federal securities regulation. Other specialized securities legislation followed:

Public Utility Holding Company Act of 1935

The Public Utility Holding Company Act of 1935 forced the breakup of holding companies in the gas and electric utility industries. The act produced a revolutionary change in the ownership structure of an industry once dominated by multi-layered groups of affiliated, highly leveraged companies. Holding company structures had bred abusive interaffiliate transactions, the flouting of state utilities regulation, and high levels of bankruptcy. The act required the SEC to administer the restructuring of the industry to limit public utility operations to a single integrated system (gas or electric) and to simplify capital structures. In this way utility company rates and capital structures became subject to state regulation. The SEC substantially completed its work in the 1950s, and today there are calls to repeal the Act.

Trust Indenture Act of 1939

The indentures (or contracts) between the issuer of debt securities and the administrator of the debt issue (the trustee, typically a bank) whose role is to protect the debt holders is regulated by the Trust Indenture Act of 1939. The act sought to address reports of mismanagement of corporate debt securities by trustees who furthered management interests at the expense of debt holders. Under the act, an indenture covering debt securities to the public of a certain size (under current SEC rules, $5 million issued over a 36-month period) must contain specified terms, and the trustee must meet criteria of independence and adhere to standards of conduct.

Investment Company Act of 1940

Mutual funds and other investment companies are subject to separate regulation. See §11.4. The Investment Company Act of 1940 requires that investment companies with more than 100 investors register with the SEC and have boards of directors composed of independent directors. The SEC oversees the operations of investment companies, which are subject to modified registration and prospectus-delivery rules when they issue securities. The Act also authorizes the SEC, in conjunction with the Financial Industry Regulatory Authority (FINRA, the successor to the National Association of Securities Dealers, NASD), to regulate the advisory fees and other charges levied by fund advisers. Once the preserve of a small number of specialized securities lawyers, regulation of mutual funds has gained broader attention (and a flurry of SEC rule-making) following the timing and pricing scandals that came to light in 2003.

Investment Advisers Act of 1940

Another act requires the registration of anyone in the business of offering investment advice. The Investment Advisers Act of 1940 requires investment advisers to disclose their interests in transactions executed for their clients and prohibits fraud.

* * *

Although these specialized acts have great importance for the industries they regulate, the broader Securities Act and Exchange Act are more important to all companies and, in particular, the securities industry. Law courses in securities regulation focus on these two acts, known by aficionados according to their year of enactment — the "1933 Act" and the "1934 Act." This book adopts the less clubby, but more descriptive, nomenclature used by the SEC — the "Securities Act" and the "Exchange Act."

§1.3.4 Securities and Exchange Commission

The Securities and Exchange Commission (SEC) is an independent agency, not part of the President's cabinet. It was created in the Exchange Act to assuage the fears of Wall Street that the FTC, which was originally assigned the task of administering the Securities Act, would be too much of a blunderbuss. The SEC is a paradigm New Deal agency. Specialized and expert, it exercises broad executive, legislative, and judicial powers:

Executive Power

The SEC administers and enforces the federal securities laws. The SEC has broad investigative powers and can issue cease-and-desist orders, impose fines, and order disgorgement of profits in administrative proceedings. The agency coordinates the enforcement of U.S. securities laws with securities administrators outside the United States in "memoranda of understanding." Additionally, the SEC can initiate court action to seek injunctive relief or refer matters involving violations of the securities laws to the Justice Department for criminal prosecution.

Legislative Powers

The SEC, pursuant to congressional authority, promulgates rules and regulations that have the force of law. For example, federal proxy rules arise entirely from SEC regulations promulgated pursuant to authority granted by Congress in §14(a) of the Exchange Act. Sometimes the SEC issues guidelines (such as the instructions that accompany disclosure forms) that have the force of law. Other pronouncements — typically *interpretive releases* — state Commission policies and viewpoints concerning statutes, rules or court decisions. Although formally lacking the force of law, these releases are avidly read and followed by securities lawyers — and law students.

The SEC also uses *interpretive letters* and so-called *no-action letters* to express its views and provide guidance to securities planners. The no-action letter process begins when an interested person (or his lawyer) outlines a proposed securities transaction to the SEC staff, with an accompanying explanation of why the transaction does not violate the securities laws. If amenable, the SEC staff will respond by letter that it "will not recommend action to the Commission" if the transaction is carried out as proposed. Although not binding on the SEC itself, no-action letters nonetheless carry significant weight with private parties and the courts. In some areas of SEC regulation, such as the resale of securities by company insiders and the exclusion of shareholder proposals from company proxy statements, no-action letters have come to constitute an impressive body of administrative common law. SEC no-action, interpretive and exemptive letters can be found on the SEC website at www.sec.gov/interps/noaction.shtml.

Judicial Powers

The SEC acts both as original tribunal, principally regarding disciplinary charges against securities professionals subject to SEC supervision, and as an appellate tribunal to review disciplinary actions taken by the stock exchanges, Financial Industry Regulatory Authority (FINRA), and other self-regulatory organizations (SROs) against their members. For example, the SEC can restrict or revoke the licenses under which broker-dealers and investment advisers operate. The SEC also reviews FINRA disciplinary actions. The SEC is headed by five commissioners, appointed by the President and confirmed by the Senate, one of whom is designated as chair by the President. The commissioners serve staggered five-year terms, with the term of one commissioner expiring each year. No more than three commissioners can be from the same political party. The President cannot remove commissioners except for misconduct, something that has not happened since the SEC was created in 1934.

The Commission meets several times each month, mostly to discuss and resolve issues the SEC staff presents. The SEC staff, currently totaling close to 3,000, is composed mostly of professionals — lawyers, accountants, economists, financial analysts, and engineers — as well as clerical and support personnel. The agency is headquartered in Washington and has 11 field offices throughout the United States.

SEC Regulation and Technology

As you can tell from the disclosure statutes the SEC administers, the agency is the "filing cabinet" of corporate America. A partial list of the SEC filing requirements illustrates the scope of the agency's information-gathering functions:

- Companies must file registration statements (which includes a prospectus) when they issue shares to the public.
- Public companies must file annual, quarterly, and special informational reports, as well as proxy statements whenever shareholder votes are solicited.
- Investors selling restricted securities (purchased in private placements) and insiders selling shares of their companies must disclose their sales.
- Bidders making tender offers for public companies must file tender offer documents, and management must file the documents responding to these bids.
- Broker-dealers must register and file annual reports.
- Securities exchanges, the FINRA (formerly NASD), and other self-regulatory organizations must file any rule changes.

All told, each year the SEC receives and processes more than 11 million pages of information from more than 28,000 corporate and investment company filers. With rare exceptions, all of this information is available to the public.

Over the last decade, the SEC has computerized its filing and disclosure system. The SEC now requires the electronic filing of disclosure documents using the EDGAR (Electronic Data Gathering, Analysis, and Retrieval) system. First opened in 1992, EDGAR became fully operational in May 1996. Today all company and individual filers must file their documents in electronic form.

EDGAR filings are available on the Internet. You might want to browse EDGAR, which can be reached from the SEC's home page at www.sec.gov or directly at www.sec.gov/edgar.shtml. With EDGAR any member of the public—that is, the whole global community—can review and obtain information in filings with the SEC. For example, how much did Tim Cook of Apple make last year in salary and bonus? What were the revenues of ExxonMobil last quarter? What does Nike's management have to say about workplace conditions for its foreign workers?

Moreover, the intersection of the federal securities laws and the Internet and other electronic media has led the SEC to reevaluate the assumptions that required disclosure be in paper form and that information published in one state or country is limited by geographic boundaries. SEC rules permit and encourage the dissemination of securities information by electronic media, subject to certain safeguards. Securities Act Rel. No. 7856 (2000) (describing how investors can consent to receive information electronically, as well as the format and content of electronic disclosure).

SEC Partnership with Securities Industry

The SEC handles its broad mandate by relying, to a large extent, on a public-private partnership. The SEC and its staff take responsibility for the "big picture" areas, while much of the day-to-day regulation of securities market participants is handled by firms themselves and by private membership organizations ("self-regulatory organizations" or SROs) under SEC oversight. This regulatory approach allows the SEC—with its relatively small staff—to oversee the dynamic U.S. securities markets that are worth more than $20 trillion (equity) and $35 trillion (debt). (By comparison, banking activities are subject to direct, comprehensive regulation by federal banking agencies, which maintain staffs seven times larger in the aggregate than the SEC's staff.)

The key to making self-regulation work effectively is SEC over-sight. As William O. Douglas, the SEC's third chairman, commented: "The SEC is a shotgun . . . behind the door, loaded, well oiled, cleaned, ready for use." The SEC inspects SROs and performs targeted oversight examinations of their broker-dealer members to determine whether the SROs are in fact effectively supervising the financial condition and business practices of their members. The SEC also must approve (and may amend) SRO rules as consistent with the public interest.

"Plain English" Initiative

The SEC has revolutionized the form and style of disclosure to investors. In the late 1990s, the agency adopted rules requiring issuers to provide investors with "plain English" disclosure in prospectuses, proxy materials, and tender offer documents. See §4.2.3 (prospectus contents); §8.4 (proxy regulation); §8.5 (tender offer regulation). Disclosure documents must include more white space, shorter sentences, greater use of tables and charts, and less jargon. *A Plain English Handbook* published by the SEC provides useful guidelines for improving the readability and appearance of disclosure documents, and can be downloaded from the SEC's website: www.sec.gov/pdf/handbook.pdf.

Despite the use of "plain English" in disclosure documents, many investors have trouble understanding the nature and risks of their securities investments. To deal with this problem, the Dodd-Frank Act of 2010 required the SEC to study and improve the financial literacy of investors, as well as consider how disclosure documents can best communicate the costs and risks of investing in securities. See Dodd-Frank §917. The SEC completed the study in 2012 and found that "U.S. retail investors lack basic financial literacy." SEC, *Study Regarding Financial Literacy Among Investors* (Aug. 2012). To improve things, the SEC recommended that retail investors — before they invest — receive information on whether or not to engage a financial intermediary (such as a stock broker or investment adviser), the fees and background of the intermediary, and investment summaries written in clear language (using bullet points and tables/charts/graphs). In particular, the SEC urged that investor.gov be the primary resource for investor information. What do you think of investor.gov?

SEC Exemptive Powers

Marbled throughout the federal securities laws, Congress gives the SEC significant authority to exempt particular persons and transactions from regulation. Securities Act §3(b)(1) (power to exempt from registration securities offerings up to $5 million, if registration is unnecessary in the public interest), §19(a) (power to define "accounting, technical and trade terms"); Exchange Act §12(h) (power to exempt issuers, and their directors, officers, and 10 percent shareholders from Exchange Act requirements as necessary or appropriate).

In 1996, Congress significantly expanded the SEC's exemptive powers. In perhaps the most sweeping aspect of NSMIA, the SEC is granted authority to exempt "any person, security, or transaction, or any class or classes of persons, securities, or transactions" from any provision of the Securities Act or the Exchange Act or any rule or regulation promulgated under those statutes. Securities Act §28; Exchange Act §36. The only matters beyond SEC exemptive authority are the rules applicable to government securities brokers and dealers, currently administered by the Treasury Department. Exchange Act §15C.

There are few limits on the SEC's exemptive authority, which may be exercised on a finding that action is "necessary or appropriate in the public interest, and consistent with the protection of investors" — a broad standard found throughout the federal securities laws. Nonetheless, judicial review of any exemptive rule is subject to NSMIA's requirement that the SEC consider the promotion of "efficiency, competition, and capital formation" whenever it engages in rulemaking under the public interest standard. See Securities Act §2(b); Exchange Act §3(f); see also *Business Roundtable v. SEC*, 647 F.3ed 1147 (D.C. Cir. 2011) (pointing out SEC's "unique obligation" to consider effect of its rules on "efficiency, competition and capital formation").

§1.3.5 Evaluation of Mandatory Disclosure

Why does securities regulation make disclosure mandatory for public companies? Don't these companies have enough incentives to provide optimal levels of information voluntarily? And do the benefits of mandatory disclosure outweigh the costs — considering both the company and its investors, as well as others outside the company?

These questions have provoked an academic debate and sometimes regulatory realignments. The conventional answer has been that without a government mandate, relevant information (which is costly to create and disseminate) would be underproduced given the lack of incentives for management to disclose voluntarily. Although some critics have suggested that market forces might accomplish indirectly what regulation imposes directly, the prevailing view is that if left to voluntary choice the creation and dissemination of securities-related information — such as company earnings, management plans, and competitive risks — would be inadequate for the functioning of a well-informed, efficient market.

Underproduction of Information

The conventional assumption has been that without mandatory disclosure private investors and traders (particularly professional securities analysts) would have to do their own research and would underproduce securities information since such information has the characteristics of a "public good." If one securities analyst undertakes to obtain relevant information (such as to verify a company's earnings), that information cannot be protected like other property rights since it becomes publicly discernible once the analyst advises clients to trade. The hard-working analyst cannot exclude "free riders" who have not paid for the information.

Even if investors and securities analysts could protect their proprietary research and exclude others from exploiting it, a world of private research would lead to duplication as rival analysts generated essentially the same data. The SEC's function of gathering and disseminating information for all securities participants avoids this wasteful duplication and increases standardization. Mandatory disclosure reduces the cost of doing business for professional securities analysts, who depend on the information "subsidy" provided by government regulation.

Evidence that mandatory disclosure increases price-sensitive information comes from a study of the imposition in 1964 of periodic disclosure requirements on OTC stocks — one of the few modern instances in which a developed securities market went from voluntary to mandatory disclosure. The study finds a dramatic reduction in the volatility of OTC stock returns with the imposition of mandatory disclosure, suggesting that improved information permits investors to more precisely value stocks — thus increasing their investment value.

Perverse Management Incentives

Some critics of mandatory disclosure have suggested that an optimal level of disclosure might occur even without a government mandate because of management's desire to establish a reputation with capital markets of honesty and trustworthiness. Under this view, the government mandate is unnecessary (and wastefully burdensome) because private incentives would produce optimal disclosure. This account of human motivations fails, however, to deal with the many circumstances in which management and investors have different interests in disclosure. Whether at the time they sell securities or on a continuing basis afterward, experience shows that issuers have incentives to hide and delay "bad" news, but overemphasize "good" news. It is only human nature.

Furthermore, mandatory disclosure assumes a disequilibrium in bargaining power between investors and issuers concerning investment information. For often self-serving reasons, corporate management will not voluntarily provide the level of information that investors collectively would have been willing to pay for. Unless compelled to reveal firm-specific information, management will underprovide it.

Nonetheless, there are times that management may be discouraged from providing information — whether on a mandatory or voluntary basis — when there are litigation risks. For this reason, the securities laws impose barriers to securities fraud litigation (see §9.3) and provide safe harbors from litigation for certain kinds of disclosures, such as predictions about the future. See §3.3.2. In addition, recognizing that disclosure is costly to prepare, there are exemptions for smaller firms from the information-gathering and full-blown disclosure requirements applicable to larger firms. See §8.3.4 (internal controls) and §5.2.3 (small offering exemptions).

Side Effects

Mandatory disclosure also produces important side effects. With mandatory disclosure comes greater accuracy of share prices, which gives investors greater confidence when they buy and sell shares — thus making it easier and less costly for companies to raise capital in the first place. By forcing management to disclose how the company is being run and how it is performing, mandatory disclosure also allows shareholders to monitor management and, when appropriate, to enforce management's fiduciary duties. Shareholders, properly informed, can also exercise their voting and liquidity rights to effect a change in control. That is, mandatory disclosure under the federal securities laws complements the exercise of shareholder rights under state corporate law. Finally, mandatory disclosure makes it harder for management to commit fraud, since "weaving a tangled web of lies" is tougher than just telling the truth.

Mandatory disclosure has effects beyond the disclosing firm. The firm's competitors can take advantage of disclosure about the firm and its products, sales, and other proprietary information. (Not surprisingly, firms may sometimes choose to not fully disclose competitive-sensitive information, and the SEC sometimes allows for such information not to be disclosed.) In addition, investors in other firms (in fact, society as a whole) can use disclosures by publicly traded firms to make investment decisions. For example, disclosures by oil and gas producers that reserves are limited might lead college graduates to invest their human capital in "renewables."

Reassurance of Oversight

Mandatory disclosure also bolsters investment confidence in securities markets by providing assurances of coercive government oversight and protection. The SEC, for example, frequently justifies its existence by pointing to its role in assuring the "integrity" of U.S. securities markets. The mandatory disclosure scheme — bolstered by the incentives in the Sarbanes-Oxley Act (see §1.4.1 below) for accountants, securities analysts, and lawyers to focus on investor protection — offers a calming reassurance that the markets are subject to oversight and that more than an "invisible hand" is at work. Although some question whether the SEC should bolster this image, there are strong institutional pressures to create the appearance of an alert watchdog.

Liability for Securities Fraud

Despite academic disagreement on the need for *ex ante* mandatory disclosure, there is general agreement that *ex post* antifraud liability enforced by courts and the SEC is an appropriate governmental role. Such liability proceeds from the theory that securities fraud is not different from theft—that is, misappropriation in a transaction to which one party, if informed, would not have consented. The social costs of fraud come not so much from the transfer of wealth from victim to defrauder, but rather the costs it forces on would-be victims to investigate on their own and demand costly assurances before parting with their money. Moreover, without a legal cost for lying, defrauders themselves would have incentives to put more resources into lying. In the end, in a world without securities antifraud protection, investors would shy from securities markets and put their money in cautious, socially less desirable investments. Private capital formation would suffer, sending shock waves through the economy and through our lives.

§1.4 BEYOND DISCLOSURE: FEDERAL INCURSIONS INTO CORPORATE GOVERNANCE

Over the last decade, the federal securities laws have taken a decided interest in the functioning of public companies, beyond their disclosure to investors and securities markets. The Sarbanes-Oxley Act of 2002 added new federal regulation of the financial auditing apparatus in public companies, with additional responsibilities for gatekeepers of the company's disclosures (outside auditors, board audit committees, company officers, lawyers, and whistleblowers). The Dodd-Frank Act of 2010, though mostly aimed to reform the U.S. financial and banking system, also introduced new corporate governance reforms aimed at greater shareholder voting rights and oversight of executive compensation in public companies. Both new laws, as you'll notice, move federal law into areas once occupied primarily by state corporate law.

In keeping with the traditional demarcation of securities regulation and corporate law in the United States, this book describes and analyzes the aspects of Sarbanes-Oxley and Dodd-Frank that deal with the reforms affecting disclosure to investors. As for those reforms that address the relationship of corporate shareholders, directors, and executives—corporate governance—you can turn to the law of corporations. See Alan R. Palmiter, CORPORATIONS: EXAMPLES & EXPLANATIONS (7th ed. 2012).

§1.4.1 Sarbanes-Oxley Act of 2002

Responding to the accounting and corporate scandals of the early 2000s, Congress passed sweeping legislation that departs in many instances from the disclosure-based philosophy of the federal securities laws. The Public

Company Accounting Reform and Investor Protection Act of 2002 (known as the Sarbanes-Oxley Act after its congressional sponsors) seeks both to strengthen the integrity of the federal securities disclosure system and to federalize specific aspects of public corporation law.

The Story of Enron

The story of Enron's rise and fall is an inextricable part of Sarbanes-Oxley. An energy trading company that started as a stodgy natural gas pipeline, Enron grew dramatically during the 1990s to become the seventh largest corporation in the United States by market capitalization. Its innovative business model, widely lauded and studied, involved the creation of a freewheeling trading market in wholesale energy and transmission (with appurtenant risk-management and financial hedging products).

At first the new market and Enron thrived. But as competitors imitated its model, Enron had to look for new ways to maintain its constantly growing profits. Its executives devised two main techniques: (1) Enron entered into paper transactions with special-purpose related entities that created the appearance of revenues on Enron's financial statements, and (2) Enron financed these related entities with loans (secured by its high-priced stock) that were not reported as debt on Enron's balance sheet. In short, Enron began trading with itself and placing bets on its common stock.

Both the related-entity transactions (in which high-placed Enron executives held personal investments) and their accounting treatment received the blessing of the Enron board of directors, its auditing firm Arthur Andersen, and its outside law firm Vinson & Elkins. Also, securities firms that participated in financing Enron's related entities pressured their securities analysts to recommend the company's stock. Rather than question anomalies in its financial statements, the investment community awarded Enron with accolades and an ever-increasing stock price.

In 2001 Enron's stock price began to slip as investors became suspicious of its related-entity dealings. As federal investigators began their probes, Enron's auditor publicly vouched for the company's financial statements, while privately shredding incriminating documents. In late 2001, Enron restated its financials for the previous four years, and with a few pencil strokes reduced its net income by $600 million and increased its debt by $628 million. Bankruptcy soon followed.

Although many in the financial (and political) community decried Enron as a "bad apple," the true impetus for legislative reform came from the almost weekly revelations in late 2001 and early 2002 of new financial scandals at other companies. Some had reported not actual earnings but predicted *pro forma* earnings. Some had treated payments for phone capacity as an investment, not a current expense — thus overstating both assets and net earnings. Some had engaged in paper buy-sell transactions, to report immediate revenues while amortizing costs. The final straw came when WorldCom, the second largest U.S. telecommunications company and operator of MCI, announced that $7 billion the company had reported as assets should have been treated as operating costs. Within weeks the company declared bankruptcy, and a few weeks later Congress passed Sarbanes-Oxley.

Sarbanes-Oxley as Pavlovian Response to Enron

Sarbanes-Oxley reads like a Pavlovian response to the stories of business and financial misconduct revealed in congressional hearings into the collapse of Enron, WorldCom, and a slew of other companies—many in the overbuilt telecom industry.

Consider the list of corporate misconduct revealed to Congress and the regulatory responses in Sarbanes-Oxley:

Misconduct	Sarbanes-Oxley response
Outside auditors failed to discover or report accounting fraud. Some attributed this failure to self-regulation of the accounting profession, which during the 1990s relied on technicalities to satisfy clients. In particular, the accounting firm Arthur Andersen (auditor for many scandal-ridden companies) was passive toward financial irregularities at many clients.	• **PCAOB.** Creates a self-regulatory, five-person Public Company Accounting Oversight Board to establish auditing standards and regulate accounting profession (Sarbanes-Oxley §101 — see §8.3.4) • **Auditor registration.** Requires accounting firms that audit public companies to register with PCAOB (Sarbanes-Oxley §102) • **Audit standards.** Authorizes PCAOB to set standards for public company audits and to enforce its audit rules (Sarbanes-Oxley §§103, 104, 105) • **Auditor sanctions.** Authorizes SEC to sanction auditors for intentional, reckless, and highly negligent conduct (Sarbanes-Oxley §602 — see §12.2.2)
Outside auditors performed nonaudit services that undermined their audit independence. For example, Arthur Andersen came to earn more from Enron for its nonaudit services than for its work as financial auditor. Outside auditors became too "cozy" with executives of audit clients. For example, many financial officers of	• **Nonaudit services.** Bans auditors from providing certain types of nonaudit services and requires preapproval by the company's audit committee of permissible nonaudit services (Sarbanes-Oxley §§201, 202 — see §8.3.4) • **Auditor rotation.** Requires rotation of audit partner every five years (Sarbanes-Oxley §203 — see §8.3.4)

Misconduct	Sarbanes-Oxley response
Enron were former principals of Arthur Andersen, its auditor.	• **Revolving door.** Closes "revolving door" for members of audit team who within one year after engagement become financial/accounting officers of audit client (Sarbanes-Oxley §206 — see §8.3.4)
Corporate boards (especially board audit committees) failed to supervise outside auditors and lacked expertise to understand company's finances. The Enron board became a symbol of directorial inattention.	• **Audit committee composition.** Authorizes SEC to have stock exchanges change their listing requirements to require audit committees composed only of independent directors, with full authority over outside auditor (Sarbanes-Oxley §301 — see §8.3.4) • **Financial expert.** Requires disclosure whether company has at least one "financial expert" on audit committee (Sarbanes-Oxley §407 — see §8.3.4)
Corporate executives failed to ascertain the truthfulness of company filings and to supervise subordinates, and pressured auditors to give "clean" reports.	• **Officer certification.** Requires SEC rules that CEO and CFO certify that SEC filings are true, complete, and fairly presented (Sarbanes-Oxley §302, Exchange Act Rules 13a-14, 13a-15 — see §8.3.3) • **Internal controls.** Requires SEC rules on disclosure of internal controls, and requires top executives to certify them (Sarbanes-Oxley §404 — see §8.3.3) • **Auditor influence.** Prohibits company officials from improperly influencing outside auditors (Sarbanes-Oxley §303 — see §8.3.4)
Companies failed to report (and the SEC failed to notice) their true financial condition, especially the potential effect of risky off-balance sheet arrangements.	• **Real-time disclosures.** Requires companies to make additional, real-time disclosures in "plain English" of current changes to financial condition (Sarbanes-Oxley §409 — see §8.3.3) • **Off-balance sheet transactions.** Mandates SEC rules requiring disclosure of all material off-balance sheet arrangements (Sarbanes-Oxley §401 — see §3.2.1) • **SEC review.** Requires SEC to review filings by reporting companies at least every three years (Sarbanes-Oxley §408 — see §8.3.3)
Corporate cultures encouraged irresponsible behavior, such as unauthorized or excessive loans to company executives. For example, at Adelphia the family of the company	• **Code of ethics.** Requires disclosure whether the company has a code of ethics applicable to senior financial officers, or justify why not (Sarbanes-Oxley §406 — see §8.3.4)

Misconduct	Sarbanes-Oxley response
founder received loans and other benefits worth $3.1 billion, while the company reported large financial losses.	• **Director and officer bans.** Authorizes SEC to remove "unfit" officers and directors from their positions, and bar them from similar offices in other public companies (Sarbanes-Oxley §§305, 1105 — see §12.3.2) • **Personal loans.** Bans "personal loans" to company directors and officers, except in regular course of company's lending business (Sarbanes-Oxley §402)
Corporate executives sold company stock while aware of accounting misinformation and while employees in company pension plan could not sell.	• **Clawbacks.** Requires forfeiture of executive pay and trading gains when company restates financials due to misconduct (Sarbanes-Oxley §304 — see §10.4.2) • **Blackout periods.** Bars company executives from selling stock during any trading blackout period imposed on employees (Sarbanes-Oxley §306 — see §10.4.1) • **Insider reports.** Requires corporate insiders to disclose their trading in company stock within two business days (Sarbanes-Oxley §403 — see §10.3.1)
Outside securities lawyers "papered" illegal transactions or failed to intercede to stop company wrongdoing.	• **Up the ladder reporting.** Mandates SEC to create rules requiring lawyers working for company to report securities violations and fiduciary breaches up the internal corporate ladder (Sarbanes-Oxley §307 — see §§8.3.4, 12.2.2) • **Lawyer malpractice.** Authorizes SEC to bring enforcement actions against lawyers for malpractice (Sarbanes-Oxley §602 — see §12.2.2)
Securities analysts prepared biased research reports for companies with which their securities firms did business.	• **Analyst reports.** Mandates SEC to adopt rules on the independence and objectivity of securities analysts, and protect them from retaliation for negative reports or ratings (Sarbanes-Oxley §501 — see §12.2.2)
Many frauds only came to light because of courageous "whistleblowers" inside the company.	• **Whistleblower protection.** Imposes criminal liability on those who retaliate against employees (whistleblowers) who provide evidence or assist in the investigation of business crimes (Sarbanes-Oxley §1107 — see §8.3.4) • **Whistleblower action.** Creates a administrative redress for whistleblowers who

Misconduct	Sarbanes-Oxley response
	experience retaliation to seek compensatory damages, reinstatement, back pay, litigation costs (Sarbanes-Oxley §806 — see §8.3.4)
	• **Hotlines.** Requires audit committees to create procedures for handling (anonymous) complaints about accounting improprieties (Sarbanes-Oxley §301 — see §8.3.4)
	• **Statute of limitations.** Extends statute of limitations in cases of securities fraud to two years from discovery, or five years from violation (Sarbanes-Oxley §804 — see §9.4.1)
Company officials and outside auditors destroyed documents to cover up wrongdoing. For example, Arthur Andersen employees destroyed Enron documents, hoping to hide the financial scandal.	• **Criminal sanctions.** Increases criminal sentences for destruction, alteration, or falsification of records in federal investigation, and for violating rules on document retention (Sarbanes-Oxley §802 — see §12.4) • **Obstruction crime.** Creates a new crime for obstructing a proceeding, including by tampering with documents (Sarbanes-Oxley §1102 — see §12.4)
Company officials did not take their oversight and disclosure responsibilities seriously.	• **Heavier sentences.** Increases criminal sentences for corporate officials who retaliate against whistleblowers, those who commit mail and wire fraud, and those who falsely certify financials (Sarbanes-Oxley §§806, 903, 906, 1107 — see §§8.3.3, 8.3.4, 12.4) • **New crime.** Creates a new crime of "knowing securities fraud," with maximum prison term of 25 years (Sarbanes-Oxley §807 — see §9.5.1)

Disclosure Versus Corporate Governance

Many of the congressional responses in Sarbanes-Oxley sought to strengthen disclosure — the heart of federal securities regulation. For example, the rules affecting auditors sought to revitalize auditor independence; the requirements for audit committees and certifications of SEC filings by company executives sought to focus corporate attention on proper disclosure; the requirements on internal controls, the encouragement of whistleblowers, and the "up the ladder" reporting by securities lawyers sought to deter and detect securities fraud. In each case, the ultimate goal was to improve the integrity of the disclosure system and to lower the risk of fraud.

Other congressional responses, however, ventured into waters previously uncharted by federal securities law. By specifying board functions and regulating specified corporate transactions, Sarbanes-Oxley moved into areas of corporate governance historically within the domain of state corporate law. For example, the provisions that specify the composition and responsibilities of board audit committees, the restrictions on loans to corporate executives, the forfeiture of executive pay after financial restatements, and limitations on trading by executives during blackout periods have traditionally been subjects of state corporate statutes and fiduciary law. The reforms aimed to reshape the corporate culture of public corporations.

Evaluation of Sarbanes-Oxley

The impact of Sarbanes-Oxley was immediate, as the business, accounting, and legal communities rushed to adopt new internal controls, ethics codes, and compliance structures called for by the legislation. Many commented on how Sarbanes-Oxley changed attitudes toward corporate governance, with both insiders and outside gatekeepers in public corporations more sensitive to their responsibilities.

Nonetheless, smaller public companies complained that the heavy compliance costs of the Act were not worth the marginal benefits. In response, first the SEC and then Dodd-Frank exempted small public companies from the Sarbanes-Oxley §404 requirement that an auditor attest to the company's internal controls. See Dodd-Frank §989G.

Also from the start, academic commentators debated the meaning and merits of Sarbanes-Oxley. Some saw the far-reaching legislation as part of the centuries-old cycle of capital market booms and busts, inevitably followed by a frenzy of regulation — which they considered unnecessary, ill-conceived, or even counterproductive. Others argued that, except for creating a new regulatory structure for the accounting profession, the legislation merely codified reforms already underway by the stock exchanges, the SEC, sentencing authorities, and state judges. Yet even if Sarbanes-Oxley was superfluous, some found value in its signaling of the government's resolve to address improper corporate behavior.

Empirical studies have generally given favorable grades to the law. According to one study, investors have shown greater confidence in the information contained in SEC filings certified by company officers (as mandated by Sarbanes-Oxley) compared to prior uncertified filings. Another study found that "management" of accounting earnings, which had increased steadily from 1987 to 2001, decreased after the enactment of Sarbanes-Oxley, with a resulting greater reliance by investors on reported earnings. In addition, as companies implemented the internal controls mandated by the Act, they increased their liquidity and corporate investments, while their cost of debt decreased. Most remarkable was the rise immediately after the Act's enactment in corporate restatements of financial results, as corporate managers and accountants sought to correct errors large and small. Then, corporate financial restatements by public companies (particularly larger companies) began to decline and have remained low, suggesting that the audit function and internal controls have been working.

§1.4.2 Dodd-Frank Act of 2010

In the fall of 2008, the U.S. financial markets nearly collapsed. Banks stopped lending, investors dumped their securities, and the U.S. economy stumbled badly. The reasons for the collapse are still being debated, but the most popular culprit has been the "housing bubble" of the 2000s. Trillions of dollars went to finance unsustainable (subprime) mortgage loans, many of which ended up in the portfolios of the leading financial institutions of this country and abroad.

In response, Congress enacted the Wall Street Reform and Consumer Protection Act (known as the Dodd-Frank Act after its principal congressional sponsors) to reform the U.S. financial system. Most of Dodd-Frank's reform agenda was focused on the systemic risks in the financial system, the stability of financial institutions, and the investment and lending practices of U.S. banks. But Dodd-Frank also took aim at corporate governance in public corporations — primarily by expanding the voting rights of shareholders and increasing the responsibilities in public companies regarding executive compensation.

Dodd-Frank is a massive piece of legislation, running 2,300 pages in length with 240 rulemaking directives to the SEC and other regulatory agencies (some of them new agencies) and 89 additional directives to these agencies to issue reports and conduct studies. Under Dodd-Frank, the SEC alone must adopt 95 new rules and prepare 22 reports — by comparison, Sarbanes-Oxley resulted in just 14 new rules and just one study by the SEC. The success of Dodd-Frank, as you might guess, depends on how the regulators are carrying out these directives.

Corporate Governance Reforms

Here is an overview of the corporate governance reforms of Dodd-Frank:

New shareholder powers

Advise on executive compensation

- **Say on pay.** Creates right of shareholders in public companies to a non-binding, advisory vote on the prior year's pay package and golden parachutes for the company's top executives — subject to a shareholder vote on whether the "say on pay" vote would occur every one, two, or three years (Dodd-Frank §951, adding Exchange Act §14A)

Nominate directors

- **Access to proxy statement.** Authorizes the SEC to give shareholders in public companies access to the company's proxy statement to nominate directors to the board (Dodd-Frank §971, amending Exchange Act §14(a); see Exchange Act Rel. No. 62,764 (2010) (adopting new Rule 14a-11 to permit shareholders holding at least 3 percent of voting shares for more than one year to nominate "short slate" to board, if consistent with company's governing documents and state law), *vacated, Business Roundtable v. SEC*, 647 F.3d 1144 (D.C. Cir. 2011) (rulemaking failed to consider cost-benefit of proxy access)

New responsibilities of corporate gatekeepers

Directors

- **Compensation committees.** Mandates that exchange listing standards require compensation committees be composed only of independent directors, with the authority to hire independent compensation consultants (Dodd-Frank §952)
- **Pay disclosure.** Mandates that SEC rules require more disclosure and charts on executive pay compared to stock performance over a five-year period, as well as a comparison of the CEO's pay and the median pay of all the company's employees (Dodd-Frank §953)

Officers

- **Pay clawbacks.** Mandates that stock exchange listing standards require that companies have (and disclose) a policy that, whenever the company restates its financials because of misconduct, CEOs and CFOs must reimburse the company for any bonuses and other stock-based incentive compensation they received, or the SEC can bring an enforcement action to enforce this "claw-back" obligation (Dodd-Frank §954)

- **Chair-CEO.** Mandates that SEC adopt rules requiring public companies to disclose whether the CEO and board chair are the same person and, if so, the reasons for doing so (Dodd-Frank §972)

Accountants

- **Internal controls exemption.** Exempts small business issuers (public companies with less than $75 million in market capitalization) from the Sarbanes-Oxley §404 requirement that an auditor attest to their internal financial controls, and calls for SEC study on how to reduce compliance burden on companies with market capitalizations of $75-250 million (Dodd-Frank §989G — see §8.3.4)

Whistleblowers

- **Increased protections.** Strengthens private action for whistleblowers against employers who retaliate against them, including remedies for rein-statement and double back pay (Dodd-Frank §924 — see §8.3.4)

- **Increased bounties.** Mandates new SEC program under which employees and others who report securities violations in a company can be rewarded between 10 and 30 percent of the funds recovered based on the information provided (Dodd-Frank §§922-924 — see §8.3.4)

One interesting aspect of these corporate governance reforms is that many of them came, for the first time, in response to the clamor of institutional investors, primarily activist pension funds.

Securities Regulation Reforms

The financial regulatory reforms of Dodd-Frank include many that affect traditional securities regulation — most them of them covered in greater detail elsewhere in this book. Some of the reforms create new regulation for financial intermediaries that had been only lightly regulated before (such as credit rating agencies, hedge funds, and private equity funds). Other reforms regulate new categories of financial instruments — such as credit-default swaps — forcing their trading on transparent exchanges.

Reflecting a concern that SEC regulation had been too lax, the agency received new enforcement powers and directives to provide greater protection to investors in private markets. The relationship between broker-dealers and their customers came under scrutiny, with a call for the SEC to consider subjecting broker-dealers to the same fiduciary standards as investment advisers and limiting the scope of pre-dispute arbitration agreements in broker-customer disputes.

To ensure that the SEC becomes more responsive to the views of investors, Dodd-Frank makes permanent the SEC's Investor Advisory Committee, which is supposed to comment on rulemakings and other regulatory initiatives from an investor's viewpoint. Dodd-Frank §911. There will also be an Office of the Investor Advocate in the SEC, charged with preparing an annual report to Congress on the most serious problem encountered by investors, with recommendations for regulatory action. See Dodd-Frank §915.

Here is a list of the Dodd-Frank provisions that reform securities regulation:

New regulation of financial intermediaries

- **Credit rating agencies.** Subjects credit rating agencies to new duties — and accompanying liabilities — similar to those of securities firms that participate in securities offerings (Dodd-Frank §§932-939 — see §11.6)
- **OTC derivatives.** Authorizes SEC regulation of OTC derivatives such as credit-default swaps (Dodd-Frank §701-774 — see §11.2.4)
- **Private funds.** Requires that advisers of "private funds" (defined to include hedge funds and private equity funds) register with the SEC (Dodd-Frank §§402, 403 — see §11.5.2)

New SEC enforcement powers

- **Aiding and abetting.** Increases aiding and abetting enforcement powers for the SEC under Securities Act, Investment Company Act, and Investment Advisers Act (Dodd-Frank §§929M, 929N — see §9.2.2)
- **Subpoena powers.** Grants broader (nationwide) subpoena authority to the SEC (Dodd-Frank §929E — see §12.1)
- **Extraterritorial enforcement.** Grants SEC enforcement powers over extraterritorial securities fraud (Dodd-Frank §929P — see §13.3.2)
- **Collateral bars**. Grants SEC authority to impose collateral bars on directors and officers committing (or aiding and abetting) securities fraud (Dodd-Frank §925 — see §12.3.2)

Protection of sophisticated investors	• **"Bad boy" issuers under Reg D.** Mandates that the SEC preclude certain "bad boy" issuers from raising capital in private markets using Regulation D (Dodd-Frank §926 — see §5.2.4) • **Asset-back securities disclosures.** Mandates that the SEC establish additional disclosures on asset-backed securities (such as debt obligations that are collateralized by mortgages — CDOs), even when offered to sophisticated investors in private markets (Dodd-Frank §943)
Broker-dealer regulation	• **Fiduciary duties of broker-dealers.** Requires the SEC to consider subjecting broker-dealers (securities firms), when they give investment advice to clients, to the same fiduciary "customer first" standards that apply to investment advisers (Dodd-Frank §913 — see §11.1) • **Securities arbitration.** Authorizes the SEC to prohibit or limit mandatory pre-dispute arbitration in broker-customer disputes (Dodd-Frank §921 — see §11.2.5)

§1.5 STATE SECURITIES REGULATION — STATE BLUE SKY LAWS

As originally enacted in 1933 and 1934, the federal securities laws reflected an important policy choice not to preempt state law. The Securities Act, while creating a registration regime for public securities offerings, left intact a parallel system of state securities registration. Former Securities Act §18. Likewise, federal regulation of broker-dealers and investment advisers contemplates parallel state regulation. Exchange Act §28; Investment Advisers Act §222.

Then, as now, every state has securities laws — known as "blue sky" laws — that regulate the offering of securities, require the licensing of securities broker-dealers and investment advisers, impose civil liability for false and misleading information, and establish state agencies for administering these laws. Recent scholarship suggests that the widespread adoption of state "blue sky" legislation was largely the product of the progressive movement of the early 1900s and lobbying by small state banks and their regulators, worried about competition from unregulated securities sellers. (Where does the term "blue sky" come from? Apparently, it was meant to describe securities sellers whose investment scams were compared to those of flim-flam rainmakers who promised rain to Midwest farmers but, after taking the farmers' money, delivered only "blue skies.")

State securities regulation, however, is not completely parallel to its federal counterpart. Unlike federal securities laws, state securities laws in many states regulate the merits of particular offerings by empowering state officials to decide whether the offering deserves the attention of investors in the state ("merit regulation"). In addition, state securities laws do not attempt to regulate securities exchanges or other interstate trading markets, or to regulate disclosures by public companies in connection with shareholder trading or voting.

State securities laws, however, are not uniform. Although 39 jurisdictions have adopted some version of the Uniform Securities Act, exceptions and variations are the rule. The result has been that issuers, broker-dealers, and investment advisers have had to comply with a largely uncoordinated and sometimes conflicting set of state and federal rules.

National Securities Markets Improvement Act of 1996 (NSMIA)

This lack of coordination, which many commentators believed threatened U.S. competitiveness in attracting issuers to our securities markets, led Congress to pass the National Securities Markets Improvement Act of 1996. NSMIA fundamentally changes the parallel system of regulation by allocating regulatory responsibility for particular securities offerings exclusively to the federal government. For offerings covered by the Act, states can no longer require registration or qualification, impose conditions on offering documents or other sales literature, or engage in any merit regulation. For "covered securities" states can only require notice filings and collect fees to finance their policing of securities fraud. Otherwise, NSMIA limits state securities regulation to small, regional, or intrastate securities offerings.

Under §18 of the Securities Act, as added by NSMIA and amended by the JOBS Act, state securities regulation of offerings is preempted in four categories of "covered securities" (see also §4.2.6):

- **Listed securities.** Securities listed on a stock exchange or quoted on NASDAQ (including debt and other securities of the same issuer equal in seniority or senior to the listed securities), no state registration, notice filings, sales reports, or filing fees are permitted.
- **Mutual funds.** Securities issued by "registered investment companies." See §11.4.
- **Private placements.** Securities sold to "qualified purchasers," as defined by the SEC (presumably sophisticated investors capable of protecting themselves).
- **Exempt offerings.** Securities exempt from Securities Act registration, unless the exemption anticipates state securities regulation. Preempted

45

is state regulation of (1) private placements under Rule 506 (see §§5.2.2, 5.2.4); (2) secondary distributions in public reporting companies by control persons and holders of restricted securities under Rule 144 and by "qualified institutional buyers" under Rule 144A (see §§7.2.1, 7.2.2); (3) "crowdfunding" offerings (see §5.2.5); and (4) Reg A+ offerings by public companies or sold to "qualified purchasers" (see §5.2.3). States retain regulatory authority over offerings subject to the intrastate exemption and the small-offering exemptions of Regulation A and Regulation D (Rules 504, 505). See §§5.2.1, 5.2.4.

NSMIA preserves certain state prerogatives. In the last three categories of "covered securities," states can require fees, consent to service of process, and filing of sales reports and other documents "substantially similar" to those filed with the SEC. In all cases, states may continue to apply their antifraud laws to securities offerings for the protection of investors.

NSMIA also created a two-tier system for the regulation of investment advisers, by requiring federal supervision for investment advisers that manage $25 million or more (now $100 million or more, as increased by Dodd-Frank) in client assets or that advise registered investment companies, and state supervision for all other investment advisers. See §11.3.3.

Securities Litigation Uniform Standards Act of 1998

Besides drawing the jurisdictional boundaries for the regulation of securities offerings and investment advisers, Congress has also attempted to define the roles of state and federal courts in class actions involving securities fraud. Concerned about abusive litigation tactics in these cases, Congress imposed significant procedural and substantive conditions in the Private Securities Litigation Reform Act of 1995. See §9.1.2.

In response to the 1995 legislation, many plaintiffs' attorneys moved securities class actions to state court, where state procedures and substantive rules were less demanding. Congress reacted by closing this circumvention in the Securities Litigation Uniform Standards Act of 1998 (SLUSA), which requires that class actions involving allegations of securities fraud in publicly traded securities be litigated exclusively in a federal court. Securities Act §16(c); Exchange Act §28(f)(2). See *Professional Management Associates, Inc. v. KPMG LLP,* 335 F.3d 800 (8th Cir. 2003) (dismissing investor's class action claims under state law arising from misrepresentation in purchase of shares).

The Supreme Court has ruled that SLUSA preempts state-based "holder" claims when shareholders allege losses because they held on to their stock, rather than selling it, in reliance on fraudulent reassurances. See *Merrill Lynch, Pierce, Fenner & Smith, Inc. v. Dabit,* 547 U.S. 71 (2006) (plaintiffs alleged that securities firm had disseminated false research reports to inflate stock price of its corporate clients and that plaintiffs held their stock in reliance on these reports). By preempting state law, the ruling effectively denies defrauded "holders" (any) class action remedy — state claims are preempted and federal claims are unavailable to non-transacting shareholders who simply held their stock. See §6.3.1 (Securities Act §11); §9.2.1 (Exchange Act Rule 10b-5). The Court also ruled that a federal district court's remand of a securities class action to state court cannot be appealed — thus leaving to state courts to decide the SLUSA preclusion issue on remand. See *Kircher v. Putnam Funds Trust*, 547 U.S. 633 (2006) (concluding that state courts are "equally competent" to decide preclusion issues).

To keep things interesting, though, the 1998 legislation makes an exception — the "Delaware carve out" — for state cases that allege fiduciary breaches under state corporate law. Securities Act §16(d); Exchange Act §28(f)(3)(A). Courts interpreting the statutory exception have permitted securities fraud class actions alleging state fiduciary breaches to be brought in federal or state court, not limited to the company's state of incorporation. *Gibson v. PS Group Holdings Inc.*, Fed. Sec. L. Rep. ¶90,921 (S.D. Cal. 2000).

CHAPTER 2

Definition of Security

The boundaries of securities regulation are drawn by the definition of "security." Securities transactions are subject to registration, mandatory disclosure, and heightened antifraud liability; intermediaries in securities transactions are subject to SEC registration, rules, and supervision; and participants in securities transactions are exposed to civil and criminal liability. Nonsecurities transactions receive none of this regulatory attention.

The federal securities laws list what constitutes a security, and the Supreme Court has developed a test for when an unorthodox investment is a security. Nonetheless, the "security" boundary has perplexed courts and securities practitioners. In fact, the definition of security regularly generates splits among lower federal courts. As the courts have discovered, many investments do not fall neatly inside or outside the regulatory boundary. But you should not despair. The elusive search for "security" can be a wonderful, even satisfying, amusement.

This chapter covers:

- the implications of calling something a "security" [§2.1]
- the statutory definition of "security" and the Supreme Court's famous *Howey* test for "investment contracts" [§2.2]
- approaches used by federal courts in various contexts: real estate interests, business interests, pension plans, notes (including sale-leasebacks), bank instruments (including synthetic investments), and sales of businesses [§2.3]

§2.1 IMPLICATIONS OF DEFINITION

A transaction that involves a "security" triggers a host of federal and state securities regulation:

- registration and disclosure requirements in public offerings of securities, including secondary distributions (Chapters 4 and 7)
- disclosure and other conditions necessary to claim an exemption from registration (Chapter 5)
- liability for selling unregistered securities, and liability for misrepresentations in a public offering (Chapter 6)
- registration by companies whose securities are publicly traded, disclosure by those who solicit votes from public shareholders, and disclosure by those who offer to buy publicly traded securities (Chapter 8)
- antifraud protection in federal court (with nationwide service of process) for those who buy or sell securities (Chapter 9)
- limits on trading by those who have inside information and disclosure by insiders and those who hold specified amounts of publicly traded securities (Chapter 10)
- registration by persons in the business of intermediating transactions involving securities (Chapter 11)
- administrative and judicial liability of persons who violate securities laws (Chapter 12)

Failing to identify a security is disastrous not only for the parties but also for the attorney, who can be liable for malpractice. *Wartzman v. Hightower Productions, Ltd.*, 53 Md. App. 656 (1983) (holding attorneys liable for $170,000 in losses for failing to advise flagpole-sitting company to register its investment interests as securities).

Special Note

Remember that just because a financial transaction is defined as a "security" does not necessarily mean it's subject to the full brunt of securities regulation. For example, the transaction may be subject to a registration exemption, because the security itself is exempt or the nature of the transaction creates an exemption (see Chapter 5); the alleged misinformation in the transaction is not material (see Chapter 3); or the security is transacted beyond the jurisdictional reach of the U.S. securities laws (see Chapter 13).

§2.2 TESTING FOR A "SECURITY"

The federal securities acts define a "security" with a list of financial instruments (stock, bonds, debentures, notes, and transferable shares) and generic catchall terms (evidences of indebtedness, investment contracts, and certificates of interest in profit-sharing agreements). Securities Act §2(a)(1); Exchange Act §3(a)(10). Even if an instrument falls in one of the enumerated categories, the statutory definitions exclude those instruments when "the context otherwise requires."

In interpreting the definitional lists, courts have focused on two questions:

- When does an unorthodox investment fall within the catchall terms, principally "investment contract"?
- When are instruments that nominally fall into an enumerated category (such as "notes" or "stocks") actually not securities?

The federal courts don't have a unified approach to these two questions. Nonetheless, you will discover that the cases turn on whether investors have entrusted their money to another's management and whether they face practical difficulties in collectively supervising the managers. Two economic concepts describe the predicament of investors in securities. First, these investors face "agency costs" as they seek to inform themselves, negotiate constraints, and monitor and discipline those who manage their money. Second, when there are many such investors, they face "collective action" problems in coordinating among themselves their supervisory control. These two concepts combine to explain many of the definitional approaches of the courts, an idea more fully developed in the examples and explanations of this chapter.

§2.2.1 Investment Contracts — The *Howey* Test

The meaning of "investment contract" — a legal term without commercial significance — reveals the judge-made boundaries of the security definition. The Supreme Court has defined an "investment contract" as any transaction in which "[1] a person invests money [2] in a common enterprise and [3] is led to expect profits [4] solely from the efforts of others." *SEC v. W. J. Howey Co.*, 328 U.S. 293 (1946). The Court's test has taken on a quasi-statutory quality, with subsequent cases adding glosses:

Investment	The investment, which can be of cash or noncash consideration, is expected to produce income or profit; the investor is looking for financial returns, not a consumable commodity or service.
Commonality	Multiple investors have interrelated interests in a common scheme—horizontal commonality. Or, according to some courts (a minority), it is sufficient if a *single* investor has a common interest with the manager of his investment—vertical commonality.
Expected profits	The expected return (whether fixed or variable) must be the principal motivation for the investment. The return must come from earnings of the enterprise or appreciation of the investment based on anticipated earnings, but not merely from additional contributions.
Efforts of others	According to *Howey*, profits must be derived "solely" from the efforts of others, though lower courts have generally accepted that the investor's efforts in the common enterprise *may* contribute to profits. The efforts of the managers, however, must be predominant; the investors must be mostly passive.

The *Howey* test, applied in light of the "economic realities of the transaction," seeks to identify transactions in which investors are counting on others to manage an enterprise that will produce financial returns on their investment. This definition identifies those transactions in which ownership is separated from control, suggesting the importance to capital markets of mandatory disclosure and higher liability standards to ensure that investors allocate capital to its highest-valued uses.

Courts have applied the "investment contract" definition in surprising contexts. The following schemes have been held to be "investment contracts" and thus securities:

- The sale of a row of 48 citrus trees when the cultivation, harvesting, and marketing of the fruit was handled by an affiliate of the seller—the facts in *Howey*.
- The sale of earthworms when the seller promised to repurchase the worms (which were to reproduce at geometric rates) and to market them to farmers. *Smith v. Gross*, 604 F.2d 639 (9th Cir. 1979).

- The sale of "participations" in a pyramid scheme (ostensibly for distributing cosmetics) when the seller conducted promotional meetings and the buyer received a "commission" for each new person brought into the scheme. *SEC v. Koscot Interplanetary, Inc.*, 497 F.2d 473 (5th Cir. 1974).

In each instance, people had given money to a promoter in the expectation of a return derived *predominantly* from the efforts of the promoter. See *SEC v. Glenn w. Turner Enterprises, Inc.*, 474 F.2d 476 (9th Cir. 1973) (holding that the managerial efforts of promoter must be "the undeniably significant ones . . . which affect the failure or success of the enterprise"). The enticement was not ownership of land, worms, or wholesale discounts ostensibly offered the investor, but rather an investment return generated by the management or marketing efforts of another.

Although the *Howey* test is applied only to unorthodox transactions that fall outside the list of enumerated instruments (such as stock and notes), courts have used its logic in deciding whether "the context otherwise requires" for instruments that fall in the list. For this reason *Howey* is (almost certainly) the first case in your casebook on the definition of security.

§2.2.2 Risk Capital Test

Some state courts have used a "risk capital" test to identify when their state's blue sky laws apply to unorthodox transactions. Unlike *Howey*'s focus on the investor's reliance on the promoter's efforts, the "risk capital" test focuses on the extent to which the investor's initial outlay is subject to the risks of the enterprise, risks over which the investor has no managerial control.

The "risk capital" test, which requires neither commonality nor that profits be derived from the efforts of others, is often easier to satisfy than the *Howey* test. For example, state courts have treated memberships in recreational clubs as securities if the memberships were to finance the club facilities. See *Silver Hills Country Club v. Sobieski*, 55 Cal. 2d 811 (1961).

§2.3 "SECURITIES" IN VARYING CONTEXTS

Not all investments are securities. Many investments fall clearly within the definition (such as publicly traded stocks and bonds), many fall clearly outside it (such as precious metals and real estate in fee simple), and many investments exist in a definitional netherworld. For example, partnership interests, employer-funded pension funds, and notes given in commercial transactions are usually not viewed as securities, even though they are meant to produce a return on an investment. On the other hand, time-share interests in resort condos, buying into a pyramid scheme, and some franchise arrangements are viewed as securities, even though they nominally involve the purchase of commodities or services.

As you will see, the definitional contours often turn on the meaning of "investment contract" — a term that has received much judicial attention. While courts once regularly sided with plaintiffs who sought an expansive definition of the term, courts over the last couple decades have been reluctant to bring all novel financing arrangements under the umbrella of the securities laws. Courts increasingly have recognized that defining a financial transaction as a security implies significant and sometimes unnecessary regulatory costs. The following subsections describe the treatment as securities of various financial transactions.

§2.3.1 Real Estate as Securities

Normally, the sale of real estate (without any collateral arrangements with the seller) is not a securities transaction. Even when the real estate is purchased as a speculative investment, there is no security if profits do not depend on "the efforts of others." But when the marketing of real estate emphasizes the economic benefits to be derived from the managerial efforts of others, such as a promoter's sharing of rents from condominium units, courts have readily found a security. Securities Act Rel. No. 5347 (1973) (establishing guidelines for when offering time-share condos constitutes an investment contract).

Thus, a security exists when a developer offers resort condos under an arrangement in which purchasers agree to make their property available for rental, with limited rights of occupancy, and to receive a pro rata share of net rental income from a pool of all rentals in the complex. In an important extension, the Ninth Circuit ruled a security could be found when a *real estate agent* offered a rental condo and helped the buyer make arrangements with an unrelated company that would manage the property. *Hocking v. Dubois*, 885 F.2d 1449 (9th Cir. 1989) (en banc) (holding that the offering of a rental condo along with collateral management agreement could constitute an "investment contract"). But if there is no pooling of rents and condo purchasers each have control over rental arrangements, the property sale does not involve a security. *Wals v. Fox Hills Development Corp.*, 24 F.3d 1016 (7th Cir. 1994) (finding no security when rents from time-share condos were not pooled and owners could rent or use property as they chose).

§2.3.2 Business Interests as Securities

As a general rule, whether ownership interests in a typical business organization are securities depends on the legal form of the business organization:

	Security	Not Security
Corporation	Common shares Preferred shares	
Limited partnership	Limited partner interests	General partner interests
Limited liability company (LLC)	Passive member interests (manager-managed LLC)	Active member interests (member-managed LLC)
Partnership (joint venture)	Passive partner interests	Active partner interests Co-venturer interests

These categories, however, are not airtight. Lower federal courts have increasingly recognized that the organizational form under state law is not always an accurate guide to the "economic realities" of the parties' relationship. Applying a framework developed by the Fifth Circuit in *Williamson v. Tucker*, 645 F.2d 404 (5th Cir. 1981), many lower courts permit a nominal general partner to claim that his interest is an investment contract by demonstrating that he was so dependent on the promoter that he actually could not exercise meaningful control. The investor must show *either*

- **No legal control.** The partnership agreement leaves so little power in the investor's hands that the arrangement in fact distributes power as would a limited partnership; or
- **No capacity to control.** The partner is so inexperienced and unknowledgeable in business affairs that he cannot intelligently exercise his partnership powers; or
- **No practical control.** The partner is so dependent on the unique managerial ability of the promoter that he cannot replace the manager or otherwise exercise meaningful partnership powers.

Applying these factors, the court in *Williamson* held that general partners "acquired securities" when they invested in a real estate development in which all management functions (planning, acquiring, rezoning, financing, developing, renting, and selling the properties) had been left to the manager by agreement. Given the economic realities of the partnership, the court treated the partnership interests as investment contracts. Not all lower courts, however, have been as willing to engage in such a broad inquiry. Some courts have ruled that a partnership interest is a security only if the partnership agreement does not give investors partner-type powers (the first *Williamson* factor). See *Rivanna Trawlers Unlimited v. Thompson Trawlers, Inc.*, 840 F.2d 236 (4th Cir. 1988) (not finding "investment contract" when partners in general partnership that engaged in commercial fishing business had power to replace managing partner, and twice exercised their power; stating that mere choice by partner to remain passive is not sufficient).

One question raised by the *Williamson* test is whether the factors must exist at the time of the investment or can also arise as the partnership evolves and operates. Applying *Williamson* to a limited liability partnership (which under state law has all the management attributes of a partnership, though with limited liability for all partners), courts have generally focused on the relationship of the parties at the time of the investment. See *SEC v. Merchant Capital, Inc.*, 483 F.23d 747 (11th Cir. 2007) (finding "investment contract" when experienced business people purchased partner interests in 28 LLPs engaged in business of purchasing fractional interests in non-performing debt pools, concluding that partnership agreements did not give partners practical ability to remove managing partner, that investors were inexperienced in debt-purchasing business, and that investors had no practical alternative but to stay with managing partner). By focusing on the investment when sold, courts avoid the messy problems of an investment relationship that begins as a nonsecurity and evolves into a security — or vice versa.

In a limited partnership, the usual approach is to treat the interests of limited partners as securities (since they share the attributes of passive corporate shareholders) and the interests of general partners as nonsecurities given their management role. Nonetheless, using the obverse of the *Williamson* test, a limited partner's interest may sometimes be seen as a nonsecurity, if economic realities indicate the limited partner has significant legal and actual control of partnership management. *Steinhardt Group v. Citicorp*, 126 F.3d 144 (3d Cir. 1997) (holding limited partner's interests are not securities if the limited partner can and does exercise "pervasive control" of the partnership). With the advent of limited liability partnerships, which offer many of the organizational features of a close corporation, some commentators have argued for abandoning the *Williamson* presumption that partnership interests are not securities.

Investment interests in limited liability companies (LLCs) present a similar set of issues. Given that LLC interests are not mentioned in the statutory definition of security, courts have mostly analyzed them using the *Williamson* test. Although a one-person LLC that takes no outside investments does not involve any securities, the analysis of a co-owned LLC depends on investor expectations and the efforts of others. LLC members who expect a return on their investment mostly from the efforts of others (the usual case in a manager-managed LLC) are deemed to have acquired a security, but LLC members who rely on their own efforts have not (the usual situation in a member-managed LLC). *United States v. Leonard*, 529 F.3d 83 (2d Cir. 2008) (focusing on "reasonable expectation" of investor control in LLC). As a number of courts have pointed out, there are no bright-line rules and the analysis will depend on the "economic realities" of each particular LLC and its members. (Remember that when an LLC has passive members, the sale of LLC interests to these members must either be registered with the SEC or satisfy an exemption from registration. See Chapters 4 and 5.)

Pyramid Schemes

A pyramid scheme attracts investors with the promise of high returns, but pays these returns using money from the original investors or new investors. Eventually, the funds run out as the promoters extract their take, and the last wave of investors is left penniless. An early such scheme, developed in 1920 by one Carlo Ponzi of Boston, promised investors 50 percent returns every 90 days by investing in his plan to convert inexpensive foreign postal coupons into U.S. stamps. Instead, Ponzi used the money (some $15 million from 40,000 people) to pay early investors and create the illusion of high returns, while pocketing the rest.

In their essence, pyramid schemes are a criminal taking of money by false pretenses. But, as structured, many operate as a facially legitimate business — such as jewelry distribution, worm farming, or inventory financing. That is, the promoters can defend themselves in criminal proceedings by asserting they had simply promoted a business that failed — hardly evidence of criminal intent. For this reason, many pyramid schemes are targeted by the SEC in civil enforcement actions in which the agency asserts that the investments offered in the scheme constitute "securities" and their unregistered sale violates the no-fault provisions of the Securities Act.

The most significant issue in these enforcement actions, and one on which the SEC has been remarkably successful, is whether investing in a scheme built on the gullibility and misfortune of later investors constitutes a "security." Using the *Howey* analysis, courts have concluded that pyramid schemes (1) seek to attract cash investments (2) in an enterprise involving multiple investors and a promoter who organizes the scheme (3) with the promise of future (usually exorbitant) investment returns (4) arising from the efforts *primarily* of the promoter in attracting new investors and providing management services related to the nominal business. See *SEC v. SG Ltd.*, 265 F.3d 42 (1st Cir. 2001) (finding a "security" when off-shore company created online investment game that allowed players to buy "virtual investments" and earn virtual "investment returns," which depended on the promoters and players luring new players into the game).

The most famous (and largest ever) pyramid scheme was pulled off for nearly 20 years by Bernie Madoff, a stock broker who promised an exclusive clientele modest (but steady) returns of around 10 to 12 percent per year by using sophisticated financial hedging techniques that were "too complicated for outsiders to understand." Like many other pyramid schemes, Madoff's scheme preyed on investors with a common affinity — in his case, mostly Jewish charities and wealthy individuals who knew of Madoff by word of mouth. Madoff kept the scheme going with a constant stream of new investors, using their funds to pay off old investors. In fact, about half of Madoff's investors were "net winners," receiving returns that exceeded their investments. All told, about $65 billion (including fabricated gains) was missing from client accounts when the fraud was revealed in 2008, though actual cash losses turned out to be less than $18 billion. Although the SEC had received repeated allegations that Madoff's investment model was "too good to be true," the agency failed to notice the red flags and uncover the fraud. It came to light only when Madoff told his sons that his investment fund was "one big lie." He eventually pled guilty to securities fraud and in 2009 was sentenced to 150 years in prison.

§2.3.3 Pension Plans as Securities

When an employee participates in an employer-funded pension plan, the question arises whether interests in the plan constitute securities and the employer's payments to fund the plan the purchase of securities. The Supreme Court applied a modified version of the *Howey* test to conclude that an *employer-funded, fixed-benefit* pension plan in which employees make no direct contributions and their participation is compulsory is not a security. *International Brotherhood of Teamsters v. Daniel*, 439 U.S. 551 (1979). Although such a plan arguably fits the *Howey* test since employees invest by exchanging their labor in the expectation of future pension benefits, which depend in part on income produced by the plan's investment managers, the Court was unwilling to subject such plans to securities regulation. The Court pointed out that an employee's plan benefits were fixed and depended not so much on the plan's investment returns as on the employee becoming eligible under the plan. In addition, the Court pointed out that employer-funded pension plans are regulated by the Employee Retirement and Income

Security Act (ERISA) — this "comprehensive legislation" suggests Congress was filling a regulatory void and its presence makes securities law protection less important.

The *Daniel* decision raises the question whether voluntary *employee-funded, variable-benefit* pension plans in which employee payroll deductions fund the plan and benefits depend on plan performance should be treated differently. On one hand, such plans involve voluntary contributions and plan benefits depend largely on the acumen of the plan's managers. On the other hand, such plans are also subject to ERISA regulation, which not only requires extensive disclosure to plan participants but also imposes standards of conduct on plan managers. *Daniel* strongly suggests that ERISA's more comprehensive scheme preempts the securities laws. The SEC, however, has taken the view that pension plans are securities when funded by employees who make the choice whether to invest — even though such plans are regulated by ERISA. Securities Act Rel. No. 6188 (1980) (limiting conclusion to defined-contribution plans, not necessarily defined-benefit plans); Securities Act Rel. No. 6281 (1981) (expanding conclusion to include all voluntary, contributory plans in which employee chooses to participate or to invest).

Lately, compensation and pension plans have taken new forms. One popular device is to compensate employees with stock appreciation rights (SARs) whose value is pegged to the company's stock price. Although it later withdrew its decision, the Eleventh Circuit has said SARs are not securities since they are not transferable and they carry no opportunity to hold or affect ownership in company stock. *Clay v. Riverwood Int'l Corp.*, 157 F.3d 1259 (11th Cir. 1998) (ruling that employees who cash in their SARs using nonpublic information are not liable for insider trading), *modified on reh'g* 176 F.3d 1381 (11th Cir. 1999) (concluding plaintiff lacked standing to pursue claims against insiders).

In addition, some charities have begun to offer "charitable gift annuities" that allow a donor to transfer money to the charity in exchange for a partial tax deduction and a lifetime stream of annual income from the charity, with any remaining money paid to the charity or another charity chosen by the donor. Such annuities, though not necessarily resulting in a net gain to the donor, have been deemed "investment contracts." See *Warfield v. Alaniz*, 569 F.3d 1015 (9th Cir. 2009) (finding charitable gift annuity to be "investment contract" given that charity's promotional literature, and the annuity contracts themselves, presented gift annuity as "opportunity for financial gain" and thus donors were "led to expect profits"). Although charitable gift annuities are generally deemed to be securities, they are exempt from registration under §3(a)(4) of the Securities Act, though they remain subject to the antifraud provisions of the securities laws. See §5.1 (Exempt Securities — Securities of Not-for-Profit Issuers).

§2.3.4 Notes as Securities

A note evidences a borrower's promise to repay a debt (extension of credit) and, as such, represents the creditor's investment in the borrower. Not surprisingly, the federal securities laws specifically define a security to include "any note." Securities Act §2(a)(1); Exchange Act §3(a)(10). Yet many extensions of credit do not have the typical attributes of an investment. When a bank lends money to a customer who gives a promissory note to the bank, it would be absurd to say the bank's investment in the customer warrants protecting the bank under the federal securities laws. Many notes given in consumer and commercial financing transactions should not be treated, and courts have not treated them, as securities because "the context otherwise requires." See introductory phrase to Securities Act §2(a)(1); Exchange Act §3(a)(10).

When is a "note" a security? The federal securities statutes provide some guidance as to Congress's thinking. Under the Securities Act, a note that "arises out of a current transaction" and that matures within nine months is *exempt* from registration under the Act. §3(a)(3). This exemption was intended to cover "commercial paper" — that is, unsecured promissory notes issued by large, financially sound companies to finance current operations and sold to institutional investors in large denominations. A similar provision in the Exchange Act *excludes* from the definition of security any note that matures within nine months (§3(a)(10)), and the Supreme Court has stated that the Exchange Act's provision's coverage is the same as that of the Securities Act.

Despite the Acts' express emphasis on when a note matures, courts have focused on the economic realities of the transaction and not merely the note's maturity. Applying a variety of tests — commercial-investment, *Howey*, risk capital — lower courts have over time identified certain classes of notes that fall outside the securities definition, and others that fall within it. Notes in traditional consumer and commercial transactions are not securities; notes sold to numerous investors seeking an investment return are securities.

In 1990 the Supreme Court adopted a "family resemblance" test to judge whether notes are securities, thus resolving a split among the circuits. *Reves v. Ernst & Young*, 494 U.S. 56 (1990). The "family resemblance" test begins with a rebuttable presumption that every note is a "security" unless it falls into a category of instruments that are not securities. Offering guidance, the Court stated that notes used in consumer lending, notes secured by a mortgage on a home, and short-term notes secured by an assignment of accounts receivable are in the "family" of nonsecurities.

For new types of "note" transactions, *Reves* set out four factors to determine the "family" into which the note fits. The factors bear an uncanny similarity to the elements of the *Howey* test:

Motivation of seller and buyer	If the issuer of the note uses the proceeds for general business purposes, it is more likely a security. If the issuer gives the note to buy consumer goods or for some "commercial" purpose, it is more likely not a security. (Compare this to *Howey*'s "investment of money.")
Plan of distribution	If the notes are widely offered and traded, it is more likely a security. If the note is given in a face-to-face negotiation to a limited group of sophisticated investors, it is more likely not a security. (Compare this to *Howey*'s "[horizontal] common enterprise.")
Reasonable expectations of investing public	If investors generally view the type of notes to be investments, it is more likely a security. (Compare this to *Howey*'s "expectation of profits from the efforts of others.")
Other factors reduce risk	If the note is not collateralized and not subject to nonsecurities regulation, it is more likely a security. If the note is secured or otherwise regulated (such as by banking authorities), it is more likely not a security. (Compare this to the gloss of the Court's decisions in *Daniel*, see §2.3.3, and *Marine Bank*, see §2.3.5 next.)

No *Reves* factor is sufficient or necessary, but together they provide a "gestalt" sense of whether a note involves an investment or merely represents part of a commercial-consumer transaction.

Sale-Leaseback Financing

Not all loans involve the giving of a note. One type of borrowing is a sale-leaseback, where a financier agrees to nominally "purchase" an asset used by a business and receive fixed "lease payments" for a specified period, after which the lease terminates and the asset must be repurchased by the business. For the financier, the lease payments are like interest payments secured by the "purchased" asset and the buyback a return of principal. For the business, the original purchase is like a loan whose proceeds can be used to acquire the asset or to otherwise use in the business.

Normally, a sale-leaseback is not viewed as a security, but instead as a form of secured financing — much like a bank loan in which the lender takes a security interest in the financed assets. This analysis, however, is less persuasive when the financier is not a commercial lender, but instead a group of individual speculators. In *SEC v. Edwards*, 540 U.S. 389 (2004), the Supreme Court unanimously concluded that a sale-leaseback arrangement for payphones can constitute an "investment contract" under the flexible *Howey* test, even when the scheme involves a contractual promise to pay a fixed (not variable) rate of return. In the case, more than 10,000 people invested $300 million in a scheme where purchasers were offered to buy a payphone, along with a five-year agreement for the management and then buyback of the payphone — an arrangement that nearly all investors chose. (The management company, in fact, never generated profits and instead funds from new investors were used to pay existing investors — a typical "Ponzi" scheme.) The purchasers, none of whom were involved in the day-to-day operation of the payphones they purchased, were promised a flat 14 percent return on their investment. The management company selected sites for the phones, installed the equipment, arranged the connections, collected coins, and maintained the phones.

The Court concluded that an investment contract could involve one that promised a fixed rate of return, even though there was no promise of capital appreciation or participation in business earnings. Nothing in the *Howey* test, according to the Court, required that "profits" be variable or derive from a particular source. The Court pointed out that a flexible interpretation of the catchall "investment contract" furthers the purpose of the securities laws to snag unscrupulous marketers who promise low-risk investments (such as "guaranteed" fixed returns) to the elderly and unsophisticated. To decide otherwise would invite fraudsters to circumvent the federal securities laws simply by touting their schemes as promising a fixed return.

Curiously, *Edwards* does not mention the family-resemblance test of *Reves*, whose approach toward "notes" would seem relevant to determining whether a fixed-rate instrument deserves securities law protection. Perhaps, as some commentators have observed, the *Reves* test represents a somewhat clumsy application of the four-part *Howey* test, and *Howey* continues to offer the most attractive analytical framework for the definition of "security."

§2.3.5 Bank Instruments as Securities

Bank savings accounts and certificates of deposit (CDs) are prevalent financial investments. Although such bank instruments are exempt from registration and private antifraud liability under the Securities Act (see §§3(a)(2) and 12(a)(2)), there is no exemption under the Exchange Act. The Supreme Court, however, has held that a CD issued by a national bank is not a security under the Exchange Act. *Marine Bank v. Weaver*, 455 U.S. 551 (1982). In the case, the Weavers pledged a bank CD as collateral to guarantee a bank loan to Columbus Packing. When the bank reneged on its promise to deliver the loan proceeds to Columbus, which later went bankrupt, the Weavers claimed the bank had defrauded them under Rule 10b-5 when they pledged their CD. (The Weavers also claimed that their agreement with the owners of Columbus to share 50 percent of the company's profits was a "profit-sharing agreement," so that their guarantee was also in connection with this security.)

The *Marine Bank* Court turned to the "unless the context otherwise requires" language of the statutory definition. The Court pointed out that, although bank CDs have many of the attributes of a long-term debt instrument, CDs are federally insured and subject to comprehensive banking regulation for the protection of depositors. That is, an alternative regulatory scheme renders securities regulation unnecessary. (The Court also decided, in a much-maligned part of its opinion, that the profit-sharing agreement was not a security since the privately negotiated arrangement gave the Weavers significant control over the operation.)

§2.3.6 "Stock" as Security

The federal securities acts define a security to include "stock," subject to the exasperating caveat "unless the context otherwise requires." Securities Act §2(a)(1); Exchange Act §3(a)(10). The courts have held that not all instruments labeled "stock" are securities.

Noninvestment Stock

The Supreme Court has emphasized that the definition of a security must reflect "economic reality." *United Housing Foundation v. Forman*, 421 U.S. 837 (1979). In the case, a cooperative housing corporation required residents to buy "shares of stock" in the corporation to secure housing. Residents were entitled to one vote in the cooperative, regardless of the number of shares they held. The shares were nonnegotiable and operated as a refundable deposit; a resident on leaving the cooperative was obliged to resell her shares at their original price to the corporation.

The Court held there could be no Rule 10b-5 action by residents alleging fraudulent rent increases since the cooperative's "shares" were not securities. The Court pointed out that the shares had none of the characteristics of a stock investment: There was no right to dividends contingent on profits; the shares were not negotiable; voting rights were not proportionate to the number of shares held; and the shares could not appreciate in value. Further, the Court applied the *Howey* test and concluded that the residents' intent in purchasing the "shares" was solely to acquire a place to live, rejecting the notion that tax deductibility, rental savings, or income to the cooperative from leasing of commercial space indicated an "expectation of profits."

"Sale of Business" Doctrine

Sometimes transactions in corporate stock involve in "economic reality" the whole business. When a corporate acquiror buys a majority block of stock, rather than buying the corporate assets or engaging in a merger, should a "stock purchase" acquisition be treated as a securities transaction?

During the early 1980s, a number of lower courts concluded that the transfer of a majority of the stock of a closely held corporation is not a securities transaction. Under the "sale of business" doctrine, the courts looked to *Howey*'s emphasis on management to conclude that the sale of a majority interest passes complete control to the purchaser, who becomes an owner-entrepreneur and not an investor. *Fredricksen v. Poloway*, 637 F.2d 1147 (7th Cir. 1981). Other courts adopted a literalist approach that stock is stock, no matter how transacted. *Golden v. Garafalo*, 678 F.2d 1139 (2d Cir. 1982).

The Supreme Court resolved this split with a literalist reading of "stock." *Landreth Timber Co. v. Landreth*, 471 U.S. 681 (1985). The case involved the purchase of 85 percent of the common stock of a closely held business that failed to live up to the purchaser's expectations. The Court pointed out that the stock in the transaction had all the traditional indicia of corporate stock: dividend rights, liquidity rights, proportional voting powers, appreciation potential. Choosing a literalist approach, the Court refused to look at the "economic substance" of the transaction or to assume the securities acts apply only to passive investors. Moreover, the Court pointed out there would be difficult line-drawing issues in acquisitions of less than 100 percent of a corporation's stock or when a purchaser arranged to have the seller stay on to manage the business, as had happened in *Landreth*.

Despite the Supreme Court's rejection of a *corporate* "sale of business" doctrine, lower courts have chosen not to treat LLC interests as "stock" and have applied the "sale of business" doctrine to LLCs. When 100 percent of the membership interests in an LLC are sold to a single buyer, courts have held that *Landreth* does not apply and have looked to the economic realities of the transaction. See *Great Lakes Chemical Corp. v. Monsanto Co.*, 96 F. Supp. 2d 376 (D. Del. 2000) (concluding that LLC gave members sufficient powers over manager so that profits did not come "solely from the efforts of others" and membership interests were not securities).

Examples

1. Identify which of the following arrangements involve a securities transaction:

   a. Alicia buys voting common shares of Citrus Corporation, a publicly traded corporation that owns citrus groves in Florida and harvests and markets citrus fruits and juices.

   b. Bob buys a row of 48 citrus trees from Howey Company. Although not required, Bob agrees to have Howey-in-the-Hills (a related company) cultivate, harvest, and market his citrus, along with that of many others who own rows like Bob's.

   c. Carlita and Carlos agree to work for Howey-in-the-Hills as orange pickers, with half their pay in cash and the other half a bonus based on a percentage of the profits of the company.

   d. David, Delilah, and Dina buy a citrus grove in Florida as tenants in common. They contract with Sam, a local farmer, to manage their farm.

   e. There is a terrible freeze in Florida, and neither Citrus Corporation, Howey-in-the-Hills, nor Sam has any smoke machines to save their groves' delicate blossoms. What remedies do Alicia, Bob, Carlita, and David have if they were never told about the lack of smoke machines?

2. First Lynch Securities offers its customers managed trading accounts, in which the brokerage firm exercises its discretion to buy and sell securities and commodities for the customers' accounts. Identify which of the following "managed accounts" involve a securities transaction:

   a. Alvine joins with investors Albert, Allen, and Aldo to pool their investments in one discretionary trading account in which First Lynch's fee is based on the profitability of the account.

   b. Brady joins with investors Bertha, Beverly, and Betty in a pooled discretionary trading account in which First Lynch is paid a flat fee based on the amount of assets in the account.

   c. Cristina gives her money to First Lynch, which sets up a discretionary trading account for her. First Lynch's fee is based on the account's performance.

   d. Daniel gives his money to First Lynch, which sets up a discretionary trading account for him. First Lynch receives a flat fee based on assets in the account.

3. Identify which of the following "real estate" transactions involve a securities transaction:

   a. Beachfront Resorts offers to sell "rooms" in its beachfront hotel. Buyers of rooms agree that all rents are pooled, and each room "owner" receives from the rental pool a pro rata payment for the hotel room she owns. Buyers cannot occupy their rooms, except

65

for two designated weeks each year. Beachfront Resorts emphasizes that rent payments will more than cover the owners' principal and interest (P&I) obligations.

b. Dubois is a real estate agent who offers privately owned Hawaii condos. To sell the condos, Dubois helps buyers arrange with Hotel Corporation (an unrelated management company) to collect rents from the condos. Under a rent-pooling agreement offered by Hotel Corporation, the rents from various condos are pooled; buyers can occupy their condos for only two weeks each year. Dubois points out to buyers that income from the pooling arrangement will cover P&I.

c. Fox Hills Golf Villas offers "weeks" at condos in its golf complex. Buyers can buy condos for any one week of the year. Fox Hills allows buyers to occupy the condo themselves or to rent the "week" on their own or through a rental arrangement with Fox Hills in which the unit's rent is passed through to the owner. Fox Hills emphasizes that buyers who choose not to occupy the condo will receive more in rent than they pay in P&I.

d. Expectations Ltd. develops a resort community near Disney World. The company offers residential lots and requires residents to pay "dues" for a country club, as well as such community facilities as a clubhouse, swimming pool, tennis courts, and water treatment. The developer emphasizes to prospective buyers the potential appreciation of their investment.

4. Identify which of the following "business" investments involve a securities transaction:

a. Albert and Amanda invest in the stock of an S-corporation formed under the New Columbia Business Corporations Act. Albert and Amanda are the only shareholders, and they enter into a shareholders' agreement in which they do away with the board of directors and agree to co-manage the business. Albert and Amanda are both sharp business people.

b. Bart and Barbara invest in a joint venture that buys apartment buildings for investment. Bart and Barbara enter into an agreement with a manager, Goodacre Investments, to develop, lease, and sell the venture's properties. Under the agreement, the buyers retain authority to approve any purchase and development of new properties and to remove Goodacre as manager. Bart and Barbara, however, lack any business or investment sophistication.

c. Carol and Carl invest with ten other investors in a limited liability company. They all are members with equal financial and management rights.

d. Donald and Dana invest with ten other investors as limited partners in a limited partnership formed in a jurisdiction that has adopted the

Revised Uniform Limited Partnership Act (RULPA). Under the partnership agreement, the limited partners can advise the general partner on partnership business, participate in partner meetings, vote to remove and replace the general partner, and amend the partnership agreement.

e. Edgar and Erin (two wealthy medical practitioners) invest in a partnership that owns an 80-acre tract of land and produces jojoba. Edgar and Erin enter into a partnership agreement with Chew, who acts as operating partner for their jojoba farm, as well as for 20 other adjoining 80-acre jojoba farms. Chew hires a foreman who does all the work. Under their agreement, Edgar and Erin (along with the other general partners) have full control of the business. In fact, though, the general partners are mostly passive.

f. Fred and Freda invest their life savings in a partnership under the New Columbia Uniform Partnership Act. Fred and Freda are the only partners, and they enter a partnership agreement in which they agree to co-manage the business. Fred is not that sharp; Freda really runs the business.

5. Identify which of the following "notes" involve a securities transaction:
   a. Gladys buys a motorcycle and gives her bank a promissory note in which she promises to repay her loan in 36 equal payments over 36 months. The note is secured by the bike.
   b. Mega Motors (an NYSE-listed company) raises capital for current operations by issuing unsecured promissory notes (maturing in six months) in $1 million denominations to institutional investors. First Lynch Securities acts as a "best efforts" underwriter.
   c. Integrated Resources raises capital by borrowing money through unsecured 30-day loans from Security Pacific Bank. The bank's commercial department resells these loans (in $1 million denominations) in a "loan participation" program to banks and institutional investors.
   d. Farmer's Co-Op raises capital for its gasohol operations by selling unsecured (and uninsured) promissory notes to its members. The notes, issued in small denominations, are payable on demand and yield variable rates of interest competitive with bank CDs.
   e. Upstart, Inc. raises capital for its operations by offering unsecured promissory notes in $1,000 denominations to many individual investors. The notes mature in six months and, if not redeemed, become payable in six-month intervals thereafter.

6. Olde College has a large endowment and looks for ways to make it grow. Identify which of the following "investments" involve a security.
   a. Olde College and other universities hire Alma Mater Campaigns (AMC) to conduct fundraising campaigns for their schools. AMC solicits donations and passes on donations to the designated schools after

deducting its commission. If any donors designate their gift for "higher education," these funds (after deducting AMC's commission) go into a pool in which all participating universities share pro rata.

b. New Age Fund offers universities its contacts with wealthy philanthropists who wish to give anonymously to higher education. If a university commits to putting money into an account for six months, New Age says its secret donors will match the same amount at the end of the six-month period — a 100 percent return. Olde College learns of this opportunity from Renowned University, which has already used New Age twice with results as promised.

c. Cougars Football, Inc. hopes to acquire a professional football franchise and offers to sell 100-seat blocks in its planned new stadium. If the Cougars get the franchise, buyers can use their seats or sell them (at a potentially sizable profit) through the Cougars' ticket office. If the Cougars do not get the franchise, the club will return the buyers' purchase price, less the promoter's expenses in seeking the franchise. Olde College, which does not have a football team, buys 20 blocks of seats for students and alumni.

d. Life Partners, Inc. identifies persons with terminal diseases who wish to use the proceeds of their life insurance policies while still alive. For a fee, Life Partners finds investors willing to purchase the insurance policies at a discount, thus giving the patients access to immediate cash and a substantial return to the investors when the patient dies. Life Partners monitors the status of the insureds, making sure their premiums are paid and then disbursing the insurance proceeds when they die.

e. Tacos Unlimited operates a taco restaurant on campus and offers to sell the business to Olde College. Tacos suggests two options: Olde College could purchase all the stock of the existing campus restaurant, which Tacos holds as a subsidiary; or Olde College could purchase the restaurant's assets. In either case, Tacos would operate the restaurant for Olde College and remit to it a fixed percentage of net revenues.

Explanations

1. a. Security. This "stock" transaction involves the prototype "security" and falls squarely within the federal securities laws' enumerated list of securities. Presumably, Alicia's shares have all the traditional indicia of corporate stock: dividend rights, liquidity rights, proportional voting powers, appreciation potential. *Landreth Timber Co. v. Landreth*, 471 U.S. 681 (1985) (applying per se test to corporate "stock"). As a passive shareholder, her ownership rights are separated from actual control of the business.

In economic terms, Alicia and the other shareholders face not only "agency costs" by entrusting management control to the company's managers, but also "collective action" obstacles if they try to organize themselves to exercise their shareholder voting rights. The securities laws seek to minimize these "agency costs" by requiring disclosure (and by imposing fraud liability) for investors so they can value their investment both when they purchase and later when they vote, tender, or otherwise transact their shares. The securities laws seek to minimize the costs when atomistic investors entrust control over their investment to another.

b. Security. These are the facts of the landmark *Howey* case. See §2.2.1. The Supreme Court looked at earlier tests developed in cases interpreting state blue sky laws in developing its definition of "investment contract." The *Howey* test fit the scheme in the case like a glove: (1) an investment of money (2) in a common enterprise (3) in which investors were led to expect profits (4) derived solely from the efforts of the promoter or its related company. The test measures whether an investor, along with other similarly situated investors, has entrusted control over the investment to another. Even if Bob had not used the Howey-in-the-Hills management services, he was *offered* a package of real estate and management. It is the *combined offer* of a 48-tree row and of cultivation, harvesting, and marketing services for that row, along with many other rows like it, that constitutes an offer of a security.

c. Probably security. Although the cash payment for orange-picking services raises no securities issues, there is a question whether the agreement to take a profit-sharing bonus is an "investment contract" under the *Howey* test. In looking at the *Howey* elements, it would seem the bonus satisfies elements (2), (3), and (4): a common enterprise (the orange-grove business) in which the orange pickers have been led to expect profits (a significant part of their compensation) based "predominantly" on the efforts of others (how well the company manages the groves and markets the orange crop, even though results will somewhat depend on the pickers' efforts). Thus, the key question becomes whether element (1) is satisfied: did the pickers "invest money" when they agreed to take half of their compensation as a profit-sharing bonus? The Supreme Court in *Int'l Brotherhood of Teamsters v. Daniel* (§2.3.3) stated that an "investment of money" need not take the form of cash only, but can include "goods and services" (footnote 12). In effect, Carlita and Carlos are giving up a significant part of their services in return for a share of company profits, a risky proposition that will depend on the abilities of the company's management.

Does this mean that all company profit-sharing or bonus plans offered to employees are securities? Generally, courts have not treated employee profit-sharing plans as "securities" since the plans are typically viewed as an "incident of employment" and thus not involving a separate investment decision by the employee. *Foltz v. U.S. News & World Report, Inc.*, 627 F. Supp. 1143 (D.D.C. 1986). The judicial reluctance to treat employee profit-sharing plans as "securities" reflects a broader reluctance to subject typical consumer and employment transactions to securities regulation — on the assumption that markets and other legal regimes provide adequate protection. Unless it is clear that an employee voluntarily gives up something specific of value in the expectation of financial returns that will flow from an enterprise managed predominantly by another, there is no "investment contract."

d. Not security. Although the three land speculators have combined and are passive investors, the success of their common investment depends on the demand and supply of a commodity, not their entrusting of control to another. Their collective ownership rights are not meaningfully separated from control — "agency costs" are minimal. The three can contract with Sam; they can replace him; they can let the farm lie fallow. Although they may face some "collective action" difficulties in making these choices, their dependency on Sam (or somebody like him) to manage their farm is no greater than someone who buys services from another or a principal who works through an agent. *Deckebach v. La Vida Charters*, 867 F.2d 278 (6th Cir. 1989) (finding no security when investors buy yacht for personal use and also enter into contract, terminable on 60-days notice, for a management company to charter the yacht when not in use). In sum, though there may be "collective action" obstacles, the relative absence of "agency costs" means there is no security.

This is not to say there are no risks in this real estate investment. The seller may have lied; the grove may become a sinkhole; Sam may prove to be crooked or shiftless. Yet the federal securities laws assume other legal regimes can deal with these risks adequately. The law of deceit, contract law, and agency law (as well as specialized laws applicable to real estate sales) provide protection against deceit and opportunism.

e. Alicia has full-blown securities remedies. If she purchased in a non-exempt, unregistered public offering, she may rescind her purchase. Securities Act §12(a)(1) (see §6.2). If she purchased in a registered offering, she may recover the loss in value of her shares if the seller made any material misrepresentations or omissions in connection with the offering. Securities Act §§11, 12(a)(2) (see §§6.3, 6.4). In addition, whether the offering was registered or not, she may recover if there was any fraud in connection with her purchase. Exchange Act Rule 10b-5 (see Chapter 9). Finally, she may have remedies under the antifraud provisions of state blue sky laws. See §9.5.2.

Bob and Carlita have the same remedies as Alicia.

David, however, has no remedies under the securities laws. He may pursue fraud remedies under state law, the elements of which are typically more demanding than the federal remedies available to Alicia, Bob, and Carlita. See §9.5.2.

2. a. Security. When an investor sets up an account with a broker for the trading of securities or commodities, the account itself has similarities to an investment if the broker has discretion over trading in the account. Courts have interpreted the *Howey* test, with sometimes surprising results, in cases involving customer claims that brokers violated the securities laws in the way they promoted or managed the accounts. The cases have turned on whether a discretionary trading account satisfies the "common enterprise" element of the *Howey* test.

In cases of multiple investors in a pooled account, like this one, courts have said that there is horizontal commonality because investors are all looking for profits from a single enterprise — the account. Investors have not only given the broker discretionary control over the account but have also diluted their individual control by sharing in the pool. No one investor can, for example, require the broker to buy only "blue chip" stocks for the account. In economic terms, the investors face not only "agency costs" by giving the broker investment discretion, but also "collective action" obstacles because of their horizontal investment relationship.

Courts have also assumed, without explanation, that there is more commonality when the broker's fee is tied to the account's performance. Although it may be true in such a case that the investors and broker have a common interest in the account's performance, the linkage to performance actually reduces "agency costs" and undermines the existence of a security. That is, there is less need for securities regulation when the broker's interests converge with those of the investors.

b. Security, probably. Although this pooled account has the horizontal commonality that most courts have insisted on, courts have viewed the fixed-fee arrangement as making it less of a common enterprise. This is a curious result because the fixed-fee structure means that the broker's incentives are less aligned with the interests of the investors — there are greater "agency costs." Seemingly mesmerized by the "common enterprise" language of the talismanic *Howey* test, courts have failed to consider the rationale for the element.

c. Not security, probably. Many courts require horizontal commonality for there to be an "investment contract." When a single investor gives a broker discretion over a trading account, there is no pooling of investments and hence no security. *Milnari v. M-S Commodities, Inc.*, 457 F.2d 274 (7th Cir. 1972) (no common enterprise because the profitability of each account did not depend on the success or failure of other accounts managed by the same broker).

A dwindling minority of courts have recognized "vertical commonality" based on the relationship between the investor and the broker. *SEC v. Continental Commodities Corp.*, 497 F.2d 516 (5th Cir. 1974). But these courts have required that the investors and brokers share the account's risk. *Mordaunt v. Incomco*, 686 F.2d 815 (9th Cir. 1982). As noted above, this is an odd requirement that means courts will refuse to find a security if the promoter can earn flat commissions even while the investor is losing money — that is, precisely when the arrangement creates the greatest "agency costs." *Meyer v. Dans un Jardin, S.A.*, 816 F.2d 533 (10th Cir. 1987).

The growing rejection of vertical commonality makes sense, since a single investor suffers none of the "collective action" problems that might arise if multiple investors sought to control the broker's discretion. The discretionary account has the appearance of the purchase of services, an arrangement whose "agency costs" are regulated by traditional agency and contract law.

d. Not security, probably. This arrangement lacks "horizontal commonality" and only a few courts have applied a broad rule of vertical commonality that is satisfied when the broker's compensation is tied merely to the size of the account, not investor profits. *Long v. Shultz Cattle Co.*, 881 F.2d 129 (5th Cir. 1989). Although it seems appropriate to find a security when broker fees are not linked to investor profits and thus "agency costs" are high, few courts have viewed the problem in these terms.

This perspective, however, animated the *Howey* analysis. In its arguments to the Supreme Court in *Howey*, the SEC argued that an investment contract exists if either (1) multiple investors rely on the *predominant* efforts of the promoter or (2) one or more investors rely on the *sole* efforts of the promoter. This recognition of the interplay of "agency costs" and "collective action" problems, long since swallowed by the vagaries of the caselaw, has great merit. The first test would find a security if "collective action" problems combine with some "agency costs" to make security law protection appropriate. The second test would find a security if "agency costs" are clear and significant, even if there are no "collective action" problems. That is, there can be an investment contract with vertical commonality if the investor is completely dependent on the promoter. The greater the dependence, the more likely the arrangement is a security.

3. a. Security. This rent-pooling arrangement is a classic real estate "investment contract." The hotel rooms are marketed to purchasers emphasizing the economic benefits to be derived from the managerial efforts of the promoter from the rental of units. Under *Howey* there is an investment of money in a rent-pooling arrangement (a horizontal common enterprise) when profits are derived from the efforts of the rental manager and personal use of the property is restricted. Securities Act Rel. No. 5347 (1973).

   b. Security. These are the essential facts of an important Ninth Circuit case. *Hocking v. Dubois*, 885 F.2d 1449 (9th Cir. 1989) (en banc). Like our example, the case did not involve a classic rent-pooling arrangement since the real estate agent, who the purchasers claimed sold them a security, had no formal relation to the management company. Nonetheless, the court concluded the condo and the rent-pooling agreement were offered as a package; the management company's pooling of rent (less expenses) from many condos indicated a common enterprise. The court noted the "collective action" problems that the many passive condo owners faced in replacing the management company and concluded that, as a practical matter, the unsophisticated (and generally absentee) owners lacked effective control of the manager.

   The *Dubois* decision reflects that when an owner faces a combination of "agency costs" and "collective action" problems, the securities laws regulate his investment as a security. Although an owner buys tangible assets, securities law protection is warranted if his assets (along with those of other owners) are to be managed by another.

   c. Not security. In this situation, there is no rent-pooling agreement (or "horizontal commonality") and thus none of the "collective action" problems of the *Dubois* arrangement. Each buyer is free to choose to occupy for her "week," to rent her "week" herself, or to hire a management company. Even though Fox Hills offers a "managed" investment, buyers have significant control over how their "week" of real estate is consumed or managed. *Wals v. Fox Hills Development Corp.*, 24 F.3d 1016 (7th Cir. 1994) (in a case involving similar facts, court decided that without "horizontal commonality" there is no security).

   d. Not security. Purchasers of resort residences who also pay community dues do not invest in an enterprise since any investment returns do not depend on the efforts of others. Although property owners join together to purchase additional community services, these services are for their own consumption—just as their residences are for their own occupancy. That is, commonality does not alone create a security. Just as investors who jointly own unmanaged property do not buy a security, so too when property owners jointly buy services.

Although they face "collective action" difficulties in procuring and supervising these services, they do not look for a financial return from the efforts of others. In this example, any investment returns on the purchasers' real estate depend only tangentially on the management of community services. Compare *Rodriguez v. Banco Central*, 727 F. Supp. 759 (P.R. Dec. 1989) (assuming existence of security if resort promoter promised to develop common facilities and services with common funds).

4. a. Security. The corporate form dictates the result. Although neither investor would seem to need the protections of the securities laws, the Supreme Court has said that "stock" is "stock." *Landreth Timber Co. v. Landreth*, 471 U.S. 681 (1985) (finding security in sale of stock in a closely held corporation). The parties' alteration of the traditional corporate structure by doing away with the board of directors does not change the answer. Even though our two investor-managers do not face the "agency" and "collective action" costs of a typical publicly held corporation, their stock presumably has the essential attributes of corporate stock: dividend rights, liquidity rights, proportional voting powers, appreciation potential. Courts have not looked at the "context" of stock ownership in a corporation, whether closely or publicly held.

   b. Perhaps a security. Although the federal securities acts do not include partnership interests on their definitional list, lower federal courts have come to use a contextual approach in assessing whether partnerships involve securities. Under this approach, a partnership interest may be a security if the context indicates the particular co-partners lacked control over their investment — suffering "agency costs" and "collective action" obstacles comparable to those faced by corporate shareholders. Following the lead of the Fifth Circuit, most courts require a co-partner claiming the existence of a security to show either (1) the arrangement legally denied partnership-type control to the investors or (2) the investors lacked the business experience and knowledge to exercise partnerlike control or (3) the investors depended, as a practical matter, on the unique expertise of the promoter or other manager. *Williamson v. Tucker*, 645 F.2d 404 (5th Cir. 1981) (see §2.3.2).

   In our example, the investors would appear to have the legal attributes of typical joint venturers — that is, co-partners in a partnership with a limited scope. Moreover, there is nothing to indicate the real estate management company has any unique attributes that would prevent the joint venturers from replacing it with another manager. Yet the investors' lack of business experience and knowledge raises factual issues about whether they could meaningfully exercise their powers. The burden would be on them to show they lacked the acumen to exercise their legally sufficient control rights.

c. **Not enough information.** Limited liability companies (LLCs) represent an organizational structure that fits neither the typical corporate nor the typical partnership mold. Most commentators (and the courts that have addressed the issue under the federal securities laws) have applied a contextual test similar to that applied to partnerships. Some state blue sky statutes, however, take the doctrinaire position that LLC interests are automatically securities, whether the LLC is managed by its members or a nonmember manager. Ohio Rev. Code §1707.01.

Applying a contextual "economic reality" analysis to an LLC, you should ask about the extent of the members' control rights under the governing state statute, the company's articles of organization and the parties' operating agreement, the business sophistication of the members, and the extent to which control rights are delegated to any particular member or manager.

d. **Probably security.** Courts have generally assumed that a traditional limited partner interest is a security since it shares many attributes with corporate common stock. Limited partners typically do not and cannot (without risking their limited liability) engage in managing the business, which is left exclusively to the general partners. Although RULPA permits limited partners to take on significant control powers, these powers are similar to the voting rights of corporate shareholders. Even armed with full RULPA powers, limited partners depend on the efforts of the general partner for a return on their investment and typically face significant "collective action" obstacles to asserting their control prerogatives. Only in a case perhaps such as ours, where the ten limited partners might easily organize and actually exercise their powers, might limited partners be likened to general partners. If our ten limited partners could, for example, use threats to remove the general partner to effectively run the business, their interests might not be securities. See *Steinhardt Group, Inc. v. Citigroup*, 126 F.3d 144 (10th Cir. 1997) (concluding that limited partner in limited partnership created so bank could "securitize" its bad loans did not acquire investment contract, since limited partner had power to veto any material actions related to loans, and to propose and approve new business plans).

e. **Security.** Although structured as a partnership, the structure in "economic reality" has few of the attributes of a typical co-partnership. The *Williamson v. Tucker* analysis (see §2.3.2) provides a useful framework. Although the "general partners" have legal control of the partnership's 80-acre farm, the analysis does not end with legal formalities. In reality, the passive partners do not appear to have the business expertise to manage a jojoba farm. Instead, the farm's operation is left entirely to the operating partner and the foreman. Moreover, the structure of the property rights (which resembles that of *Howey*) effectively divests the investing partners of control. The entire jojoba farm comprises 1600 acres, divided among 20 partnerships, and practical control resides in the operating partner and the foreman. Even if investing partners chose to exercise control, such as by converting their tract to alfalfa production, they would face significant practical obstacles. *Koch v. Hawkins*, 928 F.2d 1471 (9th Cir. 1991) (finding a security under essentially same facts).

f. Not security. As with a corporate investment where the organizational structure dictates the result, this typical partnership does not create a security because of the organizational structure. Courts have shown willingness to treat general partnership interests as securities only in nontraditional contexts. To engage in a full-blown *Williamson v. Tucker* analysis (see §2.3.2) for every partnership would generate significant business uncertainty. In our example, it should be conclusive that Fred has full partnership rights and powers — at the time of the investment. His subsequent failure to exercise them is just his tough luck.

5. a. Not security. Although the federal securities laws define a security to include "any note," the Supreme Court has held that notes may or may not be securities depending on their "family resemblance." *Reves v. Ernst & Young*, 494 U.S. 56 (1990) (§2.3.4). A note given in a consumer transaction has none of the attributes of a typical investment and is a member of the nonsecurity "family." In extending credit, the bank is not investing in a common enterprise, but rather in the borrower's ability to repay. The borrower gives her note to only one bank, and the bank's ability to protect itself (with credit checks and a security interest) undermines any argument that the bank faces "agency costs" or "collective action" obstacles that warrant securities law protection. In fact, to the contrary, federal consumer lending laws reflect a concern that borrowers in such transactions need protection from bank overreaching.

b. Security under Securities Act — but not subject to registration; not security under Exchange Act — perhaps. This typical issuance of short-term commercial paper raises some perplexing interpretive issues. The Securities Act exempts from registration any "note . . . to be used for current transactions" with a maturity of less than 9 months. Securities Act §3(a)(4). The Act's legislative history indicates the exemption's reference to "current transactions" refers to commercial paper. The exemption thus suggests that short-term commercial paper is a Securities Act security, though exempt from registration. Securities Act Rel. No. 4412 (1961) (according to SEC, exemption applies only to "prime quality negotiable commercial paper of a type not ordinarily purchased by the general public"). The exemption can be justified given the presumed quality of the issuer, the ready liquidity of "current operations" assets, and the presumed sophistication of buyers of commercial paper — typically institutional investors.

The Exchange Act, on the other hand, excludes from the definition of security "any note" maturing in less than nine months, an exclusion commentators have assumed is similar in scope to the Securities Act exemption. Exchange Act §3(a)(10). Thus, short-term high-quality commercial paper is not an Exchange Act security. *Zeller v. Bogue Electrical Manufacturing Corp.*, 476 F.2d 795 (7th Cir. 1973).

This reading of the statutory provisions is shaken by dictum of the Supreme Court that the Exchange Act definition "is virtually identical" to the Securities Act definition and "the coverage of the two Acts [in the context of a case involving notes] may be considered the same." *Reves v. Ernst & Young*, 494 U.S. 56 n.1 (1990) (see §2.3.4). It is further confounded by the Supreme Court's holding that §12(a)(2) of the Securities Act does not cover privately placed securities, which the Court assumed would be subject only to Rule 10b-5 liability under the Exchange Act. *Gustafson v. Alloyd Co.*, 513 U.S. 561 (1995) (see §6.4.1). Read literally, these decisions suggest commercial paper is not subject to private liability under the federal antifraud provisions.

c. Security, perhaps. This issue divided the Second Circuit. *Banco Español de Crédito v. Security Pacific National Bank*, 973 F.2d 51 (2d Cir. 1992). On the one hand, as the majority in the case pointed out, the "loan participations" were similar to a syndicated commercial line of credit, which standing alone is a commercial (not investment) transaction. The participations were undergirded by short-term loans made by banks for the borrower's current business operations.

On the other hand, as the dissent in the case argued, the "loan participations" were made through the bank's investment department, not its lending department. Institutional investors viewed the loan participations as investment alternatives to such instruments as commercial paper. The syndicator sold the loan participations on a nonrecourse basis, requiring the purchasers (who had no dealings with the borrowers) to look only to the borrowers in the event of default. No regulatory scheme or security interests protected the purchasers' position. See *Pollack v. Laidlaw Holdings, Inc.*, 27 F.3d 808 (2d Cir. 1994) (holding that uncollateralized participations in mortgages constitute securities, given their broad-based sales to the general investing public).

d. Security. This example presents the facts of the *Reves* case. *Reves v. Ernst & Young*, 494 U.S. 56 (1990) (see §2.3.4). The Supreme Court concluded that the Co-op's notes were securities using its four-factor test. Proceeds from the notes were for general business purposes, rather than a limited commercial purpose; they were widely offered to the co-op's 23,000 members and were sold to some 1600 investors; they were advertised as "investments"; and they were neither insured nor collateralized. As to the notes' demand feature, which arguably gave them a "zero-month maturity," the Court concluded that their maturity could just as easily be seen as exceeding nine months since demand could be postponed indefinitely. The Court avoided deciding whether there is a bright-line rule for any note with a maturity of less than nine months. Instead, the Court assumed the co-op's notes were investments that presented significant risks of fraud and abuse — and thus securities.

e. Security, probably. These notes resemble no particular "family" of notes. They, however, have many of the risks and attributes of an equity investment. In effect, investors have put at risk their capital, subject to a revolving right every six months to liquidate their investment.

The example raises the relevance of the notes' six-month maturity. Under a literal interpretation, the notes would seem to be both excluded from the Exchange Act's coverage and, at the least, exempt from Securities Act registration. The notes' automatic renewal feature does not change this result since both acts contemplate that renewable notes still fall within the exemption/exclusion if any renewal is for less than nine months. Although the Supreme Court in *Reves* did not decide whether the nine-month feature of a note is determinative, lower courts have not felt so constrained. See *SEC v. Wallenbrock*, 313 F.3d 532 (9th Cir. 2002) (finding "security" when hundreds of investors purchased promissory notes in a business that ostensibly provided short-term financing to manufacturers of medical latex gloves, where notes had a three-month maturity and then rolled over from month-to-month).

6. a. Not security. Olde College has purchased two fundraising services. The first service involves the fundraising company soliciting donors and forwarding donations earmarked for Olde College. It receives a commission for these services. Olde College neither invests money nor expects a financial return.

The second service involves the joint purchase of a service by Olde College and other universities that receive pooled donations to "higher education." Although the participating universities may face some "collective action" problems if the fundraising company mishandles pooled donations, they would be in no different position if they collectively purchased legal, accounting, or any other professional service. None of the participating universities has entrusted AMC with money from which they expect profits. Compare this to a pyramid scheme in which buyers make significant payments in the hope of gaining a return as the promoter entices others to make similar payments. SEC v. Koscot Interplanetary, 497 F.2d 473 (5th Cir. 1974).

b. A security, perhaps. You might be interested to know that this example, though seemingly far-fetched, retells the 1990s story of New Era Fund. The entity offered "double your money" deals to hundreds of universities and major charities, which deposited nearly $500 million in accounts in the covetous hope that unnamed philanthropists would mysteriously double their investment. The scheme, like a typical pyramid scheme, created the appearance of investment returns by using new investments to pay returns on old ones. New Era's house of cards collapsed when an accountant at a small university called New Era's bluff. The last wave of investors (the losers) included such notables as the Rockefeller Foundation, the Academy of Natural Science in Philadelphia, and the University of Pennsylvania.

Courts have held that comparable pyramid schemes are securities because investors are enticed to join the scheme in the hope of earning profits from the efforts of the promoters as new investors are brought into the scheme. SEC v. Koscot Interplanetary, 497 F.2d 473 (5th Cir. 1974). Pyramid schemes, however, are an uncomfortable fit with the "investment contract" paradigm. First, such schemes may not involve horizontal commonality, because often investments are not pooled and each investor's account is separate. Nonetheless, pyramid investors face significant "collective action" difficulties because the success of the scheme depends on the promotional ability of the pyramid manager to bring in new investors. In the pyramid scheme of Koscot Interplanetary, for example, all the investors depended on the glitzy efforts of the promoter at "opportunity" meetings. Likewise, New Era returns depended on the promoter adding new investors. In both cases, particular investors had little individual say in how the promoters managed the pyramid. Despite the lack of usual horizontal commonality, investors faced "collective action" problems similar to investors whose returns are pooled.

Second, pyramid schemes are not typical "investment contracts" since central to their success are the witting and unwitting efforts of the very investors who seek legal protection. Just as the Koscot Interplanetary returns depended on participants bringing in new participants, the New Era pyramid grew largely through word-of-mouth testimonials about the scheme's results. Courts, however, have not read Howey literally to require that returns come "solely" from the efforts of the promoter. See SEC v. Edwards (§2.3.4) (rejecting argument that investors' bargaining for a rate of return means return comes from efforts of investors; "any other conclusion would conflict with our holding that an investment contract was offered in *Howey* itself"). Instead, it is enough that investors face significant (not pure) agency costs. In *Koscot Interplanetary* investment returns depended on the promoter's "opportunity" meetings; in New Era investment returns depended on the scheme's smooth-talking promoter.

c. Perhaps security. The offer of a block of seats, with the attendant promise to market them later, has the elements of an investment contract. Like a promoter of an animal program that promises to market the animals after their effortless and boundless breeding, the football team offers to resell tickets if buyers wish. Although purchasers can choose to "consume" their seats, the resale option offered by the promoter ties the purchaser's return to the promoter's success in getting a franchise and then marketing the team. The many ticket buyers face "collective action" and "agency costs" comparable to those of equity investors. Those who buy blocks of seats with the resale possibility in mind are together engaged in a common enterprise, from which they may expect a financial return based on the team's success.

On the other hand, the typical purchase of a club membership, even when made before the club's facilities exist, does not involve a security under the federal securities laws since the buyer does not seek a financial return, but rather the eventual benefits of club membership. The buyer, though she takes the risk the promoter will not build the club, is much like a home buyer who takes a risk in contracting with a builder to build her house. The federal securities laws do not concern themselves with purchasing or even prepurchasing nonfinancial goods or services. (The result, however, might be different under the state "risk capital" test.)

Notice that without the resale option, the prepurchase of tickets for a new sports team is similar to "crowdfunding"—a popular fundraising method used by individuals and organizations, often on the Internet, to raise money for such things as disaster relief, citizen journalism, artist careers, motion picture promotion, software development, inventions, scientific research, and so on. Such crowdfunding does not involve a security, given that at most the promoter is only selling goods or services. But when a business uses crowdfunding to raise money from investors, the offering (whether of equity or debt) is subject to securities regulation. The JOBS Act of 2012 creates an exemption from Securities Act registration for small companies using "crowdfunding" to raise up to $1 million from small investors. See §5.2.5.

d. Perhaps security. Life Partners acts as an intermediary, bringing together cash-needy patients and cash-rich investors, and then facilitating the payment of the patient's insurance proceeds to the investor.

Does it offer investors a security? The issue raised by viatical settlements turns on whether the investment returns depend primarily on the efforts of the intermediary. One view is that the intermediary is not involved in managing an ongoing business, but has done the bulk of its work in identifying insured terminal patients to investors. These prepurchase activities, according to an interpretation of *Howey* that focuses on ongoing agency costs, do not merit protective securities disclosure. See *SEC v. Life Partners, Inc.*, 87 F.3d 536 (D.C. Cir. 1996) (concluding that value of intermediary's services are already impounded in fees and purchase price of investment).

Another view is that the intermediary's prepurchase activities, in identifying patients and assessing whether their disease is terminal and their insurance transferable, are precisely the kinds of management services requiring securities disclosure. Much as investors of closed-end mutual funds depend on an adviser's expertise in selecting and packaging a fixed portfolio of securities, investors in viatical settlements require information to assess the intermediary's ability to identify terminal patients and the risks that the insurance proceeds may not be paid. See *SEC v. Mutual Benefits Corp.*, 408 F.3d 737 (11th Cir. 2005) (concluding that returns from viatical settlement contracts are based on the efforts of the intermediary, since "there is no basis for excluding pre-purchase managerial services from the analysis" under *Howey*).

e. There are two issues. Is the acquisition a security? Even if not, is the franchise arrangement a security? As to the first issue, the structure of the acquisition makes all the difference. A sale of assets is not a securities transaction, while a stock purchase is. *Landreth Timber Co. v. Landreth*, 471 U.S. 681 (1985) (see §2.3.6).

But even if structured as a sale of assets, the subsequent franchise arrangement may involve a security if the franchisor manages the operation. Typically, the sale of a franchise does not involve a security because the franchisee undertakes to operate the business. In a typical franchise, although much of the franchise's merchandising and operations are dictated by the franchisor, the profits depend substantially on the efforts of the franchisee. "Agency costs" are not significant.

Our example describes an unusual franchise arrangement because the franchisor is to run the operation and remit a portion of net revenues to Olde College, which is cast as a passive investor. Is there commonality in a franchise arrangement? Although courts that apply a "horizontal commonality" test might say there is not, this conclusion seems wrong. If many other franchisees depend on the franchisor's acumen and marketing, Olde College faces a "collective action" problem in supervising Tacos Unlimited's many franchise-related efforts that reach beyond its own relationship with the franchisor. Properly viewed, there is commonality and a security.

3

Materiality

Securities transactions are creatures of the Information Age. When securities markets lack information, investors shy from investing — and the markets wither. But when too much information is required and disclosure becomes too costly, businesses avoid securities financing — and again the markets dry up.

To avert both informational scarcity and overload, the federal securities laws delineate mandatory disclosure with the concept of "materiality." The items of information required in SEC filings reflect the agency's views on what investors should consider material. In addition to line-item disclosure, SEC rules require that filings contain "such further *material* information . . . as may be necessary to make the required statements . . . not misleading." Rule 408 (Securities Act filings); Rule 12b-20 (Exchange Act filings). Finally, the many antifraud standards in the securities laws hinge on a finding of materiality. For example, famous Rule 10b-5 prohibits any person from making "any untrue statement of a *material* fact" or from omitting "a *material* fact necessary in order to make the statements made . . . not misleading." See §9.1.1.

Ultimately, "materiality" balances (1) the costs of mandated disclosure such as the information-gathering burden, the risk of investor confusion, the possibility of frivolous litigation, or the revelation of competitive secrets, (2) the availability of the same information through unregulated channels, and (3) the effect disclosure has on other regulatory regimes (such as environmental compliance or corporate governance).

This chapter covers:

- the definition of "materiality" [§3.1]
- application of the materiality standard to various kinds of information, such as historical data, forward-looking information, and opinions [§3.2]
- materiality in the context of cautions and disclaimers [§3.3]

---

§3.1 DEFINITION OF MATERIALITY

How to deal with parties that claim informational defects in a transaction has long been an issue in the law of deceit. Although *caveat emptor* is no longer the rule, courts are suspicious of parties that seek to use informational defects to avoid a transaction. For this reason materiality is an element of fraud — to corroborate the party's claim that she relied on the alleged misinformation in entering into the transaction. Restatement (Second) of Torts, §538(2)(a). To allow a party to shift losses to the other party just because of some misinformation in their transaction would give an easy pretext to escape any bargain later found unfavorable. The materiality element promotes certainty by testing objectively whether misinformation is likely to have induced the transaction. It also reduces unnecessary disclosure in commercial transactions by insulating parties from liability if informational defects are insignificant.

§3.1.1 "Substantial Likelihood" Test

The definition of materiality under the federal securities laws, though judge-made, has assumed the status of statutory language:

> A fact is material if "there is a substantial likelihood a reasonable investor would consider it important" in making a securities-related decision.

TSC Industries, Inc. v. Northway, Inc., 426 U.S. 438 (1976). Federal courts recite this test whether the disclosure involves shareholder voting, securities trading, a tender offer, or itemized disclosure in securities filings.

The Supreme Court has explained that the words "substantial likelihood" connote that the information "probably" would have been important to a reasonable investor, not that its importance was "merely possible." *TSC Industries, Inc. v. Northway* (rejecting earlier dictum that information is material if it "might" be considered important by investors). Yet, the false or misleading information need not have actually caused reasonable investors to change their votes or investment decisions—it is not a "but for" test. Rather, it is enough that the misinformation "would have assumed actual significance" in the investors' deliberations.

§3.1.2 Who Is a Reasonable Investor?

The federal securities laws waver on who is the object of the disclosure regime: unsophisticated investors, sophisticated securities analysts, or both. In either event, courts do not assume an *irrational* investor, even though there is significant evidence that investors (both individual and institutional) suffer from a variety of behavioral biases: hindsight bias (overestimating the probability of future events), overoptimism (exaggerating their own expertise), availability bias (unduly relying on recent events in judging risks), endowment effects (overvaluing the status quo), and "groupthink" (following the crowd). Although irrational investors may need more protection than reasonable ones, securities regulation has mostly chosen not to rehabilitate investors' irrational tendencies.

Much of the disclosure in the forms filed with the SEC is intended only for professional securities analysts, who often use the information to confirm data they already know or to enrich their overall mix of information about a company. Some cases mirror this assumption and measure the materiality of information against what a professional analyst would consider price-sensitive. *Wielgos v. Commonwealth Edison Co.*, 892 F.2d 509 (7th Cir. 1989) (concluding that omitted information about regulatory proceedings that resulted in costly delays for a utility's nuclear power plants was not material since securities analysts already knew of the proceedings and their risks).

Nonetheless, courts sometimes describe the congressional intent to protect the "average small" unsophisticated investor. *Pinter v. Dahl*, 486 U.S. 622 (1988); *Feit v. Leasco Data Processing*, 332 F. Supp. 544 (E.D.N.Y. 1971). In nonmarket transactions or when the market is not informationally efficient, it makes sense to relax the standards of materiality and demand more information since investors cannot rely on a market price and presumably will want to know more. Some courts have used a subjective standard of materiality in securities transactions in close, nonmarket settings to accommodate the parties' greater (or sometimes lesser) informational needs.

Who decides the issue of materiality? Courts in federal securities cases often intone that materiality is a mixed question of law and fact. Nonetheless, judges often take it upon themselves to decide the issue as a matter of law, assuming the role of the illusive "reasonable investor."

§3.1.3 Relationship of Materiality and Duty to Disclose

Just because information is false or misleading does not make it material. And just because information is material does not mean it must be disclosed. Under the federal securities laws, materiality and disclosure duties are different (though related) concepts. Duty relates to *whether* and *when* information must be disclosed; materiality relates to *what* information must be disclosed.

This means that the first issue in any securities disclosure context is always one of duty. Unless there is a duty to disclose, the materiality of the information is only of theoretical interest. Disclosure duties under the federal securities laws arise in essentially two ways:

- **SEC filing obligations.** Companies offering securities to the public and reporting companies that have publicly traded securities must provide line-item disclosure in SEC filings, such as registration statements by public issuers and periodic reports by reporting companies. In addition, the SEC requires these companies to include in their filings any other *material* information necessary to make required line-item disclosure not misleading. Securities Act Rule 408; Exchange Act Rule 12b-20.
- **Duty of honesty.** The antifraud provisions of the federal securities laws require complete honesty about material information whenever one speaks in connection with certain securities transactions — namely, securities trading, voting, and tender offers for publicly traded shares. The duty of honesty includes duties (a) not to make false statements about material facts, (b) not to make misleading statements about material facts, (c) to correct materially false or misleading statements, and (d) to update certain statements that have become materially false or misleading. For those in a fiduciary relationship, the duty of honesty also precludes trading on material, nonpublic information.

If a company does not speak and has no specific duty to speak, the federal securities laws permit management to keep business information confidential — no matter how material.

§3.2 MATERIALITY — TYPES OF INFORMATION

Despite the prevalence of the "substantial likelihood" test, the SEC and courts take different approaches to materiality depending on the type of information.

§3.2.1 Historical Information

Most securities disclosure is of verifiable data about such matters as past financial results, completed business transactions, executive compensation and shareholdings, and so on. For such historical information, the "substantial likelihood" test frames the materiality enquiry.

When disclosure of past information coincides with abnormal changes in public stock prices, courts often assume that the information was material since it affected the actual behavior of securities traders. The converse, however, is not necessarily true. Sometimes the disclosure of information does not result in price changes because the market has already absorbed the information through various channels prior to formal disclosure.

In addition, courts have rejected arguments that materiality depends on particular quantitative benchmarks, such as a 5 percent change in a company's stock price. *Ganino v. Citizens Utilities Co.*, 228 F.3d 154 (2d Cir. 2000) (finding that storing 1995 income to bolster 1996 income to meet analysts' expectations could be material, even though "earnings management" involved only 1.7 percent of total annual revenues). The SEC staff has taken the position that in preparing and auditing financial statements even small discrepancies (such as a 2 percent overstatement of earnings) can be *qualitatively* material if the misstatement hides an earnings trend, a failure to meet analysts' expectations, regulatory noncompliance, a default under loan covenants, increased executive compensation, or illegality. SEC Staff Accounting Bulletin No. 99 (1999).

Off-Balance Sheet Disclosures

One of the practices contributing to the collapse of Enron in 2001 was the use of special-purpose entities to move financial obligations off the company's balance sheet and thus to hide the company's true financial precariousness. As mandated by the Sarbanes-Oxley Act, the SEC has adopted rules requiring reporting companies to disclose off-balance sheet arrangements and known contractual obligations (in tabular form) reasonably likely to have a material effect on the company's financial condition in the Management Discussion and Analysis (MD&A) of the company's disclosure documents. Sarbanes-Oxley §401; Item 303(c), Regulation S-K.

The rules are meant to ensure disclosure of arrangements under which a company incurs risks not fully transparent to investors — such as guarantees, contingent interests in transferred assets, obligations under certain derivative instruments, or obligations to outside entities providing financial or risk support to the company. Although some argued that the MD&A even before Sarbanes-Oxley required disclosure of contingencies that could materially affect a company's financial position, the revised rules specify the types of contingencies that must be disclosed. Curiously, the SEC test for whether disclosure is required is less stringent than that specified in Sarbanes-Oxley. The agency adopted a "reasonably likely" standard, even though Congress had mandated a more demanding "may" standard. Securities Act Rel. No. 8182 (2003).

Market Reaction

A common test for the materiality of company information is whether the market price of the company's stock changes on the date the information is first disclosed. A significant change in price (in the indicated direction) suggests materiality; no change (or a change in the opposite direction) suggests immateriality. Although there may be other events or other disclosures on the disclosure date that confound the inference that a price change shows the market viewed the information to be material, courts have increasingly relied on this measure of materiality — in the process assuming the informational efficiency of stock markets to absorb and react to the information (see §1.2).

Thus, if a company makes an SEC filing that discloses it has been using an aggressive accounting practice to recognize as revenues certain payments to third parties, the revenue recognition is not material if the company's market price did not change with the disclosure. See *In re Merck & Co. Securities Litigation*, 432 F.3d 261 (3d Cir. 2005) (pointing out that newspaper reporter, who later wrote story about the accounting practice, was able to estimate dollar impact of revenue recognition of copayments to third-party pharmacies from filed information). Although on the day the *Wall Street Journal* reported on the accounting practice, the company's stock price declined by more than 2 percent and the company was forced to cancel an IPO for the business unit engaged in the accounting practice, the court gauged materiality and the market reaction as of the date the information was first revealed. In effect, the court assumed the informational efficiency of the market despite the evidence that the market only responded to the accounting practice when the story had been broken by the *Wall Street Journal* and not when the company had first filed a registration statement for the IPO.

Statistical Significance

Sometimes companies are faced with adverse information about their products. If the adverse events are statistically significant — more than just random chance — action by the company may be warranted or even required. But when adverse reports are not statistically significant, is the information immaterial under the federal securities laws? In *Matrixx Initiatives, Inc. v. Siracusano*, 563 U.S. _____ (2011), the Supreme Court held that companies cannot rely on statistical significance in deciding whether to disclose to investors. In the case, a pharmaceutical company that sold a popular cold remedy began to receive reports that one of the remedy's active ingredients caused users to lose their sense of smell. When the adverse reports came out, the company's stock price fell significantly, and investors sued. The company argued that the adverse reactions were not "statistically significant" from a medical standpoint, and thus not "material" from a securities standpoint. In a unanimous decision, the Court rejected the argument and held that the adverse reports might be important to investors, though not to medical researchers or even drug regulators. Thus, company statements that the company "was poised for growth" may have been materially misleading, a conclusion supported by the sharp drop in the company's stock price on news the FDA was beginning an investigation into the adverse reports and after a morning show reported how some users of the company's cold remedy had lost their sense of smell.

§3.2.2 Speculative Information

When information is relevant because it portends a future event — such as negotiations that could lead to a merger or exploratory drilling that might lead to a mining bonanza — courts have applied a special version of the "substantial likelihood" test.

> [M]ateriality "will depend on balancing of both the indicated probability that the event will occur and the anticipated magnitude of the event in light of the totality of the company activity."

Basic, Inc. v. Levinson, 485 U.S. 224 (1988), quoting *SEC v. Texas Gulf Sulphur Co.*, 401 F.2d 833 (2d Cir. 1968) (Friendly, J.). This "probability-magnitude" test measures the current value of information that bears on a future event by measuring the financial significance of the event, discounted by the chances of it actually happening. Information about activities that suggest an event with significant price ramifications might happen, even though the probability of the event is low, may be material. That is, information is material if its expected value (discounted by its uncertainty) indicates it would affect investor behavior.

The fluid "probability-magnitude" test replaces an earlier "bright line" test used by some lower courts in deciding the materiality of merger negotiations, which were deemed material only when the parties had agreed on the price and structure of the transaction. *Greenfield v. Heublein, Inc.*, 742 F.2d 751 (3d Cir. 1984). The Supreme Court rejected this "agreement-in-principle" test since denying investors information about a possible merger assumed investors could not discount the uncertainties of merger negotiations. This does not mean, however, that sensitive merger negotiations (even if material) need be disclosed. Companies in merger negotiations may remain silent so long as they do not release false or misleading information.

Puffery

One kind of speculative information is an overstatement of present circumstances, based on a hope that events will turn out well. Federal courts have been reluctant to treat optimistic statements as misleading, referring to the common law notion that puffery is not actionable. For example, when a company put itself up for sale and represented that the auction process was going smoothly, its optimism was not actionable since "*everyone* knows that someone trying to sell something is going to . . . talk on the bright side." *Eisenstadt v. Centel Corp.*, 113 F.3d 738 (7th Cir. 1997).

§3.2.3 "Soft Information"

Sometimes information — such as projections, estimates, or opinions — reflects a look into the future. This "soft information" is at once the most valuable and the most perilous for investors. On the one hand, reliable predictions by management of a company's future are highly relevant to investors who value securities by calculating the present value of future cash flows. In fact, studies show that company managers generally predict future cash flows better than even sophisticated securities analysts outside the firm. On the other hand, managers have great incentives to mold their predictions. Favorable estimates of earnings can buoy stock prices and save careers; unfavorable opinions about future competition can sink unwanted merger bids. Predictions are fraught with risk since they cannot be verified when made and almost always turn out wrong.

Voluntary Disclosure of Forward-Looking Information

The SEC once took a rigid stance against the disclosure of favorable soft information. The agency asserted that disclosure should be limited to verifiable historical information. Pressured by the investment community and chastised by contrary court opinions, the SEC gradually came to the view that forward-looking statements are not necessarily misleading. Since 1978, SEC safe harbor rules *permit* forward-looking information in SEC filings unless it is shown the statement was made "without reasonable basis" or disclosed "other than in good faith." Rule 175 (Securities Act); Rule 3b-6 (Exchange Act). What is a "reasonable basis" for forward-looking information? The SEC does not require that it be stated, though the agency has said that there may be circumstances when it would be misleading not to include the basis for a projection or estimate.

3. Materiality

This administrative safe harbor focuses on what management knows or should know when it looks to the future—a subjective test. The federal courts and Congress have created safe harbors for forward-looking statements that focus on what disclaimers and cautions accompany these statements to investors—an objective test. See §3.3.2 below.

Mandatory Disclosure of Forward-Looking Information

Since 1989, the SEC has *required* the presentation of soft information in the management discussion and analysis (MD&A) of certain SEC filings, such as annual reports and prospectuses. The MD&A must describe trends and uncertainties that are "reasonably likely to result" in material changes to the company's financial position. Item 303, Regulation S-K. The idea is to present a picture of the company's prospects through the eyes of management, particularly when historical data is not a good indicator of future results. MD&A Interpretive Release, Exchange Act Rel. No. 26,831 (1989). In the wake of the 2000s accounting scandals, the SEC has also made clear that the MD&A should not only mention known trends and risks, but also analyze their potential effects on the company using tables and numbers—"what keeps management up at night." The MD&A should also describe the quality and potential variability of earnings, so investors can determine whether past performance is indicative of future performance. MD&A Guidance, Securities Act Rel. No. 8350 (2003).

Responding to management's use of the MD&A to describe financial results through a "rose-colored" lens, the SEC has sought to constrain management's creative optimism. To prevent a company from modifying its accounting methods to bolster results, the SEC requires that the MD&A include (and update) information on the adoption of revised accounting policies and on accounting estimates underlying financial statements. Securities Act Rel. No. 8098 (2002). In the same vein, SEC rules required by Sarbanes-Oxley limit the ability of management to present "pro forma" accounting—that is, non-GAAP financial information based on non-factual assumptions—or the reporting of earnings before interest, taxes, depreciation and amortization (EBITDA). Regulation G, Securities Act Rel. No. 8176 (2003). Under Regulation G, a company that reports non-GAAP results must compare (and reconcile) them to results calculated using GAAP. Thus, a pro forma report that showed earnings without taking into account lost revenues because of a hurricane would have to compare and reconcile them to actual storm-affected earnings.

Despite the SEC's acceptance of management estimates, courts have been wary of imposing liability for omitted "soft information," even when such information as internal appraisals or financial projections would seem highly material. See *Oran v. Stafford*, 226 F.3d 275 (3rd Cir. 2000) (concluding that even though medical test data having a potential effect on future earnings was required in MD&A, it was not necessarily material in Rule 10b-5 class action). Courts have not required forward-looking information when it is unreliable, uncertain or based on speculative assumptions. Although the Supreme Court in *Basic v. Levinson* decried this paternalism and assumed investors would be able to discount uncertain future-looking information, the judicial reluctance to mandate "soft information" may reflect deeper concerns about the competitive costs of managers revealing their business secrets, as well as the risks of unwarranted liability such disclosure would engender.

Actionability of Forward-Looking Statements

For a long time, the common law took the view that opinions or predictions (no matter how baseless or malevolent) could not be material since a reasonably skeptical party should attach no importance to the other party's opinions.

In a departure from the common law, the SEC and federal courts have treated opinions, forecasts, projections, and even "general expressions of optimism" as actionable under the federal securities laws. When one party has an informational advantage, a forward-looking statement may be relevant to the other party given the other party's special credibility or expertise. Can such a statement be false? A forward-looking statement carries a number of testable factual assertions: the speaker genuinely holds her opinion; there exists a reasonable basis for her opinion; there is nothing that contradicts the opinion. Forward-looking statements can be seen as false if one of these implicit assertions is false.

The Supreme Court, however, has limited the actionability of statements of motives. *Virginia Bankshares, Inc. v. Sandberg*, 501 U.S. 1083 (1991). In the case, minority shareholders challenged the disclosure in a proxy statement of a board's motives in approving a squeeze-out merger. Specifically, the board had stated: "The Plan of Merger has been approved by the Board of Directors because it provides an opportunity for the Bank's public shareholders to achieve a high value for their shares." The shareholders alleged the directors did not believe this statement and actually approved the merger for a different reason—to protect their jobs. The Court readily found that the board's beliefs about the merger were highly relevant to shareholders, given the directors' expertise and their corporate duties to act in the shareholders' interest. The Court, however, held that disbelief or undisclosed motives could not alone make a statement misleading, because of the nebulous and manipulable nature of the factual inquiry into motives. Instead, the Court held the board must have both misstated its beliefs *and* misled about the "subject matter" of its opinion—in the case, the merger price for the shares.

Similarly, securities fraud actions based on failed predictions face high hurdles — given that no prediction has a 100 percent probability of being correct. See *City of Lavonia ERS v. Boeing Co.*, 711 F.3d 754 (7th Cir. 2013) (J. Posner) (cautioning against "securities fraud by hindsight"). Nonetheless, failure to disclose known negative trends — such as that declines in the real estate markets were likely to affect the value of mortgage-backed securities guaranteed by a company — can be actionable. See *Litwin v. Blackstone Group, L.P.*, 634 F.3d 706 (2d Cir. 2011) (finding actionable under §11 and §12(a)(2) of the Securities Act failure of investment fund to disclose in its MD&A "known" negative trends in real estate markets, even though affecting only 3.9 percent of fund revenues, where it was "reasonably likely" such trends would adversely affect fund's future financial results).

§3.2.4 Information About Management Integrity

For shareholders, management's experience and integrity are often critical to their investment. SEC line-item disclosure rules require information about management incentives (compensation, conflict-of-interest transactions, loans), management integrity (lawsuits involving personal insolvency, criminal convictions, stock fraud), and management commitment to the company (stock ownership, stock pledges as security for personal loans). Subpart 400, Regulation S-K.

The SEC has long asserted the materiality of information that bears on management integrity, as when the agency stopped a securities offering for not disclosing serious defalcations and suspicious stock pledges of the company's controlling shareholder. *In re Franchard*, 42 S.E.C. 163 (1964). Yet, in the same case, the SEC refused to require disclosure of the board's lax monitoring of the defalcating shareholder. The SEC concluded that disclosure of how the board carried out its state-mandated oversight duties was not a matter for federal securities law.

Disclosure of Obedience to Non-Securities Norms

In general, federal securities law mandates disclosure of the company's compliance with other nonsecurities norms only if noncompliance is clear and its ramifications have financial significance — a heightened test of materiality. See *SEC v. Joseph Schlitz Brewing Co.*, 452 F. Supp. 852 (E.D. Wisc. 1978) (holding that $3 million of kickbacks to beer retailers, in violation of liquor laws, was material since such kickbacks went to integrity of company's management and jeopardized liquor licenses of customers upon which company's business depended). Thus, the SEC generally does not require the disclosure of executives' criminal behavior unless it has resulted in an indictment or conviction in the last five years. Item 401, Regulation S-K; *United States v. Mathews*, 787 F.2d 38 (2d Cir. 1986) (finding criminal behavior not to be material since securities law should not impose penalties on corporate officer for failing to predict whether he will be indicted).

Likewise, courts have been reluctant to require disclosure of fiduciary breaches, unless management misfeasance is clear. *Golub v. PPD Corp.*, 576 F.2d 759 (8th Cir. 1978) (holding that failure to disclose improper board motives in sale of assets raised state fiduciary claim that should have been pursued in state court). Nonetheless, the SEC has taken the view that disclosure duties are heightened when management self-dealing is a possibility. Thus, company officers and directors must ensure proper disclosure about benefits in a retiring CEO's compensation package, even though they did not differ from the benefits that the CEO received before retirement. *In re W.R. Grace & Co.* (SEC 1997) (holding that, even though counsel had prepared the disclosure, successor CEO and outside director were subject to disciplinary proceeding since former CEO had substantial influence over company).

A related question is whether a company can withhold material information that it has a duty to disclose where the information incriminates company executives. Generally, courts have held that securities disclosure obligations are not trumped by the Fifth Amendment privilege against self-incrimination. *SEC v. Fehn*, 97 F.3d 1276 (9th Cir. 1986) (concluding that mandatory securities disclosure is not aimed at undermining the privilege since it does not target groups inherently suspect of criminal activities). Nonetheless, the SEC disclosure rules take the position that *unadjudicated* wrongdoing is not material, unless the issuer proclaims its compliance with the law or the wrongdoing involves self-dealing by company executives. Item 401, Regulation S-K.

Whether this federal deference to other regulatory schemes that address corporate wrongdoing survives the Sarbanes-Oxley Act of 2002 may be in doubt. Certainly, it would seem odd that public companies must have codes of ethics and internal controls, and whistle-blowers are protected from reprisals and securities lawyers must internally report fiduciary breaches, yet the company need not tell shareholders of uncorrected malfeasance by company insiders.

Codes of Ethics

As mandated by the Sarbanes-Oxley Act, the SEC requires that every public company (domestic and foreign) disclose whether it has a code of ethics covering its principal executive and financial officers. The disclosure requirement effectively compels such a code, which must contain standards for promoting honest and ethical conduct — including handling of conflicts between personal and professional relationships, and compliance with applicable laws. Expanding on the Sarbanes-Oxley mandate, the SEC rules also anticipate that an ethics code will address the reporting and disciplining of code violations. Any waiver of the company's ethics code, a disturbing aspect of the self-dealing discovered at Enron, must now be reported promptly on Form 8-K.

While the SEC only mandates disclosure of an ethics code, the NYSE and NASDAQ listing rules require that all listed companies actually have one and specify its contents. See §8.3.4. The code required by the NYSE goes beyond that envisioned under the SEC rules, requiring standards that address corporate opportunities, confidentiality, protection of corporate assets, and insider trading. The code required by NASDAQ simply tracks the one described in the SEC rules.

§3.2.5 Social/Environmental Disclosure

Generally, the disclosure policy of the federal securities laws focuses on the financial relevance of business information to investors, not its broader social and environmental impact on the public. In the 1970s the SEC rebuffed attempts to broaden its disclosure policies to cover business activities affecting the environment and civil rights. More recently, however, the SEC has shown greater interest in companies disclosing business risks (and opportunities) presented by social/environmental issues, particularly climate change. See Guidance on Climate Change Disclosure, Securities Act Rel. No. 9106 (2010) (explaining that existing disclosure requirements, such as management's discussion of future contingencies, may compel companies to disclose material information about business impact of climate change laws, impact of international accords on climate change, actual or indirect consequences of climate change trends (such as decreased demand for carbon-intensive products or higher demand for lower-emission products), and actual and potential physical impacts of environmental changes to company's business).

The tension between financial and social/environmental disclosure arose in the 1970s when the National Resources Defense Council asked the SEC to amend its rules to require greater environmental and civil rights disclosure. The NRDC argued that National Environmental Policy Act of 1969 (NEPA) requires every federal agency to interpret and administer federal laws "in accordance with" NEPA policies. In response, the SEC adopted a financial perspective in carrying out its NEPA responsibilities. Reporting companies must disclose *pending* environmental proceedings (private or public) that involve potential damages, penalties, and litigation costs of more than 10 percent of current assets. Instruction 5 to Item 103,

Reg. S-K ($100,000 if a government proceeding). *Potential* environmental liability need not be disclosed, nor need the company disclose actual or potential harm to the environment. That is, the SEC viewed its charge under the federal securities laws to be investor protection, not environmental protection. Securities Act Rel. No. 5627 (1975).

The SEC's view that disclosure policy, including that on environmental matters, should be limited to investor's financial interests has been criticized. Critics point out that investors are not entirely motivated by financial returns and that managers tend to minimize environmental risks and harm — both suggesting the value of a more active SEC approach on environmental disclosure. Some scholars point out that the §14(a) of the Exchange Act (supported by its legislative history) authorizes the SEC to expand proxy disclosure beyond investor protection to encompass "the public interest." Thus, the SEC could require expanded disclosure of management policies with respect to social and environmental issues. See Cynthia A. Williams, *The Securities and Exchange Commission and Corporate Social Transparency*, 112 Harv. L. Rev. 1197 (1999). In addition, many investors (both individual and institutional) have increasingly recognized that environmental and social concerns affect both the company's financial prospects and investor choice.

In a nod to the growing relevance to investors of environmental concerns, the SEC issued interpretive guidance to reporting companies on disclosures regarding climate change. Guidance on Climate Change Disclosure, Securities Act Rel. No. 9106 (2010) (pointing out that the insurance industry lists climate change as the number one risk facing the industry). While not taking a stance on the climate change debate, the SEC pointed out that under existing disclosure requirements (such as the MD&A discussion of future contingencies) companies may have to disclose material information about (1) the impact on the company's business of existing (and even pending) climate change laws; (2) the impact of international accords on climate change; (3) the actual or indirect consequences of climate change trends (such as decreased demand for carbon-intensive products or higher demand for lower-emission products); and (4) actual and potential physical impacts of environmental changes to the company's business. As some have pointed out, "what gets measured gets managed."

§3.2.6 Materiality in Different Contexts

The following table lays out the various kinds of securities-related information whose materiality may be at issue:

3. Materiality

Type of disclosure	Test	Issues
Historical facts	*TSC v. Northway* (U.S. 1976): substantial likelihood that reasonable investor would consider such facts important	• Who is reasonable investor? • How important is information to company's finances? • Did information, when revealed, affect stock price?
Speculative information	*Basic v. Levinson* (U.S. 1988): current information bears on probability and magnitude of future event	• How does information affect probability of event? • What is magnitude (price) effect? • How far along are merger talks?
Soft information (forward-looking projections, opinions)	*Virginia Bankshares v. Sandberg* (U.S. 1991): opinions actionable only if not believed and mislead about subject matter	• Is forward-looking statement voluntary or mandatory? • Was there basis for opinion or prediction? • Is there safe harbor (see below)?
Information on management integrity	*In re Franchard* (SEC 1964): management conflicts of interest highly material, though not failures in board oversight	• Does information reveal management conflict of interest? • Is noncompliance with other laws clear (criminal, state fiduciary)?
Social/ environmental information	*Guidance on Climate Change Disclosure* (SEC 2010): impact of existing or anticipated laws, and physical impacts, may be material	• Do social/environmental policies affect company's business? • Are environmental compliance proceedings pending or potential? • Is company's business potentially affected by climate change?

§3.3 MATERIALITY IN CONTEXT: "TOTAL MIX" OF INFORMATION

Disclosure is contextual. Information revealed in one part of a disclosure document may be tempered or disclaimed in another part. Or an important piece of information omitted from an SEC filing may already be widely known by investors.

§3.3.1 "Total Mix" Test

In defining materiality, the Supreme Court recognized the contextual nature of securities disclosure:

> [T]here must be a substantial likelihood that the disclosure of the omitted fact would have been viewed by the reasonable investor as having significantly altered the "total mix" of information made available.

TSC Industries, Inc. v. Northway, Inc., 426 U.S. 438 (1976). That is, an omission is not material (even if the information is important to investors) if reasonable investors already know or can infer the omitted information from other disclosure. For example, in *Northway* a TSC shareholder complained that the proxy statement for a sale-liquidation of the company had failed to disclose that National (the buyer of the assets) controlled the TSC board. The Court held the omission to be immaterial because the proxy statement disclosed that National owned 34 percent of TSC's stock and had nominated five of the ten directors.

"Total Mix" in an Efficient Market

Securities investors do not depend exclusively on mandatory disclosure. In fact, as predicted by the Efficient Capital Market Hypothesis (see §1.2), SEC filings by widely followed companies often merely confirm information that is known to securities analysts and already impounded in market prices.

Thus, omitted information that is already known to the market is not actionable, even if material. Sometimes courts assume the market is informed to avoid analyzing whether the information is material or inquiring into management's integrity. For example, when a grocery chain's alleged labor violations were widely reported in the press, the court assumed that the market was aware of them, even though the information came from the company's labor union and was denied by the company. *Longman v. Food Lion, Inc.*, 197 F.3d 675 (4th Cir. 1999).

It is even possible that false or misleading disclosure on important company matters is not material if professional securities traders who set the market price know the disclosure to be wrong. The strongest statement of this "truth on the market" doctrine comes from Judge Easterbrook. *Wielgos v. Commonwealth Edison Co.*, 892 F.2d 509 (7th Cir. 1989). The court held that optimistic cost estimates for a utility's nuclear power plants, though lacking a reasonable basis when the company issued new securities, were not materially misleading because professional securities analysts "surely deduced what was afoot" and knew to discount management's consistently biased optimism. In short, managers can lie if the market knows it's dealing with liars.

"Buried Facts" Doctrine

Not only may too little disclosure be harmless, but too much information may be unfairly misleading. Under the "buried facts" doctrine, disclosure can be misleading if it contains material information that is inaccessible or difficult to assemble. *Kohn v. American Metal Climax, Inc.*, 322 F. Supp. 1331 (E.D. Pa. 1970) (finding proxy statement to be materially misleading for prominently disclosing an investment adviser's favorable opinion, but burying in an appendix that the adviser had failed to evaluate the firm's assets).

On the other hand, if a company discloses both accurate and inaccurate information in the same document, the court will consider whether the document as a whole is misleading. Accurate specific disclosures can "cure" inaccurate general disclosures. See *DeMaria v. Andersen*, 318 F.3d 170 (2d Cir. 2003) (concluding inaccurate graphs that summarize revenues are cured by accurate financial tables). Nonetheless, truth does not neutralize falsity if the truth is hidden or discernible only by sophisticated investors.

§3.3.2 Safe Harbors for Forward-Looking Statements

Caveats and warnings are often part of the "total mix" of information that investors receive. Federal courts have recognized that cautioning statements that identify risks temper forward-looking statements, sometimes rendering them immaterial. Congress has followed suit by codifying this view in a statutory safe harbor.

"Bespeaks Caution" Doctrine

According to the judicially created "bespeaks caution" doctrine, cautionary disclosure (beyond boilerplate warnings) can negate the materiality of, or reliance on, an unduly optimistic prediction. *Luce v. Edelstein*, 802 F.2d 49, 56 (2d Cir. 1986) (dismissing claim of unrealized projections of cash and tax benefits because offering memorandum warned that the projections were "necessarily speculative" and not sure to be realized). The Supreme Court has implicitly accepted the doctrine, stating that a misleading statement can be discredited by an accompanying true statement such that "the risk of real deception drops to nil." *Virginia Bankshares v. Sandberg*, 501 U.S. 1083 (1991).

A prominent and illustrative case applying the "bespeaks caution" doctrine arose from a debt offering for an Atlantic City casino developed by Donald Trump. *Kaufman v. Trump's Castle Funding*, 7 F.3d 357 (3d Cir. 1993). Hopeful statements in a prospectus that operations "will be sufficient to cover all of [the issuer's] debt service" were, in the court's estimation, rendered immaterial by extensive cautionary statements elsewhere in the prospectus. The court pointed to numerous prospectus disclosures of the circumstances that could adversely affect the issuer's ability to pay interest, which alerted investors to the risks of the venture.

Does this mean that a company can overtly mislead about the future, so long as it accompanies its misstatements with cautionary language? Some courts have said no, concluding that cautionary language cannot be "meaningful" if management had actual knowledge that a prediction was false or misleading. See *Freeland v. Iridium World Communications*, 545 F. Supp. 2d 59 (D.D.C. 2008).

PSLRA Safe Harbor

In 1995, Congress passed the Private Securities Litigation Reform Act to reconcile the growing market demand for forward-looking information and the ease with which lawsuits (particularly class actions) are filed when projections fizzle. To encourage issuers to disclose forward-looking information, whether voluntary or not, the PSLRA immunizes public companies and their executives from civil liability (but not administrative liability) for forward-looking statements that comply with the Act's safe harbor provisions. Securities Act §27A; Exchange Act §21E.

The PSLRA contains three separate safe harbors. Satisfying any one of them precludes a shareholder lawsuit based on written forward-looking statements that later turn out to be wrong.

No actual knowledge	The plaintiff fails to prove the defendant had actual knowledge that the forward-looking statement was false. This safe harbor applies to oral or written forward-looking statements and immunizes reckless or negligent forward-looking statements from private liability.
Immateriality	The forward-looking statement was immaterial. This safe harbor focuses attention on whether the forward-looking statement is too "soft" to be material and

3. Materiality

opens the door to the judicial "bespeaks caution" doctrine as a separate basis for immunity.

Cautionary statements

The forward-looking statement "is identified as a forward-looking statement and is accompanied by meaningful cautionary statements identifying important factors that could cause actual results to differ materially from those projected in the forward-looking statement." This safe harbor provides the clearest protection because it calls for the dismissal of a lawsuit without an inquiry into knowledge or materiality, thus avoiding costly discovery and further litigation. Although the PSLRA does not define the important terms "accompanied," "meaningful," or "important factors," the Act's legislative history indicates that boilerplate cautions are not enough. Instead, the cautionary statements must "convey substantive information about factors that realistically could cause results to differ materially from those projected in the forward-looking statement" and must be "relevant to the projection."

Much like the SEC safe harbor (see §3.2.3), the PSLRA defines forward-looking statements to include: (1) projections of revenues and other financial items; (2) plans and objectives for future operations; (3) statements of future economic performance, including MD&A statements of financial condition and results of operation; and (4) assumptions underlying these statements. In addition, forward-looking oral statements are covered by the safe harbor for "cautionary statements" if the speaker identifies a readily available written document containing factors that could cause actual results to materially differ. See *FindWhat Investor Group v. FindWhat Corp.*, 658 F.3d 1282 (11th Cir. 2011) (finding that misstatements about company's "click rates" and revenues were not forward looking and thus not protected by PSLRA safe harbor).

The PSLRA's safe harbor applies only to SEC reporting *corporations* (not partnerships or limited liability companies) and excludes from its coverage recent violators of federal securities antifraud provisions, investment companies, and penny stock issuers. Significantly, the statutory safe harbors do not apply to initial public offerings, tender offers, going private transactions, beneficial ownership reports under §13(d), or offerings by blank check companies.

Courts have reacted skeptically toward the PSLRA safe harbor for forward-looking statements. On the question of whether a statement is "forward looking," courts have been reluctant to apply the safe harbor to statements that include present or historical facts, and have required that the statement have a clear predictive quality. Courts have been exacting on properly identifying forward-looking statements (such as an explanation that words like "believe" or "anticipate" are forward looking) and properly accompanying them with cautionary language (cautionary statements in prior SEC filings are insufficient). Whether the cautionary language is meaningful, courts have been inconsistent — with some demanding specificity and others accepting general warnings. In addition, perhaps inconsistent with the text of the PSLRA, courts have concluded that forward-looking statements made with actual knowledge of their falsity can be actionable, even if properly identified and accompanied by cautionary language. See *Asher v. Baxter Int'l, Inc.*, 377 F.3d 727 (7th Cir. 2004) (Easterbrook, J.) (concluding that PSLRA does not require disclosure of assumptions or "most useful caution," but only cautions about "important" risks known to company management; remanding for factual inquiry into whether management was aware of internal projections and product setbacks that contradicted overly-optimistic projections of earnings growth). Although the three PSLRA safe harbors — for immaterial statements, forward-looking statements, and statements made without actual knowledge — are disjunctive, some courts have treated them as conjunctive.

Nonetheless, some courts have taken an expansive view of the PSLRA safe harbor. For example, the Eleventh Circuit held that a corporate press release stating "challenges . . . are now behind us," while describing the ongoing risks of the company's generic drug business, was a forward-looking statement and within the safe harbor. *Harris v. IVAX Corp.*, 82 F.3d 799 (11th Cir. 1999). The court reached this result even though losses turned out to be four times greater than predicted, and the company ended up writing off $104 million of goodwill. When a statement's veracity can only be ascertained with time and investors are led to understand the volatility of the business, the court held the statement falls within the statutory definition and the issuer meets its "burden to warn under the statute."

Comparison of Safe Harbors for Forward-Looking Statements

Although the SEC, the courts, and Congress have each attempted to immunize forward-looking statements from liability, their coverage and conditions vary:

Safe harbor	Coverage	Conditions
SEC (Rules 175 and 3b-6)	Forward-looking statement by issuer in SEC filings	Statement not fraudulent, unless shown to be without reasonable basis or other than in good faith (not necessary to identify risk factors)

3. Materiality

Safe harbor	Coverage	Conditions
Judicial ("bespeaks caution")	Forward-looking statement by any person, whether or not in SEC filing	Statement not material (or presume no reliance), if statement cautions and generally describes possible risk factors
Statutory (PSLRA "cautionary language")	Forward-looking statement by issuer (subject to exceptions) in specified SEC filings	No private liability, if statement identified as forward-looking and accompanied by meaningful cautionary language that identifies risk factors

As you can see, the judicial "bespeaks caution" doctrine is broader than the SEC and statutory safe harbors. The doctrine covers issuers and nonissuers and applies whether or not the forward-looking statements are in writing or filed with the SEC. In addition, the judicial and statutory safe harbors focus on the objective disclosures made by the issuer (or those acting on its behalf) rather than on management's subjective intent under the SEC's "reasonable basis" and "good faith" tests. The judicial and statutory safe harbors thus make it easier to seek dismissal of suits on the pleadings. Nonetheless, judicial standards have not been uniform. Some courts have conditioned judicial immunity on the existence of "honestly held beliefs," exposing issuers to litigation and discovery on their state of mind.

Examples

1. Basic and Combustion are public corporations listed on the NYSE. One day, their CEOs meet over breakfast to discuss a strategic alliance, and they agree in principle to work toward a business combination. Their boards agree to an exchange of confidential information. There are meetings among the companies' top executives, but they have not agreed on a price or whether the combination will be structured as a merger, tender offer, or sale of assets. (This scenario, though based on the facts of *Basic, Inc. v. Levinson*, 485 U.S. 224 (1988), is often hypothetical; many of the specific examples did not actually occur.)

   Under these circumstances, does Basic have a duty to disclose the current negotiations
   a. under the federal securities law?
   b. under state corporate codes?
   c. under stock exchange or securities industry rules?

2. Assuming the agreement in principle reached by the companies' CEOs is material, is it fraudulent for Basic to withhold this information from its shareholders

3. Materiality

    a. under Rule 10b-5 of the Exchange Act?
    b. under state corporate law?

3. Basic's stock price fluctuates on rumors of a pending combination, even though there is no agreement on price or structure. The CEO of Basic is planning to give a newspaper interview. To throw off other potential bidders, she will tell the reporter there are no pending merger negotiations.

    a. Is it relevant whether the companies' negotiations are material?
    b. Is the agreement in principle material?
    c. Throwing off potential bidders would be consistent with her fiduciary duties. Can the CEO tell a white lie — that is, one that the company's shareholders might prefer she tell?
    d. What should the CEO say during the interview?

4. The newspaper interview falls through. Must Basic nonetheless disclose the merger discussions in light of the following:

    a. One year ago, before the CEOs' agreement in principle, Basic had issued a press release (truthful at the time) that said: "Basic is not engaged in any merger negotiations." Assuming the agreement in principle is material, must Basic now update this earlier press release?
    b. Basic plans to offer early retirement to some midlevel executives who do not know about the pending negotiations. Can the company exercise its option to buy back their stock without disclosing the negotiations?
    c. The *Wall Street Journal* has published a story based on market rumors that Combustion will buy Basic for $50 per share. The rumors are not true. Must Basic correct the false story?

5. Basic issues a press release: "The Company's management cannot explain recent price fluctuations and high trading volume in Basic stock." Technically, the release is true since management does not know who leaked the secret negotiations or how the market seems to be aware of them.

    a. Has Basic violated a disclosure duty?
    b. When Basic issues the press release, stock prices actually continue to climb compared to the market. Does this indicate the press release was immaterial?
    c. Many sophisticated analysts who read the press release note that it did not deny there were merger negotiations, and they view the release as a cagey statement about company leaks. Some unsophisticated investors who hear of the press release, however, assume that merger negotiations are off. For purposes of materiality, who is the "reasonable investor"?

    d. Is it relevant to determining the materiality of the press release's implicit denial of merger negotiations that Basic's stock price did not move on the day of the release?

6. The parties agree to terms and announce a cash-for-stock merger. Combustion will buy Basic stock in the merger for $42 a share. Basic and Combustion solicit proxies from their shareholders to approve the merger, and Basic's proxy materials state: "The Company's board approved the merger because the timing is right and, in the board's opinion, the price is fair to the shareholders."

    a. Some of Basic's directors actually approved the merger because they wanted a quick sale of their significant stock holdings. Are their real motives for approving the merger material?

    b. The board offered no supporting data for its opinion that the price is fair, besides historical financial data of the company's results. Is this a material omission?

    c. The proxy statement explains prominently that there was no independent valuation of Basic, and the $42 price was reached through negotiations of the two companies. Does this render immaterial the board's opinion that the price was fair?

    d. The proxy statement fails to disclose that the Basic-Combustion merger may violate antitrust laws and could result in the merger being voided in the future. There are no pending antitrust enforcement proceedings. Is this omission material?

7. The Basic-Combustion merger closes. The new firm, with plans to revamp its manufacturing operations, undertakes a public offering. Combustion's management is considering the inclusion of the following statement in its Form S-3 prospectus (see §4.2.2) to be filed in connection with the offering:

> The Company has developed a new refractory process, designed to replace current manufacturing processes. Management anticipates significant cost savings from energy and other efficiencies resulting from the new process. Cost savings, if they occur, will begin in the Company's next fiscal year.

The statement, however, does not specify how projected cost savings would affect cash flows or earnings.

    a. Must management disclose this forward-looking information about its new refractory process? If so, is the statement adequate?

    b. After a year, cost savings from the new process are minimal — energy prices do not climb as much as management had been anticipated. Are the projections actionable?

c. The new refractory process is actually experimental and probably unworkable. Management knew that its statement about "significant cost savings" was wishful. Are the projections now actionable?

d. During the offering, Combustion's CEO states at a trade conference, "We originally thought our new refractory process would reduce manufacturing costs by 25 percent. In fact, we expect more!" When savings fail to materialize, is Combustion liable for the CEO's exuberance?

e. When Combustion realizes that the savings will not materialize, must it update its disclosures?

Explanations

1. a. No. Even if the agreement in principle is material, there is no general affirmative duty under the federal securities laws to disclose material information. Disclosure is required only if mandated by statute, SEC rule or a specific affirmative disclosure duty.

None of the SEC forms that mandate disclosure by reporting companies under the Securities Exchange Act of 1934 (§8.3.2) requires disclosure of pending merger discussions. Form 8-K (which requires current reports of important events) mandates disclosure of merger transactions only once consummated. The requirement that annual and quarterly reports contain management discussion of "known uncertainties" is tempered by the SEC's position that reporting companies need not disclose otherwise-secret merger negotiations if management thinks disclosure would jeopardize the transaction. MD&A Interpretive Release, Exchange Act Rel. No. 26,831 (1989).

Although SEC rules require extensive disclosure of merger negotiations in connection with corporate takeovers, none applies here. Form 14D-1 requires a tender offeror to disclose any negotiations it has had with the target in the last three years. See §8.5.2. If a company is tendering for its own shares, Rule 13e-3 requires that it disclose any merger negotiations it has conducted with management.

b. No. State corporate codes impose limited notice requirements when a company holds a shareholders' meeting. Model Business Corp. Act §7.05 (notice for special meeting must describe purpose). In addition, some state statutes require management to prepare and mail to shareholders "annual financial statements." Model Business Corp. Act §16.20. Meaningful disclosure duties arise from management's fiduciary duties. Some state courts have inferred a duty of "complete candor" in management communications connected with shareholder voting or share tenders. *Lynch v. Vickers Energy Corp.*,

3. Materiality

383 A.2d 278 (Del. 1977). In addition, management has a duty to deal with shareholders honestly, even in the absence of a request for shareholder action. *Malone v. Brincat*, 722 A.2d 5 (Del. 1998).

c. No. The listing rules of the major stock exchanges, as well as the NASD, expect that traded companies will make timely public disclosure of material developments as they occur. There is a gaping exception, however, whenever there is a proper business reason for withholding the information. See NYSE Listed Company Manual 202.06.

2. a. Not necessarily. Rule 10b-5 prohibits fraud but does not compel disclosure. As the Supreme Court has made clear in the context of insider trading, silence is not actionable under Rule 10b-5 unless there is a duty to speak. *Chiarella v. United States*, 445 U.S. 222 (1980) (see §10.2.1).

   Lower courts have inferred corporate disclosure duties under Rule 10b-5 in limited situations: (1) the company trades in its own securities; (2) the company becomes aware of errors in prior disclosure, provided it is still current in the market; or (3) the company learns that insiders are trading on the basis of material nonpublic information. Otherwise, corporate silence is not fraudulent.

   b. No. Under the business judgment rule, corporate managers have almost unfettered discretion to disseminate or withhold information as they choose. *Financial Indus. Fund v. McDonnell Corp.*, 474 F.2d 514, 518 (10th Cir. 1973) (holding that company's timing of disclosure of earnings decline was matter of discretion protected under business judgment rule). Although some federal securities cases imply that management may have disclosure duties with respect to highly material information, no state court has ever held that management must break silence to reveal confidential business information.

3. a. Yes. If the CEO speaks, she must do so fully and honestly. Under Rule 10b-5, any communications that she knows will affect market trading cannot misrepresent material facts. See §9.3.1.

   b. Probably. For this speculative information, courts apply a variant of the "substantial likelihood" test that measures the expected informational value of the negotiations by combining the probability of a merger occurring (given the state of the negotiations) and the magnitude of such a merger to Basic. *Basic, Inc. v. Levinson*, 485 U.S. 224 (1988) (see §3.2.2). Although there has been no agreement on price and structure, experience shows that stock markets react vigorously and immediately to news that a merger is probable.

   According to the Supreme Court in *Basic v. Levinson*, the "probability-magnitude" test focuses on such indicia of interest as board resolutions, the hiring of outside investment bankers and lawyers to work on the deal, and negotiations among upper-level managers. An agreement in principle by the CEOs, along with the secret exchange of information, fits these indicia and suggests that the deal is moving forward. Since *Basic v. Levinson*, lower court cases have divided on whether an agreement in principle (but not on price or structure) is material. Some cases have turned on whether other impediments stood in the way of the merger. *Taylor v. First Union*, 857 F.2d 240 (4th Cir. 1989) (holding that negotiations for bank merger were not material because deal depended on regulatory approval and the adoption of an interstate banking compact).

c. No, if information about the negotiations is material. Although Basic's shareholders as a group might prefer that management give strategic misinformation, the federal securities laws are not designed to foment business but to inform securities investors.

Some earlier federal lower courts, perhaps confused about the difference between duty and materiality, sought to protect the confidentiality of merger negotiations by assuming investors would not consider such negotiations to be material until the two sides had struck a bargain. The "price and structure" standard, it was said, saved shareholders from their own overoptimism or a deluge of information from management. The standard also assured managers that they could negotiate in secret and even posture (or strategically mislead) without fear of being accused of lying. Honesty was required only when confidentiality concerns were no longer at issue — upon an agreement as to price and structure.

The Supreme Court in *Basic v. Levinson* rejected this approach as an unrealistic view of the materiality of merger negotiations. Securities traders are highly interested in acquisition rumors and know enough to discount tentative news. Indeed, a whole subindustry — risk arbitrage — subsists on speculative information about unconsummated corporate acquisitions. The stock markets quickly impound preliminary information about impending mergers through price changes.

d. She should hang up or say "no comment." Silence is not actionable, and "no comment" is treated as polite corporate silence. *Basic, Inc. v. Levinson*, 485 U.S. 224, 240 n.17 (1988). If Basic has a consistent "no comment" policy on internal company matters — whether management knows of something or not — the market will not be able to read in anything.

Under Rule 10b-5, even a truthful answer is actionable if it is evasive, misleading, or incomplete. If the CEO speaks, she must not only be truthful, but also complete. Thus, virtually any answer — whether about "rumors of negotiations" or "our corporate attitude toward mergers" — could be seen as a half-truth and materially misleading if the negotiations have passed the "probability-magnitude" threshold.

4. a. Probably not. The duty to update, to the extent it exists, lasts only as long as the prior incorrect information continues to affect prices in the market. *Backman v. Polaroid Corp.*, 910 F.2d 10 (1st Cir. 1990). The year-old disclaimer has almost certainly grown stale; it is unlikely securities traders would treat it as operative much longer after it was made. The duty to update, for example, has arisen when a company failed on Monday to update statements made on Friday that had become obsolete over the weekend. *Kamerman v. Steinberg*, 123 F.R.D. 66 (S.D.N.Y. 1988) (bidder agrees to greenmail over weekend but does not disclose the withdrawal of its bid until late Monday).

   b. No. The company has a duty to disclose or abstain when it deals in its own stock while in possession of material nonpublic information. Although materiality in such cases often has the benefit of 20/20 hindsight — the ultimate merger may appear to have been more probable if the merger negotiations turn out to be fruitful — courts protect even unwitting insiders from corporate insider trading.

      Moreover, Basic had the option to repurchase its shares from the executives — that is, the executives had not chosen to retire and force the buy-back of their shares. This mitigates the argument, accepted in some cases, that a company has no disclosure duties if the securities transaction is contractually triggered by a preexisting contract.

   c. No. Although the rumor may be highly material and drive the market price of Basic's stock, the company has no duty to respond to market rumors. A rule otherwise would make corporate issuers a kind of "rumor police."

      If, however, the company was somehow responsible for these rumors, it must correct misinformation it has allowed into the market through leaks or implicit adoption. *Elkind v. Liggett & Myers Inc.*, 635 F.2d 156 (2d Cir. 1980).

5. a. Yes. Rule 10b-5 prohibits false or misleading statements in connection with securities trading, even if the company is not trading. Once the company speaks, it has a duty to speak honestly and completely. See §9.2.2. The press release is both an "untrue statement of material fact" and an omission "to state a material fact necessary in order to make the statements made . . . not misleading." Rule 10b-5. It falsely states management's understanding of the reasons for the market variability and omits material information about the negotiations.

      The sophistic argument that the statement was technically true was made and rejected in *Basic v. Levinson.* In federal securities cases, courts look at the impact of a statement, not its precise wording. The press release implies that management has no knowledge of negotiations, not leaks.

b. Perhaps, but unlikely. The market's apparent nonreaction to the press release suggests that sophisticated securities analysts discounted management's denial of merger negotiations. These analysts may have known Basic's management was playing a corporate cat-and-mouse game. Some federal courts have been willing to assume in cases of well-followed companies that market professionals can see through management lies or omissions, rendering them immaterial. *Wielgos v. Commonwealth Edison Co.*, 892 F.2d 509 (7th Cir. 1989) (see §3.2.2).

Nonetheless, this analysis assumes the lie was transparent and a "reasonable investor" knew from other sources as much about the merger negotiations as a complete and honest press release would have disclosed. Even if professional traders knew the press release was false, it seems unlikely they would have known the exact status of the negotiations.

c. It depends. When prices as to particular securities are set by sophisticated securities traders, disclosure is to them and their trading sets prices for all who invest in those securities. In such an efficient capital market, these sophisticated traders constitute the reasonable investors for purposes of materiality. Unsophisticated "noise" investors who trade on idiosyncratic preferences, immaterial to professional traders, are protected by the market's pricing mechanism. In our example, if professional traders had full information about the merger negotiations, the information would be reflected in the stock's price and any unsophisticated shareholders who sell their Basic stock will receive a "fully informed" price.

On the other hand, if the market is not efficient as to particular securities, the "reasonable investor" standard should be that of the investor who sets prices in the market. Thus, in our example, if trading by nonprofessional traders can affect the price of Basic's stock, any information important to their trading becomes material.

d. Perhaps. Many courts look to the stock market reaction (particularly when the company and its stock price are widely followed by stock analysts) as a surrogate for materiality. In effect, the courts view sophisticated stock analysts to be better than judges in determining whether the information is important to a reasonable investor. Typically, evidence of the stock price reaction is presented as an "event study" — which looks at the company's stock prices around the date the new information is disclosed and compares any price changes to those happening in the market or relevant market segment. In this way price changes related to the new information can be isolated from price changes flowing from general market conditions. If *actual price* changes vary from *expected* price changes (given the market), the variance can be analyzed for statistical significance. If the variance is statistically abnormal, the study provides evidence that the market perceived the information to be material.

Event studies — and reliance on market reactions to new information — suffer from a number of deficiencies. First, the market in the company's stock may not be informationally efficient, and thus market prices may not accurately reflect the new information. Second, there may be confounding information about the company or in the market that drowns out the new information — that is, changes in the market price may actually be in response to other news. Third, the market may overreact to negative information, assuming that it will lead to negative publicity and spurious litigation even though the information itself is not financially significant. Fourth, the news may have already been leaked to the market, and the absence of a market response to the now-stale information may simply reflect that it had already been impounded in the stock price.

6. a. Probably. The board's unsupported views of the merger's fairness — what could be obtained in an arm's-length transaction — are significant to shareholders because of the position of the directors. Even though unsupported, the opinion comes from corporate directors who are charged with watching out for shareholder interests, generally have greater expertise, and have access to internal corporate information. Although some sophisticated shareholders might draw their own conclusions about the merger's fairness, there is no efficient mechanism for corporate voting that signals to the market the optimal vote. Shareholder voting, unlike securities pricing, is much more atomistic.

The Supreme Court rejected the argument in *Virginia Bankshares* (see §3.2.3) that shareholders could protect themselves by evaluating a merger using financial information in the proxy statement. The Court held that a misleading opinion was not necessarily neutralized by other truthful information, particularly if "it would take a financial analysis to spot the tension" between the two.

b. Perhaps they are material, but standing alone they are not actionable. Shareholders may well consider the board's motives in the transaction to be important in their vote, but the Supreme Court has also required that there be objective evidence that the dark motives were accompanied by a flawed transaction. *Virginia Bankshares* (see §3.2.3). That is, the board's unstated motives, even if material, are not misleading unless the board also deceived shareholders about the "subject matter" of its statement — namely, the value of the shares. The test treats the misstated motives to be a harmless lie that caused no loss. In a similar case in which a large shareholder recommended a quick sale of the company, failing to explain her personal need for cash to pay estate taxes, the court concluded her unstated motives were not actionable if the plaintiff could not show price unfairness. *Mendell v. Greenberg*, 938 F.2d 1528 (2d Cir. 1991) (remanded in light of *Virginia Bankshares*).

This analysis forecloses the argument that had shareholders known about the board's tainted motives, they might have turned down the merger in the hope of being offered an even "fairer" price. It forecloses to investors a method to undo or renegotiate corporate transactions when they cannot link the alleged misinformation to financial harm — the purpose for a materiality test.

c. Perhaps, but unlikely. The "bespeaks caution" doctrine may negate the significance of the board's fairness opinion, rendering it immaterial, since it is accompanied by prominent cautionary disclosure. Would a reasonable investor understand to discount the board's opinion of fairness? Although such discounting may be appropriate when sophisticated investors evaluate securities and their views are transmitted in efficient markets through the pricing mechanism, the same efficiency does not exist for shareholder voting. That is, the board's opinion may well carry great weight for some unsophisticated investors, even though other investors are able to understand its limited importance. In contrast to efficient trading markets, there is no mechanism for uninformed shareholders to learn the views of informed shareholders.

d. Not necessarily. Normally, under the "probability-magnitude" test, a looming event that could void a significant transaction would be material if the event were more than a speculative possibility. In this example, however, the antitrust enforcement proceedings have not been brought, and the company would be put in the difficult position of having to disclose potential illegality, something that state antitrust regulators might not even have noticed. To avoid this, some cases have said there is a disclosure duty concerning a company's regulatory compliance only if there are no actual enforcement proceedings or criminal indictments pending. *Roeder v. Alpha Industries, Inc.*, 814 F.2d 22 (1st Cir. 1987). In a similar vein, the SEC has required disclosure of potential environmental liability, but only when the company had already been identified by the EPA as potentially responsible.

7. a. The statement is required by SEC line-item disclosure rules and probably is adequate. The SEC reversed its historic distaste for disclosure of forward-looking information and requires such disclosure, most prominently in the Management Discussion & Analysis (MD&A)

section of prospectuses and periodic securities filings. Item 303, Regulation S-K. The extent to which management must disclose known trends and uncertainties that are "reasonably likely to result" in material changes to the company's financial position has been the subject of some controversy between the SEC and corporate filers. Company filings often contain the sort of relatively superficial, undetailed projections reflected in this example, apparently to avoid disclosing competitive-sensitive information and to minimize the risk of antifraud liability for inevitably guessing wrong. The SEC has urged issuers to provide more extensive and useful forward-looking disclosure, but with only modest success. The SEC's safe harbor rule for forward-looking statements permits forward-looking statements in SEC filings but does not require detailed projections or the disclosure of supporting data. It is enough if the forward-looking statement has a "reasonable basis" and is disclosed in "good faith."

b. Perhaps. The forward-looking statement, which is based in part on predictions about energy prices, may be immunized from liability under one of three theories:

SEC safe harbor. The SEC safe harbor rule applies only to documents filed with the SEC and specifies that a forward-looking statement is not fraudulent if made in "good faith" and with a "reasonable basis." Securities Act Rule 175 (filings under the Securities Act). On the assumption that Combustion's management believed its projections of costs savings were accurate and had supporting data that made the belief reasonable, the SEC safe harbor rules may immunize the projections. The SEC safe harbor, however, has significant shortcomings, particularly since it does not define "good faith" or "reasonable basis." As a task force of the American Bar Association has pointed out to the SEC, "the very nature of forward-looking information makes it difficult in hindsight to establish that the forward-looking statement was made with a 'reasonable basis.'"

Statutory safe harbor. The statutory safe harbor may apply to Combustion's "statement of future economic performance" included in the MD&A section. Securities Act §27A(i)(1)(C). The statutory safe harbor raises three issues. First are the questions whether the statement is "identified" as forward-looking, is accompanied by "meaningful" cautions, and identifies "important facts" that could cause actual results to differ materially from those in the statement. Although the cautionary language ("costs savings, if they occur") might be argued to fit these requirements, courts have interpreted the safe harbor narrowly and our example probably fails on all counts. It is not explicitly identified as forward-looking; its cautions lack clarity; and the contingencies that might cause savings not to occur are not identified.

The second statutory safe harbor applicable to forward-looking statements requires a plaintiff to show that Combustion's management had actual knowledge that the cost savings would not materialize as anticipated. This is the converse of the SEC safe harbor, whose immunity depends on showing an innocent state of mind. In our example, there is no indication management knew its expectations were wrong. Nonetheless, some courts have treated the PSLRA safe harbors as conjunctive, and failure to identify the statement as forward-looking might negate the "actual knowledge" safe harbor.

The third statutory safe harbor specifies that a plaintiff challenging a forward-looking statement must prove materiality, thus focusing judicial attention on whether the statement is too "soft" to be material. *In re Syntex Corp. Securities Litigation*, 855 F. Supp. 1086, 1096 (N.D. Cal. 1994). This aspect of the safe harbor thus invites courts to probe the relevance of the statement to investors and to use the "truth-on-the-market" theory if the market knew the projections were overly optimistic. In our example, it is unclear that the market was misled about management's projections of cost savings.

"Bespeaks caution" doctrine. The judicial "bespeaks caution" doctrine may be less demanding than the statutory safe harbor, particularly if sophisticated investors were the principal recipients of the disclosure. If the "if they occur" caution were sufficient to put such investors on notice that cost savings might not occur, the otherwise optimistic nature of the forward-looking disclosure might have been discounted by price-setting professional traders. "In other words, cautionary language, if sufficient, renders the alleged omissions or misrepresentations immaterial as a matter of law." *Kaufman v. Trump's Castle Funding*, 7 F.3d 357, 371 (3d Cir. 1993) (holding that sophisticated purchasers of bonds should have realized that whether casino would meet revenue expectations was uncertain).

c. Perhaps not. Although the SEC safe harbor for forward-looking statements evaporates if management lacks "good faith," which would include the knowing deception of this example, the statutory "cautionary statement" safe harbor and the "bespeaks caution" doctrine do not focus on state-of-mind issues. Rather, as articulated, they turn on objective statements to investors, not the subjective motives of management.

Do the "cautionary statement" immunities give issuers a license to lie? Some commentators have suggested the statutory safe harbor permits issuers to make misleading forward-looking statements through the expediency of including cautionary language. The legislative history, they point out, advises that courts are not to inquire into the speaker's state of mind if the cautionary language is sufficient on its face. Nonetheless, the stated requirement both in the statute and the judicial "bespeaks caution" cases that there be a "meaningful" caution arguably precludes predictions known at the time to be false or improbable. That is, it is difficult to view a cautionary statement as truly "meaningful" if the speaker knows his prediction is a bold lie. In fact, courts interpreting the PSLRA safe harbor have concluded that cautionary language does not vitiate liability if the speaker knew that a projection would not be realized. Yet, given the PSLRA's purposeful limits on discovery, the cautionary statement safe harbor may effectively immunize intentional deception if a plaintiff cannot obtain information outside of civil discovery about the issuer's actual knowledge.

d. Perhaps, assuming this forward-looking statement is not "puffery," since none of the SEC and statutory safe harbors apply.

At first blush, this statement by the CEO at a trade conference would seem to be immaterial "puffery." If the statement was aimed at touting the company's technological prowess — a plausible interpretation given that it was apparently delivered before a non-investor trade group — its materiality to investors would be attenuated. Nonetheless, public statements by company officials during a public offering are viewed through a more exacting prism. See §4.3 ("gun-jumping" rules). If stock traders noticed and reacted to the CEO's comments, the off-hand prediction that cost reductions will be greater than previously reported might well be material.

If facially material, the forward-looking statement must then look for a safe harbor. The SEC safe harbor for forward-looking statements is limited to SEC filings. Although the statutory safe harbor covers forward-looking statements both in SEC filings and made orally by the issuer's officers, directors or employees, the oral statement must (1) be identified as forward-looking and (2) be accompanied by oral cautions and make reference to a "readily available" document that satisfies the statutory "meaningful cautionary" standard. Securities Act §27A(c)(2). Neither happened here. Nor is there any indication the prediction was accompanied by cautions that would justify using the "bespeaks caution" doctrine. In our example, the issuer would have to turn to the normal defenses of lack of scienter, reliance, or causation. See §9.3.

e. Perhaps. A significant issue with respect to forward-looking statements that go wrong (an inevitability) is the duty to update or correct them. On the one hand, the statutory safe harbor expressly states that "[n]othing in this section shall impose upon any person a duty to update a forward-looking statement." Securities Act §27A(h). Yet the PSLRA leaves a number of open questions. First, it is unclear whether its "no update" policy relates only to forward-looking statements covered by the statutory safe harbor or generally negates any duty to update forward-looking statements. Second, the Act fails to address whether a company has a *duty to correct* (that is, mitigate damages) if either the forward-looking statement or cautionary language is misleading when disclosed; a number of cases have recognized a duty to correct. Third, the statutory language does not expressly negate a duty to update cautionary statements if risk information changes after the forward-looking disclosure.

Beyond the statutory safe harbor, cases that apply a duty to update hinge on whether the initial statement had a forward intent or connotation on which investors could be expected to rely. *Shaw v. Digital Equipment Corp.*, 82 F.3d 1194 (1st Cir. 1996); *Stransky v. Cummins Engine Co.*, 51 F.3d 1329 (7th Cir. 1995) (stating company has no duty to update forward-looking statements simply because changing circumstances have proved them wrong). In our example, Combustion implied that cost savings would continue into the future, thus suggesting the ongoing vitality of the original projection. Prudence suggests the company should update or correct projections that have gone awry.

Registration of Securities Offerings

The regulation of securities offerings to public investors is the cornerstone (both historically and philosophically) of federal securities regulation. With few basic modifications, the regulatory scheme enacted by Congress in the Securities Act of 1933 persists today. To ensure that investors receive material information when issuers raise capital by selling securities in public markets, the Securities Act imposes a mandatory registration system, along with heightened antifraud liability for those involved in the selling effort.

This chapter covers:

- how securities are sold to the public [§4.1]
- the process of registration — preparation of the registration statement, SEC review, postregistration activities, and state regulation [§4.2]
- the regulation of selling activities during the registration process — the gun-jumping rules [§4.3]

The chapters that follow describe exemptions from registration (see Chapter 5), the liability scheme under the Securities Act (see Chapter 6), and the regulation of secondary distributions and other postoffering transactions (see Chapter 7).

Note on Calls for Reform

As you will notice throughout this chapter, many of the cases and SEC releases on registration of securities offerings are decades old. Although the SEC in 2005 significantly revised the kinds of communications that are permitted during a registered offering, questions remain whether the expensive and time-consuming registration process — now more than 70 years old — has become outmoded.

There's reason for concern. In the past decade, the number of U.S. companies with publicly traded stock has fallen from 5,700 to 3,700 as a result of mergers and acquisitions, companies that have gone private or bankrupt, and a drop-off in new companies going public. In short, deaths of public companies have outpaced births. Part of the problem is that investment banks (the financial institutions that bring new companies to market) have been reluctant to help smaller companies gain access to public securities markets. It's just not been worth it.

Not surprisingly, there have been calls for reform to reduce (or eliminate) the underwriting fees charged by investment banks when they bring companies to market. Although direct sales of securities to the investing public would seem the solution, such sales continue to be subject to significant regulatory baggage — even after enactment of the JOBS Act in 2012, which opened the way to "crowdfunding," broader marketing of private placements under Regulation D, and mini-registrations under an expanded Regulation A. See Chapter 5. Moreover, smaller offerings have been the playground of financial swindlers, and any new markets for direct offerings to the investing public must assure investors of their fairness.

§4.1 DISTRIBUTION OF SECURITIES TO PUBLIC INVESTORS

Companies "go public" (sell securities to the public) generally to raise additional capital unavailable from private sources, such as loans from banks or additional investments by company founders. Companies whose securities are publicly traded — that is, public companies — also are more able to attract top-notch employees with stock-based compensation, such as stock grants or stock options. Going public also adds prestige to a company, giving the founders a sense they've arrived and giving the company greater exposure and access to business opportunities. Public companies also tend to sell at higher prices than private companies; studies indicate that while private companies sell at 4 to 6 times earnings, public companies average 25 times earnings.

§4.1.1 Types of Public Offerings

A typical securities offering works much like the sale of other products to the public. The issuer (the company that creates the securities) arranges with financial firms (which act as wholesalers, retailers, and brokers) for the distribution of the securities to public investors (the consumers).

The financial intermediation by investment banking firms (known as "underwriting") happens in a variety of ways.

Standby (or Old-Fashioned) Underwriting

The issuer directly offers its securities to the public, and the underwriter (acting as an insurer) agrees to purchase from the issuer any securities not purchased by the public — hence the name "underwriting." The standby underwriter is paid a fee for assuming the insurance risk. Today this true underwriting is typically used in rights offerings when companies give existing shareholders the right to purchase additional shares.

Originally in a strictly old-fashioned underwriting, the issuer would advertise for subscriptions or offers to buy. It was the method during the 1800s by which capital-intensive firms raised money from dispersed investors.

Best-Efforts Underwriting

The issuer directly offers a stated amount of its securities to the public, and the underwriter (acting as an agent for the issuer) agrees to use its best efforts to find investors. The issuer pays the underwriter a fee for helping place the issue. The issuer and the underwriter can agree to an "all or none" underwriting or a "minimum percentage" underwriting. Best-efforts underwriting is used mostly by smaller underwriters unwilling to risk buying the offered securities.

Firm-Commitment Underwriting

The issuer sells its securities to the underwriter at an agreed price. The underwriter then resells the securities to brokerage firms or to the public at a profit. The participants in the underwriting receive a spread between the purchase price and the public offering price. Typically, a group of underwriters (known as the "underwriting syndicate") acts together under the leadership of a managing underwriter. The managing underwriter negotiates with the issuer, arranges the issuance, puts together an underwriting syndicate, and receives a percentage of the spread for its efforts. Each member of the underwriting syndicate agrees to purchase a specified percentage of the total offering, and its profit or liability is based on that percentage.

Alternative: Auctioning Securities

An alternative to selling securities through an underwriter at a fixed price is to sell directly to investors through an auction. Investors bid for the number of shares they want and the price they are willing to pay. When the bidding ends, the issuer sets the price at the lowest bid that clears the offering. All the winning bidders buy the shares for which they bid at the clearing price, and the bidders at the clearing price divide the remainder. (This method, known as a "Dutch auction," was used by sellers in the early flower markets of the Netherlands.)

The U.S. government, the largest issuer of securities in the world, finances the U.S. debt using a Dutch auction. Investors place bids for U.S. notes and bonds at a stated number and price. For example, a government offering of five-year notes with a face value of $1,000 carrying a 6.5 percent interest rate might produce the following bids:

- Bid A: 10,000 notes at $1,001 (effective rate 6.48 percent)
- Bid B: 5,000 notes at $992 (effective rate 6.69 percent)
- Bid C: 12,000 notes at $987 (effective rate 6.80 percent)
- Bid D: 10,000 notes at $980 (effective rate 6.97 percent)
- Bid E: 20,000 notes at $978 (effective rate 7.03 percent)

In the Dutch auction, the government sells to the highest bidders until it fills the offer, pricing all the securities at the price that clears the whole issue. In our example, if the U.S. Treasury wanted to sell 20,000 notes, Bids A, B, and C would clear the issue, and the price would be $987 for all three purchasers (with Bid C receiving only 5,000 notes). Bids D and E would lose.

The 2004 initial public offering (IPO) by Google tested whether a Dutch auction can be used to raise equity capital on the Internet. Despite a number of hurdles — confusion about bidding procedures, objections from securities firms that helped prequalify bidders, inquiries by the SEC into prior sales of unauthorized shares to employees, and last-minute changes in the expected price range and number of shares offered — the IPO eventually raised more than $1.7 billion, the largest Internet offering to date.

§4.1.2 Pricing and Commissions in a Public Offering

The price of a public offering depends on whether there exists an established market for the offered securities. For securities already traded publicly, the offering price is typically set slightly below the prevailing market price to assure the issue clears. For securities without an existing market, the price is set in negotiations between the issuer and the underwriters. The issuer will want a high price to maximize the offering's proceeds, while the underwriters will seek to minimize their risk and negotiate a price low enough to clear the entire offering. Typically, the final offering price will be determined during the "waiting period" (after the registration statement is filed and before it becomes effective) when the underwriter will identify market demand as it "builds the book" by contacting its institutional and other sophisticated customers.

Consider the pricing (and commissions) in a typical firm commitment underwriting for an IPO:

Public offering price	$14.00
Sales price to underwriters	$13.00
Underwriting spread (divided as follows)	
Fee to managing underwriter	$0.20
Profit to underwriter that sells to dealer	$0.20
Profit to dealer that sells to public	$0.60
Total spread	$ 1.00 (approximately 7%)

Notice that an underwriter with an in-house retail department that sells directly to the public would receive $0.80 — the combined underwriter's and dealer's spread. In addition, fees for a typical IPO (which include SEC registration and state filing fees, legal and accounting fees, printing costs) are typically about 2.5 percent, or $0.35 per share in our illustration.

Inefficient Pricing of IPOs

How efficiently do stock markets and underwriters price initial public offerings? Not very well. Studies show that underwriters systematically underprice IPOs initially, to ensure the issue clears and to create profit opportunities for IPO purchasers, typically institutional investors and other favored customers of the underwriters. One study found that the average IPO gained 16.4 percent in its first day of trading. Long term, however, IPOs are systematically overpriced. Studies indicate that following the initial price spike, IPOs generally decline compared to both the overall market and other companies with comparable risk profiles. For example, prices of IPO firms were found to underperform the market by 27.4 percent over the first three years after the IPO.

Given that IPO gains happen mostly in the first day of trading, there is great demand for "hot" IPO shares among investors, who can sell the shares and make a quick and sizeable trading profit (a practice known as "flipping"). Particularly during the dotcom boom of the late 1990s, the power to allocate IPOs created a pool of instant profits for underwriters to distribute. Some underwriters allocated IPO shares preferentially to corporate executives in the hope of garnering future investment-banking business from their companies (a kickback known as "spinning"). To sustain the aftermarket price spike in an IPO, some underwriters pressured their firms' research analysts to issue "buy" recommendations after the IPO, even when the analysts privately said the stock was an overpriced "dog."

Underwriters also required customers who received IPO allocations to purchase additional shares in the aftermarket at above-IPO prices (a price manipulation known as "laddering"). To minimize flipping and its downward price pressure, underwriters also allocated IPO shares to customers on the promise they would not flip their shares. To further discourage flipping, some securities firms imposed penalties on individual brokers if their clients sold an IPO within a certain time (so-called "penalty bids").

Although the SEC has authority to regulate price-stabilization practices, including practices by securities firms in IPOs, the agency has chosen not to regulate flipping. See *Friedman v. Smith Barney, Inc.*, 313 F.3d 796 (2d Cir. 2002) (describing SEC's decisions in 1955, 1963, and 1994 not to regulate flipping). Nonetheless, the SEC took enforcement action against securities firms that engaged in laddering or that issued fraudulent analyst reports, some of these actions resulting in large financial sanctions and changes in the way securities firms divulge their research to the markets. See §11.2.1 (describing Global Settlements).

The SEC also took action against securities firms that engaged in spinning, though the theory for illegality has been unclear. When an underwriter allocates IPO shares, it simply exploits the systematic underpricing of IPOs — which is not illegal. Its allocation of shares to particular corporate executives, to generate future business, is a form of client development — which is not itself illegal. If there is illegality, it arises from the corporate executive's accepting a valuable IPO allocation for his personal benefit — the improper selling of influence. Given the unseemliness of securities firms paying kickbacks to get business, FINRA (Financial Industry Regulatory Authority) now prohibits securities firms from allocating "hot" IPO shares to executives whose companies are actual or prospective investment banking clients. FINRA Rule 5131; Exchange Act Rel. No. 63,010 (2010) (approving fourth amendment to rule).

Dutch Auction Solution?

Some commentators have argued that the use of a Dutch auction (described above) in which IPO pricing and allocation are determined by investor bids, not issuers and underwriters, can control the IPO "pop" and its corrupting effects. In August 2004 the Internet-search company Google went public using a modified Dutch auction in which it reserved the right to set the final price and to reduce allocations to high-volume bidders. By having bidders set the selling price, Google's stated purpose was to democratize the IPO process and eliminate the first-day price "pop" of most IPOs.

Although Google at first estimated that its shares were worth between $108 and $135, it later cut the estimate to between $85 and $95 along with the number of shares from 25.7 million to 19.6 million. When the bidding closed, Google set the final price at $85. On the first day of trading, surprising many, the price rose to $100 as investors who wished they had bid purchased shares in the aftermarket. In fact, more shares were traded in the first day (22.1 million) than had been sold in the IPO — suggesting that many successful bidders took their profits as the shares moved into new hands.

Google's IPO revealed that investors in an IPO expect a "pop." Without it, they have little reason to buy in the IPO since shares will be available in the aftermarket at the same price. Although Google's first-day price increase meant the company had left money on the table, the Dutch auction accomplished its purpose of distributing shares to a broad base of investors prequalified on the basis of investment experience and portfolio size.

Removed from the IPO process were underwriters spreading the instant profits of the IPO "pop" to favored customers. (The two investment bankers who advised Google and helped conduct the auction received a low 2.8 percent commission and an option to buy 2.9 million additional shares.) Many institutional investors criticized the IPO as overpriced and stayed away, leaving the question (perhaps answered with the run-up in Google's stock price) whether their view was based on a sound valuation or sour grapes.

§4.1.3 Documentation in a Public Offering

A public securities offering generates reams of paper (or word-processed documents) and lots of work for securities lawyers. The documentation in a typical public offering reveals the sequence of events and the players:

Letter of intent	Before filing a registration statement, the issuer selects an underwriter to manage the offering. The issuer and managing underwriter sign a letter of intent (or "memorandum of understanding"). The letter, which is worded not to be binding, indicates the managing underwriter's willingness to organize the offering.
Issuer housekeeping	In preparation for the offering, the issuer (its board and sometimes shareholders) must consider a number of actions to get the company ready for the offering and its status as a public company: granting officers authority for the offering, changing the issuer's capital structure, reincorporating the business in Delaware, adding independent directors to the board, establishing an audit committee with a majority of independent directors, inserting antitakeover measures into the articles and bylaws, and making sure the company's books contain the financial information the SEC will require.

4. Registration of Securities Offerings

Registration statement	The registration statement (which includes a disclosure document called a "prospectus") describes the offering and the issuer. The registration statement is filed with the SEC, and the prospectus becomes the principal selling document for the offering. The registration statement is typically prepared by counsel for the issuer, with careful review by counsel for the managing underwriter.
Comfort letters	Underwriters typically demand that the issuer's counsel write a letter to the underwriters assuring them the issuer's legal house is in order: The issuer is duly incorporated, the securities are authorized, and there are no undisclosed contingencies. (Issuer's counsel will also give an opinion letter to the issuer regarding corporate law compliance, which will be filed with the registration statement.) Usually underwriters also demand a comfort letter from the issuer's accounting firm regarding the accuracy of the financial disclosure in the prospectus.
Agreement among underwriters	Once the underwriting syndicate is assembled, the underwriters enter into an agreement among themselves. The agreement, finalized just before the registration statement becomes effective, authorizes the managing underwriter to act on behalf of the syndicate in negotiations with the issuer. The agreement specifies the managing underwriter's compensation and imposes joint liability on the underwriters for selling expenses.
Underwriting agreement	The issuer enters into an agreement with each of the underwriters, signed on their behalf by the managing underwriter. The agreement specifies the price and amount of securities to be offered and specifies each participating underwriter's allotment. The agreement may also include an over-allotment option — sometimes called the "Green Shoe option," nicknamed after a 1930s IPO where the option was first used. The over-allotment option allows underwriters to buy additional shares from the issuer if demand outstrips the initial offering supply, subject to a FINRA-imposed cap of 15 percent of the original number of shares offered. The over-allotment option gives the managing underwriter the means to stabilize the postoffering price by first overselling the offering

by up to 15 percent and then, if necessary, buying back the oversold shares so as to buttress the postoffering market price and prevent it from falling below the offering price.

Typically, the underwriting agreement is signed just before the registration statement becomes effective and the offering begins. The agreement typically specifies market-out conditions and obligates the issuer to indemnify the underwriters if they become liable for disclosure violations in the offering. Counsel for the managing underwriter drafts the underwriting agreement and negotiates with issuer's counsel such matters as the scope of representations and warranties, indemnification provisions, and covenants in the underwriting agreement.

Selling-group agreements

The underwriters often enter into agreements with securities firms that will act as retail dealers in the offering (the "selling group"). These "select dealer agreements," finalized just before the offering begins, require that all sales be at the offering price.

A public offering, particularly an IPO, is not cheap. Professional fees for issuer's counsel in a typical IPO range from $600,000 to $1,000,000, and for the auditing firm from $500,000 to $900,000. In addition, the filing and listing fees and printing costs add $200,000 to $500,000 in costs borne by the issuer. This does not include the distraction visited on the issuer's senior executives during the process, or the sales spread or commissions for the securities firms who constitute the selling group.

Examples

1. It is October 1985. A start-up company that sells software for use in personal computers (a burgeoning new industry) is considering going public. The company, Microsoft Corporation, was incorporated only five years ago and is already an industry leader in operating software for personal computers. The privately held business is led by its founder, whiz-kid CEO and 49 percent shareholder William H. Gates III. Many believe that even better days lie ahead for Microsoft and for Gates. In mid-October, after an intense courting by securities firms hoping to manage a Microsoft offering, the company's board decides to go public.

(The examples in this chapter, though based on Microsoft's actual IPO, are often hypothetical. Many did not occur. If you are interested, a journalistic account of Microsoft's going public can be found in a riveting *Fortune* article. Uttal, "Inside the Deal That Made Bill Gates $350,000,000," *Fortune*, July 21, 1986, at 23-33.)

a. What does it mean when a company "goes public"?

b. What obligations does a company assume by going public?

c. Why might a company go public?

d. How does a company interested in going public find and choose a managing underwriter?

2. Microsoft meets with a number of securities firms about acting as managing underwriter in the IPO.

a. What kind of offering would you recommend for a company going public?

b. Microsoft shares have not traded on any public market. How will the price be set for this IPO?

c. Microsoft's offering promises to be a "hot issue" — perhaps the IPO of the decade. Underwriters want to sell their allotment of Microsoft shares to their preferred institutional customers and not into retail distribution. Can they?

d. The underwriters suspect Microsoft's IPO will be a "hot issue" and convince Microsoft to increase the size of the offering to 2.5 million shares. Why will they also ask for a "Green Shoe" option?

e. Some underwriters worry that if the market turns sour on new computer offerings, they might not be able to move the whole issue. If this happens, could the underwriters sell their allotted shares at a discount?

Explanations

1. a. A company "goes public" by selling its voting common shares for the first time to unrelated investors. The sale is made by means of a registration statement filed under the Securities Act. Once sold, the shares can be traded in a public trading market — such as the New York Stock Exchange (NYSE) or NASDAQ. See §1.1. In Microsoft's case, the shares were traded on the computer-based NASDAQ.

b. When a company sells its shares to the public in a registered offering, it becomes subject to the periodic reporting requirements of §15(d) of the Securities Exchange Act of 1934. The company must file quarterly and annual disclosure documents with the SEC (Forms 10-Q and 10-K), as well as disclose specified significant events (Form 8-K). See §8.3.2.

   Since 2002, companies that go public also become subject to the many requirements imposed by the Sarbanes-Oxley Act (see §1.4.1) and the governance listing standards of the NYSE and NASDAQ (see §8.3.5). For example, the company must have a majority of independent directors, a board audit committee composed entirely of independent directors, codes of ethics, and procedures for handling whistle-blower complaints about accounting improprieties.

c. Most companies go public to raise capital for company operations or expansion. By selling to the entire investment community, a public offering usually makes it possible to raise more capital at a better price than other financing alternatives. Going public also creates a trading market in the company's stock (liquidity), thus allowing the company's founders and early investors to cash in. And if early investors sell (such as venture capitalists who typically insist on control prerogatives), management can reassert control over the business. By being public, the company will also be able to attract employees with stock-based compensation, raise capital more easily in the future, and even use its publicly traded stock to acquire other companies. And with publicly traded stock, the company's owners will know how much they're worth — useful in estate planning and enhancing their prestige.

There are trade-offs in going public. The registration process is costly. Out-of-pocket expenses for lawyers, accountants, and printing typically reach $2 million, without counting the costs of diverted executive time and energy. Ongoing SEC disclosure under the Exchange Act means these costs will continue indefinitely. The SEC's mandatory disclosure is intrusive and may prove embarrassing, give competitors an advantage, and expose the company to securities liability by investors anxious for regular, upward performance. Current owners may lose control of the company if more than a majority of the voting securities end up in the hands of outside investors. And since the Sarbanes-Oxley Act, reporting companies are subject to a variety of oversight mechanisms — independent audit committees, certification requirements for corporate executives, internal controls, codes of ethics, lawyers' professional responsibilities to report "up the ladder," protections for employee whistle-blowers, and heavy criminal sanctions for fraud.

Some of these costs, however, may be unavoidable for companies that have many shareholders. Under the Exchange Act, a company becomes a "reporting company" if it has more than 500 equity owners of record and more than $5 million in year-end assets. Exchange Act §12(g)(1). It was for this reason that Microsoft went public in 1986: not to raise capital — its pretax profits were running at 34 percent of revenues — but rather to provide a trading market for its employees who had received stock compensation. The company was approaching the 500-shareholder threshold for reporting under the Exchange Act, and company executives figured a public offering would create a deeper market in Microsoft stock.

d. The choice of a managing underwriter may make the difference between a successful public offering and a flop. In the securities investment community, the underwriter's reputation — which depends on its stability, visibility, and knowledge of the field — is critical. Securities firms that engage in underwriting (investment banks) often avoid risky issuers because of potential damage to their reputation, not to mention the exposure to liability (see §6.3). Even when investment banks make competitive bids for offerings by high-quality issuers that will be readily placed with institutional investors (so-called "bought deals"), the underwriter's status and watchdog function provide the market important assurances.

An issuer's managing underwriter often continues an investment banking relationship with the issuer in which it offers a wide range of financial planning services related to antitakeover strategies, acquisitions, and recapitalizations. The "chemistry" between the underwriter and the issuer thus becomes vital. For some issuers that intend an IPO, finding a top investment bank to handle the offering may be difficult. In Microsoft's case, it was quite the opposite. Dozens of different investment banks clamored to manage the "offering of the decade." Microsoft ruled out some larger investment banks because they lacked experience with technology stocks. In the end, Microsoft chose Goldman Sachs (one of the industry leaders) because of its contacts with institutional investors and its "chemistry" with Microsoft's management. Microsoft also chose as co-manager Alex. Brown & Sons, a smaller "technology boutique" firm.

2. a. The type of underwriting in an IPO often depends on the strength of the issuer. Firm commitment underwritings require that the underwriters purchase the entire issue and assume the risk that it cannot be resold. Best efforts underwritings only require the underwriters to broker the issue, with the risk of market rejection falling on the issuer. Standby underwritings typically are not used in IPOs because the insurance premium will be the same or more than the firm commitment discount. Another possibility is a Dutch-auction IPO in which the issuer receives bids from investors and underwriters simply provide information to investors and help the issuer sort out the bids.

Studies show that best-efforts IPOs typically are managed by less-established underwriters and tend to do poorly in the market. On average, a best-efforts IPO raises about one-third as much capital as a firm-commitment underwriting, and over time the price of stock issued in best-efforts IPOs underperforms that of firm commitment IPOs. Although a Dutch-auction IPO would seem a useful way to ensure the issuer captures the full market demand for its securities, such IPOs have not caught on since Google's successful 2004 Dutch-auction IPO. Very few companies have enough preexisting market "hype" to attract investors without selling efforts by an established securities firm.

Microsoft chose a firm-commitment underwriting. Issuers prefer such underwritings because they ensure that the whole issue will be sold and typically raise more money than best-efforts underwritings. In addition, a firm-commitment underwriting signals to the market the issuer's strength, an important consideration for Microsoft.

b. When there is no market price, the IPO price is set by negotiation between the underwriter and issuer. Typically, the issuer will want a higher price (more capital) and the underwriter a lower price (easier to clear). In the negotiations between Microsoft and Goldman Sachs, Microsoft first asked for a low price ($15) so as not to draw attention to itself! Microsoft based this price on the price-earnings ratio of other recent IPOs by comparable software companies. Later, after Goldman Sachs assembled a list of buy orders from institutional investors (known as "the book"), Microsoft sought a higher price. Eventually, the two settled on a price of $21. Within a couple months after the offering, Microsoft's stock price rose to $35.50 on the over-the-counter (OTC) market. Studies suggest that IPO pricing is not efficient — that is, the pricing by underwriters and buyers in an IPO does not reflect all the public information about companies that go public. Post-IPO stock prices systematically perform poorly compared to the broader market and to other companies with similar risk profiles. In other words, the market for IPOs does not impound fully the information eventually impounded by the trading market.

c. Not if it is a "public offering." There is no requirement that underwriters sell (or not sell) to particular buyers. Nonetheless, if underwriters were to sell only to special customers, there might be some question as to whether the offering was "public." Microsoft itself was concerned that if the offering came to rest predominantly in the hands of institutional investors, a trading market in its shares would not develop. The SEC also suggested that the Microsoft registration statement (which stated the shares would be "offered to the public") might be misleading if the offering was targeted only to preferred institutional customers.

Under FINRA Rule 5130, originally passed by the NASD in response to the abuses by underwriters in the allocation of IPO shares during the dotcom bubble, securities firms (whether acting as underwriters or retailers in a public offering) cannot sell to "restricted persons" in the securities industry. Exchange Act Rel. No. 48,701 (2003) (rule defines "restricted persons" to include broker-dealers and their personnel, portfolio managers of financial institutions, mutual funds and insurance companies, and their immediate family members). In addition, FINRA Rule 5131 prohibits "spinning"—the practice of allocating IPO shares to corporate executives whose companies are actual or prospective investment banking clients. Exchange Act Rel. No. 63,010 (2010) (approving fourth amendment to rule).

d. Yes. Typically underwriters in an IPO will ask for an over-allotment (or "Green Shoe") option to sell up to 15 percent more shares than agreed to with the issuer. Issuers are usually happy to sell additional shares at the offering price, though may not grant the option if the issuer has a need for only a fixed amount of new capital.

An over-allotment option gives the underwriters room to maneuver in the postoffering market. If demand exceeds supply, the underwriters can exercise the option to buy up to 15 percent additional shares to fill the market demand—and also to increase their compensation in the deal! If postoffering demand slackens, however, the underwriters can choose not to exercise the over-allotment option and instead to stabilize the price so it doesn't fall below the original IPO price. The underwriters accomplish this by first overselling the IPO to clients by an additional 15 percent (going "short") and then, when the postoffering price begins to fall, buying back shares in the market at the IPO price (thus "covering" or closing out the 15 percent the underwriters had oversold). The effect is to put upside "buy" pressure on the market price, without the underwriters having to actually buy the shares for their own account.

e. No. Securities offerings operate on a fixed-price system—a kind of retail price maintenance. By agreement, underwriters and members of the selling group must sell only at the offering price.

Antitrust challenges to this fixed-price system have not succeeded. *United States v. Morgan*, 118 F. Supp. 21 (S.D.N.Y. 1953); *Papilsky v. Berndt*, Fed. Sec. L. Rep. (CCH) ¶95,627 (S.D.N.Y. 1976). In addition, practices that affect pricing in a securities offering are immune from antitrust attack since the SEC either permits such conduct or has authority to regulate it. As one court pointed out, imposing antitrust liability would force underwriters "to navigate the Scylla of securities regulation and Charybdis of antitrust law." *In re Initial Pub. Offering Antitrust Litig.*, 287 F. Supp. 2d 497 (S.D.N.Y. 2003) (finding implied immunity from antitrust scrutiny for fixed-price equity underwriting and aftermarket "laddering" and "anti-flipping" arrangements that allegedly inflated prices for purchasers of IPO shares).

Nonetheless, securities firms and institutional customers have found ways to circumvent the fixed-price system. For example, underwriters give institutional customers free services or swap the security being offered for lower-valued shares in the customer's existing portfolio, both techniques effectively lowering the price to the customer. In addition, some institutional investors have simply set up broker-dealer subsidiaries to buy securities as members of the selling group, thus "recapturing" the selling group spread. Although a FINRA rule (applicable to all securities firms) prohibits such direct or indirect discounting, powerful incentives remain to cheat.

§4.2 REGISTRATION OF PUBLIC OFFERINGS

The Securities Act of 1933 regulates the public offering of securities. Before securities can be offered or sold to the public, the issuer must file a registration statement with the SEC and provide investors a detailed prospectus. Unlike registration under the Securities Exchange Act of 1934, which calls for the registration of any class of publicly traded equity securities and operates to register *public companies*, registration under the Securities Act covers only a *particular offering of securities*. It is possible that securities registered and sold once under the Securities Act may have to be registered again if resold in a new public offering, such as by a "control" person.

Note on SEC's 2005 Public Offering Reforms

In 2005 the SEC sought to modernize the public offering process by eliminating "outmoded restrictions" and by recognizing the role of the Internet in securities offerings. Securities Act Rel. No. 8591 (2005). The Public Offering Reforms, laid out in a 468-page agency release, established far-reaching exemptions that changed the permitted communications, offering methods, and delivery of information during the registration process. The reforms were meant to facilitate information flows from issuers to investors and to ensure timely information to investors before making their investment decision.

As we will see in the next section on "gun jumping" (see §4.3), the 2005 Public Offering Reforms assume that the risk of non-prospectus disclosures during the registration process varies according to the type of issuer and the investors who are targeted in the offering. Thus, companies going public in an IPO remain subject to significant restrictions on when and how they communicate to investors. On the other hand, large companies with an established market presence are mostly exempted from these disclosure restrictions. For a chart laying out the different offering activities permitted and required during the registration process, see §4.3.4 below.

One question that might have occurred to you is where the SEC gets the authority to change a regulatory scheme specified by statute. The SEC can draw from a few sources. The Securities Act gives the SEC significant leeway to define terms and specify the process and disclosure in public securities offerings. See §4.3 below. In addition, the National Securities Markets Improvement Act of 1996 gives the SEC sweeping exempting powers. The Act authorizes the SEC to exempt "any person, security, or transaction, or any class or classes of persons, securities, or transactions," from any provision of the Securities Act or any of its rules or regulations. Securities Act §28. The Act's legislative history specifically referred to new approaches to registration and disclosure suggested by an SEC advisory committee. There are few limits to this exemptive authority, which may be exercised on a finding that action is "necessary or appropriate in the public interest, and consistent with the protection of investors," a broad standard found in numerous places elsewhere in the federal securities laws.

§4.2.1 Section 5: The Heart of the Securities Act

At the heart of the Securities Act and the registration process it envisions lies §5. The section separates the registration process into three time periods, each subject to a different set of statutory rules (which, as we will see, have been significantly modified by SEC rules):

- **Prefiling period** (beginning when the issuer prepares for the offering and thus is "in registration"). The marketing and sale of any security is prohibited.
- **Waiting period** (after a registration statement is filed with the SEC, but before it becomes effective). Sales are still prohibited, and written marketing efforts are strictly regulated.
- **Posteffective period** (after the registration statement becomes effective, until the offering ends and the issuer no longer is "in registration"). Sales are permitted, but written marketing continues to be regulated; purchasers must receive a prospectus that complies with statutory and SEC specifications.

Two important exemptions temper this remarkable regulatory intrusion. Sales of securities outside a distribution (normal securities trading) and sales in nonpublic offerings (private placements) are exempt from the §5 requirements. Securities Act §4(a)(1) (see §7.1); §4(a)(2) (see §5.2.2). In addition, government securities (issued or guaranteed by the federal government or any state or municipality) are exempted from the definition of security and thus from Securities Act regulation. Securities Act §2(a)(2) (see §5.1).

§4.2.2 Contents of Registration Statement

Section 7 of the Securities Act (by reference to the list-of-disclosure item in the Act's Schedule A) specifies the information that must be included in the registration statement filed with the SEC. (Securities of foreign governments are subject to the information requirements of Schedule B.) The SEC has broad rulemaking authority to deviate from these statutory items. In addition, §10(a) specifies which of the Schedule A information must be included in the prospectus, again subject to SEC rules.

The SEC has used its rulemaking authority to create "forms" (sets of disclosure instructions) for the registration statement. In general, the forms contemplate a two-part filing: Part I is the prospectus (disseminated to investors), and Part II contains technical information, undertakings, signatures, and exhibits (available for inspection at the SEC or through the SEC's Internet-accessible database called EDGAR, as well as private information service providers). The prospectus contains information about the registration, the securities being offered, the issuer and its business, the issuer's financial history, the distribution, and the use of the proceeds.

The registration forms under the Securities Act vary in the detail they require, as well as the latitude they give registrants to incorporate by reference information contained in other SEC filings. You should browse and become familiar with the principal registration forms for domestic U.S. issuers:

Form S-1

This contains the most detailed set of instructions and must be used by companies that do not qualify to use Form S-3, either *non-reporting issuers* (making an IPO), or small or unseasoned *reporting issuers*. For reporting issuers that are current in their Exchange Act filings for the past year, the prospectus may incorporate company-related information by reference to other SEC filings. Information incorporated by reference must be accessible on the issuer's website, including by hyper-linking to EDGAR.

Form S-3

This form is available to large, seasoned companies that have been reporting companies for at least one year (see §8.3) and, if they are offering new equity securities, that have a "public float" of at least $75 million—so-called "seasoned reporting issuers." (The "public float" is the aggregate market value of the company's equity stock held by public investors who are not insiders or affiliates of the company.) In addition, issuers (that are not shell companies) with less than a $75 million public float qualify for Form S-3 if they have been a reporting company for 12 months, their common stock is listed on a national stock exchange, and they do issue more than one-third of their public float in a 12-month period. Securities Act Rel. No. 8878 (2007). The form permits the prospectus to incorporate by reference information from the company's annual report and other periodic reports filed under the Exchange Act. Investors receive only a streamlined prospectus *describing the particular offering.* Why don't they receive information about the company? The assumption for large, seasoned companies is that that the securities markets have already impounded the information found in the company's SEC filings into the price of the company's securities. See §1.2.

Other Forms

Similar forms (designated F-1 and F-3) apply to foreign companies that sell their securities in this country. Special forms govern securities issued in a merger or acquisition (Form S-4), as part of employee stock purchases plans (Form S-8), and for real estate companies (Form S-11).

You may be wondering: what about Form S-2? This form was eliminated by the 2005 Public Offering Reforms. Before 2005, it had permitted smaller, reporting companies to use a prospectus that incorporated by reference information from the company's annual report and other periodic SEC filings — but required that investors in an offering receive the company's annual report, along with the streamlined prospectus.

Special Forms for Smaller Reporting Issuers

To relieve smaller companies from the burdens of a full-fledged SEC registration, the SEC in 2007 revised the regulatory framework for small issuers. New rules create an expanded category of "smaller reporting companies" with less than $75 million in public float (or if the float can't be calculated, less than $50 million in revenues in the last fiscal year). See Securities Act Rel. No. 8876 (2007) (eliminating Forms SB-1 and SB-2, which had cap of $25 million in float or revenues).

Smaller reporting companies — estimated by the SEC to number about 1,500 of the 12,000 companies filing annual reports — are eligible to use scaled-down disclosure and financial-statement requirements. See Regulation S-K and Regulation S-X (replacing former Regulation S-B). The scaled-down disclosure is meant to reduce the burden on smaller issuers and to make information more accessible to nonprofessional investors. (Despite these advantages, smaller issuers — even those that are seasoned — do not enjoy the same leeway in marketing their offerings afforded large, seasoned reporting companies under the SEC Public Offering Reforms. See §4.3.)

Special Rules for "Emerging Growth Companies"

To reduce some of the regulatory burden on business start-ups, the JOBS Act of 2012 creates a new category of issuers known as "emerging growth companies." An emerging growth company is defined as any company that had less than $1 billion dollars in annual revenues during its most recent fiscal year. Securities Act §2(a)(19) (SEC to index dollar amount for inflation).

In their IPO, emerging growth companies:

- may file their registration statement confidentially with the SEC (at least 21 days before the start of the company's road show), thus to protect competition-sensitive information and receive SEC input before committing to an IPO.
- may "test the waters" by holding meetings with institutional investors that are "accredited investors" (see definition, §5.2.4) or "qualified institutional buyers" (see definition, §7.2.2) to gauge investor interest in their IPO, without being subjected to preoffering communication restrictions, see §4.3.1 below.
- may have research reports published about them by securities firms both before and after going public, see §4.3.1 — Permitted Activities, Research Reports.

Emerging growth companies also get a break — for up to five years after their IPO — on some of the reporting and corporate governance requirements under the Exchange Act. See §8.3.1.

§4.2.3 Preparation of Registration Statement

The registration statement is typically prepared by issuer's counsel. Part I contains the prospectus; Part II contains supplemental information, signatures, and exhibits.

The prospectus is highly stylized and has multiple personalities. First, it is written to pass SEC muster and must faithfully disclose all the information required by the relevant registration form. In an S-1 registration this includes the company's business, risk factors, financial position, management compensation and shareholdings, principal shareholders, self-dealing transactions, use of proceeds, and audited financial statements. Second, the prospectus is a selling document. It must provide investors (especially securities analysts who advise their clients whether to buy the offering) an enticing picture of the issuer and the securities offered. Third, the prospectus is written with an eye to litigation. In a first-time offering, a pessimistic emphasis on risk insulates the offering from disclosure liability. Bear in mind that investors who shy from investing because of an overly glum prospectus have no standing to sue under §11 of the Securities Act (see §6.3.1) or Rule 10b-5 of the Exchange Act (see §9.2.1).

Plain English

Since 1998 issuers must use "plain English" in writing the prospectus. Rule 421(d) (requiring "plain English" in the front and back cover pages, the summary, and the risk factor section of the prospectus). Securities lawyers have risen to the challenge and injected "plain English" throughout the prospectus. And even beyond prospectuses, the style of disclosure to investors has fundamentally changed.

What is "plain English"? The SEC rule lays out six stylistic principles: short sentences, everyday language, active voice, tabular presentation of complex material, no legal jargon, and no multiple negatives — the same admonitions that law students hear in their legal writing classes. In addition, the agency has created a wonderful *Plain English Handbook* with writing guidelines, before/after illustrations, and examples of reworked disclosure documents. (It can be downloaded at www.sec.gov/pdf/handbook.pdf.) By the way, my goal was to write this study book in plain English. How have I done?

§4.2.4 SEC Review (and Effectiveness) of the Registration Statement

Under §5 of the Securities Act, securities may be sold once the registration statement becomes effective. Although the Securities Act specifies when the registration statement becomes effective and outlines a statutory period for SEC review, the actual process is quite different. Here is the *statutory scheme*.

Effectiveness	The registration statement becomes effective automatically 20 days after its filing (or 20 days after any amendment) unless the SEC determines an earlier effective date. Securities Act §8(a).
SEC review	After the filing, the SEC has ten days to review the registration statement for incomplete or misleading disclosure and give notice of its intention to issue a *refusal order* that keeps the registration statement from becoming effective. Securities Act §8(b).
SEC oversight	Before or after effectiveness, the SEC can begin a nonpublic administrative investigation. §8(e). After

the registration statement becomes effective, the SEC can issue a *stop order* if it notices a defect in disclosure. §8(d). No offering activities are permitted when a refusal or stop order is outstanding or the SEC is investigating a registration statement. Securities Act §5(c).

In practice, the SEC only rarely uses its refusal and stop-order authority. Instead, the SEC staff selectively reviews filings, which become effective at the agency's discretion. While the SEC staff reviews all IPO filings, review of other registration statements usually depends on how seasoned the issuer is. The agency wrangles disclosure changes informally from issuers without imposing orders or undertaking formal investigations.

How does the SEC do this? First, the SEC asks each registrant to delay effectiveness indefinitely by making amendments to the registration statement as necessary to give the agency time to review the filing. (Remember that the 20-day period for automatic effectiveness restarts each time an amendment is filed.) To accomplish this, registrants stipulate to a "delaying amendment" in their registration statements. Rule 473. This stipulation creates the charade that the issuer is continuously amending the registration statement — thus continuously delaying effectiveness. The effect is that issuers must please the agency reviewers so the SEC (acting through its staff) *accelerates* the effective date and ends the indefinite administrative limbo. The delaying amendment gives the SEC time to review the registration materials, and issuers routinely include a delaying amendment to stay on the agency's good side. A noncooperative issuer risks a refusal order, an investigation, or a stop order if the SEC suspects disclosure defects.

Second, the SEC uses its acceleration power under §8(a) to extract compliance with the Act's disclosure and prospectus dissemination policies. After reviewing the registration statement, SEC staff issues a comment letter (or deficiency letter) that raises disclosure issues and suggests changes. (Since 2005 these letters are available online.) The agency makes the registration statement effective only when the registrant addresses these comments and the staff is satisfied that (1) disclosure is adequate; (2) there has been sufficient circulation of preliminary prospectuses among underwriters, dealers, and requesting investors; (3) the underwriters meet the net capital requirements of the Securities Act; and (4) the FINRA has not disapproved of the offering price or the concessions to the securities firms participating in the offering.

Shelf Registration

What if a company wants to preregister securities and then sell them when (or continuously as) market conditions dictate? Unfortunately, the Securities Act envisions a "register as you go" system. Under §6(a) the registration statement must relate to securities "proposed to be offered," which the SEC has interpreted to prohibit issuers from registering securities for the indefinite future. In 1983, however, the SEC formalized a practice called "shelf registration" to permit registration of securities for later sale if the registrant undertakes to file a posteffective amendment disclosing any "fundamental" change in the information set forth in the original registration statement. Rule 415; Item 512, Regulation S-K. The 2005 Public Offering Reforms further streamline the process for making "continuous or delayed" offerings in the future.

To ensure that investors have access to current information, Rule 415 imposes a variety of conditions on delayed or continuous offerings (whether debt or equity). The conditions vary depending on whether the issuer is a large, seasoned company. For issuers that don't qualify for Form S-3 or F-3, shelf registration is available only for offerings involving preexisting obligations (such as secondary distributions, conversion rights, warrants, collateral pledges), business combinations, and continuous offerings lasting more than 30 days. Only issuers that qualify for Form S-3 or F-3 can delay their offering and choose when to sell "off the shelf." See also Rule 415(a)(4) (limiting "at market" equity offerings to S-3 and F-3 issuers).

Rule 415 used to impose a blanket two-year time limit on shelf offerings, but the 2005 Public Offering Reforms removes the time limitation for shelf offerings involving preexisting obligations. Time limitations remain, however, for other shelf offerings:

- Two years for business combinations. See Rule 415(a)(2) (issuer must reasonably expect to take securities "off the shelf" for business combination within two years of the registration statement's initial effective date).
- Three years for mortgage-backed debt offerings, continuous offerings lasting more than 30 days, and offerings by S-3/F-3 issuers that do not relate to preexisting obligations. See Rule 415(a)(5).

Thus, S-3/F-3 issuers seeking to make equity offerings at market must reregister every three years. The SEC facilitates this renewable "company registration" by allowing the use of the prior registration statement for 180 additional days until the new registration statement becomes effective. Rule 415(a)(5)(ii)(A). In addition, any unsold allotments under the old registration statement can be rolled over into the new registration statement. Rule 415(a)(6) (also permitting rolling over of previously paid, but unused fees).

Issuers using shelf registration must also undertake to update publicly-available information when the securities are "taken off the shelf." Issuers must file a new prospectus (as a posteffective amendment to the registration statement) if there are "fundamental changes" or when securities are taken off the shelf more than nine months after the effective date. See §10(a)(3) (prohibiting use of prospectus with stale financial information more than 16 months old). In addition, any "material changes" to the plan of distribution, such as a change in the number of shares, must be included in the post-effective amendment. These updating requirements, however, do not apply to S-3/F-3 issuers — if the information is in an Exchange Act filing incorporated by reference or a prospectus supplement filed under Rule 424(b).

What is the significance that informational changes be made in a post-effective amendment to the registration statement? As we will see, §11 of the Securities Act imposes strict liability for misstatements in the registration statement *as of the effective date*. See §6.3.3. And whether the issuer files a posteffective amendment, incorporates information from Exchange Act filings, or uses a prospectus supplement — each is deemed part of the registration statement for liability purposes. See Item 512(a), Regulation S-K; Securities Act Rel. No. 8591 (2005).

Shelf offerings are even easier for well-known seasoned issuers (WKSIs, see definition at §4.3), which can check a box to file an "automatic shelf registration" on Form S-3. See Rule 405. Automatic shelf registration statements — which can register primary or secondary offerings, debt or equity securities, and even securities of majority-owned subsidiaries — become effective when filed with the SEC, without SEC review. Rule 462. The WKSI can register an unspecified amount of securities; the to-be-completed shelf prospectus (or "base prospectus") need only name the class of securities being registered. See Rule 430B (specifying the information that may be omitted in a shelf prospectus, including information unknown at the time of filing, whether primary or secondary offering, plan of distribution, and description of securities). And WKSIs can even add new classes of securities to the offering, without filing a new registration statement. Rule 413(b) (permitting automatic shelf registration of new classes by filing posteffective amendment). All that is required to take shares "off the shelf" is to file a prospectus supplement that includes any omitted information — such as the offering price and the participating underwriters — within two business days after the offering is priced and sold. Rule 424(b). Combined with the three-year refiling requirement of Rule 415 for S-3 issuers, the overall effect is that WKSIs can seamlessly sell any amount and class of securities off the shelf.

Withdrawal of Registration

When an issuer abandons a registered public offering, it is placed in a regulatory limbo. If the issuer were then to pursue a private offering, any sales effort in the public offering could be "integrated" with the private offering and violate the condition that private offerings not involve a "general solicitation." See §5.2.4. To permit easier movement from public to private markets (and vice versa), the SEC adopted rules in 2001 that permit easy withdrawal of a preeffective registration. Rule 477 (withdrawal effective automatically on filing of withdrawal application, unless SEC objects within 15 days).

If the public offering is abandoned before any sales, the issuer can go forward with a private offering by waiting 30 days. Rule 155(c) (safe harbor against integration when an abandoned registered offering is followed by a private offering; requiring disclosure in a private offering about withdrawal-of-registration statement, restrictions in private offering, and any material business or financial changes since filing of registration statement). Likewise, an issuer that has begun and abandons a private offering before making any private sales may commence a public offering by disclosing this in its prospectus and waiting 30 days to file the registration statement if any offers had been made to nonaccredited investors. Rule 155(b) (safe harbor against prefiling offers that violate gun-jumping rules when abandoned private offering followed by registered offering).

§4.2.5 Purchases During Registration

Securities sell when the markets embrace them. You might ask, then, what is to keep underwriters in a public offering from buying securities and boosting the postoffering price?

The Securities Act does not expressly address the question, but the SEC has used its rulemaking authority under the Exchange Act to prohibit manipulation during a distribution. Regulation M (replacing former Rules 10b-6 to 10b-8). Regulation M, which narrows and eliminates many prior restrictions contained in the SEC's "trading practices rules," forbids each participant in a distribution from bidding or purchasing securities that, because of their terms, can affect the price of the securities being distributed. Rule 242.101 (limits on underwriters and other nonissuer participants); Rule 242.102 (limits on issuers and selling shareholders). These restrictions generally begin the day before the issuance is priced (for smaller companies, five days before pricing) and end when the participant has completed its participation in the distribution. Rule 242.100 (definition of "restricted period"). Significantly, Regulation M exempts purchases by securities firms participating as underwriters, if the issuer is a large public company and its securities are actively traded. Rule 242.101(c) (exemption for offerings by issuers with a public float of $150 million and global daily trading that averages $1 million during a prior 60-day period).

Regulation M creates an important exception to the prohibition against purchases during a distribution and permits stabilizing purchases under narrow circumstances. Rule 242.104. Stabilizing purchases may smooth out supply-demand imbalances during an offering and, if their possibility is disclosed, may also signal the underwriters' confidence in the offering. To satisfy the rule, the stabilizing purchases must be for the purpose of preventing a decline in the market price; they must be at or below the offering price; they must be initiated generally at a price no higher than the then-current price in the stock's principal market; prior notice must be given to the market whose prices are to be stabilized; and purchasers must receive disclosure on or before their purchase of the possibility of stabilizing purchases. Rule 242.104.

Former Rule 10b-6 (replaced by Rules 101 and 102 of Regulation M) had been held to apply to purchases during a distribution even when they do not influence the market or affect the market price. *Jaffee & Co. v. SEC*, 446 F.2d 387 (2d Cir. 1971) (imposing liability on underwriter that had purchased while still holding unsold allotment). The Supreme Court's implication of a scienter requirement in actions under Rule 10b-5, however, suggests that liability under Regulation M (in part promulgated under §10(b) of the Exchange Act) may depend on a showing of "intentional or willful conduct designed to deceive . . . investors . . . artificially affecting the price of securities." *Ernst & Ernst v. Hochfelder*, 425 U.S. 185 (1976).

§4.2.6 State Regulation of Public Offerings

Lurking in the background of any securities offering are state securities laws — so-called "blue sky laws." (The term comes from a turn-of-the-century adage that securities swindlers sold no more than a "piece of the blue sky.") What must be done at the state level when securities are offered to the public?

Federal Preemption for "Covered Securities"

Originally, the Securities Act contemplated parallel federal/state regulation of securities offerings. Over time, this system of parallel regulation has proved cumbersome, particularly for national securities offerings forced to comply with a patchwork of state blue sky laws that impose inconsistent registration requirements. Calls by the investment community for reform were answered in the National Securities Markets Improvement Act of 1996 (NSMIA), which reversed the long-standing policy against preemption. Securities Act §18.

Under new §18, state authority to regulate securities offerings is largely preempted with respect to "covered securities." In offerings of these securities, states can no longer require registration or qualification, impose conditions on offering documents or other sales literature, or engage in any merit regulation. States can only require notice filings and collect fees to finance their policing of securities fraud. Otherwise, state securities regulation is limited to small, regional, or intrastate securities offerings.

Section 18 defines five categories of "covered securities":

Exchange-listed securities	For securities listed (or authorized for listing) on the New York Stock Exchange (NYSE) or the American Stock Exchange (Amex), as well as securities included in the National Market System of NASDAQ, preemption is complete. Securities Act §18(b)(1). For these securities, states can no longer require registration, notice filings, sales reports, or filing fees. The SEC has discretionary authority to extend coverage to securities listed on other national exchanges (including electronic exchanges) with listing standards similar to those of the NYSE or NASDAQ. In addition, securities equal in seniority or senior to listed securities of the same issuer are covered. This means public companies with listed equity securities can sell debt securities free of state registration.
Securities issued by registered investment companies	This preemption was a major boon to the mutual fund industry, which before had been forced to gerrymander its marketing of mutual funds to conform to the variety of state blue sky regulations. Securities Act §18(b)(2).
Securities sold to "qualified purchasers"	Congress left the SEC to define "qualified purchasers" and to tailor the definition to include securities offerings of a national character subject to federal regulation. Securities Act §18(b)(3). By preempting from state regulation offerings to qualified purchasers, presumably sophisticated investors capable of protecting themselves, NSMIA intended to create a uniform national rule for securities sold to such investors. The SEC, however, has not issued rules, and the exemption has never materialized.
Securities offered and sold pursuant to a §4 exemption	This preemption covers private placements made pursuant to exemptive rules promulgated under §4(a)(2) of the Securities Act, specifically Rule 506 of Regulation D (see §5.2.4). Securities Act §18(b)(4)(E). Notice that the preemption does not cover statutory §4(a)(2) offerings (see §5.3).

The preemption also covers exempt secondary distributions, technically exempt under §4(a)(1), by control persons and holders of restricted securities in public companies made pursuant to Rule 144 and by "qualified institutional buyers" in securities of public companies under Rule 144A (see §§7.2.1, 7.2.2). Securities Act §18(b)(4)(A).

The JOBS Act extended the preemption to cover securities sold in an exempt §4(a)(6) "crowdfunding" (see §5.2.5). Securities Act §18(b)(4)(C).

Securities offered and sold pursuant to a §3(b)(2) exemption

This preemption, added by the JOBS Act, covers extended Regulation A offerings (so-called Reg A+ offerings) provided the offered securities are traded on a national stock exchange or sold only to "qualified purchasers" — a term left to SEC definition (see §5.2.4). Securities Act §18(b)(4)(D). Notice that the preemption for these Reg A+ offerings does not extend to regular Reg A offerings, even if they meet the Reg A+ provisos.

NSMIA preserves some state prerogatives. States retain their authority to require notice filings, sales reports, consent to service of process, and the payment of filing fees with respect to "covered securities" sold within their jurisdiction. (As for listed or senior "covered securities" in the first category, however, the exemption is complete.) Failure to submit a notice filing or pay a required fee can be the basis for a state to suspend, within its jurisdiction, the offer or sale of securities.

States can also continue to police securities fraud by investigating and bringing enforcement actions under their own antifraud laws. But states cannot indirectly mandate or impose conditions on the disclosure of information concerning "covered securities." This new preemption regime raises an interesting question whether the elements of state deceit actions must hone to the current 10b-5 standards or may deviate to relax the requirements of reliance, causation, and scienter. See §9.5.2.

State Blue Sky Regulation

Many smaller and local offerings remain subject to state blue sky laws. Like their federal counterpart, these laws require registration before securities may be offered or sold in the state. There are different kinds of state registration — coordination, notification, and qualification — that vary according to the perceived risks of the offering:

Registration by coordination	For a company that makes an SEC-registered offering of other than "covered securities," state registration by coordination is simple. The issuer files a copy of the federal registration statement with the state securities administrator. State registration becomes effective automatically with the federal registration.
Registration by notification	For a seasoned issuer not in default on its debt and with a history of healthy net earnings, state registration of an offering exempt from federal registration can be by notification. This registration requires only a short-form filing, but it is little used since only seasoned, healthy issuers not making an SEC-registered offering can use it.
Registration by qualification	For other companies making non-preempted offerings (such as offerings subject to the §2(a)(11) intrastate exemption, see §5.2.1, or the small-offering exemptions of Rules 504 and 505 of Regulation D, see §5.2.3), registration by qualification is rigorous. The issuer must file a registration statement, disseminate a disclosure document to investors, and obtain administrative approval in each state where the securities are offered or sold. In many states, securities administrators can pass on whether the offering is "fair, just, and equitable" — so-called "merit regulation."

According to a 1997 study by the SEC of state merit regulation, states impose a wide range of conditions in determining whether an offering is fair to investors. To reduce this jumble, most states have adopted the Small Corporate Offerings Registration (SCOR), which uses a fill-in-the-blank form for offerings that do not exceed $1 million (complementing the SEC's Rule 504 exemption, see §5.2.4). For larger offerings some states have implemented Coordinated Equity Review (CER), allowing an issuer to file one uniform application with all the states where it wants to sell and with Arizona, which acts as CER administrator and assigns a "lead state." That state then reviews the application and SEC registration statement, and works with the issuer to resolve all regulatory questions. Once cleared by the lead state, the offering can proceed in all CER-participating states.

In 2002, a new Uniform Securities Act (USA) was promulgated by the National Conference of Commissioners on Uniform State Laws. The 2002 act displaces an earlier 1956 uniform act, revised in 1985, which had sought unsuccessfully to create a uniform body of state securities laws. Responding to the need for uniformity in global securities markets and to the changes in federal preemption, the 2002 USA seeks to promote (1) uniformity and coordination among state securities laws, (2) consistency with NSMIA, and (3) electronic filing and communications. While the 2002 act makes far-reaching changes to the registration exemptions under state securities laws (see §5.3), it leaves largely intact the registration provisions of the prior revised act. Although state merit regulation was once controversial, NSMIA's preemption of state regulation of "covered securities" offerings has largely dispelled the concerns.

Examples

1. Transport yourself to December 1985. Microsoft engages two underwriters to comanage its public offering: Goldman Sachs (a national securities firm with a strong base of institutional customers) and Alex. Brown & Sons (a firm with experience in technology issues).

   Founded in 1975, Microsoft has financed its growth almost entirely from its own revenues, derived mostly from sales to PC manufacturers of its famous MS-DOS operating software. The company has attracted top executives and programmers by offering them stock grants and options, and as the number of employee-shareholders approaches 500, the company approaches the threshold under the Exchange Act for becoming a reporting company.

   a. In preparation for the offering, what changes should Microsoft make in its corporate structure?

   b. Bill Gates, Microsoft's CEO and 49 percent shareholder, worries about revealing such sensitive matters as executive compensation, stock ownership, and strategic plans. Does he have reason to worry?

   c. Microsoft has never paid, and has no plans to pay, dividends. Francis Gaudette, Microsoft's chief financial officer (CFO), wonders whether the SEC may look unfavorably on this corporate strategy. Could it doom the offering?

   d. Microsoft incorporated only five years ago, and its financial statements do not conform to the rigorous standard of the U.S. accounting profession's generally accepted accounting principles (US-GAAP). Will Microsoft have to go back and pay to conform them?

2. Microsoft's outside law firm begins work on the registration statement.

   a. Microsoft is already well known in the investment community. (In fact, its initial offering will eventually attract more than 100 participating underwriters.) What form of registration may Microsoft use?

b. Company counsel reviews registration statements by other computer companies that have recently gone public: Lotus, Ashton-Tate, Sun Microsystems. The statements describe competitive conditions and risks in the industry. Can Microsoft's filing plagiarize?

c. Bill Gates and other senior Microsoft executives have significant shareholdings. They want to sell some of their stock into the trading market that will develop after the public offering. Can they?

3. Microsoft files its registration statement on February 3, 1986. Within a couple of weeks Goldman Sachs reports that the "book" on Microsoft — buy orders from institutional investors — is the best it has ever seen. Microsoft demands a higher price, in the $20-22 range, and investors remain interested. The underwriters eventually agree to an offering price of $21 and a relatively small 6.2 percent spread.

a. It is March 12, more than 20 days after the registration statement was filed. Can Microsoft close the deal and sell to the underwriters, who will in turn sell to their eager customers?

b. Gaudette, Microsoft's CFO, becomes impatient and suggests that Microsoft simply amend the registration statement to redact its delaying amendment. Any advice?

c. Microsoft's counsel sends a letter to the SEC requesting immediate effectiveness. Counsel points out that the offering has generated significant interest by sophisticated securities firms and institutional investors. Further SEC review would be superfluous. When will the SEC accelerate?

4. Microsoft's bylaws authorize the company to indemnify any director or officer for liabilities in his or her corporate capacity. The indemnification covers liability arising under the Securities Act.

a. What disclosure do the SEC rules require with respect to this indemnification provision?

b. What undertakings does the SEC require with respect to the provision?

c. How can the SEC justify, under its statutory authority, more than disclosure?

5. The SEC suggests some nit-picking changes to the registration statement: disclosure that Gates does not have an employment contract, clearer accounting of returned merchandise, and greater disclosure on a pending IRS investigation of the company. Microsoft amends its registration statement to make the changes. The SEC reviewers are happy with the changes, and the agency is ready to accelerate effectiveness.

a. When can Microsoft close the deal and sell to the underwriters, who will then begin to distribute the securities?

b. Must Microsoft make any further filings? Remember that the registration statement does not yet reflect the price negotiated for the offering.

c. Microsoft's stock is traded on NASDAQ. Assume that a few days after the offering Microsoft's stock price begins to fall. Bill Gates worries that if the stock price falls below $21, it would tarnish the company's reputation. Can he buy to prop up the price?

d. Goldman Sachs places a bid with market makers to buy Microsoft at the offering price. This is meant to ensure that the market price will not fall below the offering price. Can Goldman Sachs do this?

6. Jump forward (for just a second) to 2008. Microsoft anticipates the need to issue new equity securities to engage in business acquisitions or to raise money to meet the competitive threat from Google. It files a registration statement for up to 2 billion new common shares. (There are 9.4 billion currently outstanding.)

a. For how long is the registration statement effective?

b. Does the registration of shares for future sale affect the price of currently traded shares?

7. Now jump forward (if you don't mind) to 2012. Assume Microsoft, with revenues of $97 million, is going public for the first time. The company is concerned that competitors will learn how vulnerable the company is to IBM's continued use of MS-DOS.

a. Goldman Sachs wants to contact some of its institutional clients, even before Microsoft files its registration statement, and find out what they think about IBM's commitment to MS-DOS. Any problems?

b. Can Microsoft submit a draft to the SEC of those portions of its planned registration statement dealing with its relationship with IBM and ask for confidential review?

c. Goldman Sachs plans to post an analysis of Microsoft, which states that the company could become the dominant software company in the world — its stock price (after stock splits) reaching $12,300 per share by the year 2000. Can it do this?

Explanations

1. a. A company going public must typically go through a corporate "housekeeping." The company may have to amend its articles to authorize additional shares sufficient for the offering or affect a stock split so the price per outstanding share is in a marketable range of $5-25 per share. Many companies use the opportunity to amend their articles of incorporation to add antitakeover provisions and indemnification of directors and officers. In Microsoft's case, the

number of authorized shares had already been increased in 1984 from 20 million to 60 million, followed by a stock split.

b. Yes. The prospectus must disclose detailed information on executive compensation and stock ownership, and the management discussion and analysis (MD&A) section must assess any trends or uncertainties that will affect the company's future financial position. See §3.2.3. These intrusive requirements continue under the Exchange Act's periodic disclosure regime. See §8.3.

c. No. If Microsoft discloses its no-dividend policy, as it must under SEC rules, the SEC cannot prevent the registration statement from becoming effective or stop the offering. The purpose of the Securities Act is to provide investors with information to make their investment decisions. The SEC cannot pass on an investment's merit.

Microsoft's no-dividend policy, however, could draw scrutiny under some state blue sky laws. If Microsoft were not listed (or authorized for listing) on the NYSE, the Amex, or the National Market System of NASDAQ, the new preemption provisions of §18 would not apply, and the offering would be subject to state securities registration. Even if state registration is by coordination, state securities officials would retain the power to stop the offering if they found it lacked merit. If, however, Microsoft were listed or quoted (in fact, it was quoted on the NMS of NASDAQ), there could be no state registration, administrative review, or even filing requirements. Securities Act §18.

d. Yes. The accounting requirements of the SEC's integrated disclosure system are the most rigorous in the world. An offering on Form S-1 must conform to all the financial disclosure requirements, including the accounting conventions of Regulation S-X. Although the SEC offers some flexibility for "small business issuers" that register on Form SB-1 or SB-2, this option is available only if the issuer has less than $25 million in revenues. A small business registration would not have been possible for Microsoft.

2. a. Form S-1, even though Microsoft is well known. The SEC measures a company's market reputation according to whether it is a reporting company that has been filing reports under the Exchange Act. The less-burdensome Form S-3 is available only to larger, seasoned reporting companies. Form S-3 (reporting company for one year and $75 million in publicly held voting stock). Microsoft is too large to use the scaled-back disclosure rules for "smaller reporting issuers," available to issuers with less than $75 million in public float.

b. Yes. In fact, it might border on legal malpractice for a securities lawyer to attempt to write a registration statement from scratch. Junior securities lawyers are often advised, before drafting, to consider which other offerings are most similar to the one at hand. Selecting and revising appropriate language from comparable disclosure documents not only saves time and lawyers' fees, but may expedite SEC review.

c. Yes, but with limits. Sales of their shares would be a secondary distribution by "control persons" of the issuer. As such, these sales must either be registered under the Securities Act or be sold pursuant to Rule 144, an SEC exemptive rule that permits sales into trading markets under specified conditions. Under Rule 144, control persons can sell shares they acquired from the issuer only if the shares have been held for at least six months and then are sold through broker transactions in limited quantities. See §7.2.1. (The holding period was two years at the time of the Microsoft IPO in 1986.)

To avoid these restrictions, the Microsoft registration statement also registered a total of approximately 800,000 shares sold by "Selling Stockholders," Microsoft insiders and others related to them. In addition, to avoid a postoffering glut of Microsoft shares, the underwriters extracted a promise from the Selling Stockholders that they would not sell additional shares under Rule 144 during the 90-day period after the company went public.

3. a. No. Sales can begin only when the registration statement becomes effective. Under §8(a) the registration becomes effective 20 days after filing, unless the registrant has filed an amendment. Although more than 20 days have passed since Microsoft first filed, its registration does not become effective because Microsoft filed a "delaying amendment" with its original filing. This has the effect of continuing to amend the registration statement and thus postponing the 20-day period for automatic effectiveness until the SEC exercises its discretion to accelerate the effective date. A company that fails to include a delaying amendment garners immediate SEC attention and wrath.

Although §2(a)(3) defines "offer" to permit "preliminary negotiations and agreements" between the issuer and underwriters prior to effectiveness, the SEC and securities bar have understood "preliminary" to modify "agreements," as well as "negotiations." Any binding contract between the issuer and underwriter — a final sale — remains prohibited by §5(a)(1). Otherwise, underwriters could assume the full financial risk of an offering before effectiveness with nobody to sell to, a temptation too dangerous for the regulatory scheme to countenance. Only preliminary deals (like letters of intent) are permitted while the delaying amendment is working its magic.

b. Don't annoy the bureaucrats. The SEC has the authority to investigate the filing and issue a refusal order prior to effectiveness or issue a stop order after the registration is effective. §8(b) (refusal order); §8(d) (stop order). Under §5(c), if the SEC pursues either course, there can be no sales efforts and the offering is effectively doomed. *Las Vegas Hawaiian Development Co. v. SEC*, 466 F. Supp. 928 (D. Hawaii 1979) (upholding discretion of SEC to investigate a company in registration, and thus halt the offering, when the company withdrew a delaying amendment to avoid SEC review). For this reason, issuers cooperate with the SEC staff, which works closely and informally with the company in "suggesting" disclosure changes.

c. Acceleration is at the agency's discretion. Securities Act §8(a). Under the SEC's current policy of selective review, the agency reviews all initial registrations and grants acceleration of effectiveness only after it completes its review. That the market has embraced an offering is not relevant, at least explicitly, to the agency's review.

In addition to reviewing disclosure in the registration statement, the SEC conditions acceleration on (1) FINRA approving the compensation for securities firms participating in the offering, (2) wide distribution of the preliminary prospectus, (3) the underwriters satisfying the financial capacity requirements of the Exchange Act, and (4) measures to ensure compliance with the rules on stabilizing purchases during a distribution. Rule 461.

4. a. Form S-1 requires disclosure of the indemnification provision in Part II of the registration statement on the theory that indemnification of directors and officers against liability, including for liability under the Securities Act, dilutes their monitoring and "watchdog" functions. Item 14, Form S-1; Item 702, Regulation S-K. The SEC has adopted the view that indemnification of Securities Act liability is against public policy and is unenforceable. Prospectus disclosure of indemnification of the issuer's directors and officers is not required, however, if the issuer gives the undertaking described in 4b next.

b. Any issuer that seeks SEC acceleration of the effectiveness of its registration statement *must* undertake not to indemnify its officials for liability arising under the Securities Act, unless a court rules that such indemnification would not violate public policy. Item 512(h), Regulation S-K.

c. This indemnification undertaking is a dramatic departure from the SEC's limited mandate under the Securities Act to ensure full and honest disclosure, but not substantive review. The SEC justifies conditioning acceleration on the undertaking as a proper exercise of its discretion to accelerate effectiveness. §8(a) (SEC may accelerate "having due regard . . . to the public interest and the protection of investors"). The undertaking ensures the vitality of the liability scheme of §11, which was meant to impose a watchdog function on all directors and any officers who sign the registration statement. See §6.3.

It is curious that the agency does not extract a similar undertaking with respect to issuers' usual indemnification of underwriters for Securities Act liability they may incur in an offering. On the one hand, indemnification of underwriters dilutes the watchdog function that §11 envisions for them. On the other hand, such indemnification is of no value when the issuer is insolvent, and the underwriters can be exposed to full liability. The effect of the issuer's indemnification is to make the underwriters secondarily liable. This may actually be consistent with the §11 liability scheme, which makes the issuer strictly liable yet gives underwriters a "due diligence" defense and specifically limits the liability of nonmanaging underwriters to the price of their allotment.

5. a. Only after the SEC declares the registration statement to be effective. Under current rules, however, final pricing of cash offerings can occur after the SEC makes the registration statement effective, provided the issuer files a final prospectus with pricing information within 15 days after the effective date. Rule 430A (failure to file within 15 days triggers an obligation to file a posteffective amendment). This allows the issuer and underwriter to obtain SEC acceleration of effectiveness, and then price the offering and begin sales on their own schedule. Under current rules, the issuer can even reduce (though not increase) by up to 20 percent the amount of securities being offered without amending the registration statement. Rules 413, 430A.

In 1986, prior to Rule 430A's adoption in 1987, the practice was to negotiate the terms of the deal, immediately file a preeffective amendment with pricing-related information, and then begin sales once the SEC accelerated effectiveness. In Microsoft's IPO, the company negotiated price terms with its underwriters on March 12 and then prepared an amendment to the registration statement incorporating information on pricing and the underwriting syndicate. This pricing amendment was filed the next morning, and SEC staff (acting pursuant to delegated authority) declared the registration statement effective as of 9:15 A.M. on March 13.

b. Under Rule 430A the issuer need only file a prospectus supplement that contains information on price and the underwriting syndicate. This filing must be made within two business days after pricing. Rule 424(b)(1). This posteffective filing window avoids the logistical problems of filing a preeffective pricing amendment and hoping for immediate SEC action. Most issuers now use Rule 430A for bringing their securities to market.

c. Probably not, unless the distribution has been completed. To avoid manipulation of the postoffering market, Regulation M prohibits purchases by participants in an offering (issuers, selling shareholders, underwriters, and participating dealers) during the person's "participation in such distribution." Rules 242.101, 242.102. The prohibition also extends to "affiliated purchasers," who act in concert with the participant or who control the participant. Thus, Gates is prohibited both by virtue of his own sales and as a control person of Microsoft.

According to Regulation M, the prohibition against purchases by the issuer and selling shareholders continues until the distribution is completed. That is, participating underwriters and dealers must have finished selling their allotments. Securities Act Rel. No. 7375 (1996). If the distribution is complete, there are no limitations on Gates's purchases. Although the SEC once proposed to regulate all stabilizing activities, even outside a distribution, it never adopted the rule. In fact, the new Regulation M seeks to provide greater leeway to participants in distributions on the theory that modern markets are more transparent, self-regulating organizations (like the FINRA) are more effective in disciplining wayward securities firms, and antimanipulation liability under Rule 10b-5 provides strong disincentives. In any event, it is unlikely that Gates's motives would be relevant. Whether his purpose was to move the offering or to preserve the company's reputation, his purpose was to artificially affect the market. *Jaffee & Co. v. SEC*, 446 F.2d 387 (2d Cir. 1971) (see §4.2.5).

d. Yes, if the possibility of this stabilizing activity was disclosed in the prospectus. Item 502, Regulation S-K. Although Regulation M generally bars participants in a distribution from bidding to buy the securities being distributed during their participation in the distribution, Rule 104 of Regulation M creates an exception for stabilizing purchases. Under Rule 104, purchasers may buy or bid for securities during the distribution to stabilize the market price so long as the purchase or bid does not exceed the offering price, the stabilizing activity is disclosed to the market in which it occurs, and the possibility of stabilization is disclosed in the prospectus. Rule 104, in effect, allows market manipulation in the name of creating a floor so that demand can coalesce.

6. a. For three years, and easily indefinitely. The 2005 Public Offering Reforms simplify the shelf registration process for well-known

seasoned issuers (WKSIs), such as Microsoft with more than 12 months as a registered company and a public float well in excess the $700 million needed to qualify as a WKSI. The registration statement filed by Microsoft, as a WKSI using Form S-3 or F-3, is deemed an "automatic registration statement," which becomes effective immediately upon filing, without prior SEC staff review. Rule 462(e). The filing can be as short as two pages through the use of extensive incorporation by reference.

The registration statement remains in effect for three years, even though it registers securities that may be used as consideration in business combinations. Rule 415(a)(2) (requiring that securities to be used in business combination must be expected to be taken from shelf within two years, unless registered on Form S-3 or F-3); Rule 415(a)(5) (permitting S-3/F-3 issuers to make an offering within three years after effectiveness). And Microsoft can extend the effectiveness for another three years, and thus indefinitely, by filing another (streamlined) registration statement.

b. Yes, an equity shelf registration typically results in the drop of the market price of the issuer's equity shares — a phenomenon known as "shelf overhang." There are two explanations. One is that the market anticipates (and prices) the possibility that the impending offering may dilute existing shareholders, if the shelf offering is at or below market — that is, at a price below the value placed on the shares by current holders. Another is that the market fears management will issue shares only when the market is overvalued, a distinct possibility given the superior informational position of management. And when the company floods the market with new shares, the price will fall — thus preventing existing shareholders from selling (or realizing fully any gains) in an overvalued market.

7. a. No problems. As a company with less than $1 billion in revenues that is planning an IPO, Microsoft is an "emerging growth company" (see §2(a)(19)) and thus not subject to the usual gun-jumping rules during the prefiling period. See §5(d) (permitting emerging growth companies and those acting on their behalf to contact, orally or in writing, accredited investors and qualified institutional buyers to gauge their interest in contemplated securities offerings). Thus, Goldman Sachs (acting on Microsoft's behalf) can contact institutional investors to determine their interest in the Microsoft offering — provided the investors are banks, insurance companies, or registered investment companies; or pension plans, corporations, or partnerships holding more than $5 million in assets. Although these communications need not be filed as "free writing prospectuses," they are subject to liability under §12(a)(2), if materially false or misleading.

b. Yes. An "emerging growth company" planning to make an equity IPO may submit a draft of its planned registration statement for confidential SEC review. §6(e). Technically, the submission is not a "filing" and thus does not affect the gun-jumping rules on prefiling communications. See §4.3.1 below. But the draft—and any amendments—will eventually have to be filed with the company's registration statement. See §6(e). And when the company files its registration statement, it must then wait for 21 days before it begins its road show. SEC, JOBS Act FAQs—Confidential Submission Process for Emerging Growth Companies (2013).

c. Yes. Even though Goldman Sachs is expecting to participate in the Microsoft offering, it may post research reports about the company and its IPO, without the reports being treated as "offers" or "prospectuses." See §2(a)(3) (revised by JOBS Act); see also §4.3.1 below. The prediction of Microsoft's future stock price, which actually turned out to be correct, would be subject to the antifraud rules of §12(a)(2).

§4.3 MANAGED DISCLOSURE DURING REGISTRATION — "GUN JUMPING"

Disclosure in a public offering is regulated by the carefully crafted prohibitions (and conditions) of §5 of the Securities Act. Violations of §5 during the registration period are known as "gun jumping." Paraphrased, §5 says the following:

- You cannot make "offers" until a registration statement is filed with the SEC. §5(c).
- Once the registration statement is filed, you cannot use a "prospectus" unless it contains specified information. §5(b)(1).
- You cannot make "sales" or "deliveries" until the registration statement becomes effective, and then "deliveries" must be accompanied by a formal prospectus. §§5(a), 5(b)(2).

If §5 is the heart of the Securities Act, the section's terms of art are the chambers and valves that make it work. Only by understanding such terms as "offer," "sale," and "prospectus" can you hope to make sense of the highly technical (sometimes diabolical) disclosure regime of the Securities Act.

Section 5 regulates disclosure during three periods. The following chart is worth committing to memory:

	Filing	Effective
Prefiling period After the company is "in registration," but before the registration statement is filed	**Waiting period** After the registration statement is filed, but before it becomes effective	**Posteffective period** After the registration statement becomes effective, until the distribution ends and the issuer is no longer "in registration"
§5(a)(1) — no "sales" §5(a)(2) — no "deliveries"		
	§5(b)(1) — no "prospectus" unless complies with §10	
		§5(b)(2) — no delivery, unless accompanied by §10(a) prospectus
§5(c) — no "offers"*		

* The prohibition against offers also applies after filing if the SEC issues a refusal order or commences an investigation, and after effectiveness if the SEC issues a stop order.

The statutory scheme creates a "quiet period" before the issuer files the registration statement. After filing and before the SEC clears the registration, the sales effort is limited to a preliminary prospectus. Once the registration is effective, sales must be accompanied by a final prospectus.

Jurisdictional Means

In 1933, when Congress passed the Securities Act, federal power over economic activity not involving the movement of goods or people across state lines stood on uncertain constitutional ground. For this reason, each of the regulatory provisions of §5 reaches only activities that use "means or instruments of transportation or communication in interstate commerce or of the mails."

Technically, none of the §5 prohibitions reaches face-to-face offers or hand delivery of securities within a state. But it will be almost impossible to carry out a public offering without at some point using jurisdictional means. Some courts have indicated intrastate phone calls involve the use of an "instrument of communication in interstate commerce." *Kerbs v. Fall River Industries, Inc.*, 502 F.2d 731, 737-738 (10th Cir. 1974); *Lennerth v. Mendenhall*, 234 F. Supp. 59, 63 (N.D. Ohio 1964). And payment for securities by check (which entails normal clearance through the mails) will doom the sale to the §5 prohibitions. Except on law school exams, the jurisdictional issue can be virtually ignored.

Electronic Offerings

The Internet has changed not only securities trading, but also how information is made available to investors. Increasingly, issuers and securities firms provide information to investors using electronic means. E-disclosure not only allows faster dissemination of information, but often at lower cost. The SEC has encouraged this development and has provided guidance on using electronic means to deliver documents required under the federal securities laws, as well as on the liability of issuers for the content on their websites and the basic principles that govern online securities offerings. Securities Act Rel. No. 7856 (2000).

The SEC allows electronic delivery of documents to investors, such as prospectuses and sales literature, if the investors have consented to it (including by telephone). This consent may cover a particular issuer or transaction, or apply "globally" on a multiple-issuer basis. The SEC advises that documents should be delivered in a format that the investor can readily access and print. Further, hyperlinking can be used to satisfy any requirement that a particular document, such as a §10 prospectus, accompany a particular communication. The SEC has also clarified that merely including information on a website in close proximity to a §10 prospectus does not, by itself, make that information an "offer to sell" within the meaning of §2(a)(3) of the Securities Act.

Issuers remain fully responsible for the contents of their electronic communications. The 2005 Public Offering Reforms treat "graphic communications" (such as audiotapes, videotapes, faxes, e-mails, websites, and "blast" voicemails) as forms of written communication. See Rule 405. And an issuer can even become responsible for third-party information if its website links to that information. For example, during a registered offering an issuer's links to third-party sites that tout the issuer or its securities may be considered prohibited "gun jumping." Although the SEC permits regular Web advertising of the issuer's products and services, as well as links to answers to unsolicited inquiries from securities analysts, it discourages website communications for issuers in registration that give more than ordinary business and financial information.

As for online offerings, the SEC has recognized their potential (and risk) for investors. The agency has outlined two fundamental legal principles to guide participants in online public offerings. First, participants remain subject to the prohibition against securities sales before effectiveness of the registration statement. Second, the offering remains subject to the usual rules against "gun jumping."

Issuer Categories Under the 2005 Reforms

The 2005 Public Offering Reforms identify four categories of issuers. The activities permitted during the registration period vary greatly depending on which category the issuer falls — on the theory that investors will learn about new issuers only through disclosure during registration, while investors (and markets) will already have significant knowledge about issuers with an established market presence. The issuer categories are:

- **Non-reporting issuers** — companies that are not required to file under the Exchange Act (such as issuers going public in an IPO)
- **Unseasoned reporting issuers** — companies that are required to file Exchange Act reports, but not eligible for Form S-3
- **Seasoned reporting issuers** — reporting companies that are eligible for Form S-3 (more than one year since going public and a $75 million public float)
- **Well-known seasoned reporting issuers (WKSIs).** Seasoned reporting companies that have either (a) $700 million worldwide public float or (b) if issuing non-convertible debt, $1 billion in debt issues in the last three years. (According to the SEC, WKSIs constitute about 30 percent of listed issuers, and accounted for 95 percent of US market capitalization.)

Some companies are ineligible to use the communication exemptions available under the 2005 Public Offering Reforms: reporting companies that are *not current* in their Exchange Act filings; *blank-check companies* that are in a development stage with no specific business plan or purpose, or only a plan to combine with an unidentified company (see Rule 419(a)(2)); *penny stock issuers* that issue stock at less than $5 per share and have few net tangible assets and minimal revenue (see Rule 419(a)(2), Exchange Act 3a51-1); *shell companies* with essentially no operations and no non-cash assets (see Rule 405).

As we will see, offering restrictions ease progressively as a company moves from being non-reporting to reporting, reporting to seasoned, seasoned to well known. For a chart summarizing the different offering activities permitted (and required) during registration, see §4.3.4 below.

Liability for Offering Misinformation

Most investors in a public offering make their investment decision before delivery of the final prospectus. Recognizing this, the 2005 Public Offering Reforms attach liability for material misstatements and omissions under §12(a)(2) (private liability) and §17(a)(2) (SEC liability) made before the investor decides to purchase — regardless of postsale corrections or modifications. Rule 159 (see Chapter 6, Liability under Securities Act). Thus, contrary to prior practice, liability under these provisions can arise from a preliminary prospectus, base prospectus, or other offering materials available to investors when they made their investment decision;

information disseminated to the investor after the sale is not taken into account. For this reason, the SEC provides guidance to securities firms on terminating a sales contract based on faulty disclosures and entering into a new contract, thus extinguishing any liability for misinformation. Securities Act Rel. No. 8591 (2005).

Section 11 of the Securities Act imposes liability for material misinformation in the registration statement when it "became effective." See §6.3. The 2005 Public Offering Reforms treat prospectus supplements filed after the effective date as being part of the registration statement for purposes of §11 liability. Likewise, each takedown of securities in a shelf registration creates a new effective date for purpose of issuer and underwriter liability under §11. Rule 405B(f) (but not liability for directors, officers, and experts).

§4.3.1 Prefiling Period

Prohibited Activities

Two statutory prohibitions apply during the prefiling period (sometimes called the "quiet period"):

No Sales or Deliveries

Section 5(a) prohibits sales of unregistered securities or deliveries for purposes of sale. The prohibition is straightforward: Section 2(a)(3) defines a "sale" in the normal sense as including every contract of sale or disposition of a security for value.

No Offers

Section 5(c) prohibits any person to "offer to sell" or "offer to buy" any security, unless a registration statement has been filed. The definition of "offer" is tricky!

What is an "offer"? As with many of the terms of art used in federal securities law, you have to peel a definitional onion. Section 2(a)(3) defines "offers to sell" and "offers to buy" to include "every attempt or offer to dispose of, or solicitation of an offer to buy, a security or interest in a security for value." Notice how much broader this is than the common law definition of "offer," which generally means a communication that, when accepted, forms a contract. The SEC has issued an interpretive release that states any publicity that may "contribute to conditioning the public mind or arousing public interest" in the offering can be seen as part of a selling effort and thus constitute a prohibited "offer." Securities Act Rel.

No. 3844 (1957). Among the factors in deciding whether a communication constitutes an "offer" is whether it was arranged after a financing decision, was broadly disseminated (in writing or using electronic media), included forward-looking information about the issuer or its business, and mentioned the planned offering.

Why prohibit publicity of an offering if securities regulation is all about getting information to investors? The problem, in the eyes of the SEC and the drafters of the Securities Act, is that early, incomplete, or misleading information may poison the disclosure well. Consider *In re Carl M. Loeb, Rhoades & Co.*, 38 S.E.C. 843 (1959), a disciplinary proceeding against two underwriters that issued press releases concerning a land development company that proposed a public offering before the company had filed a registration statement. The releases, which appeared in newspapers and major wire services, announced a "full scale program for the orderly development of lands" held by Arthur Vining Davis. The press releases said that the nationwide public offering would provide a capital infusion for the development project. The SEC sanctioned the two firms for violating §5 and "arousing and stimulating investor/dealer interest" before a registration statement had been filed. The releases had painted an incomplete picture, and the registration statement later revealed that the acreage owned by Davis was "remote in time and distance" from the development and that most of the proceeds of the financing would not be used to develop the properties, but rather to discharge mortgage debt.

Permitted Activities

To give issuers and securities firms some leeway to continue conducting business and to announce prospective offerings, the Securities Act and the SEC provide a handful of exceptions and exemptions for companies in registration. (Many of these provisos were added or amended in the 2005 Public Offering Reforms.)

Preregistration Communications

The 2005 Public Offering Reforms create a bright-line starting point for when an issuer is "in registration"—and thus when "offers" are prohibited. Communications by issuers and those acting on their behalf (other than prospective underwriters or dealers) are permitted when made more than 30 days before the registration statement is filed, provided the proposed offering is not mentioned. Rule 163A (excluding such communications from definition of "offer"). The issuer must take reasonable steps to ensure these preregistration communications are not further distributed or published within the 30 days before filing.

Regularly Released Information

Issuers "in registration" need not go completely quiet. In guidelines to issuers in registration, the SEC has cautioned issuers not to initiate publicity, but to continue to advertise products and services, to make periodic and other disclosures required by the Exchange Act, to issue factual press announcements, and to respond to regular inquiries — all while avoiding future-looking statements and valuation opinions. Securities Act Rel. No. 5180 (1971).

The 2005 Public Offering Reforms clarify and expand the types of regularly-released information excluded from the definition of "offer." All issuers can continue to release factual business information to their customers, suppliers, and other non-investors. Rule 169. Issuers that are already reporting companies under the Exchange Act can also continue to release not only factual business information, but also forward-looking information (FLI) about the company's operations and finances — including to investors. Rule 168 (no information about offering).

Preliminary Negotiations

Section 2(a)(3) exempts from the definition of "offer" preliminary negotiations or agreements between the issuer and the underwriters, or among underwriters, that will be in privity with the issuer. This means the issuer can negotiate with prospective underwriters and enter into a "letter of intent."

Research Reports

The §5(c) prohibition of "offers" puts a damper on the securities business. When can a securities firm tout an industry, highlight a company, or suggest particular securities without its recommendations becoming illegal "offers"? SEC safe harbor rules give guidance to securities firms and their analysts to permit the flow of information to securities markets when an issuer has taken preregistration steps or has filed a registration statement (when it is "in registration"):

Research reports by nonparticipants. A securities firm not participating in the distribution may publish research reports about an issuer in registration if: (1) the report is in the regular course of the firm's business, (2) the issuer (which need not be a non-reporting company) is not a blank-check, shell, or penny-stock company, and (3) the securities firm has received no special compensation from the issuer (or anyone interested in the offering) related to the report. Rule 137 (exemption from the definition of "underwriter").

Research reports on issuer's non-offered securities. Any securities firm (including one participating in the distribution) may publish research reports about the issuer's common stock, if the offering is for fixed-income securities. Rule 138 (exemption from the definition of "offer"). Conversely, any securities firm may publish research reports about an issuer's fixed-income securities, if the offering is for common stock. The rule recognizes that the market for fixed-income securities (preferred stock or debt) is largely institutional, and it assumes investor interest in the market for common stock will not affect the fixed-income market, and vice versa. The report can cover the securities of domestic reporting companies current in their Exchange Act filings, as well as certain large foreign issuers. But the securities firm must have previously issued reports on similar securities in the regular course of business.

Research reports by participants. A securities firm that participates in the distribution may issue *company-specific research reports* about an issuer if the report appears in a regular publication and either: (1) the issuer is a large, seasoned reporting company that meets the requirements of Form S-3 or F-3, (2) the issuer is a WKSI, or (3) the issuer is a large, foreign issuer that is either seasoned on a foreign stock market or has a $700 million global public float. Rule 139(a)(1) (exemption from definition of "offer"). The securities firm must have previously covered the issuer or its securities, and cannot reinitiate coverage of the issuer during registration. The research report can, however, be more favorable than previous reports. But if the report contains financial projections, they must have already been published on a regular basis.

In addition, participating securities firms are permitted to publish (in the regular course of business) *industry research reports* that include reporting companies that are in registration. Rule 139(a)(2). These research reports must have included the issuer in previous reports and must include a substantial number of other issuers, giving no greater prominence to the issuer. Any reports with financial projections for the issuer must also include projections for a substantial number of issuers.

For emerging growth companies (see §4.2.2), the JOBS Act specifies a different set of rules. Under revised Securities Act §2(a)(3), analyst reports (whether written or oral) by securities firms about an emerging growth company's IPO are not considered a "prospectus" under §2(a)(10) or an "offer" under §5(c). Thus, securities firms (even those participating in the offering) may issue reports both before and after the company goes public.

Company Announcements

If securities firms (sometimes) can talk about a company in registration, what can the company say? Rule 135 permits the issuer (as well as selling shareholders and those acting on behalf of either of them) to announce the issuer's intention to make a public offering by stating (1) the amount and type of security to be offered, and (2) the timing, manner, and purpose of the offering. The announcement must state that the offering will be by prospectus, but cannot identify prospective underwriters or the expected offering price.

Before the 2005 Public Offering Reforms, Rule 135 was the only way an offering could be publicized during the prefiling period. See *Chris-Craft Industries, Inc. v. Bangor Punta Corp.*, 426 F.2d 569 (2d Cir. 1970) (en banc), rev'd on other grounds, 430 U.S. 1 (1977) (announcement by underwriter that company would offer a package of securities valued at "$80 or more" violated §5 because it went beyond disclosure permitted by Rule 135).

WKSI Communications

The 2005 Public Offering Reforms permit some offering-related communications by well-known seasoned reporting issuers (WKSIs) during the prefiling period. Rule 163 (exempting such communications from §5(c), though still treating them as "offers" for antifraud purposes). Under this rule, WKSIs may make any "oral offers" during registration. WKSIs can also make "written offers" that bear a legend (where to get prospectus, along with admonition to read it) and are filed with the SEC — that is, when the written offer meets the criteria for a "free writing prospectus" (FWP).

In effect, the SEC has decided that WKSIs (whose securities are assumed to trade in informationally efficient markets) are unlikely to be able to condition the market with prefiling disclosures. Nonetheless, prefiling communications by WKSIs remain subject to the prohibitions against selective disclosures under Regulation FD. See §10.2.5.

Gun-jumping Exemptions (Prefiling Period)

Prefiling period	Filing Waiting period	Effective Posteffective period
Rule 135: offering announcements[**] • allows notice of public offering (exempted from definition of "offer") • limited information: issuer, security, amount offered, timing, manner, and purpose (special requirements for rights offerings, offerings to employees, exchange offers, mergers) • applicable only to issuer; cannot name underwriter		

Prefiling period	Filing Waiting period	Effective Posteffective period
Rules 163: "free writing prospectus"* • permits written communications, if they contain legend (where to get copy of prospectus once available and instructions to read it) and are filed with SEC after filing RS • available only to WKSIs in prefiling period; not available to underwriters (UWs) or other participants		
Rule 163A: preregistration communications* • permits communications 30+ days before filing RS; cannot reference offering • creates safe harbor for issuers, but not UWs or other participants		

Rule 168: regular communications (by reporting issuers)*
- permits factual info and SEC-filed FLI, provided timing, manner, and form are similar to past releases (excluded from definition of "offer"); may not reference offering
- applies to domestic reporting issuers (and seasoned reporting foreign issuers), but not UWs or other participants

Rule 169: regular communications (by new issuers)*
- permits regularly released factual info, but not FLI (excluded from definition of "offer"); may not reference offering; must be intended only for non-investors
- applies to non-reporting issuers, but not UWs or other participants

* Added by 2005 Public Offering Reforms
** Amended by 2005 Public Offering Reforms

§4.3.2 Waiting Period

Prohibited Activities

Two prohibitions apply during the waiting period — that is, after filing, but before the registration becomes effective.

No Sales or Deliveries

The §5(a) prohibition against sales is tricky during the waiting period. Since a "sale" is any finalized contract, offers cannot be accepted during the waiting period. To avoid creating a binding contract, any solicitation of interest must be phrased not to constitute a common-law offer capable of acceptance. Even if an offer has a condition subsequent (such as effectiveness of the registration statement), any acceptance would create a binding contract and thus violate the prohibition against preeffective sales. The usual practice is for participants in an offering to collect *indications of interest* from investors, but not to take checks or otherwise accept orders.

No Prospectuses

On its face, the prohibition of §5(b)(1) against using a "prospectus," unless it meets the requirements of §10, seems simple enough. But in the world of securities regulation, words are often not what they seem. Section 2(a)(10) defines a "prospectus" as any communication "written or by radio or television, which offers any security for sale." In other words, a "prospectus" is defined as any selling effort in writing. (Compare this to the interpretation given "prospectus" by the Supreme Court for purposes of §12(a)(2) liability. *Gustafson v. Alloyd Co.*, 513 U.S. 561 (1995) (see §6.4.1).)

Permitted Activities

During the waiting period the issuer and the other offering participants will want to gauge investor interest. Basically, four types of market-testing and selling activities are permitted during the waiting period: (1) oral communications; (2) §10(b) prospectuses; (3) identifying information about the offering; and (4) "free writing prospectuses."

Oral Communications

Once the registration statement is filed, the §5(c) prohibition on "offers" no longer applies. And the §5(b)(1) prohibition relates only to written offers. Thus, oral selling efforts during the waiting period are permitted, subject only to the antifraud prohibitions of the Securities Act and the Exchange Act. See §§6.4, 9.2.

Prospectus Under §10(b)

Preliminary Prospectus. According to §5(b)(1), the prohibition against using a prospectus during the waiting period does not apply to any prospectus that meets the requirements of §10. What prospectus works? Typically, the prospectus filed as part of the registration statement will be incomplete. The underwriting syndicate is seldom established by the time of filing, and pricing issues will still be open. To address this problem, §10(b) authorizes the SEC to permit the use during the waiting period of an incomplete prospectus. Rule 430 allows a preliminary or "red herring" prospectus, which is filed with the registration statement and includes a marginal legend that cautions the securities cannot yet be sold. (The name "red herring" comes from the special legend typically printed in red ink that the SEC requires on the front of the preliminary prospectus.) The preliminary prospectus contains the information found in the final prospectus but omits information on the offering price and the underwriting. During the waiting period investors have available the same disclosure document under review by the SEC. The preliminary prospectus should be distinguished from the final prospectus (sometimes known as the "statutory" prospectus) called for by §10(a) and used in the posteffective period to confirm sales. See §4.3.3.

Summary prospectus.   The SEC has also exercised its §10(b) authority to permit the use of a summary prospectus during the waiting period, though this is rarely used. Rule 431.

Identifying Information

Tombstone ads.   Section 2(a)(10) excepts from the definition of "prospectus" advertisements (typically made in the financial press using a tombstone-like border) that state from whom a §10 prospectus may be obtained and then do no more than identify the security, state its price, and name the underwriters who will execute orders.

Identifying statements (and solicitations of investor interest).   Section 2(a)(10) permits the SEC to expand the tombstone-ad exception. The SEC has established guidelines that allow expanded (though still bland) identifying information about the offering. Rule 134. The rule says:

(a) you can give specified written information about the issuer, the underwriters, and the offering (more detailed than a tombstone ad and expanded by 2005 Public Offering Reforms), **if**

(b) you include a legend if the registration statement is not yet effective and explain who is selling the securities and where to obtain a preliminary prospectus, **but**

(c) you need not give explanation (b) if (1) you include only the information of a tombstone ad (including a URL for where to obtain a prospectus), or (2) you send (or hyperlink to) a preliminary prospectus, **or**

(d) you can ask investors to indicate their interest in the offering by return card, if you also send (or hyperlink to) a preliminary prospectus and explain there is no commitment.

In short, you can do (a) if you do (b); but you need not do (b) if you do either (c)(1) or (c)(2); or you can do (d) alone under specified circumstances. Any communication that complies with Rule 134 is deemed not a "prospectus" for purposes of §5(b)(1).

"Free Writing Prospectus"

The 2005 Public Offering Reforms permit issuers and other participants in an offering to use something known as a "free writing prospectus" (FWP). (The term comes from the posteffective practice of "free writing" — the use of brochures, news clippings, and other non-prospectus sales materials, provided they are accompanied or preceded by a final prospectus.)

A "free writing prospectus" is any written or graphic communication by the issuer or in its behalf (including Web postings, mass e-mails, but not live PowerPoint presentations) that satisfies certain conditions:

Consistent information and legend	The "free writing prospectus" may include information beyond that found in the prospectus, but it must not conflict with information in the registration statement or any other SEC filings incorporated by reference. Rule 433(c)(1). The "free writing prospectus" must also include a legend that advises the investor to read the preliminary prospectus and how to obtain a copy. Rule 433(c)(2).
Filing	The "free writing prospectus" must be filed with the SEC (and thus made available on EDGAR) on or before the day first used. Rule 433(d). There are exceptions for previously filed information, non-final terms, offerings of asset-backed securities, and business combinations. (If not filed, the issuer or offering participant must retain the "free writing prospectus" for three years.)
Prospectus accompaniment	For offerings by non-reporting and unseasoned issuers, the "free writing prospectus" must be accompanied or preceded by a preliminary prospectus. Rule 433(b)(2) (in IPO must include price range). If the "free writing prospectus" is electronic, the preliminary prospectus can be hyperlinked. The prospectus accompaniment condition, however, is eliminated for seasoned and well-known seasoned issuers (WKSIs). Rule 433(b)(1) (preliminary prospectus or base prospectus must be on file with SEC).

Under Rule 164, a FWP that satisfies these conditions is deemed a "prospectus" under §10(b), thus permitting its use during the waiting period. See §5(b)(1).

The SEC has made the "free writing prospectus" a veritable workhorse. Media companies (like newspapers and TV networks) can disseminate press stories based on interviews of the issuer and other offering participants without them being considered a prohibited "prospectus." Rule 164(a). So long as the publisher or broadcaster is in the media business and has not been compensated by the issuer or other offering participants, the media story is treated as a "free writing prospectus." Rule 433(f) (exempting media companies from information/legend and filing requirements). The issuer or offering participants, however, must file the media story (and include a legend) within four business days of becoming aware of it. Rule 433(f)(1), (f)(2) (unless information in story has previously been filed; permitting the filing requirement to be satisfied by filing the "transcript of interviews" given to the media source). If the media story has any misstatements, the issuer is under no duty to correct the information (assuming that it was not responsible for the misinformation, see §9.3.2), but may choose to include additional information in its filing to correct the story. Rule 433(f)(2)(ii).

The "free writing prospectus" concept has also been put to work with "road shows" — meetings in various cities arranged by the underwriter during the waiting period — at which the issuer's executives make presentations and answer questions for institutional and wealthy, individual investors. Any written material used at a road show, such as a handout or PowerPoint presentation, is specifically treated as a "free writing prospectus." Rule 433(d)(8). The legending and prospectus-accompaniment conditions apply to road-show presentations, though filing is generally not required. Rule 433(d)(8) (requiring filing of road-show presentations only in equity offerings by non-reporting issuers, unless the latest version of the road show with management presentations is posted on the issuer's website). In addition, road shows posted on the issuer's website are considered "graphic communications," but are treated as a "free writing prospectus" if the consistency, legending, and prospectus-accompaniment conditions are met. Filing is not required if the online road show is "bona fide," that is, if it contains presentations by the issuer's management.

All of this is complicated! What if the issuer or underwriter fails to comply with the many conditions for a "free writing prospectus" — would it constitute a §5 violation that could sink the whole offering? See §12(a)(1) (permitting investors to recover their investment, if the offering violates §5, described in §6.2). The SEC allows non-compliant issuers and offering participants to cure "immaterial or unintentional" failures to legend or file a "free writing prospectus." Rule 164 (b), (c). To qualify, the issuer or offering participant must originally have made a "good faith and reasonable effort" to comply with the legending and filing requirements, and must take corrective action "as soon as practicable" once the failure is discovered. See Rule 164(d) (also forgiving failures to comply with record retention requirements, though not requiring corrective action). Notice, however, that the SEC is unforgiving when it comes to communications that are inconsistent with the prospectus (or other SEC filings) or that do not comply with the prospectus-accompaniment condition.

Note on Prospectus Dissemination

Notice the gaping regulatory hole left by the §5(b)(1) scheme. It is entirely possible for an investor to get an oral offer during the waiting period, place an order (written or oral) contingent on the registration statement becoming effective, but never receive a preliminary prospectus! Remember that §5(b)(1) only permits, but does not require, the use of a preliminary prospectus during the waiting period.

Besides the prospectus-accompaniment condition for free writing in the waiting period, the SEC has sought to plug this regulatory hole by making prospectus dissemination a condition to acceleration of the effective date. First, the agency cajoles the issuer to ensure that preliminary prospectuses have been made available to all participating underwriters and dealers. Rule 460 (condition for acceleration). Second, using its Exchange Act authority to prohibit securities firms from engaging in deceptive practices, the SEC requires participating underwriters and dealers to furnish copies of preliminary prospectuses to their salespeople, as well as to any investor who makes a written request for a copy. Rule 15c2-8(c), (e). Third, under this same authority, the SEC requires offering participants (if the issuer has not been a reporting company) to send a preliminary prospectus to any investor who is expected to receive a confirmation of sale upon effectiveness — that is, investors who have indicated an interest in buying during the waiting period. The preliminary prospectus must be sent at least 48 hours before such investors are sent confirmations of their purchase. Rule 15c2-8(b); Securities Act Rel. No. 4968 (1969) (condition of acceleration). In the end, however, an investor could decide to invest without ever having seen the prospectus.

Gun-jumping Exemptions (Waiting Period)

Filing		Effective
Prefiling period	Waiting period	Posteffective period

	Rule 134: identifying statement[**]
	• permits identifying information about issuer (exempted from definition of "prospectus")
	  • (a) permitted: issuer info, info about security, issuer's business, price of security, use of proceeds, identity of sender, names of UWs, schedule, and nature of offering
	  • (b) during waiting period: must include legend and where to obtain preliminary prospectus
	  • (c) can avoid (b), if tombstone ad or accompanied by preliminary prospectus
	  • (d) can seek investor interest, if accompanied by preliminary prospectus and includes statement that interest is not binding, but is fully revocable
	• available to issuer, UW, or other participant	

Rule 135: offering announcement[**] [see prefiling period]		

	Rule 164: free writing[*]
	• permits "free writing prospectus" (FWP) (deemed to satisfy §10(b) if Rule 433 conditions are satisfied)
	• excuses immaterial or unintentional failure to file or legend FWP, if (1) it was good-faith attempt, (2) filing or legend happens as soon as practicable after discovery, (3) properly legended FWP is resent
	• available to issuer, UW, or other participant
	• not available to ineligible issuers (Rule 405): not current with Exchange Act filings, "bad boys," or subject to SEC investigation
	Rule 433: conditions[*]
	• FWP can include info not in RS, but cannot conflict with RS or SEC filings
	• FWP must include legend (read prospectus, how obtain)
	• FWP must be accompanied by (or link to) preliminary/final prospectus
	  • applies to non-reporting, unseasoned issuers: if by issuer (or someone paid by issuer) or other participants
	  • does not apply to seasoned issuers, WKSIs
	• must file with SEC (on date of first use)
	  • issuers must file FWP and issuer info (press interview)
	  • other participants must file FWP if "broad unrestricted dissemination"
	• must retain FWP for three years, if not filed	

Filing		Effective
Prefiling period	Waiting period	Posteffective period
Rule 168: regular communications (by reporting issuers)[*] [see prefiling period]		
Rule 169: regular communications (by new issuers)[*] [see prefiling period]		
	Rule 405/433: road shows[*] <ul><li>treats live or real-time webcast road shows as oral communications</li><li>permits PowerPoint (PPT) presentations at show (deemed "graphic communications"), subject to FWP consistency and legending conditions, and must be accompanied by prospectus</li><li>filing of PPT or other handouts generally not required, except for equity offering by non-reporting issuers: must file PPT unless "bona fide electronic road show" (officers present, similar info as other road shows) and available online</li></ul>	
	Rule 433: press interviews[*] <ul><li>specifies conditions for media-disseminated FWP (such as press interview) originating from issuer or other participant</li><li>must be consistent with RS, other SEC filings</li><li>must file within four days after issuer becomes aware of publication (filing can include corrections or simply give transcript of what was provided to media)</li><li>not subject to prospectus-accompaniment rules, need not be legended provided no payment was made</li></ul>	

[*] Added by 2005 Public Offering Reforms
[**] Amended by 2005 Public Offering Reforms

§4.3.3 Posteffective Period

Prohibited Activities

Two prohibitions apply after the registration statement becomes effective.

No Prospectus, Unless Final Prospectus

Section 5(b)(1) prohibits use of any "prospectus," unless it complies with §10.

No Deliveries, Unless Accompanied by Final Prospectus

Section 5(b)(2) prohibits any deliveries of securities, unless accompanied (or preceded) by a §10(a) prospectus.

Permitted Activities

The regulatory game in the posteffective period is *prospectus delivery.* The statutory prohibitions and the definition of "prospectus," given their references to the final prospectus, seek to require the posteffective delivery of a final prospectus. In this way, investors will finally receive a disclosure about the offering — thus to discover whether they bought a security or a lawsuit!

The 2005 Public Offering Reforms, however, make physical delivery to investors of the final prospectus a relic of the past. The reforms specify that "access equals delivery" — that is, the mere filing of the final prospectus and its availability on the SEC website is deemed to be delivery! The idea is to deemphasize prospectus delivery *after* the investment decision and to encourage prospectus delivery *before* investors actually decide.

Expanded "Prospectus" Types

During the posteffective selling period, §5(b)(1) permits dissemination of a prospectus that complies with §10. Although the statutory scheme envisions the use of a final §10(a) prospectus, the SEC has expanded the repertoire available to offering participants: (1) "not-yet-final prospectus," Rule 430A (for cash offerings, can omit price-related and offering-related information, provided this information is filed within 15 days after effectiveness); (2) "shelf-registration prospectus," Rule 430B (see §4.2.4); and (3) "not-yet-final prospectus," Rule 430C (for non-cash offerings).

Free Writing

The statutory scheme loosens the regulatory grip on written sales efforts during the posteffective period. Even though the §5(b)(1) prohibition against written offers continues, the definition of "prospectus" has a curious wrinkle in the posteffective period. Section 2(a)(10) excepts from the definition of "prospectus" any written sales literature if it is accompanied (or preceded) by a final §10(a) prospectus. Securities lawyers call this "free writing."

The free writing possibilities are further expanded by the 2005 Public Offering Reforms, which permit the use of a "free writing prospectus" at any time after the registration statement is filed, thus including the posteffective period. Rules 164, 433 (see §4.3.2). For non-reporting and unseasoned issuers, the "free writing prospectus" must be accompanied by a §10 prospectus, which in the posteffective period is the final §10(a) prospectus, if available. Rule 433(b)(2)(i).

Confirmations

The statutory scheme seeks to place a final prospectus in the hands of purchasers when their sale is confirmed. Remember that the convoluted
§2(a)(10) definition of "prospectus" includes any writing that "confirms
the sale of any security." A confirmation is necessary to finalize sales under
Exchange Act rules and applicable state statute of frauds. Rule 10b-10
(requiring securities firms to confirm securities transactions in writing
"at or before completion" of transaction); UCC §8-319 (requiring a writing
for sales of securities).

At first glance, this definition would seem to require — to avoid the
§5(b)(1) prohibition against non-prospectus writings — that confirmations be in the form of a §10(a) prospectus. But the drafters of the Securities
Act solved the problem by crafting an exception to the definition of "prospectus." Under §2(a)(10)(a), a confirmation is not a "prospectus" if it is
preceded or accompanied by a final §10(a) prospectus. This statutory
finesse was intended to compel delivery of a final prospectus with every
confirmation in the posteffective period.

The 2005 Public Offering Reforms, however, effectively eliminate the
prospectus-delivery requirements for confirmations (including allotment
notices to offering participants). Purchaser confirmations that meet the
Rule 10b-10 informational standards are exempt from §5(b)(1), though
they may include a Rule 173 notice and incidental information about offering allocations, pricing, and settlement procedures. Rule 172(a)(1).
The issuer need only have filed (or plan to file) a final prospectus.
Rule 172(c) (provided there are no pending SEC proceedings against the
offering, the issuer or other offering participants). The assumption is that
"access" to the final prospectus equals "delivery."

In addition, any sale by an issuer, an underwriter, or a dealer that is subject
to prospectus-delivery obligations under §4(3) (see duration rules below),
must provide the purchaser a notice within two days after the sale. Rule 173
(or provide a final prospectus). The notice must state that the sale was made
pursuant to a registration statement; and the purchaser who receives the notice
has the right to request physical delivery of a final prospectus. The effect is to
substitute notice-delivery for prospectus-delivery. (Rule 173 notices, however,
cannot be used for employee benefit offerings registered on Form S-8, or
business combinations or exchange offers registered on Form S-4.)

Securities Delivery

The statutory scheme also requires prospectus delivery when the securities
are delivered. Under §5(b)(2) the delivery of securities is prohibited unless
accompanied (or preceded) by a prospectus that meets the requirements of
§10(a) — a final prospectus.

The 2005 Public Offering Reforms effectively dispense with the prospectus-delivery requirements for securities delivery. For those with prospectus-delivery obligations during the posteffective period (see the duration rules below), prospectus delivery can be accomplished with a Rule 173 notice (see above), which usually will be sent with the confirmation. Otherwise, the prospectus-delivery obligations of §5(b)(2) are satisfied if the issuer has filed (or is planning to file) a final prospectus — again "access equals delivery." Rule 172(b) (provided there are no pending SEC proceedings against the offering, the issuer, or other offering participants). And for non-participating securities firms, prospectus delivery is deemed to happen simply upon effectiveness — even if the issuer never files a final prospectus. Rule 172(c).

For transactions *between* securities firms (which technically are also subject to the prospectus-delivery requirements), "access equals disclosure" also applies. Once the issuer has filed (or plans to file) a final prospectus, the SEC deems prospectus delivery to occur between securities firms for purposes of §5(b)(2), whether or not they actually participated in the offering, provided the securities are traded on a stock exchange or other stock-trading system (such as NASDAQ or one registered under Regulation ATS, see §8.1). Rule 153 (provided also there are no pending SEC proceedings against the offering, the issuer, or other offering participants). There is no need, however, for a Rule 173 notice. See Rule 173(f) (excluding from the notice requirement dealer transactions under Rule 153).

Form of Final Prospectus

As originally conceived by the statute, the prospectus-delivery requirements were to be satisfied by a full and final prospectus contained in the effective registration statement. This placed issuers (and underwriters) under significant pressure to time effectiveness to coincide with market conditions. To allow flexibility on when offerings are brought to market, the SEC now permits the "final prospectus" to omit price-related information. Rule 430A (available for all-cash, firm-commitment offerings). Issuers have 15 business days after the effective date of the registration statement to file a prospectus containing the price-related information. Rule 424(b). If the issuer waits more than 15 business days, the price-related information must be filed as a posteffective amendment to the registration statement. Rule 462. In either event, the price-related information is treated as part of the registration statement for liability purposes. See Item 512(i), Regulation S-K.

This means that purchasers in an offering will, in most situations, *not receive* the prospectus containing the final price terms. Instead, in most instances, the final prospectus is deemed to be delivered ("access equals deliver") when the registration statement becomes effective. Rule 172(b). All that is required is that issuers, underwriters, and participating dealers provide their purchasers a notice (which says the securities are part of a registered offering) within two days after completing the sale. Rule 173. Purchasers can request a copy of the final prospectus from the person who sent the notice.

Duration of Notice/Confirmation or Prospectus-Delivery Obligations

How long must participants in an offering deliver either the Rule 173 notice or the final prospectus if "access equals delivery" is not applicable? The answer lies at the boundary between distribution and market trading, and thus dwells in the wonderful world of §4 of the Securities Act. According to the §4 statutory scheme, the prospectus-delivery requirements imposed by §5 during the posteffective period continue as follows:

Issuer	The issuer must deliver notices (or prospectuses) indefinitely for any sales it makes. §4(a)(1) (formerly §4(1), renumbered in JOBS Act of 2012).
Original allotment	An underwriter or securities firm that is a member of the selling group must deliver notices (or prospectuses) indefinitely for any sales from its original allotment. §4(a)(3)(C) (formerly §4(3), renumbered in JOBS Act of 2012).
Resales by securities firms	Resales by non-participating securities firms (or those that have sold their allotment) that transact the offered securities in the postoffering market must deliver notices (or prospectuses) for a specified period. The statute imposes this obligation on all "dealers" (by definition, firms in the securities business), thus including those not in the selling group. §§4(a)(3)(B), 2(a)(12).

How long must securities firms continue to deliver notices (or prospectuses)? The answer varies depending on how much information is available about the issuer:

- zero days, if the issuer was a reporting company when it filed its Securities Act registration statement — Rule 174(b)
- 25 days, if the securities are to be listed on a stock exchange or NASDAQ — Rule 174(d)
- 40 days, if the issuer has made other registered offerings — §4(a)(3)(B)
- 90 days, if it is the issuer's first registered offering — §4(a)(3), last sentence.

There is no prospectus-delivery obligation for sales by a securities firm acting as a broker on customer orders — the so-called "broker exemption." Securities Act §4(a)(4) (formerly §4(1), renumbered in JOBS Act of 2012).

Incorrect Disclosure

What happens when posteffective events, like the departure of the issuer's CEO or an adverse court judgment, make the prospectus misleading? If the change is "substantive" though minor, the registrant can place a sticker on the prospectus with the new information. Rule 424(b)(3) (requiring "stickered" prospectus be filed within five business days). If the event is considered "fundamental," not just "substantive," the issuer must amend the registration statement and wait for the SEC to declare the amendment effective.

What if information in the prospectus turns out to be wrong, perhaps on purpose? The Second Circuit concluded, in a largely discredited opinion, that such misinformation has the effect of voiding the prospectus. *SEC v. Manor Nursing Centers, Inc.*, 458 F.2d 1082 (2d Cir. 1972) (prospectus failed to mention that participating securities firms were to be paid special commission, that some of the securities would be sold for other than cash, and that less than all securities would be sold in an ostensibly "all or nothing" offering). The court implied that purchasers could rescind under §12(a)(1) on the theory that a fundamentally deficient prospectus cannot comply with §10(a), and thus sales violate §5. The decision would render superfluous the defenses and limits on damages under §11, the liability scheme for misrepresentations in a registration statement. See §6.3.

What if information in an EDGAR-filed prospectus contains incorrect information, while the printed prospectus delivered to investors is correct? The Second Circuit rejected the argument that a registration statement is negated just because the filed prospectus contains inaccuracies and does not conform to the printed prospectus, as required by SEC rules. *DeMaria v. Andersen*, 318 F.3d 170 (2d Cir. 2003). Instead, the court concluded that an inaccurate, nonconforming prospectus can satisfy the filing requirements, though it may be subject to antifraud liability.

Stale Information

How long can a prospectus be used in a public offering? Section 10(a)(3) says that if a prospectus is used more than nine months after the effective date, the information in the prospectus cannot be more than 16 months old. This means that a prospectus may have to be stickered with new financial information if it is used more than nine months after the registration statement became effective.

Gun-jumping Exemptions (Posteffective Period)

Filing	Effective	
Prefiling period	**Waiting period**	**Posteffective period**
	Rule 134: identifying statement[see waiting period]	
		Rule 153: prospectus delivery for securities firms • for broker-dealer confirmations, access equals prospectus delivery • securities trading on stock exchange, NASDAQ or ATS • provided issuer files or plans to file final prospectus • provided no pending SEC proceedings against the offering, the issuer, or other offering participants
	Rules 164/433: free writing and press interviews[see waiting period]	
Rule 168: regular communications (by reporting issuers)[see prefiling period]		
Rule 169: regular communications (by new issuers)[see prefiling period]		
		Rule 172: prospectus delivery • for confirmations, access equals prospectus delivery (provided issuer files or plans to file final prospectus) • confirmation *must* include information required by Rule 10b-10 • confirmation *may* include Rule 173 notice and incidental information about offering • for deliveries of stock certificates, access equals prospectus delivery (provided issuer filed or plans to file final prospectus) • provided no pending SEC proceedings against the offering, the issuer, or other offering participants **Rule 173: notice of registration** • for issuers, underwriters, or dealers selling securities subject to prospectus-delivery requirements • must give purchaser, within two days of sale, either notice or final prospectus • notice must state sale made pursuant to registration statement • purchaser can request final prospectus • notice requirement independent of "access equals delivery"

* Added by 2005 Public Offering Reforms

** Amended by 2005 Public Offering Reforms

§4.3.4 Summary of Gun-jumping Rules

As you can see, "managed disclosure" during the registration process shuffles together multiple and overlapping elements: (1) the three registration periods: prefiling, waiting, and posteffective; (2) the four types of issuers: non-reporting, reporting, seasoned, and well-known seasoned (WKSI); and (3) the three levels of regulation: prohibited, permitted, and required. And to make sure this is the most complex topic of securities regulation, you have to remember whether the disclosure rules arise from the statute, the regulations (Securities Act or Exchange Act), or agency pronouncements. No wonder students turn to study guides!

The following chart identifies the permitted and required disclosures to investors for non-reporting issuers and WKSIs — the two most common issuers. Remember that many permitted activities are subject to important conditions (described above in more detail), such as the requirements that any "free writing prospectus" include a legend, be accompanied or preceded by a preliminary or final prospectus, and be filed with the SEC (or retained) — unless, of course, one or more exceptions applies.

Prefiling Period	Waiting Period	Posteffective Period
Non-Reporting Issuers		
Permitted:	**Permitted:**	**Permitted:**
• Preliminary negotiations and agreements with/among underwriters (§2(a)(3))	• Oral offers	• Oral offers
	• Preliminary negotiations and agreements with/among underwriters (§2(a)(3))	• Distribution and sale of securities
• Issuer announcements of proposed offering (Rule 135)	• Tombstone ads, identifying statements, requests for interest (§2(a)(10)(b), Rule 134)	• Tombstone ads, identifying statements, requests for interest (§2(a)(10)(b), Rule 134)
• Issuer communications 30+ days before offering (Rule 163A)	• Preliminary (red-herring) prospectus (§10(b), Rule 430)	• Free-writing communications (§2(a)(10)(b))
• Regularly released information (Rule 169)	• Summary prospectus (§10(b), Rule 431)	• Final prospectus (§10(a))
	• "Free writing prospectus," accompanied/preceded by preliminary prospectus (§10(b), Rules 164 and 433)	**Required:**
		• Written confirmations for sales from allotment and dealer sales (§5(b)(1), Rules 172 and 174, Rule 10b-10)
	Required:	• Filing by issuer of final prospectus (§§5(b)(1), 5(b)(2), Rules 153, 172)
	• Distribution of preliminary prospectus (Rule 15c2-8)	• Delivery of notice within two days after sale (Rule 173)

Prefiling Period	Waiting Period	Posteffective Period
Well-Known Seasoned Reporting Issuers (WKSI) Same as Non-reporting Issuers, except:		
Permitted: • Oral offers (Rule 163) • "Free writing prospectus" need not be accompanied/preceded by any prospectus (Rule 163) • Regularly released, forward-looking information (Rule 168)	**Permitted:** • "Free writing prospectus" need not be accompanied/preceded by preliminary prospectus (Rule 433)	**Permitted:** • Free-writing communications need not be accompanied/ preceded by preliminary prospectus (Rule 433) **Required:** • Delivery of notice only applies to sales from allotment (§4(a)(3), Rule 174)

Examples

1. It is January 1986, though assume the current gun-jumping rules apply. Microsoft's board has approved a public offering. The company engages its outside corporate law firm in Seattle to begin work on a registration statement, but it has not yet filed anything with the SEC. Identify any violations of §5.

    a. Microsoft sends an e-mail to its principal customers that announces, "The company contemplates it will go public within the next few months."

    b. Francis Gaudette, Microsoft's CFO, telephones Goldman Sachs in New York to set up a meeting in Seattle about the securities firm becoming the managing underwriter for the planned offering.

    c. After some discussions, Goldman Sachs sends a letter to Microsoft indicating its willingness to manage the offering.

    d. Bill Gates tells his housekeeper about the offering. The next day the housekeeper telephones Gates and says, "I would like to buy 100 shares."

    e. Goldman Sachs mails letters to 80 national and regional brokerage houses asking them to join an underwriting syndicate for the upcoming offering. Cable, Howse & Regan (a prominent Seattle securities firm) is not asked but mails a request to participate in the offering.

    f. Cable, Howse & Regan circulates its regular monthly newsletter to its clients. The newsletter continues to give glowing reports of Microsoft and speculates that "an IPO between $15 and $20 is in the offing."

    g. Microsoft places an ad in a national computer magazine announcing a seminar it will hold in March on PC operating-system technology.

The ad states, quite truthfully, that Microsoft is "the industry leader in operating-systems software."

h. Goldman Sachs issues a press release: "Microsoft will offer 2.5 million shares of common stock to be sold in a registered offering. Goldman Sachs and Alex. Brown & Sons will be the managing underwriters." There is no mention of an offering price.

i. In April 1985, several months before the board's decision to go public, Bill Gates told a reporter for the *Puget Sound Business Journal* that Microsoft would go public in 1986. The *Journal's* story, distributed on wire services, stated that Bill Gates "publicly pegged the date of such an offering as 1986."

2. On February 3, 1986, Microsoft files a registration statement for 2 million shares to be sold by the company and another 500,000 shares to be sold by Microsoft insiders. The preliminary prospectus states an anticipated price range of $16-19 per share. Identify any violations of §5.

a. Microsoft's vice president of marketing runs a first-time ad in *Business Week* captioned "Microsoft: the industry leader in operating-systems software."

b. Microsoft's personnel department sends a company-wide e-mail to employees: "The company will sell 2 million shares of its common stock to the public in the $16-19 range."

c. Microsoft adds a new banner to its website that announces: "Microsoft to go public — click here to read the prospectus and learn about this milestone for the company and the PC industry." When anybody clicks on the banner there is a click-through screen before arriving at an electronic version of the preliminary prospectus: "MS has filed a registration statement (and prospectus) with the SEC for this IPO. Before you invest, you should read the prospectus and other documents MS has filed. Go to www.sec.gov or call toll-free 1-800-555-1234."

d. Goldman Sachs places an ad in *The Wall Street Journal*:

This announcement is neither an offer to sell nor a solicitation of an offer to buy securities. The offering is made only by prospectus.

New issue   February 3, 1986

2,000,000 Shares of Common Stock
Microsoft Corporation

Price range: $16.00-19.00

Goldman Sachs & Co.
Alex. Brown & Son

---

e. Bill Gates talks to securities analysts at "dog and pony" meetings set up by the underwriters. At one of these road shows, Gates volunteers that Microsoft management expects "revenues to keep growing, perhaps doubling every year into the foreseeable future."

f. A *New York Times* reporter attends one of the road shows and interviews Gates. The next day the newspaper runs a story quoting Gates on Microsoft's performance, plans, and prospects.

g. Microsoft posts an electronic version of its road show on the company's website, with online videos showing presentations by company management, links to PowerPoint presentations and the preliminary prospectus, and warnings that investors should read the prospectus.

h. Janice, a sales rep of Goldman Sachs' brokerage department, calls Robert and strongly recommends buying Microsoft. Robert says he is interested, so Janice sends him an e-mail that has a link to Microsoft's "red herring" prospectus. In the message line she jots, "Microsoft looks really good."

i. Robert looks over the prospectus and mails a note to Janice: "Put me down for 1,000 shares." He attaches a check for $19,000.

j. Janice e-mails Clara and asks her to e-mail back a card indicating how many Microsoft shares she wants to purchase. The e-mail has a hyperlink to the preliminary prospectus. The card states: "No offer to buy or money can be accepted before Microsoft's registration statement becomes effective, and any offer to buy can be withdrawn before acceptance after the effective date. Returning this card creates no commitment to buy."

k. Janice calls William about Microsoft, and he says, "Buy me 1,000 shares when they're available." Janice does not send William a prospectus, but tells the Order Desk to confirm William's order as soon as the offering begins.

l. Goldman Sachs sends a mass e-mail to its customers that has attached a reprint of a *Business Week* article that describes the growing PC market and concludes "Microsoft will have an ever-increasing role in the PC market." The e-mail includes a hyperlink to the preliminary prospectus.

m. Goldman Sachs calls Cable, Howse & Regan (not a member of the underwriting syndicate) and offers to set aside 5,000 Microsoft shares for the firm to resell to their retail customers once the registration statement becomes effective.

n. Cable, Howse & Regan circulates its monthly newsletter, which continues to recommend Microsoft.

o. On March 10, the SEC finishes its review of the registration statement. Before seeking acceleration, the members of the underwriting syndicate sign an agreement among themselves on their participation in the Microsoft offering.

3. On March 10, Microsoft registers its common stock under the Exchange Act, becoming a reporting company. On March 12, Microsoft agrees with its underwriters on a $21 price for the offering. At 9:15 A.M. on March 13, the SEC accelerates effectiveness of the registration statement. Some investors who purchased at $21 sell almost immediately into a trading market that opens at $25. Identify any violations of §5 regarding these posteffective events.

   a. Microsoft sends an e-mail to the company's employees: "Today the company sold 2 million of its shares in a public offering at $21. The stock closed the day at $27.75, a hefty 32 percent bump."

   b. On March 18 *Business Week* runs another Microsoft ad with the caption "Microsoft: the industry leader in operating-systems software."

   c. Cable, Howse & Regan (a participating securities firm) adds a link on its website to a wire story that reports on the success of the Microsoft offering. It later sends e-mails attaching the final prospectus to its customers who buy Microsoft shares.

   d. Goldman Sachs e-mails confirmations of sales to customers who bought from its allotment. All of these customers had received a preliminary prospectus during the waiting period.

   e. After sending the confirmations, Goldman Sachs mails Microsoft share certificates to a handful of purchasers who requested certificates. It includes in the mailing printed copies of the final prospectus.

   f. Goldman Sachs sends a confirmation of 10,000 shares to a securities firm that wants to be a market maker in Microsoft stock. Goldman Sachs fails to send a prospectus with the confirmation.

   g. On March 20, Goldman Sachs has sold its entire allotment. Janice (a Goldman Sachs trader) calls an institutional investor and says at current trading prices of $27, Microsoft is still a good buy. The customer buys 10,000 shares. Goldman Sachs fills the order through NASDAQ and mails a confirmation of the order.

   h. Microsoft discovers a major omission in the final prospectus. The company misstated the status of pending litigation concerning rights to MS-DOS by failing to mention that a court had ruled against Microsoft's motion for summary judgment.

   i. On January 15, 1987, Goldman Sachs finds that it somehow failed to sell 5,000 shares of its allotment. The firm sells the shares, sending a confirmation and notice that the sales are pursuant to a registration statement. The final prospectus, which was originally filed on March 13, has not been updated. The prospectus covered financial results through December 31, 1985, though audited financials were as of June 30, 1985.

Explanations

1. a. Violation. When a company is "in registration," §5(c) prohibits the making of any "offer" (using jurisdictional means) until the company files a registration statement. Section 2(a)(3) defines "offers" broadly to include every "attempt . . . to dispose" of securities, and the SEC has interpreted this to mean any activity that conditions the investment market. Microsoft customers are potential purchasers in the new offering. Since Microsoft sent the announcement by e-mail (thus using the nationwide and global Internet), it used jurisdictional means. The SEC has made clear that it views electronic communications in the same way as other forms of communication under the gun-jumping rules. Securities Act Rel. No. 7856 (2000).

   The only significant issue is whether Microsoft is "in registration." Although the SEC has described the process of registration as beginning when the issuer reaches an understanding with a managing underwriter, Securities Act Rel. No. 5180 (1971), it would seem anomalous that a company planning an offering could condition the market so long as it has not found a managing underwriter. Instead, the registration process should be seen as beginning once the issuer has taken concrete steps toward an offering.

   The 2005 Public Offering Reforms provide guidance when an issuer is "in registration" with a bright-line rule for issuer communications that occur more than 30 days before the filing of the registration statement, provided they do not mention the offering. Rule 163A. In this case, although the e-mail suggests filing of the registration statement is more than 30 days away, the e-mail mentions the proposed offering — the safe harbor is lost.

   The SEC also allows issuer announcements during the prefiling period, but only if the announcement complies with specified informational conditions. Rule 135. Microsoft's announcement would satisfy the rule had it stated that "the offering will be made only by means of a prospectus." This cautionary statement suggests to potential investors (including customers) that they not get their hopes up until they and the market have absorbed the prospectus.

   WKSI note: The answer would be the same if Microsoft (a well-known seasoned issuer or WKSI) were making the offering today. WKSI written announcements during the prefiling period must satisfy either Rule 135 (see above) or Rule 163, which imposes "free writing prospectus" conditions — including a legend (where to get prospectus once filed and an admonition to read it) and eventual SEC filing (with the registration statement). Here the e-mail to customers was apparently oblivious to these conditions, making the "immaterial and unintentional" proviso unavailing. See Rule 163(b)(1)(iii), (b)(2)(iii) (excusing failures when "good faith and reasonable effort" to comply with legending and filing conditions).

Even if Microsoft's announcement complied with Rule 163, it would remain subject to the prohibitions against selective disclosure. See Regulation FD, Rule 100(b)(2)(iv) (excluding Rule 135 announcements, but not "free writing prospectuses" in the prefiling period). Thus, when Microsoft (as a reporting company) makes a prefiling announcement of the anticipated offering that goes beyond Rule 135, it must not only comply meet the "free writing prospectus" conditions, but also the Reg FD requirement that any such announcement to securities professionals and likely investors be made simultaneously to the investing public. See §10.2.5.

b. No violation. Although the broad statutory definition of "offer" covers Microsoft's efforts to set up a selling group, the definition excepts "preliminary negotiations . . . between an issuer . . . and any underwriter . . . to be in privity of contract with an issuer." Securities Act §2(a)(3). (The definition of "underwriter" includes any person "who has purchased from an issuer with a view to . . . the distribution of any security." Securities Act §2(a)(11).) Since Goldman Sachs may become an underwriter in contractual privity with Microsoft, this contact is not an "offer."

What about the Reg FD prohibition against selective disclosure — which as we saw in 1a may apply in the prefiling period? See §10.2.5. Although selective disclosure by an issuer to a securities firm of non-public material information (here, Microsoft's plan to make a public offering) would normally be prohibited under Reg FD, there are two exceptions that apply in this case. First, Microsoft is not yet a reporting company under the Exchange Act, and thus not subject to Reg FD. See Rule 101 (definitions). Second, even if Microsoft were a reporting company, the disclosure is exempt since it is made to a person with a duty of trust or confidence (underwriters are specifically mentioned in the rule) and to a person who expressly agrees to maintain the confidence. Rule 100(b)(2)(i), (ii).

c. No violation. The letter of intent should be worded carefully so as not to be a binding "sale," which is prohibited during the prefiling and waiting periods. Securities Act §5(a). If (as is typical) the letter merely states Goldman Sachs' intent to put together an underwriting syndicate and to negotiate the terms of the offering, it is a "preliminary negotiation or agreement" between the issuer and an underwriter and excepted from the definition of "offer." Securities Act §2(a)(3). (There is some disagreement among securities connoisseurs whether "preliminary" in §2(a)(3) modifies both "negotiations" and "agreements" or only "negotiations." Nonetheless, whether a letter of intent is an "agreement" or merely a "preliminary agreement," universal consensus says it is not prohibited.)

d. Violation. There were two "offers" for purposes of §5: first, Gates's initial communication to the housekeeper about the offering — an "offer to sell" — and second, the housekeeper's showing of interest — an "offer to buy." Both are prohibited during the prefiling period by §5(c), the former because it conditioned an investor's mind and the latter because offers to buy evidence (as here) prohibited conditioning.

And don't forget the jurisdictional issue. Gates's communication, though an "offer," did not violate §5(c) if he did not use jurisdictional means. The housekeeper's offer, however, was by telephone (no doubt connected to an interstate grid) and thus arguably used a "means . . . of communication . . . in interstate commerce." Although §2(a)(7) defines "interstate commerce" to include communication "among the several States," most courts hold that even intrastate use of the telephone may confer Securities Act jurisdiction. *Dupuy v. Dupuy,* 511 F.2d 641 (5th Cir. 1975); but see *Rosen v. Albern Color Research, Inc.,* 218 F. Supp. 473 (E.D. Pa. 1963) (concluding that telephone call between persons within the same city did not constitute a means of communication in interstate commerce).

WKSI note: The answer would be slightly different if Microsoft (a WKSI) were making the offering today. Gates's oral offer to sell made on behalf of the issuer would be exempt from §5(c). See Rule 163. But, curiously, the rule — which is limited to offers "by or on behalf" of the WKSI — might not cover the housekeeper's offer to buy. Although the rule exempts issuer offers from the §5(c) prohibition against "offers to sell, offers for sale, or offers to buy," the rule forgot (or consciously chose not) to exempt offers to buy made by potential investors.

e. Possible violation. Putting together an underwriting syndicate falls under the §2(a)(3) exception for "preliminary negotiations and agreements" among potential privity underwriters. The letter by Goldman Sachs must make clear that it is asking securities firms to act as underwriters, who will purchase from Microsoft, and not as retail dealers.

The letter from the Seattle firm, however, may be problematic. If the letter asks no more than to join the underwriting syndicate, it would be a "preliminary negotiation" among potential underwriters. But if the Seattle firm seeks to participate as a retail dealer in the offering, the §2(a)(3) exception would not apply. (Securities firms that receive only a retail seller's "usual and customary" commission in a distribution are excepted from the §2(a)(11) definition of "underwriter.") The Seattle firm's letter would be a prohibited "offer to buy." The Securities Act regulates buying interest during the prefiling period for fear that securities firms will start lining up customers before the prospectus is disseminated.

WKSI note: The answer would be the same if Microsoft (a WKSI) were making a public offering today. The exemption from §5(c) for WKSIs during the prefiling period only applies to oral and written sales efforts *by the issuer or on its behalf.* See Rule 163 (written offers must also satisfy "free writing prospectus" conditions). Here the letter from the potential retail dealer is not by or on behalf of the issuer.

f. Violation. The CHR newsletter is a prohibited "offer" because it "arouses public interest" in the issuer. Securities Act Rel. No. 5009 (1969). The newsletter would appear to be a research report — which the SEC defines to include information, opinions, and recommendations to help with investment decisions — but none of the SEC safe harbors applies. Although nonparticipating securities firms can issue research reports about non-reporting companies, the problem here is that CHR may be planning to participate in the offering. Rule 137(a) (safe harbor not available to securities firms that "propose to participate in the distribution"). Nor does the safe harbor for research reports on equity in a debt offering (and vice versa) apply to this newsletter. Rule 138. And the safe harbor for company-specific and industry research reports applies only to reporting companies under the Exchange Act, which Microsoft is not. Rule 139(a). The securities firm cannot tout the securities of a company "in registration."

WKSI note: The answer would be different if Microsoft (a WKSI) were making a public offering today. Even if CHR were planning to participate in the offering, the newsletter would be a regularly published research report about a WKSI — and thus exempt from the definition of "offer." Rule 139(a)(1).

g. Perhaps no violation. Once an issuer is "in registration," any publicity that arouses public interest in the issuer's securities may be a prohibited "offer." Securities Act Rel. No. 5180 (1971) (permitting normal corporate advertising and publicity). By saying that Microsoft is "the industry leader," the company walks a fine line between advertising its business and promoting its upcoming securities offering. Out of caution, company counsel often urges the issuer (as was true for Microsoft) to discontinue public statements about its industry prowess.

The 2005 Public Offering Reforms, however, may change the answer. Regularly released factual information is excluded from the definition of "offer," so long as it is aimed at customers, suppliers, and other non-investors. Rule 169 (issuer must have previously distributed same type of information in ordinary course of business). Here the ad in a national computer magazine would seem to be aimed at non-investor customers, but it is unclear whether this is a new kind of advertising. If so and particularly if the ad were a subterfuge to create investor interest, it would not fit under the SEC safe harbor.

WKSI note: The answer would be the same if Microsoft (a WKSI) were making a public offering today. Issuers that are already reporting companies under the Exchange Act can continue to release not only factual business information, but also forward-looking information about the company's operations and finances—including to investors. Rule 168 (no information about offering). But the timing, manner, and form of the release must be consistent with similar past releases. Here, again, it is unclear whether this is a new kind of advertising and whether the ad was intended to excite interest in the offering.

h. Violation. This press release arouses interest in the upcoming offering and is a prohibited "offer." It does not fall within the safe-harbor Rule 135 for two reasons. First, Goldman Sachs made the announcement. Although the announcement can state the amount and type of security to be offered, as well as the manner and purpose of the offering, Rule 135 is limited to announcements by the issuer. Second, even if it can be said Goldman Sachs acted for Microsoft, the announcement goes beyond Rule 135 by identifying the managing underwriters. In the eyes of the SEC, it overstimulates public interest.

Nor does the press release fall into the exempting rules added by the 2005 Public Offering Reforms. The press release is not a communication by an issuer made more than 30 days before the registration statement is filed. Rule 163A (not available to non-issuer offering participants). Nor is the press release regularly released information by an issuer. See Rule 168 (business information released by any issuer); Rule 169 (business and forward-looking information released by reporting issuer).

WKSI note: The answer would be similar if Microsoft (a WKSI) were making a public offering today. Although WKSIs have more latitude in the prefiling period to make written announcements about upcoming offerings, any such communication must satisfy the legending and filing conditions applicable to a "free writing prospectus." Rule 163 (permitting prefiling communications by or on behalf of WKSI, provided the issuer or its representative approves any communications by another offering participant). Thus, the press release by the underwriters would have to have been approved by the issuer or issuer's counsel, would have to have included a legend about how to obtain a prospectus and urging investors to read it, and would have to be filed with the registration statement. There is no indication any of this happened or was attempted.

i. Probably no violation. Reports that Microsoft planned to go public circulated widely before the company filed its registration statement in February 1986. The April 1985 news story seems to have occurred before Microsoft was "in registration" (see answer 1a) and thus is not covered by the §5(c) prohibition against offers. It is not unusual for the press to uncover and report more about public offerings than the Securities Act scheme contemplates.

If the news story had run when Microsoft was "in registration," one question would be whether it was Microsoft that violated §5(c) or the newspaper. Although it might be argued that the newspaper is not by an issuer, underwriter, or dealer — and thus exempt under Securities Act §4(a)(1) (see §7.1) — this argument fails under extant case law on two grounds. First, the newspaper can be seen as an unwitting agent of the issuer. That is, Gates and Microsoft violated their §5 duties by using the newspaper to tell about Microsoft's plans to go public. Second, the newspaper might itself be seen as an "underwriter" by acting on behalf of the issuer in promoting the offering. *SEC v. Chinese Consolidated Benevolent Association*, 120 F.2d 738 (2d Cir. 1941) (the benevolent association urged, without compensation, the purchase of bonds of the Republic of China and therefore acted as "underwriter" in the bond issue).

If so, isn't §5(c) a prior restraint — arguably at odds with free press rights? Under current First Amendment doctrine, "commercial" speech enjoys less protection than "political" speech, on the assumption that constitutional free-speech protections are aimed at "effective self-government" and "individual self-fulfillment" — neither of which are thought to be implicated when government seeks to protect against marketplace fraud. In fact, the Supreme Court has observed in dicta that "exchange of information about securities" in corporate proxy statements can be regulated apparently regardless of the First Amendment. *Ohralik v. Ohio State Bar Ass'n*, 436 U.S. 447, 456 (1978).

2. a. Violation. During the waiting period, §5(b)(1) prohibits use of any "prospectus" — defined to include written "offers" that "arouse public interest" in the issuer's securities. This first-time ad in a business magazine, as opposed to a computer publication, may relate more to selling securities than selling Microsoft's products. Securities Act Rel. No. 5180 (1971).

The SEC safe harbor for regularly released factual information does not change the answer. Even if the "industry leader" ad is factually correct, it does not fall within the Rule 169 safe harbor because (1) it is not the type of information previously distributed in the ordinary course of business, and (2) it is arguably directed at potential investors.

WKSI note: The answer would be the same if Microsoft (a WKSI) were making a public offering today. The safe-harbor Rule 168 allows reporting issuers to continue to release factual business and forward-looking information—including to investors. But the timing, manner, and form of the release must be consistent with similar past releases. Here, advertising in a new investor-oriented publication would seem to be intended to create interest in the offering.

b. Violation. The e-mail message is a prohibited "prospectus" because it might arouse investment interest, unless it falls within an exception. The message is not a §2(a)(10) "tombstone ad" (no mention of how to obtain prospectus), a Rule 134 identifying statement (no legend or preliminary prospectus attached), or a Rule 135 company announcement (cannot mention price). And there are no special safe harbors or exceptions for communications to employees.

Although the 2005 Public Offering Reforms permit free writing in the waiting period, this e-mail does not satisfy the conditions of a "free writing prospectus." It did not include a legend or accompanying prospectus, and it was not filed with the SEC on the day it was sent. Rules 164, 433. But if these conditions had been met and since the information in the e-mail was consistent with the registration statement, it would have been a "free writing prospectus"—that is, a §10(b) prospectus useable in the waiting period.

One important (and easily overlooked) issue is whether the company e-mail involved jurisdictional means, an element of the §5(b)(1) prohibition. Any message delivered outside of Washington State would involve interstate communication, and if the company's e-mail system is connected to interstate phone (or data) lines, even messages delivered in Washington State might be seen as using "means of communication in interstate commerce."

WKSI note: The answer would be the same if Microsoft (a WKSI) were making a public offering today. Although WKSIs can use a "free writing prospectus" during the waiting period without complying with the prospectus-accompaniment condition, the legending and filing conditions still apply. Rules 164, 433. Unless there had been a good faith and reasonable effort in this regard, the exempting rule is unavailable.

c. No violation, if the banner is filed with the SEC. The banner meets the conditions of a "free writing prospectus" and as such is treated as a permitted §10(b) prospectus during the waiting period. Go down the checklist for a "free writing prospectus."

(1) The statement that the offering is a "milestone," even if not found in the prospectus, does not appear to conflict with anything in the registration statement. Rule 433(c)(1).

(2) Although the legend is not a verbatim version of that found in the rule (probably not a good idea), it is nonetheless "substantially" the same. Rule 433(c)(2)(i).

(3) The banner has a hyperlink to the preliminary prospectus, thus satisfying the prospectus-accompaniment condition. Rule 433(b)(2)(i); Securities Act Rel. No. 7856 (2000).

(4) All that remains is to file the banner using the SEC's electronic filing system, EDGAR. Rule 433(d)(1) ("free writing prospectus" not deemed to be part of registration statement).

Although not subject to §11 liability for misstatements in the registration statement (see §6.3), the banner and its "milestone" statement remain subject to the antifraud rules of §12(a)(2) (see §6.4) and Exchange Act Rule 10b-5 (see Chapter 9).

WKSI note: The answer would be the same if Microsoft (a WKSI) were making a public offering today — although the prospectus-accompaniment condition would not apply. Rules 164, 433(a).

d. No violation. This is a classic tombstone ad, a long-standing tradition in the securities industry that the Securities Act blessed in §2(a)(10)(b). Notice, though, that it does not satisfy the conditions of Rule 134(c)(1), which since 2005 requires that the ad include a URL where the preliminary prospectus may be obtained. Thus, the "statutory" tombstone ad — unlike the "regulatory" tombstone ad — harkens back to a time before the Internet when investors were expected to use telephones and the mail to obtain information about securities offerings.

e. No violation of §5, but the antifraud rules apply. Road shows with securities analysts and larger investors, common for an IPO, are mostly oral. Oral sales efforts are not prohibited during the waiting period.

Nonetheless, Gates's statements about management expectations are forward-looking statements (see §3.2.3) subject to the antifraud rules. Securities Act §12(a)(2) (see §6.4) and Exchange Act Rule 10b-5 (see §9.2). Company counsel often advises executives during the registration process to keep to a script that parrots the mostly historical information contained in the prospectus. Moreover, Gates's statements do not satisfy the safe harbor for oral forward-looking statements. To fall within the safe harbor of the Private Securities Litigation Reform Act of 1995, the speaker must accompany his oral forward-looking statement with a caution that results could differ materially from the statement and identify a readily available written document that contains additional information concerning risk factors. Securities Act §27A(c)(2).

What about the selective disclosure rules of Regulation FD? The road show, traditionally made available exclusively to securities analysts and institutional investors, would seem to violate Reg FD, which prohibits selective disclosure to favored investors or their representatives. Nonetheless, Reg FD does not apply here for two reasons. First, Microsoft is not a reporting company under the Exchange Act. Second, Reg FD expressly excludes oral communications in connection with registered non-shelf offerings. Rule 243.100(b)(2)(iv)(F).

f. No violation, so long as the story is consistent with the prospectus and the issuer files the news article within four days after becoming aware of it. Notice that the newspaper article can be seen as a §2(a)(10) "prospectus" — a written "offer" that conditions the market. As such, absent an exemption, §5(b)(1) prohibits its interstate distribution. (In fact, an interview given by the founders of Google to *Playboy* magazine during their 2004 IPO led the SEC to insist that the IPO be delayed until the interview was reprinted in an amended prospectus and distributed to investors who had shown an interest in the offering.)

The 2005 Public Offering Reforms provide a safe harbor for media publications that contain press interviews of the issuer or other offering participants. If the interview is consistent with the registration statement (including any SEC filings incorporated by reference), it is treated as a "free writing prospectus" so long as (1) it is published by an unaffiliated media company and (2) the issuer files it with the SEC (along with the usual legend) within four days after becoming aware of it. Rules 164, 433(f) (filing not required if substance of interview has already been filed). The filing can make corrections or simply include a transcript of what was provided the media. The media company is not subject to any legending or prospectus-accompaniment conditions, provided the issuer did not make any payments for the story.

The 2005 Public Offering Reforms seek to avoid (at least in the postfiling period) the argument that subjecting the press to the gun-jumping rules constitutes a government-imposed prior restraint. See explanation 1i above. The 2005 Reforms resolve the argument by placing the disclosure obligations on the offering participant that was the source of the information, not the media company that runs the story.

g. No violation. The 2005 Public Offering Reforms specifically exempt the posting of road shows on a company website. Although websites are treated as "graphic communications" (thus falling within the §2(a)(10) definition of "prospectus"), the audio/video/written content from the road show, such as handouts or a PowerPoint presentation, is treated as a "free writing prospectus." Rule 433(d)(8). The legending and prospectus-accompaniment conditions apply to road show websites, and filing by non-reporting issuers in an equity offering (such as Microsoft's IPO) is not required if the issuer posts the latest version of the road show with management presentations on its website. Rule 433(h)(5) (defining "bona fide electronic road show" to include presentations by one or more officers of the issuer).

h. Violation. Everything was perfectly proper until Janice jotted the note in the message line of the e-mail. A phone call followed by the sending of the preliminary prospectus (or "red herring" prospectus) is precisely the selling sequence envisioned by §5(b)(1). If Robert consented to receiving the prospectus by e-mail, Janice satisfied her obligations by linking to the prospectus, assuming it was accessible and printable. Furthermore, oral communications during the waiting period are permitted, so long as there is no binding "sale." And §5(b)(1) permits prospectuses that conform to §10 — here a preliminary prospectus that conforms to §10(b), which permits a prospectus during the waiting period even though it does not have final price or underwriting information.

The problem comes from the e-mail message line. This writing, which states a view about Microsoft's prospects and promotes the offering, is not a tombstone ad (§2(a)(10)(b)), an identifying statement (Rule 134), a company announcement (Rule 135), or a brokerage research report (Rules 137-139). See *In re Franklin, Meyer & Barnett*, 37 S.E.C. 47 (1956) (concluding that business card from securities salesman with notes urging customer to act quickly constituted illegal "prospectus").

Nor is the e-mail message line a "free writing prospectus" — it does not include the required legend and there is no indication that it has been retained. Rule 433(c)(2), (g). (Filing with the SEC may not be required since non-issuer offering participants need not file communications unless there is "broad unrestricted dissemination." Rule 433(d)(1)(ii).) Nor can these failures be excused as "immaterial or unintentional" since there is no indication there was any effort to comply with them. See Rule 164 (c), (d). As sent, the e-mail is a prohibited "prospectus," as defined by §2(a)(10).

What should Janice (and Goldman Sachs) have done? If the e-mail message had (1) included the proper legend, (2) been retained by the securities firm, and (3) been hyperlinked to the preliminary prospectus so Robert could download and print it, the message would satisfy the conditions of a "free writing prospectus." See Rules 164, 433. In fact, Janice could have written much more in the e-mail message, subject only to the requirement that her communication be consistent with the registration statement (including the prospectus) and the antifraud rules. If offering participants comply with the SEC checklist, the 2005 Public Offering Reforms permit free writing during the waiting period.

Why don't underwriters (and other non-issuers) have filing obligations when they use a "free writing prospectus," like those for issuers? The SEC rules require a filing only if the underwriter is distributing the materials in a "broad unrestricted dissemination" (such as a mass mailing to non-customers or a posting on its website). Rule 433(d)(1)(ii). The idea is that the underwriter should not be compelled to file, and thus to disclose on EDGAR, information to its customers that may contain proprietary analysis or advice. Securities Act Rel. No. 8501 (2005).

i. Violation. Section 5(a) prohibits "sales" (that is, contracts) during the waiting period. Robert has made a common-law offer, capable of being accepted to form a binding contract. The broker cannot accept the customer's check and would be well advised to return it to avoid any question that there was a "sale" during the waiting period.

j. No violation. The sales rep followed the script of Rule 134(d) for soliciting indications of interest during the waiting period. The card contains substantially the disclaimer of Rule 134(d) and attaches a preliminary prospectus.

k. No violation, at least of §5. Such oral contingent offers to buy are possible during the waiting period. So long as there is no binding acceptance, there is no §5 violation.

Participants in an offering, however, have obligations to provide preliminary prospectuses to customers who are anticipated to invest. The SEC requires participating securities firms to send a preliminary prospectus to any customer who is expected to receive a confirmation of sale once the registration becomes effective. The firm must send this prospectus at least 48 hours before it sends the customer the confirmation. Rule 15c2-8(b) (prospectus-delivery obligations of participating broker-dealers); Securities Act Rel. No. 4968 (condition of acceleration). This obligation applies to offerings in which the issuer has not been a reporting company, as was the case for Microsoft.

l. No violation, if the e-mail with the reprint meets the "free writing prospectus" conditions. The reprinted *Business Week* article is a "prospectus" under §2(a)(10) when used to solicit investor interest. Before the 2005 Public Offering Reforms, the reprint (even though accompanied by a preliminary prospectus) would have been prohibited under §5(b)(1).

"Free writing," however, is now possible during the waiting period if it meets the conditions of a "free writing prospectus." For this non-issuer "free writing prospectus" used in an S-1 offering, the magazine article must be consistent with information in the prospectus, the e-mail must be properly legended, it must be accompanied by or linked to the preliminary prospectus, but it need not be filed (though it must be retained). Rule 433.

While all issuer "free writing prospectuses" (those prepared or used by the issuer) must be filed, see Rule 433(d)(1)(i)(A), (h)(1), the filing requirements for written communications disseminated by non-issuer offering participants, such as underwriters, is trickier. If the communication was prepared by another person on the basis of information from the issuer *and* it is not sent in a manner that could lead to "broad unrestricted dissemination," then the underwriter need not file it. Rule 433(d)(1)(i)(B), (d)(1)(ii), (h)(2). Here the e-mail and reprint were sent to customers of the securities firm, which the SEC has explained does not constitute a "broad unrestricted dissemination." Securities Act Rel. No. 8591 (2005). The underwriter, however, will have to retain the e-mail and reprint for three years after the offering. Rule 433(g). Thus, underwriters can provide investors their views about the issuer and the offering, without having this proprietary information filed with the SEC.

WKSI note: The prospectus-accompaniment condition would not apply if Microsoft (a WKSI) were making a public offering today — though the information-consistency, legending, and retention conditions still would. Rules 164, 433(b)(1).

m. No violation. The creation of a selling group is permitted during the waiting period, so long as the underwriters make no binding commitments ("sales") and the communications are oral.

n. Violation. The newsletter is a "prospectus," and the safe harbors for "research reports" do not apply. Although the newsletter may qualify as a research report, the safe harbor available to non-participating securities firms does not apply since CHR plans to participate in the distribution. Rule 137 (though allowing nonparticipating securities firms to issuer research reports on non-reporting companies). The safe harbor for research reports on equity in a debt offering (and vice-versa) is inapplicable to this newsletter. Rule 138. The safe harbor for participating securities firms applies only if the issuer is a reporting company, and in some situations only if the issuer is a large, seasoned company able to use Form S-3. Rule 139(a).

o. No violation. This is standard practice in the industry. Although the "Agreement Among Underwriters" is part of a selling effort and technically a "prospectus," it is viewed as a "preliminary negotiation or agreement" among those who will be in privity with the issuer and is thus excepted from the definition of "offer." Securities Act §2(a)(3).

3. a. Violation. This graphic communication (if it used jurisdiction means — see explanation 2b above) could be construed to be a "prospectus," a written effort to excite potential investor interest. As such it is covered by §5(b)(1), which continues to prohibit written sales

efforts during the posteffective period unless they take the form of a final §10(a) prospectus.

None of the exceptions apply to the e-mail because it includes the information on the amount of shares sold and the market price, and favorably characterizes the first day's closing price. It thus goes beyond the information permitted in a tombstone ad, see §2(a)(10)(b) (permitting mention only of "price thereof"), and identifying statement, see Rule 134 (permitting "information" on amount being offered and offering price). And the e-mail fails to satisfy the legending, prospectus-accompaniment, and filing conditions to be considered a "free writing prospectus." Rule 433(b)(2), (c)(2). Even if these conditions were met, there is also some question whether the e-mail satisfies the information-consistency condition, which requires that the "substance" of the free writing not "conflict" with information in the registration statement. Arguably, the "hefty bump" language implies that Microsoft is a "hot IPO" and that further price increases are likely, information well beyond that of the staid prospectus.

WKSI note: The answer would likely be the same if Microsoft (a WKSI) were making a public offering today. Although WKSIs can use a "free writing prospectus" without complying with the prospectus-accompaniment condition, the information-consistency, legending, and filing conditions still apply. Rules 164, 433. The "hefty bump" language may be an insurmountable obstacle.

b. Probably violation. The §5(b)(1) prohibition against the use of "prospectuses" continues into the posteffective period. If the ad arouses investor interest, it would be a prohibited "prospectus" — so long as the issuer is still in "registration." (Notice the exemption for "free writing prospectuses" would not apply since the legending, prospectus-accompaniment, and filing conditions are not met.)

When is an issuer no longer "in registration"? The SEC has assumed that this period ends once participants in the offering no longer have prospectus-delivery obligations. Securities Act Rel. No. 5180 (1971). In Microsoft's offering, this would have happened on April 8, 1986 (25 days after the initial offering date) on the assumption the underwriters and other participants had sold their allotments by that time. See Rule 174(d) (25 days for non-reporting companies whose securities are listed on a stock exchange or authorized on NASDAQ). Thus, Microsoft was still "in registration" when it placed the magazine ad.

WKSI note: The answer would likely be different if Microsoft (a WKSI) were to make a public offering today. The issuer is "in registration" only as long as offering participants have unsold allotments; the prospectus-delivery obligations for nonparticipating securities firms last for *zero days* for issuers that were Exchange-Act-reporting companies before filing the registration statement. See Rule 174(b). Typically, allotments are sold within the first few days. Thus, there would be only a short window during which a reporting issuer would have to "remain quiet." And a WKSI could avoid any problems by treating the magazine ad as a "free writing prospectus," requiring only that the ad not be inconsistent with the prospectus, be legended, and be filed with the SEC. See Rule 433(a) (no prospectus-accompaniment for WKSI free writing).

c. Violation. By linking to the wire report, CHR has adopted the content of the wire story. Securities Act Rel. No. 7856 (2000). Free writing during the posteffective period requires that the final prospectus precede or accompany written sales material. Otherwise, the wire report is a "prospectus," prohibited by §5(b)(1). (The information-consistency, legending, prospectus-accompaniment, and filing conditions also apply if the wire story is considered a "free writing prospectus." Rule 164, 433.) The later sending of final prospectuses does not cleanse this violation since customers will receive and perhaps act on the wire report without a chance to review the chastening disclosure of the prospectus. CHR should have included a link to the final prospectus along with its link to the wire report.

d. No violation, assuming the confirmation meets Rule 10b-10. Section 2(a)(10) defines "prospectus" in an odd way to include sales confirmations. The effect is that a naked confirmation is itself a "prospectus." Under the statute, the confirmation is permitted only if accompanied or preceded by a final §10(a) prospectus. But the 2005 Public Offering Reforms change this by eliminating the prospectus-delivery obligation for confirmations. Instead, access to a final prospectus is deemed to equal delivery, requiring only that the issuer have filed (or plans to file) a final prospectus. See Rule 172(a) (exempting confirmations from §5(b)(1) that meet the information requirements of Rule 10b-10 and the issuer-filing condition). Of course, the underwriter could deliver a final prospectus — but why bother?

The 2005 Reforms, in addition, impose an independent notice obligation on offering participants that sell while they have a prospectus-delivery obligation. Rule 173(c) (notice not a condition to relying on "access equals delivery" rule). The notice, which must be sent within two days after the sale, must state the sale was made pursuant to a registration statement. Rule 173(a). The purchaser can request physical delivery of a final prospectus. Rule 173(d).

WKSI note: The answer would be the same if Microsoft (a WKSI) were making a public offering today. Although offerings by WKSIs receive many regulatory dispensations, the "access equals delivery" conditions are the same as for other issuers.

e. No violation, assuming Microsoft will file its final prospectus under Rule 424(b). In the posteffective period, offering participants have prospectus-delivery obligations when they deliver securities. See §5(b)(2). But this obligation is satisfied under the "access equals delivery" rule if the issuer (assuming neither the offering nor the issuer is subject to any pending SEC proceedings) has filed a prospectus and will make an effort to file a final prospectus under Rule 424(b). See Rule 172(b) (providing that the prospectus-delivery obligations of §5(b)(2) are satisfied).

The underwriter remains subject to the Rule 173 notice requirement, though satisfying this notice obligation is not necessary to relying on the "access equals delivery" rule. Rule 173(c). Why completely dispense with any requirement for underwriters and other offering participants in connection with securities delivery? For one, delivery of share certificates is mostly a thing of the past, since securities ownership is now universally documented through electronic record-keeping systems, including for brokerage customers who hold shares as beneficial owners. For another, there's little point in requiring a disclosure document *after* investors have purchased the securities.

f. No violation. Although notices of dealer allocations constitute "confirmations" that the statute requires be accompanied or preceded by a final prospectus, the "access equals delivery" rule covers the allocation notice. Rule 172(a) (exempting allocation notices from §5(b)(1) if they contain the confirmation information required by Rule 10b-10, as well as identifying (CUSIP numbers), pricing, allocation, and settlement information. This changes prior law that imposed a prospectus-delivery requirement for allocation notices, which could not be satisfied with postconfirmation prospectus. *Diskin v. Lomasney & Co.*, 452 F.2d 871 (2d Cir. 1971) (essentially the facts of the example). The 2005 Public Offering Reforms assume that participating dealers will have had a chance to review the prospectus before accepting their allocation; a final prospectus with the allocation notice would come too late.

g. No violation. The statute assumes that securities firms selling to customers in the posteffective period must confirm with a final prospectus. See §5(b)(1). This obligation continues so long as (1) the firm is selling its allotment and (2) the firm fills solicited customer orders on the market during the §4(a)(3) "registration" period. See Rule 174. Even though Goldman Sachs is no longer selling from its allotment, the "registration" period continues for Microsoft's IPO until April 8 (see 3b above). Thus, Goldman Sachs has prospectus-delivery obligations when it sells non-allotment shares before this date. To satisfy §5(b)(1) and its prospectus-delivery obligation, its confirmation must satisfy the "access equals delivery" conditions of Rule 172(a). And it also is subject to the notice requirements of Rule 173.

The 2005 Public Offering Reforms assume that the investor will have received the prospectus as part of the selling effort, and that delivery of a final prospectus comes too late. This reverses prior law, which assumed all purchasers should have a chance to review a final prospectus before being bound on their purchase. See *Byrnes v. Faulkner, Dawkins & Sullivan*, 550 F.2d 1303 (2d Cir. 1977) (market maker did not know it was buying stock from control person).

h. Probably no §5 violation. Although the prospectus misstates information that is arguably material, this does not necessarily create §5 liability. If the offers and sales during the offering otherwise complied with §5, the use of a materially misleading prospectus at most creates §11 or §12(a)(2) liability (see §§6.3, 6.4). The issuer has an obligation to sticker the prospectus and file it within five business days of using it. Rule 424(b)(3).

If, however, the misinformation was so critical that one could view the final prospectus as essentially nonexistent — voiding its use to confirm sales or accompany stock deliveries — there exists some judicial precedent for finding a §5 violation. *SEC v. Manor Nursing Centers*, 458 F.2d 1082 (2d Cir. 1972) (see §4.3.3). But merely failing to include information that should have been included under the SEC line-item disclosure rules does not constitute a §5 violation. *DeMaria v. Andersen*, 318 F.3d 170 (2d Cir. 2003) (inaccurate summary of graphs in EDGAR-filed prospectus, but included in printed prospectus, not a violation of registration rules).

i. No violation, barely. Even at this late date, the confirmation of the sales from the underwriter's allotment must satisfy the "access equals delivery" conditions of Rule 172, in particular that the issuer has filed a final prospectus meeting the requirements of §10(a). See Rule 172(c)(3). According to §10(a)(3), any prospectus used more than nine months after the effective date (for Microsoft, after December 13, 1986) may not have financial information that is more than 16 months old. In this case, the financial information (even though unaudited) is as of December 31, 1985, and thus less than 13 months old. The final prospectus satisfies the requirements of §10(a) and thus those of Rule 172. Nonetheless, if there have been any "substantive" changes since March (whether financial or otherwise), the prospectus must be "stickered" and then filed under Rule 424(b).

Exemptions from Securities Act Registration

Registering a securities offering under the Securities Act of 1933 is intrusive, expensive, and perilous. The costs of disclosure, underwriting, and potential liability in a registered public offering often outweigh the benefits of new capital. In recognition of this, the Securities Act exempts from registration those offers and sales (that is, *transactions*) for which full-blown registration may be unduly costly given investor sophistication, state securities regulation, or the issuer's small capital needs. For many securities lawyers, avoiding Securities Act registration is the grist of their practice.

The Securities Act also exempts specified kinds of securities from the §5 registration requirements when other market or regulatory protections make SEC registration superfluous. *Exempt securities* constitute a huge part of the securities markets: government securities, short-term commercial paper, securities issued by banks, and insurance policies issued by state-regulated insurance companies.

This chapter covers:

- the securities whose sale and resale are exempt from SEC registration [§5.1]
- the offerings (or transactions) that are exempt from SEC registration, including intrastate offerings, private placements, small offerings, crowdfunding offerings, and issuer exchanges [§5.2]
- the exemptions from state "blue sky" regulation [§5.3]

Preliminary Points

You should keep a couple points in mind. First, even if an offering satisfies an exemption, it remains subject to the antifraud provisions of the securities laws. The SEC can proceed against any seller of securities under §17 of the Securities Act. See §6.6. Purchasers of securities (other than exempt government securities) may have a private §12(a)(2) rescission remedy for misrepresentations in an offering (whether or not registered) that can be viewed as a "public offering." See *Gustafson v. Alloyd Co.*, 513 U.S. 561 (1995) (§6.4.1). And always lurking in the background is Rule 10b-5 of the Exchange Act, which exposes all securities sales and purchases to potential antifraud liability, including those exempt from Securities Act registration. See §9.2.

Second, although Congress has preempted large swaths of state securities regulation ("blue sky" rules) under the National Securities Markets Improvement Act of 1996 (see §1.5), many small and intrastate offerings exempt from federal registration remain subject to state regulation. In addition, all securities offerings (whether or not exempt from state registration) are subject to state *antifraud* rules and liability.

§5.1 EXEMPT SECURITIES

The first group of Securities Act registration exemptions focuses on the issuer and the type of securities being offered — these are called *exempt securities*. An exempt security is always exempt from registration, both when issued and later when traded.

Government Securities

The most significant category of exempt securities includes securities issued or guaranteed by governmental organizations. §3(a)(2). Thus, U.S. notes and bonds (as well as those of states and municipalities) are exempt from §5 registration when issued and subsequently traded. Federal, state, and municipal governments are spared the political embarrassment of mandatory disclosures about their executive officers, flagrant spending, shaky revenues, and so on.

Nonetheless, the SEC has imposed a disclosure regime on municipal securities through the back door by requiring that securities firms that deal in municipal securities provide investors an "official statement" for offerings above $1 million. Exchange Act Rule 15c2-12 (extended in 1994 to apply to industrial development bonds).

Commercial Paper

One of the trickier categories of exempt securities covers "notes . . . arising out of a current transaction" that mature in less than nine months. §3(a)(3). The SEC and the courts have understood this to mean "commercial paper" — that is, short-term, high-quality negotiable notes issued by companies for their current business operations and typically purchased by banks and other institutional investors, not the general public. *Reves v. Ernst & Young*, 494 U.S. 56 (1990) (see §2.3.4). The Securities Act exemption assumes that the sophistication of commercial paper markets, along with potential anti-fraud liability, adequately protects investors in short-term commercial paper. Although short-term commercial paper can be issued and transacted without §5 registration, issuers and securities firms that participate in a "public offering" of short-term paper may face potential §12(a)(2) liability. *Gustafson v. Alloyd Co.*, 513 U.S. 561 (1995) (see §6.4.1).

Curiously, the Exchange Act completely *excludes* short-term commercial paper from the definition of "security" and thus from Exchange Act regulation, including liability under Rule 10b-5.

Securities Subject to Non-SEC Regulation

The Securities Act exempts some securities on the theory that other regulations offer adequate protection to investors: securities issued by banks (§3(a)(2)); securities issued by federally or state-regulated S&Ls (§3(a)(5)); insurance policies and annuity contracts issued by state-regulated insurance companies (§3(a)(2)); tax-qualified employee pension plans, which are generally regulated by the Employee Retirement and Income Security Act (ERISA) (§3(a)(2)); certificates issued by bankruptcy trustees pursuant to court approval (§3(a)(2)); and participation interests in railroad cars of a federally regulated common carrier (§3(a)(6)).

Securities of Not-for-Profit Issuers

Not-for-profit issuers need not register their securities (often sold as bonds) so long as none of the issuer's net earnings benefit "any person, private stockholder, or individual." §3(a)(4). The exemption is available to issuers organized and operated exclusively for religious, educational, benevolent, fraternal, charitable, or reformatory purposes — typically tax-exempt organizations. The exemption assumes that mandating registration by not-for-profit issuers would indirectly raise costs to investors who themselves may have charitable motives.

Non-profit organizations, such as churches, often pay higher interest rates on their bonds than for-profit organizations, given that non-profits' bonds are not rated by ratings agencies and usually must be held to maturity because there is no trading market. Non-profits are often the first hit in an economic downturn as charitable donations decline, adding a special risk to investments in non-profits.

§5.2 TRANSACTION EXEMPTIONS

The second group of Securities Act registration exemptions focuses on the nature of the offering — these are called *transaction exemptions*. Securities sold under a transaction exemption do not themselves become exempt. This means that each time such securities are transacted, the seller must find a transaction exemption to avoid registration.

It is useful to keep in mind that most offerings of securities (particularly by smaller companies seeking to raise less than $20 million in capital) are structured as exempt offerings. Thus, the bulk of work for many securities lawyers lies in identifying and helping clients navigate the registration exemptions created by statute and SEC regulation.

Primary Offerings by Issuers

The transaction exemptions apply to primary offerings by issuers — intrastate offerings, private placements, certain small offerings, crowdfunding offerings, and exchanges by the issuer. These exemptions do not cover subsequent trading by investors or secondary offerings by control persons of the issuer. Instead, the §4(a)(1) "market trading" exemption, which applies to any transaction by a person "other than an issuer, underwriter, or dealer," demarcates the line between securities "distributions" and securities trading. See Chapter 7.

Burden to Establish Exemption

It is important to remember that the party seeking a transaction exemption bears the burden to show it has met the exemption's conditions. If this burden is not met, the exemption is lost, and rescission liability for selling unregistered securities is automatic under §12(a)(1). See §6.2.1.

Integration

To be exempt under a transaction exemption, the offering must meet all the exemption's conditions. Under the *integration principle*, an issuer cannot slice and dice an offering so that different parts fit separate exemptions, if the offering as a whole fits none. This principle is prophylactic and compels issuers to be meticulous in structuring an exempt offering.

When do multiple offers and sales constitute an integrated offering? The SEC has articulated a five-factor test that considers whether the multiple transactions (1) are part of single plan of financing, (2) involve the same class of security, (3) took place at about the same time, (4) involved the same consideration, and (5) were made for the same general purpose. See Securities Act Rel. No. 4552 (1962). In effect, the test asks whether there was *one financing*. See *In re Kunz*, Exchange Act Rel. No. 45290 (2002) (upholding NASD disciplinary sanctions arising from unregistered offerings of various notes with different maturities and secured by different assets, since all offerings made "at about the same time" with the same general purpose to finance issuer's mortgage lending business).

To alleviate uncertainty, many SEC exemptions contain a "safe harbor" from integration under a test that focuses on the timing of the sales. Under this test, sets of sales separated by six months are considered separate offerings and are not subject to integration. See Rule 502(a) (Regulation D); Rule 147(b)(2) (intrastate offerings). In addition, the SEC permits an issuer to first complete a private placement under §4(a)(2) (including under Rule 506) and then to "subsequently" initiate a public offering, without the two offerings being integrated. Rule 152.

In 2001 the SEC promulgated a rule to allow issuers to shift from a private to registered offering (and vice versa) without the two being integrated. Rule 155. To help issuers respond to changing market conditions, Rule 155 creates two integration safe harbors. The first permits an issuer that begins a qualified, bona fide private offering (but sells no securities) to abandon it and begin a registered offering. A 30-day waiting period applies, unless the private offering was only to accredited or sophisticated investors. Rule 155(b). The second safe harbor permits an issuer that started a registered offering to withdraw the registration statement before any securities are sold and then begin a private offering, again after a 30-day waiting period. The issuer must disclose this withdrawal in the private offering, as well as describing the unregistered nature of the offering and any material changes that occurred after the registration statement was filed. Rule 155(c).

§5.2.1 Intrastate Offerings

The Securities Act exempts from registration purely intrastate offerings — that is, those by an in-state issuer to in-state residents. §3(a)(11). The exemption, linked to constitutional concerns in 1933 about the extent of federal legislative power, covers local offerings capable of regulation by state securities law.

The SEC and the courts have interpreted the §3(a)(11) statutory intrastate exemption narrowly and strictly, and issuers rely on it at their peril.

To temper the statutory exemption, the SEC has promulgated a safe harbor rule that creates bright-line standards defining (1) the scope of the offering, (2) whether the issuer and offerees are in-state, and (3) when out-of-state resales are permissible. Rule 147. The safe harbor rule is not exclusive. An offering that fails the Rule 147 standards can still be exempt under the §3(a)(11) statutory standards.

The intrastate exemption does not limit the amount of money that can be raised, how often the exemption can be used, or the number or sophistication of offerees and purchasers. An intrastate offering exempt from Securities Act registration, however, remains subject to state "blue sky" laws. See §4.2.6.

In-State Issuer

Under the statutory §3(a)(11) exemption, the issuer must be "a person resident and doing business within" the state of the offering. A corporation, according to the statute, "resides" in the state of its incorporation. Courts have held that an issuer "does business" in a state if its revenues, assets, principal office, and use of the offering's proceeds are principally in-state.

Consistent with the statutory purpose to avoid federal regulation when state regulation is feasible, the issuer's in-state nature often turns on whether the state's securities administrator could exercise jurisdiction to investigate the issuer and its use of the proceeds. *SEC v. McDonald Investment Co.*, 343 F. Supp. 343 (D. Minn. 1972) (rejecting exemption when state administrator could not attach out-of-state real estate developed from offering's proceeds).

Rule 147 provides some clarity. It defines the "residence" of a noncorporate issuer as the state where the issuer is organized or, if an unorganized partnership, where it has its principal business. Rule 147(c)(1). It also specifies quantitative guidelines for the "doing business" requirement. Rule 147(c)(2). An issuer is deemed to be doing business within a state if its principal office is in-state, and 80 percent of its gross revenues, 80 percent of its consolidated assets, and 80 percent of the intended use of the offering's net proceeds are all within the state.

In-State Offering

The statutory exemption specifies that the issue may be "offered and sold only to persons resident within a single State." §3(a)(11). Otherwise, there are no qualitative or numerical limits on in-state offerees or purchasers.

The SEC and the courts have interpreted the statutory exemption to require that *all* offerees and purchasers have actual residence and domiciliary intent in the issuer's state. Securities Act Rel. No. 4434 (1961). The statutory exemption is lost if any sale or any offer (even one that does not result in a sale) is made to an out-of-state resident. The exemption also evaporates if any purchaser acts as a statutory underwriter by offering or reselling to out-of-state investors. The issuer cannot rely on "investment representations" by in-state purchasers who buy with a view to distribute to out-of-state investors. In-state purchasers, however, can resell to out-of-state purchasers if the securities have "come to rest" with them prior to their resale. See §7.2.

Again, Rule 147 provides some helpful clarity. Under the rule, an individual's in-state residence can be established by her actual principal residence, without regard to ephemeral domiciliary intent. Rule 147(d)(2). The residence of business entities tracks their principal office. Rule 147(d)(3). Moreover, the rule permits in-state purchasers to resell after a nine-month holding period—a "come to rest" safe harbor. Rule 147(e). But even one out-of-state offer or resale voids the rule's exemption if it occurs during the nine-month period after the issue is completed.

Scope of In-State Offering

Section 3(a)(11) specifies that offers and sales that are "part of an issue" must satisfy all the conditions of the statutory exemption. This means an intrastate offering cannot be part of a larger offering to out-of-state investors—remember the *integration principle*.

When are transactions "part of an issue"? In general, the SEC's five-part test provides the answer. See §5.2. But for offerings covered by Rule 147, there is a six-month safe harbor. Offers and sales made six months before the intrastate offering begins, as well as offers and sales made six months after it ends, are not integrated with the intrastate offering. Rule 147(b)(2).

	§3(a)(11)	Rule 147
Scope of offering (integration)	All securities offered as "part of an issue" are integrated	Sets of sales separated by six months are not integrated
In-state issuer	"Resident and doing business" within the state	Principal office within state, and 80% of gross revenues, assets, and proceeds used are within the state
In-state offerees	Offerees must be domiciled within the state	Offerees must have principal residence within the state
Restriction on resales	Securities must "come to rest" prior to being resold	Nine-month safe harbor holding period

§5.2.2 Private Placements

Section 4(2) of the Securities Act—numbered as §4(a)(2) by the JOBS Act of 2012—exempts from registration any offering "by an issuer not involving any public offering." Although Congress conveniently forgot to define "public offering," courts and the SEC have interpreted the §4(a)(2) *private placement exemption* to embody a congressional judgment that registration is unnecessary when investors on their own have adequate sophistication and information to protect themselves.

Private placements are significant to capital formation in this country. For example, more than two-thirds of all debt issues are privately placed. Without the private placement exemption, Securities Act registration would burden (and even squelch) capital formation in offerings to investors whose informational or bargaining position is comparable to the issuer's.

The private placement exemption exists in two forms:

- **Statutory exemption**. The §4(a)(2) statutory exemption completely exempts issuers from all Securities Act disclosure and registration requirements.
- **Safe harbor rule**. A regulatory safe harbor exemption (Rule 506 of Regulation D) provides clear guidance for issuers, though mandates disclosure to certain investors.

Here we explore the elements of the statutory §4(a)(2) exemption. The safe harbor Rule 506 is addressed below in connection with Regulation D.

Courts have interpreted the §4(a)(2) exemption not to limit the dollar size of a private offering or the number of investors. Instead, courts have focused on investor qualification, formulating a "sliding scale" of investor sophistication and access to information about the issuer. The burden of establishing the exemption rests on the person claiming it.

Ralston Purina

During the first two decades of its existence, uncertainty abounded about the §4(a)(2) private placement exemption. The section's legislative history mentioned "specific or isolated" sales, and a 1935 opinion by the SEC's general counsel had suggested a cap for the exemption of 25 investors.

In 1953, the Supreme Court resolved this uncertainty and supplied the exemption an operative philosophy. *SEC v. Ralston Purina Co.*, 346 U.S. 119 (1953). The case involved Ralston Purina's policy of selling its common stock to employees—without registration. Hundreds of employees in a variety of positions (including chow-loading foreman, stock clerk, and stenographer) had purchased unregistered stock on their own initiative.

The SEC sued, demanding that future sales be registered. The Court held that the §4(a)(2) exemption applies when offerees and investors, regardless of their number, are "able to fend for themselves." Who are these vaunted investors? The Court gave as an example "executive personnel" with access to the same kind of information as would be available in a registration statement. In the case, the Court held that many of the Ralston Purina stock purchasers lacked this access, and registration was required.

Investor Qualification

When can investors "fend for themselves"? Lower courts interpreting §4(a)(2) have focused both on the investor's *ability to evaluate* the investment (given his business and investment sophistication) and on his *access to information* about the investment (based on the availability of information or the issuer's actual disclosure). The less sophisticated the investor, the more disclosure is required; the more sophisticated, the less disclosure is required.

A line of Fifth Circuit cases dating from the 1970s wrestled with the balance between investor sophistication and information access:

Sophisticated, but not informed	The court denied a §4(a)(2) exemption when sophisticated investors in a franchise received no disclosure document or other access to information. The court said the exemption requires that investors (no matter how sophisticated) have access to information about the issuer. *Hill York Corp. v. American International Franchises, Inc.*, 448 F.2d 680 (5th Cir. 1971).
Not sophisticated, but informed	The court denied a §4(a)(2) exemption when investors received information comparable to that of a registration statement, but many lacked investment sophistication. The court suggested qualified investors must have personal contact with corporate officers, making them tantamount to insiders. *SEC v. Continental Tobacco Co.*, 463 F.2d 137 (5th Cir. 1972).
Sophisticated, but not insider	The court clarified that the §4(a)(2) exemption does not depend on insider status — sophisticated outsiders can be qualified. *Wolfe v. S. D. Cohn & Co.*, 515 F.2d 591 (5th Cir. 1975).

Access to information, but no actual disclosure	The court held that investors must either receive or have access to information comparable to that found in a registration statement. Access can be shown by the investor's insider status, family, or privileged relationship with the issuer, or the investor's economic bargaining power. *Doran v. Petroleum Management Corp.*, 545 F.2d 893 (5th Cir. 1977).

The person claiming the §4(a)(2) exemption must show that each purchaser and each offeree (even one who does not purchase) meets the sliding scale test. Absent this showing, the exemption is lost for the entire offering. *Doran v. Petroleum Management Corp.*

Prohibition Against General Solicitations

A natural corollary to the §4(a)(2) requirement that all *offerees* be qualified is a prohibition against general solicitations. Public advertising or open-to-the-public investment seminars eviscerate the exemption because not all offerees can be shown to be qualified. (Remember the burden of showing all elements of the exemption are met is on the person claiming the exemption.) For this reason, issuers making a private placement often rely on securities firms to prescreen potential investors. This prohibition is also a main reason many issuers prefer to use the Rule 506 exemption under Reg D for their private placements, given that offers to non-qualified investors do not eviscerate the SEC exemption and especially since the JOBS Act of 2012 permits broad marketing of Rule 506 offerings, so long as the issuer ends up selling only to accredited investors. See §5.2.4 below.

Resale Restriction

Investors who purchase in a private placement cannot resell to unqualified investors. Such resales transform the whole offering into a public distribution and the reselling investors into statutory underwriters. See §2(11). For this reason, issuers seek to restrict the transferability of privately placed securities, known as "restricted securities." Typically, the purchase agreement in a private placement will contain transfer restrictions (noted on the security certificates), and the issuer will instruct its transfer agent (often a bank that keeps records on shareholder ownership) not to record any transfer unless it complies with or is exempt from the Securities Act's registration requirements.

§5.2.3 Small Offerings

Congress has a special place in its heart for small business, and the Securities Act contains a variety of exemptions for small offerings.

Offerings up to $5 Million

Since 1933, the Securities Act has given the SEC authority to exempt offerings to the public that do not exceed a specified amount. In 1996, Congress set the limit at $5 million. §3(b)(1). The SEC has used its §3(b)(1) authority in a variety of ways:

Regulation A

The SEC has promulgated a regime of miniregistration for offerings during any continuous 12-month period having an aggregate price up to $5 million. Regulation A; Rules 251-264 (insiders can sell up to $1.5 million).

Under Reg A, offerings are exempt from registration if the issuer uses an "offering circular" and complies with filing and circular delivery requirements that mimic those of §5. The offering circular is a simplified disclosure document that can use either a registration-type or question-and-answer format. Financial information is required, though it need not be audited. See Form 1-A (Part F/S). Sales may commence 20 days after the filing or any amendment. Rule 252(g). During the waiting period before the offering qualifies for sale, preliminary offering circulars may be used. Rule 255. In addition, Reg A permits issuers to "test the waters"—that is, to solicit investor interest before filing an offering statement. Rule 254 (compare to §5 gun-jumping prohibition; see §4.3).

Reg A is available only to nonreporting U.S. and Canadian issuers that are not disqualified under detailed "bad actor" provisions: (1) issuers under pending SEC administrative review; (2) issuers subject to SEC orders in the last five years; (3) issuers convicted or enjoined for federal or state securities violations or postal fraud in the last five years; (4) issuers whose executives or 10 percent shareholders have been subject to similar SEC sanctions or court orders; (5) issuers who use an underwriter with a comparable tainted past. Rule 262. In addition, as mandated by the Dodd-Frank Act of 2010, the SEC amended Rule 262 to further disqualify (1) issuers barred from engaging in the business of securities, insurance or banking; (2) issuers subject to a final order for fraudulent, manipulative or deceptive conduct within the 10 years before the offering; and (3) issuers convicted of any felony or misdemeanor in connection with the purchase or sale of any security or involving false filings with the SEC. Dodd-Frank §926; Rule 262. As mandated by Dodd-Frank, the SEC has also imposed similar (though slightly broader) "bad actor" disqualifications for Rule 506 offerings. Rule 506(d).

Reg A's use has been eclipsed by Regulation D (below) and the streamlined registration for "smaller reporting companies" (see §4.2.1). Nonetheless, it has proved useful for a handful of small, national offerings to many investors over the Internet. Unlike Reg D, there are no limitations on general solicitations in a Reg A offering.

Regulation D (Rules 504 and 505)

The SEC has used its §3(b)(1) authority to exempt small offerings up to $1 million (Rule 504) and nonpublic offerings up to $5 million with 35 or fewer "nonaccredited investors" (Rule 505). The SEC amalgamated these two exemptions, along with a safe harbor §4(a)(2) exemption (Rule 506), into a highly successful set of rules known as Regulation D. See §5.2.4.

Small Business Stock Compensation Plans

In 1999, the SEC used its §28 exemptive authority (see §1.5) to revise the exemption available to nonreporting companies that offer employee stock compensation plans. Rule 701. The maximum value of securities that can be sold under these plans is $1 million, 15 percent of the issuer's total assets, or 15 percent of the outstanding securities of that class — whichever is greater. Offers (as opposed to actual sales) do not count against these price ceilings. If more than $5 million worth of securities are sold, the issuer must provide to each employee-purchaser specific disclosure that includes a summary of the compensation plan, risk factors, and financial statements used in a Reg A offering. The rule can be used to give stock compensation to consultants and advisers.

In addition, to make it easier for small companies to compensate employees and consultants with stock — without increasing their shareholder base for purposes of §12(g) Exchange Act registration (see §8.3.1) — the JOBS Act of 2012 specifies that stock "held of record" does not include any shares issued pursuant to an employee compensation plan exempt from §5 registration. See Exchange Act §12(g)(5).

Small Business Investment Companies

In 1958, Congress extended the SEC's exemptive authority to offerings by small business investment companies — that is, investment funds that invest in many small businesses. §3(c). The SEC has used this authority to exempt offerings up to $5 million by such investment companies. Regulation E; Rules 601-610a.

Offerings up to $50 Million: New Reg A+

The JOBS Act of 2012 adds another avenue for small- and medium-sized companies to raise money without having to undertake a registered offering. Under new §3(b)(2) of the Securities Act, Congress directed the SEC to create a new exemption from §5 — often referred to as "Reg A+" — for companies raising up to $50 million over a 12-month period. In 2013, the SEC proposed rules to implement the exemption — though at the beginning of 2014 the Reg A+ regime has yet to be finalized.

The congressional call for a new Reg A+ exemption reflected the view that the existing Reg A had not fulfilled its purpose. A GAO study required by the JOBS Act confirmed the obvious: small issuers have tended to prefer Reg D over Reg A, given the SEC delays in reviewing Reg A offering statements, the absence of disclosure requirements in Reg D offerings made to only accredited investors, and the time-consuming and expensive process of complying with state "blue sky" laws (which are preempted for Rule 506 offerings, but not Reg A offerings). GAO, *Factors that May Affect Trends in Regulation A Offerings* (July 2012).

The new Reg A+ exemption is supposed to function similarly to Reg A. Issuers are to be subject to the disqualification provisions of Rule 506 (see §5.2.4 below). The issuer must file with the SEC and distribute to investors an offering statement with audited financial statements. An issuer is allowed to gauge the interest in the offering prior to filing an offering statement. And securities issued in a Reg A+ offering are not restricted and can be traded.

Besides its higher offering amount, Reg A+ is to be different from Reg A in a few important respects. First, the Reg A+ $50 million ceiling is subject to upward adjustment by the SEC every two years. Second, companies making a Reg A+ offering become subject to on-going disclosure requirements, including the filing of annual audited financials. Third, in limited circumstances, state "blue sky" laws are preempted for Reg A+ offerings: when the securities are offered and sold on a national securities exchange or when the securities are offered and sold only to "qualified investors" (a term left for SEC definition). See Securities Act §18(b)(4)(D) (see §4.2.6).

Importantly, the JOBS Act explicitly subjects companies and intermediaries that offer and sell securities in a Reg A+ offering to §12(a)(2) liability. See §6.4.

§5.2.4 Regulation D

In 1982 the SEC amalgamated its exemptions for small and private offerings in a set of rules known as "Regulation D" — affectionately "Reg D." Securities Act Rel. No. 6389 (1982). These rules give detailed guidance on when an offering qualifies for the §4(a)(2) private placement exemption (Rule 506) and create additional exemptions for "small offerings" as authorized by §3(b)(1) (Rules 504 and 505).

Rule 504: *Small Offerings (Subject to State Blue Sky Laws)*

Companies seeking to raise capital for specific purposes can sell up to $1 million in securities in any 12-month period. (The exemption is not available to reporting companies, investment companies, or development stage companies that lack a specific business plan—sometimes called "blank check" companies.) To reduce fraud in the sale of low-priced (or "microcap") securities, the exemption does not permit general advertising or solicitations, and the securities issued under the exemption become "restricted"—which means that any resales are subject to at least a six-month holding period or the securities must be registered. See Rule 144 (§7.2.1). To avoid these marketing and liquidity constraints, small issuers have two options: (1) register the offering under a state "blue sky" law that requires public filing and pre-sale delivery to investors of a substantive disclosure document, or (2) limit the offering only to "accredited investors" (as defined in Reg D) under a state law exemption that permits general solicitations. If the issuer registers the offering in one state, it can expand the offering to other states that do not require registration, so long as all investors are delivered the disclosure document before sale.

Rule 505: *Medium-Sized Offerings (Subject to SEC Conditions)*

Companies can sell up to $5 million in securities in any 12-month period. (The exemption is not available to investment companies or to "bad actors" under the criteria of Reg A, see §5.2.3.) No general advertising or solicitations are permitted. The offering can be sold to an unlimited number of "accredited" investors, "but there can be no more than 35 'nonaccredited' investors." All nonaccredited investors must receive specified written disclosure and have an opportunity to ask questions of the issuer. Securities acquired pursuant to Rule 505 become "restricted securities."

Rule 506: *Private Offerings (Subject to SEC Safe Harbor Conditions)*

Companies—both public and private companies, though not "bad actors" under criteria broader than those of Reg A, see Rule 506 Disqualifications below—can sell an unlimited amount of securities under much the same conditions as Rule 505, with one added condition. If any sale is made to nonaccredited investors, each nonaccredited investor (alone or with an independent purchaser representative) must have sufficient knowledge and experience in business and financial matters so she can evaluate the merits and risks of the investment. (This requirement can be satisfied if the issuer reasonably believes the nonaccredited investor is sophisticated.) Rule 506 is a nonexclusive safe harbor; an offering that does not satisfy all the rule's conditions may still be exempt under §4(a)(2).

Integration

Reg D offerings are governed by the integration principle. This means all offers and sales that are part of a Reg D offering must meet all the conditions of the relevant exemption. Transactions are integrated if they meet the SEC five-part test. See §5.2. Regulation D, however, creates a safe harbor against integration for offers and sales occurring six months before the start (and six months after the completion) of the Reg D offering. Rule 502(a). (An exception applies to offerings pursuant to an employee benefit plan, which are not integrated even within the six-month windows.)

Aggregation

Rules 504 and 505, adopted pursuant to the §3(b)(1) small offering exemption, cap the aggregate dollar amount that an issuer may raise in any 12-month period. The cap is calculated by aggregating

- the offering price of all securities sold pursuant to the Rule 504 or 505 exemption, *plus*
- the offering price of all securities sold within the previous 12 months in reliance on any §3(b)(1) exemption — Rule 504, Rule 505, Reg A, Rule 701 (small business stock compensation plans), *plus*
- the offering price of all securities sold in the previous 12 months in violation of the §5 registration requirements — so nonexempt unregistered offerings also count against the §3(b)(1) cap.

This aggregate cannot exceed $1 million (Rule 504) or $5 million (Rule 505).

Students (and securities lawyers) often confuse aggregation with integration. The two are distinct. *Aggregation* involves a simple calculation of whether the amount to be financed in a 12-month period exceeds the Rule 504 or 505 dollar limit. *Integration* involves treating different offers and sales as a single offering — treated together they may (or may not) satisfy the conditions of the relevant exemption. Integration can happen, for example, without there being an aggregation problem. Suppose a $1 million intrastate offering to 20 in-state purchasers in January is followed by a $2 million Rule 505 offering to 20 out-of-state purchasers in March. If integrated, the combined offering would not satisfy the intrastate exemption (because of the out-of-state purchasers) or the Rule 505 exemption (if the

40 purchasers were nonaccredited). But, even if we aggregate the January and March offerings, the $5 million cap of Rule 505 would not be exceeded.

Accredited Investors

Rules 505 and 506 permit an unlimited number of "accredited" purchasers, but only 35 "nonaccredited" purchasers. Neither rule requires disclosure to accredited purchasers, but both mandate significant disclosure to nonaccredited purchasers. Rule 506 imposes sophistication criteria on nonaccredited purchasers, but none on accredited purchasers.

Rule 501(a) sets out categories of accredited investors, which as of 2013 include:

Institutional investors	Banks, savings institutions, brokerage firms, insurance companies, mutual funds, and certain ERISA employee benefit plans.
Big organizations	Tax-exempt organizations and for-profit corporations with more than $5 million in assets.
Key insiders	The directors, executive officers, and general partners of the issuer.
Millionaires	Individuals who have a net worth (along with their spouse) of over $1 million, not counting the value of their primary residence — with the threshold to be adjusted periodically by the SEC. See Dodd-Frank §413(a) (adjustment every four years beginning in 2014).
Fat cats	Individuals who have had for two years, and expect to have, an annual income of $200,000 (or $300,000 with their spouse) — with the thresholds to be adjusted periodically by the SEC. See Dodd-Frank §413(b) (adjustment every four years beginning at least by 2014).
Venture-capital firms	Firms that invest in start-up companies to which they make available "significant managerial assistance."
Sophisticated trusts	Trusts with over $5 million in assets and run by a sophisticated manager.
Accredited-owned entity	An entity in which all the equity owners are accredited investors.

Reg D assumes that investors in these categories either have the sophistication to fend for themselves or the financial resources to pay for a sophisticated investment adviser. An investor is "accredited" either by fitting in one of the categories or if the issuer reasonably believes the investor is accredited. For this reason, issuers and their financial advisers often demand that purchasers supply "suitability letters" warranting their qualifying characteristics.

Counting Nonaccredited Purchasers

The cap of 35 nonaccredited investors in Rules 505 and 506 is not immediately evident from reading the rules. Both rules set a limit of 35 "purchasers" with no limits on the number of offerees. Although this would seem to limit both accredited and nonaccredited purchasers, Rule 501(e) computes the number of purchasers by excluding "accredited investors." The effect is that the 35-purchaser limit is really a 35-nonaccredited investor limit.

Reg D also avoids double counting related purchasers. When an investor (whether accredited or not) buys for himself, additional purchases by his spouse or relatives who live with him or purchases for a trust, estate, or other organization in which he has a significant interest are not counted. Thus, a single nonaccredited investment decision, carried out through different channels, gets counted as one nonaccredited purchaser.

Prohibition Against General Solicitations

In a departure from §4(a)(2), Reg D does not prohibit *offers* to nonaccredited investors, but does prohibit "general solicitations or general advertising" in a Rule 505 or 506 offering, as well as Rule 504 offerings not subject to state law that permits such solicitations. Rule 502(c). Reg D gives some examples of prohibited solicitations: newspaper, magazine, television or radio ads, public websites, and open seminars or investment meetings.

When is a solicitation not general? The SEC has interpreted the prohibition as requiring that the issuer (or a person acting on its behalf) have a "pre-existing relationship" with each offeree. Under this interpretive gloss, the actual sophistication or financial wherewithal of the offerees is irrelevant. See *In re Kenman Corp.* (SEC 1985) (finding that issuer had no preexisting relationship with executives, professional, and investors who were identified from lists purchased or created by issuer, including executives from "Fortune 500" companies, physicians in the state of California, and large real estate investors). In theory, the preexisting relationship test is meant to ensure that the issuer (or its financial adviser) knows the investment sophistication and financial circumstances of *all offerees*. In effect, it mandates that suitability screening occur before any Reg D solicitation — not as a part of the solicitation. This gloss has been criticized for forcing issuers to hire securities firms to market their Reg D offerings since issuers rarely have their own lists of prescreened qualified investors.

To make it easier for companies seeking to raise capital, the JOBS Act directed the SEC to remove the prohibition on general solicitations in Rule 506 offerings to accredited investors. JOBS Act §201. Under new Rule 506(c), general solicitations (including "cold calls") are permitted provided the issuer verifies that all of the investors who end up purchasing in the offering are accredited. See Securities Act Rel. No. 9415 (2013) (verification rules required by JOBS Act). The issuer can verify an investor's income using tax forms/returns and an investor's net worth using recent bank/brokerage statements (assets) and a recent credit report (liabilities). The issuer can also obtain confirmations from securities firms, investment advisers, attorneys, and CPAs that the investor meets the accredited investor standards. (Notice that self-verification by investors of their "accredited investor" status is available for Rule 506 offerings that do not involve general solicitations.)

The prohibition on general solicitation, however, still applies to offerings under Rules 504 and 505, as well as offerings under Rule 506 that include nonaccredited investors.

Resale Restrictions

Securities sold in a Rule 505 or 506 offering, as well as a Rule 504 offering not subject to state law that allows resales, have the status of §4(a)(2) "restricted securities" and cannot be resold without registration or further exemption. Rule 502(d). Reg D requires issuers to take "reasonable care" to prevent unregistered, nonexempt resales, such as by (1) having purchasers sign letters of investment intent, (2) disclosing the securities' restricted nature, and (3) legending the securities as restricted. Other actions, such as establishing stop order procedures with transfer agents, may also satisfy the provision.

Disclosure Obligations

There is no disclosure requirement in Rule 505 and 506 offerings made exclusively to accredited investors, though such offerings remain subject to general antifraud provisions. But, disclosure becomes mandatory if there are any nonaccredited investors. See note to Rule 502(b)(1) (suggesting general antifraud provisions may require that accredited investors receive same information as nonaccredited investors).

If the issuer is a reporting company, it must furnish nonaccredited investors its most recent annual report, its proxy statement, and any subsequent Exchange Act filings, along with a brief description of the particular offering. Rule 502(b)(2)(ii) (or, alternatively, Form S-1 or Form 10-K, plus updating and offering information).

Disclosure requirements for nonreporting companies vary with the size of the offering. Rule 502(b)(2)(i)(A), (B); Regulation S-B, item 310(a).

Size of offering	Disclosure required
Up to $2 million	Regulation A offering circular, with financials required of small business issuers.
Between $2 million and $7.5 million	Part I of registration form for which issuer is eligible, with financials required of small business issuers.
More than $7.5 million	Part I (and financials) of the registration form for which the issuer is eligible.

Typically, nonreporting issuers must provide their most recent balance sheet, as well as income statements for the last two years. For offerings of less than $2 million, only the balance sheet need be audited. For offerings larger than $2 million, all the financials must be audited—often a significant additional expense. If audited financials would entail an "unreasonable effort or expense," the rule allows for only the balance sheet to be audited. Rule 502(b)(i)(B)(2), (B)(3).

Besides getting mandated disclosure, nonaccredited investors (whether the issuer is reporting or nonreporting) are entitled to a summary (or a copy, if requested) of any information given accredited investors. Both accredited and nonaccredited investors can ask questions and demand verification. Rule 502(b)(2)(v). Accredited investors have no right to the information given nonaccredited investors, though the securities antifraud rules (such as Rule 10b-5) may have the practical effect of compelling it. See Note, Rule 502(b)(1).

Notice to SEC — Form D

Reliance on any of the Reg D exemptions requires that notice be filed with the SEC within 15 days after the first sale. Rule 503(a). The SEC uses the notice to keep track of Reg D usage.

In 2008 the SEC significantly revised Form D and required that it be filed electronically. Securities Act Rel. No. 8891 (2008). Among the important changes, the revised Form D need not disclose 10 percent beneficial owners or how the proceeds will be used (for competitive and privacy reasons), but it must disclose the amount and recipients of sales commissions/finder fees. Generally, Form D must be filed on the date of the first sale, which is defined as when an investor has become "irrevocably contractually committed" to invest. And an amended Form D must be filed whenever the offering size or sales commissions/finders' fees increase by more than 10 percent, whenever the company has a change in management, and annually so long as the offering is continuing.

In addition, Form D calls on the company to identify (among other things) which Reg D exemption is being claimed, whether the offering is intended to last more than one year, the company's industry group (including whether the company is a hedge fund, private equity fund, or venture capital fund), the range of the company's revenue (for operating companies) or aggregate net asset value (for investment funds), the types of securities being offered, whether the offering is in connection with a business combination, the minimum investment amount, and the company's principal place of business.

Finally, for Rule 506 offerings accomplished through general solicitations, as permitted by the JOBS Act, issuers must also check a box on Form D indicating whether they are claiming this new exemption. In addition, in such offerings, Form D must be filed before general solicitations begin and again when the offering closes. Failure to file results in a one-year "time out" from using Rule 506. In addition, the company must file solicitation materials with the SEC.

Incomplete Compliance

Even if an issuer fails to comply with Regulation D, the exemption is not lost if the issuer shows the failures were insignificant:

- the noncompliance did not undermine the protection available to the particular investor seeking to avoid the exemption; and
- the noncompliance did not involve the ban on general solicitations, the Rules 504 and 505 dollar limits, or the Rules 505 and 506 limits on the number of nonaccredited investors; and
- the issuer made a good faith and reasonable attempt to comply with the rule.

Rule 508(a). You should also remember that Reg D sets out safe harbor rules. Even when an offering does not comply with the rule, it may still fit another exemption, such as the §4(a)(2) private placement exemption or the intrastate exemption.

"Bad Actor" Disqualification

An issuer is disqualified from using Rule 506 if the issuer or persons connected with the issuer are "bad actors." See Rule 506(d), (e) (implementing §926 of Dodd-Frank); see also SEC, *Small Entity Compliance Guide — Disqualification of Felons and Other "Bad Actors" from Rule 506 Offerings and Related Disclosure Requirements* (2013). Disqualification happens because of specified criminal convictions, regulatory or court orders, or other disqualifying events affecting the issuers or persons connected with the issuer, where the event happened after September 23, 2013 (the effective date of the rule amendments). Under the new rule, events before this date that would be disqualifying must be disclosed to investors. Rule 506(e).

Besides the issuer, the rule covers the issuer's insiders (directors, general partners, and managing members, executive officers, and 20 percent owners), investment managers (for pooled investment funds, such as hedge funds), and intermediaries (promoters and others compensated for soliciting investors). Rule 506(d)(1).

The rule specifies disqualifying events —

- securities-related *criminal convictions* (in the last 5/10 years)
- securities-related *court injunctions* and restraining orders (in the last 5 years and still in effect)
- *final regulatory orders* of financial-related state and federal regulators that bar a person or are based on fraudulent conduct (in the last 10 years)
- *SEC disciplinary orders* that suspend, revoke, limit, or bar securities-related entities or their professionals (while order is still in effect)
- *SEC cease-and-desist orders* based on fraudulent conduct (while order is still in effect)
- *SEC Reg A orders* stopping or suspending the exemption (in the last 5 years)
- *SRO suspension or expulsion*, such as by FINRA (while order is still in effect)
- *U.S. Postal Service false representation orders* (in last 5 years).

The issuer can avoid disqualification if it shows it did not know and reasonably could not have known that a covered person with a disqualifying event participated in the offering, or obtains a waiver from the court or regulatory authority that entered the order. Rule 506(d)(2).

Summary Charts

The following is a chart showing the operation of Reg D:

	Rule 504	Rule 505	Rule 506
Issuer qualification	No reporting companies, investment companies, "development stage companies"	No investment companies, "bad actor" issuers disqualified under Reg A	No "bad actor" issuers (broader than criteria under Reg A)
Dollar ceiling	$1,000,000 (12 months)	$5,000,000 (12 months)	No limit
Number of investors	No limit	35 + unlimited accredited investors (AIs)	35 + unlimited accredited investors (AIs)
Investor qualification	None	None	Non-AI must be sophisticated (alone or with rep)
Manner of offering	General solicitations OK, if shares issued (1) in state(s) that require registration and disclosure doc, (2) in state(s) where purchasers receive disclosure doc, (3) exclusively to AIs	No general solicitations	General solicitations allowed, but limited
Resale limitations	Resales OK, if issuance meets conditions for general solicitations (see "Resale Restrictions" above)	Restricted	Restricted
Info requirements	None (other than state law)	None, if all purchasers are AIs. If some non-AIs, issuers must furnish information (see "Disclosure Obligations" above)	None, if all purchasers are AIs. If some non-AIs, issuers must furnish information (see "Disclosure Obligations" above)
Notice of sale	Form D required (file five copies with SEC ten days after first sale)		

Despite the SEC intention that smaller issuers would use Rule 504, medium-sized issuers Rule 505 or Reg A, and large issuers Rule 506, experience under the SEC exemptive rules has been quite different. In a study of exempt securities offerings during 2008-2010, Professor Rutherford Campbell found that only a handful of issuers used Reg A and most used Rule 506 (and then generally only with accredited investors):

Number of Exempt Offerings (2008-2010)

	Number	Percent	Only AI*
Reg D	27,234		
Rule 504	1,196	4.4%	59.3%
Rule 505	447	1.6%	56.5%
Rule 506	25,591	94.0%	91.2%
Reg A	46		

* Based on sample of 1,000 Reg D offerings

Notice that Rule 506—with its preemption of state "blue sky" laws (see §4.2.6)—was the predominant exemption used by issuers, regardless of the size of the offering:

Size of Exempt Offerings (2008-2010)

	Number	Percent	Only AI*	Fin Interm*
<$1MM	7,880	30.8%	82.4%	5.8%
Rule 504	1,125	14.3%		
Rule 505	559	7.1%		
Rule 506	6,196	78.6%		
$1MM - $5MM	7,059	27.6%	88.3%	12.7%
Rule 505	276	3.9%		
Rule 506	6,487	91.9%		
>$5MM	12,295	48.0%	91.2%	13.8%
Rule 506	12,295	100.0%		

* Based on sample of 1,000 Reg D offerings

In short, issuers used Rule 506 most of the time—whether the offering was small, medium-sized, or large—and generally limited their offering to accredited investors. Interestingly, issuers did not use financial intermediaries that often—for example, less than 15 percent of the time even in large offerings. See Rutherford Campbell, Jr., *Wreck of Reg D*, 66 Bus. Law. 919 (2011).

Proposed Exemption for Large Accredited Investors

There have been complaints that Reg D is overly restrictive, denying to issuers access to capital. In 2007 the SEC proposed a new exemption for private offerings to "large accredited investors." Securities Act Rel. No. 8828 (2007) (proposing to add new Rule 507). Under the proposal "large accredited investor" would be defined as:

- individuals with $2.5 million in investments, or annual income of $400,000 or aggregate income of $600,000 with their spouses;
- entities with $10 million in investments, or financial institutions without regard to monetary thresholds; and
- directors, executive officers, and general partners of the issuers.

Under this proposed exemption, there would be no investor sophistication requirements, and issuers could do limited advertising, similar to "tombstone" ads. The exemption would arise under the SEC's exemption-granting power under §28 of the Securities Act, thus limiting its usefulness to private equity and hedge funds, since they must use §4(a)(2) offerings to maintain their exemption under the Investment Company Act.

Notice that the dollar thresholds of the proposal effectively adjust for inflation the Reg D dollar thresholds, which were originally set in 1982. Dodd-Frank addresses the inflation-adjustment question for individual accredited investors by calling on the SEC to adjust these thresholds every four years. Dodd-Frank §413 (beginning at least by 2014 for annual income amount and beginning in 2014 for net worth amount). In some ways, therefore, Dodd-Frank moots any move by the SEC to create a new exemption for "large accredited investors."

§5.2.5 Crowdfunding

As a practical matter, the Securities Act registration exemptions provide only limited options to businesses looking for new investors. If the issuer can raise money from accredited investors, then Rule 506 of Reg D (particularly with the recent loosening of the rules on general solicitations) opens the door to new financing. If the issuer is willing to register under state "blue sky" laws, then the intrastate exemption, Reg A and Rules 504 and 505 of Reg D also open the door. But otherwise, for issuers seeking money from nonaccredited investors or without having to comply with the "blue sky" laws, the door is mostly closed. Only a public offering gives such businesses access to public investors.

The JOBS Act of 2012 aimed to change this by allowing small issuers to raise capital from many small investors — via the Internet. The law includes an exemption for so-called crowdfunding offerings, under which U.S.

companies can raise money from public investors in securities offerings of $1 million or less. New §4(a)(6). The exemption imposes individual investment caps based on investors' annual income and net worth, and requires the issuer to sell the securities through an intermediary — either an SEC-registered securities firm or funding portal. Further, securities sold in an exempt crowdfunding are subject to strict limits on advertising and to resale restrictions. But most state "blue sky" regulation is preempted.

The crowdfunding exemption is in its infancy. In October 2013, the SEC proposed rules that specify the conditions for such offerings — but until the rule is finalized, no crowdfundings can occur. See Proposed Crowdfunding Rules, Securities Act Rel. No. 9470 (Oct. 23, 2013). Further, given the regulatory hurdles imposed on crowdfunding intermediaries, it is unclear the extent to which the new exemption will be used. Also, given the significant rate of failure for small businesses, it is unclear whether public investors (particularly after the likely stories of early flops and scandals) will be willing to assume the investment risk.

Nonetheless, maybe crowdfunding will work! The following is a quick survey of the elements required for a crowdfunding offering as laid out in new §4(a)(6) and §4A of the Securities Act, as well as the new (proposed) SEC "Regulation Crowdfunding (CF)."

Qualified Issuers

To use the §4(a)(6) exemption, the issuer must be organized in the United States. Proposed CF Rule 100(b); §4A(f)(1). Reporting public companies, investment companies, and "bad actor" issuers are ineligible. See §4A(f)(2)-(4); SEC Rule 227.503 (generally tracking the "bad actor" disqualifications of Reg A, see §5.2.3). Also disqualified are companies that had a prior crowdfunding and are not in compliance with the annual reporting requirements, and companies that do not have a defined business plan.

Amount Limitations

Issuers are limited to $1 million in crowdfunding sales during any 12-month period. Proposed CF Rule 100(a)(1); §4(a)(6)(A); §4A(h) (SEC must adjust $1 million limit every 5 years for inflation). This dollar limit only looks backward in time, so subsequent crowdfunding sales do not jeopardize the exemption for prior sales that were within the limit. Nonetheless, sales before or after the crowdfunding offering can raise integration issues, but unless integrated they do not retroactively reduce the §4(a)(6) limit.

Issuers must state a target amount for their crowdfunding — and then meet the target. The issuer can receive the offering proceeds only when the amount raised equals or exceeds its stated target. Until then, investors can cancel their commitments to invest. See Proposed CF Rule 201(g), (h), (j).

223

However, failure to comply with the stated deadline could constitute fraud, since the deadline could be construed as a representation that the issuer will not continue the offering beyond the deadline if the goal is not reached.

The SEC estimates compliance and marketing costs of $14,000–$19,000 for offerings less than $100,000; $40,000–$70,000 for offerings between $100,000 to $500,000; and $75,000–$150,000 for offerings between $500,000 and $1 million.

Qualified Intermediaries and Permitted Advertising

A crowdfunding offering must be conducted online through a single SEC-registered intermediary — either a registered broker or a "funding portal." Proposed CF Rule 100(a)(3); §4A(a). The intermediary, which cannot own any securities of the issuer, must make sure investors are provided the issuer's crowdfunding offering statement, must enforce the investor education requirements, and must limit the issuer's access to investor funds. Proposed CF Rules 300(b), 301, 302, 303.

Advertising in a crowdfunding offering is strictly regulated. Proposed CF Rule 204. The intermediary can provide notices of the offering on its website and add communication channels to its platform for online discussion about the offering. The issuer cannot advertise the offering, except by providing a bare-bones notice that directs investors to the intermediary's website. Nor can the issuer (or the intermediary) pay others to promote the offering, except through (and as disclosed on) the intermediary's website. Proposed CF Rule 205.

Crowdfunding intermediaries must register with the SEC (and any applicable self-regulatory organization) either as securities brokers or as funding portals. Proposed CF Rule 300; §4(a)(6). This means that intermediaries that do not register (or are already registered) as securities brokers must register as "funding portals" — a new kind of animal. See Proposed CF Rules 401-404. Funding portals are subject to a number of additional restrictions, including a ban on soliciting investors for a particular offering or giving investment advice or recommendations. The idea is that funding portals will advertise their website and there provide investors offering statements for crowdfunding offerings. Registered brokers, on the other hand, may give investment advice — something that many believe will lead most funding portals to become affiliated with registered brokers.

Crowdfunding intermediaries — both registered brokers and funding portals — must undertake a variety of policing roles. Proposed CF Rule 100(a)(1). They must check the background and regulatory history of the issuer and its officers, directors, and 20 percent shareholders. They must make sure the issuer is complying with the crowdfunding rules, including the rule that the issuer's offering statement must be available to investors at least 21 days before securities are sold. In addition, the intermediaries must make sure investors review required investor-education materials, answer a mandatory quiz, and affirm that they understand the risks.

Investor Caps

Each crowdfunding investor is subject to investment caps, which depend on the investor's annual income and net worth (as calculated under the "accredited investor" rules of Reg D). Proposed CF Rule 100(a)(2).

- For investors with annual income and net worth less than $100,000, the cap for a single crowdfunding is $2,000 or 5 percent of the investor's annual income or net worth — whichever is greater.
- For other investors (with an annual income or net worth of at least $100,000), the cap is 10 percent of the investor's annual income or net worth — whichever is greater, up to $100,000.

These investment caps also apply to investors who purchase in multiple crowdfundings during a 12-month period. Proposed CF Rule 100(a)(2); §4A(a). A violation of the single-issuer cap causes the §4(a)(6) exemption to be lost. §4(a)(6)(B). But a violation of the aggregate cap does not affect the §4(a)(6) exemption, but may lead the SEC to take action against intermediaries that fail to enforce it.

Required Disclosures

Crowdfunding issuers must prepare an offering statement that is filed with the SEC and provided to intermediaries (and thus made available to investors). Proposed CF Rules 201, 203 (and Proposed Form C); §4A(b). Potential investors must have access to the offering statement at least 21 days before the issuer begins selling securities — thus creating a built-in 21-day waiting period for crowdfunding offerings.

The offering statement must include:

- general information about the company — name, legal status, physical/website address; directors and officers; description of business and business plans; number of employees; financial information that varies with "targeted" size of the offering;
- information about the offering — purpose of the offering; intended use of the proceeds; the "target" offering amount and the deadline for meeting the target; whether the issuer will accept capital in excess of the target; the offering price and how the securities were valued; and
- information about company's ownership and capital structure — classes of securities; how the offered securities might be modified or their rights diluted; information about 20 percent shareholders; and the risks to minority shareholders of future offerings, sale of the company, and related-party transactions.

Importantly, the financials for crowdfunding offerings with a target amount above $500,000 must be audited by an independent public accountant — making crowdfundings above $500,000, as a practical matter, prohibitively expensive. For offerings with a target amount between $100,000 and $500,000, the financials need not be audited, but must be reviewed by an independent public accountant. For offerings with a target amount of $100,000 or less, the financials need only be certified by the company's principal executive officer (and the company must provide its most recent income tax return). The disclosure standards, however, do not "ramp up" if an issuer ends up selling more than the target amount.

In addition, crowdfunding issuers must file annual reports with the SEC and provide them to investors. The reports generally update the information in the offering statement. This annual reporting obligation continues until the issuer becomes a public reporting company, buys back all crowdfunding securities, or dissolves. Proposed CF Rule 202.

Resale Restrictions

Purchasers in a §4(a)(6) offering may not resell the securities for a year from the date of purchase. Proposed CF Rule 501. During this time, sales can be made only in a registered offering, to the issuer or accredited investors, or to a family member or family trust.

Preemption of State "Blue Sky" Law

States are preempted from requiring registration or qualification of §4(a)(6) crowdfundings. See §18(c)(2)(F) (defining securities in §4(a)(6) offering to be "covered securities" under §18(b)(4)). Nor may states require the filing of crowdfunding documents, the reporting of crowdfunding sales, or the payment of filing or registration fees — with two exceptions. Such filing, reporting, or fee requirements can be imposed in (1) the state of the issuer's principal place of business, and (2) any state where 50 percent or more of the investors reside, based on the offering's dollar amount.

Nonetheless, states retain their authority to "take enforcement action with regard to an issuer, funding portal, or any other person" using the §4(a)(6) exemption. Thus, states can go after fraud or unlawful conduct by crowdfunding issuers, brokers, and funding portals. To facilitate this state role, the SEC is required to make §4(a)(6) disclosures available to the states.

Crowdfunding: Unresolved Issues

The JOBS Act and proposed SEC rules fail to resolve a number of issues. For example, the SEC added an "insignificant deviations" provision (Proposed CF Rule 502) to protect issuers from innocent and immaterial violations, but does not define what is "insignficant." It is unclear how investors will actually be solicited, and whether a non-portal website that collects information about crowdfunding offerings is engaged in soliciting investors. It is unclear whether an issuer can sell additional securities outside the crowdfunding (pursuant to another exemption) to investors in the crowdfunding. It is unclear whether separate companies, under common ownership, are each subject to the $1 million cap. And there will certainly be other questions.

Note On Non-Securities Crowdfunding

Even before the JOBS Act, many entrepreneurs and creative folks have been raising money on the Internet by asking for donations to back their business or artistic plans, or by offering prepurchases in which funders are promised the "product" being developed. Others offer non-financial rewards to funders, such as including their names in the credits of a movie they will make. A well-known "crowdfunding" site, kickstarter.com, allows people to pool their money to back new artists, film producers, musicians, designers, novelists, and so on. None of these crowdfunding methods involve a security, so the federal securities laws are not a problem. (Think about it . . . maybe law school and becoming a securities lawyer isn't the right path for you.)

§5.2.6 Issuer Exchanges

In 1933, Congress was solicitous of financially troubled businesses that sought to make internal capital adjustments without having to bear the costs of registration.

When an issuer adjusts its capital structure by exchanging its securities with existing holders, §3(a)(9) exempts such exchanges provided "no commission or other remuneration is paid . . . for soliciting such exchange." In a similar vein, §3(a)(10) exempts securities issued in exchange for bona fide legal claims, securities, or property interests if, after an adversary proceeding, a court approves the transaction's fairness. Although intended for use by struggling businesses, the §3(a)(10) exemption is sometimes used by solvent businesses to issue securities in settlement of private lawsuits or in court-approved business reorganizations.

§5.3 STATE BLUE SKY EXEMPTIONS

For many offerings, perfecting a federal exemption is only half the game. State securities laws also impose their own registration requirements. See §4.2.6.

Preemption

The effect of state securities laws is significantly tempered by the preemption regime created in the National Securities Markets Improvement Act of 1996 (NSMIA), as amended by the JOBS Act. See §1.5. Under revised §18 of the Securities Act, state blue sky registration is preempted for certain offerings exempt from federal registration. The assumption is that federal exemption requirements and conditions are sufficient for investor protection, and that state registration adds unnecessary burdens and costs to the process of capital formation. Preemption of state law applies to the following offerings exempt under federal law:

Exempt securities	Offerings of exempt securities under §3(a), including offerings of government, bank and insurance securities, but not including offerings by charitable or religious organizations, offerings of municipal securities in the issuer's state, and §3(a)(11) offerings (see §§5.1, 5.2.1 above)
Secondary distributions	Resales by control persons and holders of restricted securities in public reporting companies exempt under Rule 144 (see §7.2.1) and by "qualified institutional buyers" under Rule 144A (see §7.2.2)
Private placements	Offerings exempt under Rule 506 (see §5.2.4 above)
Crowdfundings	Offerings exempt under the new crowdfunding rules (see §5.2.5 above)
Reg A+ offerings	Offerings exempt under the new Reg A+ rules by public companies or sold to "qualified purchasers" (see §5.2.3 above)

Importantly, states retain regulatory authority over offerings subject to the intrastate exemption (see §5.2.1) and the small-offering exemptions of Reg A and Reg D (Rules 504, 505). See §5.2.4.

Even for the exempt offerings listed above for which state registration is preempted, NSMIA preserves state authority to require the filing of documents also filed with the SEC, the consent to service of process, and the payment of filing fees. §18(c). In addition, for Rule 506 offerings, states may continue to require notice filings "substantially similar" to those required under Reg D as of September 1, 1996, even if SEC requirements change.

State Exemptions

Even after NSMIA, many offerings exempt from federal registration remain subject to state regulation — namely those subject to the §3(b)(1) small offering exemption (such as Rule 504, Rule 505, and Reg A offerings), the statutory §4(a)(2) private placement exemption (until the SEC defines the "qualified purchaser" preemption), and the §3(a)(11) intrastate exemption. Although NSMIA does not preempt state registration of these offerings, state exemptions may still be available. These exemptions, which vary from state to state, are typically more restrictive than the federal exemptions and often impose the controlling conditions on the offering.

State exemptions largely parallel those of the federal Securities Act. The Uniform Securities Act (USA), originally promulgated in 1956 and re-promulgated in 2002 by the National Conference of Commissioners on Uniform State Laws, exempts classes of securities similar to (and sometimes broader than) those exempted by the Securities Act. Exemptions under the USA cover U.S., state and municipal government securities; bank and savings and loan securities; securities of insurance companies qualified to do business in the state; securities listed on national exchanges; securities issued by not-for-profit organizations; and short-term commercial paper. USA §402(a) (1956 version); §201(1) (2002 version).

Many states exempt issuer "limited offerings" made pursuant to *offers* directed to no more than 10 persons (revised in many states to 25 persons) within the state in any 12-month period. USA §402(b)(9) (1956 version); §202(14) (2002 version would cover both preorganization and operational financing). The exemption has no dollar ceiling, and specified institutional investors are often excluded from the 10-person (or 25-person) numerical limits. Some states, consistent with Regulation D, have revised their limited offering exemption to cap the number of actual *purchasers*, not *offerees*.

About half the states have adopted the Model Accredited Investor Exemption, developed in 1997 by the North American Securities Administrators Association. Designed to fit with Rule 504, the exemption has no dollar limit and permits "general announcements" (including Internet notices) and telephone solicitations—but only to accredited investors. The issuer must reasonably believe all purchases are for investment; unregistered resales within 12 months may be made only to accredited or institutional investors. The exemption is not available to development stage companies or "bad actor" issuers, and a filing must be made with the state regulator.

In 1983, to facilitate the use of Regulation D, the North American Securities Administrators Association (NASAA) promulgated the Uniform Limited Offering Exemption (ULOE) to create a uniform state exemption for Rule 505 and 506 offerings. As promulgated and adopted in many states, the ULOE is more demanding than Regulation D. While generally exempting offerings that meet the federal Rules 505 and 506 conditions, the ULOE contains investor "sophistication-suitability" requirements for Rule 505 offerings and "bad actor" disqualifiers for Rule 506 offerings. The future of the ULOE remains uncertain since NSMIA preempts any conditions imposed on Rule 506 offerings and Rule 505 offerings have become (by comparison) less attractive.

5. Exemptions from Securities Act Registration

One effect of the state limited offering exemptions is that small intrastate offerings, as well as Rule 504 offerings that are not broadly marketed, which comply with the numerical limits of the various applicable state exemptions escape both federal and state registration requirements. Nonetheless, issuers remain subject to state and federal fraud provisions, whose effect is to compel disclosure of material information in offering circulars and similar disclosure documents so as to avoid fraud liability. The following table shows the fit of Regulation D and current state exemptions:

	Federal exemption	**State exemption**
Small offerings	Rule 504 • no reporting companies, investment companies, or "blank check" companies • $1 million or less (12 months) • no general marketing • limits on resales • marketing and resale limits not applicable, if offering is state-registered or state-exempt because sold only to accredited investors	"Limited offering" exemption • less than 10 (or 25) investors • no restrictions on marketing • no limits on resales Model Accredited Investor Exemption • no "bad actor" issuers and no "blank check" companies • sold only to accredited investors • general announcements to accredited investors
Medium offerings	Rule 505 • no investment companies or "bad actor" issuers • $5 million or less (12 months) up to 35 nonaccredited investors (must receive disclosure document) • no general marketing • limits on resales	"Limited offering" exemption • less than 10 (or 25) investors • no restrictions on marketing • no limits on resales Uniform Limited Offering Exemption • similar conditions as Rule 505 • all investors must meet sophistication and suitability requirements
Large offerings	Rule 506 • no "bad actor" issuers (as required by Dodd-Frank) • unlimited amounts • up to 35 nonaccredited investors (must receive disclosure document, and must be sophisticated or have investor rep) • no general marketing • limits on resales	NSMIA preempts state conditions

Examples

1. Burnhill Inc. is in the furniture mail-order business. The company has offices and a small showroom in Orange, New Columbia, where its sales reps take furniture orders by phone. The company fills the orders through furniture manufacturers that ship directly to mail-order buyers. Burnhill's management wants to raise $5 million in a common stock offering. Identify any problems if Burnhill claims an intrastate exemption for its offering.

   a. Is the issuer qualified?
      (1) Burnhill, incorporated in New Columbia, fills 60 percent of its orders through New Columbia manufacturers. But 90 percent of its orders come from out-of-state customers.
      (2) Burnhill plans to use the proceeds of the offering to put its catalog on the Internet and build a new warehouse in New Columbia for next-day shipments.
      (3) Two months after the offering, Burnhill changes its plans and uses the proceeds to build a warehouse in Old Columbia.
      (4) Edward, Burnhill's largest shareholder, wants to sell $2 million of his own shares to a family friend, Colonel Jim, who lives in New Columbia.

   b. Are the investors qualified?
      (1) First Lynch Securities, incorporated in Delaware with its headquarters in New York, agrees to be a "firm commitment" underwriter of the offering.
      (2) First Lynch puts a notice of the offering on its website and solicits investor inquiries, but "only from New Columbia residents."
      (3) Carl, an investor solicited by First Lynch, spends six months each year at a Florida golf resort, though his principal residence is in New Columbia.
      (4) Burnhill finds a sophisticated and wealthy venture capitalist from California who will buy $2 million in common stock, thus reducing the amount to be raised in the separate intrastate offering.
      (5) Burnhill prepares an offering circular, and First Lynch sends copies to its customers with New Columbia addresses.
      (6) Burnhill's offering circular goes only to New Columbia residents and includes financial statements which, though prepared by an accountant, have never been audited.

   c. Are resales permitted?
      (1) Carl buys 1,000 shares on October 1 in the in-state offering. The following April 1, his daughter is admitted to a prestigious law school. To raise cash for this new circumstance, Carl sells his Burnhill shares to a sophisticated out-of-state investor.

       (2) Burnhill completes its offering to only residents of New Columbia and figures what they do with their shares is their business.

2. Big Strike, a limited partnership set up to drill for oil and gas in the West, looks for investors to buy limited partner interests. Identify any problems if Big Strike claims a private placement exemption.
   a. Are the investors qualified?
      (1) Jake, a seismologist, formed Big Strike and is its managing partner. He has been in the oil business for 20 years. He has worked and invested in 10 oil and gas ventures, most of them losers. Jake invests in Big Strike.
      (2) Reginald, a city slicker, is out West to find himself. He signs on as a hired hand of Big Strike and then invests as a limited partner.
   b. Is disclosure sufficient?
      (1) Dora, an experienced petroleum engineer worth more than $1 million, already owns oil and gas properties worth $850,000. She reviews drilling logs of properties on which Big Strike holds options, and asks Jake some questions. She receives no disclosure document. Dora invests in Big Strike.
      (2) Reginald, the city slicker, receives a massive disclosure document from Big Strike about the venture, complete with expert statements about drilling logs and chilling disclosures about business risks. Reginald says, "Looks like a prospectus!" Reginald still invests in Big Strike.
   c. Given the disclosure, are the investors qualified?
      (1) Marge, a recent winner of the state lottery's $20 million jackpot, receives the same document that Reginald thought was a prospectus. Marge invests in Big Strike.
      (2) Maurice, a wealthy and aggressive investor, wants to include some oil and gas investments in his portfolio. He asks Dora to look over Big Strike Ltd. On her advice, he invests about 1 percent of his portfolio.
      (3) Martha, who runs a registered mutual fund that specializes in oil and gas limited partnerships, invests the fund in Big Strike but never receives any drilling logs, though she had requested them.
   d. Has the issuer met its burden?
      (1) Martin, a mystery investor about whom little is known, invests in Big Strike. There is no indication whether he is sophisticated or whether he received information from Jake. After investing, Dora says she wants out of the deal on account of Martin.
      (2) Madeline, another mystery investor, signed an investment letter before investing in Big Strike. The letter contained a number of representations:

The Purchaser:

(a) is a substantial, sophisticated investor having such knowledge and experience in financial and business matters, and in particular in such matters related to securities similar to the Securities, that she is capable of evaluating the merits and risks of investment in such business and the Securities,

(b) is able to bear the economic risks of such an investment,

(c) has been furnished with, and has had an opportunity to review, all financial data and other information relating to the Issuer and the Securities requested by the Purchaser, and

(d) has had any questions relating to such review answered to the satisfaction of the Purchaser.

Madeline

---

3. Laugh House Inc. runs a chain of comedy clubs in New Columbia. Its three owners — Larry, Curley, and Moe — want to expand and add new clubs in other states. Banks won't lend more money unless the company raises new capital. Laugh House hires Keystone Securities to help it raise $6 million in a common stock offering. Identify any Reg D problems.

   a. Keystone has identified 50 investors who may be willing to buy $6 million in Laugh House stock. Twenty are millionaire entertainment moguls. The Laugh House owners think it is silly to give anyone a formal disclosure document.

   b. Laugh House is under investigation by the SEC for trying to sell unregistered stock last year to Stan and Oliver, two unsophisticated (but wealthy) comics from California.

   c. Laugh House's accountant, Cantinflas, has helped the three owners keep their company's books but has never performed an audit of its financial statements.

   d. Curly and Moe give each nonaccredited investor an investment circular, with audited financials. But they do not bother to give anything to accredited investors.

   e. Larry, the company's president and largest shareholder, wants Keystone Securities to help him sell some of his Laugh House stock in the offering.

4. Laugh House proceeds with a Rule 505 offering. Many of the millionaires turn serious and abandon the offering. But Laugh House has identified exactly 35 nonaccredited investors who are still interested. Identify any problems with adding the following investors.

    a. Ivan, a home builder with limited investment experience, wants to add some mirth to his life and has his bank buy the stock.

    b. Iris, Laugh House's vice president for sales who has been with the company for six months, invests her life's savings.

    c. Imelda, who owns a $1.3 million collection of antique porcelain and has been heavily sedated since she began turning gray, will sell half her collection to buy the stock.

    d. Introductions Ltd., a venture-capital firm with $4 million in assets, will invest and put one of its principals on the Laugh House board.

    e. New Columbia's Public Bureaucrats Pension Fund, with assets of $30 million and run by a political yahoo, will buy up to its 5 percent statutory limit.

    f. Wolf Television, an upstart television network that is looking for young comedy talent, after a thorough investigation, will buy.

    g. Irene and Irwin, a married professional couple who each have had an annual income of $160,000 for the last two years, will buy $250,000 worth. Keystone Securities, however, failed to investigate or document their income.

5. Laugh House plans to proceed using Rule 506. Imogene lacks investment experience, but wants to invest in the offering. She considers getting investment help. Identify any problems if the following people advise her about her Laugh House investment.

    a. Rochester, Imogene's former husband, is an experienced stock broker. Laugh House does not know that Rochester is helping Imogene with her investments.

    b. Curly and Moe, officers of Laugh House, are helpful to a fault and disclose to Imogene the risks of the investment and their possible conflicts of interest.

    c. William Claude, a professional investment counselor and long-time patron of Laugh House, is friends of the Laugh House owners and has invested in the offering.

    d. Laugh House considers restructuring the offering to satisfy Rule 505. William Claude continues to advise Imogene, without disclosing his interests in Laugh House.

    e. Ramona, Imogene's lawyer and an experienced CPA, has often assisted her clients in identifying investment opportunities.

6. Laugh House has many potential investors — perhaps more than 35 — for its Rule 506 offering. How many nonaccredited investors must Laugh House count in the following cases?

    a. Investors Henry and Wilma are married. Neither is an accredited investor. Each invests in Laugh House.

    b. Harold and Wendy are married, and they live together. Wendy is a director on the Laugh House board. Harold is not accredited. Each invests in Laugh House.

    c. Bobby and Sissy, brother and sister, live in different states. Neither is an accredited investor. Each owns 50 percent of Family Corporation, which invests in Laugh House.

    d. This time all three — Bobby, Sissy, and Family Corporation — invest in Laugh House.

7. Laugh House proceeds with its offering under Rule 506. Identify any problems.

    a. Laugh House places newspaper ads in cities where Laugh House will expand. The ads show a laughing Greek drama face and the caption "LAUGH HOUSE, Laugh House, laugh house — soon." The ad is meant to titillate patron interest.

    b. Laugh House prepares a cover letter, an offering circular, and a reply card that it mails to all members of the New Columbia bar association, figuring the lawyers would appreciate a good laugh. Laugh House plans to sell only to lawyers who are accredited investors.

    c. Laugh House sends the same mailing as before to executives (50 in all) of the state's most prominent restaurants and dinner clubs.

    d. Laugh House hires Keystone Securities, a registered broker-dealer, to help solicit interest in its offering. Keystone posts the Laugh House information on its password-protected Internet website, which is accessible only to customers it determines are accredited under Reg D.

    e. Keystone representatives call individuals who live in expensive neighborhoods in New Columbia. They mention an "exciting entertainment investment" and ask those interested to complete a questionnaire describing their financial status and investment objectives. Keystone then gives them access to its website describing the Laugh House offering.

    f. Keystone mails its regular investment newsletter to its customers, some of whom do not qualify as "accredited investors." The newsletter, as usual, describes start-up private offerings handled by the firm and includes Laugh House for the first time.

    g. Tom Paine writes a newsletter for financial planners who advise clients about investment options. After interviewing Laugh House executives and analyzing the company's disclosure documents, Tom rates the company in his newsletter comparing it to other start-up investments.

8. Laugh House considers some possibilities to raise money for its expansion plans. Identify any problems.

a. On April 1, the company sells $4 million under Rule 505 to 30 purchasers, many of whom are out-of-state residents. On March 1, Laugh House had sold $2 million in stock to 50 purchasers in a Rule 147 intrastate offering.

b. On April 1, the company begins and completes a Rule 504 offering for $500,000. On May 1, Laugh House sells $100,000 to unsophisticated investor Stan. On March 1 of the next year, Laugh House wants to begin another Reg D offering.

c. On May 1 Laugh House begins a Rule 504 offering for $750,000. On January 1 of the prior year, it had begun a Rule 505 offering, which it had completed on June 1 after selling $4.5 million.

9. Laugh House completes a $7 million offering under Rule 506 to 10 accredited investors, but in a somewhat cavalier fashion. Identify any problems.

a. Laugh House sells only to accredited purchasers. It places no limits on resales, figuring that what the purchasers do with their stock is their business.

b. Laugh House fails to notify the SEC of its offering, but otherwise complies scrupulously with all the Rule 506 conditions.

c. One of the purchasers, Chevy, is not accredited and did not have a purchaser representative. The other investors, all accredited millionaires, seek to rescind their purchases.

d. As part of the offering, Laugh House had sent a letter to Stan and Ollie — two individuals with no pre-existing relation to the company or its underwriter — but neither ended up purchasing. Four of the accredited investors, however, seek to rescind.

10. Laugh House runs through all of its money — no joke! It decides to do an online offering of "magic debt" that will pay 12 percent interest and entitle investors to 5 shares of common stock (that "will appear like magic") for every $1,000 of debt they hold, if the company ever goes public. Laugh House contacts Crowds-R-Us, a brand-new "crowdfunding" portal, to help set things up. Identify any problems:

a. Laugh House is planning to raise $900,000 in its "magic debt" crowdfunding in two phases, one at the beginning of the year and the other at the end — though it still does not have any audited financials.

b. Laugh House posts an offering statement on its website, describing its business, management, financial summary, and how it will use the proceeds of the offering. This document is similar to one Laugh House used when it first approached "angel investors."

c. Crowds-R-Us posts the offering document (after making the revisions you suggested) and includes on its website: "No kidding, you'll laugh all the way to the bank with Laugh House."

    d. Crowds-R-Us receives inquiries from a number of investors. One of the investors, Louis, has income of $125,000 and a net worth of $200,000. He wants to invest $15,000 in Laugh House's "magic debt." Louis also has invested in other crowdfundings.

    e. The Laugh House crowdfunding is quite successful. By December 31, the target date set by the company for the offering to close, the company had raised $500,000 of its $600,000 target.

    f. After the crowdfunding, Laugh House turns things around. Some of the investors in the crowdfunding want to sell their "magic debt." Crowds-R-Us — to create a market in Laugh House's "magic debt" — sets up a trading platform for the investors to sell their securities. Crowds-R-Us asks Laugh House to post its most recent tax return.

Explanations

1. a. 1. Problem. Under the intrastate exemption, a corporate issuer must be incorporated in and "doing business" in the state of the offering. §3(a)(11); Rule 147(c)(1). Since Burnhill is incorporated in New Columbia, the only issue is whether Burnhill is "doing business" in the state. The SEC and courts have both focused on whether the company's in-state operations are "substantial" or "predominant." The essential question is whether the state's securities authorities would have jurisdiction to inspect the company's records, books, and operations and take corrective action against a fraudulent offering. *Chapman v. Dunn*, 414 F.2d 153 (6th Cir. 1969) (not enough that company with out-of-state oil and gas wells could be served with process in the state). The intrastate exemption assumes Securities Act registration is unnecessary if the issuer and offering are subject to comprehensive state jurisdiction.

    Are the company's operations in-state? On one hand, its purchasing of furniture from out-of-state manufacturers and selling to out-of-state mail-order buyers suggests not. Yet, in our example, the company's revenue-producing activities are conducted in New Columbia, and state securities authorities could (to the same extent as the company) inspect the company's records and operations and deal with the company's suppliers and customers. Thus, any jurisdictional difficulties are comparable to those faced by the company itself. Securities Act Rel. No. 5450 (1974) (giving example of mail-order business with in-state office, warehouse, and manufacturing plant as "doing business" within state even though most sales are out-of-state); SEC No-Action Letter, WKD Corp. (Sept. 13, 1972) (purchasing of out-of-state supplies does not negate intrastate exemption).

The objective 80 percent in-state tests of the Rule 147 safe harbor do not necessarily resolve the question. Whether Burnhill's mail-order revenues are "derived from operations in the state" (Rule 147(c)(2)(i)) or whether its likely principal asset (mail-order accounts payable) is "located within" the state (Rule 147(c)(2)(ii)) essentially rephrases the question that arises under the statute.

a. 2. Problem, depending on how much goes out-of-state. If the issuer plans to use the proceeds substantially or predominantly to pay for an out-of-state warehouse, the statutory "doing business" requirement would not be met. The SEC and the courts have required that state securities authorities have jurisdiction over the use of the offering's proceeds. *SEC v. McDonald Investment Co.*, 343 F. Supp. 343 (D. Minn. 1972) (denying intrastate exemption for notes offering by company that developed land outside Minnesota, even though development contracts were subject to Minnesota law, interest payments were in Minnesota, and notes were registered in Minnesota).

The conclusion might be different if the issuer planned for the proceeds to go predominately towards the Internet catalog. Under the analysis of question 1a(1), this catalog would seem to exist in the state where state authorities could most readily investigate and attach the assets—most likely at the company's offices in New Columbia. Moreover, if more than 80 percent of the net proceeds were to be used for the catalog and thus "in connection with . . . the rendering of services within such state," Rule 147 would be conclusive that the use of the proceeds met the "doing business" requirement.

a. 3. Problem, perhaps. At least one court found the issuer's intent at the time of the offering to be controlling. *Busch v. Carpenter*, 827 F.2d 653 (10th Cir. 1987) (no exemption if company "covertly" planned to invest proceeds out-of-state). This, however, would permit an issuer to change its plans and move assets from the offering beyond the reach of state securities authorities. Arguably, an issuer seeking to use the intrastate exemption must follow through on its in-state investment plans.

a. 4. No problem, perhaps. The SEC has taken the view that the statutory §3(a)(11) exemption permits secondary distributions that are "part of an [intrastate] issue." See Securities Act Rel. No. 4434 (1961). The control person's offers and sales must be only to residents, and the issuer must otherwise meet the exemption's residence and doing business requirements. To ensure the state's jurisdictional authority, the control person should also be a resident, and the proceeds should be used to acquire in-state assets. But there is contrary authority, based on the language of §3(a)(11), which exempts only "issues." *SEC v. Tuchinsky*, 1992 WL 226302 (S.D. Fla. 1991).

The SEC, however, has taken a contrary view with respect to secondary distributions by control persons under the safe harbor Rule 147. See Rule 147, note 4 (safe harbor rule "provides an exemption for offers and sales by the issuer only (and) is not available for offers or sales of securities by other persons").

1. b. 1. No problem, if the underwriter uses an in-state branch office. Although §3(a)(11) requires that all purchasers in an intrastate offering be in-state residents, the SEC has taken the view that a firm commitment underwriter that purchases from the issuer may be a nonresident if it conducts the underwriting through an in-state branch office. Presumably, state securities authorities would have jurisdiction over the office's representatives, their activities, and their records.

If, however, the underwriter carried out the offering from New York with its sales representatives making phone calls or mailings from New York to residents in New Columbia, these activities would void the §3(a)(11) exemption. Such out-of-state phone calls would involve offers by an out-of-state seller to in-state investors and would violate §5 as nonexempt offers made by jurisdictional means. In such a case, state securities authorities would lack jurisdiction over the New York persons and their activities, undermining the assumption of the intrastate exemption that in-state offerings will be subject to local oversight.

b. 2. Problem. The intrastate exemption is lost if any "offer" is made to a nonresident, whether that person ends up purchasing or not. Rule 147 (unlike Regulation D) provides no safe harbor relief for offers and requires that all offers and sales be to residents. If the underwriter's Internet message reaches just one nonresident — which seems certain — limiting sales to residents does not cleanse the taint. Again, the concern is jurisdictional. New Columbia authorities would have jurisdictional difficulties regulating out-of-state offers, and out-of-state authorities would have trouble regulating offers coming from New Columbia.

b. 3. No problem. Although Carl's domiciliary intent might be debatable, Rule 147 provides some comfort with a more objective standard of residence that looks to the "principal residence" of the investor. Rule 147(d)(2). Issuers using the safe harbor rule must ask customers for a written representation of in-state residence and often seek additional proof of principal residence, such as copies of their driver's license. See Rule 147(f)(1)(iii).

The Rule 147 safe harbor, however, remains perilous: An offer to even one person whose principal residence is out-of-state destroys the exemption. The safe harbor is also an all-or-nothing proposition. An issuer relying on it must comply with all the rule's conditions, such as that no other related financing occur within the six-month windows before and after the offering, that the issuer meet the various 80 percent "doing business" tests, and the issuer take precautions to prevent resales to nonresidents. Rule 147, note 3.

b. 4. Problem. Under §3(a)(11) every "part of an issue" must comply with the intrastate offering requirements. The issuer's understanding that the California transaction is separate from the intrastate offering is not controlling. Under the integration principle of the Securities Act, an issuer cannot divide a financing effort into separate parts and seek an exemption for each one. If the sale to the California investor is part of the issue, the sale to this one nonresident would invalidate the entire exemption. The SEC has identified five integration factors: single plan of financing, same class of securities, contemporaneous transactions, same type of consideration, and same general purpose. From appearances, the contemporaneous sale of the same common stock for the same financing purposes as the intrastate sales is part of "one issue." Rule 147 does not provide safe harbor relief, unless the California transaction were to occur either six months before or after the intrastate offering.

b. 5. Problem, perhaps. Soliciting potential investors based on their address does not ensure that they are in-state residents. This example illustrates the danger of an intrastate offering. If just one offeree is a nonresident, the entire exemption is lost. This is true under both the statute and safe harbor rule. The statute, as interpreted, requires that each offeree have in-state domiciliary intent. Rule 147 requires that all offerees have their principal residence in-state. Rule 147(d). This means the exemption would be lost if an offeree on the underwriter's mailing list actually had her principal residence out-of-state. The issuer and the underwriter act at their own risk.

b. 6. No problem, under federal securities law. The intrastate exemption imposes no disclosure conditions. The offering, however, will have to comply with state securities blue sky law. For an intrastate offering that does not comply with the state's "limited offering" exemption (which places a cap on the number of offerees or purchasers that varies from 10 to 35), state securities law requires full-blown registration by qualification, which includes preparation of a disclosure document and in many states administrative review of the merits of the offering. See §4.2.6.

1. c. 1. **Problem.** If Carl's shares had not "come to rest," he would have acted as an underwriter — that is, someone who "purchased from the issuer with a view to . . . the distribution." Securities Act §2(11). The issuer's intrastate exemption would be lost on the theory it sold, albeit indirectly, to nonresidents.

When do securities "come to rest"? The answer turns on the purchaser's investment intent, as measured by the purchaser's specific plans to resell when he invested. Some courts (though not the SEC) look at subsequent changes in the investor's circumstances that explain why the investor is reselling and negate an inference that he planned a quick resale. See §7.1.2.

Rule 147 makes a safe harbor presumption that securities in an intrastate offering have come to rest when held by a resident purchaser for at least nine months. Rule 147(e). The safe harbor, though not available to Carl because he held for only seven months, is not exclusive. A person challenging the validity of the intrastate exemption would have to show that Carl's securities had not come to rest with him. *Busch v. Carpenter*, 827 F.2d 653 (10th Cir. 1987) (issuer has burden to show sold to in-state purchasers, then burden shifts to challenger to show purchaser lacked investment intent).

c. 2. **Problem.** The issuer cannot be cavalier about resales, because any resales to nonresidents jeopardize the issuer's intrastate exemption. Until the securities have come to rest, original purchasers may resell only to other residents. Rule 147, for example, requires the issuer to legend stock certificates, place stop transfer instructions with its transfer agent, and notify all investors of the resale restrictions. Rule 147(f).

2. a. 1. **No problem.** The essence of the §4(a)(2) exemption for offerings "by an issuer not involving any public offering" is that investors can fend for themselves. As manager of the business, Jake has as much information about the venture and its risks as anyone. Moreover, his business and investment background suggests he has the ability to process this information. In short, he is at "full" on both gauges of the §4(a)(2) sliding scales: investor sophistication and information access. To require registration for him would impose an unnecessary (and ludicrous) cost on capital formation.

a. 2. Problem. Not all insiders can fend for themselves. Reginald does not have a position in the venture that provides him either actual information or access to information about the business and its risks — comparable to that found in a registration statement. And even with this disclosure, he seems to lack the ability and experience to process it. In short, Reginald is at "empty" on both gauges of the §4(a)(2) sliding scales.

2. b. 1. No problem. This example is drawn from the facts of an important Fifth Circuit decision on the scope of the statutory private placement exemption. *Doran v. Petroleum Management Corp.*, 545 F.2d 893 (5th Cir. 1977). Although not an insider, Dora in our example received actual disclosure and was a sophisticated, well-to-do investor. It is unnecessary, according to the Fifth Circuit, that such an investor be an insider or receive actual prospectus-like disclosure. It is enough that the investor, by virtue of her relationship to the issuer or her bargaining position, have access to such information.

b. 2. Problem. "Registration-like" disclosure does not alone render unsophisticated investors able to fend for themselves. Remember that registration comes attached with a variety of other protections: SEC review, due diligence by §11 defendants, and §11 misrepresentation liability for listed defendants (including strict liability for the issuer).

2. c. 1. Problem, probably. Money does not buy sophistication, at least according to courts interpreting §4(a)(2). Marge's wealth does not necessarily mean she has the financial acumen to evaluate an investment or to hire somebody who will evaluate it for her. Although the case law refers to an investor's ability to take investment risks, this factor alone does not mean the investor can fend for herself. This judicial interpretation is at odds with the SEC's accreditation of wealthy investors under Reg D. Nonetheless, courts have shown reluctance to stretch the §4(a)(2) concept of investor acumen to investor risk capacity.

c. 2. No problem, probably. Although judicial guidance is scarce, an investor would seem able to fend for himself if he gets the right investment advice and assistance. This is the theory behind registration under the Securities Act, which assumes securities professionals will evaluate the investment and help investors interpret the mandated disclosure. It is also the theory behind the "purchaser representative" concept of Rule 506, the SEC's safe harbor interpretation of the private placement exemption. To deny issuers access to an investor like Maurice would limit capital formation without substantial justification.

c. 3. No problem, probably. The example raises the issue whether access to information — without actual disclosure — satisfies the information component of the §4(a)(2) sliding scale, when the investor meets the sophistication test. Although some earlier cases suggested that nothing short of actual "registration-type" disclosure could satisfy §4(a)(2), this standard is rarely met in many private placements to corporate insiders. The critical §4(a)(2) test is investor sophistication. The sufficiency of information should be in the eyes of such an investor, rather than after-the-fact judicial second-guessing. That Martha thought her fund had enough information should be conclusive.

2. d. 1. Problem. The issuer (or other person relying on the statutory §4(a)(2) exemption) bears the burden of showing that the entire offering was private. This means the issuer must show that each *offeree* and *purchaser* met the §4(a)(2) sliding scales. Any one offeree or purchaser who does not destroys the entire exemption. In such a case, any investor (sophisticated or not) may assert a §12(a)(1) put on the theory the sale to her violated §5.

You might ask why one errant offer should undermine an issuer's entire exemption and allow investors who can fend for themselves to gain a windfall from regulatory protection meant for another? The answer is deterrence. Absent the harsh "one offer" rule, issuers would be tempted to make unregistered offerings, knowing their only liability would be to *purchasers* later discovered to be unqualified. Issuers would have far less incentive to limit their private offerings to qualified investors. Private placements would catch in their unregistered nets far more victims than the §4(a)(2) exemption contemplated. The "one offer" rule makes private placements more likely to be "simpleton-free."

d. 2. Problem. An investor cannot become sophisticated by unsubstantiated representations. The statutory §4(a)(2) exemption, unlike Rule 506 of Regulation D, does not permit the issuer to rely on a "reasonable belief" about the investor's sophistication. See Rule 506(b)(2)(ii). Only if it turns out that all of Madeline's representations were correct would Madeline satisfy the sophistication and access requirements of the §4(a)(2) sliding scales.

Why then do issuers ask for such representations from purchasers? The answer lies outside the federal securities laws. Issuers hope the representations, if false, will create grounds to countersue investors who falsely represent their investment sophistication or receipt of disclosure.

3. a. Problem. The offering fits none of the Reg D exemptions:

   Rule 504 has a $1 million cap during a 12-month period. Even if the size of the offering were scaled back, it would still face significant hurdles. It would be subject to the Reg D prohibition against general solicitations and restrictions on resales — unless the issuer limits the offering to accredited investors under a state blue sky exemption or registers the offering under state blue sky laws that mandate a formal disclosure document. In short, Rule 504 does not permit a widely marketed offering, if it includes any nonaccredited investors who will not receive a disclosure document.

   Rule 505 has a $5 million cap. Even if the offering were conducted in stages so that no more than $5 million were sold in any 12-month period, Rule 505 places limits on the method of solicitation, resales, the number of nonaccredited investors, and disclosure to nonaccredited investors. Rule 505 requires a disclosure document for nonaccredited investors. Rule 505(a); Rule 502(b). In addition, every Rule 505 offering must comply with applicable state blue sky regulation. Under the preemption regime of §18 of the Securities Act, states retain full registration authority over offerings exempted pursuant to rules promulgated under §3(b)(1) of the Securities Act, including Rule 505. An offering to more than 30 nonaccredited investors would not meet the ULOE exemption and in most states would require the filing and dissemination of a disclosure document. See §5.3.

   Rule 506 has no dollar ceiling, but imposes the same conditions as Rule 505 — namely, limits on solicitation method, resale restrictions, and numerical caps on (and disclosure to) nonaccredited investors. In addition, Rule 506 requires that nonaccredited investors either be sophisticated or receive investment advice from a qualified "purchaser representative." See Rule 506(b)(2)(ii). Not only would nonaccredited investors have to receive a disclosure document, they would also have to satisfy the sophistication condition of Rule 506. If these conditions were met, however, the Rule 506 offering would not be subject to state registration. Under §18, states have only limited authority over offerings exempted by rules promulgated under §4(a)(2) of the Securities Act, specifically Rule 506. In such offerings, states can require only the filing of a Form D, a consent to service of process, and a filing fee. See §18(b)(4)(D). This makes Rule 506 offerings more attractive than Rule 505 offerings.

   b. Not a problem under Reg D or state law. Since the offering is for $6 million, it would have to be made under Rule 506. Although Rule 506 (as required by Dodd-Frank) includes "bad actor" disqualifications, the grounds for disqualification under Rule 506(d) do not include a pending administrative review of non-registered sales. See §5.24 — "Bad Actor" Disqualification (final convictions and regulator orders).

The only other limitation on a Rule 506 offering is the Reg D condition that a company not use the regulation if a court has enjoined it from using Reg D for failing to notify the SEC of its offering as required by Rule 503. See Rule 507. Any state blue sky law disqualification, which could well apply to a Rule 504 or 505 offering, would be preempted if the offering satisfied the conditions of Rule 506.

c. Problem, probably. Laugh House's books must be audited for it to use Reg D to raise $6 million — if there are any nonaccredited investors. For offerings between $2 million and $7.5 million by reporting companies, Reg D parallels the "small business" registration requirements of Reg S-B. See Rule 502(b)(1), (b)(2)(i)(B)(2). Nonaccredited investors must receive (1) an audited balance sheet as of the end of the most recent fiscal year, and (2) audited income statements for the two preceding fiscal years. See Form SB-2 (item 22); Item 310 of Reg S-B (financial information).

Audited financials are expensive, and Reg D allows issuers making an offering of less than $7.5 million that cannot obtain full audited financials "without unreasonable effort or expense" to use only an audited balance sheet as of some date within 120 days of the offering.

Even if Laugh House raises less than $2 million, the company cannot avoid an audit if it gets financing from nonaccredited investors. Reg D specifies that the disclosure document, in such circumstances the most recent balance sheet, must be audited. See Rule 502(b)(2)(i)(A). There is no exception for issuers who find the audit burdensome or expensive.

d. No problem, but not wise. Even though Reg D does not require that accredited investors receive any information (see note to Rule 502(b)(1)), such investors might later use this informational gap to argue under §12(a)(2) or Rule 10b-5 that they were misled.

e. Problem. So-called secondary distributions by control persons are not possible under Reg D. The Reg D exemptions are available only to issuers, not control persons or holders of restricted stock. Reg D, note 4. The exemptions were meant to encourage capital formation, not to facilitate stock trading. Reg D, however, is not exclusive, and Larry can look to other exemptions if he wishes to sell. For example, Larry could sell to sophisticated investors who can fend for themselves under the "§4()" exemption. See §7.2.2. Or, if a trading market develops in

Laugh House stock, he might use Rule 144 to sell limited amounts of stock into the market. See §7.2.1.

4. a. Problem, perhaps. The issuer has reached its 35 "purchaser" limit of Rules 505 and 506. But Reg D, in a bit of drafters' gamesmanship, does not count accredited investors as "purchasers" — that is, the limit on "purchasers" applies only to nonaccredited investors. Rule 501(e)(1)(iv). The question is whether the bank's purchase for Ivan adds another nonaccredited investor.

Reg D defines an accredited investor to include a bank that invests in its own capacity or as a fiduciary. Rule 501(a)(1) (clause 1). At first glance, this suggests the purchase by the bank for Ivan was by an accredited investor. But this reading would create an untoward Reg D loophole, permitting issuers to use Reg D to sell to unsophisticated investors who invest by having a bank make their purchases. Reg D closed this loophole for purchases made through broker-dealers, who are accredited only when they buy for their own account. Rule 501(a)(1) (clause 2). The SEC's release accompanying its Reg D definitions do not give any reason to believe that a bank acting as purchaser for an investor offers more protection than a broker-dealer. Rather, the SEC release indicates that the fiduciary capacity envisioned in Reg D is one in which the bank has traditional investment discretion, as when it administers a trust or estate. Arguably, Ivan needs the protections accorded nonaccredited investors and cannot use the bank to be his purchaser; he should be counted as nonaccredited.

b. No problem. Reg D defines an accredited investor to include "executive officers" of the issuer, which is meant to include those with policymaking positions and presumably access to information about the company's operations and risks. Rule 501(a)(4). There are no requirements on how long the insider has held her position or on how much an accredited investor may invest. Iris seems to fit.

c. Problem, perhaps. Reg D defines an accredited investor to include individuals with a net worth of $1 million, not including their principal residence. Rule 501(a)(5). Imelda's vaunted porcelain collection is problematic. First, the collection may not be worth what she says it is. For nonliquid assets, an issuer may have difficulties showing it had a "reasonable belief" about the investor's accredited status unless it obtains an independent appraisal. Second, even if the porcelain is worth $1.3 million, Reg D looks at "net assets." Any debts Imelda has (other on her principal residence) must be subtracted from her assets.

If Imelda's net worth, excluding her principal residence, exceeds (or reasonably appears to exceed) $1 million, Reg D assumes that her wealth enables her to assume risks and buy investment advice. Despite Imelda's seeming personal incapacity as an investor, the definition does not require that she have a purchaser representative. Reg D's bright-line tests provide certainty, even at the cost of some investor protection.

d. No problem, perhaps. Reg D defines an accredited investor to include venture-capitalist firms, though not by name. In our example, Introductions Ltd. may be a "private business development company" if organized to invest in nonpublic companies (such as Laugh House) and "makes available significant managerial assistance" to these companies. Rule 501(a)(2); Inv. Adv. Act §202(a)(22); Inv. Co. Act §2(a)(48). In addition, the firm may qualify as a "Small Business Investment Company" if licensed and partially financed by the Small Business Administration. Rule 501(a)(1) (clause 4).

e. No problem. Reg D defines an accredited investor to include state and local employee pension plans, if the plan has more than $5 million in assets. See Rule 501(a)(1) (clause 5). The definition offers certainty and assumes the plan administrator's sophistication is a matter for state or local, not federal, supervision.

f. No problem, almost certainly. Reg D defines an accredited investor to include business organizations (including corporations) with total assets above $5 million and not organized to acquire the offered securities. See Rule 501(a)(3). It seems almost certain Wolf Television has assets (not necessarily net assets) above $5 million; and it was organized to run a television network, not invest in Laugh House. As with individual millionaires, the theory is that money can buy investment acumen.

g. No problem, perhaps. Reg D currently defines an accredited investor to include spouses with joint income above $300,000 for the last two years who reasonably expect at least the same income in the current year. See Rule 501(a)(6) ($200,000 for individual). (Remember that Dodd-Frank calls on the SEC to adjust these dollar thresholds by 2014. See §5.2.4.) Thus, so long as Irene and Irwin expect to make together more than $300,000 this year, they seem to fit under the dollar thresholds as of 2010. Under the current Reg D, the size of their investment is irrelevant. See Securities Act Rel. No. 6758 (1988) (eliminating category of accredited investors who buy at least $150,000 of securities when the purchase price is no more than 20 percent of the investor's net worth). Furthermore, the issuer's reasonable belief is not necessary for the exemption. Remember a person qualifies as an accredited investor either by actually fitting one of the Reg D categories (which seems the case for Irene and Irwin) or when the issuer "reasonably believes" the person fits. The issuer (alone or through its financial adviser) need not undertake an investigation to form a reasonable belief, but it would be foolish not to.

5. a. No problem, if Imogene acknowledges in writing that Rochester is her purchaser representative. Reflecting its §4(a)(2) roots, Rule 506 requires that each nonaccredited investor "alone or with a purchaser representative" have a financial and business background that allows her to evaluate the risks and merits of the Reg D investment. Rule 506(b)(2)(ii). Rochester's background would appear to be such that he can help Imogene evaluate the Laugh House offering. Rule 501(h)(2). To act as her purchaser representative and "qualify" Imogene under Rule 506, Imogene must acknowledge his role in writing — not necessarily to Laugh House. Rule 501(h)(3). Although Reg D does not permit purchaser representatives who are insiders of the issuer or have had a material relationship with the issuer, Imogene's prior marriage to Rochester is irrelevant. Rule 501(h)(1), (4).

That Laugh House does not know about Rochester, let alone whether he has acknowledged his role, is not fatal to the issuer using Rule 506. Meeting the regulatory criteria is enough. But Laugh House's failure to investigate is imprudent. Reg D treats a person as a purchaser representative if either (1) the person meets the regulatory criteria or (2) the issuer "reasonably believes" the person meets them. See Rule 501(h).

b. Problem. Insiders of the issuer, including officers, cannot act as purchaser representatives because of the obvious conflict of interest. Rule 501(h)(1). Reg D disqualifies any insider from acting as purchaser representative, unless the representative has a specified family or fiduciary relationship to the purchaser that suggests the representative will put this relationship ahead of any interest in the issuer.

c. Problem, if conflict not disclosed. A person who has a "material relationship" with the issuer (or has had one in the last two years) cannot act as a purchaser representative, unless he discloses the relationship and any compensation involved. Are William Claude's friendship with the issuer's owners, his patronage, and his investment in Laugh House material? Although the friendship and patronage standing alone might not be, because they do not oblige W. C. to the issuer, his actual investment creates a financial interest in the offering that a reasonable investor in Imogene's position should consider important in deciding to invest.

d. No problem, under Reg D. Rule 505, whose source is the small offering exemption of §3(b)(1), does not require that nonaccredited investors have a purchaser representative. Nonetheless, W. C. remains subject to the antifraud requirements of the federal securities laws and must act in the interest of the purchaser. In particular, he may well be a statutory seller under §12(a)(2) and potentially a primary violator under Rule 10b-5. In addition, he may also be treated as a securities broker, subject to SEC registration and regulation. See §11.2.1. Finally, W. C. may be an "investment adviser" by virtue of his activities and subject to registration and regulation under the Investment Advisers Act. See §11.3.1.

e. No problem under Reg D, but this presents a professional problem for Ramona. There is potential confusion if she assumes the roles as business adviser and legal counselor. At the least, she should explain this to her client. Moreover, she may risk falling outside the coverage of her legal malpractice insurance.

6. a. One, if they have "the same principal residence." Rule 501(e)(1)(i). Reg D counts nonaccredited purchasers by counting the number of *nonaccredited investment decisions*. If two nonaccredited investors are "related" and live in the same household, the rule assumes that their separate purchases reflect one investment decision. The rule would count only Henry (or only Wilma) as a purchaser for purposes of the 35-nonaccredited investor cap. In this way an "investing unit" can structure an investment decision to accomplish the unit's family, tax, estate, or business purposes without undermining the issuer's Reg D exemption.

b. None. As a director, Wendy is accredited and does not count against the 35-nonaccredited investor cap. Rule 501(e)(1)(iv). Harold, as Wendy's spouse who shares the same principal residence, does not count either. Rule 501(e)(1)(i). The rule assumes there is only one investment decision, presumably an accredited one. Notice, though, that Harold is treated as a nonaccredited purchaser for purposes of disclosure under Rule 501(b)(1) and the sophistication requirement of Rule 506(b)(2)(ii). Note to Rule 501(e).

c. One, provided Family Corporation was not "organized for the specific purpose of acquiring the securities offered." Rule 501(e)(2). The corporation is counted as one purchaser, avoiding multiple counting where there is only one joint (albeit nonaccredited) investment decision.

d. Perhaps, three — whether or not Family Corporation was organized to acquire the securities offered. Under the normal counting rule for corporations, Family Corporation counts as one purchaser. Rule 501(e)(2). Bobby and Sissy count as two separate purchasers because they live separately and the family counting rule does not apply to them. Rule 501(e)(1)(i). This makes some sense. There were three investment decisions: Bobby's, Sissy's, and their joint decision with respect to the corporation.

It might also be argued the answer is two — reflecting the two investment decisions, one by Bobby and the other by Sissy. Just as Reg D's counting rule for corporate purchasers does not count shareholders as separate purchasers when a corporation invests, it should not count the corporation's investment when all shareholders also invest. This analysis has some textual support. Reg D's counting rule disregards a corporation "of which a purchaser and any of the persons related to him as specified in paragraph (e)(1)(i) . . . collectively are beneficial owners of more than 50 percent of the equity securities." Rule 501(e)(1)(iii).

On the one hand, Bobby and Sissy are related and collectively hold more than 50 percent of the corporation's shares. By virtue of their family relation, their joint decision is treated as an extension of each of their individual decisions. On the other hand, neither of them alone owns more than 50 percent of the corporation's shares, and they are arguably not related "as specified in paragraph (e)(1)(i)" because they do not share a principal residence. That is, without the commonality that the rule assumes for relatives living together, Bobby and Sissy's corporate decision is arguably separate from their individual investment decisions.

7. a. Potential problem. Offerings made pursuant to Rule 504 (if they don't satisfy the blue sky conditions) and Rule 505 and 506 are subject to the Reg D prohibition against "general solicitations." Rule 502(c). This prohibition parallels the "gun-jumping" prohibitions of §5(c). In our example, if the ads are meant to produce patrons, not investors, they are not solicitations. But the line may be hazy, and Reg D issuers are often advised to trim back on advertising during the solicitation period. If these ads are viewed as soliciting investors, they are "general" because there is no prior family, investment, or business relationship that would ameliorate their market-softening effects.

b. Problem. This is a general solicitation, which precludes the use of Rule 506. See Rule 502(c). This Reg D condition is intended to deter broad promotional efforts that fuel uninformed investor speculation. Even though (as in our example) only accredited investors eventually buy, a wide offering risks that some nonaccredited investors will be overcome by a speculative fervor — without adequate disclosure or investment advice. The prohibition parallels that of

§4(a)(2) against offers (even if unconsummated) to investors who cannot fend for themselves.

c. Problem. The SEC has interpreted the "general solicitation" prohibition to cover those solicitations in which the issuer has no "pre-existing relationship" — whether family, investment, or business — with those solicited. SEC No-Action Letter, E. F. Hutton & Co. (Dec. 3, 1985). The theory is that such prior relationships evidence that the investor has knowledge of the issuer and perhaps access to issuer information, and that the issuer can gauge whether the investor is accredited or capable of evaluating the investment and assuming the investment risk. In our example, absent a prior relationship between the issuer and the furniture executives, the SEC would view the solicitation as general, thus ruining the Rule 506 exemption.

This interpretation makes the Rule 506 exemption more demanding than the statutory private placement exemption of §4(a)(2), which does not depend on investors having a prior relationship with the issuer so long as they have sufficient sophistication and access to information to fend for themselves.

d. No problem. The SEC permits solicitations of investors who have a pre-existing relationship with the *issuer's securities firm*. See Securities Act Rel. No. 6455 (1983) (question 60). In fact, this mailing to the firm's *existing* customers is precisely the solicitation method envisioned by the SEC "pre-existing relationship" gloss. The securities firm, acting for the issuer, has identified the customers for this particular offering.

In addition, the SEC has accepted the marketing of private offerings through an Internet website accessible only to a securities firm's accredited customers. See SEC No-Action Letter, IPOnet (July 26, 1996) (limited to offerings posted after broker-dealer determines customer is accredited). According to the SEC, the customer cannot be told of the particular offering before his or her qualification.

Notice that the practical effect of the "pre-existing relationship" gloss to the ban on general solicitations is to force issuers using Reg D to obtain (and pay for) the intermediation of a securities firm. The SEC interpretation of its rule has been criticized for narrowing the pool of potential investors in Reg D offerings.

e. Problem. The securities firm can solicit only existing customers and not those "developed" for the offering. In fact, even if the customers were solicited prior to the offering, the SEC has taken the view that there must be a waiting period after the investors have been qualified before they can be solicited.

Although the SEC has generally shown solicitude toward dissemination of securities information using the Internet, the underlying concerns of investor protection have not changed. The SEC has warned that private issuers cannot give preliminary information about an offering on its website to potential investors before assessing investor qualifications. Securities Act Rel. No. 7904 (2000).

f. Problem. The securities firm has not qualified the customers who receive the newsletter, which makes it a prohibited general solicitation. The prohibition of Rule 502(c) against general solicitations extends to the issuer and "any person acting on its behalf." By contrast, a securities firm participating in a *public offering* is permitted to provide information or investment recommendations in a regularly circulated newsletter about a public company whose stock it is selling, so long as the information or recommendation is given no greater prominence than that of other companies and is no more favorable than that given in prior newsletters. See Rule 139.

g. Problem. The SEC has taken the stance in circumstances similar to those of our example that such a newsletter constitutes a general solicitation on behalf of the issuer. Even though the issuer did not pay for it, the newsletter involved a symbiotic relationship between the issuer and the newsletter publisher. The publisher had interviewed Laugh House officials, had disclosed information selectively, and had rated the offering favorably.

8. a. Integration problem. If the March and April sales are parts of one "offering," neither exemption applies to the whole. The intrastate exemption fails because some of the April sales were to out-of-state investors; the Rule 505 exemption fails because the combined sales exceeded $5 million (and may have been to more than 35 nonaccredited investors, none of whom received the mandated disclosure).

Should the two offerings be integrated? The Reg D safe harbor does not help because the March and April sales occurred within six months of each other. Rule 502(a). Many of the SEC factors bode poorly: The offerings were for the same consideration, for the same purpose, and involved the same securities. To maintain the integrity of the Securities Act's exemption scheme, the March and April sales would likely be integrated. The financing scheme would either have to be readily subject to state jurisdiction (intrastate offering) or meet all the criteria of the limited offering exemption (Rule 505).

b. Aggregation problem. There is no risk that the prior April or May offerings will be integrated with the new March offering. Rule 502(a) (six-month safe harbor). The problem is the §3(b)(1) dollar cap — $5 million under Rule 505 and $1 million under Rule 504.

The amount Laugh House can raise on March 1 pursuant to Rule 504 or 505 depends on how much it raised after March 1 of the previous year pursuant to a §3(b)(1) exemption or in violation of §5. In our example, the prior Rule 504 offering of April 1 reduces by $500,000 the amount Laugh House can raise on March 1 of this year — whether under Rule 504 or 505. In addition, if the May offering violated §5, it would further reduce by $100,000 the amount that Laugh House could sell in March. (This is only fair. Otherwise, issuers who complied with the particular §3(b)(1) exemption might be worse off than those who violated the act.) All told, the prior offerings reduce the dollar caps under Rule 504 or 505 by $600,000.

There is no aggregation issue, however, if Laugh House uses Rule 506 in March. Rule 506, a §4(a)(2) safe harbor, has no dollar limit. So long as there is no integration, prior or contemporaneous offerings (exempt or not) do not limit the use of Rule 506.

c. Potential aggregation problem. The May 1 offering under Rule 504 has a $1 million cap. The earlier Rule 505 offering, to the extent there were sales after May 1 of the prior year, reduces the amount that can be sold in the current Rule 504 offering. If, for example, $400,000 of the prior Rule 505 offering was raised after May 1, Rule 504 could be used only up to $600,000.

9. a. Problem. Reg D seeks to prevent purchasers in exempt offerings from being conduits to nonaccredited public investors. (An exception in Rule 504 arises when the offering is registered under state blue sky laws.) A condition of exemption is that the issuer must take resale precautions by finding out whether investors plan to resell, notifying investors that they cannot resell unless the stock is registered or there is an exemption, and legending the stock to this effect. (There may even be a requirement to tell nonaccredited investors this in person or in a conspicuous way in a cover letter.)

b. Minor problem. Reg D requires an informational filing with the SEC that describes the issuer; its business; its directors, officers, general partners, promoters, 10 percent owners; number of nonaccredited investors; any underwriters in the offering; total offering price, number of investors, expenses, and use of proceeds. See Rule 503, Form D. The failure to file does not affect the exemption, though an issuer risks the SEC seeking a court injunction against the issuer's further use of Reg D. See Rule 507.

c. No problem. Reg D takes some of the sting out of immaterial and insignificant noncompliance. Rule 508. Unless the noncompliance goes to the heart of the exemption, purchasers cannot back out of an investment on the pretext of a noncompliance that affects another. (This is a change from the strict court-made rule of §4(a)(2) that one glitch in a private placement ruins the exemption for all investors.)

Here the exemption as to the accredited millionaires is not lost just because the issuer failed to comply with the "purchaser qualification" requirement for Chevy. Under Rule 508, the requirement of a purchaser representative for Chevy was not meant to protect the accredited purchasers, and the purchaser representative requirement of Rule 506 is not one of the listed "significant" requirements of Reg D. If Laugh House made a good faith, reasonable effort to have a purchaser representative for Chevy, the other purchasers cannot complain.

d. Problem. Although Reg D does not limit the number or qualification of offerees, the prohibition against "general solicitations" has such an effect. See Rule 502(c). In our example, the offers to Stan and Ollie would be considered general solicitations because they had no pre-existing relationship to the issuer. The prohibition on general solicitations, however, does not apply to Rule 506 offerings where the issuer (or its agent) has *verified* that all the actual purchasers are accredited investors. Here, though, there was no indication that the issuer had undertaken a verification — thus making its offering subject to the general-solicitation prohibition.

If the general-solicitation prohibition applies, the savings provisions of Rule 508 would not apply because any violation of the general solicitation prohibition is deemed significant. Thus, Laugh House would lose its Rule 506 exemption, and all the purchasers in the offering (including those accredited and unaffected by the solicitations of Stan and Ollie) can claim a §5 violation. This result under Reg D gives issuers (and any underwriters in the offering) strong incentives to avoid a general solicitation — or to ensure verification of the accredited status of all purchasers.

10.a. Problem, because the financials are not audited. Laugh House — assuming it is incorporated in a U.S. state — is eligible to use the §4(a)(6) crowdfunding exemption. In addition, its proposed $900,000 offerings does not exceed the cap for "crowfunding" offerings — an aggregate of $1 million every 12 months. But if the company offers more than $500,000 in a 12-month period, its financials must be audited. Given the costs of an audit, most companies using the "crowdfunding" exemption are likely to prefer to keep their offerings under $500,000.

Notice that offering debt (with contingent rights to equity) is allowed under the crowdfunding rules. In fact, many predict that offerings of such hybrid securities will be common. Current owners may be reluctant to bring in unsophisticated equity shareholders, and venture capital firms would likely view the company as less attractive if there were a large number of un-accredited investors.

b. **Problem.** The offering statement does not include the information required by Form C:

- a description of the company's officers, directors, and 20 percent shareholders;
- a description of the company's business, business plan, and number of employees;
- the intended use of proceeds from the offering;
- the offering price (and how the price was calculated);
- the target offering amount and deadline to reach this amount, whether the company will accept investments in excess of the target offering amount, and how an oversubscription will be allocated;
- how investors can cancel their commitments before the target deadline;
- the company's ownership and capital structure, including its debt load;
- risk factors related to the company and the offering;
- the intermediary and how it's being compensated;
- any earlier exempt securities offerings, and certain related-party transactions
- the company's tax returns for the past two years — audited, if the offering is for more than $500,000.

  In short, the offering statement goes well beyond what would be sufficient for a sophisticated "angel investor" and instead is much more like a prospectus!

c. **Problem.** A "crowdfunding" issuer may not advertise its own offering, which can only be done through a registered broker or crowdfunding portal — here, Crowds-R-Us. The company could refer potential investors the Crowds-R-Us website, but no more.

d. **Perhaps problem.** For investors with net worth or annual income of $100,000 or more, the individual cap is 10 percent of their net worth or annual income — whichever is greater. Here, Louis could invest an aggregate of up to $20,000 (10 percent of his net worth) in crowdfundings in any 12-month period. The funding portal must ensure that investors do not exceed this overall cap. If Louis had already invested more than $5,000 in crowdfundings in the previous 12 months, the $15,000 investment in Laugh House would not be allowed. Whether inadvertent noncompliance with the investor caps puts at risk the whole §4(a)(6) exemption for Laugh House is not clear.

e. **Problem.** Crowdfundings must be conducted as an "all or nothing" offering. Crowds-R-Us must ensure that Laugh House receives the offering proceeds only when investor commitments equal or exceed

255

the issuer's target amount by the target date. Until then, investors can cancel their commitments. According to the SEC rule, the issuer cannot change the target amount or date.

f. Problem. Investors cannot resell for 12 months after the offering. But even if the new trading platform were set up a year after the offering, Laugh House has ongoing disclosure obligations beyond posting its tax returns. Under the SEC rule, a company using the "crowdfunding" exemption must continue to file basic information with the SEC, including names of directors and officers and holders of more than 20 percent of the company's shares, plus a description of its business and financial condition. This information would not be required of companies that obtain funding through other exemptions.

Securities Act Liability

The Securities Act of 1933, reflecting a congressional distrust of state remedies for securities purchasers, imposes heightened standards of liability on those who offer and sell securities.

The Securities Act arsenal is imposing:

- **Liability for noncompliance with registration rules — §12(a)(1).** If a seller or offeror violates the registration or gun-jumping requirements of §5, securities purchasers can rescind their investment. [§6.2]
- **Liability for fraudulent registration statement — §11.** If a registration statement (including the prospectus) contains a materially false or misleading statement, purchasers in a registered offering can recover damages from specified participants in the offering. [§6.3]
- **Liability for other fraud in registered offering — §12(a)(2).** If sales or offers in a registered offering (not subject to §11 liability) are accomplished by means of materially false or misleading information, purchasers can rescind their investment. [§6.4]
- **Control person liability — §15.** Investors can also recover, on a joint and several basis, from persons (individuals or corporations) who control any person liable under §11 or §12. [§6.5]
- **Crowdfunding liability — §4A(c).** If the issuer (including its top managers) or any intermediary in a crowdfunding makes a materially

false or misleading statement, investors can rescind their investment or recover damages. [§6.6]

- **Government civil enforcement — §17.** The SEC has broad authority under §17, which prohibits offerings (whether registered or not) accomplished by false or misleading means. [§6.7] Under §20, the SEC can seek civil injunctions and penalties in court for violation of the Securities Act or its rules. Under §8A, the SEC can issue administrative cease-and-desist orders.
- **Government criminal enforcement — §24.** Willful violations of the Securities Act, such as the antifraud provisions of §17 or the registration requirements of §5, are punishable by up to five years in prison and fines of $10,000. [§12.5]

This chapter focuses on the civil liability scheme of the Securities Act and how its carefully crafted provisions depart from common law rules against misrepresentation [§6.1]. It also describes liability for misrepresentations in securities sales under state "blue sky" law [§6.8]. Civil liability for securities fraud under Rule 10b-5 of the Securities Exchange Act of 1934 is the subject of Chapter 9. SEC civil and criminal enforcement is the subject of Chapter 12.

§6.1 COMMON LAW OF MISREPRESENTATION

The civil liability scheme of the Securities Act (like those of the other federal securities laws) draws on and often modifies the elements for common law deceit and contractual rescission. Although the rules governing misrepresentations are neither static nor uniform, and modern courts in other contexts have relaxed some of the traditional elements, the following summary describes the prevalent common law rules — both as to fraud and rescission — at the time the Securities Act was enacted.

§6.1.1 Common Law Deceit

One who intentionally makes a material misrepresentation is liable for the losses caused by the other's justifiable reliance. Restatement (Second) of Torts, §§525-551. There is no requirement of privity. The tort of *deceit* (*fraud*) has five elements, all of which must be proved by the party who seeks to recover.

Here are the elements of common law deceit:

Misrepresentation of material fact

The misrepresentation must be material—that is, a reasonable person would attach importance to it in deciding whether to enter into the transaction. The common law demanded that the misrepresentation be affirmative and factual; opinions and puffing were not actionable. According to the common law, failing to disclose material information was not actionable unless the silent party had a fiduciary or similar "confidential" relationship that triggered a duty to disclose.

Scienter

The maker of the misrepresentation must have been culpable—that is, he either knew or believed the facts were otherwise or lacked a reasonable basis for the representation. Under the common law, a representation that was literally true (though failed to state relevant additional or qualifying matters) was not necessarily fraudulent. That is, incomplete or misleading half-truths were not actionable.

Reliance

The person who seeks to recover must have actually and justifiably relied on the fraudulent misrepresentation.

Causation

The pecuniary loss of the person who seeks to recover must reasonably have been expected to result from the reliance. Not only must the misinformation have induced the transaction ("transaction causation" or "reliance"), but the misinformation must have related to the cause of the loss ("loss causation").

Damages

In general, recovery includes (1) "out-of-pocket" damages—the difference between what the person who seeks to recover received in the transaction and the purchase price, (2) any consequential damages, and (3) punitive damages in flagrant cases. In a business transaction, damages may also include the "benefit of the bargain" if future damages can be proved with reasonable certainty.

These elements act as legal sieves or filters. One who claims losses in a commercial transaction because of alleged misinformation can shift her losses to another responsible for the misinformation only when there is a high level of confidence that the misinformation drove the transaction and led to the losses, and that the person who supplied the misinformation was better positioned to prevent the harm.

§6.1.2 Equitable Rescission

Rescission, an invention of equity, seeks to undo misinformed deals. A contracting party may rescind the contract if he justifiably relied on a misrepresentation, whether it was fraudulent or simply material, when he entered into the contract. Restatement of Contracts, §§159-167. The person who seeks to rescind must prove all the elements.

Rescission may be based on one of two types of misrepresentation, either "material misrepresentation" or "fraudulent misrepresentation." Here are the elements of common law rescission:

Material misrepresentation	One ground for rescission is a material misrepresentation of fact, one that a reasonable person would attach importance to in deciding whether to enter into the transaction. The culpability (or scienter) of the person making the misrepresentation need not be proved if the misrepresentation is material.
Fraudulent misrepresentation	Another ground for rescission is a fraudulent misrepresentation of fact, one known to be false or to lack a factual basis. If the misrepresentation is fraudulent — that is, made with scienter — its materiality need not be proved.
Reliance	The person who seeks to rescind — whether the misrepresentation was innocent or fraudulent — must have relied actually and justifiably on the material or fraudulent misrepresentation.
Damages	Recovery in a rescission action seeks to put the plaintiff in a position as though the contract had never happened. If the object of the contract can be returned, rescinding the transaction is the remedy. If the object of the contract is gone, such as when a purchaser has resold the goods, the remedy is rescissionary damages equal to all the losses arising out of the contract. Consequential and punitive damages are not available.

In a rescission action, unlike one for deceit/fraud, the plaintiff must establish a causal link between the misrepresentation and any loss. Rather, the contract can be avoided even if the plaintiff suffered no harm or extraneous circumstances made the deal commercially unattractive.

Normally, privity of the parties is required for rescission. Nonetheless, some modern courts permit rescission if the actionable misrepresentation came from a nonparty, unless the nonrescinding party had already given value in reliance on the transaction and did not know (or have reason to know) of the nonparty's misrepresentation. At the time of the Securities Act, rescissionary damages were generally not available against nonparties.

§6.2 SECTION 12(a)(1): VIOLATIONS OF §5

Section 12(a)(1) — which before 1995 was numbered §12(1) — sets out a simple and powerful private remedy to enforce the registration and gun-jumping requirements of §5. When securities are offered or sold in violation of §5, the purchaser may rescind the transaction and get his money back with interest or recover rescissionary damages if he has resold his stock. Although the section's purpose is ultimately to promote full disclosure in offerings subject to Securities Act registration, §12(a)(1) does not require proof of any misrepresentation.

§6.2.1 Strict Liability

Section 12(a)(1) imposes strict liability against "sellers" of unregistered securities when no exemption applies. In effect, purchasers receive a "put" (an option to sell back their securities) if there is a §5 violation during an offering. See §4.3 (description of activities that violate §5).

Once there is a violation of §5, later compliance does not retroactively cure the defect. For example, courts have held that a noncomplying "offer" during the waiting period allows for §12(a)(1) rescission, even though the offer leads to a sale that complies with the prospectus delivery requirements. *Diskin v. Lomasney & Co.*, 452 F.2d 871 (2d Cir. 1971).

§6.2.2 "Statutory Sellers"

Who may be sued under §12(a)(1)? The language of the statute is not a model of clarity. It says that any person who "offers or sells" a security in violation of §5 is liable to the "person purchasing such security from him." On one hand, this language suggests that only persons from whom the plaintiff purchases (that is, the seller who passes title) can be liable. On the other hand, the section talks of any person who "offers or sells" securities.

The Supreme Court sought to clarify this ambiguity in *Pinter v. Dahl*, 486 U.S. 622 (1988). In the case, investors in an unsuccessful oil and gas venture (Black Gold Oil Company) sued under §12(a)(1) to get their money back from the venture's promoter (Pinter). Pinter then counterclaimed for contribution from a major investor in the venture (Dahl) who had told the other investors about the venture and had assisted them in filling out subscription forms. Dahl claimed he could not be liable in contribution because he was not a "statutory seller" for purposes of §12(a)(1).

Even though Dahl had not passed title to the securities — nor had Pinter, for that matter — the Supreme Court held that a §12(a)(1) statutory seller includes not only the person who passes title, but any person who solicits securities sales. The Court reached this conclusion by looking at the "offers or sells" language of §12(a)(1), as well as the broad definition of "offer" in §2(3) and the Securities Act's concern with the flow of information to potential investors. The Court, however, assumed that the purpose of §12(a)(1) did not extend to persons who give gratuitous advice — not for their "own financial interests" or for those of the seller. The Court remanded the case on the issue whether Dahl's solicitation efforts were meant to further his or Pinter's financial interests.

The Supreme Court's narrow focus on solicitation for financial gain departed from earlier lower court decisions. The Court rejected a "proximate cause" or "substantial factor" test, which had been employed by lower courts to impose §12(a)(1) liability on collateral participants, such as lawyers and accountants, who contributed proximately to the offering's success but did not necessarily solicit sales. The Court concluded that §12(a)(1)'s strict liability should not reach persons who neither solicit sales nor have control over conducting the offering.

§6.2.3 Limitations Period

The §12(a)(1) "put" is not indefinite. Purchasers must bring their §12(a)(1) action within one year after the alleged §5 violation. §13.

§6.3 SECTION 11: MISREPRESENTATIONS IN REGISTRATION STATEMENT

The most controversial innovation of the Securities Act was the §11 liability scheme for registered distributions. Even today, commentators criticize §11 and its potential for heavy liability for distorting the pricing of public offerings, particularly initial public offerings. Although Wall Street's predictions that §11 would ruin the market for public offerings proved exaggerated, the section continues to shape the way company executives, directors, underwriters, accountants, and lawyers play their roles in a registered offering.

Section 11 creates a civil remedy for purchasers in a registered offering if they can point to a material misrepresentation or omission in the registration statement. Joint and several liability falls on the issuer and specified defendants associated with the distribution, subject to nonculpability ("due diligence") defenses for nonissuer defendants, a limited reliance defense, a "negative causation" defense, and a special rule of proportionate liability for unwitting outside directors.

Thus, §11 changes the elements of common law fraud (and Rule 10b-5 liability, see §9.2) to require only that the plaintiff show a material misstatement or omission — without having to show scienter, reliance, or causation. Instead, culpability, reliance, and causation become defenses that must be established by the defendants.

§6.3.1 Section 11 Plaintiffs

All purchasers of registered securities have standing to sue. §11(a) (by reference to §10, "any person acquiring [security registered under Act]"). Left ambiguous in the statutory text, however, is when the registered security must have been acquired. Some courts have limited Section 11 standing to those who acquired the registered securities in the original distribution. Others courts, looking at the liability scheme of Section 11 and in particular the section's damages formula, have extended Section 11 standing to those who acquired registered securities in the post-offering aftermarket. See *Hertzberg v. Dignity Partners, Inc.*, 191 F.3d 1076 (9th Cir. 1999).

The requirement that §11 plaintiffs acquired registered securities imposes on them a tracing requirement. If the plaintiff purchased directly from an underwriter or a dealer selling its allotment, tracing is possible. But if the plaintiff purchased in the aftermarket, tracing becomes problematic. See *Krim v. pcOrder.com*, 402 F.3d 489 (5th Cir. 2005) (denying §11 standing to plaintiffs who could not trace shares purchased in aftermarket back to IPO, despite 99.85 percent chance their shares came from IPO). If a secondary market in fungible shares existed at the time of the public offering or unregistered shares were sold in the aftermarket by employees or others, tracing may be impossible given the absence of any numbering or other identification of securities in U.S. markets.

Although disclosure in a registered offering may impact investors even though they did not purchase the securities offered, courts have limited §11 standing to actual purchasers. Those who relied on misrepresentations in a prospectus and traded in other securities of the issuer have no §11 standing. Likewise, nonpurchasers who rely to their detriment on false statements in a prospectus have no standing under §11. *Barnes v. Osofsky*, 373 F.2d 269 (2d Cir. 1967) (denying standing to sellers who relied on pessimistic information in a registration statement).

To discourage §11 strike suits, the statute permits courts to require the plaintiff to post a bond to cover the defendant's defense costs. After judgment, the court may assess litigation costs against the plaintiff if the suit was "without merit." §11(e).

§6.3.2 Section 11 Defendants

Section 11 lists potential defendants:

- **Signers** — those who signed the registration statement (the issuer and its chief executive, financial, and accounting officers)
- **Directors** — all the issuer's directors at the time of filing (whether or not they signed the registration statement)
- **Underwriters** — all underwriters participating in the offering
- **Experts** — any expert who consents to his opinion being used in the registration statement, such as an accounting firm that audited the company's financial statements or a credit rating agency who agrees to the issuer using its rating of debt securities (see §11.6) — with the expert's liability limited to the information prepared or certified by him

To promote full and honest disclosure to investors, §11 loosens many of the common law elements and purposely puts fear in the hearts of potential defendants in the hope of creating a diligent pack of "information watchdogs." As you notice, §11 defendants need not be (and often are not) in privity with the purchasing investor and need not have actually created or disseminated the challenged misinformation.

Generally, liability under §11 for each defendant is joint and several. There are two exceptions. First, underwriters' liability is limited to the amount of their participation in the offering. §11(e) (except for managing underwriter). Second, for outside directors, the director's liability is proportionate to the damages he caused, unless the trier of fact determines the director knowingly violated the securities laws. §11(f)(2)(A).

§6.3.3 Material Misinformation in Registration Statement

A purchaser makes out a prima facie case simply by showing either material untruths or omissions of material facts in the registration statement. Silence is not a defense in a §11 action.

When a §11 plaintiff's allegations of false or deceptive statements "sound in fraud," some courts have required that the circumstances constituting fraud be pleaded "with particularity." See *Indiana State District Council of Laborers & Hod Carriers Pension & Welfare Fund v. Omnicare, Inc.*, 719 F. 3d 498 (6th Cir. 2013) (interpreting heightened pleading requirements of FRCP Rule 9(b) to apply to §11 allegations where plaintiff's claims "could be construed as alleging fraud or intentional or reckless misconduct").

Section 11 liability arises from misinformation in the registration statement at the time it became effective. This generally means that liability attaches to the final prospectus (or prospectus supplement) and not the preliminary prospectus. See §4.3.3. What happens if there is a discrepancy between the version filed electronically through EDGAR and the final, printed prospectus sent to investors? The Second Circuit, accepting the view of the SEC, decided that §11 liability can lie if either version is misleading or if the two taken together are misleading. *DeMaria v. Andersen*, 318 F.3d 170 (2d Cir. 2003).

In addition, forward-looking statements that predict or estimate future activities, or that state opinions or company motives, may be actionable. The Private Securities Litigation Reform Act of 1995 creates a safe harbor from §11 liability for forward-looking statements if the defendant establishes that either (1) there was a lack of actual knowledge that the forward-looking statement was false, (2) the forward-looking statement was immaterial, or (3) the forward-looking statement "is identified as a forward looking statement and is accompanied by meaningful cautionary statements identifying important factors that could cause actual results to differ materially from those projected in the forward looking statement." Securities Act §27A. The first two safe harbors become relevant only if the third "cautionary statement" safe harbor is unavailable. These statutory safe harbors are in addition to the SEC's safe harbor for forward-looking statements in SEC filings (see Rule 175) and the judicial "bespeaks caution" doctrine. See §3.3.2.

§6.3.4 Culpability — Defenses and Limitations on Liability

Under §11 the plaintiff generally need not plead or prove the defendants' culpability. Instead, §11 places on nonissuer defendants the burden to establish their nonculpability — the "due diligence" defense. The issuer, on the other hand, has no defense and is strictly liable regardless of its knowledge or negligence.

Reflecting concerns about abusive securities litigation, the Private Securities Litigation Reform Act of 1995 changes the §11 culpability standards in two respects. First, if liability is asserted against an outside director, the director's liability is proportionate to the damages he caused, unless the trier of fact determines that the director knowingly violated the securities laws. §11(f)(2)(A). Second, if liability is based on a forward-looking statement by (or on behalf of) a reporting company in a non-IPO offering, the plaintiff must prove the person making the statement had actual knowledge that it was false or misleading. §27A(c)(1)(B).

What does a §11 plaintiff have to allege in the case of a false statement of opinion or belief? In a case arising under §14 of the Exchange Act (proxy fraud), the Supreme Court held that statements of opinions and beliefs are actionable if the statement misstated the speaker's actual belief *and* misled about the subject matter of the opinion. See *Virginia Bankshares, Inc. v. Sandberg*, 501 U.S. 1083 (1991) (see §3.2.3). Nonetheless, the Sixth Circuit has held that a §11 plaintiff claiming a materially false opinion need only plead that the stated opinion was objectively false, without having to plead that the defendant knew it was untrue when made. See *Indiana State District Council of Laborers & Hod Carriers Pension & Welfare Fund v. Omnicare, Inc.*, 719 F. 3d 498 (6th Cir. 2013) (upholding §11 claim that opinion by health care company that its contracts were "legally valid" was materially false where company had actually been paying illegal kickbacks to drug manufacturers, even though plaintiffs did not allege company management knew about kickbacks).

Due Diligence

What is due diligence, besides something junior securities lawyers are told they will enjoy? It is the investigation by potential §11 defendants of information contained in the registration statement and prospectus. The due diligence task is often delegated to outside law firms and, within those firms, to junior lawyers.

The level of due diligence depends on whether the defendant is an expert and whether the alleged misinformation had been *expertised*. Here is a chart of the defendants' due diligence defenses:

	Expertised portion	Nonexpertised portion
Expert	Actually and reasonably believes, after reasonable investigation, that information is true (ignorance is no excuse)	No liability
Nonexpert	No reason to believe that information false (ignorance is excuse)	Actually and reasonably believes, after reasonable investigation, that information is true (ignorance is no excuse)

Expertised Information

The portions of the registration statement prepared or certified by an expert — such as financial information audited by an accounting firm or legal opinions given by a lawyer — are referred to as "expertised." As to expertised portions, the responsible expert has a higher standard of diligence than nonexperts. The expert must show she conducted a reasonable investigation and had reasonable grounds to believe (and did believe) that the expertised portions were *true and not misleading* — ignorance is no excuse. §11(b)(3)(B). Nonexperts, however, make out their defense as to expertised portions if they can show that they had no reasonable grounds to believe (and did not believe) that the expertised disclosure was *not true or misleading* — good faith, reasonable ignorance is an excuse. §11(b)(3)(C).

Nonexpertised Information

Those portions of the registration statement not prepared or reviewed by an expert (usually most of it) are referred to as "nonexpertised." See In re WorldCom, Inc., 346 F. Supp. 2d 628 (S.D.N.Y. 2004) (concluding that underwriters in $11 billion debt offering had due diligence obligations as to unaudited interim financials). As to nonexpertised portions, the stated standard is the same for all nonexperts. (Experts are liable only with respect to the portions they expertised.) To establish a due diligence defense, the defendant must show that he conducted a reasonable investigation and had reasonable grounds to believe (and did believe) that the nonexpertised portions were *true and not misleading* — ignorance is no excuse. §11(b)(3)(A).

Reasonableness

When is an investigation or a belief reasonable? The statute is circular: Reasonableness is that "required of a reasonable [person] in the management of his own property." §11(c). The SEC, by rule, explains that reasonableness is a sliding scale that depends on "relevant circumstances" that relate to the defendant's access to the contested information. Rule 176 (circumstances include type of issuer and security, defendant's background and relationship to the issuer, and defendant's responsibility for information in the registration statement). For example, it has been argued that in an offering of investment-grade debt, an underwriter would bear less responsibility for information incorporated by reference that it had not helped prepare. Nonetheless, underwriters have been required to conduct an "equally thorough" due diligence in a shelf registration, in which securities are brought to market under a compressed schedule (see §4.2.4). The underwriter should have a "reservoir of knowledge" about the issuer gained by (among other things) keeping abreast of analyst reports on the company and hiring a law firm that has acted as underwriters' counsel for prior offerings of the issuer. See *In re WorldCom, Inc.*, 346 F. Supp. 2d 628 (S.D.N.Y. 2004) (concluding underwriter had not met its "reasonable investigation" duties under Rule 176 in a shelf registration; finding that jury could conclude that underwriters were aware of "red flags" of improper accounting of expenses in audited financials and should have made additional inquiries about similar accounting in unaudited financials).

Due Diligence Applied — *Escott v. BarChris Construction*

Judicial guidance on the due diligence defense is scant because most §11 cases are settled. Nonetheless, the leading case illustrates how due diligence varies with the defendant's role in the offering and his relationship to the issuer. *Escott v. BarChris Construction Co.*, 283 F. Supp. 643 (S.D.N.Y. 1968). BarChris built bowling alleys and suffered a big downturn in its business during the early 1960s when the bowling industry became overbuilt. To raise capital, the company issued debentures under a registration statement that seriously misstated the company's financial position and its exposure to losses.

Material Misstatements

There was little question that the false and misleading information was material. The audited financial statements (expertised by the company's accounting firm) overstated the number of bowling alleys BarChris had sold. The prospectus did not disclose that BarChris stood to lose money on guarantees it had made when it "factored" (resold) shaky notes that cash-strapped customers had given BarChris when they bought on credit. The prospectus misstated backlog orders; it omitted that some construction jobs had no customers; it did not disclose that proceeds from the offering would be used not for expansion but to repay BarChris's existing debt; and it failed to state that certain insiders had not repaid company loans. The case turned on the various defendants' due diligence defenses.

Officer and Director Due Diligence

According to the *BarChris* court, due diligence varies in relation to two factors: (1) the director's access to inside company information and (2) the director's position as a company insider or as a nonemployee outsider:

Inside insiders	The court held that company insiders who perpetrated the coverup of the company's faltering finances (Vittolo, the company founder and president; Russo, executive vice president) had no defense as to either the expertised or

nonexpertised portions. One insider (Kircher, the company treasurer) claimed ignorance as to the expertised audited financials. The court rejected his defense because he was thoroughly familiar with the company's finances and knew the facts underlying the false audited financials. The court also concluded that Kircher, given his position, "must have known" of the nonexpertised inaccuracies as well. Like the perpetrators of the fraud, Kircher became a virtual guarantor of the accuracy of the registration statement.

Outside insiders

Another insider (Birnbaum, the company's in-house lawyer and relatively new director) was generally ignorant of the company's finances. The court accepted his defense as to the expertised financials but not as to the nonexpertised portions of the prospectus. Birnbaum had failed to investigate information in the prospectus despite his position and access to documents such as board minutes and contracts for bowling alleys. The court did not require complete verification, but instead an investigation commensurate with Birnbaum's position.

Inside outsiders

One outside director (Grant, the company's outside lawyer and drafter of the registration statement) had access to inside information. The court rejected his defense under a standard approximating that of an insider. Grant had failed to investigate sufficiently the correspondence, contracts, and corporate minutes that would have revealed the inaccuracies of the nonexpertised portions. Nonetheless, the court accepted Grant's defense as to the expertised financials because he had no reason to doubt their accuracy.

Outside outsiders

Another outside director (Auslander, the CEO of BarChris's bank) had no special access to company information. The court accepted that he had justifiably relied on the auditor's reputation as to the expertised financials. But Auslander could not simply rely on assurances by company insiders as to the nonexpertised portions. Due diligence required him at least to read and familiarize himself with the registration statement.

Underwriter Due Diligence

The *BarChris* court treated the offering's managing underwriter (Drexel & Co.) much as an "inside outsider." Drexel had delegated its due diligence work to "underwriter's counsel" and was bound by the deficiencies of its agent's investigation. The court rejected Drexel's defense as to the nonexpertised portions because counsel had failed to uncover the same board minutes and contracts that had rendered Grant's investigation inadequate. The other underwriters, represented by Drexel, were bound by Drexel's failed diligence. The court accepted the underwriters' defense as to the expertised financials because Drexel and the other underwriters could rely on the accounting firm.

Accountant (Expert) Due Diligence

The court held BarChris's accounting firm (Peat Marwick) to the standards of an "inside outsider" as to the expertised audited (or certified) financials. The court faulted Peat Marwick's inexperienced, non-CPA auditor for not discovering (from accounting entries on costs and accounts receivable) that BarChris had not actually sold some bowling alleys reported as sold. In addition, the court faulted the firm's "S-1 review" of the unaudited financial information. Although under §11(a)(4) an expert is liable only for expertised information, the court accepted that the auditor must review the unaudited financials to ensure that the certified financials were not rendered misleading. In this regard, the Peat Marwick auditor had (like Grant and underwriter's counsel) accepted the insiders' answers at face value—an effort inadequate to establish its due diligence defense.

No Liability for Innocent Forward-Looking Statements

The Private Securities Litigation Reform Act of 1995 (PSLRA) exempts from §11 liability innocent (nonculpable) forward-looking statements in the registration statement for a reporting company under the Exchange Act. §27A(c)(1)(B). To recover under §11, the plaintiff must show the person making the forward-looking statement (whether a natural person or business entity) had "actual knowledge" that the statement was false or misleading. Excluded from this exemption are forward-looking statements in the financial statements (prepared according to generally accepted accounting principles) or in an initial public offering. §27A(b)(2).

Proportionate Liability for Outside Directors

The PSLRA also takes some of the bite out of §11 liability for *outside directors* by carving an exception to the rule of joint and several liability for such defendants. Under the PSLRA, any "outside director" (a term yet to be defined by the SEC) sued under §11 can become jointly and severally liable for damages only if the trier of fact specifically determines the director "knowingly" committed a violation of the securities laws. Otherwise, the director is liable only for the portion of damages he caused. §11(f)(2)(A) (incorporating by reference the proportionate liability scheme of §21D of the Exchange Act).

An outside director "knowingly commits" securities fraud when he has "actual knowledge," whether of the material misrepresentation or material omission. In addition, the outside director must have actual knowledge that persons are "likely to reasonably rely on that misrepresentation or omission." According to the definitions, "reckless" conduct is not to be construed as a knowing commission of a securities law violation. See Exchange Act §21D(f)(10).

An "outside director" without actual knowledge can be liable only for the portion of the judgment that corresponds to the percentage of his responsibility. See Exchange Act §21D(f)(2)(B). The court is required to instruct the jury to answer special interrogatories (or, in a bench trial, the court makes the findings) with respect to each defendant and any other person claimed to have contributed to the plaintiff's loss concerning each person's violation of the securities laws, the responsibility of the person as a percentage of total fault, and whether the person knowingly committed a violation. See Exchange Act §21D(f)(3). Special, complex provisions apply to uncollectible shares.

§6.3.5 Reliance

In the usual §11 case, proof of reliance is unnecessary. The plaintiff need not have read the registration statement or prospectus, much less have known of the false or misleading information.

Reliance becomes relevant under §11, however, in two limited cases. First, there can be no recovery if the defendant proves the plaintiff knew the alleged misinformation was false. §11(a) (first sentence). Second, reliance becomes an element of the plaintiff's case if he bought the security after the issuer had released an earnings statement for the one-year period after the registration statement's effective date. §11(a) (last sentence).

Nonetheless, the presumption of reliance may not apply when sophisticated investors made a "legally binding commitment" to take stock in a corporate merger months before the filing of a defective registration statement. See *APA Excelsior III LP v. Premiere Technologies Inc.*, 476 F.3d 1261 (11th Cir. 2007) (pointing out that sophisticated investors had failed to exercise due diligence). The court did not explain how a preregistration commitment could be legally binding given that §5(a) prohibits any "sales" of securities until the registration statement has become effective. See §4.3.

§6.3.6 Loss Causation

The §11 plaintiff need not prove that the challenged misinformation caused his loss. Instead, the statute gives the defendant a "negative causation defense" if he can show how other factors besides the misinformation explain (or contributed to) the depreciation in value. For example, if the defendant can show that an oil company's stock price collapsed not because of the revelation that the prospectus overstated earnings but because of a worldwide oil glut, the plaintiff cannot recover.

The courts have been less than consistent in applying the negative causation defense. In *Ackerman v. Oryx Communications, Inc.*, 810 F.2d 336 (2d Cir. 1987), the court upheld a "negative causation" defense when the issuer showed that the price of its stock had actually risen when it disclosed publicly the allegedly false information.

Date	Event	Stock price
6/30	IPO	$4.75
10/15	Disclosure to SEC	4.00
11/10	Disclosure to public	3.25
11/25	Suit filed	3.50

According to the §11 damages formula (see §6.3.7), plaintiffs' recovery in the case should have been the difference between $4.75 (the offering price) and $3.50 (the value at time of suit). The court held, however, that any price decline before disclosure could not be charged to the issuer. See *Beecher v. Able*, 435 F. Supp. 397 (S.D.N.Y. 1977). And since the plaintiffs had not shown that the trading market had become aware of the alleged misinformation prior to public disclosure, the court held that the issuer had sustained the defense by showing that the price had risen after disclosure. Like other courts, the *Oryx* court seemed reluctant to impose damages for declines in value not clearly related to the alleged misinformation.

§6.3.7 Damages

Section 11 caps recovery at the aggregate offering price. The §11 formulas for computing damages depend on whether (and when) the plaintiff resold his securities:

Formula #1 (securities held at time of judgment)	Damages equal purchase price (not greater than public offering price) minus value at time suit brought. §11(e)(1)
Formula #2 (securities sold before suit)	Damages equal purchase price (not in excess of public offering price) minus sales price. §11(e)(2)
Formula #3 (securities sold after suit, but before judgment)	Damages equal purchase price (not greater than public offering price) minus sales price, but not more than damages under Formula 1. §11(e)(3)

This means that a §11 plaintiff's recovery is capped by the offering price, and defendants are not liable for the extra damages if the plaintiff purchased registered securities in a trading market above the offering price. See also §11(g) (total recovery capped at aggregate offering price).

Section 11 also caps the liability of nonmanaging underwriters. An underwriter that does not receive special compensation in the offering cannot be liable for more than the aggregate offering price of its allotment. §11(e).

§6.3.8 Periods of Limitations and Repose

According to §13 of the Securities Act, §11 actions are subject to relatively short limitations and repose periods. A §11 action must be brought within one year after the plaintiff discovers (or should have discovered) the alleged misinformation. And the action must be brought within three years after the security was first "bona fide" offered to the public, thus promising repose after three years to §11 defendants. See *P. Stolz Family Partnership LP v. Daum*, 355 F.3d 92 (2d Cir. 2004) (concluding that repose period begins with first bona fide public offer).

An interesting question arises whether the Sarbanes-Oxley Act expands the limitations and repose periods for §11 actions. Under Section 804 of Sarbanes-Oxley, codified at 28 U.S.C. §1658(b), uniform limitation/repose periods apply to any "private right of action that involves a claim of fraud, deceit, manipulation, or contrivance in contravention of a regulatory requirement concerning the securities laws." Under §1658(b), such actions must be brought within two years after the plaintiff discovers the facts constituting the violation, and the action must be brought within five years after the "violation." See §9.4.1.

Lower courts, however, have rejected the argument that the expanded limitations period of §1658(b) applies to §11 actions, which "sound in negligence, not fraud." See *Amorosa v. Ernst & Young LLP*, 672 F. Supp. 2d 493 (S.D.N.Y. 2009). This reading is confirmed in Justice Scalia's concurrence in a case construing the term "discovery" under §1658(b), where he pointed out that misrepresentations in a registration statement covered by §11 are easier to detect than market deceptions covered by §10(b) and Rule 10b-5 of the Exchange Act — justifying a longer limitations period for the latter. See *Merck & Co. v. Reynolds*, 130 S. Ct. 1784 (2010) (§9.4.1).

The conclusion that §1658(b) does not apply to §11 actions is confirmed by a close reading of §1658(b). First, the phrase "fraud, deceit, manipulation, or contrivance" in §1658(b) tracks the language of §10(b) of the Exchange Act, which makes it "unlawful" to use "any manipulative or deceptive device or contrivance" in connection with the purchase or sale of a security. Given that the Supreme Court has interpreted the language of §10(b) to require proof of scienter (see §9.3.2), and since §11 does not require proof of scienter, it would seem a §11 action does not involve a "claim of fraud, deceit, manipulation, or contrivance." Second, §11 liability does not technically turn on a "violation" of the securities laws, but rather a predicate finding that a registration statement includes a materially false or misleading statement.

§6.4 SECTION 12(a)(2): MISREPRESENTATIONS IN "PUBLIC" OFFERINGS

Section 12(a)(2) — which before 1995 was numbered §12(2) — takes over where §11 leaves off. Purchasers in an offering may seek rescission from "statutory sellers" if the offering was carried out "by means of a prospectus or oral communication" that is materially false or misleading. Sellers have a "reasonable care" defense if they show they did not know (and reasonably could not have known) of the misinformation.

§6.4.1 Coverage of §12(a)(2)

Section 12(a)(2) applies to sales that involve the use of instruments of transportation or communication in interstate commerce or the mails — jurisdictional means. As we have seen, this will rarely present a problem. At some point in nearly all securities sales, the parties will use a telephone or the mails. See §4.3 (Jurisdictional means).

By its terms, §12(a)(2) applies to sales and offers of securities (except government securities) "by means of a prospectus or oral communication." Reading "prospectus" broadly to include all written sales efforts, lower courts had long assumed the section applies to both public offerings and private placements. Some lower courts even said that this liability extends to sales in trading markets.

The *Gustafson* Bombshell

In 1995, the Supreme Court addressed the scope of §12(a)(2) in a surprising, sweeping, and strained 5-4 decision. *Gustafson v. Alloyd Co.*, 513 U.S. 561 (1995). In the case, shareholders of a closely held corporation sold all their shares to an investor group. The investor group claimed that the sellers had misrepresented the company's financial position in the contract of sale and sought rescission under §12(a)(2). The Court majority held the parties' contract of sale could not constitute a "prospectus" under §12(a)(2) because it was not the prospectus described in §10 and filed in a registered public offering.

What about the Securities Act's carefully crafted definitions? The majority construed the Act's definition of "prospectus" in §2(10) to refer simply to widely disseminated sales materials used in a public offering. The Court noted various interpretive and policy anomalies if §12(a)(2) created liability for misrepresentations in sales documents used in trading transactions, and then assumed that if the section did not apply to secondary market trading, it must be limited to *public* offerings. The majority also pointed to the Securities Act's sparse legislative history, which suggested that §§11 and 12 created complementary liability in public offerings.

Analysis of *Gustafson*

The Court's decision in *Gustafson* surprised the securities law community. While reaching the plausible conclusion that §12(a)(2) distinguishes between issuer transactions and aftermarket trading, the decision abandoned decades of uniform case law that §12(a)(2) covers both registered public offerings and exempt private placements. The decision swept broadly beyond the ostensible issue in the case — the application of §12(a)(2) to a secondary market transaction — to hold that the section applies only to public offerings.

The Court's strained analysis casts dark interpretive shadows over the Securities Act.

- The Court's reading of the §2(a)(10) definition of "prospectus" to mean widely disseminated sales literature significantly undermines many of the "free writing" strictures of §5. See §4.3.2.
- The Court's suggestion that §12(a)(2) covers "oral communications that relate to a prospectus" in a public offering might mean that oral misstatements (that relate to a public offering, but are limited in scope) are actionable even though they would not be if made in writing.
- The Court's reading of §12(a)(2) to cover only "public" offerings is laden with ambiguity. For example, many small offerings made

pursuant to §3 exemptions (such as intrastate offerings and smaller offerings under Reg A or Rules 504 and 505 of Reg D) are technically exempt "public" offerings. See §5.2.3.

- The Court's understanding that "prospectus" in §12(a)(2) refers to a §10 prospectus that "must include the information contained in the registration statement" suggests the section might cover "prospectus-like" offering circulars in a private placement.

The Court's agenda to limit the scope of the Securities Act seemed clear enough, but what remains is anyone's guess.

§6.4.2 Section 12(a)(2) Defendants

Lower courts have assumed that §12(a)(2) — which covers the identical class of defendants as §12(a)(1) — imposes liability on the same class of "statutory sellers" as §12(a)(1). Thus, not only is the seller who passes title potentially liable, but also any collateral participant who solicits purchasers for his own or the issuer's benefit. See *Pinter v. Dahl*, 486 U.S. 622 (1988) (§6.2.2). In a registered public offering this would include retail broker-dealers and selling shareholders, but not the issuer itself. *Rozenzweig v. Azurix Corp.*, 332 F.3d 854 (5th Cir. 2003) (holding that issuer in the "usual case" is not a "solicitor" liable under §12).

Since *Pinter v. Dahl*, lower courts have rejected §12(a)(2) liability on an aiding and abetting theory, pointing out that it would be anomalous that nonselling collateral participants are insulated under *Pinter* yet liable as §12(a)(2) aiders and abettors. *Wilson v. Saintine Exploration & Drilling Corp.*, 872 F.2d 1124 (2d Cir. 1989). This view is bolstered by the Dodd-Frank Act, which amended §15 of the Securities Act (as well as the "control person" provisions of the other securities laws) to clarify that the SEC can bring an enforcement action against a person who aids and abets, either knowingly or recklessly, a violation by another person. Dodd-Frank §929M.

§6.4.3 Elements of §12(a)(2) Rescission Action

Section 12(a)(2) hones close to equitable rescission, abandoning the more demanding elements of common law deceit.

Misrepresentation of Material Fact

A purchaser makes out a §12(a)(2) misrepresentation claim by showing either a material untruth or the omission of a material fact necessary to make what is said not misleading.

Culpability of Seller

Section 12(a)(2) modifies equitable rescission and makes the defendant's nonculpability a defense. The seller must show he did not know and "in the exercise of reasonable care" could not have known of the misinformation.

Does "reasonable care" create a due diligence duty? In *Sanders v. John Nuveen & Co.*, 619 F.2d 1222 (7th Cir. 1980), the Seventh Circuit rejected a "reasonable care" defense by a securities firm that acted as underwriter for a commercial paper offering exempt from Securities Act registration. Applying a §11 "due diligence" analysis, the court faulted the underwriter for failing to investigate the issuer's financial soundness, even though the issuer's seemingly healthy financials had been audited by an outside accountant. When the Supreme Court denied certiorari, Justice Powell dissented on the ground that the lower court's reading of §12(a)(2) imposed an even greater investigation duty than did §11 for nonexperts with respect to expertised portions of the registration statement.

Reliance of Purchaser

Under §12(a)(2) the purchaser need not show that he relied on the alleged misinformation. Rather, the section conditions recovery on "the purchaser not knowing" of the challenged misinformation.

Nonetheless, courts have made reliance an issue by insisting on "transaction causation" — that is, proof of some causal connection between the misinformation and the transaction. See §12(a)(2) ("by means of" false or misleading prospectus or oral communication). Although the purchaser need not have received the misinformation — such as false reports distributed by a commercial paper seller — the misinformation must have been "instrumental" in the sale. This can be established if the misinformation bolsters a market in the purchased securities. See *Sanders v. John Nuveen & Co.*, 619 F.2d 1222 (7th Cir. 1980) (finding sufficient link, even though some plaintiffs were unaware of defendant's "risk-free" representations, because had the market known the truth it would have collapsed).

What information can be the basis for §12(a)(2) liability in a public offering where investors often make their investment decision based on preliminary sales efforts, not the final prospectus? The SEC addressed this problem as part of its 2005 Public Offering Reforms (see §4.2). Under Rule 159, an investor can assert §12(a)(2) liability only as to false or misleading information that arose *before the sale occurred*. Post-sale information "will not be taken into account." Rule 159(a). Similarly, any defense that the investor knew of the allegedly false or misleading information can only be based on information that the investor knew *at the time of the sale*. Rule 159(c). Thus, there can be neither liability nor a reliance defense based on post-sale information.

Loss Causation

Loss causation — a causal link between the misinformation and the plaintiff's loss — has become an affirmative defense in §12(a)(2) actions. See §12(b) (added by the Private Securities Litigation Reform Act of 1995). Before 1995, courts interpreted §12(2) to be modeled on equitable rescission and not to require that the plaintiff suffered *any* loss. Under this interpretation, §12(2) allowed investors to rescind an investment tainted by misinformation, whether or not other factors contributed to a decline in the value of the investment.

The PSLRA, however, creates a "loss causation" defense similar to the "negative causation" defense of §11 that permits a defendant in a §12(a)(2) action to prove that a portion (or all) of the amount recoverable "represents other than the depreciation in value . . . resulting from" the false or misleading statement on which liability is based. §12(b). Rejecting a pure rescission theory of recovery, Congress concluded in the PSLRA that rescission provided "an unfair windfall to shareholders who have not in any way been harmed by the misstatement or omission."

§6.4.4 Periods of Limitations and Repose

According to §13 the Securities Act, actions under §12(a)(2) are subject to essentially the same limitations and repose periods as §11 actions. The action must be brought within one year after the plaintiff discovers (or should have discovered) the alleged misinformation. In no event may an action be brought more than three years after the sale.

As we have seen, the Sarbanes-Oxley Act extends the limitations period for fraud-type securities law claims. Sarbanes-Oxley §804, codified at 28 U.S.C. §1658(b) (covered actions must be brought two years after the plaintiff discovers the facts constituting the violation, and within five years after the violation). Nonetheless, as with claims under §11, it can be argued that §12(a)(2) claims do not fall within §1658(b) — given its apparent focus on securities fraud claims brought under §10(b) of the Exchange Act. Like §11, but unlike §10(b), §12(a)(2) does not require a showing of scienter. Moreover, §12(a)(2) does not use the language of "unlawfulness" — technically, liability under §12(a)(2) is not predicated on a violation, but instead conduct specified in the section.

§6.5 SECTION 15: LIABILITY OF CONTROL PERSONS

Persons (whether individual or corporate) who control any person liable under §11 or §12 are jointly and severally liable to the same extent as the controlled person. §15. Control persons — such as major shareholders, directors and officers of a corporate seller — have a limited defense if they did not know (and had no reason to know) of the facts on which liability is based.

The question of control is sometimes straightforward, such as when an issuer is a majority-owned subsidiary of a parent corporation. But often the question will necessitate a fact-intensive inquiry into the alleged control person's influence over the violator — often a jury question. The good faith defense, which the alleged control person must prove, also raises factual questions that usually must go to trial.

§6.6 SECTION 4A(c): LIABILITY IN CROWDFUNDING

As part of the new crowdfunding regime (see §5.2.5), the JOBS Act of 2012 creates a liability scheme for issuers and intermediaries participating in an exempt crowdfunding offering similar to that of §12(a)(2).

§6.6.1 New §4A(c) Action

Under new §4A(c) of the Securities Act, crowdfunding purchasers can bring an action in federal or state court to rescind their investment or seek damages from crowdfunding defendants that make materially false or misleading statements (oral or written) in the offering, provided the purchaser did not know of the untruth or omission. §4A(c)(1), (2)(A).

Crowdfunding defendants include the issuer, its top managers who participate in the offering (including directors or partners, principal executive officers, principal financial officers, and principal accounting officers), intermediaries participating in the offering (including securities brokers and crowdfunding portals), and any other "person who offers or sells" securities in the offering. §4A(c)(3).

There is a "due care" defense for crowdfunding defendants (including the issuer) similar to the defense under §12(a)(2). Defendants can avoid liability by proving that they did not know, and in the exercise of reasonable care could not have known, of the deception. §4A(c)(2)(B).

Finally, a crowdfunding action is subject to the "loss causation" defense and the limitations periods applicable to a §12(a)(2) action. §4A(c)(1)(B). Thus, crowdfunding defendants can avoid liability to the extent that they prove the plaintiff's losses resulted from other than the claimed false or misleading statements. See §12(b). And crowdfunding claims must be brought within one year after the plaintiff discovers (or should have discovered) the alleged misinformation — but in no event more than three years after the purchase. See §13.

§6.6.2 Unresolved Issues in §4A(c) Action

The crowdfunding liability scheme raises some interpretive issues. It will be interesting to see how courts resolve them:

- Will subsequent purchasers (that is, purchasers who acquire crowd-funding shares from an original purchaser) have a cause of action?
- What disclosures, beyond those specified in the SEC rules, will be "material" to crowdfunding investors — such as disclosures about how the offering price (for equity) or interest rate (for debt) was determined?
- Will crowdfunding defendants — particularly brokerage firms and funding portals — be able to enter into indemnification agreements with the issuer or its principals?
- Will parent companies of participating intermediaries (brokers and portals) be liable as control persons (the JOBS Act did not amend §15 to include persons liable under new §4A(c))?
- Will class actions be feasible — given the relatively small amounts involved in any one crowdfunding?
- Will a website that describes crowdfunding offerings — such as by listing pending offerings — be subject to liability as a "person who offers or sells" in a crowdfunding?

§6.7 SECTION 17(a): LIABILITY IN SEC ENFORCEMENT ACTION

Section 17(a) is a catch-all provision that makes unlawful fraudulent and deceptive conduct in the offer or sale of securities — whether in a public offering, a private offering, or even an offering of exempt securities. See §17(c) (see §5.1). The Supreme Court has concluded that the §17(a) prohibition also extends beyond distributions to cover cases where a broker defrauded a customer. See *United States v. Naftalin*, 441 U.S. 768 (1979) (finding that Congress sought to ensure honesty "in every" facet of securities business).

Specifically, §17(a) prohibits the sale of securities using jurisdictional means that (1) employ an "artifice to defraud," (2) obtain money by means of a material misstatement or misleading omission, and (3) engage in actions that "operate as a fraud." Courts have interpreted the provision's broad language (which was copied into Rule 10b-5 under the Exchange Act, see §9.1.1) to create liability for negligent misrepresentations. See *Aaron v. SEC*, 446 U.S. 680 (1980) (upholding SEC injunction based on negligent misrepresentations by broker-dealer's sales representatives).

Some courts once took the view that §17(a) creates an implied private cause of action not only for willful misrepresentations but also for negligent misrepresentations whose "*effect* is to deceive." Over time the federal circuit courts have come to the uniform view that §17 does not create an implied private cause of action. See *Finkel v. Stratton Corp.*, 962 F.2d 169 (2d Cir. 1992). Nonetheless, §17 is an important tool in the SEC's enforcement of full disclosure in securities offerings.

§6.8 LIABILITY UNDER STATE BLUE SKY LAWS

State securities law has become an increasingly popular basis for purchasers seeking relief in securities offerings — particularly since the narrow construction of §12(a)(2) in *Gustafson*. Most states have enacted some version of §410 of the Uniform Securities Act (as promulgated in 1956 and revised in 1985), which allows *buyers* in any securities sale (whether a public or private offering, and whether a primary or secondary market transaction) accomplished by means of materially false or misleading statements to recover the consideration they paid. Though modeled on §12(a)(2), §410 goes well beyond its Securities Act parent in a number of respects:

	USA §410	Securities Act §12(a)(2)
Plaintiff	Purchaser	Purchaser
Defendant	Seller, controlling person, and partners; directors, officers, and employees; broker-dealers and agents who "materially aid" in sale. An attorney who meets with potential investors and promotes investment can be liable. *Johnson v. Culp*, 658 N.E.2d 575 (Ind. 1995).	Seller and "statutory seller" (person who solicits sales for own financial interest)
Predicate	Purchase by means of materially false or misleading statement	Sale or offer by means of "prospectus or oral communication" that includes materially false or misleading statement. Sale or offer must be

	USA §410	Securities Act §12(a)(2)
Plaintiff	Purchaser	Purchaser
		part of a "public offering." *Gustafson* (see §6.4.1).
Culpability	Seller: strict liability (no defense) Non-seller: defense if did not know or could not have known in exercise of reasonable care Partners, officers, and directors are strictly liable, even if they did not aid in sale. *Taylor v. Perdition Minerals Group, Ltd.,* 766 P.2d 805 (Kan. 1988).	Defense if defendant did not know or could not have known in exercise of reasonable care
Reliance	Purchaser does not know of "untruth or omission." Reliance is not an element. *Ritch v. Robinson-Humphrey Co.,* 748 So.2d 861 (Ala. 1999).	Purchaser does not know of "untruth or omission"+ sale "by means" of prospectus or oral communication
Causation	[not specified]	Defense if seller shows damages to be other than from depreciation due to false or misleading statement [§12(b)]
Liability	Joint and several + right of pro rata contribution among liable persons	[not specified]
Damages	Consideration paid + 6 percent annual interest + costs and attorney's fees (less any income received) OR damages if purchaser no longer owns securities	Consideration paid +"interest thereon" OR damages if purchaser no longer owns securities
Limitations/ repose	Two years after purchase [under new 2002 Act, two years after discovery but five years after purchase]	One year after discovery of false or misleading statement, but three years after purchase [perhaps longer under 28 U.S.C. §1658(b)]

In 2002, the National Conference on Commissioners of Uniform State Laws promulgated a new USA that specifies that civil liability is subject to the Securities Litigation Uniform Standards Act, which preempts class actions based on state securities law. The 2002 Act, however, largely leaves intact the provisions of USA §410, which are renumbered as §509(b). The only significant change is the Act's adoption of a uniform statute of limitations/

repose to correspond to that created in the Sarbanes-Oxley Act — namely, two years after discovery of the false or misleading statement, but no more than five years after the purchase.

Examples

The Plymouth-Davenport Tramway Company was formed to carry passengers in trams from Plymouth to Davenport. The company offered common stock to investors, and toward that end the company's directors authorized a prospectus that stated in part:

> One great feature of this undertaking is that by special act of the legislature the company will have the right to use steam power, instead of horses. It is fully expected this will result in considerable savings compared with other tramways worked by horses.

The offering was a success. But alas! The legislature had never authorized steam power for the Tramway Company. In fact, the law was quite the opposite: "All carriages used on any tramway shall be moved by animal power only, unless a special Act prescribes otherwise." When the Tramway Company finally asked for special permission, the legislature refused. The company eventually wound up its affairs — an investment and business failure.

Investors sue the directors of Tramway Company, "five men of good character and conduct" — and of means.

1. Consider liability under common law theories of deceit and equitable rescission. Which of the following are relevant under each theory?
   a. Investors in the offering bought shares from the company, not the directors.
   b. Many investors, relying on what they had heard from acquaintances and stock brokers, bought shares without ever receiving or reading a prospectus.
   c. The prospectus had added that the matter of steam power was before the legislature, but omitted that the legislature had never before permitted a steam-powered tramway.
   d. The directors, before authorizing the prospectus, had honestly thought the legislature was about to approve steam power for the Tramway Company.
   e. Some investors knew there had been no legislative approval for the steam-powered tram but hoped the company would get one eventually.

     f. A flood struck Plymouth and Davenport soon after the company was to have begun operations. The tram would have failed, whether powered by steam or not.

     g. Experts opine that there was a 40 percent chance, at the time of the offering, that the company would obtain permission to use steam power and that the shares were originally worth $8. Assume the offering price was $20, and shareholders received $2 in liquidation of the company.

     h. Tramway Company's board chairman bribed the other directors to approve the deceptive prospectus, and shareholders want to make an example of him.

     i. After the offering, the shareholders remain hopeful the company will turn itself around. They sue the directors once the company winds up its business and dissolves, three years after the offering.

2. Consider liability against Tramway Company under the Securities Act of 1933.

     a. Assume the Tramway Company never registered its securities with the SEC. When the Tramway Company goes bust, the investors consider their options. What claims might they pursue under the Securities Act?

     b. Why might investors prefer to sue under the Securities Act, rather than state law?

     c. In addition to their Securities Act claims, investors want to pursue claims under state law and other federal securities laws. Can they?

     d. The investors live in a federal district with a clogged civil docket. Can they bring their Securities Act claims in state court? Could the defendants then force them to federal court?

     e. A provision in the investors' subscription agreement requires that they submit any claims arising from the offering to binding arbitration. Must the investors arbitrate their Securities Act claims?

3. Consider liability under the Securities Act in an unregistered offering. Assume the Tramway Company offering is exempt from the filing requirements of the Securities Act, but sold through underwriters who used a written offering circular containing the misinformation stated in the prospectus.

     a. Investors claim the offering circular was misleading. What Securities Act claim should they pursue?

     b. Many investors never received the offering circular; many others did not read it. Can they recover?

     c. The company and the directors never solicited investors themselves, a task left to the underwriters. Can the company or the directors be liable?

     d. Before the company made the offering, the company's outside attorney told the board the legislature "would most certainly approve the use of steam power." The board proceeded with the offering on this basis. Can investors sue the attorney?

e. The directors claim they relied on the attorney and honestly believed the legislature had approved steam power. Does their reliance absolve them?

f. A flood struck Plymouth and Davenport soon after the company was to have begun operations. The trams could not have run, whether powered by steam or not. Does this make a difference?

g. Albert purchased in the original offering at $20. Two weeks later Albert resold to Bertha at $12. When the company announced it had never gotten legislative approval, the price dropped to $3. Can Bertha recover from the company, and how much?

h. Eventually the company was wound up and liquidated. Many shareholders took a tax write-off, ameliorating their loss. Does this affect their recovery?

i. Soon after the offering, some savvy investors learned of the difficulties the company was having getting legislative permission. They waited to sue until the company had wound up its affairs, which happened two years later. Can they recover?

4. Consider liability under the Securities Act in an offering registered with the SEC. Tramway Company hired First Lynch Securities to advise it and advertise the offering on a "best efforts" basis. Sales were directly by the company.

a. Some investors never received the false prospectus when they bought their shares. What Securities Act claim should they pursue?

b. Purchasers who never received a prospectus sue First Lynch, even though they had bought directly from the issuer. Is the underwriter strictly liable?

c. Shareholders who received a prospectus seek rescission from the issuer for its failure to provide prospectuses to all purchasers. Can the issuer be liable to purchasers who actually received a prospectus?

d. Soon after the offering, Tramway sent letters to all shareholders who had not received a prospectus and offered to buy back their shares at the offering price, plus interest. The shareholders refused, hoping their investment would work out. Later they sued the company for rescission. Can they recover?

e. Barth (a First Lynch sales representative) sends Farley a prospectus and tells him Tramway "can't miss with its steam-powered trams." Can Farley, a longtime customer of First Lynch, sue Barth for this false statement?

f. Fifteen months after the offering, some investors contact a lawyer and for the first time realize they should have received a prospectus. Can they rescind their purchases?

5. Consider the liability under the Securities Act in a registered offering.
   a. Most investors received a copy of the misleading prospectus before investing. What claim should these investors pursue?
   b. Some shareholders bought their shares in the thin market that developed after the offering. They never saw a prospectus, nor were they required to receive one. Can they sue because of misinformation in the prospectus?
   c. Investors sue all the directors, even though some of the directors had not signed the registration statement. Which of the directors can be liable?
   d. After the offering, one of the directors has second thoughts about misleading investors. He resigns from the board. Does he escape liability?
   e. The company's outside attorney misled the directors into believing the legislature had approved the use of steam power. Can the attorney be liable?
   f. One of the directors is the company's outside counsel. She asserts that the plaintiffs cannot prove that she knew the legislature had not approved steam power. Can she be liable?

6. Consider defenses in a registered offering. Before Tramway went public, Lillian (the company's head of legislative affairs) had written a memo to the file: "After meeting today with the chair of the Transportation Committee, I now realize the political muscle of the horse lobby. The legislature will never let us use steam." She was right. The company fails, and disgruntled shareholders sue the usual suspects under §11.
   a. The directors claim they never knew of Lillian's memo. They were convinced of the truthfulness of the statements in the prospectus that the legislature would soon approve steam power for the company. Is their honest belief relevant?
   b. Lillian had told the directors she was sure the legislature would approve the use of steam power. Relying on this, none of the directors checked further. Can they be liable?
   c. The directors assigned to company counsel the task of writing and assuring the accuracy of the prospectus. Company counsel did not ask to look through Lillian's files. Can the directors be liable?
   d. Lillian had not circulated the memo for fear that it would "complicate" financing. She was not a director, but she signed the registration statement even though she was not required to. Can she be liable?
   e. The managing underwriter had asked Lillian if they could look through her files, but she refused. Does this absolve the underwriters from liability?

7. Consider an expert's report in a registered offering. A transportation engineer had prepared a report stating that operating a steam-powered

tramway would be technologically feasible and would cost half as much as a horse-powered tramway. This report was quoted in the prospectus.

   a. Is the engineer liable for the prospectus's misstatements about legislative approval of steam power?

   b. The engineer's report seriously misstated the savings of steam-powered tramways by failing to take into account the cost of coal used for such trams. This defect should have been obvious, even to a nonexpert. Can Tramway's underwriter be liable for the defects of the engineer's report?

8. Consider the mechanics of the §11 suit.

   a. Investors in the registered offering sue once Tramway Company winds up its business and dissolves, two years after the offering. A few sophisticated investors knew soon after the offering of the legislative roadblock. Other investors learned of it only when the company wound up its business. Who can recover?

   b. A couple of weeks after the company began operations, a flood struck Plymouth and Davenport and tramway use dropped by half. Does this affect plaintiffs' recovery?

   c. The offering at $20 per share was fully subscribed, and a thin market developed in Tramway shares. At the time of suit, shares were selling for $12. During the litigation, Tramway was wound up and liquidated, with shareholders receiving $2. What will shareholders who bought at $25 in the market recover?

   d. Should §11 plaintiffs sell before suit, sell during suit, or hold their shares to judgment?

   e. First Lynch, worried about its liability, had set up a separate subsidiary "First Lynch-Tram" to be the underwriter for the Tramway offering. The subsidiary uses First Lynch executives and facilities. In these circumstances, can §11 plaintiffs pierce the corporate veil?

   f. First Lynch pays the entire judgment and then points an accusing finger at Derry, a director who knew all along that the legislature had not approved and would not approve steam power. Can First Lynch seek contribution from Derry? How much?

Explanations

1. a. Relevant for rescission, not deceit. Privity is not required for common law deceit, and the investors may recover against any person who intentionally misstated the truth to induce their reliance, if the misstated facts were related to the cause of their loss. See Restatement (Second) of Torts §531.

      Privity is, however, relevant to a rescission action. Since the investors did not purchase from the directors, there is nothing between

287

them to rescind. See Restatement of Contracts §164(2). Although the transaction with the issuer can be rescinded if the investors relied on the misrepresentations of the directors, who acted for the issuer, the directors are not liable for the obligations of the issuer.

b. Relevant for both deceit and rescission. The investors must have relied, even if indirectly, on the prospectus's misrepresentations. Reliance is an element of common law deceit and equitable rescission. See Restatement (Second) of Torts §537; Restatement of Contracts §164. If the investors were unaware of the misrepresentation, it could not have induced their purchases, and there can be no common law liability.

c. Perhaps relevant for both. The common law of deceit traditionally treated as fraudulent only actual misstatements, but was beginning to encompass misleading or incomplete representations when Congress enacted the Securities Act of 1933. See Restatement (Second) of Torts §551. In rescission actions, the traditional approach has been to permit rescission for an omission, if materially misleading. See Restatement of Contracts §161.

d. Relevant for deceit; relevant for rescission based on fraudulent misrepresentation. Scienter makes a false statement into a fraudulent one. It establishes the defendant's culpability and can be shown if the defendant (1) knew the representation was false, (2) acted without belief in its truth, or (3) was reckless as to whether it was true or false. See Restatement (Second) of Torts §526. A defendant who honestly believes a representation to be true, however, lacks scienter.

The scienter element indicates the defendant was in a superior informational position than the plaintiff. Thus, under the common law of deceit, there can be no liability if both parities were ignorant or careless. Although this culpability standard may reward indifference to the truth, it serves the greater purpose of preventing easy shifting of losses on the basis of informational defects in the bargain. Scienter is also relevant in a rescission action. A false statement, even if not material, can be the basis for rescission if the statement was made fraudulently. Restatement of Contracts §164.

You might be interested to know that the facts of this example are drawn from the famous British case that established the scienter requirement in British common law of deceit. *Derry v. Peek*, 14 App. Cases 335 (House of Lords 1889). Since the case, however, British courts have abandoned a strict scienter requirement and permit recovery on a showing of negligence. Most U.S. courts, however, have stayed the course and continue to require scienter in deceit actions, notably in Rule 10b-5 cases.

e. Relevant for both deceit and rescission. The plaintiffs' knowledge of the true state of affairs thwarts their claim of reliance. See Restatement (Second) of Torts §546; Restatement of Contracts §167.

f. Relevant for deceit, not rescission. The common law of deceit requires a causal link between the transaction induced by the defendant's fraud and the plaintiff's losses — "loss causation." See Restatement (Second) of Torts §525. This element ensures that losses are shifted only to the extent of the misinformation, not extraneous causes.

Loss causation, however, is not an element in a rescission action. The theory of rescission is to restore the plaintiff to her position prior to the transaction induced by misinformation. There is no need to prove the plaintiff was injured or to prove the transaction caused any losses.

g. Relevant for deceit, not rescission. The computation of damages varies significantly in a deceit and rescission action. Common law deceit measures out-of-pocket damages based on the value of securities at the time of offering compared to their price. In this case, damages for fraud would be the purchase price ($20) less the shares' value ($8 according to the experts) — or $12.

In a rescission action, although rescission is not possible because the shareholders received $2 in liquidation, rescissionary damages will restore the investors to their preinvestment position. In this case, rescissionary damages would be the original purchase price ($20) less realized salvage value ($2) — or $18.

h. Relevant for deceit, not rescission. Punitive damages may be recovered, in appropriate circumstances, in a deceit action — an action in tort. Punitive damages are not available in a rescission action, which seeks to undo a contracting mistake.

i. More relevant for deceit than rescission. Statutes of limitations and repose periods vary from state to state. Generally, actions based on common law fraud have shorter statutes of limitations (typically, one to four years) than actions based on contractual rescission (typically three to ten years).

2. a. There are four possibilities for civil liability against the Tramway Company under the Securities Act. (Remember that negligence-based liability for material misstatements and omissions under §17(a) is not available in private actions, but only in SEC enforcement actions. See §6.6.)

§12(a)(1): If registration was required and the company used jurisdictional means in the offering, investors may seek rescission under the strict liability scheme of §12(a)(1). The investors need only show unregistered sales of securities. No showing is needed of any misrepresentation, any culpability, or any relationship between disclosure defects in the prospectus and their losses. Compare §12(b) ("loss causation" defense applies only in §12(a)(2) actions).

The only issue would be whether the company was a "statutory seller" in the offering — which may depend on the type of underwriting. If a best-efforts underwriting, the company would be a seller for passing title. If a firm-commitment underwriting, the issuer would be liable if it engaged in "solicitations" (obviously for its benefit). Although some cases suggest preparing a disclosure document is not a solicitation under §12, it would seem odd that the issuer in an unregistered offering would escape liability.

§11: If the offering was not registered, there can be no §11 liability, even though the circular contained prospectus-like information. Purchasers have a §11 claim only when misinformation appears in a registration statement that becomes effective after being filed with the SEC. See §11(a).

§12(a)(2): Whether exempt or not, investors might seek rescission for misinformation in the self-styled prospectus. By its terms, §12(a)(2) permits investors to rescind their investment if the offering was accomplished by means of a "prospectus" containing materially false or misleading information. Arguably, the statements about legislative permission to operate steam-powered trams would trigger this liability.

The Supreme Court's decision in *Gustafson v. Alloyd Co.*, however, creates doubts about the applicability of §12(a)(2) to unregistered offerings, exempt or not. See §6.4.1. Under one reading of the case, an unregistered offering does not trigger liability under §12(a)(2). Simply because the selling document was described as a "prospectus" does not make it one under §12(a)(2). Under this understanding of *Gustafson*, the "prospectus" referred to in §12(a)(2) is limited to the document filed with the SEC in a registered offering.

Nonetheless, *Gustafson* might also be read to require only that the offering be "public" in nature — such as an exempt public offering under Regulation A or even an illegal, unregistered public offering. If so, investors might sue Tramway to rescind their investment under §12(a)(2) for the false or misleading statements in the "prospectus." (If §12(a)(2) applies to this offering, there would again be a question about the company's status as a "statutory seller" — see above.)

Interestingly, the understanding that §12(a)(2) covers exempt "public" offerings was adopted by Congress in the JOBS Act for so-called Reg A+ offerings, which are explicitly made subject to §12(a)(2) liability. See Securities Act §3(b)(2)(D) (see §5.2.3 — Offerings Up To $50 Million). It remains to be seen whether this congressional extension of §12(a)(2) liability to "public" offerings exempt under Reg A+ affects judicial interpretation of the scope of the §12(a)(2) generally.

§15: Those individuals or entities who control any person liable under §11 or §12 are also liable. Some of the directors and officers of Tramway might be considered "control persons."

b. The Securities Act's liability scheme offers investors a number of substantive advantages. Defects in the registration process that violate §5 create a no-fault "put" for investors, which allows them to rescind their transaction against the seller and those who solicited the sales. §12(a)(1).

Information defects in a registered offering give rise to a "relaxed fraud" action that permits purchasers to recover merely by identifying material misinformation in the registration statement. §11. The section effectively eliminates any need to prove reliance, scienter, or causation. Instead, nonissuer defendants bear the burden of showing their nonculpability, the purchaser's actual knowledge, or the absence of a causal link between the misinformation and the plaintiff's losses. Information defects outside the registration statement, such as oral communications or sales literature used in a registered offering, give rise to a "relaxed rescission" action that permits purchasers to recover merely on a showing their purchases were induced by material misinformation. §12(a)(2). Liability may also extend to some communications in an unregistered "public" offering. *Gustafson v. Alloyd Co.* (§6.4.1). Scienter and causation are not elements of a plaintiff's §12(a)(2) action, though defendants have a due care and loss causation defense.

Finally, the Securities Act's liability scheme annuls traditional corporate limited liability by imposing liability on any person who controls a person liable under §11 or §12. See §15. Controlling shareholders and corporate insiders become liable for corporate violations, unless they can show their nonculpability.

c. Yes, unless brought as a class action.

Federal court. Investors can sue in federal court and join their Securities Act claims with Exchange Act (particularly Rule 10b-5) claims, as well as any pendent state claims that arise under state common law or state securities laws (blue sky laws). Before 1995 when the Supreme Court decided *Gustafson*, there were few advantages to suing under Rule 10b-5, when Securities Act claims were available. Courts have interpreted Rule 10b-5 actions to require a showing of scienter, reliance and causation. (Rule 10b-5 actions, once subject to the same 1-year/3-year limitations and repose periods as §12(a)(2) actions, are now subject to the longer 2-year/5-year periods created by §804 of the Sarbanes-Oxley Act. See §9.4.1.) Nonetheless, the Supreme Court's decision in *Gustafson* revives the importance of

Rule 10b-5 for sales not made "by means of a prospectus or oral communication," as those terms are now interpreted by the Supreme Court.

State court. Investors can also sue in state court and join their Securities Act and state claims. They cannot, however, add any Exchange Act claims in a state action since federal courts have exclusive jurisdiction over Exchange Act claims.

Class actions based on state law. Securities disclosure claims based on state statutory or common law cannot be brought as a class action. The Securities Litigation Uniform Standards Act of 1998 precludes class actions, whether brought in federal or state court, based on state law allegations of "an untrue statement or omission of a material fact" in a securities transaction. §16(b). The 1998 Act, however, permits class actions involving the corporate law of the issuer's state of incorporation — the so-called "Delaware carve out" — in situations involving shareholder voting, tender offers, and appraisal rights. §16(d).

d. The investors can bring their Securities Act claims in state court, and the claims cannot be removed by the defendant to federal court. See §22(a). The Securities Act gives the plaintiff an immutable choice of forum. The Securities Litigation Standards Act of 1998, however, limits the plaintiff's choice when securities claims are brought as a class action. The Act provides that any damages class action brought in state court involving publicly traded securities can be removed to federal court. §16(c). This means that a Securities Act claim brought in state court involving, for example, false statements in a registered public offering could be removed to federal court at any defendant's request.

e. Yes. The Supreme Court has interpreted the Securities Act to permit arbitration of claims arising under the act, despite the choice-of-forum provisions of §22. *Rodriguez de Quijas v. Shearson/American Express, Inc.*, 490 U.S. 477 (1989). Although the Court had once read the Securities Act's policy against stipulations that waive the Act's provisions as voiding any arbitration agreement, *Wilko v. Swan*, 346 U.S. 427 (1953) (interpreting §14 of the Act), the Court has shown a remarkable willingness to permit arbitration of federal claims. The Federal Arbitration Act (FAA), according to the Court, "mandates" enforcement of agreements to arbitrate federal claims, unless Congress has explicitly exempted such claims from arbitration or there exists "an inherent conflict between arbitration and the statute's underlying purposes." *Shearson/American Express, Inc. v. McMahon*, 482 U.S. 220 (1987).

Today, investors with Securities Act claims may avoid an arbitration clause only if they show the clause is unconscionable, was induced by fraud, or involved overreaching. See FAA §2 (arbitration contracts enforceable "save upon such grounds as exist at law or in equity for the revocation of any contract").

3. a. Perhaps a §12(a)(2) claim. Although lower courts had before 1995 uniformly interpreted §12(a)(2) to cover informational defects in *any* nongovernmental securities offering (whether exempt or registered), the Supreme Court's decision in *Gustafson v. Alloyd Co.* has created significant uncertainty about the reach of the section. See §6.4.1.

   The *Gustafson* Court stated that §12(a)(2) is limited to "public offerings" — sometimes referring to them confusedly as "initial public offerings." Yet, some offerings that are exempt from the registration requirements of §5 still have a public character. For example, offerings that fit within the Act's intrastate exemption or comply with the "mini-registration" requirements of SEC rules, such as under Regulation A or Rule 505 of Regulation D, can be seen as exempt "public offerings." In addition, the Court concluded that the "prospectus" referred to in §12(a)(2) is the one described in §10, which states a "prospectus shall contain the information contained in the registration statement." If so, a widely disseminated document (such as a private placement circular) that contains the information one would normally find in a registration statement can also be seen as falling in the category of a §10 prospectus. That is, if §12(a)(2) covers documents that are "prospectus-like," the section could well cover some exempt offerings.

   In addition, §12(a)(2) could well have some vitality as to non-exempt unregistered public offerings for which the one-year statute of limitations has run for a §12(a)(1) claim. The period for bringing a §12(a)(2) suit is one year after discovery or notice of the misrepresentation, but within three years after the sale. §13. (Or perhaps the 2-year/5-year periods of 28 U.S.C. §1658(b), as added by the Sarbanes-Oxley Act, applies. See §6.4.4). The world after *Gustafson* has been weird and promises to remain that way.

   b. Perhaps. Section 12(a)(2) requires that sales be "by means" of a false or misleading communication — here the misleading offering circular. Although courts have concluded that individual reliance is not an element of a §12(a)(2) action, the "by means" language suggests that misinformation must have been instrumental in the offering. Courts have accepted a showing of a general link between the misinformation and the transaction — a "transaction causation" requirement satisfied by a relaxed "but for" showing. That is, but for the misleading offering circular, the underwriters or others who read the circular would have refused to participate in the offering, and their reluctance would have precluded the offering from happening. *Sanders v. John Nuveen & Co.*, 619 F.2d 1222 (7th Cir. 1980) (finding reliance on false commercial paper reports, even though many purchasers had not read them, on theory that publication of issuer's "true financial condition would have caused a total collapse of the market for its notes").

c. Perhaps — assuming §12(a)(2) covers this unregistered offering. Liability of the issuer is clear if it passed title and sold the securities — for example, in a best-efforts underwriting. But if the issuer did not sell directly to investors — as in a firm-commitment underwriting — the company's liability would depend on whether it could be seen as a "statutory seller" under §12(a)(2). According to some courts, a non-selling issuer is a "statutory seller" by virtue of its preparing the offering materials. A growing number of other courts, however, have concluded that merely preparing offering materials or engaging in other normal promotional activities does not make the issuer a "solicitor" under the *Pinter v. Dahl* analysis. See *Shaw v. Digital Equipment Corp.*, 82 F.3d 1194 (1st Cir. 1996). Instead, there would have to be shown a direct communication between the issuer and the purchasers.

Directors could become liable in two ways. First, the directors might be liable as "statutory sellers" on the theory their activities constituted "solicitations." Although it might be argued that their authorization of the offering circular qualified the directors as statutory sellers, the judicial focus on actual "solicitation" activities suggests more would be needed. If the directors were involved in communications with investors, these activities would seem sufficient to qualify them as statutory seller, particular if their purpose would be to secure financing for the issuer. See *Pinter v. Dahl* (imposing §12(a)(1) liability on any person who solicits investors "to serve his own financial interests or those of the securities owner"). Second, even if the directors are not seen as statutory sellers, they nonetheless may be liable as control persons of the issuer under §15. That is, the directors could become vicariously liable if the issuer is liable under §12(a)(2).

d. No. The attorney did not pass title or solicit investors and is not a "statutory seller" under §12(a)(2). Although the lawyer may have been a collateral participant who was a substantial factor in the deception of investors and may even have aided and abetted the fraudulent transaction, courts have rejected these grounds of liability. Lower courts have uniformly followed *Pinter v. Dahl* in §12(a)(2) cases, since the section contains the identical "offers or sells" language of §12(a)(1). In addition, lower courts have rejected aiding and abetting liability on the theory that the "offers or sells" language of §12(a)(2) defines the range of §12(a)(2) defendants. Although there is criminal liability for one who aids and abets by substantially assisting a primary violator and being aware that his role is part of an improper activity, there is no civil liability under the Securities Act.

e. Not necessarily. The directors' honest belief does not establish their §12(a)(2) "due care" defense. Some lower courts have required a "due diligence-like" investigation to establish the defense, particularly if the defendant is in a position comparable to one who would have had §11 "due diligence" duties in a registered offering. *Sanders v. John Nuveen & Co.*, 619 F.2d 1222 (7th Cir. 1980). Other lower courts have permitted §12(a)(2) defendants to rely on others' assurances. Whether the directors have made out their "due care" defense should turn on how reliable the attorney was and how difficult it was for the directors to confirm the attorney's statement.

f. Yes. Section 12(a)(2) actions now include a "loss causation" defense. See §12(b). Congress in the Private Securities Litigation Reform Act of 1995 reversed the prior judicial approach that allowed §12(2) recovery without proof of any loss at all. Although a §12(a)(2) plaintiff may still seek rescission of an investment tainted by misinformation, the defendant may minimize its exposure by proving that the loss was due to intervening factors, including floods or acts of God.

g. Perhaps not. The company could assert it was not a "statutory seller" because it neither passed title to Bertha nor solicited her investment. Bertha purchased from Albert, and it was Albert, not the company, who solicited Bertha's purchase. Nonetheless, if Bertha heard of the offering through the company's original marketing effort, it could be argued that the company solicited Bertha. *Abell v. Potomac Insurance Co.*, 858 F.2d 1104 (5th Cir. 1988). In fact, it could even be argued that the company solicited Bertha through Albert, who is potentially a "statutory" underwriter in this transaction. Remember that the SEC has interpreted "offer" broadly to cover "arousal of public interest" and "conditioning of the market." (§4.3.1). On policy grounds, it would seem that Bertha should be able to recover from the issuer, but the Supreme Court's decision in *Gustafson* makes any assumptions about §12(a)(2) problematic. If Bertha can recover from the company, rescissionary damages would be the difference between her purchase price ($12) and the amount she could realize by "tendering" the shares on the market ($3) — or $9.

The SEC has sought to resolve the conundrum that issuers might technically not be statutory sellers under §12(a)(2) when investors purchase from intermediaries in an offering. Under Rule 159A, added by the 2005 Public Offering Reforms (see §4.2), issuers are considered "sellers" for purposes of §12(a)(2) if the sale was accomplished by a prospectus filed under Rule 424(b), a "free writing prospectus" (sales material) prepared by or for the issuer, or any other sales communication by the issuer to the investor. Rule 159A(a). In our example, the company would be a statutory seller under the rule if

Bertha had received any sales information (written or oral) from the company.

h. No. Although the §12(a)(2) formula for calculating damages requires an offset for "any income received," the Supreme Court has held that §12(a)(2) does not treat tax benefits as "income received" in determining the investor's rescissionary recovery. *Randall v. Loftsgaarden*, 478 U.S. 647 (1990). This means that the rescission remedy of §12(a)(2) may leave some investors better off than if they had not invested.

i. Not under §12(a)(2). The investors must sue within one year of learning of the misinformation. See §13.

4. a. A §12(a)(1) claim. Section 5(b)(2) requires that securities in a registered offering be delivered with an accompanying final prospectus. This requirement applies to any sales by the issuer. The issuer's failure to deliver the prospectus violates §5 and gives purchasers who did not receive the prospectus an automatic rescission remedy under §12(a)(1).

b. Probably no strict liability. Section 12(a)(1) arguably requires a link between the §5 violation and the defendant. Although First Lynch became a "statutory seller" by soliciting investors for financial gain, §12(a)(1) imposes liability only on those who "offer or sell a security in violation of section 5." In our example, the underwriter was not the one that violated §5, instead it was the issuer. Although this "best efforts" underwriter may have effectively solicited all purchasers when it "conditioned the market," a strict reading of §12(a)(1) limits a statutory seller's liability to its own §5 violations.

Keep in mind that the underwriter might be liable under §12(a)(2) if it participated in disseminating the false information in the prospectus and propping up the market in Tramway stock. Some courts have suggested that §12(a)(2) broadly imposes liability for creating a market in stock through the use of false information, even when some purchasers were not actually aware of the tainted disclosure. *Sanders v. John Nuveen & Co.*, 619 F.2d 1222 (7th Cir. 1980).

c. No. Section 12(a)(1) gives standing only to purchasers who bought in transactions that violated §5. The section imposes liability on any person who "offers or sells a security in violation of section 5 . . . to the person purchasing such security from him." Thus, the section links the security as to which there was a §5 violation with the security for which the plaintiff seeks rescission. Purchasers who bought securities in transactions that did not violate §5 cannot seek §12(a)(1) rescission.

Contrast this to the situation where a sophisticated investor seeks rescission in an offering that fails the private placement exemption because other investors lacked the requisite sophistication. In that case, each purchaser has a rescission right since all sales violated the §5 prohibition against sales of nonexempt, unregistered securities. See §5.2.2.

d. No. Although §14 voids any stipulation that waives compliance with any Securities Act provision, courts have recognized the ability of issuers to make binding "rescission offers." *Meyers v. C&M Petroleum Producers, Inc.,* 476 F.2d 427 (5th Cir. 1973) (finding purchasers estopped to pursue §12(a)(1) claim if they reject issuer's unconditional tender of purchase price together with interest). This approach assumes that purchasers can waive a §12(a)(1) claim, much like settling a court case, if they are offered and refuse their §12(a)(1) "put." Issuers often make "rescission offers" to remove a liability cloud when there is doubt about an offering's exemption from §5.

e. Perhaps, under §12(a)(2). The sales representative is a statutory seller because he solicited an investor presumably to earn a commission. *Pinter v. Dahl.* To make out a §12(a)(2) claim, the customer must prove only that the sale was "by means of a prospectus or oral communication" that was materially false or misleading. Because the customer considered the letter's false representations about steam-powered trams, there would seem to be §12(a)(2) liability. The sales representative could avoid liability only by proving a due care defense.

The lurking question is whether the letter is a §12(a)(2) "prospectus." At first glance, it fits the §2(10) definition of a written communication that attempts to sell a security. But the "free writing" provisions of §2(10)(a) seem to except it from the definition — though this definitional wrinkle can be seen as limited to the §5(b)(1) prohibition against prospectuses that do not comply with §10. Further, the Supreme Court's decision in *Gustafson* can be read to limit §12(a)(2)'s coverage only to §10 prospectuses and related oral communications. This reading produces the odd result that §12(a)(2) would have covered the broker's misrepresentations if they had been oral, but not if written. This seems ludicrous. At the least, and consistent with *Gustafson's* analysis of the Securities Act's structure, §12(a)(2) should fill the liability gaps in a registered offering left by §11.

Notice that neither §12(a)(1) nor §11 applies in our example. If the offering is registered, the sales representative's letter does not violate §5. According to the §2(10)(a) definition, free writing accompanied by a final prospectus is permitted during the posteffective period. Moreover, there can be no §11 liability because the misrepresentation in the letter was not a part of the registration statement.

f. No. Purchasers must bring their §12(a)(1) claims within one year of the violation. §13. This differs from the limitations period for §12(a)(2) violations, which permits investors to bring claims within one year after the *discovery* of the misinformation.

5. a. A §11 claim. Section 11 permits purchasers to sue if any part of the registration statement contained a materially false or misleading statement.

   b. Yes. Purchasers in the aftermarket have §11 standing, if they can trace their securities to the registered offering. *Hertzberg v. Dignity Partners, Inc.*, 191 F.3d 1076 (9th Cir. 1999) (aftermarket purchasers); *Barnes v. Osofsky*, 373 F.2d 269 (2d Cir. 1967) (tracing requirement). In an initial public offering where only the issuer sells shares, this presents little difficulty.

      If the plaintiffs meet their tracing burden, they need only point to materially false or misleading statements in the registration statement (which includes the prospectus). Unless the plaintiffs acquired their shares more than a year after the offering, they need not show they read the prospectus or otherwise relied on the information in the registration statement. This avoids problems of individual proof and ensures that §11 operates as designed to deter misinformation in the registration statement.

   c. All of them. Section 11(a) provides that *every* person who was a director of the issuer at the time of the filing of the false registration statement is liable to the purchaser. As a result, all directors become guardians of the veracity and completeness of the registration statement.

   d. No, not if he knew of the registration. A whistle-blowing director may avoid §11 liability before the registration becomes effective by resigning and then notifying the SEC and the issuer. §11(b)(1). After the registration statement has become effective, a director may escape §11 liability only if he shows the registration statement became effective without his knowledge and he immediately advised the SEC and gave public notice of his lack of knowledge. §11(b)(2). Otherwise, directors vouch for the veracity and completeness of the registration statement, subject to their due diligence defenses.

   e. Not under §11. The only persons liable under §11 for misinformation in the registration statement are those enumerated in §11(a) — namely, the issuer, signing officers, directors, experts, and underwriters. There is no §11 liability for an attorney in his capacity as company counsel, even if he misleads the board or knowingly prepares a false registration statement. Courts have rejected any aiding and abetting liability under §11. *In re Equity Funding Securities Litigation*, 416 F. Supp. 161 (C.D. Cal. 1976).

      Nor is the attorney liable under §12(a)(2). Since the attorney has not solicited investors, he cannot be a statutory seller. The Supreme Court in *Pinter v. Dahl* commented that extending liability to collateral participants in an offering (such as attorneys and accountants) would chill their participation, with a resulting reduction in professional assistance.

A fraudulent attorney may be liable to the issuer, however, under general principles of agency, tort, and contract. Some courts have even suggested that the attorney may be liable under these theories to investors, the third-party beneficiaries of the attorney's professional services.

f. Yes. Nonissuer defendants under §11 have the burden of showing their nonculpability. (Compare this to the common law, which makes culpability one of the elements the plaintiff's case.) This §11 defense, known as the "due diligence" defense, varies depending on whether the defendant is an expert or nonexpert and whether the alleged misinformation was prepared by an expert (that is, "expertised") or not.

In our example, the attorney-director would have to establish, as to the nonexpertised misinformation about legislative approval, that she made a reasonable investigation and had reasonable grounds to believe (and did believe) that the misleading portion of the registration statement was true. The reasonableness of her investigation and of her beliefs would be affected by her status as a lawyer, which gives her special competence to evaluate the truthfulness of any statements concerning legislative action. As a lawyer she might be considered an "outside insider" under the analytical framework of *Escott v. BarChris*, with a higher burden than that of a nonlawyer-director to make out her due diligence defense. Whether a defendant makes out a due diligence defense, courts have often held, is a matter of law for determination by the judge, not a jury. See *In re Software Toolworks Securities Litigation*, 38 F.3d 1078 (9th Cir. 1994) (summary judgment appropriate when historical facts are undisputed and no rational jury could find otherwise).

6. a. Not relevant. The §11 due diligence defense places the burden on the directors to show their nonculpability. Because disclosure of the company's prospects for using steam power would have appeared in the nonexpertised part of the registration statement, the directors must show a "reasonable investigation" and an actual and reasonable belief that the disclosure was true. It is not enough that the directors subjectively believed the information was true; they must have performed an investigation to meet the objective standard of a reasonable belief. Even if a reasonable investigation would not have turned up the "smoking gun" memo, the directors' due diligence defense fails if they did not conduct any investigation.

Notice that the alleged misstatement concerned the likelihood of legislative approval — a forward-looking statement. Under the PSLRA, when §11 liability is predicated on a false or misleading forward-looking statement, an issuer (or a person acting on behalf of the issuer) is not liable if the plaintiff fails to prove the person making the forward-looking statement lacked actual knowledge that the statement was false or misleading. §27A(c)(1)(B). This effectively shifts the burden of showing culpability in cases involving forward-looking statements, making the defendants' ignorance relevant. In this case, however, this liability limitation would not apply since Tramway was making an initial public offering. The PSLRA shifts the burden only for offerings by seasoned, reporting companies. §27A(b)(2).

b. Perhaps. It may depend on the particular director's position. For outside directors who read the registration statement and had grounds to trust the president's confident prediction, their reliance might well be sufficient. These directors' access to information about legislative approval, in all likelihood, would have been through company officials. Moreover, even if the outside directors had reason to doubt the president, their liability would not be joint and several, but rather proportionate to their culpability, if they did not have "actual knowledge" of the falsity of the president's prediction. See §11(f) (proportionate liability scheme for outside directors).

For inside directors — particularly those who supervised the lobbyist — the story could well be different. If they had access to information about the legislative process, particularly as revealed in the lobbyist's files, their unquestioning reliance would not constitute a "reasonable investigation." Their position would have made it easier for them to ask the lobbyist about the reasons for her confidence and to demand access to her files. See Rule 176 ("relevant circumstances" relate to the defendant's access to the challenged information).

c. Yes. Although §11 defendants can delegate their "due diligence" task to others, they are bound by the failures of the person assigned the job. Thus, if inside directors should have asked more questions of the lobbyist or looked through her files, the failure of company counsel to do this binds them. The directors' delegation of their §11 responsibilities is not of itself a reasonable investigation or belief of the registration statement's truth.

d. Only if the lobbyist fits into one of the categories of a §11(a) defendant. If she does, her liability would be inescapable. She knew of the true state of affairs and failed to correct the misleading statement in the prospectus. It is irrelevant that she withheld the information for a valid business purpose because it is precisely this expedient secrecy the Securities Act is aimed against. Nor is it relevant that she had not read the registration statement, something required of every nonexpert defendant who seeks to establish a due diligence defense.

e. Not necessarily. In *BarChris*, the court held the managing underwriter (which acted on behalf of all the underwriters) to the standard of an "inside outsider." Despite the position of underwriters as arm's-length financial intermediaries in the offering, courts have placed on them significant investigatory responsibility. The lobbyist's refusal to turn over her files suggested something was amiss. Although the underwriter may have conducted due diligence under these circumstances, it would be difficult for the managing underwriter to hold a "reasonable belief" about the registration statement's veracity. All the underwriters would be bound by the managing underwriter's lack of skepticism.

7. a. Probably not. An expert, assuming he consented to the use of his report in the registration statement, has no due diligence responsibilities except as to the part of the registration statement that "purports to have been prepared or certified by him." §11(a)(4). Thus, the expert is responsible only for the veracity and completeness of his report. Some courts have also assumed the expert must conduct due diligence to ensure that the registration statement's nonexpertised parts do not contradict or render misleading the expert's statements. See *BarChris* (accountant must also review events after certified financials to "prevent the balance sheet figures from being misleading"). In this case, the engineer's general statement comparing horse-powered and steam-powered tramways might be seen as reflecting a specific assumption that the company had legislative approval to use steam power. But the argument is weak if the report's tenor was not company-specific.

   b. Perhaps, but under §12(a)(2). The underwriter has no due diligence duties as to the expertised portions of the registration statement. See §11(b)(3)(C). Even if it failed to read or investigate the report, its ignorance of the report's deficiencies constitutes a §11 defense.

   Nonetheless, §12(a)(2) does not create separate standards of "due care" with respect to alleged defects in a "prospectus." Although it might seem anomalous that §12(a)(2) liability may be broader than the carefully crafted liability scheme of §11, the Supreme Court's *Gustafson* decision creates significant uncertainty. The Court seemed confused about the nature of a registration statement and stated: "Section 11 provides for liability on account of false registration statements; §12(a)(2) for liability based on misstatements in prospectuses." The Court seemed not to understand that §11 liability is almost always based on misstatements in prospectuses that are contained in the registration statement.

8. a. Perhaps none. The one-year statute of limitations for §11 actions begins to run when the plaintiff discovers or should have discovered the challenged misinformation. §13. Therefore, investors who knew

of the misinformation soon after the offering did not sue in time. Other investors who learned of the misinformation only after the company's insolvency, though not barred by the statute's three-year repose period, may nonetheless be barred for not suing within one year after they should have learned of the misinformation.

b. Yes. Although the §11 plaintiffs need not prove that the misinformation caused their loss, the defendants have a "negative causation defense." The defendants must prove that other factors, besides the misinformation, caused all or some of the decline in value of the securities. Thus, if the defendants can show the extent to which the flood hurt business and share value, they are not liable for these losses.

c. Recovery will be $8 per share, assuming that the price at suit reflected the value of the shares. Under the §11(e)(3) pricing formula for shares held at suit, but sold before judgment, recovery is equal to the purchase price (but not greater than the public offering price) minus the sales price — but this cannot exceed the recovery computed under §11(e)(1). Compare the two formulas:

§11(e)(3) formula		§11(e)(1) formula	
Purchase price	$25	Purchase price	$25
(offering price cap)	$20	(offering price cap)	$20
Sales price*	$ 2	Value at suit	$12
Damages	$18	Damages	$ 8

* For purposes of §11, payment in liquidation is treated as a sale.

Notice that by capping the purchase price at the offering price, the §11(e) formulas cap total damages at the aggregate offering price. See §11(g).

d. The damages formula of §11(e) encourages plaintiffs to sell before suit. Assume the following sequence:

public offering price	$20
sell before suit	15
price at suit	12
sell during suit	7
value at judgment	2

Selling before suit produces a judgment of $20 minus $15. §11(e)(2) (offering price minus sales price). In all, the plaintiff recovers the $20 offering price — $15 from the sales proceeds and $5 from judgment. The formula approximates rescissionary damages.

Selling during suit produces a judgment of $20 minus $12. §11(e)(3) (offering price minus value at suit, provided less than offering price minus value at suit). In all, the plaintiff recovers $15 — the $7 sales proceeds and the $8 judgment. If the price rises after suit above $12, judgment will be even less.

Holding until judgment produces a judgment of $20 minus $12. §11(e)(1) (offering price minus value at suit). In all, the plaintiff recovers $10 — the $2 value at judgment and the $8 judgment. If the stock price at judgment rises above $12, the plaintiff theoretically can recover more than her purchase price. But this is a highly risky strategy.

Not surprisingly, once a fraud is revealed, securities lawyers advise potential §11 plaintiffs to sell before suit. This was the objective of the §11 damages scheme, to encourage potential plaintiffs to sell before suit and thus to cap the defendants' liability at the difference between the offering price and the plaintiffs' sales price. This then sets the exposure of §11 defendants (particularly securities firms) since any purchasers who buy after the fraud is revealed become subject to a reliance defense. §11(a). By limiting liability to predisclosure purchasers who sell their shares before suit, the §11 damages scheme transfers the bulk of postdisclosure losses from participants in the underwriting to market investors.

e. No need to. Section 15 imposes liability on the parent corporation of any person liable under §11, thus supplanting state corporate law on limited liability. The parent corporation has an ignorance defense, if it did not know (or have reason to know) of the facts that gave rise to the subsidiary's liability. If the subsidiary is a paper shell, First Lynch would be fully liable.

f. Yes, perhaps for the full amount if it did not know of the legislative roadblock. Section 11(f) imposes joint and several liability on §11 defendants and provides that any person becoming liable may recover contribution from anyone who would have been liable for the same payment if sued separately. Contribution is not available, however, "if the person who became liable was, and the other was not, guilty of fraudulent misrepresentation." §11(f) (last sentence).

This presents an interesting question whether a person liable under §15 (by virtue of a subsidiary's §11 liability) has the same contribution rights as the subsidiary. Because the purpose of §15 is to place controlling persons in the liability shoes "to the same extent" as those they control, it would seem §11 and §15 should be read together. It would be anomalous to deny contribution rights and impose greater liability on controlling persons than on those they control.

Under the section, contribution is computed "as in cases of contract." This creates some ambiguity. Is contribution per capita (total judgment divided by number of defendants) or based on relative fault? Arguably, the section's denial of contribution to fraudulent defendants against nonfraudulent defendants suggests contribution is fault-based. Moreover, in our case, it might even be argued that First Lynch should recover 100 percent from Derry, and any other fraudulent defendants, on the theory that in the converse circumstances the fraudulent defendants would have been denied contribution against First Lynch.

Secondary and Other Postoffering Distributions

The Securities Act of 1933 aims at public offerings of securities, not post-offering securities trading. The boundary between regulated "distributions" and unregulated "market trading" is found in §4(1), which was renumbered in the JOBS Act of 2012 to be §4(a)(1). The provision exempts from Securities Act registration "transactions by any person other than an issuer, underwriter, or dealer."

Some postoffering transactions, with informational dangers comparable to those of public offerings, fall within the Securities Act's regulatory boundary and are subject to full-blown registration. In particular, the Act focuses on resales to public investors by (1) persons who previously purchased securities from the issuer in private transactions ("restricted securities"), and (2) persons in a control position who hold securities of the issuer ("control securities"). The common denominator, in each case, is a resale by a person with informational advantages similar to those of the issuer — that is, a transaction that presents many (if not all) of the risks of a public offering by the issuer. For this reason, resales of restricted or control securities are known as "secondary distributions."

As all securities lawyers know, the statutory definitions of the securities laws carry much of the regulatory baggage. This is especially true for secondary distributions, whose regulation hinges on the layered definition of "underwriter" in §2(a)(11).

This chapter covers:

- the definitions of "issuer," "dealer," and "underwriter" [§7.1]

305

- postoffering resales exempt from registration, either by virtue of SEC rules (particularly Rules 144 and 144A) or the niceties of the statutory "underwriter" definition [§7.2]
- other postoffering transactions by the issuer (such as corporate reorganizations and recapitalizations) that, like secondary distributions, reside at the definitional boundary of Securities Act regulation [§7.3]
- resales under state blue sky laws [§7.4]

Introductory Definitions

To understand the boundary between regulated "distributions" and unregulated "market trading," you must understand the concepts of "control securities" and "restricted securities."

Control Securities

Control securities are those owned by a *control person*, who the SEC rules refer to as an "affiliate" of the issuer. See Rule 405 (defining "affiliate" to include any person that, directly or indirectly, controls the issuer; defining "control" to mean the possession, direct or indirect, of the power to direct management and policies of the issuer, whether through ownership of voting securities or otherwise). When a control person sells his securities to public investors, there is the understandable concern that he can exploit his superior informational position. For this reason, the Securities Act regulates sales by control persons in much the same way it regulates sales by issuers. The theory is that public investors need the protection of Securities Act registration when they purchase control securities as much as when they purchase from an issuer.

Restricted Securities

Securities originally acquired in a nonpublic distribution, either from the issuer or a control person, may not be resold into a public trading market without registration or another exemption — and thus are "restricted." Absent such a restriction, the purchaser-reseller could act as a conduit for the issuer or control person. Restricted securities may be acquired in (1) a §4(a)(2) private placement (see §5.2.2), (2) a Regulation D offering subject to resale limitations (see §5.2.4), and (3) a transaction meeting the conditions of Rule 144A (see §7.2.2 below).

Securities acquired in a nonpublic transaction retain their restricted character whether acquired directly from the issuer, from a control person, or in a chain of transactions subject to restrictions on public resale. The theory is that, although qualified purchasers of restricted securities may not need Securities Act registration, public investors who cannot fend for themselves need the protections of registration when they purchase restricted securities. See §5.2.2.

§7.1 DEFINITIONS OF ISSUERS, UNDERWRITERS, AND DEALERS

Section 4(a)(1), the boundary between regulated public offerings and unregulated market trading, is a simple and powerful double negative:

> The provisions of section 5 shall <u>not</u> apply to . . . transactions by any person other than an issuer, underwriter, or dealer.

Stated in the affirmative, transactions by issuers, underwriters, and dealers are subject to Securities Act registration.

Thus, transactions between investors (Investor A → Investor B) are not subject to §5 since it is unlikely there is any informational advantage on either side of the transaction. But transactions (that is, offers and sales) by issuers, underwriters, and dealers carry an informational risk.

Definitions of "Issuer" and "Dealer"

The definitions of "issuer" and "dealer" are straightforward. An "issuer" is what the word implies: "every person who issues or proposes to issue any security." Securities Act §2(a)(4). That is, the issuer is the person or entity that becomes bound to the package of rights that inhere in the ownership of a security.

The Securities Act defines "dealer" broadly as "any person who engages . . . in the business of . . . dealing or trading in securities." Securities Act §2(a)(12). But the exemption for "dealers" under §4(a)(3) lifts the regulatory burdens created by §4(a)(1) once the registration period ends. Securities Act §4(a)(3); Rule 174 (see §4.3.3). The combined effect of §4(a)(1) and §4(a)(3) is that "dealers" are essentially those securities firms engaged in an offering subject to registration.

Definition of "Underwriter"

The real contours of §4(a)(1) arise from the definition of "underwriter" found in horrific §2(a)(11), which before 1996 was numbered §2(11):

> The term "underwriter" means any person who has purchased from an issuer with a view to, or offers or sells for an issuer in connection with, the distribution of any security, or participates or has a direct or indirect participation in any such undertaking, or participates or has a participation in the direct or indirect underwriting of any such undertaking; but such term shall not include a person whose interest is limited to a commission from an underwriter or dealer not in excess of the usual and customary distributors' or sellers' commission. As

used in this paragraph the term "issuer" shall include, in addition to an issuer, any person directly or indirectly controlling or controlled by the issuer, or any person under direct or indirect common control with the issuer.

What do these two (awful) sentences mean? Let's first extract the exception: the second clause of the first sentence that begins "but such term . . ." According to this exception, one is not an underwriter if his participation in a distribution involves earning a usual and customary retail commission. That is, a securities firm is not a statutory underwriter merely by participating as a retail broker-dealer in a public offering.

Next we can parse the first clause of the first sentence, which enumerates four categories of "underwriters":

1. "any person who has purchased from an issuer with a view to . . . the distribution of any security"
2. any person who "offers or sells for an issuer in connection with . . . the distribution of any security"
3. any person who "participates or has a direct or indirect participation in any such undertaking" — namely, participants in (1) or (2)
4. any person who "participates or has a participation in the direct or indirect underwriting of any such undertaking" — namely, underwriters in (1) or (2).

What does the second sentence of §2(a)(11) mean? It's a definition within a definition: if someone performs the activities of (1)-(4) for a "control person," that person becomes an underwriter. (For simplicity's sake, we will use the shorthand *control person* to refer to the statutory "any person directly or indirectly controlling or controlled by the issuer, or any person under direct or indirect common control with the issuer.")

The second sentence thus indicates four additional categories of "underwriters":

5. "any person who has purchased from [a control person] with a view to . . . the distribution of any security";
6. any person who "offers or sells for [a control person] in connection with . . . the distribution of any security";
7. any person who "participates or has a direct or indirect participation in any such undertaking" — namely, participants in (5) or (6); and
8. any person who "participates or has a participation in the direct or indirect underwriting of any such undertaking" — namely, underwriters in (5) or (6).

Before considering the important operative phrases of §2(a)(11), we can put aside categories (3)-(4) and (7)-(8). These categories deal with persons who agree to offer or sell securities (such as those who make standby commitments) or who guarantee the placement of the offering. As a practical matter, their significance is marginal.

We are left with essentially three categories of "underwriters," which we discuss separately in the following three subsections:

Agent "for issuer"	Those who offer or sell "for an issuer" in connection with a distribution of securities — category (2). This category deals with assistance in *de facto* distributions. [§7.1.1]
Purchaser from issuer "with a view" to distribute	Those who purchase from an issuer "with a view to" the distribution of securities — category (1). This category deals with the resale of restricted securities. [§7.1.2]
Underwriter for "control person"	Those who perform either of these distribution activities in connection with a "control person" — categories (5) and (6). This category deals with the resale of control securities. [§7.1.3]

Definition of "Distribution"

You will notice that the meaning of "underwriter" in each instance turns on specified activities in a "distribution." Curiously, "distribution" is defined neither in the Securities Act nor by SEC rule. From context and as understood by the courts and by the SEC, its meaning is any offer or sale to public investors. See Rule 144. The prototype distribution is a public offering by an issuer. But a distribution also includes secondary transactions with public investors — such as offers or sales of control or restricted securities through a broker on a stock exchange or to an investor unable to fend for himself.

§7.1.1 Agent "for Issuer"

One category of "underwriter" is the person who sells or offers "for an issuer." The obvious example is an investment banker in a "best efforts" offering, who, for a fee, entices investors who then purchase directly from the issuer. We can diagram this as:

$$\text{Issuer} \rightarrow [\text{Agent}] \rightarrow \text{Investor}.$$

Compensation from the issuer is not a condition to being an underwriter "for an issuer." In a famous case that illustrates the scope of both the "underwriter" definition and regulation under the Securities Act, a not-for-profit association of Chinese Americans sought to encourage the purchase of bonds of the Republic of China through mass meetings, newspaper ads, and personal appeals. *SEC v. Chinese Consolidated Benevolent Ass'n*, 120 F.2d 738 (2d Cir. 1941). At the request of individual purchasers, and without compensation or specific authorization by the Chinese government, the association remitted subscription applications and payments to the Chinese government's agent in New York.

The Second Circuit held that these activities by the association constituted "transactions by an underwriter" and, because the bonds were not registered, were illegal under §5 of the Securities Act. The court reasoned that purchasers deserved the information and protection of registration, whether or not the issuer authorized or compensated the selling activities made on its behalf. The court also concluded that even if the association was not an underwriter, the sales efforts by the Chinese government were regulated "transactions by an issuer" and any "steps necessary to the distribution" (including those by the association) were subject to regulation.

The decision drew a spirited dissent that criticized the majority's broad reading of the term "underwriter" in §2(a)(11). The dissenter reasoned that because the association had no relationship with the issuer, the Chinese government, it should not be deemed an "underwriter." He pointed out that the words "for an issuer" implied some relationship between the person making solicitations and the issuer of the securities. He worried that the majority's broad reading could have First Amendment implications, for example, by rendering a newspaper a statutory "underwriter" if it printed an editorial urging the purchase of bonds in the name of patriotism.

§7.1.2 Purchaser from Issuer "with a View" to Distribute

Another category of "underwriter" is the person who purchases securities from an issuer with the purpose of reselling them to public investors. The obvious example is the investment banker in a "firm commitment" underwriting who purchases from the issuer and resells his or her allotment to retail dealers or directly to investors. We can diagram this as:

Issuer → Purchaser → Investor

But to fall in the category of a statutory underwriter, the intermediary need not be a securities firm or even a major investor. A person who purchases securities in a private placement and then resells in a public trading market is an "underwriter" if she purchased "with a view" to resell to public investors. (For this reason, issuers often place resale restrictions on privately placed securities — that is, restricted securities — to avoid having the issuance converted into a public distribution subject to Securities Act registration.)

When does a purchaser have a "view" to distribute? As understood by the courts and the SEC, the question is one of the purchaser's "investment intent." An important indication of intent has been a holding period before resale, evidence that the purchaser had assumed the investment risk and was not acting as a scheming conduit of bad securities. An early influential court decision concluded that a holding period of two years provided sufficient proof of investment intent to avoid "underwriter" status. *United States v. Sherwood*, 175 F. Supp. 480 (S.D.N.Y. 1959). Although at first the SEC intimated that two years was not enough, the SEC revised Rule 144 in 1997 to provide a two-year holding period and then again in 2008 to provide a one-year holding period for the unlimited sale of restricted securities held by a noncontrol person. See §7.2.1.

Besides looking to holding periods as evidence of investment intent, many securities lawyers have advised purchasers wishing to resell that the holding period could be shortened if the purchaser could point to a "change in circumstances." A change in circumstances indicates that the purchaser's reason for reselling is to obtain liquidity and not to act as a conduit for bad securities, thus buttressing a claim of original investment intent. The SEC, however, has taken the tenuous position that the investing public deserves disclosure whether or not the seller's circumstances have changed. Securities Act Rel. No. 5223 (1972) (adopting Rule 144).

In the end, the question of whether an investor is an "underwriter" should turn on whether the investor who resells is likely to be in a *better* informational position based on a relationship with the issuer than her buyer. An investor interested in a quick resale is suspicious because she predictably knows something her buyers do not, but an investor who has held for a significant period or can explain her desire for quick liquidity seems an unlikely scoundrel.

Pledges

An interesting problem arises when a bank or other lender receives securities as a pledge securing a loan and then resells the securities after the borrower defaults on the loan. Did the bank acquire the securities from the holder "with a view" to distribute? This depends on whether the bank received the pledged securities expecting that the borrower would default. *SEC v. Guild Films Co.*, 279 F.2d 485 (2d Cir. 1960) (holding banks to be "underwriters" for foreclosing on securities held as collateral for loans to major shareholder).

§7.1.3 Underwriter for "Control Person"

The convoluted definition of "underwriter" also closes a loophole in the regulatory structure of the Securities Act. Notice the §4(a)(1) exemption by its terms limits the Act's registration requirements to an issuer making a public offering, along with the issuer's agents, resellers and dealers participating in the distribution. But what of a person who controls the issuer (or is controlled by the issuer) who dumps his securities into a public market? The regulatory concern for such activity should be at least as great as that for public offerings by an issuer because the control person has presumably the same informational advantages as the issuer and often greater incentives to exploit them. We can diagram these two situations as:

Control Person → **[Agent]** → **Investor**
Control Person → **Purchaser** → **Investor**

As we have seen, §2(a)(1)) defines "underwriter" to include those persons who act for a "control person" in a distribution or who purchase from a "control person" with a view to distribute — that is, "underwriters" of "control persons." The effect is to make securities professionals who assist control persons in dumping their stock into public markets, without registration, liable as statutory underwriters by virtue of their participation. In re *Ira Haupt & Co.*, 23 S.E.C. 589 (1946) (concluding that broker-dealer had acted as a statutory underwriter in a distribution, not as a broker in exempt brokers' transactions, when it assisted controlling shareholders sell a 38 percent interest in their company over the course of six months).

Meaning of "Control Person"

Who is a "control person" of an issuer? There are two alternative meanings of "control person," both fact-dependent. One meaning is that a control person is one who directs (or has the power to direct) the management and policies of the issuer, whether through stock ownership, position, contract, or otherwise; this is the SEC's understanding. See Rule 405 (definitions). The second meaning focuses on the person's power to obtain the signatures of those required to sign a registration statement; this second meaning seems to have been the one that Congress had in mind in §2(a)(11). See H.R. Rep. No. 85, 73d Cong., 1st Sess. 13-14 (1933) ("distributor would be in the position of controlling the issuer and thus able to furnish the information demanded by the bill").

Each meaning has something to recommend it. A management/power meaning catches those persons (such as executives and controlling shareholders) who are likely to have inside information that would give them an informational advantage in any dealings with public investors. A registration/power meaning hones closely to the congressional understanding that control persons have sufficient control "to furnish the information demanded by the bill."

§7.2 EXEMPTIONS FOR CONTROL AND RESTRICTED SECURITIES

How can holders of restricted shares and control persons resell their shares?

Noncontrol holders of restricted securities who wish to sell their holdings have essentially three ways to avoid Securities Act registration:

- wait until the securities have "come to rest" (a vague and uncertain concept)
- avoid a "distribution" and sell in a nonpublic transaction, subject to the criteria of the §4(a)(2) private placement exemption
- comply with Rule 144, the SEC's safe harbor for secondary distributions

Control persons who wish to sell without registration also have essentially three choices:

- claim that isolated and sporadic sales into public trading markets are not a "distribution" (highly risky)
- avoid using an "underwriter" either by selling in a nonpublic transaction or by selling directly on their own without assistance (very tricky)
- comply with SEC Rule 144

Bottom line in both situations: use Rule 144 to be safe!

Registration Rights

Of course, persons holding restricted or control shares can also arrange to have the issuer register the shares — a possibility often covered by contract rights. Registration rights typically come in three varieties: (1) "piggyback" rights that require the issuer to register the shares for resale the next time it files a registration statement for other shares; (2) "demand" rights that require the issuer to register the shares when the holder wants them registered, whether or not the shares are being registered and whether or not the issuer wants to be in registration; and (3) "S-3" rights which require the issuer, once it is eligible, to use Form S-3 (see §4.2.2), to register the shares as part of the S-3 offering. Sometimes these rights are intertwined. For example, the issuer may give piggyback rights triggered by an S-3 offering or demand rights only in an S-3 offering.

§7.2.1 Rule 144: Secondary Distributions in Public Markets

Given the SEC's stingy views on investment intent and the blanket prohibition against control persons using intermediaries to sell into public markets, how can holders of restricted shares or control persons ever sell? In 1972 the SEC answered this nagging question by adopting Rule 144. The rule defines when a person is an "underwriter" and thus clarifies when control persons, as well as holders of restricted securities, may sell into public trading markets. Most securities professionals view Rule 144 as the exclusive means for control persons to sell into a public trading market without registration.

Operation of Rule 144

The rule, revised most recently in 2008, specifies the conditions when restricted securities and control securities can be resold. The conditions — which include holding periods, amount sold, availability of public information, method of sale, and SEC informational filing — vary depending on whether the resale is by a noncontrol person or by a control person selling restricted or nonrestricted securities.

- **A noncontrol person who sells restricted securities** is deemed not to be an "underwriter" under §2(a)(11), provided the person was not a control person for the three months before the sale. The noncontrol person is subject only to a holding period, which is set at six months for securities of reporting companies current in their periodic filings under the Exchange Act. The holding period is extended to 12 months if the issuer was not a reporting company for the 90 days before the sale or was not current in its periodic filings for the 12 months before the sale.
- **A control person who sells restricted or nonrestricted securities** (as well as any person, such as a broker, who assists in the sale) is deemed not to be an "underwriter" under §2(a)(11), provided the sale meets the conditions specified in the rule on holding period, amount sold, information availability, manner of sale, and SEC filing. (These conditions also apply to any person who was a control person during the 90-day period before the resale.)

In each case, since there is no "underwriter," there can be no "transaction by an underwriter" and thus no need for Securities Act registration. Fantastic! Rule 144 has been a regulatory success, establishing the regulatory standards for secondary distributions. Few court cases have interpreted the rule, and the law comes mostly from more than 2,000 no-action letters from the SEC staff giving guidance on who is covered by the rule, how holding periods are computed, how many securities can be sold in a given period, and so on. See also Securities Act Rel. No. 8869 (2007) (revising holding periods under Rule 144 and codifying various SEC staff positions).

Conditions of Rule 144

The Rule 144 conditions (many of which were significantly relaxed in 2008 for noncontrol persons) are convoluted: (1) availability of current public information, Rule 144(c); (2) holding periods for restricted securities, Rule 144(d); (3) limitations on the amount of control securities that can be sold, Rule 144(e); (4) the manner of sale of control securities, Rule 144(f), (g); and (5) required filings with the SEC that give notice of the sale by control persons, Rule 144(h).

As the following chart makes clear, the Rule 144 conditions vary depending on who is making the sale, whether the securities are restricted, and whether the issuer is a reporting company.

Noncontrol persons selling restricted stock[*]

Holding period	six months (for securities of reporting companies); 12 months (for securities of non-reporting companies)[**]
Trickle	not applicable
Sale method	not applicable
Information	publicly available information for reporting issuer (during 12 months before resale)
Filing	not applicable

Control persons selling restricted stock

Holding period	six months (for securities of reporting companies); 12 months (for securities of non-reporting companies)[**]
Trickle	greater than 1 percent of outstanding equity securities or average weekly trading in any three-month period; greater than 10 percent of tranche of debt securities in any three-month period
Sale method	brokers' transactions (after filing Form 144); not applicable to resale of debt securities
Information	publicly available information about issuer[***]
Filing	disclosure on Form 144 (if sell more than 5,000 shares or more than $50,000)

Control persons selling nonrestricted stock (through brokers)

Holding period	None
Trickle	greater than 1 percent of outstanding equity securities or average weekly trading in any three-month period; greater than 10 percent of tranche of debt securities in any three-month period
Sale method	brokers' transactions (after filing Form 144); not applicable to resale of debt securities
Information	publicly available information about issuer[***]
Filing	disclosure on Form 144 (if sell more than 5,000 shares or more than $50,000)

---

[*] Provided the noncontrol person was not a control person for the three months before the sale.

[**] Before 2008, the Rule 144 holding period was one year (and before 1997, two years), and resales of restricted stock by noncontrol persons were subject to trickle, manner-of-sale, public information, and filing conditions. The 2008 revisions shortened the holding period for securities of up-to-date reporting companies and lifted the other conditions for resales by noncontrol persons "to increase the liquidity of privately sold securities . . . without compromising investor protection." The SEC noted that holding securities of a reporting company for six months was a reasonable indication the investor had assumed the economic risk of the investment. Before 2008, the other conditions were lifted only if the noncontrol person had held the securities for at least two years (before 1997, at least three years.)

[***] The issuer must be subject to (and current with) periodic filing requirements under the Exchange Act, or there must otherwise be publicly available information comparable to that found in such reports. (For noncontrol persons to sell securities after a six-month holding period, the issuer must be a reporting company that has been current in its Exchange Act filings for the previous 12 months.)

Rule 144 can be summarized as follows:

Resales of restricted securities (reporting companies). There is a six-month holding period for both noncontrol and control persons who resell restricted securities of reporting companies. After six months, noncontrol persons can resell on the sole condition that the issuer is a reporting company current with its Exchange Act filings; and after one year, noncontrol persons can resell without limitation. Control persons who have held restricted securities for six months can resell but are subject to the trickle, sales method, information, and filing limitations of Rule 144.

Resales of restricted securities (non-reporting companies). There is a longer, one-year holding period for both noncontrol and control persons who resell restricted securities of non-reporting companies. After one year, noncontrol persons can resell without limitation. But control persons who have held for one year can resell only subject to the other Rule 144 limitations.

Resales by control persons of nonrestricted securities. There is no holding period for nonrestricted securities held by control persons. But resales of such control securities are always subject to the other Rule 144 limitations.

§7.2.2 Exemptions for Secondary Private Placements

The resale of securities originally purchased in a private transaction (exempt under §4(a)(2) or one of the small-issue exemptions) and then resold in another private transaction is not a "distribution" and does not trigger "underwriter" status. Such resales are exempt under §4(a)(1) because, by definition, they involve no transaction by an issuer, underwriter, or dealer.

"§4(a)(1½) Exemption"

Securities lawyers and law professors have chosen to complicate this simple principle by inventing an imaginary statutory provision to describe the exemption for private resales. An illustrative case shows how this confusion has even spread to the courts. *Ackerberg v. Johnson*, 892 F.2d 1328 (8th Cir. 1989). In the case, one Johnson (a founder and largest shareholder of Vertimag) sold a block of his shares to one Ackerberg, an investor bursting with wealth and sophistication. The two had been brought together by one Petrucci, an executive at a brokerage firm, who furnished Ackerberg a detailed private placement memo about Vertimag.

When Ackerberg sought to cancel his sale on the ground that it was subject to registration, the court viewed the problem as whether Johnson had acquired the shares "with a view" to distribute or "for an issuer." It concluded Johnson's acquisition five years before the Ackerberg sale negated his "underwriter" status. But, as we have seen, there are eight categories of "underwriter" imbedded in the §2(a)(11) definition, and the court only focused on categories (1) and (2). More significant under the facts of the case was whether the role of broker Petrucci rendered Johnson's sale a "transaction by an underwriter" given Petrucci's sales activities for a control person — category (6). The court, to its credit, addressed this point in a footnote and correctly concluded that "the definition of underwriter . . . depends on the existence of a distribution." In the end, though, the case could have been quickly and easily dismissed. All of the "underwriter" definitions require a "distribution" and because the private sale to sophisticated Ackerberg was not a distribution (a term the court correctly understood to mean a "public offering"), the transaction was not one by an issuer, underwriter, or dealer — and thus was exempt under §4(a)(1).

Securities *cognoscenti* refer to this situation as the "§4(a)(1½) exemption" — that is, a §4(a)(1) exemption in which there is no distribution under the §4(a)(2) criteria for private placement by an issuer. These *cognoscenti* know that the "§4(a)(1) exemption" is just a shorthand expression for a §4(a)(1) exemption when offers and sales are to nonpublic investors: no distribution, no underwriter, and no registration — you're done!

Rule 144A

The SEC has partially codified the "§4(a)(1½) exemption" to facilitate trading in securities privately placed with institutional investors. Rule 144A (adopted in 1990). Like Rule 144, the rule's operative precept is that persons who satisfy its conditions are deemed not to be engaged in a "distribution" and therefore not to be "underwriters," and any securities firm that serves as intermediary is deemed neither a "dealer" nor an "underwriter." Rule 144A(b), (c).

The rule's guiding condition is that resales of unregistered privately placed securities be to "qualified institutional buyers" (QIBs), defined generally as any institutional investor with at least a $100-million securities portfolio or a securities firm with a $10-million securities portfolio. See §13.2.3. In addition, the securities cannot be traded on any U.S. securities exchange or NASDAQ, but rather the rule anticipates the creation of a private market in "144A securities." Information about the issuer must be available to QIBs. Issuers must either be reporting companies, foreign issuers with an exempt ADR program in the United States, foreign governments, or a company that has undertaken to provide current financial information (audited if possible).

What if an offer is made to a non-QIB? Before 2013, such offers jeopardized the entire Rule 144A exemption. To make the exemption less perilous, the SEC (as mandated by the JOBS Act of 2012) revised Rule 144A to permit sellers to make offers — including general solicitations — that might include non-QIBs, so long as sales are eventually made only to investors that the seller (and those acting on its behalf) reasonably believe to be QIBs. See Rule 144A(d)(1); Securities Act Rel. No. 9415 (2013).

When the SEC originally adopted Rule 144A, the hope was that the exemption (combined with the safe harbor Regulation S for international offerings, see §13.1.2), would induce foreign issuers to make private placements in U.S. capital markets with the confidence that both their offerings and subsequent trading by institutional investors would be exempt from Securities Act registration. The hope has been realized, as foreign issuers have issued twice as much debt in the private trading market facilitated by Rule 144A than any other market.

In addition, Rule 144A has often been used extensively in offerings of high-yield debt to institutional shareholders, often followed by a registered exchange of the unregistered securities for registered securities — known as an *A/B exchange*. The SEC has blessed such exchanges, but only for nonconvertible debt, preferred stock, and IPOs by foreign issuers — not placements of U.S. common stock. Exxon Capital Holdings Corp., SEC No-Action Letter (May 13, 1988). Increasingly, QIBs purchasing in Rule 144A placements insist on promises from the issuer to make an A/B exchange in the future. In the registered offering, the exchanging QIB must be named as a "selling shareholder," subjecting it to the due diligence obligations of an under-writer for purposes of §11 liability. See §6.3.4. But securities firms that participate in the initial Rule 144A placement are not liable under §11 for misstatements in the subsequent registered offering. See *American High Income Trust v. AlliedSignal Inc.*, 329 F. Supp. 2d 534 (S.D.N.Y. 2004).

§7.3 CORPORATE REORGANIZATIONS AND RECAPITALIZATIONS

§7.3.1 Issuer Exchanges

Companies often find it advantageous to issue new securities in exchange for outstanding securities, issued either by the company or by another company. The offer and subsequent exchange, which alter the nature of the investment held by the exchanging securities holder, are treated as an "offer" and "sale" under the Securities Act. If the exchange offer is made to public investors, the offering is subject to registration and the regular gun-jumping rules.

The Securities Act exempts exchange offers that are made as "no pressure" recapitalizations in which the issuer exchanges its own securities with current holders without paying a commission to anyone for soliciting the exchange. Securities Act §3(a)(9). In addition, consistent with the political compromise in the Securities Act not to regulate insurance or the bank industry, the Act exempts from registration any exchange offers approved after a hearing by a state bank or insurance authority. Securities Act §3(a)(10).

§7.3.2 Fundamental Corporate Transactions — Rule 145

The automatic exchange of outstanding securities for new securities in a merger, sale of assets, or recapitalization accomplished by the vote of share-holders is difficult to categorize under the "offer" and "sale" concepts of the Securities Act. On the one hand, the corporate transaction, once approved by the shareholders, does not give individual shareholders any further sale-purchase discretion; once the transaction is approved, the company makes no offer or sale. On the other hand, the transaction can be seen as the disposition of new securities; the company offers these new investment rights when it proposes the transaction.

How should such fundamental corporate transactions be categorized? The choice seems to depend on the perceived adequacy of federal proxy regulation and corporate voting protections in such transactions. Before 1972, the SEC took the view that fundamental corporate transactions were not "sales" by the issuer because, once approved, such transactions did not involve shareholder volition. The result was that voting shareholders received only the disclosure mandated by the federal proxy rules. In 1972, the SEC reversed its stance and announced its current interpretation that such transactions involve the issuer's "offer" of a new investment interest. In the end, the interpretive about-face is less dramatic than it may seem. In the usual case, the company will file a single document that is both a Securities Act registration statement and an Exchange Act proxy statement. Under the integrated disclosure regime, the disclosure requirements for each will generally overlap. See Form S-4 (special disclosure form for business combination transactions).

In 1999 the SEC revised its approach to business combinations to update and simplify the federal securities laws' application to mergers, tender offers, and going-private transactions. Securities Act Rel. No. 7760 (adopting Regulation M-A). Significantly, for purposes of Securities Act regulation, the SEC eased the disclosure rules surrounding the announcement of a business combination that involves a stock offering. Rule 165 puts stock deals on the same footing as cash deals, by creating a safe harbor for deal-related disclosures prior to and after the filing of a registration statement. Specifically, the rule exempts business combinations from the "gun-jumping" prohibitions that generally apply to prefiling announcements and post-filing "free-writing." See §4.3. This means a prospective acquirer can propose a stock deal without first filing a registration statement or waiting for SEC review. Unlike the narrow disclosures permitted under Rule 135, the safe harbor places no restrictions on the content of public disclosures about a business combination so long as any written communications are promptly filed with the SEC and the prospectus eventually reminds investors to read documents filed with the SEC.

§7.3.3 Downstream Sales and Spinoffs

Stock splits and stock dividends, though they involve the issue of new securities to existing holders, are not treated as offers or sales "for value" and are thus excluded from the registration requirements of the Securities Act. See §2(a)(3) (definition of sale and offer).

The "for value" exclusion, however, has its limits. In the 1960s some companies, many with little or no business activity, sought to go public without registration and thus create a market for insiders to dump their shares. The device, known as a *spinoff*, worked like this: (1) the company would issue its shares to a publicly traded company that would then distribute the shares as a special dividend to its public shareholders; (2) the public company would take some of the shares as compensation for its trouble; and (3) the public company's shareholders would find themselves the unwitting owners of new *unregistered* securities. Over time, courts closed the spinoff loophole. *SEC v. Datronics Engineers, Inc.*, 490 F.2d 250 (4th Cir. 1973) (holding that spinoff distribution was "sale" because public company received "value" in the form of stock from private company and distributing company was an "underwriter" by participating in an undertaking to distribute stock to public investors). The SEC has also prohibited broker-dealers from quoting securities of "shell" corporations that go public in a spinoff without adequate disclosure. See Exchange Act Rule 15c2-11.

Not all spinoffs, however, are treated as attempts to exploit a regulatory loophole. For example, if a seasoned company spins off a subsidiary by issuing the subsidiary's shares as a dividend to the company's public shareholders, no sale occurs. *Isquith v. Caremark Int'l, Inc.*, 136 F.3d 531 (7th Cir. 1998) (concluding shareholder interest had changed from owning one to owning two companies with the same pool of assets).

§7.3.4 Warrants, Options, and Conversion Privileges

Issuers often find it easier to place new securities offerings by adding rights to acquire additional securities in the future. The SEC takes the view that warrants, options, or conversion rights (though themselves defined in §2(a)(1) as securities) do not represent offers or sales "for value" unless they are immediately exercisable. Securities Act Rel. No. 3210 (1947); see also §2(a)(3) (defining "offer" and "sale" not to include rights that "cannot be exercised until some future date"). But if the rights may be exercised immediately, both the rights and the underlying securities must be registered when issued, even before they are exercised.

§7.4 RESALES UNDER BLUE SKY LAWS

State securities law requires registration of sales of securities, including resales. To a significant extent state regulation of resales is undercut by the National Securities Markets Improvement Act of 1996, which preempts state regulation of certain offerings exempt from federal registration — and thus resales of securities acquired in the exempt offering. Securities Act §18 (preempting state regulation of offerings to specified §3(b)(2) offerings, §4(a)(2) offerings pursuant to Rule 506, and §4(a)(6) "crowdfunding" offerings); see §5.3. Federal regulation of resales of securities acquired pursuant to one of these exemptions is exclusive.

Still subject to state registration, however, are resales of securities acquired in certain offerings exempt from federal registration: (1) offerings by charitable or religious organizations; (2) offerings of municipal securities in the issuer's state; (3) intrastate offerings exempt under §3(a)(11); (4) small offerings exempt pursuant to §3(b)(1) — Rule 504 or 505, Rule 701, and Regulation A; and (5) small offerings pursuant to §3(b)(2) — Reg A+ (nonaccredited investors). This means that resales of securities acquired under one of these exemptions must satisfy not only the federal resale conditions, but must also seek its own blue-sky exemption. In most situations, however, the federal conditions are more demanding than the state exempting conditions. Thus, satisfying the conditions of Rule 144 will typically be sufficient to satisfy state requirements.

Most states offer "nonissuer" exemptions for resales by both control persons and noncontrol persons. USA §402(b). These include:

- **Exemption for "isolated transactions."** Though ambiguous, the exemption is understood to permit a single resale not for the benefit of the issuer. USA §§402(b)(1), 401(h).
- **Exemption for "manual" securities.** This often-used exemption permits resales of securities listed in a "recognized securities manual" that identifies the issuer's officers and directors, and includes its current financial statements. USA §402(b)(2). Manuals such as Moody's Industrial Manual and S&P's Corporate Record contain this information for publicly listed companies, as well as companies that pay a fee to be included. The information is significantly less complete than that required under Rule 144 for the resale of securities of publicly traded companies.
- **Exemption for "unsolicited offers."** Nonissuer resales may be accomplished through a registered broker-dealer that buys for its own account or fills unsolicited buy orders. USA §402(b)(3). The exemption goes well beyond §4(4), which only exempts the broker-dealer's participation in an unsolicited buy order and not the customer's resale.
- **Exemption for "small offerings."** Nonissuers who acquire securities from an issuer with investment intent can make offers to resell their shares to up to ten potential investors within the state. USA §402(b)(9) (seller must have reasonable belief of offeree's investment intent, and no fees may be paid to solicit offerees). Technically, a nonissuer could make 500 personal offers, ten in each of the 50 states.

Examples

1. The Russian American Society is a nonprofit association in the United States dedicated to helping the "new" Russia. The group seeks to foment cultural, political, and commercial relations between the two countries. Recently, the Society included in its member newsletter a prominent story about new mutual funds that invest in securities of Russian companies, complete with the funds' websites and overseas phone numbers. In one newsletter the Society intoned that "an investment in these Russian funds is a convenient way for U.S. investors to help capitalize the second Russian revolution." The Russian funds operate mostly outside the United States and are not registered with the SEC.

   a. The SEC sues to enjoin the Society from running further stories about the Russian funds. On what theory?

   b. The Society asserts that it is not in the securities business and is merely providing free information to its members. Is the Society exempt?

   c. The *New York Times* runs a story on the Russian funds. Is the newspaper subject to the registration requirements of the Securities Act?

   d. Your business clients who consult you for legal advice often ask you about overseas investment opportunities. You suggest they consider the new Russian funds and give them a copy of the Society's newsletter. Are you liable under §12(a)(1)?

2. Robert buys preferred shares in a private placement of Hale Limited, a start-up shipping company. After four months, Robert contemplates selling his stock on the over-the-counter market, without registration.

   a. Hale Limited had imposed no restrictions on Robert about whether and when he might resell his shares. Robert assumes selling his shares would merely be "trading" in nonrestricted stock. Can he sell?

   b. Robert asserts Hale Limited would never agree to file a registration statement for his shares. Anyway, Hale and the SEC cannot abolish his liquidity rights. Can he sell?

   c. Robert has come to dislike the way Hale's revenues bob up and down. Although he claims his original purpose was to "hold for the long term," Robert says that Hale's fluctuating revenues are an unanticipated change in circumstances that justifies his selling. Can he sell for this reason?

   d. Robert says he wants to sell because his niece has been admitted to law school and he had promised to pay her tuition, which was more than anyone expected. Can he sell for this reason?

   e. Robert asks for your advice. When can he sell for sure without registration?

   f. Does your advice change if Robert originally bought the shares in an exempt intrastate offering?

3. Rather than sell his Hale Limited preferred stock, Robert borrows money for his niece's tuition from his bank, Howell Trust & Co. As collateral for the loan, Robert pledges his Hale stock. At the time of the pledge, Hale faces a liquidity crisis and has failed to file its 10-Q quarterly report on time.

    a. Howell Trust claims that Robert illegally pledged the Hale stock because it was not registered under the Securities Act. The bank seeks to rescind the transaction and call the loan. Can it?

    b. Seven months after talking out the loan, Robert defaults. Howell Trust is shocked; Robert seemed an excellent credit risk. The bank wants to sell the preferred stock into a public trading market, without registration. Can it sell?

    c. Again assume that Robert defaults. Howell Trust expected it; Robert's loan application showed little chance of him being able to repay the loan. The bank wants to sell the preferred stock into a public trading market, without registration. Can it sell?

4. Wolfson is the largest shareholder and chief executive of Continental Enterprises. He has held his stock for ten years, but the company is in trouble and he wants to sell. Wolfson lines up six brokerage firms to sell 55 percent of his holdings in Continental on the market, without registration.

    a. One of the brokerage firms, First Lynch Securities, was aware that it was selling shares owned by Wolfson. Wolfson, however, claims that he was not an issuer, underwriter, or dealer in the transaction. Are these sales legal?

    b. The other brokerage firms were unaware of who they were selling for. Wolfson claims that these firms were merely acting as brokers in exempt brokers' transactions. Are these sales legal?

    c. Wolfson claims that he was a busy executive, with no time for the details of securities regulation. Can he be convicted criminally?

5. Apex is a large company whose shares are listed on the New York Stock Exchange (NYSE). The following questions focus on Rule 144.

    a. Rule 144 permits the sale of restricted securities and the sale by control persons, both of which implicate "underwriter" status for either the seller of the restricted securities or the person assisting in the sales by the control person. Where does the SEC get the authority to exempt transactions subject to the regulatory regime of the Securities Act?

    b. Bertha bought shares from Apex in a Rule 506 offering ten months ago. The Apex attorney who structured the deal screwed up, and there were more than 35 nonaccredited investors. Can Bertha sell under Rule 144?

    c. Copernicus owns a control block of Apex. He plans to sell his stock to Ruby Powers (a qualified "Ralston Purina" investor).

  (1) Can Copernicus sell to Ruby without registration?

  (2) Copernicus grows restless in his negotiations with Ruby and wants to sell his control block on the NYSE using a group of brokers, without registration. Can he sell his control block this way?

d. Daniella holds a large quantity of restricted Apex stock. She's held it for ten months. Trading in Apex stock is thin.

  (1) Can she sell without registration?

  (2) Does your advice change if Apex has not filed its latest 10-Q, as required.

e. Ellen is a director of sales for Apex and a member of the company's board of directors. She bought 10,000 shares on the NYSE three months ago and now wants to dump them.

  (1) Is she a control person?

  (2) Can she sell without registration?

f. Frank, a sophisticated investor, bought restricted stock from Apex 16 months ago.

  (1) Frank gave Apex a full recourse personal note to finance his purchase and pledged the shares to Apex as collateral. The note is a full recourse obligation. Last month Frank paid off the note and wants to sell his shares on a public trading market without registration. Can he?

  (2) Frank took out a bank loan to purchase the Apex stock. He gave the bank a note for the purchase price, collateralized by a pledge to the bank of his Apex shares. When Frank defaults on the note, can the bank sell without registration?

g. Gail is a control person. Apex had average weekly trading of 150,000 shares for the last month, and there are 18 million shares outstanding.

  (1) Gail sells 50,000 shares in January and 50,000 shares in February. How many can she sell in March?

  (2) What if Gail had given 120,000 shares to Gonzo State University six months ago? Can GSU sell its shares in March?

h. Henry, another Apex control person, wants to sell his Apex stock using his broker, First Lynch Securities.

  (1) First Lynch called Newey & Co., a market maker in Apex stock, and asked if Newey had any unfilled buy orders for Apex near market. Newey said it did. Can Henry sell to Newey's customers?

  (2) Henry calls ten different brokers and sells through each. His total sales exceed 1 percent of Apex's outstanding shares. Are the brokers in trouble?

  (3) Henry also sold some stock to Ruby Powers, our "Ralston Purina" investor. Will the sale to Ruby limit Henry's sales through the broker?

6. Starstruck Software, a company whose shares are traded on NASDAQ, raises money for a new line of educational software with a private placement of its bonds. The bonds are placed with a variety of domestic and international institutional investors. One of the investors, Banca di Fatica (an Italian bank), purchased $5-million worth of the bonds. Later in the year it is interested in selling. Trota Fratelli, an international securities firm, learns that the College Retirement Equity Fund (CREF, the largest private pension fund in the United States) is interested in buying Banca di Fatica's position. There have been no SEC filings.

   a. Without doing anything more, Banca di Fatica sells to CREF. What is the risk it has run?

   b. Has Banca di Fatica complied with Rule 144A?

   c. Banca di Fatica fails to comply with Rule 144A. Can CREF rescind the transaction?

7. Amalgamated Motors is a car manufacturer whose shares are listed on the NYSE. Amalgamated enters into negotiations to acquire Modesta, a rapidly-growing automobile design company whose shares are closely held by 20 individuals.

   a. Modesta will sell all of its assets to Amalgamated in exchange for Amalgamated common stock. Modesta will then dissolve and distribute the Amalgamated stock to the Modesta shareholders. The Modesta shareholders approve the plan. Is Securities Act registration required? If so, when?

   b. On dissolution, many of the Modesta shareholders wish to sell their Amalgamated shares at market. Are there any restrictions on their resales?

Explanations

1. a. The SEC might assert that the Society has violated §5 of the Securities Act by conditioning the market for the sale securities of the Russian funds before the filing or effectiveness of a registration statement. The SEC would argue these offers are "transactions by . . . an underwriter" because the Society was acting "for" the Russian funds. Although the Society is receiving no compensation for its efforts and has no relation to the Russian funds, its actions create a danger that investors will invest without the disclosure and other protections of SEC registration. See *SEC v. Chinese Consolidated Benevolent Ass'n*, 120 F.2d 738 (2d Cir. 1941) (§7.1.1). That many of the funds operate outside the United States does not exempt them from U.S. securities regulation if their sales are to U.S. investors. See §13.2.1.

   b. No. The §4(a)(1) exemption does not turn on whether a person involved in a securities offering is in the securities business, but whether the person is assisting the issuers (the Russian funds) in the distribution of their securities to the public. The argument that the Society is merely providing information to its members does not negate its role in assisting issuers to find investors. It is a close question, however, whether the Society's dissemination of information has crossed the line of "offers . . . for an issuer."

On the one hand, the Society's actions are remarkably similar to that of a Chinese Benevolent Association that encouraged and actively assisted its members in their purchase of unregistered Chinese bonds. See *SEC v. Chinese Consolidated Benevolent Ass'n*, 120 F.2d 738 (2d Cir. 1941). By providing addresses and phone numbers and urging Society members to consider investing, the Russian American Society may have made "offers . . . for an issuer" and thus crossed the line. See §4.3.1. On the other hand, the Supreme Court, in a related context, concluded that securities regulation and a person's regulated status depend on whether the person has a pecuniary interest in the transaction. See *Pinter v. Dahl*, 486 U.S. 622 (1988) (interpreting the "for value" element of the §2(a)(3) definition of "offer") (see §6.2.2). In the case, the Supreme Court held that there could be no civil liability for uncompensated securities advice under §12(a)(1) of the Securities Act. The Court's apparent assumption was that federal securities regulation should not intrude into gratuitous investment tips.

In the end, there may be a different standard of what constitutes an "offer . . . for an issuer" depending on whether the SEC is seeking to enjoin further selling efforts by a third party and a private party is seeking monetary liability from the same party. The Society is playing in an uncertain (and dangerous) gray zone created by the §4(a)(1) exemption.

c. Probably not. If the newspaper merely provides a journalistic account of the Russian funds without an intention of inducing investor interest or purchases, it is difficult to argue that the newspaper was acting "for" the issuers. In fact, such a reading of the §4(a)(1) exemption may be compelled by First Amendment concerns that to impose the prior restraint regulatory regime of the Securities Act on news stories would abridge free speech rights.

d. Probably not. *Pinter v. Dahl* teaches that §12(a)(1) liability depends on a person who solicits investments acting for his own financial interests or for those of the issuer. See §6.2.2. If your business does not include giving investment advice and you did not expect compensation for the advice, there would seem to be little risk of liability. Nonetheless, the broad reading given the meaning of an "underwriter" acting for an issuer should raise some concern. Although you may not be civilly liable, the SEC has authority to seek injunctive relief in federal court under §21 of the Securities Act for violations of the Act. See §12.3.

This reveals the apparent incongruence of the §4(a)(1) exemption and §12(a)(1) liability. That is, it might be possible for an activity not to trigger "seller" liability under §12(a)(1), yet violate §5 for purposes of SEC injunction.

2. a. No, he cannot sell into a public trading market. Rule 144 is not yet available, since Robert has not held his stock for at least six months. See Rule 144(c)(1). And no other exemption applies for resales into public trading markets.

   If investors like Robert could purchase stock and resell it without registration, there would be a gaping hole in the registration scheme of the Securities Act. The Act plugs the hole by treating such purchaser-resellers as "underwriters" if they purchased from an issuer "with a view" to distribution in a public trading market. As such, offers and sales by holders of nonrestricted stock are not exempt by the §4(a)(1) market trading exemption. Robert would violate §5 by selling his nonexempt, unregistered stock.

   b. No, he cannot sell. The registration requirements of the Securities Act limit liquidity rights, whatever the parties' understanding. Robert should have obtained a registration undertaking from the issuer for his privately placed, and thus "restricted," stock. The other alternative for Robert is to sell his stock pursuant to the conditions of Rule 144, which require that he hold the stock for at least six months. See §7.2.1. Given the restrictions on liquidity for securities purchased in a private placement, such stock has sold at a significant discount compared to readily marketable stock. The 2008 revisions to Rule 144, which reduce the holding period and resale limitations for privately placed stock, seek to reduce the amount of this discount — and thus make capital formation less expensive for companies.

   c. No, he cannot sell for this reason. The "change in circumstances" doctrine derives from the §2(a)(11) definition of "underwriter," which turns on whether a purchaser-reseller bought "with a view" to resell into a public market. An investor who resells because of a change in his personal circumstances can argue that the resale is consistent with his original intention not to resell and that the resale is occasioned for reasons other than to exploit an informational advantage. In our example, however, the increased volatility and riskiness of his investment suggests that Robert is acting as a conduit of securities to public investors in circumstances where the disclosure and other protections of registration are called for. Courts have rejected similar arguments that changes in the issuer's business justified an early resale. See *Gilligan, Will & Co. v. SEC*, 267 F.2d 461 (2d Cir. 1959). Otherwise, an investor could "unload on the unadvised public what he later determines to be an unsound investment without the disclosure sought by the securities laws."

The SEC has gone one step further and has rejected the "change in circumstances" doctrine, even when the investor's changed circumstances evidence that she is selling for reasons not inconsistent with an original investment intention. The agency has assumed that investors have informational needs whether or not the seller is selling in a distress sale.

d. Perhaps, if the "change in circumstances" doctrine could be used. Despite the SEC's views, courts have suggested that a seller's change in circumstances is relevant to the §2(a)(11) inquiry into whether he purchased originally "with a view" to distribute. The question is whether the securities "came to rest" with him. This depends on a number of factual factors, including whether he had assumed the full investment risk when he purchased, whether he had held them for a significant period, and whether the change in circumstances explains his reason for selling.

In all, Robert can make a case for not being seen as a statutory "underwriter." There is no indication Robert intended to act as a conduit and exploit an informational advantage. He assumed full investment risk, and his niece's unanticipated high tuition offers a plausible reason for his selling. Moreover, if Hale Limited is a reporting company that is current in its Exchange Act filings, it could argued that the market had enough time to absorb any non-public news to which Robert was privy four months ago when he purchased in the private placement. In the past ten years, the SEC has reduced the "come to rest" period under Rule 144 from two years to one year, and then to six months. See §7.2.1.

e. Rule 144 offers some bright-line answers. The rule creates a safe harbor for holders of restricted securities, which became even easier to navigate after the 2008 revisions to Rule 144. If Robert assumed full investment risk when (and after) he purchased the securities and holds them for six months, he may resell them into a public trading market subject only to the condition that Hale Limited be a reporting company current in its Exchange Act filings. Rule 144(c), (d). After the 2008 revisions to Rule 144, he need not worry about the amount he sells or the manner in which he sells the securities. Rule 144(e), (f), and (g). Nor does he have a filing requirement with the SEC. Rule 144(h). And if Robert waits one year from the time of his purchase, he may resell even if Hale Limited is not a reporting company or is not current in its Exchange Act filings. Rule 144(k).

f. Curiously, the advice does change. The holding period for resales of securities acquired in an exempt intrastate offering — that is, the presumptive time during which the securities come to rest — is nine months according to Rule 147, not the six months and one year of the current Rule 144. See §5.2.1. In other words, an investor in an exempt intrastate offering must wait for nine months to act as a conduit, but need wait only six months to sell into a trading market under Rule 144 (assuming the company is a reporting company current in its Exchange Act filings). Why this difference? The SEC has never explained.

3. a. Not on this basis. Although the pledge of securities is viewed as a "sale," the transaction is with a sophisticated investor — the bank. As such, the pledge is exempt from registration under §4(a)(1). Robert is not an issuer or dealer, and his pledge was not a transaction by an "underwriter" because the sale to the bank was not a "distribution." In effect, the transaction with the bank was subject to the "§4(1½) exemption."

   b. Probably. If the bank accepted the pledged securities without an expectation that it would have to sell the collateral, it did not purchase "with a view" to distribute and cannot be a statutory underwriter.

      To be certain, however, the bank should consider holding for one more month to satisfy the 12-month holding period applicable to resales of restricted securities by noncontrol persons under Rule 144 —

      recall that Robert had held the securities for four months and his default came seven months after taking out the loan. (The bank must use the 12-month holding period, not the six-month holding period, because Hale Limited is not current in its Exchange Act filings.) The period of Robert's initial four-month holding would be tacked on to the bank's holding period. Rule 144(d)(1) (holding period runs from "the date of acquisition . . . from the issuer" to "any resale . . . for the account of . . . any subsequent holder" if the original acquirer paid the full purchase price). Notice that a slightly different tacking rule applies for stock pledged by a control person. Rule 144(d)(3) (holding period for stock pledged by control person begins with such person's original acquisition, unless the securities were pledged without recourse).

   c. Probably not. If the bank expected the default, and thus understood it was acting as a conduit for Robert, it acquired the securities from Robert "with a view" to distribution. That is, the bank itself becomes a statutory underwriter if Robert's sale to the market would have rendered him a statutory underwriter. Rule 144, however, permits the bank to tack any period that Robert had held the stock, even if the bank took the pledge with the expectation that it would foreclose on the loan and sell the securities into a public trading market. If Robert had held the stock for four months and the bank for seven months, the bank could wait for one more month and immediately sell the stock pursuant under Rule 144. (Compare this to the tacking rule for pledges by control persons, which must be "bona fide" before tacking is allowed. See Rule 144(d)(3).)

4. a. No. Wolfson himself was neither an issuer (his company was), a dealer (he was not in the securities business), nor a statutory underwriter (he had purchased ten years before and the securities had "come to rest" with him). The question then becomes whether First Lynch was acting as a statutory underwriter. Remember that intermediaries who assist a control person selling securities into a public trading market are defined in §2(a)(11) as "underwriters." If Wolfson was a control person and First Lynch offered or sold the securities on his behalf, the unregistered transactions are illegal.

Was Wolfson a control person? Wolfson's status as the largest shareholder and chief executive makes him an unquestioned control person. Whether measured by his ability to demand the registration of his shares or by his access to inside information, the Securities Act views his transactions with the same suspicions as an issuer transaction. The likelihood of him exploiting his informational advantages, if the company were failing, suggests the importance of investor protection.

Did First Lynch become a statutory underwriter? Under the definition of §2(a)(11), an underwriter includes any person who acts "for" a control person or who purchases from a control person "with a view" to distribute. Whether First Lynch was acting as an agent (a broker) in finding purchasers for Wolfson or as a principal (a dealer) by buying and reselling his shares, First Lynch acted as a statutory underwriter. Although Wolfson himself was not an issuer, underwriter, or dealer, the transactions in which he sold his stock were "transactions by an underwriter" and, thus, subject to registration.

b. No. This example is drawn from the facts of *United States v. Wolfson*, 405 F.2d 779 (2d Cir. 1968). It raises the question whether registration is required when the control person is not an issuer, underwriter, or dealer (see above), and the transactions are arguably subject to the §4(4) exemption for brokers' transactions. The Second Circuit solved this conundrum by brilliantly splitting hairs. First, the court concluded the brokers were acting as statutory underwriters, and the §4(a)(1) exemption did not apply to Wolfson's sales. Next, the court held that the §4(4) exemption for brokers' transactions provided an exemption for the brokers' activities, but not for Wolfson's sales.

How could the brokerage firms be underwriters if they didn't know they were acting for a control person? Although the brokerage firms were unaware of the status of the seller, their lack of awareness does not negate that they were acting as conduits for a control person. The §2(a)(11) definition does not turn on whether the person acting for a control person knows of this. The sales of Wolfson's shares were transactions by unwitting statutory underwriters and thus were non-exempt sales in violation of §5. Why doesn't the §4(4) exemption for brokers' transactions exempt the transaction from registration? The exemption was designed to provide comfort to securities firms that act as brokers by executing customer orders on trading markets, though without soliciting the orders. The SEC has interpreted the exemption to include transactions involving control persons' shares only if "the broker is not aware of circumstances indicating that the transactions are part of a distribution of securities on behalf of his principal." Rule 154(a)(4). The exemption was not designed as a way for control persons to hide behind unwitting brokers. Wolfson, as principal, violated §5 by selling his shares in transactions by a statutory underwriter.

   c. Yes. Wolfson made such an argument before the Second Circuit and was roundly rebuffed. The court pointed out that the criminal conviction was based on a finding by the jury of his willfulness (see §11.3.2) and the court expressed doubts about whether a "busy executive" defense could be any defense at all.

5. a. The operation of Rule 144 turns on the meaning of "underwriter" under §2(a)(11), which requires that there be a "distribution." The SEC's authority to define the circumstances that constitute a "distribution" and thus the presence of an "underwriter" comes from its authority in §19(a) to define "accounting, technical, and trade terms used in this subchapter." In effect, Rule 144 represents the SEC's conclusion that sales by control persons are not a "distribution" if made into a public trading market through a broker, in limited amounts, and when the market has up-to-date information about the issuer. Moreover, sales of restricted securities are not a "distribution" after a six-month holding period under specified circumstances and are not a "distribution" after a one-year holding period under all circumstances. In each case, the SEC has concluded that the activities prescribed by Rule 144 do not present significant risks of informational asymmetries.

   b. Yes. Rule 144 is concerned not with whether securities were properly issued, but whether they may be properly resold. The rule provides certainty for holders of "restricted securities," which it defines as including securities subject to resale limitations under Reg D. Rule 144(a)(3). Bertha received her securities in an offering subject to the Reg D resale limitations. She has held for more than six months, but less than one year, and can sell her securities into the market so long as Apex is current in its Exchange Act periodic reporting.

c. 1. Yes, but not under Rule 144. The SEC's rule, which deals with sales into public trading markets, is not exclusive. See Rule 144(j). Other statutory and regulatory exemptions remain available, and a control person can sell securities (whether restricted or not) to sophisticated investors under the §4(a)(1) exemption. In our example, Copernicus is neither the "issuer" of the securities nor a "dealer" in the securities business. Moreover, he is not an "underwriter" (nor is anyone connected to the transaction an underwriter) because there is no "distribution" when he sells to Ruby Powers, someone who can fend for herself. That this transaction is exempt under the §4(a)(1) exemption depends on the conclusion that there was no distribution according to the criteria of §4(a)(2). For this reason, securities lawyers call this a "§4(a)(1½) exemption."

c. 2. No. Control persons who wish to sell into a public trading market have two choices: They can register their shares or comply with Rule 144. In our example, it is unlikely that Copernicus could use Rule 144 to "trickle" his entire control block into the market at once. Instead, Copernicus will have to register or sell a bit every three months, subject to any holding periods applicable to his restricted shares.

d. 1. Yes, assuming Apex is current with its periodic filings under the Exchange Act. Rule 144(b)(1)(i), (c). If so, there are no trickle or other requirements. Holders of restricted stock for more than six months, but less than one year, are subject only to the current information requirement. For this reason, buyers of restricted stock will often insist on promises by the issuer to keep its SEC filings current.

d. 2. Yes, Deborah should seek to have Apex become current in its Exchange Act filings. Even if Apex does not become current, Daniella can wait for two more months and then sell under Rule 144 without being subject to the "current public information" condition. See Rule 144(b)(1)(i) (previously Rule 144(k)). If the one-year holding requirement is satisfied, there are no public-information, trickle, manner-of-sale, or filing requirements for noncontrol holders.

e. 1. Probably. As an apparent member of management's inner circle, it seems likely that Ellen has access to inside information about the company that places her in an advantageous informational position compared to other investors. Moreover, as a member of the board, it is likely she could ask for and obtain the registration of her shares. Although the SEC has recognized the possibility that nonemployee, outside directors may sometimes not satisfy the definition of control persons, SEC staff in no-action letters have stated that employee-directors are presumptively control persons.

e. 2. Yes, if the resale satisfies the Rule 144 conditions. Ellen's shares are not restricted because they were acquired on a public trading market. The concern is not that she will be acting as a conduit for the issuer, but rather that as an insider she may exploit information unavailable to the public trading markets. Her sales are regulated because of her status as a control person. Rule 144 permits "affiliates" to sell nonrestricted shares on public trading markets without being subject to a holding period, so long as there is current public information about the issuer and the sale is made through a broker and in small amounts.

f. 1. No. Frank has not held the shares for a sufficient time, and Rule 144 assumes he is acting as a conduit for the issuer because he never assumed an investment risk for his shares. Under the rule, the holding period for restricted shares does not start until the purchaser pays "the full purchase price." Rule 144(d)(1). Although the rule deems full payment to occur when a shareholder purchases from the issuer on credit, the loan must provide for full recourse against the shareholder, be fully secured by collateral other than the shares, and be paid off before the shares are sold. Rule 144(d)(2). In our example, Frank's loan was collateralized only by his shares. As such, it was as though the issuer had shelved some securities with Frank, who would have paid fully for them only a month before reselling them into a public trading market. Frank's purchase lacks the economic earmarks of one in which the shares had "come to rest" with the original purchaser.

f. 2. Yes. Frank's holding period of 16 months is tacked on to the bank's holding period, and Rule 144 permits the bank to sell without restriction. See Rule 144(b)(1)(i) (one-year holding period). Frank paid Apex the full purchase price when he acquired the shares. As a subsequent holder, the bank can tack on Frank's holding period. See Rule 144(d)(1). The difference between this example and the prior example is that Frank assumed the full investment risk by borrowing from the bank. Even if the bank expected that it would have to foreclose on its loan — in effect, it was purchasing the shares from Apex — it assumed the full investment risk when it lent Frank the purchase price. Frank and the bank fully absorbed any loss during their 16-month holding period; they were not acting as conduits for Apex.

g. 1. 80,000 shares. Rule 144 defines "trickle" for a control person's sale of *equity securities* (during a three-month period) as the greater of 1 percent of the company's outstanding equity shares of the class sought to be traded and the average weekly reported trading volume for the prior four calendar weeks. See Rule 144(c)(1). In this example, 1 percent of 18,000,000 (180,000) is larger than the average trading volume of 150,000. Since Gail has already sold 100,000 shares in the last two months, she can sell an additional 80,000 shares.

g. 2. No. Rule 144 does not permit a person subject to the rule to dump shares into a market using a donee; shares sold by any donee (who received them in the last six months) are aggregated with those sold by the donor. See Rule 144(e)(3)(C). This prevents a donor from dumping with her donee. Gail and GSU together can only sell up to 80,000 shares in March.

h. 1. Perhaps. The inquiries of Newey may fit the definition of "brokers' transactions," the only method for control persons to dispose of equity securities under Rule 144. See Rule 144(g)(2). The rule seeks to prevent a control person's broker from creating interest in buyers who did not exist before. Although Newey did not expressly indicate an interest to First Lynch in the Apex securities, its status as a market maker suggests a standing interest in buying or selling Apex securities. In the end, First Lynch did not solicit the offers to buy standing on Newey's books; they already existed from customers who had relayed them to Newey.

h. 2. Probably. To obtain a §4(4) exemption for their activities in connection with control-person sales, the brokers must make reasonable inquires whether "the transaction is a part of a distribution of securities of the issuer." See Rule 144(g)(3). If the issuer becomes aware of circumstances that indicate it is selling for a control person, it loses its §4(4) exemption.

h. 3. No. The "§4(a)(1½)" sales to qualified investors — that is, "sales exempt pursuant to Section 4 of the Act and not involving any public offering" — are not counted against the amount of sales permitted under Rule 144. See Rule 144(e)(3)(G).

6. a. Like any other purchaser-reseller, the institutional investor runs the risk of being treated as a statutory underwriter. If its resale is a "transaction by an underwriter" and thus a nonexempt, unregistered sale of securities, the investor would be subject to §12(a)(1) liability in a suit by its purchaser. It would also risk SEC enforcement action and even criminal liability.

b. Not quite. To comply with Rule 144A, the bank must sell securities that are not publicly traded on a stock exchange or NASDAQ (which these private bonds are not) in a company for which current information is available (which is satisfied by Starstruck's status as an Exchange Act reporting company) to a qualified institutional buyer (which CREF is) and take "reasonable steps" to ensure the purchaser is aware that the seller is relying on an exemption from Securities Act registration. This last step can be accomplished by giving the buyer notice that the seller is relying on Rule 144A.

In addition to Rule 144A's current information requirement, the private Rule 144A market has come to require issuers to provide extensive disclosures in an offering memorandum, often including warranties and representations to assure institutional buyers. To give additional comfort, the securities firm that helps place the securities often has its counsel provide investors a "10b-5 opinion" that after an investigation of the issuer's disclosures there is nothing to suggest actionable fraud. These disclosures and opinions have become common practice in private placements both in the United States and Europe, even when the jurisdictional reach of Rule 10b-5 is doubtful. See §13.3.1.

c. Not necessarily. Rule 144A is not exclusive. The bank may rely on the statutory §4(a)(1) exemption if its sale to CREF was not a distribution. Neither the bank nor the intermediary securities firm can be an underwriter if CREF is a qualified buyer under the standards for a private placement. Just as there would be no reason to insist on registration if Starstruck had sold directly to CREF, there can be no reason to insist on registration if a purchaser resells to CREF.

In fact, some of the Rule 144A conditions go beyond the criteria for a qualified private placement. Notice to buyers that the transaction is exempt (Rule 144A(d)(2)) and the requirement that the issuer either be subject to the Exchange Act reporting requirements or provide specified information (including a description of its business, products, and services; its most recent balance sheet; and its financial statements for the past two years) (Rule 144A(d)(4)) go well beyond the requirements of §4(a)(2) of the Securities Act and presumably the §4(a)(1) exemption for transactions not involving a distribution.

7. a. Perhaps. Rule 145 specifies when shareholder approval of a corporation acquisition constitutes, in effect, a decision to acquire a new investment — that is, to exchange an existing security for a new or different security. See Preliminary Note, Rule 145. As such, Rule 145 is not an exemption from registration but a clarification of when there is a "sale" under §2(a)(3) for which registration is required. This example illustrates the "transfer of assets" transaction described in Rule 145(a)(3): Shareholders of Modesta are asked to vote on a plan in which assets of their corporation are transferred to Amalgamated in consideration of Amalgamated shares, and such plan calls for the dissolution of Modesta and the pro rata distribution of Amalgamated

shares to the Modesta shareholders. In effect, Amalgamated has sold its shares to Modesta shareholders in exchange for their shares.

That the sale of assets is a securities sale does not resolve whether registration is needed. If the Modesta shareholders are all sophisticated and will be taking executive positions with Amalgamated, the transaction is arguably exempt under §4(a)(2). See §5.2.2. If, however, there are shareholders who cannot fend for themselves, registration will be required. If Amalgamated is a large, seasoned public company, it may be able to use Form S-3 registration, requiring only minimal additional disclosure to the Modesta shareholders. See §4.2.2 (Exchange Act filings incorporated by reference in Form S-3 registration statement).

b. It depends. If the shares were acquired in a private placement, they become restricted securities subject to limitations on resale. In such a case, the former Modesta shareholders would be subject to certain modified conditions drawn from Rule 144. See Rule 145(d). For example, if the former Modesta shareholders do not become "affiliates" of Amalgamated they could resell their securities within one year after they acquired them, without any limitation on the manner of sale or the amount sold, if Amalgamated was current with its public reporting obligations. See Rule 145(d)(2).

In addition, the resales may be subject to state blue-sky registration, absent a state exemption. If Amalgamated is a public company whose shares are listed in a "recognized securities manual," the resales would be exempt from state registration. See §7.4.

If the securities are acquired in a registered offering, no resale restrictions apply. It may behoove the Modesta shareholders to negotiate for registration, even if under Form S-3, to avoid liquidity constraints.

Securities Exchange Act of 1934

The Securities Exchange Act of 1934 takes up where the Securities Act of 1933 leaves off. Building on the Securities Act philosophy of "truth in securities offerings," the Exchange Act reaches ambitiously for "integrity in securities trading markets."

The Exchange Act recognizes that information, processed by securities intermediaries, is the lifeblood of securities trading markets. The Act establishes a system of administrative supervision (including supervision of *self-regulation* by the securities exchanges and the financial industry), regulation of certain industry practices, and *mandatory disclosure* for companies whose securities are publicly traded on stock exchanges. To carry out its ambitious programs, the Exchange Act created the Securities and Exchange Commission (SEC).

The Exchange Act, the bedrock of U.S. securities regulation, has been amended on a number of occasions:

1938   **Maloney Act.** Congress makes associations of broker-dealers that trade over-the-counter subject to SEC supervision comparable to that of stock exchanges. The National Association of Security Dealers, Inc. (NASD) was the first and remained the only association to register with the SEC. In 2007, the Financial Industry Regulatory Authority (FINRA) became the successor to the NASD — at the same time taking on the member, enforcement, and arbitration functions of the NYSE.

1964   **Securities Acts Amendments of 1964.** Congress systematically brings over-the-counter markets (and companies whose stock is traded on such markets) within the Exchange Act's coverage.

1968   **Williams Act.** Congress amends the Exchange Act to add new substantive and disclosure regulation of corporate control changes, particularly tender offers.

1975   **Securities Acts Amendments of 1975.** Congress gives the SEC significant additional oversight authority over self-regulatory organizations (SROs) and the securities industry, and adds two new SROs: clearing agencies and the Municipal Securities Rulemaking Board.

1978   **Foreign Corrupt Practices Act.** Congress imposes record-keeping requirements on public companies and forbids their bribery of foreign government officials.

1986   **Government Securities Act.** Congress eliminates the exemption for broker-dealers in government securities, thus bringing this aspect of commercial banking under the supervision of the SEC, the Federal Reserve, and the Treasury Department.

1990   **Securities Enforcement Remedies and Penny Stock Reform Act.** Congress buttresses the SEC's enforcement powers, authorizing administrative civil penalties and cease-and-desist orders; Congress also takes aim at high-pressure marketing of low-cost, high-risk penny stocks.

1995   **Private Securities Litigation Reform Act.** Congress addresses perceived abuses in investor class actions brought under the antifraud provisions of the Securities Act and the Exchange Act.

1996   **National Securities Markets Improvement Act.** Congress, besides preempting state securities laws for a variety of securities offerings, substantially limits state regulation of broker-dealers.

1998   **Securities Litigation Uniform Standards Act.** Congress seeks to avoid circumvention of the PSLRA standards by requiring that class actions involving allegations of securities fraud be litigated exclusively in federal court.

2002   **Sarbanes-Oxley Act.** Congress responds to a spate of corporate accounting and financial scandals, and creates a new accounting board to oversee audits of public companies, increases responsibilities for those making corporate disclosures, introduces numerous reforms to corporate governance in public companies, and imposes new professional duties for securities lawyers.

2010   **Dodd-Frank Act.** Congress responds to the financial crisis of 2008 with sweeping reforms of U.S. financial regulation, primarily affecting the banking industry. Securities reforms include regulation of over-the-counter derivatives to bring their trading onto exchanges, registration of hedge funds and private equity funds, greater regulation of credit rating agencies, greater point-of-sale disclosure by broker-dealers, increases in SEC enforcement authority (including a new "whistleblower bounty" program), and corporate governance reforms (including share-holder votes on executive pay).

2013   **Jumpstart Our Business Startups Act (JOBS Act).** Congress seeks to promote business start-ups by easing securities regulatory burdens — both in the offering process and subsequent trading. General solicitations are permitted in offerings to accredited investors and qualified institutional buyers; small companies can make online "crowdfunding" offerings to public investors; and the dollar limit is increased for mini-registrations. Small companies can have more shareholders and give stock-based compensation to employees without risking becoming a public company; and reporting and corporate governance requirements are relaxed for "emerging growth companies."

This chapter covers:

- the Exchange Act's regulation of securities markets, including new trading systems [§8.1]
- the Exchange Act's regulation of specific market practices, such as market manipulation and short selling [§8.2]
- the Exchange Act's disclosure requirements and regulation of companies whose securities are traded on public markets, including the corporate governance listing standards of the NYSE and NASDAQ [§8.3]
- summaries of the Exchange Act's regulation of proxy voting in public companies [§8.4] and regulation tender offers in public companies [§8.5]

Other chapters deal more fully with some of these topics: fraud liability under Rule 10b-5 (Chapter 9); insider trading (Chapter 10); regulation of broker-dealers and other market intermediaries (Chapter 11); and SEC enforcement (Chapter 12).

Some aspects of the Exchange Act, particularly those related to corporate governance in public companies, are only summarized in this book. For a fuller treatment of these topics, you may want to refer to Alan R. Palmiter, CORPORATIONS: EXAMPLES & EXPLANATIONS (7th ed. 2012).

§8.1 REGULATION OF SECURITIES TRADING MARKETS

Trading of equity and debt securities in the United States occurs in three major markets: stock exchanges (principally the New York Stock Exchange), over-the-counter markets (principally NASDAQ), and direct trading among institutional investors (the "third market").

§8.1.1 Regulation of Stock Exchanges

A centerpiece of the Exchange Act was to bring U.S. stock exchanges and their long-standing tradition of self-regulation under federal oversight. The Act requires the registration of national securities exchanges, unless the SEC grants an exemption. Exchange Act §5. To give teeth to the requirement, the section also prohibits broker-dealers from effectuating securities transactions on an unregistered exchange.

Self-Regulation

To register with the SEC, exchanges are required to file an application and adopt a variety of rules of self-regulation. Exchange Act §6. Self-regulation exists at two levels: (1) rules involving trading: what securities can be listed, bids and offers on the exchange floor, activities of specialists, trading by members for their own account, off-exchange trading by members, and clearing and settlement of exchange trades; (2) rules involving the qualifications of members: member firm organization, qualification of partners and salespeople, handling of customer accounts, and financial condition of members. In addition, exchange rules are supposed to "prevent fraudulent and manipulative acts and practices" and provide that exchange members and their associates be "appropriately disciplined for violations" of the Exchange Act, its rules, and the rules of the exchange. Exchange Act §§6(b)(5), 6(b)(6).

The idea was and continues to be that the stock exchanges will take the lead in policing themselves, under the watchful eye of the SEC. The SEC has significant supervisory authority:

- **Exchange rules.** The stock exchanges must file proposed rule changes with the SEC. Exchange Act §19(b). After notice and hearing, the SEC may approve or disapprove the proposed change or modify it as the agency deems desirable. The SEC can also add, delete, or modify exchange rules on its own initiative. Exchange Act §19(c).

The exchanges (as well as NASDAQ) regulate the corporate governance structures of listed companies through listing standards. These standards, which complement state corporate law, have become more extensive since Sarbanes-Oxley. See §8.3.5.

- **Disciplinary actions.** The SEC can review disciplinary actions taken by the stock exchange against its members or when the exchange denies membership to a firm. Exchange Act §19(d). The SEC on its own initiative can sanction any exchange, its members, or persons associated with the exchange. Exchange Act §19(h).

Anticompetitive Tendencies

Despite its broad supervisory authority, the SEC has permitted the stock exchanges significant freedom of action, particularly in exchange rules that restrict competition among members. For example, the rules of the NYSE prohibit its members (that is, all of the major securities firms) from effectuating trades for their own accounts in NYSE-listed securities on other exchanges or in other markets — an *exclusive-dealing requirement*. Compare SEC Rule 19c-3 (prohibiting restrictions on off-exchange trading in stock listed on an exchange after April 26, 1979).

Challenges to such practices on antitrust grounds have not fared well. The Supreme Court, for example, upheld an earlier exchange rule that mandated minimum commissions by member firms on the theory that the SEC had regulatory power over commission rates. See *Gordon v. New York Stock Exchange*, 422 U.S. 659 (1975). In 1975, Congress amended the Exchange Act to prohibit this rate fixing. The end of fixed commission rates came on May 1, 1975 — Wall Street's famous "May Day." Exchange Act §6(e).

What Is an "Exchange"?

The Exchange Act defines the term broadly to include any facility "for bringing together purchasers and sellers of securities" or that performs "the functions commonly performed by a stock exchange as that term is generally understood." Exchange Act §3(a)(1). The act's definition and regulation assumes a "private club" structure typical of traditional U.S. stock exchanges, such as the NYSE: a not-for-profit corporation whose members (securities firms seeking a mechanism to buy and sell securities) have exclusive access to the exchange's trading facilities; the members share in the costs of the exchange and elect the exchange's board of directors.

The Exchange Act's regulatory reach has been tested by new proprietary trading systems that use computer technology to permit buyers and sellers to exchange information and transact securities. The SEC and the Seventh

Circuit faced this definitional question when a securities broker (along with a bank and clearing agency) created an electronic trading system in options on government securities. See *Board of Trade v. SEC*, 923 F.2d 1270 (7th Cir. 1991). The system allowed an options trader to place a buy or sell order in the broker's computer; the clearing agency would check for possible matches, completing the transaction whenever it found a match and notifying the buyer and seller of the completed transaction. Established exchanges concerned about unregulated competition claimed the trading system was an "exchange." But the SEC took the view (and the Seventh Circuit deferred to its judgment) that the system was not an "exchange" on the ground an "exchange" must involve some kind of centralized trading and provide buy or sell quotations on a regular or continuous basis. That is, an "exchange" is a place where investors have a reasonable expectation they can regularly execute buy and sell orders at stated price quotations.

Even if electronic trading systems are not exchanges, the systems remain subject to significant SEC supervision under the agency's authority to regulate broker-dealers (including their trading activities), as well as "securities information processors" and "clearing agencies." Moreover, the SEC has authority (which it has used) to exempt electronic trading systems if they involve a "limited volume of transactions." See Exchange Act §5 (last clause).

§8.1.2 Regulation of Over-the-Counter Market

The 1964 Amendments to the Exchange Act extended the self-regulatory scheme applicable to stock exchanges to the over-the-counter (OTC) market—the decentralized buying and selling of securities by broker-dealers using telephone and computer linkages. See Exchange Act §12(g). Although broker-dealers must register with the SEC and their activities are subject to regulation by the SEC and self-regulation by the FINRA (formerly the NASD), the OTC markets are not registered. See §11.2 (regulation of broker-dealers).

Market Makers

Before 1971, trading on the OTC was accomplished by telephone calls among broker-dealers using "commercial" sheets published by securities firms making a market in a particular security. Just as the stock exchanges depend on specialists to facilitate trading in a particular security, the OTC depends on *market makers*—securities firms that hold themselves out as willing to buy (at a bid price) and sell (at an asked price) particular securities. As a market maker, the firm indicates its willingness to buy or sell from its own account in reasonable quantities.

NASDAQ

In 1971, the NASD set up an electronic automated quotation system (NASDAQ) for selected OTC securities. Broker-dealers registered with the NASD (now FINRA) place "bid" and "ask" computer-based quotes for assigned securities—an electronic stock exchange. In 2001, NASDAQ was spun off by the NASD and became a stand-alone for-profit corporation, now regulated by FINRA.

§8.1.3 Alternative Trading Systems

New trading systems that compete with the NYSE and NASDAQ allow securities buyers and sellers to deal directly with each other through online trading systems—known as electronic communication networks (ECNs). The ECNs eliminate the usual intermediaries by allowing investors (both individuals and institutions) to place their orders online, for example, a limit order to buy 2,000 shares of General Electric at $19.50. Once placed, the ECN electronically matches the buy order with pending sell orders and executes the trade. If there are no matching sell orders, the buy order is posted until a matching sell order is received. The ECN receives a commission for its online matching service. See Exchange Act Rel. No. 40,760 (1998) (authorizing ECNs, to be regulated either as stock exchanges or broker-dealers). Some ECNs, such as Archipelago, are linked to NASDAQ and display the current high bids and low offers in NASDAQ's system, thus giving traders on the ECN a sense for current prices. Some ECNs, such as Instinet, are widely used by to institutional investors and account for a significant proportion of overall trading volume— 5 percent on the NYSE and 30 percent on NASDAQ.

§8.1.4 Regulation of Collateral Market Participants

The SEC has regulatory authority over collateral market participants. Firms that process and communicate information about transactions and quotes in securities must register with the SEC. Exchange Act §11A(b)(1). Transfer agents, clearinghouses, and others who help complete securities trades must also register with the SEC. Exchange Act §17A.

§8.2 REGULATION OF MARKET PRACTICES

The Exchange Act takes aim at some specific market practices identified as abusive during the legislative hearings following the 1929 stock market crash. Some provisions impose statutory prohibitions for specific conduct (price manipulation); other provisions authorize the SEC to create fine-tuned rules (short-selling and market manipulation); and yet other provisions leave the regulation to other regulatory agencies (trading on margin).

§8.2.1 Market Manipulation

One of the most sensational securities abuses of the 1920s, at least according to testimony in legislative hearings leading to the federal securities laws, was market manipulation by securities firms and corporate insiders. According to this testimony, market manipulation occurred when a pool of investors holding securities in a particular stock would effectuate real and sham transactions to create the appearance of rising prices in that stock. When investors enticed by this price movement began to buy at the inflated prices, the pool would sell. Eventually, the emptiness of the price rise would be exposed and prices would collapse. The pool would show handsome profits ("buy low, sell high") while the investors would bear the loss ("buy high, sell low").

The Exchange Act addresses market manipulation in a variety of ways:

Specific prohibitions

The Exchange Act expressly prohibits purposefully creating misleading appearances of active trading in all securities, other than government securities. Exchange Act §9(a) (originally limited to listed securities, but amended by Dodd-Frank to include all securities, including OTC securities). Specifically, the Act prohibits a variety of activities that create the misleading appearance of trading in securities, among them: wash sales and matched orders when the same person (or an affiliate) is essentially both buyer and seller; a series of transactions to induce the purchase or sale by others; and the false or reckless "touting" or spreading of rumors by broker-dealers or other traders to induce trading in such securities. See Exchange Act §9(a).

Express private action

The Exchange Act authorizes a private action for persons injured by market manipulation prohibited by §9. Exchange Act §9(e). The plaintiff must prove that the defendant acted "willfully" and that the price of the stock was affected by the prohibited manipulative acts. In addition, the court may require the posting of a bond to cover the defendants' attorneys' fees.

General antifraud prohibition

Courts have interpreted Rule 10b-5 to pick up where §9 leaves off. In particular, courts have read Rule 10b-5's broad prohibition against securities fraud to prohibit market manipulation in the OTC market. See *SEC v. Resch-Cassin & Co.*, 362 F. Supp. 964 (S.D.N.Y. 1973) (concluding that Rule 10b-5 incorporates the prohibitions of 9(a) with respect to OTC securities). Moreover, courts have interpreted Rule 10b-5 to cover a broader range of manipulative activities, such as trading in securities aimed at increasing the price for the benefit of a *different* seller. See *United States v. Mulheren*, 938 F.2d 364 (2d Cir. 1991) (applying Rule 10b-5 to market purchases allegedly intended to raise market price to benefit unrelated seller whose contract price was set at market; holding that evidence insufficient on issue of intent).

Issuer Repurchases

Issuers have incentives to buy their own stock and manipulate the trading price. An artificially high stock price serves to deter hostile takeovers or increase the value of stock-based executive compensation. An artificially low price reduces the cost of a management buyout. Yet, issuers also have completely legitimate reasons to trade in their stock, such as funding a pension plan or employee stock ownership plan or giving shareholders additional liquidity. The SEC has promulgated safe harbor Rule 10b-18 to distinguish between evil-hearted and good-hearted issuer repurchases. An issuer can repurchase its common shares in a "trickle in" process (analogous to the "trickle out" process for insiders under Rule 144, see §7.2.1) under specified circumstances:

- the issuer uses only one broker-dealer;
- their purchases must be part of regular midday trading, neither the opening trade of the day nor a trade in the last half hour of trading;
- the price may not exceed the lowest contemporaneous market bid or trading price; and
- the stock must be repurchased on an exchange or NASDAQ.

Special rules apply to issuer repurchases made in response to a hostile takeover bid. See Rule 10b-13.

Price Stabilization During Public Offering

The SEC has also used its broad §10(b) authority (along with other statutory authority) to promulgate rules that prohibit manipulation during a public distribution. See Regulation M (see §4.2.5). The SEC rules generally prohibit purchases during a distribution, but permit price stabilization activities under specified circumstances.

§8.2.2 Short Selling

Short selling allows an investor to make money in a falling market. A short sale is accomplished when the investor sells securities that he does not own, but has borrowed. Typically, the investor will borrow from a securities firm or institutional investor that has a long-term position in the securities. If the price falls between the time the investor sells the borrowed securities and the time the investor must deliver them to the buyer — under current SEC rules, no more than three business days — the seller can make money. On the delivery date, the seller simply buys equivalent securities at the lower price to return the borrowed securities to the lender. An example illustrates:

	Short seller . . .	Market Price
Day 1	borrows securities (usually broker-dealer) sells borrowed securities at market price	$25
Day 4	delivers borrowed securities (T+3) buys equivalent securities at current market	$22
Day 7	receives delivery of securities (T+3) returns borrowed securities to lender (broker-dealer)	

The short seller makes $3, less the cost of borrowing the securities for six days — usually at interest rates that the broker-dealer charges customers for carrying securities on margin. See Exchange Act §3(b); Rule 200, Regulation SHO (definition of short sale, former Rule 3b-3).

During legislative hearings leading to enactment of the Exchange Act, short selling was criticized for accelerating the decline in stock prices during the crash of 1929 as professional speculators made large profits by selling heavily without actually owning stock. Short-selling was also purportedly used by "pool operators" to drive down the price of a stock and then buy the artificially-depressed stock for a profit. Congress responded equivocally in 1934, authorizing the newly created SEC to deal with the matter. Exchange Act §10(a) (amended by Dodd-Frank to cover all securities, except government securities).

Up-Tick Rule: Ebb and Flow

To prevent free falls in stock prices, Congress authorized the SEC to regulate short selling. Exchange Act §10(a)(1). In 1938, the SEC used this authority to prohibit short selling in a falling market. Under the so-called "up-tick" rule, no short sale using borrowed securities could occur in exchanged-listed stock at a price lower than the last previous trade. Former Rule 10a-1. In other words, if the previous market price in our example had been $25.15, our short seller could not have sold at $25.14. She would have had to wait and sell to somebody at $25.16 or more.

Over time, many questioned the premise that short selling exacerbates market declines, instead pointing to the benefits of short selling to increase market liquidity and price efficiency. In 2007, after a one-year pilot program suspending the up-tick rule for certain securities, the SEC reviewed the results and determined that imposing price tests on short selling was unnecessary to protect against market volatility — even for thinly traded securities. Exchange Act Rel. No. 55,970 (2007). The SEC eliminated the up-tick rule (and also barred stock exchanges from imposing one). The agency pointed out that short selling by those who would try to improperly influence securities prices remains subject to general antifraud and antimanipulation rules. See Dodd-Frank §929X(b) (adding short selling to the list of manipulative practices covered by §9 of the Exchange Act).

Then the financial crisis of 2008 hit. The SEC again focused its attention on short sellers, who some blamed for the precipitous drop in the prices of bank and other stocks. Accepting the premise that short sellers exacerbated market pessimism, the SEC in late 2008 temporarily banned short selling in 799 financial stocks — with the purpose to stanch their free fall. Most observers believed the effort was ill-advised, arguing that short sellers helped the market to identify mispriced securities, as well as to uncover misleading accounting and other valuation mistakes about bank fundamentals.

Even after the temporary ban, short sellers continued to get a bad rap. In 2010, accepting the argument that short selling can cause stock prices to go into a free fall, the SEC adopted a variation of the up-tick rule. Exchange Act Rel. No. 61,595 (2010) (amending Regulation SHO). Under Rule 201, whenever a stock has an intra-day price decline of 10 percent or more from the previous day's closing price, short selling is banned in that stock except at a price above the current best bid. This ban, which applies to National Market System (NMS) securities, applies for the remainder of the day that the stock had fallen 10 percent, as well as the following day.

The SEC explained that its rule — which only bans short selling in a stock after a "circuit breaker" is triggered by a one-day price decline of 10 percent — would prevent abusive short selling, thus restoring investor confidence in the market. Some questioned the explanation and argued that the rule would actually weaken investor confidence because a declining stock might be seen as still overvalued given the absence of "corrective" short selling. A recent study supports this argument and finds that stocks suffering a one-day 10 percent decline actually recovered more quickly before the rule than after the rule. In short, Rule 201 (like the up-tick rule before it) just makes it harder for the messenger to deliver bad news.

Broker-Dealer Obligations

SEC rules (amended in Regulation SHO) impose duties on broker-dealers that effect sell orders on equity securities, wherever traded. The broker-dealer must mark each sell order either "long" (customer owns security) or "short" (customer does not own, but will borrow). Rule 200(g), Regulation SHO. The mark rules are meant to restrict "naked" short selling by price speculators who neither own nor have borrowed the sold securities.

In addition, if the customer must borrow to sell short, the broker-dealer must "locate" securities available for borrowing. Rule 203 (replacing former Rule 10a-1(d)). Broker-dealers are also subject to additional delivery requirements for securities for which there have been delivery problems in the past. Rule 203(b). In addition, Dodd-Frank requires broker-dealers, subject to specific SEC rules, to notify customers that they may elect not to allow their fully paid securities to be loaned to cover others' short sales. Dodd-Frank §929X.

Dodd-Frank further requires the SEC (1) to study the incidence of naked short selling and the effect of mandating real-time disclosure by short sellers, and (2) to adopt rules that require institutional investors subject to Section 13(f) of the Exchange Act to disclose publicly (at least every month) the amount of their short sales. Dodd-Frank §§417, 929X. As of 2013, the SEC has neither issued a study (though it has sought public comments) nor has it proposed a rule.

§8.2.3 Purchasing Securities on Margin

In its hearings on the collapse of financial markets that began in 1929, Congress identified the purchase of securities on margin as driving the speculation in securities in the 1920s and as explaining the precipitous collapse of securities prices during the crash of 1929. During the speculative 1920s, many securities firms and their affiliated banks pushed customers to buy securities by borrowing up to 90 percent of the purchase price. These loans, collateralized by the securities purchased, created business for the bank and more sales for the securities affiliate, which often sold newly issued securities for which it acted as underwriter. When stock prices began to fall, the value of the collateral fell and banks made "margin calls" demanding that customers sell securities to reduce the balance on their loans so that their fallen collateral would cover their loan balance. This selling exacerbated the decline in stock prices, leading to new margin calls. Prices spiraled downward.

The Exchange Act does not prohibit the purchase of securities on margin, but rather authorizes the Federal Reserve Board to set margin levels. Exchange Act §7. Regulation T of the Federal Reserve governs the extension of credit by securities market intermediaries, such as broker-dealers. (Other regulations govern lending by banks, other lenders, and foreign lenders). For many years, the margin requirement has been set at 50 percent — that is, an investor who buys on margin can borrow only up to 50 percent of the market value of the securities being purchased.

Although the Federal Reserve is authorized to mandate maintenance levels of margin after the initial purchase of securities with borrowed money, it has not done so. This means that margin calls — a demand that additional cash be added to the account or securities sold when the loan value exceeds a specified percentage of the aggregate securities value — are regulated by stock exchange rules and the practices of individual broker-dealers.

In addition, broker-dealers are subject to "truth in lending" requirements when they extend credit to a customer in a margin transaction. Rule 10b-16 (requires both initial and periodic written disclosure of the credit terms of margin loans).

§8.3 REGULATION OF PUBLIC COMPANIES

The Exchange Act completes the "truth in securities" regime started with the Securities Act's regulation of public securities offerings. To ensure the vitality and integrity of securities trading markets, the Exchange Act extends the disclosure regime for public offerings to public trading of securities. Companies whose shares are publicly traded must register with the SEC thus making them subject to a panoply of Exchange Act regulation:

- Registered companies must file *periodic disclosure* documents with the SEC, which makes them available to securities trading markets. Such companies (including companies that have made a public offering of securities under the Securities Act) are known as "reporting companies."
- Registered companies, to carry out their periodic reporting obligations, must *keep records* and maintain a system of internal accounting controls.
- Registered companies are subject to SEC proxy regulation when management (or others) *solicit proxies* on matters requiring shareholder

voting, such as the election of directors and fundamental corporate transactions. See §8.4.

- Any person who makes a *tender offer* for the equity securities of a registered company must make disclosures to the SEC, to the company's management, and to solicited shareholders. See §8.5.
- The directors, officers, and 10 percent shareholders of registered companies must *disclose their trading* in the company's publicly traded *equity* securities and are liable to the company if they make profits (or avoid losses) from such trading during any six-month window. See §10.3.

§8.3.1 Registration with the SEC

The Exchange Act requires companies with publicly traded securities to register their securities with the SEC; this registration operates for all practical purposes as a registration of the company. See Form 10 (disclosure comparable to that required in Securities Act registration statement).

There are two triggers that compel a company to register with the SEC and plug itself into the extensive Exchange Act regulation:

Companies with exchange-listed securities

Companies whose securities (*debt* or *equity*) are listed on a stock exchange must register with the exchange, with copies to the SEC. Exchange Act §12 (prohibiting trading by broker-dealers on the stock exchange in securities not registered). Stock exchange rules specify the qualifications that issuers must satisfy to have their securities "listed" for trading on the exchange. The "listing" rules serve a gatekeeper function that assures traders on the exchange that companies meet certain sales, assets, and net worth thresholds.

Companies that meet size thresholds

In 1964 Congress amended the Exchange Act to bring into its regulatory regime companies whose *equity* securities are publicly traded on the OTC markets. A company must register if it has a class of equity securities held of record by more than 2,000 shareholders (or more than 500 shareholders who are not accredited investors) and has total assets exceeding $10 million. Exchange Act §12(g); Rule 12g-1 (asset threshold increased to $10 million in

1996; shareholder thresholds revised in JOBS Act of 2012). In addition, securities held by persons who received the securities pursuant to an employee compensation plan are not counted as shareholders of record. Exchange Act §12(g)(5) (added by JOBS Act). The issuer must register within 120 days after the end of the fiscal year in which it first crosses both these thresholds.

Once registered, a company may *deregister* only under specified conditions. A company listed on a stock exchange can deregister upon the voluntary or involuntary delisting of its securities. Exchange Act §12(d). Deregistration of a company with OTC stock is more difficult, some calling it a "lobster trap." An OTC company can deregister only if it falls significantly below the thresholds that originally triggered registration — fewer than 300 equity shareholders of record, or a combination of fewer than 500 equity shareholders of record and less than $10 million in assets for its last three fiscal years. Rule 12g-4 (termination occurs 90 days after company makes certification).

Exemptions from Registration

A number of companies are exempt from Exchange Act registration, including registered investment companies (mutual funds), state-regulated insurance companies (provided they are not listed on a stock exchange or subject to §15(d) reporting), and nonprofit charities. Exchange Act §12(g)(2). Banks are subject to Exchange Act registration, whether their stock is listed or unlisted, but the panoply of regulation under the Act is administered by federal bank regulators.

Special Rules for "Emerging Growth Companies"

"Emerging growth companies" — companies with less than $1 billion dollars in annual revenues — receive regulatory dispensations under the Securities Act in their IPO. See JOBS Act §§101-108; see §4.2.2.

In addition, after their IPO, emerging growth companies are subject to reduced reporting and corporate governance requirements under the Exchange Act. Such companies may choose to include only two years of pre-IPO audited financial statements, instead of the usual three (see §8.3.2 below), may omit shareholder "say-on-pay" votes and related executive-pay disclosures, need not rotate their auditing firm as required by the PCAOB (see §8.3.4 below), and need not have an auditor attest to the company's internal controls (see §8.3.4 below). See JOBS Act §§102, 103.

"Emerging growth company" status continues for five fiscal years after the company's IPO or until the company (1) has $1 billion or more in annual revenues, (2) becomes a large accelerated filer by virtue of having at least $700 million in public float (same as a WKSI), or (3) raises more than $1 billion in nonconvertible debt over a three-year period. Securities Act §2(a)(19).

§8.3.2 Periodic Disclosure

Companies whose securities are registered under §12 of the Exchange Act become "reporting companies" and must make two kinds of filings with the SEC: (1) filings to keep their registration current, and (2) filings of annual, quarterly, and special reports that provide ongoing information to the SEC and securities trading markets. Exchange Act §13(a). Historically, the SEC has not carefully scrutinized these filings, but Sarbanes-Oxley now mandates that SEC staff perform "regular and systematic" review of the filings of each reporting company at least every three years. Sarbanes-Oxley §408.

These disclosure documents, filed with the SEC, are at the heart of the Exchange Act's regime of periodic disclosure. Unlike the prospectus in a registered offering under the Securities Act, which must be delivered to investors, periodic disclosure is not sent to shareholders. Instead, investors and securities professionals are *indirect* users of this SEC-filed information, now readily available on the SEC's website and on the websites of reporting companies.

The three important Exchange Act filings are:

Annual report (Form 10-K)	Reporting companies must file annually (within 90 days of the close of their fiscal year) an extensive disclosure document that contains much the same information as required in a Securities Act registration statement when a company goes public.
Quarterly report (Form 10-Q)	Reporting companies must file quarterly (within 45 days of the close of each of the company's first three fiscal quarters) a report that consists mostly of quarterly financial statements and updated risk-factor disclosure.
Special reports (Form 8-K)	Reporting companies must file (within 4 business days) a special report on specified, material developments.

Each of these disclosure forms gives detailed instructions, many of them contained in Regulation S-K. Besides disclosing itemized information, companies must avoid half-truths and are obligated to include material facts (even if not required by the forms) as necessary to make facts stated not misleading. Rule 12b-20.

Reporting companies must file their reports with the SEC in electronic form using the agency's electronic filing system — Electronic Data Gathering, Analysis, and Retrieval (EDGAR). Regulation S-T. The EDGAR system, which became required for U.S. registrants in 1996, automates the receipt, processing, and dissemination of disclosure documents filed with the SEC under the Securities Act, the Exchange Act, and the Investment Company Act. Company filings are available through the SEC website (http://www.sec.gov).

Certification of SEC Filings

As mandated by Sarbanes-Oxley, the SEC has adopted rules requiring corporate officers of reporting companies to certify the annual and quarterly reports filed with the SEC. Sarbanes-Oxley §302. Under SEC rules, the CEO and CFO must each certify that he reviewed the report and, based on his knowledge, that (1) it does not contain any material statements that are false or misleading, and (2) it "fairly presents" the financial condition and results of operation of the company — regardless of formal compliance with GAAP. Exchange Act Rules 13a-14, 15d-14 (certification not applicable to 8-K reports); see *United States v. Simon*, 425 F.2d 796 (2d Cir. 1970) (holding that auditor could be criminally liable for certifying false financials when accounting of self-dealing transaction was consistent with GAAP, but did not "fairly present" transaction).

In addition, the certifying officers must certify that they are responsible for establishing and maintaining "disclosure controls and procedures" that ensure material information is made known to them, and that these internal control were evaluated before making the report. If there are any significant deficiencies or changes in the internal controls, or any fraud by those who operate them, the certifying officers must disclose this to the company's auditors and the board's audit committee. Exchange Act Rules 13a-15, 15d-15, 15d-14.

To impress upon certifying officers the gravity of these tasks, Sarbanes-Oxley enhances the criminal sanctions for certifications that are knowingly or willfully false. Sarbanes-Oxley §906, 18 U.S.C. §1350 (requiring CEO and CFO to certify that periodic report "fully complies" with Exchange Act and "fairly presents" material financial condition and results). Knowing violations carry penalties up to $1 million and 10 years imprisonment, and willful violations up to $5 million and 20 years imprisonment.

According to the SEC, these provisions apply only to annual and quarterly reports, not special reports on Form 8-K.

Real-Time Disclosure

Once required for only a short list of significant events — such as bankruptcy, merger, or a director's non-amicable resignation — Form 8-K has been expanded by the SEC in response to post-Enron concerns that reporting companies often delay disclosing material developments between quarters. See Sarbanes-Oxley §409; Exchange Act §13(l) (requiring reporting companies to disclose material changes on "rapid and current" basis, as specified by SEC rule). As revised, Form 8-K moves closer to a continuous disclosure system. Exchange Act Rel. No. 49,424 (2004). Coupled with the incentives for broad-based disclosures created by Regulation FD (which prohibits selective disclosure by public companies, see §10.2.5), Form 8-K channels company disclosure of material developments into EDGAR on a real-time basis.

Form 8-K now requires disclosure of the following:

- **Operational events:** entry into (or termination of) definitive material agreements, loss of significant customer, bankruptcy or receivership
- **Financial events:** acquisition or disposition of assets, results of operations and financial condition (such as interim earnings statements), direct financial obligations or obligations under an off-balance sheet arrangements (or events triggering such obligations), restructuring charges, material impairments under existing agreements
- **Securities-related events:** delisting or transfer of listing, unregistered sales of equity securities, changes in debt rating, material modifications to rights of securities holders
- **Financial-integrity events:** changes in registrant's certifying accountant, non-reliability of previously issued financial statements or audit report
- **Governance events:** changes in corporate control, changes affecting directors or principal officers (departure, resignation, removal, election, appointment), amendments to articles or bylaws, waivers of company's code of ethics
- **Executive pay:** compensation agreements (attached to filing), compensation arrangements outside ordinary course of business

Significantly, Form 8-K reports must now be filed 4 days (not 15 days, as before) after the relevant event occurs. There is a curious wrinkle in the filing requirement when a reporting company voluntarily issues new or updated financial data, or voluntarily releases information pursuant to Regulation FD (see §10.2.5). In such event, the company must only "furnish" a Form 8-K to the SEC. By being furnished, not filed, the report does not trigger fraud liability under §18 of the Exchange Act (§8.3.3 below) or become incorporated by reference in other filings — thus encouraging interim financial disclosures.

The SEC created a safe harbor from Rule 10b-5 liability (but not SEC enforcement) for reporting companies that miss a Form 8-K filing, but disclose the information in the next periodic report. The safe harbor covers items that may not be immediately apparent: entry into (or termination of) definitive material agreements, direct financial obligations or obligations under an off-balance sheet arrangement (or events triggering such obligations), restructuring costs, material impairments, and nonreliability of previously issued financial statements or audit report.

Public Issuers — §15(d) Reporting Companies

The reporting requirements also apply to any company that has issued securities (debt or equity) in an offering registered under the Securities Act, even though the securities are not listed on a stock exchange and the company does not satisfy the size thresholds for Exchange Act registration. See Exchange Act §15(d); Rules 15d-1 to 15d-17 (requiring annual, quarterly, and special reports comparable to those required of companies registered under the Exchange Act). Such companies must commence reporting once the Securities Act registration is effective and may cease reporting only when at the beginning of a fiscal year the company has fewer than 300 record holders of the class of registered securities, see Exchange Act §15(d), or the company has fewer than 500 such record holders and less than $10 million in assets for each of the three most recent fiscal years. See Rule 12h-3.

Companies subject to reporting by virtue of §15(d), however, escape the Exchange Act regulation applicable to other activities of registered companies: proxy solicitations, tender offers, insiders' short-swing profits, and takeover bids.

Mandatory Disclosure

In theory, the mandatory reporting of the Exchange Act represents a "public good" that can be used by all participants in securities markets. Without a system of mandatory disclosure, management might not be inclined to provide for free such fulsome information, and traders would be reluctant to pay for it if others could use price signaling to "pirate" their information. To assure an adequate supply of company information, the system is mandatory and the information it produces is available to all.

Whether this system of mandatory disclosure is worth the costs has been a topic of ongoing debate. See §1.3.5 (evaluation of mandatory disclosure).

Supporters of the system point to the lower volatility and greater liquidity (and thus value) in securities markets when company disclosure is mandatory, as well as the greater opportunities for investors to monitor management compared to voluntary disclosure. Critics have pointed to the direct costs of compliance, the competitive costs of revealing company secrets, and the distortion of management behavior. For example, as the system moves toward one of continuous disclosure, some have observed that corporate executives myopically focus on short-term results.

§8.3.3 False or Misleading SEC Filings

The Exchange Act creates an express private cause of action against any person who makes a false or misleading filing under the Exchange Act. Exchange Act §18(a). The express remedy, however, erects for plaintiffs a number of significant hoops. Plaintiffs must show they purchased or sold securities in reliance on a defective filing, the price at which they transacted was affected by the defective filing, and such false filing caused their damages. See *Cramer v. General Telephone & Electronics*, 443 F. Supp. 516 (E.D. Pa. 1977) (dismissing complaint for failing to allege reliance and causation). Defendants can avoid liability by showing they acted in good faith and without knowledge that the filing was defective. In addition, courts can require the plaintiff to undertake to pay the defendant's costs and attorneys' fees and can assess these costs against the plaintiff if the defendant succeeds.

Courts have refused to imply a remedy for defective filings. See *In re Penn Central Securities Litigation*, 494 F.2d 528 (3d Cir. 1974) (holding that "§18(a) is the exclusive remedy for alleged violations of §13(a)"). Not surprisingly, plaintiffs have opted for the more developed, and sometimes less-demanding, route of the implied Rule 10b-5 action (see §9.1.3). For example, the fraud-on-the-market theory creates a presumption of reliance in the case of misinformation disseminated in developed trading markets. Moreover, plaintiffs in a Rule 10b-5 case are not limited to misinformation contained in Exchange Act filings but may base their claims on false press releases, statements by company officials, and even silence in the face of duties to correct or update prior information.

§8.3.4 Oversight of Corporate Misconduct

Public companies are subject to an array of regulations dealing with their oversight of illegal conduct and financial fraud. The regulations are the product of two congressional reform efforts, one following the revelation of widespread foreign bribery by U.S. companies in the 1970s and the other in response to accounting and financial scandals in the early 2000s.

Foreign Bribery

In 1978 Congress passed the Foreign Corrupt Practices Act (FCPA) in response to U.S. companies doctoring their books and setting up slush funds to pay bribes to high-placed foreign government officials. The FCPA prohibits reporting companies (and their executives) from making payments to foreign government officials to influence their official actions or decisions. Exchange Act §30A(a). In recognition of the way the world works, however, the FCPA excludes from its coverage "routine" payola to lower-level government officials to facilitate their performing their duties. Exchange Act §30A(b).

With expanding global commerce, U.S. companies are increasingly exposed to foreign corruption — which appears to be widespread according to a recent survey in which 32 percent of business managers worldwide reported that "firms like theirs" pay bribes to secure government contracts, particularly in low-income countries. Enforcement actions under the FCPA by the SEC are on the rise, as are prosecutions by the Department of Justice against individuals. See *In the Matter of Oil States Int'l, Inc.*, Exchange Act Rel. No. 53732 (2006) (finding that Oil States violated FCPA by reporting kickbacks to Venezuelan oil officials as ordinary business expenses, thus rendering company's books, records, and accounts not fairly and accurately reflecting financial transactions of issuer). In addition, shareholders now regularly sue directors, seeking reimbursement for penalties paid in FCPA settlements with the SEC and DOJ.

As you can see, the FCPA enlists U.S. public companies to deal with corruption in foreign countries. Dodd-Frank goes one step further, requiring the SEC to create rules for the disclosure by companies in the oil, gas, and minerals industries of any "payments" made to the U.S. and foreign governments. Dodd-Frank §1504 (requiring disclosure in company's annual report and online). The SEC adopted a rule requiring resource extraction issuers to include annual-report information about such payments, but the rule was vacated. Exchange Act Rel. No. 67,717 (2012), *vacated American Petroleum Inst. v. SEC*, 2013 WL 3307114 (D.D.C. 2013) (finding SEC misinterpreted law by forcing public disclosure detailing payments to foreign governments, and not exempting payments where foreign countries prohibit payment disclosure was arbitrary and capricious).

Recordkeeping and Internal Controls

As part of its crackdown on foreign bribery, the FCPA also addresses lax internal controls by reporting companies. The FCPA amended the Exchange Act to require reporting companies (1) to maintain financial records in "reasonable detail" to accurately reflect company transactions, and (2) to put into place internal accounting controls sufficient to provide "reasonable assurances" of internal accountability and proper accounting. Exchange Act §13(b)(2).

The open-ended nature of the FCPA record-keeping provisions was met with waves of alarm and protest from corporate executives, accountants, and lawyers. The corporate community pointed out that the reporting requirements of the Exchange Act already impliedly mandated that companies have internal controls, and the FCPA's vague standards invited administrative overreaching. Sensitive to this concern, the SEC has shown restraint in enforcing the FCPA provisions, using them to take action against lax or corrupt management, not inadvertent record-keeping mistakes. See *SEC v. World-Wide Coin Investment Ltd.*, 567 F. Supp. 724 (N.D. Ga. 1983) (ordering company and its officials, charged with lax accounting controls, to hire independent auditor to perform full accounting of company's operations and make full disclosure to shareholders); see also Exchange Act §13(b)(7) (reasonableness measured by standards of "prudent officials in the conduct of their own affairs").

Sarbanes-Oxley increased the scope (and burden) of internal controls on reporting companies beyond financial accountability. As required by Sarbanes-Oxley, the SEC has adopted rules that reporting companies include in their annual report a statement of management's responsibility over internal controls, a statement of how those controls were evaluated and an assessment of their effectiveness (or weaknesses) over the past year, and a statement that the company's auditors attested to management's assessment. Sarbanes-Oxley §404; Items 307 and 308, Reg. S-K; Exchange Act Rel. No. 47,986 (2003).

"Up the Ladder" Reporting by Lawyers

The SEC has promulgated a rule, as commanded by Sarbanes-Oxley, that requires lawyers "appearing and practicing before" the SEC to report evidence of a material violation of securities law or breach of fiduciary duty (or similar violation) to the company's general counsel or CEO. Sarbanes-Oxley §307. Failing an appropriate response, the lawyer must then report to the company's audit committee, another committee composed exclusively of outside directors, or the full board. This "up the ladder" reporting obligation applies both to inside and outside lawyers who represent or advise on securities matters — whether the company is public or going public. 17 C.F.R. §205 (see §12.5).

Auditor Regulation

Sarbanes-Oxley created the Public Company Accounting Oversight Board (PCAOB), a self-regulatory body modeled on the NASD (whose functions have since been assumed by the Financial Industry Regulatory Authority,

FINRA) and funded by public companies, with responsibility to register and inspect accounting firms that audit the financial statements of public companies. Sarbanes-Oxley §101. In addition, the PCAOB is charged with specifying the quality control, independence, and other standards of public company audits, and with investigating and disciplining violations of its audit rules.

Like the other securities SROs, the PCAOB and its rules are subject to SEC oversight. To avoid capture by the accounting profession, the five members of the Board (only two of which may be accountants) are appointed by the SEC. See *Free Enterprise Fund v. PCAOB*, 561 U.S. _____ (2010) (upholding Sarbanes-Oxley provisions on PCAOB appointment, but striking down and severing for-cause removal provision).

Sarbanes-Oxley promotes auditor independence in a number of ways. It requires that the company's audit committee approve in advance all audit services provided to the company. Sarbanes-Oxley §202, adding Exchange Act §10A(i). It lists non-audit services that auditors are prohibited from performing for their audit clients. The nine-item list of prohibited services is daunting: bookkeeping, financial information systems design, appraisal or valuation services, fairness opinions, actuarial services, internal audit outsourcing services, human resources functions, securities and investment-related services, legal or other expert services unrelated to the audit, and other services prohibited by the PCAOB. Sarbanes-Oxley §201, adding Exchange Act §10A(g) (any non-audit services not prohibited, such as tax services, must be preapproved by company's audit committee). In addition, the audit partner must be rotated every five years, and for one year after an audit no member of the audit team can become a financial/accounting officer of the issuer. Sarbanes-Oxley §§204, 206, adding Exchange Act §§10A(j),10A(l).

Company officials, or others acting under their direction, are prohibited from attempting to improperly influence an auditor in performing its duties. Sarbanes-Oxley §303, Exchange Act §13(b)(2). The SEC has explained that improper influence (which may be knowing or negligent) includes actions that lead to a misleading audit report, as well as actions that lead an auditor not to fully perform its duties. Rule 13b2-2(b); Exchange Act Rel. No. 47,890 (2003). The SEC has "exclusive authority" to enforce these prohibitions, including against lawyers who provide legal opinions to auditors.

Audit Committee Regulation

Extending federal securities law into corporate governance, Sarbanes-Oxley mandates that U.S. stock exchanges adopt listing standards on the composition and functions of the audit committee of listed companies. Sarbanes-Oxley §301, adding Exchange Act §10A(m). Under these new standards, the audit committee of listed companies (including foreign issuers and small business issuers) must be composed entirely of independent directors, as defined by the SEC. In addition, all reporting companies must disclose whether at least one member of the committee is a financial expert. Sarbanes-Oxley §407, Reg. S-K, Item 401 (defining "audit committee financial expert" as one with significant auditing, accounting, financial or comparable experience).

The governance listing standards must also specify that the audit committee of listed companies be responsible for appointing, compensating, and overseeing the company's independent audit firm—a curtailment of the power of the full board and shareholders over outside accountants. The audit committee (not the board) must have the authority to hire independent counsel and other advisers, their fees paid by the listed company. Rule 10A-3; Exchange Act Rel. No. 47, 654 (2003).

Whistleblower Protections and Bounties

Sarbanes-Oxley sought to "protect whistleblowers in public companies." Under the Act, individuals who report securities fraud to a federal agency, Congress, or a company supervisor cannot be retaliated against. Sarbanes-Oxley §806; 18 U.S.C. §1514A (public company and specified individuals cannot "discharge, demote, suspend, threaten, harass, or in any other manner discriminate" because of lawful reporting). If there is retaliation, the whistleblower can file a complaint with the U.S. Department of Labor within 90 days. OSHA then investigates the complaint, and civil penalties (back pay and attorney fees) can be imposed by the agency or in a court action against retaliating individuals and the company. Retaliation can also result in criminal penalties, including fines and prison terms up to 10 years. Sarbanes-Oxley §1107; 18 U.S.C. §1513(e).

Federal courts were not receptive to claims by whistleblowers under the Sarbanes-Oxley whistleblower scheme. In response, Congress in Dodd-Frank expanded the reach and rewards under an existing SEC whistleblower program, hoping to encourage more whistleblowers to come forward. Dodd-Frank §924 (requiring SEC to create new office to process whistleblower claims and to issue new rules); see Rule 21F, Exchange Act Rel. No. 64,545 (2011) (defining terms, outlining application procedures and decisionmaking on claims, and explaining program). Congress took note of an internal SEC report that the agency's existing program to reward whistleblowers in insider trading cases, which had been mandated by the Insider Trading Sanctions Act of 1988, had resulted in payments of only $160,000 to five whistleblowers over more than two decades.

Dodd-Frank changes the SEC program to reward whistleblowers for tips ("original information") leading to any type of SEC enforcement action, not just insider trading cases, where the monetary sanction exceeds $1 million. Dodd-Frank §922(a), adding Exchange Act §21F. In addition, Dodd-Frank raises the reward cap from 10 percent to 30 percent, with the rewards coming from an SEC fund (itself funded by monetary sanctions collected by the SEC). Dodd-Frank §922(b). To make sure the SEC takes the expanded program seriously, Dodd-Frank makes the SEC determination on whistle-blower claims subject to judicial (appellate) review and requires the agency to make an annual report on the program to Congress.

Dodd-Frank also strengthens the protections for whistleblowers from retaliation, adding an express private action (rather than the Department of Labor procedure) against employers who retaliate against them, with remedies including reinstatement and double back pay. Exchange Act §21F(h). Dodd-Frank also specifies that the whistleblower protection extends to subsidiaries of public companies.

Some have questioned whether the new whistleblower program will have untoward side effects. For example, employees charged with maintaining internal controls in public companies may well find it more lucrative to report financial discrepancies to the SEC, rather than corporate management. As one critic noted, "Every day compliance officers will have to decide whether they're working for the company or for themselves."

Codes of Ethics

Sarbanes-Oxley commands the SEC to require reporting companies to disclose whether they have adopted a code of ethics applicable to their top financial and accounting officers—and if not, explain why. Sarbanes-Oxley §406; Item 406, Reg. S-K. Any changes or waivers of the ethics code for such officers must be promptly disclosed on Form 8-K. Exchange Act Rel. No. 47,235 (2003).

Not to be outdone, the stock exchanges have *mandated* ethics codes—disclosure is not enough. NYSE §303A(10); NASDAQ Rule 4350(n). Under the NYSE rules, for example, listed companies must adopt and disclose (including on the company's website) a code of business conduct and ethics for directors, officers and employees, and promptly disclose any waivers of the code for directors or executive officers. The code should address conflicts of interest, corporate opportunities, confidentiality of information, fair dealing, protection and proper use of company assets, compliance with law (including insider trading rules), and encouraging the reporting of any illegal or unethical behavior. The code must include compliance standards and procedures to facilitate its effective operation. Exchange Act Rel. No. 48,745 (2003).

§8.3.5 Corporate Governance Listing Standards

The stock exchanges have long sought to assure the "quality" of companies whose securities are listed on the exchange. In response to the financial and accounting scandals that precipitated Sarbanes-Oxley, the stock exchanges revised (sometimes voluntarily and sometimes as required by statute) the corporate governance standards that apply to listed companies. Here are the corporate governance listing standards for the NYSE and NASDAQ (updated through 2010):

Corporate Governance Listing Standards (NYSE and NASDAQ)

Board independence	• Majority of directors must be "independent" • Board must determine directors have no "material relationship" with company (NYSE) or no "relationship that would interfere with independent" judgment (NASDAQ) • Determination of director qualifications disclosed in proxy statement (or annual report if company not subject to proxy rules)
"Independence" defined	Director not "independent" if • director is company employee, or director's family member is company executive (past three years) • director (or family member) receives annual payments from company (more than $120,000, past three years) • director (or family member) is affiliated with current or past auditor (past three years) • company executives sit on compensation committee of outside director's company (past three years) • company has significant dealings with outside director's company (NYSE: $1,000,000 or 2% of outside company's revenues; NASDAQ: $200,000 or 5% of outside company's revenues)
Executive sessions	• Independent directors must meet at regularly scheduled meetings without management • Company must have method for internal and shareholder communications to independent directors (NYSE only)
Audit committee	• Composed solely of three or more independent directors who are "financially literate," as required by Exchange Act §10A-3 • One non-independent, non-officer director allowed in "exceptional and limited" circumstances (NASDAQ only) • Members must meet SEC standards on independence; at least one member must meet SEC "financial expert" standard • Committee must have written charter delineating its purpose, an annual performance evaluation of the committee, and the committee's responsibilities

8. Securities Exchange Act of 1934

Nominating and compensation committee	• Composed solely of independent directors (NYSE and NASDAQ) or determined by majority of independent directors on board (NASDAQ only) • One non-independent, non-officer director allowed in "exceptional and limited" circumstances (NASDAQ only) • Committee must have a written charter delineating its purpose and responsibilities, available on the company's website
Shareholder approval of equity pay plans	• Shareholders must have "say on pay" of all equity-compensation plans, though not those plans adjusted or acquired in a merger (NYSE only) • Shareholders must also have say on any material revisions to equity-compensation plans
Code of conduct	• Company must adopt and disclose code of conduct that meets requirements of Sarbanes-Oxley • Any waivers for directors and officers must be approved by board and disclosed on Form 8-K
Corporate governance guidelines	• Company must adopt and disclose guidelines on director qualifications, compensation, education, responsibilities, management succession, annual evaluation, access to management (NYSE only) • Foreign private issuers must disclose how their corporate governance practices differ from those of domestic listed companies (NYSE only)
Audits	• Company must have internal audit function, cannot be outsourced to company's outside auditor (NYSE only) • Company must disclose receipt of audit opinion with "going concern" qualification (NASDAQ only)
Related party transaction	• Audit committee, or group of independent directors, must approve related party transactions (NASDAQ only)
Certification	• CEO must certify annually that company in compliance with governance listing standards (NYSE only) • Company must notify NYSE or NASDAQ if company executives become aware of material non-compliance • Independent director requirements not applicable to companies controlled 50% or more by individual, group, or another company
Exceptions	• Investment companies generally not subject to governance listing standards • Foreign private issuers not subject to governance listing standards, except SEC standards on audit committee independence

§8.4 PROXY REGULATION (A SUMMARY)

The Exchange Act authorizes the SEC to promulgate rules to curb management abuses in the solicitation of proxies identified during congressional hearings leading up to the Exchange Act. Exchange Act §14(a). The hearings revealed that permissive state corporate rules for proxy voting permitted management of public companies to obtain open-ended (sometimes indefinite) proxies from shareholders without informing them of the issues for shareholder decision or how their proxies would be cast. The result was that management effectively had come to wield a "rubber stamp" on all matters put to shareholder vote.

Exercising the authority granted by §14(a), the SEC has created a regime of proxy regulation for public companies registered under the Exchange Act. The unabashed goal is "corporate democracy." (A fuller description of shareholder voting in public corporations, including the regulation of proxy solicitations and the nature of proxy litigation) can be found in Alan R. Palmiter, CORPORATIONS: EXAMPLES & EXPLANATIONS (7th ed. 2012) (Chapter 6 — Shareholders' Role in Corporate Governance; Chapter 7 — Voting Structure; Chapter 9 — Federal Regulation of Proxy Voting; Chapter 10 — Proxy Fraud).

§8.4.1 Mandatory Disclosure in Proxy Solicitation

Any person (including management) who solicits proxies from public shareholders must file with the SEC and distribute to shareholders (whether record or beneficial owners) specified information in a stylized "proxy statement." Rule 14a-3(a). Fraudulent or misleading proxy solicitations (a term broadly defined in the SEC rules) are prohibited. Rule 14a-9.

Definitive copies of proxy materials must be filed with the SEC when first mailed to shareholders. In addition, preliminary proxy materials must be submitted for SEC review at least 10 days before being sent to shareholders. Rule 14a-6. (There is no prior SEC review when management solicits proxies for a routine annual meeting.) Over the last decade, the SEC has eased the restrictions on shareholder communications before and during a proxy solicitation. For example, SEC rules now permit any written and oral communications about a voting issue *before* the filing of a proxy statement, so long as actual voting authority is not sought and any written communications are filed. Rule 14a-12. This means that shareholders are free to talk to each other on corporate governance matters without first preparing, filing, and disseminating a disclosure document.

Management's proxy statement must contain information about the corporation, the background of all director nominees, management's compensation and conflicts of interest, and any other matters being voted on. Schedule 14A. If the solicitation is for the annual election of directors, management also must send the corporation's "annual report to share-holders"—the typically glossy document that summarizes the company's direction, its operations, and current financial information. Rule 14a-3(b) (specifying content of "annual report to shareholders"). The proxy rules ensure a flow of information from public companies to their shareholders. In fact, for many public companies, the rules represent the only state or federal regulation that requires periodic corporate communications to shareholders.

§8.4.2 No Open-Ended Proxies

SEC rules regulate the form and content of the actual proxy card on which shareholders authorize their proxy to cast their votes. Rule 14a-4. The card must specify who is making the solicitation and can relate to only one specific meeting; it must specify the matters and directors on which share-holders are expected to vote; it must give shareholders a chance to vote for or against (or abstain from) each matter; and it must give shareholders a chance to withhold their vote for any and all directors. The proxy holder must follow the shareholder's instructions.

§8.4.3 Shareholder Access

The SEC proxy rules give shareholders access to public companies' proxy machinery in two ways. First, the rules impose a "common carrier" obli-gation on management to mail, either separately or together with the com-pany's proxy materials, any shareholder's solicitation materials if the shareholder pays for the costs of the mailing. Rule 14a-7. Management can avoid this "common carrier" obligation by giving the soliciting share-holder a current list of names and addresses of shareholders and any nomi-nees who hold shares on behalf of beneficial owners.

Second, management must include at corporate expense "proper" shareholder proposals with the company-funded proxy materials sent to shareholders. Rule 14a-8. The rule specifies which shareholders may make proposals, the procedures for their submission, management's obli-gations to include proper proposals, the grounds for management to exclude improper proposals, and procedures for the SEC to review management's decision to exclude. The exclusions serve three broad purposes: (1) to preserve management prerogatives over corporate decisionmaking; (2) to protect from interference management's usual solicitation efforts; and (3) to filter out illegal, deceptive, and crackpot proposals. Lately, the shareholder proposal rule has become an important device for shareholders (particularly institutional shareholders) to place corporate governance reforms on the corporate voting agenda.

In addition, the SEC promulgated a rule — as authorized by §971 of Dodd-Frank — that would require public companies to give shareholders access to the company-funded proxy materials for the nomination of directors. Rule 14a-11; Securities Act Rel. No. 9136 (2010). Under the rule a nominating shareholder (or group of shareholders) that held at least 3 percent of the company's voting shares (and had held this qualifying percentage for at least three years) could nominate a "short slate" of up to one-fourth of the company's board. The nominating shareholder had to give the company 150 days notice and provide full disclosure of its candidates, whose presence on the board could not violate state or federal law, or stock exchange rules.

This "proxy access" rule was challenged in court, and the D.C Circuit vacated it under the Administrative Procedure Act on the ground that the SEC had "neglected its statutory responsibility to determine the likely economic consequences of Rule 14a-11 and to connect those consequences to efficiency, competition, and capital formation." *Business Roundtable v. SEC*, 647 F.3d 1144 (D.C. Cir. 2011). As of 2013, the SEC has not addressed the court's concerns or tried to repromulgate the rule. Nonetheless, proxy access is permitted under state law on a company-by-company basis, and activist shareholders have used the shareholder proposal rule to initiate bylaw amendments creating proxy access at specific companies.

§8.4.4 Liability for Proxy Fraud

Federal courts have inferred a private cause of action for shareholders to seek relief for violations of the SEC proxy rules, particularly the proxy antifraud rule. See *J. I. Case Co. v. Borak*, 377 U.S. 426 (1964). Over time, federal courts have laid out the elements of a federal proxy fraud case:

Element	Supreme Court interpretation
Misrepresentation or omission	There must be a misrepresentation or misleading omission of fact. Opinions are also actionable if they misstate the speaker's true beliefs *and* mislead about the subject matter of the statement. *Sandberg v. Virginia Bankshares*, 501 U.S. 1083 (1991).
Materiality	The misrepresentation or omission must be material. See *TSC Industries, Inc. v. Northway, Inc.*, 426

	U.S. 438 (1976) (substantial likelihood that "reasonable shareholder" would consider the information important in how to vote).
Culpability	The Supreme Court has not addressed the question, and lower courts are split on whether the speaker must have known the misstatement was false or misleading. Some cases suggest negligent misstatements are actionable; others require a showing of scienter.
Reliance	Reliance is presumed, and actual reliance by shareholders need not be shown, if the allegedly false or misleading information was material. See *Mills v. Electric Auto-Lite Co.*, 396 U.S. 375 (1970).
Causal link to transaction	The proxy solicitation must be "an essential link to the accomplishment of the transaction." *Mills v. Electric Auto-Lite Co.*, 396 U.S. 375 (1970). There is no causal link if the vote of minority shareholders was unneeded to accomplish the challenged transaction. *Sandberg v. Virginia Bankshares*, 501 U.S. 1083 (1981).

Both injunctive relief (enjoining a vote or calling for a new vote) and damages are available to remedy proxy fraud. Federal courts often inquire into the fairness of a completed transaction on which shareholders voted and impose damages that effectively reformulate the terms of the transaction. The Supreme Court has endorsed the awarding of attorneys' fees to successful plaintiffs on the theory that proxy fraud suits benefit the body of shareholders. *Mills v. Electric Auto-Lite Co.*, 396 U.S. 375 (1970).

§8.5 REGULATION OF TENDER OFFERS (A SUMMARY)

In 1968 Congress passed the Williams Act to plug gaps in the regulation of corporate acquisitions. While federal proxy rules apply to voting contests and to negotiated acquisitions requiring a shareholders vote, and Securities Act registration applies when securities are issued in a merger or tender offer, no federal securities regulation prior to 1968 applied to the buying of a *control block for cash* in open-market purchases or a tender offer.

The Williams Act, which grafted new provisions onto the Exchange Act, regulates corporate control changes. (A fuller description of the mechanics, defenses and regulation involving corporate takeovers can be found in Alan

R. Palmiter, Corporations: Examples & Explanations (6th ed. 2009) (Chapter 34 — Takeover; Chapter 38 — Federal Regulation of Tender Offers; Chapter 39 — Takeover Defenses.)

§8.5.1 Disclosure of 5 Percent Ownership

To signal to the market (as well as target management) that the company may be in play, any person (or group) that acquires beneficial ownership of more than 5 percent of a registered company's equity securities must file a disclosure document with the SEC. Exchange Act §13(d). The filing, known as a Schedule 13D, must disclose (1) the identity and background of the acquirer and any group member, (2) the source and the amount of funds for making the purchases, (3) the number of the target's shares held by the acquirer, (4) any arrangements that the acquirer has with others concerning shares of the target, and (5) the acquirer's purposes for the acquisition and his intentions with respect to the target. The Schedule 13D must be filed within 10 days after the 5 percent threshold is passed, thus giving an acquirer a 10-day window during which to buy stock on the open market.

Passive investors, including institutional investors that acquire shares for portfolio investment, owning less than 20 percent of a company's equity securities qualify for a simplified Schedule 13G. For passive investors whose holdings change 5 percent or less, this disclosure is filed at year's end. An investor that initially qualifies for Schedule 13G, but whose objectives change, must file a Schedule 13D within 10 days.

§8.5.2 Disclosure in Tender Offer

To ensure shareholders make informed buy-sell-hold decisions in response to a bid for their shares, any tender offer for a registered company's equity securities that would result in the bidder holding more than 5 percent of the target's securities is subject to disclosure requirements. Exchange Act §14(d). The bidder must file a disclosure document, known as Schedule TO (formerly Schedule 14D-1), with the SEC on the day it commences the tender offer — that is, typically when the actual offer is first published. Rule 14d-2 (amended 2000). The bidder then transmits the offer to shareholders, with the compulsory cooperation of the target, usually by mailing the formal offer, along with a cover letter and summary term sheet.

Schedule TO (and the summary term sheet) include much the same information about the bidder and its plans as Schedule 13D, describing the terms of the tender offer, past negotiations between the bidder and the target, the bidder's financial statements (if material), and any regulatory requirements that may be applicable to the bid.

So shareholders hear the other side of the story, target management must make a statement responding to any third-party tender offer within 10 business days after the bid. Rule 14e-2 (management must in Schedule 14D-9 either oppose or support the bid, take a neutral position, or take no position at all).

The SEC has equalized the regulatory treatment of cash and stock bids. Regulation M-A (adopted in 1999). Before, a bidder that proposed to acquire a target's shares in a stock-for-stock exchange first had to register its securities under the Securities Act before commencing its exchange offer — while a bidder offering cash faced no such delay or uncertainty. The SEC now permits a bidder to solicit tenders in a stock-for-stock exchange offer before the registration statement is effective, so long as the actual exchange of securities occurs only after effectiveness. Rule 162. This allows the bidder to distribute one information document that combines the preliminary prospectus and tender offer disclosure. The deal can then be closed after 20 business days, the minimum time a tender offer must be kept open. The SEC staff has committed itself to approve effectiveness of the registration statement within this 20-day period.

§8.5.3 Regulation of Substantive Terms of Tender Offer

To safeguard shareholders against being stampeded into tendering, the tender offer rules depart from the "disclosure-only" philosophy of federal securities regulation by prescribing certain terms for third-party tender offers. As of 2010, the combination of statutory and administrative rules require:

- The tender offer must be open to all shareholders of the same class for at least 20 business days. Rules 14d-10(a)(1), 14e-1(a).
- The offer must remain open for an additional 10 business days after any change in the offering price or the percentage of securities being sought. Rule 14e-1(b).
- Shareholders can withdraw their shares (revoke their tenders) at any time while the tender offer is open. Rule 14d-7. The shareholder must be paid the best price paid to any other shareholder during the tender offer, and if the bidder offers consideration alternatives (such as a choice of cash or debentures), each shareholder can choose. Rules 14d-10(c)(1), 14d-10(a)(2).
- When the bidder seeks less than all the shares and shareholders tender more shares than the bidder seeks, the bidder must purchase the tendered shares on a pro rata basis and return the unpurchased shares. Exchange Act §14(d)(6); Rule 14d-8.

- The bidder must promptly pay for or return securities when the tender offer expires. Rule 14e-1(c).
- While the bid is pending, the bidder cannot purchase outside the tender offer. Rule 14e-5.

In 1998 the SEC used its rulemaking authority under Exchange Act §14(e) to impose some of these terms on mini-tender offers of 5 percent or less, which are not regulated under §14(d). Regulation 14E. On the theory that incomplete disclosure in a mini-tender offer would violate the §14(e) antifraud provisions, the SEC also "recommended" to bidders in a mini-tender offer to disclose—and disseminate to shareholders—information on the bidders' and acquisition plans, its ability to finance the offer, the bid price (particularly if below market), any withdrawal rights, any procedures for pro rata acceptance if the offer is oversubscribed, and any other conditions placed on the offer.

§8.5.4 Liability for Deception in Tender Offers

The Williams Act also contains a broadly worded antifraud provision, which courts have read to imply a private cause of action. Section 14(e) prohibits any false or misleading statement, as well as any fraudulent, deceptive, or manipulative act, in connection with any tender offer or any solicitation for or against tenders. Although modeled on §10(b), §14(e) does not contain the "sale or purchase" language of the latter, suggesting that nontendering shareholders and nonpurchasing investors who lack standing under Rule 10b-5 may be protected by §14(e). Nonetheless, "unfair" bids are not regulated by §14(e), which the Supreme Court has interpreted to mandate only full disclosure. *Schreiber v. Burlington Northern, Inc.*, 472 U.S. 1 (1985). See §9.3.1.

The avowed purpose of the Williams Act was to give shareholders the means to evaluate takeover bids and assure a level playing field in the take-over game between bidders and management. Nonetheless, many commentators have criticized the Act as having a pro-target bias. In fact, studies indicate that in the years immediately after the Act was passed in 1968, takeover premiums increased from 32 to 53 percent, while the frequency of takeovers declined. By imposing disclosure and timing impediments on bidders, without limiting the defensive arsenal of targets, the Act may actually tilt the playing field in favor of the target's management. During the mandated pendency of a tender offer, management has the opportunity to mount a defense whose substantive terms are beyond federal review under the Williams Act's antifraud prohibitions.

Examples

1. Bombastic Brewery is a microbrewery with macro plans. It wants to expand the marketing of its special Upper Ukrainian beers and create a chain of Pompous Pubs at which customers can enjoy their favorite Bombastic brews. The company raises $3.5 million from 1500 investors in a Regulation A offering made on the Internet (§5.2.3).

   a. The company specifies that stock issued in its Reg A offering must be held in "street" name with brokerage firms specified by Bombastic as "qualified nominees." The idea is to keep the number of record shareholders below 500. Does this allow Bombastic to avoid registration under the Exchange Act?

   b. Bombastic abandons its street-name ploy. At year's end, with the successful completion of its Reg A "mini registration" offering, Bombastic has 1600 record shareholders and its books reflect total assets of $7 million. Is Bombastic subject to the SEC reporting requirements?

   c. Bombastic's shares begin to trade in a thin OTC market, though Bombastic does not register with the SEC. Management, however, wishes the company had. Remember that Rule 144 permits insiders to sell their shares into trading markets if the company is subject to Exchange Act reporting requirements. See §7.2.1. Can Bombastic register voluntarily?

   d. Bombastic also considers getting investor attention by listing its stock on the New York Stock Exchange. Can Bombastic list voluntarily on the NYSE? What about being quoted on NASDAQ?

2. Bombastic Brewery grows, registers with the SEC, and begins filing periodic reports under the Exchange Act. With over half of U.S. households owning a computer and connected to the Internet, Bombastic plans to use this new marketing avenue to individual investors. Any problems with the following under the federal securities laws?

   a. Bombastic seeks to increase the depth of trading in its Internet-issued stock. The company sets up an online message board for investors to specify "bid" and "ask" offers. Investors can trade on the posted terms and have the deal closed by an independent clearing agency (registered with the SEC) that Bombastic has hired.

   b. Bombastic announces on its website an unregistered "dividend reinvestment plan." The announcement has a hypertext link to the website of the company's independent agent, which posts a brochure describing the plan and how to get an enrollment card.

   c. Trading by investors using Bombastic's online message board is slow. To make it easier for shareholders to trade, Bombastic sets up something akin to a Dutch auction. It revises its website to permit shareholders to leave "buy" and "sell" orders that specify price and amount. At the end of each day, Bombastic matches the orders to arrive at a "median" price that clears most of the orders.

d. Bombastic decides against its trade-matching system and begins another Reg A offering on the Internet. To ensure that its stock price doesn't dip during the offering, Bombastic places "bid" offers on its bulletin board, always above the offering price.

e. The Reg A offering closes, and Bombastic's stock price sags. So Bombastic insiders begin to purchase company stock using the online bulletin board to raise the price and discourage any hostile buys of the company stock.

f. Some investors expect a downturn in the overbuilt microbrewery industry. They borrow Bombastic shares using the online bulletin board and then sell "short" on the bulletin board.

3. As large, established brewers enter the microbrewery business, Bombastic is squeezed by the new competition. Its earnings, which had before trended upward, begin to slip. Bombastic's management worries that for the first time its next quarterly earnings will be negative. Bombastic wants to revalue its accounts receivable (mostly from its Pompous Pubs), which its current auditor believes should reflect an allowance of 50 percent for doubtful accounts. Identify whether Bombastic has any disclosure obligations:

a. Bombastic management would like to replace its current outside auditor with a new auditor that management believes would accept a valuation of accounts receivable at 85 percent of face value — a plausible result under GAAP.

b. Bombastic management would prefer to delay telling its shareholders that earnings have dropped and might be negative, at least until the end of the current quarter.

c. Bombastic management plans to ask its new auditing firm, which offers to provide non-auditing services at reduced rates, to establish a system of internal controls to assure accurate financial reporting and compliance with legal requirements.

d. Bombastic hires you as its outside lawyer to advise on disclosure issues. In the course of talking to company executives, you learn that Bombastic has a policy that executives can reserve the company's Pompous Pubs for personal parties — without paying. When you ask about this policy, the company's CEO explains that it is "just good marketing."

e. Bombastic is listed on NASDAQ. You sit on the company's audit committee and, as the company's outside lawyer, receive an annual retainer of $150,000. Your legal background and financial literacy makes you an ideal member of the committee.

f. Bombastic is about to file its quarterly report with the SEC. The CEO asks you what disclosure obligations she has in connection with the filing.

4. Bombastic reports lower earnings and begins to look for ways to cut expenses. In particular, it notices the printing and distribution costs of fulfilling its SEC disclosure obligations. Any problems with the following cost-cutting measures?

a. Bombastic's annual shareholder's meeting is approaching. Bombastic proposes to e-mail those shareholders who have previously consented to electronic delivery of company disclosures electronic notice. The e-mail would contain links to the company's proxy statement and annual report to shareholders on its website.

b. The e-mail would also link to a corporate website where shareholders could enter a password and vote their shares online.

c. Bombastic includes a video in its electronic annual report to shareholders, not available in the paper version, that shows the company's new brewery facilities and has interviews with company executives and employees. The video is accessible on the company's website.

d. Among the interviews in the video is one with Bombastic's CEO, who grandiloquently says, "I'm sure we'll double our barrel shipments over the next two years."

5. The microbrewery business begins to really boom and Bombastic leads the way, becoming the nation's largest microbrewer and the owner of a burgeoning chain of Pompous Pubs. Norman Ventures Ltd., a thirsty takeover firm, focuses its sights on Bombastic. Identify any regulatory problems with the following.

a. Since most of Bombastic's shareholders are computer literate, Norman posts a message on Bombastic's electronic bulletin board announcing that Norman plans to vote against management's slate of directors.

b. After a couple of weeks, Norman posts a new message urging fellow shareholders to also vote against management's slate of directors.

c. After a few more weeks, Norman announces that it might propose its own slate of directors and asks Bombastic shareholders to send e-mail messages saying whether they would support a Norman-led insurgency.

d. Norman receives some favorable responses to its proposal for an insurgency, including from a handful of larger Bombastic shareholders who together with Norman hold more than 10 percent of Bombastic's shares.

e. Norman opens a website of its own to further its growing proxy insurgency. Under the heading "Disquieting News about Bombastic," it states. "Bombastic's directors have received sizeable undisclosed fees." This is not true.

6. Norman Ventures loses its proxy fight; Bombastic's incumbent directors are reelected. Bombastic makes another successful public offering of its securities on the Internet, and its electronic bulletin board becomes one of the most heavily used financial websites. Norman has not lost its thirst for Bombastic and begins buying Bombastic stock.

    a. Norman makes purchases of Bombastic stock, but hides its identity and intentions using a variety of e-mail accounts around the country. If Bombastic shareholders knew the reason for the rising Bombastic stock prices, it is unlikely any would want to sell at current prices. Must Norman disclose its holdings and intentions?

    b. After acquiring 4.9 percent of Bombastic, Norman tests the waters for a $65 takeover of Bombastic. Norman asks The Karla Fund, a mutual fund specializing in the so-called spirits industry, which already owns 2 percent of Bombastic, whether Karla would be willing to sell into a $65 tender offer for Bombastic. Karla says $65 would be acceptable. Must Norman report this contact?

    c. Norman passes the 5 percent threshold and within 10 days acquires 11 percent of Bombastic. Norman discloses to the SEC that "we are considering our options, including gaining control of Bombastic." At 2:00 P.M. on a Friday afternoon, Norman sends identical e-mail messages to 30 of Bombastic's largest shareholders (mostly institutional investors) asking them to sell privately at $60. Norman explains to each shareholder that it is making the same offer to other large shareholders and must receive an answer by 5:00 P.M. Is this legal?

7. Norman Ventures abandons its market purchases and instead plans a conventional tender offer. Norman outlines its proposal and asks you to point out any problems.

    a. Any shareholder will be allowed to tender, though Norman will buy only 75 percent of Bombastic's stock, which would bring its total holdings to a comfortable 86 percent.

    b. The offer will be open on a first-tendered, first-purchased basis until the 75 percent threshold is reached.

    c. Consideration will be $65 cash or $70 in subordinated notes of Norman, at the option of each tendering shareholder, provided that no more than 50 percent of those tendering choose cash.

    d. The offer will be open for 20 business days, and tendering shareholders can withdraw their shares during the first 7 business days after the offer.

    e. Norman will follow the tender offer with a back-end merger in which the remaining shares will be acquired for subordinated notes of Bombastic worth $50.

    f. Norman will disclose: "If the offeror succeeds in gaining control of Bombastic, it will study Bombastic's business operations and prospects, and may decide to implement an alternative plan of operations."

    g. Norman will purchase shares on the open market, at prevailing prices, and only after disclosure, both during and after the tender offer.

    h. Norman will not buy any shares pursuant to the tender offer unless Bombastic's board redeems its poison pill and Norman obtains a commitment to sell junk bonds to finance the deal.

Explanations

1. a. No. If Bombastic's year-end assets surpass $10 million, it cannot avoid registration by manipulating the number of record shareholders. Companies whose shares are traded on the OTC market must register when the company is large enough to be of market interest and can afford SEC registration ($10 million in assets) and has enough equity shareholders so there is a likely trading market in its shares (500 record shareholders). Exchange Act §12(g); Rule 12g-1. The size standard refers to "record" shareholders so management can know with certainty when it has passed the numerical threshold. But if management manipulates the manner in which shareholders hold their shares to circumvent registration, SEC rules provide that "beneficial" owners count as record owners. Rule 12g5-1(b)(3).

   b. No, not yet. Company reporting is required under the Exchange Act only if the company's securities are listed on a stock exchange, it meets certain size criteria, or it has had a registered offering under the Securities Act of 1933. See §§12(a), 12(g), 15(d). In our example, Bombastic does not have securities traded on a stock exchange. Nor does it meet the current size thresholds for registration. Exchange Act §12(g); Rule 12g-1 (asset threshold increased in 1996 to $10 million). Although it issued its securities in a Reg A offering, which is sometimes referred to as a "mini-registration," this offering does not involve the filing of a registration statement under the Securities Act. Instead, a Reg A offering is accomplished under an exemption from registration pursuant to the SEC's exemptive authority under §3(b)(1) of the Securities Act. See §5.2.3.

   c. Yes. Voluntary registrations are permitted. Exchange Act §12(g)(1) ("Any issuer may register any class of equity security"). Some companies do this so insiders and others with restricted securities can trade under the safe harbor Rule 144 without being subject to the Securities Act registration requirements for secondary

377

distributions. See Securities Act Rule 144(c) (condition that issuer be registered under the Exchange Act and a reporting company for at least 90 days).

d. No. Listing on a stock exchange and quotation on NASDAQ is not available to all companies. Both the NYSE and NASDAQ have their own minimum listing requirements for equity securities.

As of 2013, the NYSE permits listing of companies with a minimum $4 stock price that satisfy the following general criteria:

- Distribution and size criteria (all of following)
  - 400 U.S. round lot holders (100 shares/lot)
  - 1,100,000 publicly held shares outstanding
  - $40 million market capitalization
- Financial criteria (any of following)
  - $10 million in aggregate *pretax earnings* for last three years (minimum $2 million annually)
  - $12 million in aggregate *pretax earnings* for last three years (minimum $5 million most recent year)
  - $25 million in aggregate *cash flow* for last three years (plus $500 million in global market value and $100 million in revenues in most recent 12 months)
  - $75 million in *revenues* in most recent fiscal year (plus $750 market capitalization)
  - $75 million in *total assets* in most recent fiscal year (plus $50 million in shareholder equity and $150 million market capitalization)

As of 2013, to be eligible for quotation through NASDAQ (Global Market), the issuer must have at least 400 shareholders (round lot holders of 100 shares/lot) and 1,100,000 publicly held shares outstanding, as well as a $4 minimum stock price and meet one of the following standards:

- Income standard
  - $1 million pre-tax income (latest fiscal year)
  - $15 million in shareholders' equity
  - $8 million public float
  - Three market makers
- Equity standard
  - $30 million in shareholders' equity
  - $18 million public float
  - Three market makers
- Market value standard
  - either $75 million market capitalization
  - $20 million public float
  - Four market makers

- Total assets/revenues standard
  - $75 million total assets + $75 million total revenues
  - $20 million public float
  - Four market makers

2. a. Problem. This example illustrates the two regulatory issues that arise whenever a person facilitates securities trading:

(1) Is the Bombastic electronic bulletin board a "securities exchange"? The Internet-based bulletin board is probably not a securities exchange because there is no centralized trading on stated buy-sell quotations on a regular or continuous basis. Investors can only post "bid" and "ask" offers; they have no expectation that these orders will be regularly executed at quoted prices. See *Board of Trade v. SEC*, 923 F.2d 1270 (7th Cir. 1991).

(2) By setting up the bulletin board, is Bombastic acting as a broker-dealer? On comparable facts, the SEC concluded an issuer is not a "broker-dealer" if it does not effectuate trades. See State Spring Brewery, SEC No-Action Letter (Mar. 22, 1996). There the issuer created an Internet website (called Wit-Trade) to facilitate trading by its shareholders after the company completed the first-ever Internet public offering. In an unusually quick decision that evidenced the SEC's agenda to encourage noncentralized and electronic markets, the SEC permitted Wit-Trade, conditioned on the issuer:

- using an independent agent, such as a bank or escrow agent, to directly handle the money used to buy and sell shares;
- publishing warnings on the online system regarding the risks involved in investing in illiquid securities; and
- disclosing a complete history of recent trades that showed the price and number of shares transacted.

SEC staff has blessed other issuer-created electronic bulletin boards in which the issuer remains passive. See PerfectData Corp., SEC No-Action Letter (Aug. 5, 1996) (issuer only assists in posting information, and any trades are effected by direct contact between users).

b. Problem. Bombastic's hypertext link to its agent may involve too much issuer involvement, transforming the transaction from a market reinvestment into an issuer distribution. The SEC has taken the position that dividend reinvestment plans must be registered under the Securities Act if the issuer's involvement in the plan goes beyond administrative or ministerial functions. See Securities Act Rel. No. 4790 (1965), Rel. No. 5515 (1974), Rel. No. 6188 (1980) (permitting such plans if issuer does no more than provide name and address of independent agent from whom additional information can be obtained). That is, if the independent agent handles the transaction, it is treated as the equivalent of a shareholder cashing a dividend check to buy additional shares on the market. Anticipating situations similar to our example, the SEC staff has taken the view that an issuer cannot use its website to advertise a dividend reinvestment plan, such as by providing a hypertext link directly to the plan materials. See Use of Electronic Media by Broker-Dealers, Transfer Agents, and Investment Advisers for Delivery of Information, Exchange Act Rel. No. 37,182 (1996).

c. Problem. Bombastic has perhaps crossed the line to become both a broker-dealer and a securities exchange. By assisting users to match orders, Bombastic has probably stepped across the boundary into the "regular business" of effecting securities transactions for the accounts of others, making it a "broker." Exchange Act §3(a)(4) (see Chapter 11). In addition, the matching system creates a centralized trading facility in which investors can expect that trades will be effectuated at or near daily quotes. The SEC has taken the view that a similar electronic matching system constituted a "securities exchange," though the SEC granted an exemption to the system "by reason of the limited volume of transaction effected on such exchange." Exchange Act Rel. No. 28,899 (1991) (granting exemption to Wunsch Auction Systems pursuant to authority under §5 of the Exchange Act to exempt an exchange when regulation is unwarranted by reason of exchange's small volume). The exemption applied to a computer-arranged auction for trading by institutional customers and broker-dealers that entered "bid" and "ask" orders in NYSE securities after NYSE-trading hours. The computer reviewed the orders and determined an optimal price for clearing the submitted bids. For example, if the computer determined that 25.48 was the optimal price for matching supply and demand, then all "bid" orders at or above 25.48 would be matched with "ask" orders at 25.48 or below. The orders would all be filled at 25.48, a price satisfying all matched sellers and buyers.

d. Problem. The issuer has engaged in stabilizing transactions during a distribution, which are generally prohibited under SEC antimanipulation rules unless they comply with strict standards. See Regulation M, Rule 242.104. In our example, the stabilizing bids do not satisfy the rule because they are above the offering price. See Rule 242.104(f). Moreover, the prior notice must be given to the market whose prices are to be stabilized, and purchasers must receive disclosure on or before their purchase of the possibility of stabilizing purchases. Rule 242.104(h).

e. Problem. Although the activity is not prohibited by the express prohibition against manipulation under §9, and thus does not trigger §9(e) liability, it is probably actionable under the broad implied Rule 10b-5 action. None of the express §9 prohibitions apply to unlisted OTC securities. In fact, none of the prohibitions prevent actual sales or purchases whose purpose is to *discourage* investors from trading. Nonetheless, courts have interpreted §10(b) more broadly than §9 to cover trading activities in OTC securities, including activities that create false or misleading appearances not specifically prohibited by §9. See §9.1.1. In some sense, the insiders' trading created the appearance of market interest in Bombastic similar to that of a press release falsely announcing higher earnings.

Some academics have questioned whether trading to manipulate prices is a feasible strategy and thus whether apparent manipulative trading should be prohibited. See Daniel R. Fischel and David J. Ross, *Should the Law Prohibit Manipulation in Financial Markets?*, 105 Harv. L. Rev. 503 (1991). Their doubts about the efficacy of manipulation arise principally in developed informational efficient markets where trading by investors, assuming it does not alter fundamental information, does not move the price. In a thinner market — such as that of an Internet bulletin board — this assumption may not be empirically valid. That is, trading patterns by others may be important for traders who lack full information. Thus, the trading by Bombastic insiders might well lead to artificial confidence in the company and could allow them to later sell in a market originally buoyed by their trading. See Steve Thel, *$850,000 in Six Minutes — The Mechanics of Securities Manipulation*, 79 Cornell L. Rev. 219 (1994).

f. No problem, from a regulatory standpoint. As a practical matter, short selling is difficult in a thinly traded security. Short sellers must be able to borrow the security at the time of the sale so the sequence "sell high, buy low" can work. Unless there are securities firms or other large traders that hold Bombastic stock and are looking for short-term interest revenues by lending their stock, short selling is unlikely.

With the elimination of the up-tick rule in 2007 (see §8.2.2), trading on the Bombastic electronic bulletin board would not be subject to pricing rules. If it were subject to such rules, however, short selling in Bombastic stock would face a significant (and perhaps insurmountable) impediment. For example, if the former up-tick rule applied, it would be a virtual show stopper for a bulletin-board trading system — since no investor could ever know with certainty whether her trade was at or above the last trade. To allow information (both good and bad) to be efficiently transmitted into market prices, the SEC no longer regulates the price at which short selling can occur.

3. a. Must disclose. Form 8-K requires disclosure of any change in independent auditor. Item 4.01. The report must be filed within four days after the event. In addition, disclosure of the reasons for the change would seem material (to wrangle a more favorable

financial statement) and would have to be disclosed, as well. Rule 12b-20 (requiring of material information beyond line-item disclosure).

In addition, company executives should tread carefully if their purpose is to hire a new auditor that will certify financial information that is potentially false. As mandated by Sarbanes-Oxley, the SEC has adopted rules that forbid corporate directors or officers (or persons under their direction) to fraudulently influence or pressure the company's auditor, if the official knew or should have known that the action could result in the issuer's financial statements becoming misleading. Rule 13b2-2; Exchange Act Rel. No. 47,890 (2003). Violations can result in SEC cease-and-desist orders or court injunctions, as well as civil or criminal penalties.

b. Need not disclose, for a while. Form 8-K requires disclosure of interim financial data that is *voluntarily* disclosed, but creates no duty to update financial results. Item 2.02 (requires disclosure only if company makes public announcements or updates quarterly or annual financial information). But the next quarterly report, which must be filed 45 days after the quarter ends, will have to disclose the negative earnings.

c. Perhaps must disclose. A public company's independent auditor cannot provide "financial information systems design" — otherwise, the auditor would be designing internal controls intended to check on the auditor itself. Exchange Act §10A(g). Moreover, any non-audit services must be approved by the company's audit committee. Although Form 8-K does not require real-time disclosure of events merely because they violate the securities laws, it does require that public companies disclose "material definitive agreements" not in the normal course of business. Item 1.01. It could be argued that an agreement for the company's outside auditor to provide an illegal service is both material and not in the normal course of business. Reasonable investors would likely consider it important that the auditor was designing the company's internal controls, thus undermining the controls' integrity. Moreover, although out-sourcing the design of internal controls might be within the normal course of business, it could be argued that it is not when done illegally.

d. Must disclose — but only internally. Under the "up the ladder" reporting required of securities lawyers, you must report evidence of a fiduciary breach to the company's general counsel, alone or with the CEO. 17 C.F.R. §205. Thus, reporting to the CEO alone is insufficient under the SEC rule. Rule 3(b)(1). If the general counsel takes the same tack as the CEO and says the "free party" practice is a form of marketing, you must determine whether this response is adequate. Absent some indication that the company was getting its money's worth, you would then be required to report the practice to the company's audit committee, another committee composed solely of independent directors, or the board of directors. If the question remains unresolved, you would have to consider resigning. Under current legal ethics rules, disclosing this information to the SEC or making a public announcement might violate your duty of confidentiality to your corporate client.

e. Must disclose, but only to NASDAQ. Under NASDAQ's listing standards, all members of the audit committee must be independent, which you are not. "Independence" is defined to exclude persons who receive payments of more than $60,000 per year from the company. (Curiously, you would be considered independent under the NASDAQ standard if the retainer were paid to your law firm, since it falls below the $200,000 level specified in the standard.) Company executives aware of this arrangement must report to NASDAQ the company's failure to comply with the listing standard.

f. After Sarbanes-Oxley, CEOs and CFOs must certify annual and quarterly reports (but not special reports on Form 8-K). Their certification must cover six points: (1) they reviewed the report, (2) they believe in the accuracy of the report, (3) they believe the report fairly presents the company's financial information, (4) they are responsible for setting up and evaluating the company's disclosure controls and procedures, (5) they have disclosed any problems to auditors or the audit committee, (6) they have disclosed any significant changes in internal controls that could affect controls in future.

Many CEOs and CFOs, recognizing that they cannot know everything about their company, have required lower-level executives to provide certifications to them of matters within these executives' competence — thus avoiding later allegations that the certifying executives were aware the reports were false or misleading or the internal controls inadequate. Whether lower-level certifications insulate CEOs and CFOs from 10b-5 liability or charges of criminal willfulness remains to be seen.

4. a. No problem. Over the last decade, the SEC has come to promote the use of electronic media (including the Internet) to deliver securities information so long as investors receive information "substantially equivalent" to what they would have received with paper delivery. See Securities Act Rel. No. 7233 (1995) and 7856 (2000) (applicable to prospectuses, offering documents under Reg A, disclosure documents under Reg D, tender offer materials, proxy statements and other proxy materials, and reports to shareholders). In its interpretative releases on electronic delivery of securities documents, the SEC has noted the many benefits of electronic distribution of information and

the growth of the media in the securities industry. The SEC set out guidelines for issuers (as well as third parties making tender offers or soliciting proxies) that wish to deliver securities information electronically — including by e-mail with links to Internet websites.

- *Notice*. The intended recipient should be on notice that an electronic document is available, to the same extent investors are on notice when they receive postal mail. Receipt of a computer disk, CD-ROM, audio tape, videotape, or e-mail is generally sufficient. For documents posted on a website, separate notice alerting the investor to the posting would normally be necessary. In our example, the e-mail must give notice of the availability of the proxy statement and annual report.
- *Access*. The recipient should be able to access, use, download, and store the electronic document with an ease comparable to that of a paper document received in the postal mail. This will often be a question of the electronic format's ease of use and compatibility with current technology. Access should continue through the period the document might be used by investors.

In our example, the proxy statement and annual report should be available at least through the date of the annual meeting and perhaps beyond.

- *Receipt*. The sender should have evidence the intended recipient actually received the electronic document, just as a postal mailing (in this country) is an assurance of receipt. According to the SEC, such evidence includes (1) informed consent from the investor to receive electronic disclosure; (2) electronic mail return-receipt or confirmation that the investor accessed, downloaded, or printed the information; or (3) making forms usable only after the investor has accessed the information. In our example, the shareholders' consent evidences receipt so long as their consent was informed. The shareholders must have been told which documents would be delivered electronically, the specific electronic medium to be used, potential online costs, and the period for which the consent was effective.
- *Withdraw consent*. The SEC has also said that investors can withdraw their consent to receive disclosure electronically and instead request documents in paper form.

b. Proxy voting is governed by state law. In its release laying out the framework for electronic delivery of disclosure documents, the SEC assumed shareholders who received proxy materials electronically would print the proxy card, sign it, and then mail it to the company. See Exchange Act Rel. No. 37,182 (1996) (example 28). Nonetheless, the practice of electronic voting has grown. The main issues are (1) whether electronic notice of a shareholders' meeting satisfies the state statutory requirement of "written" notice of such meetings, (2) whether state law permits electronic transmission of proxies, and (3) what is sufficient for shareholder authorization of electronic proxy voting.

Many corporate lawyers have interpreted state law to permit electronic notice and voting, so long as the voting shareholders have consented to electronic delivery of the proxy materials. Some states, including Delaware, permit shareholders to receive notice and authorize a proxy by electronic means, as long as there is evidence the shareholder consented to electronic communications. Other states are ambiguous, merely requiring "written notice" of meetings and that a proxy be "signed" without specifying what constitutes notice and a signature. Nonetheless, many states have digital signature acts that allow signature in electronic form. See Stephen I. Glover & Lanae Holbrook, *Electronic Proxies*, Nat. L. J. (Mar. 29, 1999).

c. No problem, so long as the issuer files both versions with the SEC and describes the omitted multimedia information for investors receiving the paper report and how to access it. The SEC has provided guidance on translating its rules premised on paper (type size, red ink, bold face, mailing) to new electronic formats. For example, electronic documents that contain manipulable graphics, audio, and video information are now acceptable, even if paper versions of the same document omit the information. See Exchange Act Rel. No. 37,182 (1996). The paper version sent to shareholders need only include a fair and accurate narrative description of the omitted multimedia information. The issuer must file both versions with the SEC or may file only the paper version (or an EDGAR filing) that contains the narrative description and a transcript of the multimedia version.

d. Problem. The liability provisions of the federal securities laws apply equally to electronic and paper-based media. In this example, the antifraud provisions of §10(b) of the Exchange Act and §17(a) of the Securities Act apply to the unsubstantiated forward-looking statement in the video as though it were made in writing on paper. See Securities Act Rel. No. 7233 (1995).

In addition, selective disclosure of this prediction to shareholders who received the annual report in electronic format could run afoul of Regulation FD and its requirement that material information be disseminated broadly, not to select securities analysts or investors. See §10.2.5.

5. a. No problem. The SEC proxy rules, as amended in 1992 to facilitate shareholder communications, *exclude* from the definition of "solicitation" (and thus even the proxy fraud rule) a public announcement by

a shareholder on how she intends to vote and her reasons. Rule 14a-1(l)(2). If the company's bulletin board can be seen as a "broadcast media . . . or other bona fide publication disseminated on a regular basis," then Norman's announcement is excluded from regulation so long as it gives the reasons for its decision to vote against management.

b. No problem, assuming Norman is neither planning its own proxy solicitation nor otherwise seeking control. The amended proxy rules *exempt* from the filing, disclosure, and dissemination requirements any communication in which the speaker neither seeks authority to act as a proxy nor requests a proxy card. Rule 14a-2(b)(1). Although such a communication is still treated as a "solicitation," it is subject only to the SEC proxy fraud rule.

c. No longer a problem. This is a proxy solicitation, but is now permitted. The communication is a proxy solicitation because it can be seen as part of a "continuous plan" leading to the formal solicitation of proxies — a broad notion under the cases. See *Studebaker Corp. v. Gittlin*, 360 F.2d 692 (2d Cir. 1966). Before 1999 this proxy solicitation would have required the filing of a proxy statement with the SEC and its dissemination to all shareholders. The notion was that shareholders should be informed even in the preliminary stages of voting contests, so they could exercise their franchise knowingly. In 1999, however, the SEC eased the restrictions on preliminary shareholder communications to permit voting-related communications *before* the filing of a proxy statement, so long as actual voting authority is not sought. Rule 14a-12. Under this rule, Norman would be required only to identify himself and his interest, as well as including a caveat in the communication that shareholders should not vote until reading the actual proxy statement, and to file the written communication with the SEC.

d. Problem. The SEC has interpreted the formation of a "group" under the §13(d) disclosure requirements for 5 percent shareholders to include the formation of a *voting* understanding among shareholders who together own more than 5 percent of a registered company's equity securities. See Exchange Act §13(d); Rule 13d-5(b)(1). Even if the group does not acquire any securities, the voting agreement itself triggers the reporting obligation. See *GAF Corp. v. Milstein*, 453 F.2d 709 (2d Cir. 1971). As a 5 percent group, the shareholders must disclose their group status, their individual stock holdings, and any financing or acquisition plans. Currently under §13(d) of the Exchange Act, disclosure must be made within 10 days of the group's agreement to act together to affect control.

e. Problem. False statements in connection with a proxy solicitation, whether made by management or by an insurgent, are prohibited by the SEC proxy rules. See Rule 14a-9. Management, acting for the cause of full and honest shareholder communications, may have standing to claim violation of the proxy rules and seek corrective disclosure or other equitable relief. See, e.g., *Greater Iowa Corp. v. McLendon*, 378 F.2d 783 (8th Cir. 1967); *Studebaker Corp. v. Gittlin*, 360 F.2d 692 (2d Cir. 1966).

6. a. No. Despite Norman's control intentions, it has no disclosure obligations so long as its holdings do not exceed 5 percent of Bombastic's common stock. The Williams Act requires disclosure of open-market purchases only when a person (or group) acquires beneficial ownership of more than 5 percent of a class of registered equity securities. Exchange Act §13(d). Further, no disclosure is required under Rule 10b-5 because Norman has no fiduciary relationship with Bombastic or its shareholders and developed its purchase plan on its own. See §9.2.2.

   b. Perhaps. If Norman and Karla are members of a "group" for purposes of §13(d), their holdings must be aggregated to determine whether the 5 percent threshold is exceeded. As interpreted, §13(d) contemplates the existence of a group even though none of its members make additional stock purchases. If Norman and Karla agreed to "hold, acquire, or dispose" of their Bombastic stock for purposes of affecting control in Bombastic, §13(d) would require them to report their identity, their holdings, their intentions, and their arrangement within 10 days after their agreement.

      Was Karla's stated willingness to sell at $65 such an agreement? On the one hand, Karla did not commit to sell to Norman or to otherwise further Norman's takeover plans. Arguably, there was no agreement to affect control. On the other hand, Karla's implicit commitment to sell its 2 percent into a $65 tender offer effectively meant that Norman could count on acquiring a total of 6.9 percent of Bombastic's stock. Arguably, the 5 percent threshold had been reached, and Bombastic shareholders are entitled to information about the possibility of a takeover. Much depends on the firmness of Karla's commitment to sell.

   c. Perhaps not. It may be a "tender offer" and, as such, would be subject to (and effectively prohibited by) the Williams Act's tender offer rules, which require that every tender offer be open to all holders for a minimum of 20 days. The term "tender offer" is not defined either in the Williams Act or in the SEC rules. Usually this is not a problem because an orthodox tender offer is easy to recognize: a bidder publicly announces an offer to buy a specified number of shares at a premium within a specified period, subject to specified terms. But problems arise when a purchase program involves the same kinds of high-pressure tactics that led to the passage of the Williams Act.

Did Norman engage in an *unorthodox tender offer* by imposing a deadline on a select group of shareholders? The cases have taken a variety of approaches. Some courts have held that a tender offer occurs only when solicited shareholders lack information and are subjected to coercive pressure akin to that of an unregulated tender offer. In *Hanson Trust PLC v. SCM Corp.*, 774 F.2d 47 (2d Cir. 1985), a bidder terminated its tender offer and, on the same day, purchased 25 percent of the target's stock in a series of five privately negotiated transactions and one open-market purchase. The Second Circuit, focusing primarily on the five negotiated purchases from institutional investors and arbitragers, held that the sellers had not been publicly solicited, that they were securities professionals aware of the essential facts concerning the target, and that they were not coerced to sell because the bidder bought at the market price without imposing any contingency that a specified number or percentage be acquired and without imposing any time limits. Accordingly, the court found the bidder's purchases did not constitute a tender offer.

Other courts, and the SEC, have articulated an eight-factor "taste" test that describes the ingredients of an orthodox tender offer and seeks to gauge how orthodox the challenged purchase program tastes. Under the test, a "tender offer" exists if there is (1) active and widespread solicitation of public shareholders (2) for a substantial percentage of the target's shares (3) at a premium price above market (4) where the offer is firm and nonnegotiable, (5) contingent on a fixed number of shares being tendered, and (6) open for a limited time. All of this (7) subjects offerees to pressure to sell their stock and (8) usually results in rapid, large accumulations of the target's shares. *SEC v. Carter Hawley Hale Stores, Inc.*, 760 F.2d 945 (9th Cir. 1985) (facts similar to our example). Although Norman directed his offer at larger shareholders, it seems to have involved the kind of coercion that the Williams Act and SEC tender offer rules are aimed at curbing.

7. a. No problem. Partial tender offers are possible under the tender offer rules. The "all holders" rule only requires that the tender offer be open to all shareholders. Exchange Act §14(d)(6); Rule 14d-8. If the offer is oversubscribed, the "pro rata" rules require that the bidder buy from each shareholder in proportion to the ratio of the number of shares sought and the number of shares tendered.

b. Problem. The "pro rata" rules specify how shares are to be purchased if the tender offer is oversubscribed. Buying shares on a first-come, first-served basis pressures shareholders to make ill-considered, rushed decisions — the main evil addressed by the tender offer rules. Although the open withdrawal rights provided for by the SEC rules largely ameliorate the problem of a first-come, first-served tender offer, the statute nonetheless requires pro rata purchases. Exchange Act §14(d)(6); Rule 14d-8.

c. No problem. The bidder can offer alternative forms of consideration and condition the tender offer in any way that does not violate the tender offer rules. Rule 14d-10. The 50 percent cash condition does not create a "stampede" problem and acts much like a financing condition. If Norman is worried about the tender offer being too cash-heavy, it can make this a condition of its offer.

d. Problem. The withdrawal period must be as long as the tendering period — here the minimum 20 business days. To prevent fraudulent, deceptive, or manipulative tender offers, the SEC has required that the tendering period be at least 20 business days. Rule 14e-1. Although the statute contemplates that shareholders may withdraw tendered shares (in the normal case) only for the first seven business days of the offer, SEC rules expand withdrawal rights to extend through the entire period the offer is open. Rule 14d-7.

e. No problem. Even though a two-tier bid is coercive and "stampedes" shareholders into tendering, the Williams Act does not require that all the shares be acquired pursuant to a tender offer. In fact, there will always be some shareholders who will fail to tender into even the most generous tender offer because of stubbornness, lack of initiative, loyalty to management, or ignorance. If Norman acquires control (usually a condition of the tender offer) and wants 100 percent ownership (particularly if it contemplates self-dealing transactions to pay off the takeover debt), it can accomplish this in a back-end merger.

As far as the federal tender offer rules are concerned, nontendered shares (as well as shares returned if the partial tender offer is oversubscribed) can be squeezed out in a merger for whatever consideration Norman decides to pay — subject to the shareholders' state appraisal rights. The "best price" rule does not apply to the merger, nor does §14(e) require that the price or other terms of the merger be fair. The only Williams Act requirement is that the bidder not misrepresent its intentions or say anything false or misleading about the merger during the tender offer. See Exchange Act §14(e). The only significant constraint on Norman are the state fiduciary rules applicable to controlling shareholders in a squeeze-out merger.

f. No problem. If this is true and not misleading, the tender offer rules do not require detailed disclosure of the bidder's plans. In fact, courts have held that it is not even necessary for the bidder to have its financing for the offer lined up when it commences a tender offer, as long as this is disclosed.

g. Problem. Tender offerors, including third-party bidders, are prohibited from making purchases outside a pending tender offer. Rule 14e-5. This keeps a bidder from starting a low-priced tender offer that artificially depresses the stock price and then buying at the manipulated price. Under current rules, third-party bidders are not prohibited from making purchases after the tender offer ends. If this possibility was disclosed and the tender offer unequivocally withdrawn, postbid purchases would not be a continuation of the original tender offer. See *Hanson Trust PLC v. SCM Corp.*, 774 F.2d 47 (2d Cir. 1985).

h. No problem. A tender offer, like any other contractual offer, can be conditioned on particular events occurring. So long as Norman does not make an illusory offer because (for example) it knows it cannot obtain financing, it may attach whatever conditions it chooses, subject to the federal tender offer rules. *Gilbert v. El Paso Co.*, 575 A.2d 1131 (Del. 1990). The bidder does not breach its implied covenant of good faith under contract law unless it deliberately causes a condition precedent not to occur.

Rule 10b-5

Rule 10b-5, the securities antifraud rule promulgated under the Securities Exchange Act of 1934, is a bedrock of U.S. securities regulation. Every securities transaction lives under its protective shade and its menacing shadow. For those who enter into securities transactions, the rule assures that relevant securities information is not purposefully false or misleading. For purveyors of securities information, it imposes standards of honesty that carry risks of heavy liability.

This chapter covers:

- the history and basics of a Rule 10b-5 private action [§9.1]
- the persons and activities to which the rule applies [§9.2]
- the fraud elements that must be shown to establish liability [§9.3]
- the defenses that apply in a Rule 10b-5 action [§9.4]
- a comparison with other antifraud remedies [§9.5]

The next chapter (Chapter 10) examines the high-profile use of Rule 10b-5 as the principal regulatory tool against insider trading.

§9.1 RULE 10b-5 OVERVIEW

§9.1.1 History of Rule 10b-5

Rule 10b-5 has been aptly described as "the judicial oak which has grown from little more than a legislative acorn." The rule's origins are humble.

In 1942, faced with reports that a company president was making pessimistic statements about company earnings while at the same time buying his company's stock, the SEC sought to fill a regulatory gap. The antifraud provisions of the Securities Act of 1933 prohibited fraudulent *sales* of securities, but there was no specific prohibition against fraudulent *purchases*.

Using its catchall authority to promulgate rules that prohibit "manipulative or deceptive devices or contrivances . . . in connection with the purchase or sale of any security" under §10(b) of the Securities Exchange Act of 1934, the SEC borrowed the language of §17 of the Securities Act to fill the "purchase" gap. Rule 10b-5 states:

> It shall be unlawful for any person, directly or indirectly, by the use of any means of instrumentality of interstate commerce, or of the mails or of any facility of any national securities exchange,
>> (a) to employ any device, scheme, or artifice to defraud;
>> (b) to make any untrue statement of a material fact or to omit to state a material fact necessary in order to make the statements made, in light of the circumstances under which they were made, not misleading; or
>> (c) to engage in any act, practice, or course of business which operates or would operate as a fraud or deceit upon any person,
> in connection with the purchase or sale of any security.

The SEC approved the rule without debate or comment, with one SEC commissioner asking rhetorically: "Well, we are against fraud, aren't we?"

The regulatory "acorn" sprouted and became a liability "tree" in 1946 when a federal district court in Pennsylvania first inferred a private cause of action under Rule 10b-5. See *Kardon v. National Gypsum Co.*, 69 F. Supp. 512 (E.D. Pa. 1946). The implied 10b-5 action then grew and branched out in the 1960s as federal courts aggressively used it to regulate not only securities fraud, but negligent securities practices and corporate mismanagement as well. In the 1970s, the Supreme Court pruned back this judicial activism and effectively limited the private 10b-5 action to cases of *intentional deception* in connection with securities trading. The pruning continued, though less dramatically, in the 1980s and 1990s as the Court dealt with issues concerning the coverage and procedures of the 10b-5 action.

Through all of this judicial shaping, the resilient 10b-5 action has become a centerpiece of U.S. securities regulation. In 1995 Congress enacted the Private Securities Litigation Reform Act to limit perceived abuses in federal securities litigation, particularly 10b-5 class actions. In 2002, responding to Enron and other accounting scandals, Congress enacted the Sarbanes-Oxley Act and signaled a renewed commitment to securities fraud liability. See §1.4.1. Then in 2010, responding to the financial crisis of 2008, Congress enacted the Dodd-Frank Act and expanded the SEC's enforcement powers, including in 10b-5 actions. See §1.4.2.

Note on Madoff Scandal

One of the most high-profile securities frauds—a Ponzi scheme orchestrated by Bernie Madoff (see §2.3.2)—illustrates the reach and limits of Rule 10b-5. Madoff was a stockbroker who promised his clients, mostly wealthy individuals and large charities, steady returns using sophisticated hedging techniques. The scheme lasted for nearly 20 years as new investors invested in the Madoff funds, thus providing money for the returns to old investors. All told, about $65 billion (including fabricated gains) was missing from client accounts when the fraud was revealed in 2008. Although the SEC received complaints that Madoff's investment model was "too good to be true," the agency failed to unearth the fraud. Instead, it came to light only when Madoff told his sons that his investment scheme was "one big lie."

Here is a partial list of the more than 250 cases spawned by the Madoff fraud (many as reported by "The D&O Diary" blog):

- Federal prosecutors brought a criminal case against Madoff, charging him with securities fraud (including under Rule 10b-5); Madoff pled guilty in 2009 and is serving a prison term of 150 years.
- Investors in the Madoff funds sued in federal court (including under Rule 10b-5) claiming fraud in their investments in the Madoff funds, seeking to recover a portion of their losses from the bankrupt funds.
- Investors in "feeder funds" that invested in the Madoff funds brought federal various class suits (including under Rule 10b-5) against the feeder funds, their advisers, and their accounting firms.
- Non-profit institutions that invested their endowments in Madoff funds sued in federal court (including under Rule 10b-5) investment advisers who recklessly directed the investments to Madoff.
- Pension funds sued (under ERISA) investment advisory firms that, despite "red flags," had directed fund investments to the Madoff funds.
- Investors in the Madoff funds sued the SEC (under the Federal Tort Claims Act) for "sheer incompetence" in failing to investigate the Madoff scheme.
- Investors in feeder funds sued (under Florida law) the funds, along with their auditors, for investing in the Madoff funds.
- The Massachusetts secretary of state brought similar suits (under Massachusetts law) against different feeder funds, which had recorded phone calls from Madoff that began "this conversation never took place, okay?"
- Investors in variable annuity policies that invested in mutual funds that invested in Madoff funds sued in federal court (1) the insurance company offering the variable annuities and (2) the investment firm managing the mutual fund.

- Investors in the Madoff funds sued in federal court (under state law) to collect under their homeowners' insurance policy, which insures against "loss of money . . . resulting from fraud . . . perpetrated against the policy holder."
- A divorced man sued his former wife (under state law) to recover payments he made in their divorce to buy her share of their Madoff investment, now worthless.
- A pro se plaintiff sued Britney Spears and Kevin Federline, on behalf of Madoff, alleging (under who knows what law) that Spears had "secret affairs with Madoff in return for Saks Fifth Avenue gift certificates."

Interestingly, although many of the claims involve fraud in connection with investments that ended up with Madoff, the claims often avoid Rule 10b-5. Why is this? You will discover that claims based on Rule 10b-5 face a number of hurdles. Class actions under Rule 10b-5 are subject to discovery stays and limits on plaintiff representatives; and 10b-5 plaintiffs must prove the defendant's knowledge of the fraud and the victim's reliance on false information. In short, although Rule 10b-5 casts a large shadow, there are numerous ways to get at securities fraud.

§9.1.2 Some Essential 10b-5 Pointers

In your study of Rule 10b-5, some preliminary pointers are in order:

Pointer	Elaboration
1. Look to the language of the statute, not the rule.	You will notice that the operative language of §10(b) is different from that of the rule. Over time, courts have interpreted the enabling statute and its phrase "manipulative or deceptive device or contrivance" as being narrower than the rule. The statute controls, and the phrasing of the rule's prohibitions has become largely irrelevant. The Supreme Court has repeatedly turned to the statutory language to fashion the 10b-5 action.
2. Identify a securities purchase or sale.	Both §10(b) and Rule 10b-5 apply to "the purchase or sale of any security." Thus, once you have identified a "security" (see Chapter 2), you must identify a purchase by an investor, or a sale by an existing holder. Rule 10b-5 applies whether the security is publicly traded or closely held, and whether it is subject to registration or exempt. Securities exempt

Pointer	Elaboration
	from registration under the Securities Act and the Exchange Act — significantly federal, state, and local government securities — are subject to the antifraud coverage of Rule 10b-5. See Exchange Act §3(a)(12) (definition of exempted securities).
3. Identify deception "in connection with" the securities transaction.	Both §10(b) and Rule 10b-5 apply to "any person" who engages in prohibited behavior "in connection with" a securities transaction. There is no requirement of privity. Rule 10b-5 applies to persons (such as companies that issue false or misleading press releases) even if they are not parties to securities transactions — so long as their behavior affects the transactions.
4. Check (quickly) for the use of jurisdictional means.	Both §10(b) and Rule 10b-5 hinge on specified jurisdictional means — that is, the use of an instrumentality of interstate commerce, the mails, or a national securities exchange. In most situations, this raises essentially a nonissue. Rarely will a securities transaction not involve the mails or interstate facilities at some point. If a check must clear or a letter confirms a transaction, the mail will be used. Further, the Exchange Act explicitly treats *intrastate* phone calls as involving the use of an instrumentality of interstate commerce. Exchange Act §3(a)(17). It is difficult to imagine, outside of a law school exam, a securities purchase or sale not involving jurisdictional means at some point in its formation or performance.
5. Check (with care) for procedural limitations imposed by the PSLRA.	Class actions claiming securities fraud under federal law (including Rule 10b-5) are disfavored under the Private Securities Litigation Reform Act of 1995. To discourage frivolous securities litigation, the PSLRA requires that the lead plaintiff in a 10b-5 class action be the "most adequate plaintiff," presumed to be the shareholder or investor with the largest financial stake in the class relief. The PSLRA imposes significant burdens on lead plaintiffs and their counsel: heightened pleading requirements, stay of discovery while any dismissal motion is pending, shifting of attorneys' fees if the complaint lacks substantial legal or factual support, payment of a bond to cover any fees that may eventually be shifted, full and detailed disclosure of any settlement, and limits on the awarding of attorneys' fees.
6. Check whether the action is brought in federal court.	Actions claiming 10b-5 violations must be brought in federal district court. Exchange Act §27 (exclusive

Pointer	Elaboration
	jurisdiction of "violations of this Act or the rules and regulations thereunder"). In addition, class actions alleging fraud involving publicly traded securities — whether under federal or state law — must be brought in federal court. Securities Act §16(c); Exchange Act §28(f)(2).

This jurisdictional mandate was added by the Securities Litigation Uniform Standards Act of 1998, which responded to a perceived loophole that allowed plaintiffs to avoid the PSLRA limitations by bringing securities fraud class actions in state court, where state procedures and substantive rules were less demanding. Under the 1998 legislation, however, class actions that allege fiduciary breaches under state corporate law may still be brought in state court — the "Delaware carve-out." Securities Act §16(d); Exchange Act §28(f)(3)(A); *Gibson v. PS Group Holdings Inc.*, Fed. Sec. L. Rep. ¶90,921 (S.D. Cal. 2000) (permitting securities fraud class action that alleges state fiduciary breaches to be brought in state court, not limited to the company's state of incorporation).

§9.1.3 Private 10b-5 Actions and SEC Enforcement

Section 10(b), unlike other antimanipulation and antifraud sections of the Exchange Act, does not specify a private remedy for violations of its rules. Despite the absence of a statutory mandate, it is now beyond question that Rule 10b-5 implies a private cause of action. See *Kardon v. National Gypsum Co.*, 73 F. Supp. 798 (E.D. Pa. 1947) (first case to recognize a private 10b-5 action, holding corporate insider liable for misrepresenting that business would not be sold when in fact the insider planned to sell it at a substantial profit). See also *Superintendent of Insurance v. Bankers Life & Casualty Co.*, 404 U.S. 6 (1971) (confirming existence of private action). Such claims may be brought only in federal district courts, which have exclusive jurisdiction over actions arising under the Exchange Act. See Exchange Act §27.

Originally, federal courts justified an implied 10b-5 private action on a broad tort theory that "where there is a legal wrong, there must be private remedy," an interpretive theory since rejected by the Supreme Court. See *Touche Ross & Co. v. Redington*, 442 U.S. 560 (1979) (rejecting implied cause of action for securities firm customers under §17 of the Exchange Act, which requires securities firms to make annual informational filings with the SEC); *Piper v.*

Chris-Craft Industries, Inc., 430 U.S. 1 (1977) (denying standing to a frustrated bidder that challenged tender offer disclosures under §14(e) of the Exchange Act, which prohibits false and misleading disclosures in tender offer documents). Nonetheless, the long-standing recognition of an implied 10b-5 action, both by the courts and by Congress, supports its existence.

Rule 10b-5 is also a potent tool in SEC enforcement. Section 21 of the Exchange Act gives the SEC broad enforcement powers to sue in federal court to enjoin violations of its rules, including Rule 10b-5. Using this authority, the SEC has sought injunctions and other equitable remedies. See *SEC v. Texas Gulf Sulphur Co.*, 401 F.2d 833 (2d Cir. 1968) (judicial order establishing a fund from which contemporaneous investors could recover lost profits from illegal insider trading). The SEC can also recommend that the U.S. Justice Department institute a 10b-5 criminal action, a common occurrence in insider-trading cases. See §12.4.

§9.1.4 Typical 10b-5 Cases

There are six basic patterns of private Rule 10b-5 actions. This chapter looks at the first three; later chapters deal with the second three, though the ground rules of this chapter (such as materiality and scienter) also apply to 10b-5 actions in these other contexts. Notice that the underlying constant in each pattern is that securities trades arise out of an informational asymmetry involving deception or other unfairness. Rule 10b-5 serves as an equalizer.

Securities Trading

A party to a securities transaction gives false or misleading information to induce the other party to enter into the transaction, or remains silent when he has a duty to disclose. The dupe sues the swindler.

Corporate Trading

A corporate manager induces her corporation to enter into a disadvantageous securities transaction. The corporation (or a shareholder or other representative on behalf of the corporation) sues the venal manager.

Corporate Disclosures

A corporation (without trading) issues false or misleading information to the public about its securities, or it remains silent when it has a duty to disclose. Contemporaneous purchasers or sellers (often in a class action) sue the corporation for their trading losses, which often run into the millions of dollars. (Perceived abuses in this kind of litigation, such as the routine filing of lawsuits following unexpected fluctuations in an issuer's stock price, motivated the PSLRA.)

Insider Trading

Corporate insiders either use confidential corporate information to enter into securities transactions or tip the information to others who, though knowing it is confidential, trade on the tip. Contemporaneous traders sue the insiders and their tippees. See §10.2.

In addition, outsiders with no relationship to the corporation use confidential information about the company entrusted to them by others (such as corporate raiders) and trade on this information. Contemporaneous traders, as well as the holders of the confidential information, sue the outsiders and their tippees. See §10.2.

Customer-Broker Disputes

Securities professionals engage in deceptive or other unprofessional conduct in connection with securities trading by or for their customers. The customers bring claims against the brokers and their firms, often in arbitration proceedings. See §11.2.4.

§9.2 SCOPE OF PRIVATE 10b-5 ACTION

Although grounded in the elements and terminology of the law of deceit, the judicially crafted private 10b-5 action varies in significant respects from a garden-variety fraud action. Courts have interpreted §10(b) to impose limits on who can sue, who can be sued, and what counts as securities fraud (the subject of this subsection). Moreover, courts have conservatively honed the elements of a private 10b-5 action to resemble a decidedly old-fashioned action for deceit, except to relax significantly the normal requirement of reliance (see §9.3). Finally, courts have fashioned defenses to a private 10b-5 action that go beyond those of a typical fraud action (see §9.4).

Layered on this court-created 10b-5 profile are the provisions of the Private Securities Litigation Reform Act of 1995. Among other things, the PSLRA revamped 10b-5 class action procedures, called for the shifting of attorneys' fees as a sanction for baseless complaints, largely replaced joint and several liability with proportionate liability, and confirmed the elimination of aiding and abetting liability in private actions.

§9.2.1 Purchasers and Sellers: 10b-5 Standing

Only actual purchasers or sellers may recover damages in a private action under Rule 10b-5. This standing requirement, generally called the *Birnbaum* rule after the Second Circuit case from which it came, avoids speculating whether and how much a plaintiff might have traded. See *Birnbaum v. Newport Steel Corp.*, 193 F.2d 461 (2d Cir. 1952). Even if a false or misleading statement leads a person not to buy or not to sell a security, with financial results as damaging as if the person had been induced to trade, there is no 10b-5 liability.

In 1975 the Supreme Court affirmed the purchaser-seller requirement in a case as famous for its holding as the Court's virulent doubts about 10b-5 litigation. *Blue Chip Stamps v. Maynard Drug Stores*, 421 U.S. 723 (1975). The case involved the unusual allegation that a corporate issuer had made overly pessimistic statements to discourage potential purchasers. A trading stamp company was required by an antitrust consent decree to offer its shares at a discount to retailers harmed by prior anticompetitive activities. One of the retailers that did not buy sued to recover damages on the theory that the prospectus offering the stock was intentionally pessimistic to discourage retailers from purchasing.

Speaking for the Court, Justice Rehnquist said the language of §10(b) and the Exchange Act's definitions did not cover offers to sell but only actual sales or purchases. He pointed out that for nearly 25 years Congress had let stand the consistent judicial application of the *Birnbaum* rule. Justice Rehnquist then launched into a diatribe against potential abuse of Rule 10b-5 litigation. In general, he speculated that an indeterminate class of non-purchasers would bring vexatious litigation to extract settlements, in the process disrupting business and abusing civil discovery. In addition, liability would be staggering if nonpurchasers could base a claim on the speculative assertion that they *would have purchased* had disclosure been less discouraging.

Blue Chip Stamps left open the question whether the purchaser-seller standing rule extends to injunctive relief. Although an injunctive action does not present the risk of speculative or runaway liability, lower courts have read the *Blue Chip Stamps* concern for vexatious 10b-5 litigation as precluding any exceptions to a flat purchaser-seller rule. See *Cowin v. Bresler*, 741 F.2d 410 (D.C. Cir. 1984).

Securities Fraud Actions by "Holders" in State Court

The 10b-5 purchaser-seller requirement has led "holders" of securities to bring securities fraud class actions in state court alleging that false or misleading statements led them *not to sell* their shares. These "holder" cases ran into the Securities Litigation Uniform Standards Act of 1998 (SLUSA), which requires that all class actions alleging fraud "in connection with the purchase or sale" of securities be brought in federal court. See §1.5. In 2006, the Supreme Court held that state law "holder" class actions are preempted by SLUSA, even though they are also precluded in federal court under the *Birnbaum* rule. *Merrill Lynch, Pierce, Fenner & Smith, Inc. v. Dabit*, 547 U.S. 71 (2006).

The principal issue in the case was whether "holder" claims were "in connection with the purchase or sale" of securities. The Court, resolving a split in the circuits, decided they were. Noting that the policy against "vexatious" litigation articulated in *Blue Chips Stamps* also motivated the PSLRA restrictions on securities class actions, the Court concluded that SLUSA was intended to funnel such actions into federal court — and squelch them. The Court pointed out that "holder" claims (whether in federal or state court) raise factual issues of whether and how much the holders would have sold, the precise speculation *Blue Chips Stamps* had sought to avoid.

Lead Plaintiff (and Counsel) in 10b-5 Class Actions

The PSLRA, a successor to the *Blue Chip Stamps* antagonism toward private 10b-5 actions, sought to contain 10b-5 class actions instituted by "professional plaintiffs" who own a nominal number of shares in many public companies and lend their names (for a bounty) to securities lawyers who sue whenever there are unexpected price swings in a company's stock. The PSLRA establishes procedures for the appointment of the lead plaintiff (and thus lead counsel) in securities fraud actions. After the filing of a securities fraud class action, the plaintiff must give public notice to potential class members inviting them to serve as lead plaintiff. The court then is to appoint as lead plaintiff the "most adequate plaintiff," presumed by statute to be the investor with the largest financial interest in the action. Exchange Act §21D(a)(3).

These provisions envision a prominent role for institutional shareholders, which typically will have the largest financial interest in securities litigation involving public companies. The provisions specifically exempt them from limits on the frequency a particular investor can serve as lead counsel. See Weiss & Beckerman, *Let the Money Do the Monitoring: How Institutional Investors Can Reduce Agency Costs in Securities Class Actions*, 104 Yale L.J. 2053 (1995) (cited prominently in PSLRA's legislative history).

Class actions under Rule 10b-5 are typically lawyer-driven, with lawyers investigating instances of securities fraud, identifying potential named plaintiffs, and handling the presentation and settlement of the case — all with the hope of garnering sizeable attorneys' fees. An interesting question is whether courts should auction the role of the lead plaintiff and counsel — the winner being the one offering the most cost-efficient litigation services. Although an auction might reduce the unseemly practices of law firms seeking to assemble the largest group of injured shareholders, courts have concluded the PSLRA does not countenance the procedure. See *In re Razorfish, Inc. Securities Litigation*, 143 F. Supp. 2d 304 (S.D.N.Y. 2001). Instead, courts have created competition by requesting law firms seeking lead counsel status to submit their proposed fee arrangements before class certification, permitting the court to compare fees and "negotiate" changes or reductions.

Studies of securities fraud class actions and the procedures mandated by the PSLRA indicate that the presence of lead plaintiffs yields better settlements and lower attorneys' fees awards.

§9.2.2 Primary Violators: 10b-5 Defendants

There is no privity requirement under Rule 10b-5. Any person who makes false or misleading statements and induces others to trade to their detriment (a primary violator) can become liable. Significantly, corporate officials who make statements about the corporation or its securities expose the corporation to 10b-5 liability, even though the corporation does not trade.

Control Persons

The Exchange Act imposes joint and several liability on any person who controls a primary violator — such as the parent corporation of a subsidiary that engages in illegal activity — unless the control person shows it "acted in good faith and did not . . . induce . . . the violation." Exchange Act §20(a). To be liable, the person must not only have the general power to control the primary violator, but must exercise actual control. See *Lustgraaf v. Behrens*, 619 F.3d 867 (8th Cir. 2010) (holding that financial services firm may be liable as "control person" where the firm had "actual control" over specific acts of registered representative who ran Ponzi scheme). Courts have interpreted the "good faith" defense as requiring the showing of an affirmative effort by a control person to prevent subordinates from committing securities fraud. See *Arthur's Children's Trust v. Keim*, 994 F.2d 1390 (9th Cir. 1993) (holding that member of issuer's management committee who was aware of, and did nothing to prevent, false marketing of securities could be liable as control person).

Courts have wrestled with whether, aside from the control person liability of §20(a), the general rule of *respondeat superior* applies to a corporate defendant when an employee of the corporation commits securities fraud in the regular scope of her employment. See *Pugh v. Tribune Co.*, 521 F.3d 686 (7th Cir. 2008) (refusing to find *respondeat superior* liability under Rule 10b-5 when employee who gave false newspaper circulation figures was not executive officer and false figures were meant to deceive advertisers, not shareholders). The Exchange Act imposes liability on "persons," defined to include a corporation, an entity that can only become liable through its agents. Thus, as some courts have persuasively pointed out, the Act already makes corporate principals liable under traditional agency principles, regardless of the corporate defendant's "good faith" efforts to supervise its employees. See *Belmont v. MB Inv. Partners*, 708 F.3d 470 (3rd Cir. 2013) (applying state agency law to impose 10b-5 liability on principal for actor acting within scope of agency). Viewed in this light, §20(a) is an additional ground for vicarious liability beyond traditional agency principles.

In SEC enforcement actions, Dodd-Frank clarifies (thus resolving a split in the circuits) that the SEC has authority to sue control persons under §20(a). Dodd-Frank §929O(c) (adding SEC to list of persons to whom control person is liable).

Aiders and Abettors

Until 1994, lower courts had uniformly upheld aiding and abetting liability under Rule 10b-5 for secondary participants, such as accountants who certified false financial statements or lawyers who advised and gave "substantial assistance" to securities swindlers. Based on criminal and tort principles, this liability expanded the circle of 10b-5 watchdogs and made compensation for defrauded investors more likely by increasing significantly the pool of solvent (often professional and insured) 10b-5 defendants.

Despite its long and seemingly established place in 10b-5 jurisprudence, the Supreme Court in 1994 rejected aiding and abetting liability. *Central Bank of Denver v. First Interstate Bank of Denver*, 511 U.S. 164 (1994). In a 5-4 decision, the Court read the "manipulative or deceptive device or contrivance" language of §10(b) to require that 10b-5 defendants engage in actual fraudulent or deceptive behavior upon which the plaintiff relied, not merely collateral assistance — thus disallowing private actions based on a theory of aiding and abetting. The Court pointed out that none of the other express private causes of action under the Exchange Act impose aiding and abetting liability and that, in any event, such liability has never been widely accepted under tort law.

Even though lower courts had uniformly assumed the existence of aiding and abetting liability under Rule 10b-5 before *Central Bank*, the Court concluded Congress had never approved these cases and suggested Congress could remedy the problem if the Court's reading were in error. Congress accepted the Court's invitation in a limited way, permitting aiding and abetting liability in SEC enforcement actions. The PSLRA expressly authorizes the SEC to seek injunctive relief or money damages against those who aid and abet a 10b-5 violation by knowingly giving "substantial assistance" to the primary violator. Exchange Act §20(e).

Dodd-Frank fosters the SEC's authority to challenge aiding and abetting. Responding to lower court decisions that required a showing of "actual knowledge" for such liability, Dodd-Frank adopts a "recklessness" standard in SEC aiding and abetting actions. Dodd-Frank §§929M, 929N, 929O (also giving SEC authority to bring aiding and abetting claims and seek civil penalties under Securities Act and Investment Company Act, and expanding such liability to include civil penalties under Investment Advisers Act). Thus, securities professionals (such as attorneys, investment banks, accountants, financial analysts, and credit rating agencies) that may not meet the definition of "primary violator" in a private action may be subject to liability in an SEC enforcement action. See §12.3.1.

What must the SEC show to establish aiding and abetting? Consider a recent SEC enforcement action against one Apuzzo, the former CFO of Terex, who allegedly helped United Rentals ("UR") carry out fraudulent "sale-leaseback" transactions to inflate UR's profits. The district court held this was not "substantial assistance," given that Apuzzo had not proximately caused the primary violation (the misstatement of UR's profits). Reversing the district court, the Second Circuit held that proximate cause and proof of injury, though required in private 10b-5 actions, were not required in "aiding and abetting" enforcement actions, which are meant to deter, not compensate. Instead, it was enough for the SEC to show "substantial assistance" — namely, that Apuzzo had associated himself with the venture, helped with the fraudulent transactions, and designed them to avoid detection. See *SEC v. Apuzzo*, 689 F. 3d 204 (2d Cir. 2012).

Scheme Liability

Central Bank holds that peripheral actors who engage in fraudulent (or deceptive) conduct on which a purchaser or seller of securities relies may be liable as a primary violator. Since *Central Bank*, a recurring question has been whether the "primary violator" standard extends to those who facilitate the fraud. Some lower courts since *Central Bank* held secondary participants (such as lawyers, accountants, and underwriters) could be liable as primary violators for their role in drafting and editing documents that contain misrepresentations, even though the participants were not mentioned and the documents were disseminated to investors by others. See *In re Software Toolworks, Inc. Securities Litigation*, 50 F.3d 615 (9th Cir. 1994). Other courts have held that primary violators must actually make the misstatement to investors or have it attributed to them. See *Wright v. Ernst & Young LLP*, 152 F.3d 169 (2d Cir. 1998) (refusing to hold liable an auditor that privately approved false press report, since report stated financials were unaudited and did not mention auditor).

And what about 10b-5 liability for those who participate in fraudulent schemes by, for example, entering into sham transactions used to generate false financial results — so-called "scheme liability"? In 2008 the Supreme Court rejected scheme liability in private 10b-5 litigation. *Stoneridge Investment Partners LLC v. Scientific-Atlanta Inc.*, 522 U.S. 148 (2008). In a 5-3 decision, the Court held that suppliers/customers who allegedly helped a cable TV company artificially inflate its earnings could not be liable as primary violators in a 10b-5 action by the company's investors. Even though the suppliers/customers had misled the issuer's auditors by documenting sham transactions with the issuer, their misdeeds were held not to be actionable in a private 10b-5 action.

The Court pointed out that the suppliers/customers owed no duty to the company's investors and the sham transactions were not disclosed to the public — and thus investors could not have relied on the deception, a requisite for 10b-5 liability. Furthermore, the Court concluded that the suppliers/customers' deception of the auditors was "too remote" from the issuer's fraudulent financial statements to support primary liability. In short, liability for the investors' full trading losses would have been disproportionate to their attenuated involvement in the company's fraud.

The *Stoneridge* Court noted that Congress in the PSLRA had placed various limits on private 10b-5 actions, including the authorization of aiding and abetting liability only in SEC enforcement actions. Although the Court did not address whether private 10b-5 liability extends to "behind the scenes" lawyers and accountants who engineer securities deception without an attribution of their role, the case reflects the Court's misgivings about expanding the implied private 10b-5 action to cover additional parties and situations.

Lower courts have followed the *Stoneridge* lead, denying secondary liability for lawyers and other professionals who created or facilitated fraudulent transactions — provided they were unknown to the victims of the fraud. See *Affco Investments 2001 LLC v. Proskauer Rose LLP*, 625 F.3d 185 (5th Cir. 2010) (refusing to hold law firm liable in disallowed tax avoidance scheme because investors did not allege investors' awareness of or reliance on firm); *Pac. Inv. Mgmt. LLC v. Mayer Brown LLP*, 603 F.3d 144 (2d Cir. 2010) (finding "behind the scenes" law firm not liable for facilitating fraudulent loan transactions or drafting false offering documents, where false statements were not attributed to firm). In short, lawyers can orchestrate a securities fraud and escape private 10b-5 liability — so long as they hide themselves from view. *Stoneridge* thus puts pressure on the SEC and state regulators to investigate and bring enforcement actions against secondary participants.

Makers of False or Misleading Statements

In a 5-4 decision with significant ramifications for 10b-5 private actions, the Supreme Court held that only those who "make" a false or misleading statement can be liable under Rule 10b-5. *Janus Capital Group, Inc. v. First Derivative Traders*, 564 U.S. _____ (2011). The case arose from a 10b-5 claim against a mutual fund adviser for false statements in the prospectus of the mutual funds that it advised. (The fund investor claimed the prospectus had falsely stated that the fund adviser would implement policies to restrain abusive market-timing practices.) The Court concluded that only the entity with "ultimate control" over the statements in the prospectus — the mutual fund itself — could be liable under Rule 10b-5.

Deviating from its 10b-5 jurisprudence, the Court focused on the language of Rule 10b-5 — which makes it unlawful for "any person . . . to make any untrue statement of material fact" in connection with securities trading — and determined that the investment adviser had not "made" the untrue statements in the prospectus, even though it was "substantially involved" in its preparation. The Court said it was bound to interpret Rule 10b-5 with "narrow dimensions," likening the relationship of the fund and fund adviser to that of speaker and speechwriter.

The Court seemed not to understand that mutual funds themselves have no staff or employees, but outsource all of their operations to the fund adviser. It is the fund adviser, in turn, that makes all investment decisions for the fund and prepares all fund disclosures, including prospectuses. Nonetheless, the Court concluded that "corporate formalities were observed" and that the investment adviser had a corporate board different from the board of trustees of the mutual fund, thus making them "separate legal entities." The Court stated that redistributing securities liability based on a "close relationship" between investment advisers and the mutual funds they advise was not the responsibility of the courts, but rather Congress.

Despite what to many seemed a misguided result, the outcome might well have been different if the plaintiffs had alleged that the fund adviser was the "control person" of the fund. Under Exchange Act §20(a) (described above), control persons assume the liability of the entities they control, which is the case in a typical mutual fund structure where the fund adviser controls all aspects of the fund's operations, including the drafting of disclosure documents. Any 10b-5 liability of the fund would thus become the liability of the fund adviser, and the "good faith" defense would be unavailable if the fund adviser's actions satisfied the 10b-5 culpability standard.

Calls for Reform

In summary, only those who "make" false or misleading statements that investors rely on can be liable in a private 10b-5 action. Secondary participants who merely draft falsehoods or participate in a behind-the-scenes scheme so that others can make false statements are not subject to private 10b-5 liability. Nonetheless, such secondary participants can be liable in an enforcement action by the SEC claiming aiding and abetting — that is, for giving substantial assistance to those engaged in securities fraud. Although Dodd-Frank called on the GAO to study and report on the impact of not permitting aiding and abetting liability in private 10b-5 actions, the GAO report essentially punted — providing only a summary of the arguments pro and con. See Dodd-Frank §929Z; GAO, *Securities Fraud Liability of Secondary Actors* (2011) (stating that proponents of aiding and abetting liability in private actions assert such liability is necessary to compensate investors and deter securities fraud, while opponents maintain the current system is adequate).

§9.2.3 Fraud "in Connection with" Securities Transactions

Section 10(b) and Rule 10b-5 prohibit deception "in connection with" the sale or purchase of securities. How close must the deception be to the securities transaction?

No Privity Requirement

Courts have not required privity in 10b-5 actions. Thus, corporate misstatements in situations when the corporation itself is not trading are actionable if it is foreseeable that the misstatements will affect securities transactions. The "in connection with" element is established even when a company makes disclosures to a public trading market that it does not actually envision will trigger reliance. For example, when a bidder makes a tender offer for another company's stock and misrepresents its own financial condition, the misrepresentations have been held to be "in connection with" purchases of the target company's stock. *Semerenko v. Cendant Corp.*, 216 F.3d 315 (3d Cir. 2001).

Beyond Privity

Courts have had more difficulty interpreting the "in connection with" requirement when securities transactions are part of a scheme of corporate misdeeds or professional malpractice. If the securities transactions are tangential to the fraudulent scheme, some courts have assumed the matter is better left to traditional state fiduciary, corporate, agency, and contract law — a federalism concern. Nonetheless, on the three occasions that the Supreme Court has addressed the "in connection" requirement, it has construed the 10b-5 "in connection" requirement broadly and flexibly to further investor protection.

- **Stockbroker Embezzlement.** Misstatements may both be actionable as a breach of fiduciary duty and as a fraud "in connection with" securities transactions. *SEC v. Zandford*, 535 U.S. 813 (2002). In the case, the SEC brought an enforcement action against a stockbroker who had sold his customer's securities and pocketed the proceeds without the customer's knowledge or consent. The stockbroker argued that any deception of the customer lacked the requisite connection with the sales of securities from the customer's account, because he had never misrepresented the value of the securities in the account. The Court rejected the sophistry and concluded the securities sales and the stockbroker's fraudulent practices coincided — with each sale furthering the stockbroker's fraudulent scheme.

- **Outsider Trading (Misappropriation).** The fraudulent misappropriation of material, nonpublic information is "in connection with" securities trading based on that information. *United States v. O'Hagan*, 521 U.S. 642 (1997). In the case (discussed more fully in §10.2.1), a lawyer used information about a client's planned takeover bid and purchased stock in the target before the bid was announced. The Court concluded that the lawyer's unauthorized use of client confidences was deceptive and "in connection with" his securities trading. The fraud was consummated, according to the Court, when the lawyer traded on the information entrusted to him — thus, the securities transaction and the breach of duty coincided. Significantly, the Court commented that its interpretation furthered "an animating purpose of the Exchange Act: to insure honest securities markets and thereby promote investor confidence."

- **Fraudulent Takeover Scheme.** A complex scheme to acquire an insurance subsidiary by using the subsidiary's assets to finance the acquisition stated a 10b-5 claim. *Superintendent of Insurance v. Bankers Life & Casualty Co.*, 404 U.S. 6 (1971). The purchasers acquired the subsidiary's shares and then, to pay for them, had the subsidiary's board authorize the sale of approximately $5 million of U.S. Treasury bonds owned by the subsidiary. To cover their tracks, the purchasers engaged in an elaborate cover-up: they had the subsidiary purchase a $5 million bank certificate of deposit, which they then used in a series of transactions with other intermediaries as collateral to finance the CD's purchase. In short, the purchasers used the subsidiary's Treasury bonds to finance their acquisition and left a mortgaged CD on the subsidiary's books. The Court held the scheme, which effectively misappropriated reserved assets meant to cover the subsidiary's insurance obligations, to be "in connection with" a securities transaction — namely the sale of the Treasury bonds. Part of the fraudulent scheme, according to the Court, was the deception practiced on the subsidiary's board when it authorized the sale of the bonds without the subsidiary receiving fair compensation. The subsidiary "suffered an injury as a result of deceptive practices *touching* its sale of securities as an investor."

Sale of Business

The Supreme Court has held that Rule 10b-5 applies to stock transactions in the sale of a business even when the purchaser is not investing as a shareholder, but buying the business outright. *Landreth Timber Co. v. Landreth*, 471 U.S. 681 (1985) (see §2.3.6). The Court rejected a "sale of business" doctrine, adopted by some lower courts, that a securities transaction is not involved when a company is sold in a 100 percent stock sale. The Court read Rule 10b-5 literally to apply to any purchase or sale of securities, including the sale of a business structured as a stock sale.

§9.3 FRAUD ELEMENTS OF PRIVATE 10b-5 ACTION

Neither §10(b) nor Rule 10b-5 specifies the elements a plaintiff must show to be entitled to relief. The Supreme Court has looked to the statutory language of §10(b) and insisted that Congress meant "fraud" when it said "any manipulative or deceptive device or contrivance." Since the mid-1970s, the Court has understood a 10b-5 action to bear a strong resemblance to its forbearer — old-fashioned common law deceit.

The plaintiff has the burden of showing the following elements, each of which tests whether the supplier of misinformation should bear another's investment losses:

Material misinformation	The defendant affirmatively misrepresented a material fact, or omitted a material fact that made his statement misleading, or remained silent in the face of a fiduciary duty to disclose a material fact.
Scienter	The defendant knew (or was reckless in not knowing) the true state of affairs and recognized that the plaintiff might rely on the misinformation.
Reliance	The plaintiff relied on the misrepresentation. In 10b-5 cases involving a duty to speak, courts dispense with reliance if the undisclosed information was material. In 10b-5 cases involving transactions on impersonal trading markets, courts infer reliance from the dissemination of misinformation in the trading market.
Causation	The plaintiff suffered actual losses proximately caused by the misrepresentation.
Damages	The plaintiff suffered damages. Courts use a variety of theories to measure damages under Rule 10b-5. Punitive damages, though, are not available under Rule 10b-5.

The PSLRA modifies the court-made rule of joint and several liability in 10b-5 actions and specifies proportionate liability in some circumstances. Exchange Act §21D(g). Although "knowing" defendants remain jointly and severally liable for the plaintiff's full losses, "unknowing" (reckless) defendants are generally liable only for that portion of damages attributable to their share of responsibility.

§9.3.1 Material Deception

Rule 10b-5 prohibits false or misleading statements of material fact. Not only are outright lies prohibited, so are half-truths. This means a true, but incomplete, statement can be actionable if it omits material information that renders the statement misleading. Under the PSLRA, a 10b-5 complaint that alleges half-truths must specify which statements were misleading and why they are misleading. Exchange Act §21D(b)(1). Further, opinions can be actionable, provided the speaker did not actually hold the opinion and the opinion was in fact incorrect. See §3.2.3.

Deception in securities markets comes in many packages, encompassing far more than false or misleading statements. It includes securities trading that creates false impressions, as well as silence in the face of a duty to speak. Deception can also occur when a statement, though true when made, is superseded by new information that triggers a duty to update. Confirming the breadth of Rule 10b-5, the Supreme Court has held that Rule 10b-5 covers deception in an oral contract for the sale of securities, despite the difficulties of proof. *Wharf (Holdings) Ltd. v. United International Holdings Inc.*, 532 U.S. 588 (2001). In the case, the seller of a securities option who secretly intended not to honor the option argued that there had been no deception as to the option's value. The Court brushed aside the argument and held the seller's secret reservation was misleading since "the option was, unbeknownst to [the buyer], valueless."

Materiality

Not all deception is actionable. To prevent allegations of bad information from being used as a pretext for shifting trading losses, courts require that the misinformation be material. The Supreme Court has held that a fact is material for purposes of Rule 10b-5 if there is a substantial likelihood that a reasonable investor "would" (not "might") consider it as altering the "total mix" of information in deciding whether to buy or sell. *Basic, Inc. v. Levinson*, 485 U.S. 224 (1988) (adopting a "probability plus magnitude" test for disclosures pertaining to possible future events, such as merger negotiations, by considering probability that event might occur and the magnitude of its effect on stock price). In general, if disclosure of the information would affect the price of the company's stock, the information is material. See Chapter 3.

To obtain class certification in 10b-5 actions, plaintiffs need only allege (but need not prove) the materiality of the alleged misrepresentations.

See *Amgen Inc. v. Connecticut Retirement Plans & Trust Fund*, 133 S. Ct. 1184 (2013). In the case, Amgen had argued that in the class certification phase (after the plaintiff's complaint had withstood a motion to dismiss) the plaintiff should be required to prove materiality — an essential element of the "fraud on the market" theory under *Basic, Inc. v. Levinson* (see §9.3.3 below — Fraud on Market). Amgen argued that because the class plaintiff was required to show the market in which the class had traded was "efficient," the plaintiff should also be required to prove that the alleged misinformation had affected the market — that is, that it was material. In a 6-3 decision, the Court held that materiality is a "question on the merits" and could await summary judgment or trial. If the plaintiff failed to prove materiality at this later stage, the Court explained that the suit would be dismissed for lacking a necessary element. Nonetheless, the corporate bar came away with a tantalizing morsel: four justices in the case questioned whether the "fraud on the market" theory was still good law, given that it has no common law or statutory basis.

Manipulation

Rule 10b-5 prohibits securities activities that manipulate the price of securities by creating false appearances of market activity. Artificial market activity can have the same effect on securities prices as false statements about a company or its securities. For example, a stock trader who buys securities to raise artificially the market price can violate Rule 10b-5, even though his purpose is not to induce others to buy or sell. See *United States v. Mulheren*, 938 F.2d 364 (2d Cir. 1991) (refusing to infer from the evidence that securities trader purchased stock in a company to raise the market price for the benefit of a corporate greenmailer whose contract called for the company to buy back its stock "at market"). Thus, securities transactions whose purpose is to manipulate prices may give rise to 10b-5 liability, even though they do not violate the specific antimanipulation provisions of the Exchange Act. See §9(a)(2) (stock trading that raises or depresses stock prices actionable if "for the purpose of inducing the purchase or sale of such security by others").

Duty to Speak

Normally, silence is not actionable under Rule 10b-5. Nonetheless, courts have imposed a duty to speak when defendants have a relationship of trust and confidence with the plaintiff. See *Chiarella v. United States*, 445 U.S. 222 (1980) (duty to disclose is predicate to 10b-5 insider trading liability). For example, bank employees who failed to tell shareholders that they could sell their shares for higher prices in a resale market, instead of the primary market offered through the bank, breached their duty to disclose.

The bank, as transfer agent for the shareholders' corporation, had a relationship of trust that compelled it to speak fully about the shareholders' selling options. *Affiliated Ute Citizens v. United States*, 406 U.S. 128 (1972). A duty to speak also arises when a closely held corporation deals with its shareholder-employees. See *Jordan v. Duff & Phelps, Inc.*, 815 F.2d 429 (7th Cir. 1987) (holding securities firm liable for remaining silent when the firm repurchased the shares of an employee who resigned on the eve of a lucrative merger offer).

Silence is also actionable in connection with corporate activities in a limited number of circumstances: when the company is trading, when the company fails to correct misinformation it begot and that is actively circulating in the market, or when the company knows that insiders are trading based on information not available to the public. This means, for example, that a company need not comment on analysts' forecasts unless the company has become entangled with the analysts. See *Elkind v. Liggett & Myers, Inc.*, 635 F.2d 156 (2d Cir. 1980) (no duty to disclose projections by investment analysts if the company had not in some way created or validated them).

Duty to Update

In some situations, statements that were accurate when made become inaccurate or misleading because of subsequent events. Most federal circuits have held that there is a duty to update when forward-looking statements still "alive" in the market have become inaccurate. The notion is that a projection carries an ongoing assurance of validity and thus an implicit duty to supply new information as it becomes available. For example, the Second Circuit has held that the public announcement of a plan to find a financial partner to mend an over-leveraged capital structure triggered a duty to update when the company began to consider a dilutive stock offering as an alternative financing plan. *In re Time Warner Securities Litigation*, 9 F.3d 259 (2d Cir. 1993). In a similar vein, the Third Circuit has held that a company that had stated its policy to maintain a stable debt-equity ratio came under a duty to disclose negotiations of a merger that would have added significant new debt. *Weiner v. Quaker Oats Co.*, 129 F.3d 310 (3d Cir. 1997).

Some have criticized the "duty to update" as the judicial imposition of an amorphous continuous disclosure requirement. Nonetheless, judicial approaches are mixed. Although some courts have said a duty to update arises only when subsequent events contradict specific prior projections, others have inferred such a duty whenever subsequent facts indicate the original projection was misleading. For companies that make forward-looking statements, whether voluntarily or in SEC filings, this case law imposes an ongoing duty to gauge whether the market continues to rely on the statements and to disclose material developments affecting the validity of the original statements. See also NYSE Listed Company Manual

§202.05 (stating that listed companies are "expected to release quickly" material information that might affect the market for securities, subject to business exigencies).

Corporate Mismanagement

Mismanagement by corporate officials can violate Rule 10b-5 if the mismanagement involves fraudulent securities transactions that can be said to injure the corporation. For example, when corporate insiders buy stock from the corporation and deceive those with whom they deal, a derivative suit can be used to enforce the corporation's 10b-5 rights.

But not every corporate fiduciary breach involving a securities transaction gives rise to a 10b-5 action. The Supreme Court has held that Rule 10b-5 only regulates deception, not unfair corporate transactions or breaches of fiduciary duties. *Santa Fe Industries, Inc. v. Green*, 430 U.S. 462 (1977). In the case, a parent company merged with its majority-owned subsidiary after giving minority shareholders notice of the merger and an information statement that explained their rights to a state appraisal remedy. The parent stated that a valuation of the subsidiary's assets indicated a $640 per share value, even though the parent was offering only $125 per share, an amount slightly higher than a valuation of the subsidiary by the parent's investment banker. The Court held that unless the disclosure had been misleading (which plaintiffs did not claim was the case) no liability could result. An unfairly low price could not amount to fraud.

Santa Fe has led to the clever argument that Rule 10b-5 applies when management *fails to disclose* that a particular corporate transaction is unfair or constitutes a breach of fiduciary duties. It would seem that *Santa Fe* precludes such claims. First, they are essentially state fiduciary claims dressed up in federal disclosure clothing. The ruse is transparent, and *Santa Fe* makes clear that Rule 10b-5 is not a source of federal fiduciary law. Second, even if corporate insiders in some abstract sense "deceived the corporation" by failing to disclose the unfairness of a transaction involving securities, it is unclear whether disclosure would have changed anything since the directors still might have approved the transaction.

Nonetheless, several lower courts have upheld a "fraud on the corporation" claim. In the leading case, the Second Circuit accepted that minority shareholders could bring a derivative action on behalf of the corporation under Rule 10b-5 claiming that the company's directors had failed to disclose the unfairness of certain self-dealing stock transactions between the corporate parent and the corporation. *Goldberg v. Meridor*, 567 F.2d 209 (2d Cir. 1977). In the case, the court focused on a press release to minority shareholders that failed to mention the inadequacy of the transactions' consideration. The court's theory was that if noninterested directors or minority shareholders could have used the disclosure to disapprove or enjoin the stock transactions under state law, the disclosure could be seen as deceiving the corporation in its "decision" to enter into the transactions. The theory is limited to fiduciary breaches in connection with securities transactions.

§9.3.2 Scienter — "Manipulative or Deceptive Device or Contrivance"

A plaintiff in a 10b-5 action must plead and prove the defendant's *scienter*, a "mental state embracing intent to deceive, manipulate, or defraud." *Ernst & Ernst v. Hochfelder*, 425 U.S. 185 (1976). In *Hochfelder*, an accounting firm negligently failed to audit a company's accounting practices, which would have revealed that the company president had induced investors to put money into nonexistent escrow accounts and pocketed the money himself. Defrauded investors claimed the accounting firm's negligence enabled the fraud. The Supreme Court rejected the argument, previously accepted by several lower courts, that negligence is actionable under Rule 10b-5. It based its holding not on the language of Rule 10b-5, which actually supports such a construction, but instead on the enabling "manipulative or deceptive device or contrivance" language of §10(b).

This culpability standard is the same whether the suit is brought by the SEC or a private plaintiff and whether the suit seeks injunctive relief or damages. *Aaron v. SEC*, 446 U.S. 680 (1980) (scienter required in SEC injunctive actions). Nonetheless, in SEC enforcement proceedings, the agency has used a lower negligence standard based on the language of Rule 10b-5.

Meaning of Scienter

What is scienter? Scienter in a fraud sense means the defendant was aware of the true state of affairs and appreciated the propensity of his misstatement or omission to mislead. See *Sundstand Corp. v. Sun Chemical Corp.*, 553 F.2d 1033 (7th Cir. 1977) (defining scienter as involving "not simple negligence," but an extreme departure from ordinary care). Showing scienter, which requires evidence of the defendant's state of mind, is often difficult.

The Supreme Court in *Hochfelder* left open the question whether a showing of recklessness can satisfy the 10b-5 culpability standard. Lower courts have uniformly concluded that recklessness is sufficient, when misrepresentations were so obvious that the defendant must have been aware of them. See *Greebel v. FTP Software, Inc.*, 194 F.3d 185 (1st Cir. 1999) (summarizing approaches in various circuits). Under this view, recklessness exists when circumstantial evidence strongly suggests actual knowledge. Some courts have even said the plaintiff must show "deliberate recklessness." See *In re Silicon Graphics Inc. Securities Litigation*, 183 F.3d 979 (9th Cir. 1999) (interpreting the

PSLRA to compel 10b-5 plaintiffs to plead "facts that constitute circumstantial evidence of deliberately reckless or conscious misconduct").

Scienter also assumes the defendant had some sense that his statements or omissions would mislead. Some lower courts have interpreted Rule 10b-5 to permit the defendant a "good faith" defense on the theory that a defendant cannot intend to deceive if she acted in good faith with an empty mind. Thus, a corporate defendant who was objectively reckless by disregarding information with an obvious danger to mislead lacks scienter if she simply forgot to disclose the information or it never came to her mind. See *Backman v. Polaroid Corp.*, 893 F.2d 1405 (1st Cir. 1990). Courts, however, have rejected a "business judgment" defense. A knowingly or recklessly false disclosure is not excused on the ground that it advanced some corporate purpose. Although the business judgment doctrine of state corporate law may excuse corporate decisions that on balance promote shareholders' interests, Rule 10b-5 regulates knowing or reckless misinformation whatever the justification.

Pleading Scienter

Most 10b-5 cases are dismissed or settled. Frequently, dismissal turns on whether the plaintiff has adequately pled scienter. In general, allegations of fraud must be pleaded "with particularity." Fed. R. Civ. P. 9(b). More specifically, the PSLRA requires a complaint alleging securities fraud to "state with particularity facts giving rise to a strong inference that the defendant acted with the required state of mind." Exchange Act §21D(b)(2); *In re Cabletron Systems, Inc.* 311 F.3d 11 (1st Cir. 2002) (permitting pleader to use unnamed "confidential sources," provided identified sufficiently to support factual inferences).

Lower courts have jostled on the PSLRA pleading standard.

- The Second Circuit has taken the position that the PSLRA "did not change the basic pleading standard for scienter." *Novak v. Kasaks*, 216 F.3d 300 (2d Cir. 2000). The court reasserted its long-standing view that a strong inference of fraudulent intent can be made by (1) alleging facts showing the defendant had both motive and opportunity to commit fraud or (2) alleging facts that constitute strong circumstantial evidence of conscious misbehavior or recklessness.
- The Ninth Circuit, on the other hand, has taken to heart the PSLRA message to curb securities fraud cases and has required 10b-5 plaintiffs to plead "facts that constitute circumstantial evidence of deliberately reckless or conscious misconduct." *In re Silicon Graphics Inc. Securities Litigation*, 183 F.3d 970 (9th Cir. 1999) (rejecting a motive and opportunity pleading standard).

- Other circuits, including the First and Sixth Circuits, have sought to synthesize these views, holding that the PSLRA contemplates that scienter can be shown by inferences, provided they are reasonable and strong. See *Greebel v. FTP Software, Inc.*, 194 F.3d 185 (1st Cir. 1999). According to these courts, one kind of relevant evidence (among many) is the motive and opportunity of company executives to deceive. See also *In re Comshare Inc. Securities Litigation*, 183 F.3d 542 (6th Cir. 1999) (adopting "middle ground" under which motive and opportunity alone are not sufficient).

The pleading standard a court adopts appears to affect dismissal rates. In a study of 10b-5 cases brought since 1995, courts in the Ninth Circuit dismissed 10b-5 cases 61 percent of the time, while in the Second Circuit the dismissal rate was only 37 percent. To test whether the Second Circuit hears stronger 10b-5 cases than the Ninth Circuit, the study looked at particular types of allegations. Again the Second Circuit seemed more friendly to 10b-5 claims. The study found that allegations of violations of accounting principles, improper revenue recognition, and false forward-looking statements have been more likely to survive dismissal in the Second Circuit, compared to the Ninth Circuit. Curiously, the Ninth Circuit was more willing than the Second Circuit to entertain claims under the Securities Act, which does not require allegations of scienter. See Pritchard & Sale, *What Counts as Fraud? An Empirical Study of Motions to Dismiss under the Private Securities Litigation Reform Act*, J. Empirical Legal Studies 125 (2005).

In 2007 the Supreme Court entered the fray and interpreted "strong inference" to mean "more than merely plausible or reasonable — it must be cogent and at least as compelling as any opposing inference of nonfraudulent intent." *Tellabs Inc. v. Makor Issues & Rights Ltd*, 551 U.S. 308 (2007). In the process the Court rejected the Seventh Circuit's "middle ground" approach to look at all the allegations collectively, without comparing them, and then determine whether they created a "strong inference" of scienter. The Court said that a comparison of "plausible inferences" (of both nonculpability and fraudulent intent) was necessary, and the inference of scienter must be "at least as likely as" any plausible opposing inference.

The Supreme Court thus accepted that the PSLRA pleading standard can be satisfied by pleaded facts that create "cogent and compelling" inferences of scienter, provided these inferences are at least as strong as inferences of nonculpability (a gloss on the First and Sixth Circuit approach). Significantly, the Court added that, as in any dismissal motion, the court must accept "all factual allegations in the complaint as true" and the complaint must be read as a whole. The majority also rejected the approach of two concurring justices who argued that the inference of culpability must be "more plausible" than the inference of innocence, or "more likely correct than not correct." That is, a tie goes to the plaintiff!

Corporate Scienter

In a corporation, where the corporate actor acts only through human agents, corporate scienter is tricky. It is not uncommon that one individual in the organization is aware of the true state of facts, but another individual unwittingly makes false or misleading statements. The SEC and the courts have looked at the sum of the knowledge of corporate agents, for example holding the corporation liable when a press spokesman misstated the intentions of the company's merger team. See *In re Carnation*, Exchange Act Rel. No. 22,214 (SEC 1985).

Duty to Correct

Sometimes a speaker learns only later that prior statements were incorrect. Although there is no private liability if the speaker did not originally know or recklessly disregard the truth, failing to correct a misstatement once the error is known supports a finding of scienter. The duty to correct exists as long as the incorrect statements remain "alive" in the market, which depends on whether the mistaken information is still affecting prices or has been supplanted by subsequent information. But if disclosure was originally correct or not misleading, there is no duty to update prior information. See *Gallagher v. Abbott Laboratories, Inc.*, 269 F.3d 806 (7th Cir. 2001).

§9.3.3 Reliance and Causation

Reliance and causation, elements of traditional common law deceit, are also elements of a private 10b-5 action. The reliance requirement tests the link between the alleged misinformation and the plaintiff's buy-sell decision — it weeds out claims where the misinformation had little or no impact on the plaintiff's decision to enter the transaction. The causation requirement, like proximate cause in tort law, tests the link between the misrepresentation and the plaintiff's loss — it weeds out claims where the securities fraud was not "responsible" for the investor's loss.

Reliance and causation are related. Each serves as a filter to ensure that the misrepresentations or omissions alleged by the plaintiff are causally linked to the plaintiff's actions and losses.

Reliance

Courts treat reliance as an element in all 10b-5 cases, but relax the requirements of proof in a number of circumstances. What is left is a requirement that a plaintiff in a face-to-face, arms-length transaction will have to show familiarity with the information alleged to be false.

Nondisclosure

When the defendant fails in a duty to speak — whether in a face-to-face transaction or an anonymous trading market — courts dispense with proof of reliance if the undisclosed facts were material. *Affiliated Ute Citizens v. United States*, 406 U.S. 128 (1972) (no reliance need be shown in face-to-face transactions when bank employees violated position of trust by failing to make material disclosures). The materiality of the undisclosed information indicates a reasonable investor would have considered it important, suggesting the plaintiff may have acted differently had he known the information. To require proof of reliance in a case of nondisclosure would impose a nearly insuperable burden on a plaintiff to prove reliance on something not said.

Omitted Information

In cases of half-truths — omitted information that renders a statement misleading — courts are divided on whether reliance must be shown. *Abell v. Potomac Insurance Co.*, 858 F.2d 1104 (5th Cir. 1988) (requiring a showing of reliance); *Sharp v. Coopers & Lybrand*, 649 F.2d 175 (3d Cir. 1981) (not requiring reliance if there are practical difficulties in proof).

Fraud on the Market

In cases of false or misleading representations on a public trading market — "fraud on the market" — courts have created a rebuttable presumption of reliance. *Basic, Inc. v. Levinson*, 485 U.S. 224 (1988) (plurality decision). The theory is that those who trade on public trading markets rely on the integrity of the stock's market price. In an open and developed stock market, the Efficient Capital Market Hypothesis (§1.2) posits that market prices reflect all publicly available information about a company's stock. On the assumption that material misinformation artificially distorts the market price, courts infer that investors have relied on the misinformation. This "fraud on the market" theory assumes that if the truth had been disclosed, investors would not have traded at the prevailing nondisclosure price.

To obtain class certification in a case based on "fraud on the market," the plaintiff must show that the market in which the class traded was efficient and that the alleged misstatements were made to the public. See *Erica P. John Fund, Inc. v. Halliburton Co.*, 131 S. Ct. 2179 (2011) (interpreting FRCP Rule 23, which requires in damages class actions that common legal/factual issues "predominate" over individual issues). The showing of an efficient market has turned on a variety of factors. See *Freeman v. Levinthol & Horwath*, 915 F.2d 193 (6th Cir. 1990) (identifying five factors, including trading volume, number of analyst reports, presence of market makers and arbitrageurs, whether company is S-3 filer, and historic movement of stock prices in reaction to unexpected events). After the plaintiff has made this showing, a defendant can then rebut the presumption of reliance and avoid the "fraud on the market" theory by showing either (1) the challenged misrepresentation in fact did not affect the stock's price, or (2) the particular plaintiff would have traded regardless of the misrepresentation. *Basic, Inc. v. Levinson*, 485 U.S. 224 (1988).

The "fraud on the market" presumption rests on a questionable theoretical base. As Justice White pointed out in dissent in *Basic*, investors demonstrably do not believe that stock prices reflect true value. Sellers believe the stock is overpriced and will soon fall; buyers believe that it is underpriced and will soon rise. Yet, even though the market is driven by varying perceptions of value, the "fraud on the market" theory may be desirable regulatory policy. Without it, each investor would have to prove her individual knowledge and reliance on alleged misinformation — for most public investors an impossible burden. The "fraud on the market" presumption makes possible 10b-5 class actions involving material misinformation on public trading markets. See Macey & Miller, *Good Finance, Bad Economics: An Analysis of the Fraud on the Market Theory*, 42 Stan. L. Rev. 1059 (1990).

The "fraud on the market" theory, which makes possible the 150-200 securities fraud class actions filed each year, has been a bane for the corporate community. Despite arguments to abandon the theory, the Supreme Court has said that whether the theory's presumption of reliance results in vexatious litigation is a matter for Congress, not the courts. See *Amgen Inc. v. Connecticut Retirement Plans & Trust Fund*, 133 S. Ct. 1184 (2013) (pointing out that PSLRA had already "homed in on the precise policy concerns" of non-meritorious securities fraud litigation). Nonetheless, in 2013, the Supreme Court agreed to hear a re-appeal in *Halliburton* on the continuing vitality of the "fraud on the market" theory. A decision is expected in 2014.

Causation

Courts have required that 10b-5 plaintiffs show two kinds of causation.

Transaction causation requires the plaintiff show that "but for" the defendant's fraud, the plaintiff would not have entered the transaction or would have insisted on different terms — a restated reliance requirement. Many courts equate transaction causation with reliance.

Loss causation requires the plaintiff show that the alleged misrepresentations or omissions resulted in the claimed losses to the plaintiff — a foreseeability or proximate cause requirement. See *AUSA Life Insurance Co. v. Ernst & Young*, 206 F.3d 202 (2d Cir. 2000) (noting that findings of foreseeability turn on fairness, policy and "rough sense of justice"). It is not enough for an investor who suffers an investment loss to identify a securities-related misrepresentation. If the investor's losses arise from extraneous causes, such as a spike in oil prices or the bursting of a stock bubble, there is no 10b-5 liability. See *Bastian v. Petren Resources, Inc.*, 892 F.2d 680 (7th Cir. 1990) (refusing to find loss causation when losses were attributable to market crash, not fraud).

Loss causation under 10b-5 is the converse of the negative causation defense of §11(e) of the Securities Act, which allows a defendant to prove which part of the plaintiff's damages represents losses other than those arising from misstatements in the registration statement. Under the PSLRA, plaintiffs in all 10b-5 actions have the burden of proving that the alleged misrepresentations or omissions caused their losses. Exchange Act §21D(b)(4). This may well place on plaintiffs the burdensome task of negating extraneous causes for their losses. See *In re Merrill Lynch & Co. Research Reports Securities Litigation*, 289 F. Supp. 2d 416 (S.D.N.Y. 2003) (dismissing complaint for failure to link deceptively favorable analyst reports and "artificial inflation" of stock prices). Courts have generally not permitted plaintiffs to use the "fraud on the market" presumption to show the alleged fraud produced an effect on stock prices.

Normally, plaintiffs can establish loss causation by showing a change in stock prices when the misrepresentations were made and then an opposite change when disclosure corrects the false or misleading information. What if there is no price change when the corrective disclosure happens — is it enough to allege and prove that the purchase price was inflated? The Supreme Court has held that the plaintiff cannot simply allege losses caused by an artificially inflated price due to "fraud on the market," but must allege and prove actual economic loss proximately caused by the alleged misrepresentations. *Dura Pharmaceuticals, Inc. v. Broudo*, 544 U.S. 336 (2005). In the usual case, this will be done by showing a drop in price at the time of corrective disclosure, creating a logical link between the misrepresentation and the loss. If there is no price drop or even a price rebound, however, the plaintiff still may be able to survive a motion to dismiss, if there is reason to think the price was affected by factors unrelated to the alleged fraud. See *Acticon AG v. China North East Petroleum Holdings, Ltd.*, 692 F.3d 34 (2d Cir. 2012) (price decline after corrective disclosure, followed by price rebound).

Despite the plaintiff's burden to prove loss causation at trial, the Supreme Court has held that 10b-5 plaintiffs need not establish loss causation to obtain class certification. Instead, a showing of materiality — which creates a presumption of reliance under the "fraud on the market" theory — justifies a finding under FRCP Rule 23 that common legal issues "predominate" over individual issues. Thus, for purposes of class certification, it is enough that the plaintiffs have pled that their investment losses were the result of the alleged fraud. *Erica P. John Fund, Inc. v. Halliburton Co.*, 131 S. Ct. 2179 (2011) (finding sufficient plaintiff's pleading that losses resulted from falsified earnings reports, understatements of asbestos-liability risk, and overstatements of benefits of merger).

§9.3.4 Damages

Proof of damages is also an element of a private 10b-5 action. The Supreme Court has held, however, that a 10b-5 plaintiff need not establish a price impact to show commonality in a class certification. *Erica P. John Fund, Inc. v. Halliburton Co.*, 131 S. Ct. 2179 (2011).

Private 10b-5 plaintiffs have a full range of equitable and legal remedies. The Exchange Act imposes only two limitations. Under §28 the plaintiff's recovery cannot exceed actual damages, implying that the goal of liability is compensation and effectively precluding punitive damages. Under §21D(e), added by the PSLRA, damages are capped according to a formula that seeks to discount posttransaction volatility in prices unrelated to any misinformation.

Courts have adopted various damages theories, though with no clear guidelines as to when each applies. To illustrate, consider a typical 10b-5 case involving a corporate statement that overstates sales of a new product:

Event	Trading price
Pre-announcement price	$24
Press release misstating product	28
Insiders sell stock	28
Pre-correction price	25
Corrective disclosure	20
One week later	19
90-day period after disclosure (average)	24
Suit filed (current price)	18

Assume further the experts say that the market overreacted to the false press release, and the stock price (given the false sales figures) should have been only $26. Compare the compensatory and deterrent value of the following liability schemes.

- *Rescission.* Rescission allows the defrauded plaintiff to cancel the transaction. If the plaintiff sold, he gets his stock back; if he purchased, he returns the stock, and the seller refunds the purchase price. Rescission is suited only to face-to-face transactions where the parties can be identified. In our example, if the insiders had sold to identifiable investors, a rescission remedy would force the insiders to buy back at $28, producing for the plaintiffs a paper gain between $28 (the purchase price) and $18 (the current price) — $10.

- *Rescissionary (disgorgement) damages.* If rescission is not possible because the stock has been resold, rescissionary damages replicate a cancellation of the transaction. A defrauded seller recovers the purchaser's profits — the difference between the purchase and resale price. A defrauded purchaser recovers his losses — again the difference between the purchase and resale price. In our example, if the purchasers had resold a week after corrective disclosure, the insiders would be liable for the difference between $28 (the sales price) and $19 (the resale price) — $9.

- *Cover (conversion) damages.* Cover damages, like those in a tort conversion action, assumes the plaintiff mitigates her losses by selling or reinvesting. They are the difference between the price at which the plaintiff transacted and the price at which the plaintiff could have transacted once the fraud was revealed. In our example, the purchasers would recover the difference between $28 (the purchase price) and $20 (the market price immediately after corrective disclosure) — $8.

- *Out-of-pocket damages.* This is the most common measure of damages in 10b-5 cases. The plaintiff recovers the difference between the purchase price and the true "value" of the stock at the time of purchase. This measure does not take into account any posttransaction price changes. In our example, accepting the expert opinions on "value," the purchasers would recover the difference between $28 (the purchase price) and $22 (the stock's "but for" value) — $6.

  Valuing stock in the abstract is often speculative, and many courts (including the Supreme Court in *Dura Pharmaceuticals,* above) look to the price at the time of corrective disclosure as a measure of the "but for" price. In our example, the purchasers would recover the difference between $28 (the purchase price) and $20 (the price immediately after corrective disclosure) — $8. Other courts are more exacting and look at the price *change* at the time of corrective disclosure to gauge the losses caused by the misinformation. In our example, recovery would be the difference between $25 (the price immediately before corrective disclosure) and $20 (the price after corrective disclosure) — $5.

- *Contract damages.* Contract damages compensate the plaintiff for the loss of the benefit of the bargain. They are the difference between the value received and the value promised. In our example, accepting the expert opinions on value, the purchasers would recover the difference between $26 (the "real" value of the stock, assuming the truth of the sales figures) and $22 (the "real" value of the stock, but for the false figures) — $4.

The theory of damages, not surprisingly, can significantly affect recovery. No one theory is always advantageous to the plaintiff, as recovery can vary depending on changes in the post-transaction prices. For example, rescissionary damages in a rising market might be negligible or nonexistent, while out-of-pocket damages that ignore post-transaction changes can be significant.

In face-to-face securities transactions courts have generally applied rescissionary damages — thus assuming that the transaction would not have occurred but for the fraud. In open-market transactions, such as false corporate filings or press releases, courts have preferred an out-of-pocket measure of damages — thus assuming that investors would have transacted, but at a more accurate price.

Damages Cap

When recovery is based on the market price of the stock — as with out-of-pocket and cover damages — the PSLRA imposes a damages cap. Congress created the cap on the assumption that damages are typically computed as the difference between the transaction price and the market price on the date of corrective disclosure — a rough out-of-pocket computation. Concerned that this "crash price" might substantially overstate plaintiffs' losses for a company with highly volatile stock, Congress required that courts consider a longer 90-day window for determining the market price. In theory, prices during this longer window will more accurately impound the corrected disclosure. See Baruch Lev & Meiring de Villiers, *Stock Price Crashes and 10b-5 Damages: A Legal, Economic, and Policy Analysis*, 47 Stan. L. Rev. 7 (1994). Under §21D(e), damages are capped at the difference between the transacted price and the average of the daily prices during the 90-day period after corrective disclosure.

In our examples, the cap imposed by the PSLRA might well affect the damages computations. Assuming that the average of daily prices during the postdisclosure period is $24, the cap would be the difference between $28 (the purchase price) and $24 (the 90-day average) — $4. As our examples illustrate, the statutory cap would significantly limit plaintiffs' recovery when prices generally rise during the 90 days after corrective disclosure. Notice, though, that the cap does not apply to a rescissory theory of damages.

Which Damages Theory?

Courts have not developed a unified theory of 10b-5 damages, except to say that the damages theory should fit the facts of the case. In cases involving claims by customers against securities firms, courts often impose rescissionary damages on the theory the customers would not have transacted had they known of the fraud. But in cases involving false corporate reports or press releases that affect trading in the company's shares, courts have been reluctant to use rescissionary damages because doing so overpunishes the corporate defendant in a falling market. *Green v. Occidental Petroleum Corp.*, 541 F.2d 1335 (9th Cir. 1976) (Sneed, J., concurring in denial of class action certification). Moreover, even though out-of-pocket damages excludes the effects of extraneous price changes, aggregating such damages may result in a significant recovery that penalizes nontrading defendants and exceeds that necessary for deterrence.

Despite the lack of clarity, plaintiffs will often prefer a 10b-5 action and its malleable damages theories over the more rigid damages formulas of the express actions of the federal securities laws. See *Wherehouse Entertainment Inc. v. McMahon & Co.*, 65 F.3d 1044 (2d Cir. 1995) (awarding plaintiff benefit-of-bargain damages under Rule 10b-5, even though not available under §11 of the Securities Act).

Circularity of Corporate Damages

When a corporation pays damages in a 10b-5 class action, the effect will often be the subsidization of one group of shareholders (or investors) by current shareholders. For example, if the class action involves falsely optimistic statements by management, class members induced to purchase overpriced stock will receive compensation from the corporation—that is, current shareholders, including the class members and existing shareholders. Rarely do managers themselves contribute significant amounts to the settlement of 10b-5 class action claims.

The result is that one group of investors (current shareholders) subsidizes another group of investors (purchasing shareholders)—net of the litigation expenses paid to class counsel and the defense counsel. For investors who are diversified, as most individual and institutional investors are, 10b-5 class action litigation imposes costs, but not necessarily net financial gains. Only to the extent that corporate managers (specifically and generally) respond to 10b-5 litigation by improving disclosure and corporate governance might the system be seen as cost-effective. Although studies indicate that companies that settle 10b-5 class actions subsequently undertake corporate governance reforms and then financially out-perform their peers, it is unclear whether the benefits of class litigation are worth the costs. Each year approximately 150-200 securities fraud class actions are filed in the United States, most of them "classic" cases alleging corporate misrepresentations that resulted in dramatic stock price declines. See Stanford Securities Class Action Clearinghouse, available at securities.stanford.edu (includes pleadings, court filings, dismissals, and settlement data in all post-PSLRA securities fraud class actions).

§9.3.5 Nature of 10b-5 Liability

Courts in 10b-5 cases have traditionally imposed liability on a joint and several basis—each culpable defendant becomes liable for all of the damages awarded. Joint and several liability serves to deter securities fraud and assures compensation for its victims. Potentially liable persons, facing the risk of full liability, feel compelled to guard against securities fraud. And plaintiffs are assured full recovery if they can identify at least one deep-pocket defendant.

The PSLRA, however, eliminates joint and several liability for defendants who do not "knowingly" commit violations of the securities laws. Exchange Act §21D(f). Instead, the Act creates a system of proportionate liability based on each "unknowing" defendant's proportion of responsibility. This liability scheme responds to concerns that tangential defendants in securities fraud cases (such as outside directors, lawyers, and accountants) with little or no responsibility for the fraud are coerced by joint and several liability into settling out of fear that they might be found liable and forced to bear all the damages awarded the plaintiffs. According to the PSLRA, a person commits "knowing" securities fraud when he makes an untrue statement or factual omission, on which others are likely to reasonably rely, with "actual knowledge" of the falsehood. Reckless conduct, by definition, does not constitute a knowing violation. In 10b-5 actions, the PSLRA liability system thus places significant importance on whether a defendant's scienter was knowing or merely reckless.

This system of proportionate liability requires that the judge instruct the jury to make specific determinations as to the "knowing" nature of each defendant's 10b-5 violations and each defendant's percentage of responsibility. Exchange Act §21D(d). "Unknowing" defendants are then liable only for their share. The PSLRA creates two wonderfully complex exceptions to proportionate liability if there are uncollectible shares:

- "Unknowing" defendants become jointly and severally liable as to plaintiffs with a net worth less than $200,000 and whose recovery exceeds 10 percent of their net worth.
- "Unknowing" defendants become liable for the uncollectible amounts in proportion to their responsibility, subject to a cap of 50 percent of whatever their original proportionate share.

To encourage settlements, the PSLRA bars contribution claims against any 10b-5 defendant who settles before final judgment, subject to any indemnification obligations for litigation costs.

§9.4 DEFENSES IN PRIVATE 10b-5 ACTION

Not only do the procedures and elements of private 10b-5 actions reflect a judicial and legislative caution about permitting investors to shift their trading losses on the basis of claimed misinformation, but additional defenses (some of recent vintage) further limit the advantages of 10b-5 litigation.

§9.4.1 Limitations and Repose Periods

The Sarbanes-Oxley Act adopts a statute of limitations for private 10b-5 actions. Sarbanes-Oxley §804. Under §1658(b) of the federal code applicable to federal courts, "a private right of action that involves a claim of fraud, deceit, manipulation, or contrivance in contravention of a regulatory requirements concerning the securities laws" may be brought two years after the discovery of facts constituting the violation (the limitations period), but no later than five years after such violation (the repose period). 28 U.S.C. §1658(b). The statute effectively codifies and extends the prior judicially imposed statute of limitations in 10b-5 actions: one year after discovery of facts constituting the violation, but no later than three years after the violation. *Lampf, Pleva, Lipkind, Prupis & Petigrow v. Gilbertson*, 501 U.S. 350 (1991) (announcing uniform federal limitations period for 10b-5 actions, which before had borrowed applicable state limitations periods).

So when is a plaintiff deemed to have "discovered" facts constituting the 10b-5 violation — thus beginning the §1658 two-year limitations period? At first, lower courts were divided. Some said the period began when the plaintiff became "constructively aware" of possible fraud, others when the plaintiff had specific evidence establishing the elements of a 10b-5 claim. The Supreme Court resolved this split in *Merck & Co. v. Reynolds*, 559 U.S. 633 (2010). In the case, the Court permitted Merck shareholders to pursue a 10b-5 claim against the company for misrepresenting the safety and commercial viability of Vioxx, a pain reliever ultimately withdrawn from the market. The Court concluded that the two-year limitations period of §1658 accrues either (1) when the plaintiff actually discovers the violation or (2) when a reasonably diligent plaintiff would have discovered the facts constituting the violation — including the fact of scienter. The Court rejected the argument that the limitations period begins to run when the plaintiff was put on "inquiry notice" that something was amiss, requiring further inquiry. Thus, the limitations period did not begin with information indicating concerns about Vioxx's safety — based on a study showing troubling cardiovascular side effects, the filing of products liability suits, and an FDA warning letter — but only when there was information indicating that Merck's statements were false and made with scienter.

The *Reynolds* decision thus clarifies the meaning of "inquiry notice." According to the Court, plaintiffs must sue within two years of having information that indicates that *all elements* of a 10b-5 claim are present, including that the defendant knew (or was reckless in not knowing) that its statements were false or misleading. Although this standard is not as forgiving as the "actual notice" standard (applicable to private actions under §18(a) for willful misrepresentations in SEC filings), the Court's interpretation gives 10b-5 plaintiffs some ability to wait and see whether apparently false statements were made knowingly. For example, fluctuations in a company's stock price (which some lower courts had held constitute "inquiry notice" of company misstatements) are not enough under *Reynolds*, which insists that the plaintiff also have notice of the defendant's scienter.

§9.4.2 *In Pari Delicto* Defense

According to the Supreme Court, a 10b-5 defendant can raise an *in pari delicto* defense when the plaintiff bears "substantially equal responsibility" for the violations he seeks to redress. *Bateman, Eichler, Hill Richards, Inc. v. Berner*, 472 U.S. 299 (1985). The defense, however, may exist more in theory than in practice since rarely will a swindled investor be equally at fault with the swindler. In *Bateman*, the Supreme Court held that a tipper of inside information could not use the defense when a tippee sued him for giving a false tip; the Court apparently viewed the giving of the tip for personal gain as more blameworthy than trading on it. Lower courts have been similarly diffident. The Second Circuit, for example, denied the defense when a plaintiff in a "joint venture" formed to trade illegally on an inside tip sought to collect certain promissory notes from a fellow venturer when the tip turned out wrong. The court denied the defense even though the plaintiff and defendant were implicated equally in the illegal venture. See *Rothberg v. Rosenbloom*, 808 F.2d 252 (2d Cir. 1986).

§9.4.3 Contribution and Indemnification

Securities fraud often implicates a number of actors. Contribution permits a defendant liable for more than his share to compel other responsible persons (whether or not sued) to pay their share of the total liability. Indemnification permits a defendant who has become liable to compel another person bound by contract to assume some or all of defendant's liability. Both sharing mechanisms have the effect of encouraging settlements and thus expediting compensation to fraud victims.

Contribution

The PSLRA expressly authorizes contribution actions by parties jointly and severally liable under Rule 10b-5 — typically "knowing" defendants. Contribution shares, like proportionate liability, are computed according to the percentage of responsibility. Exchange Act §21D(g)(8). The PSLRA also authorizes contribution by "unknowing" defendants who become subject to proportionate liability but are forced to pay other parties' uncollectible shares. Exchange Act §21D(g)(5). Contribution may be sought from any person, whether or not joined in the original action, who would have been liable for the same damages. These statutory rights clarify a contribution right earlier recognized by the Supreme Court. *Musick, Peler, and Garrett v. Employers Insurance of Wausau*, 508 U.S. 286 (1993).

Under the PSLRA, contribution claims must be brought within six months after a final nonappealable judgment, though "unknowing" defendants who make additional payments beyond their proportionate share have six months after payment to seek contribution. Exchange Act §21D(g)(9).

Indemnification

Courts have recognized the right of indemnification by "passive" or "secondary" 10b-5 defendants against more culpable participants. Such indemnification, courts have pointed out, increases deterrence by shifting liability to deliberately deceptive participants.

Whether participants in securities transactions may enter into indemnification agreements is an open question. The SEC has adopted the position that contractual or other provisions that purport to indemnify corporate directors and officers against §11 liability under the Securities Act are void as against public policy. See §6.3.2. Such indemnification, the SEC believes, undermines the watchdog role the Securities Act envisions for such corporate officials. Yet, the SEC permits indemnification of §11 liability for underwriters and accountants, suggesting that private allocations of risk may sometimes supersede the statutory scheme. The PSLRA, though not conclusively resolving the issue, gives a nod to private allocations in its express validation of indemnification agreements that deal with attorneys' fees awarded as punishment for unfounded securities claims.

§9.4.4 Contract Defenses

Although Rule 10b-5 in theory abolishes *caveat emptor* — the principle that the parties' agreement governs — courts since the 1980s have increasingly introduced concepts borrowed from state contract law to trump 10b-5 protection. Focusing on the parties' contractual relationship and the terms of their bargain, courts have denied 10b-5 recovery on such grounds as statute of frauds, merger clauses, choice of law clauses, and releases. See Margaret Sachs, *Freedom of Contract: The Trojan Horse of Rule 10b-5*, 51 Wash. & Lee L. Rev. 879 (1994).

This quiet transformation, coming mostly in 10b-5 cases involving private securities transactions, reverses an earlier, well-established attitude that 10b-5's remedial purposes preempt any defenses based on contrary state law. Moreover, this trend seemingly flouts §29(a) of the Exchange Act, which voids any stipulation that waives the protections of the Act. See Robert Prentice, *Contract-based Defenses in Securities Fraud Litigation: A Behavioral Analysis*, 2003 U. Ill. L. Rev. 337 (arguing that contract-based defenses be permitted only when objective evidence supported investor's lack of reliance on oral representations).

These decisions reflect a federal retrenchment and an emerging privatization of 10b-5 law. Courts have denied 10b-5 standing to plaintiffs who assert misrepresentations in oral contracts for the sale of securities, importing state statutes of frauds into 10b-5 jurisprudence. See *Pommer v. Medtest Corp.*, 961 F.2d 620 (7th Cir. 1992). Courts have applied merger clauses (the parties' written agreement supersedes any prior oral communications) to reject 10b-5 allegations of oral misrepresentations, in disregard of the common law rule that such clauses are irrelevant in fraud actions. See *Jackvony v. RIHT Financial Corp.*, 873 F.2d 411 (1st Cir. 1989).

The continuing validity of these defenses, however, has been brought into question by the Supreme Court's decision that 10b-5 liability extends to oral securities contracts. *Wharf (Holdings) Ltd. v. United International Holdings Inc.*, 532 U.S. 588 (2001) (noting that Exchange Act applies to "any contract" for the purchase or sale of a security and that oral securities contracts are common under UCC and recognized under state statutes of fraud). The Court also rejected an argument that the dispute, arising from a securities seller's secret intent not to honor the sales contract, merely stated a state claim for breach of contract. The Court said the seller's secret intent "went well beyond . . . a simple failure to perform." That is, securities fraud under Rule 10b-5 is not constrained by contract principles.

§9.5 COMPARISON TO OTHER SECURITIES FRAUD REMEDIES

Rule 10b-5 is not the only game in town. Victims of securities fraud have available other federal and state remedies, many offering advantages over the 10b-5 action. Some relax the demanding 10b-5 scienter and reliance requirements, without the procedural hurdles erected by the PSLRA. Others avoid the procedures and delays of court litigation. Yet the breadth of the 10b-5 action, its avoidance of state procedures in derivative litigation, its presumption of reliance in certain contexts, the availability of broad discovery rules in federal court, the possibility of worldwide service of process, and a developed case law ensure that the 10b-5 action will remain a cornerstone of U.S. securities regulation.

§9.5.1 Express Federal Remedies for Securities Fraud

The federal securities laws create express remedies in specific contexts for securities fraud. In general, courts have held that the choice of action (and its attendant elements) is the plaintiff's, even when the same conduct is covered by both an express private action and the implied 10b-5 action. See *Herman and Maclean v. Huddleston*, 459 U.S. 375 (1983) (upholding 10b-5 action, even though challenged conduct was also actionable under §11 of the Securities Act). Courts have rejected the argument, accepted in other cases involving implied private actions, that specific liability schemes negate an inference of broad implied liability. The implied 10b-5 action has a venerated status in federal securities regulation.

Express Actions Under the Securities Act

The private antifraud remedies of the Securities Act focus narrowly on misinformation in public securities offerings. Section 11 of the Securities Act provides investors a damages remedy against specified defendants in cases of material misinformation in the registration statement filed in a public offering. Section 12(a)(2) of the Securities Act provides for rescission relief in cases of material misinformation in a public offering outside the registration statement or by statutory sellers not subject to §11 liability. As interpreted, §12(a)(2) provides no private relief for securities fraud in market trading or private offerings. See *Gustafson v. Alloyd Co.*, 513 U.S. 561 (1995) (interpreting §12(a)(2) to be limited to public offerings). Both §§11 and 12(a)(2) relax the traditional elements of scienter, reliance, and causation. And since the equalization of the statutes of limitations in federal fraud actions and the demise of aiding and abetting liability in private 10b-5 actions, the private remedies of the Securities Act are relatively more advantageous than 10b-5 litigation in cases of securities fraud in a public offering.

For private offerings, since the Supreme Court's ruling in *Gustafson* limiting §12(a)(2) to public offerings, the only federal private action is that under Rule 10b-5. Likewise, it is the only means for private redress against fraud in sales of government securities, which are excluded from §12(a)(2) coverage and exempt from Securities Act registration and §11 liability. In both situations, it is remarkable that a cryptic section of the Exchange Act should fill gaps in the Securities Act.

Express Private Actions Under the Exchange Act

The Exchange Act authorizes express private actions to buttress the Act's regulation of securities trading markets and to enforce its system of periodic disclosure for publicly traded securities. Section 9 prohibits schemes to manipulate stock prices and creates a private action for victims of stock manipulation to recover damages. Exchange Act §9(e). In addition, false or misleading statements made in filings with the SEC trigger a cause of action for investors who can prove they relied on them, subject to a defense of good faith ignorance. Exchange Act §18(a).

The express antifraud remedies of the Exchange Act have proved less advantageous than Rule 10b-5. Section 18(a) is rarely used, despite its relaxed culpability standard, because of its confined focus on filed documents and its arguably more exacting reliance requirement. Section 9(e) is also disfavored because of its narrower coverage on specified manipulative behavior and its significant procedural requirements, such as the posting of a bond to cover defendant's attorneys' fees. The procedural burdens added by the PSLRA, though aimed at curbing 10b-5 litigation, generally apply to private actions under the Exchange Act. See Exchange Act §21D(a), (b); cf. §21D(g) (proportionate liability applies only to actions involving false or misleading statements, arguably not including §9(e) manipulation). Thus, the relative advantage for plaintiffs of 10b-5 litigation persists even after the PSLRA.

Criminal Securities Fraud

Section 807 of Sarbanes-Oxley creates a crime for fraud in connection with trading in securities of reporting companies, potentially broader than Rule 10b-5. Under Section 1348 of the federal criminal code any person who "knowingly" (1) defrauds any person in connection with any security of a reporting company or (2) obtains by means of false or fraudulent pretenses, representations, or promises, any money or property in connection with the purchase or sale of any security of a reporting company. Violations are subject to stiff fines or jail sentences. In addition *attempts* to defraud or obtain money by false pretenses are also covered. 18 U.S.C. §1348.

Some comparisons to the 10b-5 action are immediate. Section 1348 only covers activities involving securities of reporting companies — transactions involving non-public companies are not covered. Section 1348 requires a "knowing" violation — reckless violations may not be covered. Section 1348(1) covers fraud "in connection with any [reporting company] security" without mentioning purchases or sales — by negative implication fraudulent mismanagement may be covered.

Whether §1348 implies a private cause of action is not clear. Unlike other provisions added by Sarbanes-Oxley that foreswear a private action, §1348 is silent on whether there exists a private cause of action for violating its criminal norms. Compare Sarbanes-Oxley §303 (no private action for inducing fraudulent audit) and §307 (no private action for violations of "up the ladder" reporting by company lawyers).

Comparison of Federal Securities Fraud Remedies.

The chart that follows compares the elements of the various federal fraud actions.

Federal Securities Remedies

	Exchange Act		
	Rule 10b-5	**§18(a)**	**§9(e)**
Coverage	"purchase or sale" of securities	SEC filing	trading in securities listed on stock exchange
Plaintiff	"purchaser" or "seller"	"purchaser" or "seller" of affected securities	"purchaser" or "seller" of manipulated securities
Defendant	primary violator	person who makes false statements in filing	"willful participant" in manipulative conduct
Violation	misrepresentation or omission of material fact "in connection with" purchase or sale of any security	false or misleading statement with respect to material fact in SEC filing	specified manipulative practices (wash sales, matched orders, false or reckless touting, etc.)
Culpability	scienter required (includes recklessness)	defense: good faith and no knowledge of falsity	required ("willful participation")
Reliance	reliance required (unless case involves duty to speak or omission)	reliance required	N/A
Causation	loss causation	"price affected by statement"	"price affected" by violation
Remedy	generally out-of-pocket damages	damages caused by reliance	damages sustained as result of violation
Limited liability	proportional liability for unknowing violators	N/A	N/A
Contribution	available	available ("as in cases in contract")	available ("as in cases in contract")
Limitations period	2 years after discovery/ 5 years after violation	2 years after discovery/ 5 years after violation	2 years after discovery/ 5 years after violation

	Securities Act		
	§11	**§12(a)(1)**	**§12(a)(2)**
Coverage	registered offering	unregistered, nonexempt offering	"public offering"
Plaintiff	"acquiror" of registered securities	"purchaser" of unregistered securities	"purchaser" of securities
Defendant	issuer, directors, specified officers, experts, underwriters	statutory seller (person who "solicits" for personal gain)	statutory seller (person who "solicits" for personal gain)
Violation	untrue statement or misleading omission of material fact in registration statement	violation of §5 (sale or offer of unregistered securities or gun-jumping)	offer or sale "by means of prospectus or oral communication" containing materially false or misleading statement
Culpability	strict liability: issuer due diligence defenses: non-issuer defendants	N/A	defense: reasonable care and no knowledge
Reliance	not required (defense if income statement filed 12 months after offering)	N/A	defense if purchaser knows untruth or omission
Causation	defense (negative causation)	N/A	defense (negative causation)
Remedy	damages formula (capped at aggregate offering price)	rescission or rescissionary damages	rescission or rescissionary damages
Limited liability	proportional liability for unknowing outside directors	N/A	N/A
Contribution	available ("as in cases in contract")	N/A	N/A
Limitations period	1 year after discovery/ 3 years after offering (perhaps 2 years/ 5 years, if fraud)	1 year after violation	1 year after discovery/ 3 years after offering (perhaps 2 years/ 5 years, if fraud)

§9.5.2 State Law Remedies

State law provides several alternatives to a federal 10b-5 action. Shareholders deceived by corporate managers can claim a breach of fiduciary duty, or bring a common law action of deceit, and state blue sky laws provide statutory remedies for fraudulent sales and (sometimes) fraudulent purchases.

In most situations, plaintiffs need not choose between state or federal remedies. State claims arising out of the same facts as a 10b-5 claim can be brought in federal court as pendent claims.

Duty of Honesty

Shareholders can sue corporate managers for violating their "duty of honesty" if they knowingly disseminate false information that results in corporate injury or damage to individual shareholders. See *Malone v. Brincat*, 722 A.2d 5 (Del. 1998). Although the Delaware courts have yet to clarify the elements of a "duty of honesty," one immediate advantage is the absence of a "purchaser or seller" standing requirement.

State Law of Deceit

State common law of deceit offers some advantages over Rule 10b-5, its federal counterpart. Many states have relaxed scienter requirements; most states permit punitive damages in egregious cases; and none imposes the pleading and class action barriers created by the PSLRA. In addition, state statutes of limitations for fraud actions are sometimes longer than the two-year/five-year federal limitations periods. But see *Weinstein v. Ebbers*, 336 F. Supp. 2d 310 (S.D.N.Y. 2004) (interpreting Georgia law to not create standing for shareholders who did not trade, but held their stock in reliance on corporate misinformation).

Blue Sky Laws

Many state blue sky laws (named after scams where farmers who were promised rain got nothing but blue skies) impose civil liability for fraudulent *sales* under provisions modeled on §12(a)(2) of the Securities Act. See Uniform Securities Act §410 (see §6.6). In addition, some states impose civil liability for fraudulent *purchases* under provisions following the same pattern as §410.

Since the Supreme Court's narrow reading of §12(a)(2) in *Gustafson*, the civil liability scheme of §410 has assumed importance for aggrieved securities purchasers. Section 410 provides for rescission of securities sales (public or private) made by means of materially false or misleading statement, subject to a "due care" defense. Cases have held that causation is not an element of the plaintiff's case. Thus, compared to 10b-5 liability, the traditional elements of scienter, specific reliance, and causation are all relaxed. See Branson, *Collateral Participant Liability under State Securities Law*, 19 Pepp. L. Rev. 1027 (1992). Moreover, §410 extends to sellers (and their controlling persons, partners, directors and officers), as well as employees, broker-dealers, and agents who aid in the sale — significantly broader than the "primary violator" category under Rule 10b-5. Finally, the §410 liability scheme provides for recovery of attorneys' fees.

The blue sky liability scheme is carried forward in the revised Uniform Securities Act, promulgated in 2002 by the National Conference of Commissioners on Uniform State Laws. Under the liability provisions of the revised Act, which attracted much attention during the drafting process, private liability arises both for fraudulent sales and fraudulent purchases. USA §§509(b), (c). In both situations, the elements for establishing a cause of action are significantly relaxed compared to those under Rule 10b-5:

	USA §509(c), (d)	Rule 10b-5
Plaintiff	Purchaser (or seller)	Purchaser or seller
Defendant	Seller (or purchaser) + controlling person + partners, directors, officers + employees, broker-dealers and agents who "materially aid" in sale (or purchase)	"Primary violator" — person who engages in fraudulent (or deceptive) conduct on which purchaser or seller relies
Predicate	Purchase (or sale) "by means" of materially false or misleading statement	Purchase or sale of materially false or misleading statement (or silence when under duty to speak)
Culpability	Defense — purchaser (or seller) did not know or could not have known in exercise of reasonable care	Element — defendant's scienter (knowledge or reckless disregard of truth)
Reliance	Element — seller (or purchaser) does not know of "untruth or omission"	Element — actual and reasonable reliance, unless actionable silence or "fraud on market"
Causation	[not element]	Element — deception proximately caused losses
Damages	Rescission (upon tender of purchase price) OR out-of-pocket damages, with interest AND attorneys' fees	Rescission, cover, out-of-pocket or contract damages BUT no attorneys' fees

	USA §509(c), (d)	**Rule 10b-5**
Liability	Joint and several + right of pro rata contribution among liable persons	Joint and several + right of contribution
Limitations/ repose	Two years after discovery of facts constituting violation, but no more than five years after violation	Two years after discovery of facts constituting violation, but no more than five years after violation

§9.5.3 Racketeer Influenced and Corrupt Organizations Act (Private RICO)

The Racketeer Influenced and Corrupt Organizations Act (RICO), the famous 1970 federal legislation aimed at curbing organized crime, created a private civil action for persons injured by racketeering activities. RICO broadly defined the predicate acts of racketeering to include fraudulent sales of securities and generously mandated trebled damages and attorneys' fees to successful plaintiffs. Over time, plaintiffs claiming securities fraud came to include RICO allegations as a matter of course.

In 1995 the PSLRA amended RICO to eliminate securities fraud as a predicate act of racketeering. Congress concluded that RICO claims distort the incentives and remedies in securities litigation. In addition, the legislative history states plaintiffs may not allege other predicate acts, such as mail or wire fraud, if the conduct is actionable as securities fraud. The PSLRA, however, leaves intact private RICO securities claims brought against a person criminally convicted of securities fraud.

§9.5.4 Arbitration and Private Ordering

Parties to securities transactions have significant latitude to specify the substantive terms of their relationship and the procedures by which the terms are to be enforced. Claims of misinformation in securities transactions, particularly when they involve sophisticated investors, are increasingly guided by the terms of the parties' contract.

Arbitration of 10b-5 Claims

Claims of securities fraud can be arbitrated, if the parties so agree. The Supreme Court has upheld the validity of predispute and postdispute arbitration agreements under the Exchange Act, particularly of 10b-5 claims.

Shearson/American Express, Inc. v. McMahon, 482 U.S. 220 (1987). The Court recognized the right of parties to securities transactions to choose a forum for resolving their disputes, despite provisions of the Exchange Act that give federal courts exclusive jurisdiction over claims arising under the Act (§27) and that invalidate any contract that waives compliance with any provision of the Act (§29(a)). See also *Rodriguez de Quijas v. Shearson/American Express, Inc.*, 490 U.S. 477 (1989) (upholding arbitration of Securities Act claims, overruling prior decision that arbitration agreements illegally waived access to judicial relief).

Although the Supreme Court premised its acceptance of securities arbitration on the SEC's power to oversee arbitration administered by the NASD or the stock exchanges (now administered by FINRA), the Court assumed that arbitration offers essentially the same rights and protections as court litigation. This assumption, at least for customer-broker disputes, was called into question by Dodd-Frank §921, which authorized the SEC to prohibit or limit the use of mandatory arbitration in customer-broker disputes. See §11.2.5. As of 2013, the SEC has not taken up the congressional invitation except to solicit comments on the costs and benefits of such arbitration. Meanwhile, nearly all customer-broker disputes continue to end up in FINRA-administered arbitration.

Contracting Around 10b-5 Elements

Not only can parties to securities transactions choose the forum for resolving their disputes, they can also by private agreement set the standards for judging their behavior. The parties can specify greater protection than provided by Rule 10b-5, using such contractual devices as warranties regarding the truth of specified information, admissions of reliance and causation, representations of information the parties deem material, specification of liquidated damages, and indemnification clauses. These contractual provisions often modify the normal materiality, culpability, reliance, causation, damages, and liability standards that would otherwise apply in a 10b-5 action.

Viewed in this light, Rule 10b-5 is a default term that provides a baseline of protection to those who enter into securities transactions. Parties to securities transactions, particularly sophisticated investors, may choose to agree to terms that add or subtract from the 10b-5 baseline.

Examples

Rule 10b-5 litigation is highly fact-intensive, as are the following (mostly real-life) examples drawn from a case of garden-variety securities fraud. The various deceptions described in the examples were practiced in Arkansas in the early 1980s. They spawned a host of litigation and left a trail of federal court decisions, including three by circuit courts and two by the Supreme Court. See *United States v. White*, 671 F.2d 1126 (8th Cir. 1982); *Arthur Young & Co. v. Reves*, 856 F.2d 52 (8th Cir. 1988); *Reves v. Ernst & Young*, 494 U.S. 56 (1990); *Arthur Young & Co. v. Reves*, 937 F.2d 1310 (8th Cir. 1991); *Reves v. Ernst & Young*, 507 U.S. 170 (1993). The legal community in Arkansas, as you can see, takes fraud seriously.

Farmer's Cooperative (Co-op) helps area farmers finance their farming operations and offers various farming outreach programs. Four years ago the Co-op's manager, Jack White, started his own company to build and operate a gasohol plant that would convert corn into fuel. The company, known as White Flame, was endemically short of capital, so White approached the Co-op board for a loan. The board, composed of 12 Co-op members elected annually, had the highest confidence in White and approved $4 million in unsecured, low-interest loans by the Co-op to White Flame, for which White gave personal guarantees.

As problems at the gasohol plant mounted, White Flame was unable to pay its debts as they came due. White looked for a way to sell White Flame to the Co-op in return for a release of his personal guarantees. White's lawyers, Ball & Mourton, devised an ingenious plan to which the Co-op board agreed. The plan called for the Co-op's general counsel, Brookmore, to resign and immediately file a lawsuit on behalf of the Co-op against White. The suit alleged that White had promised to transfer his White Flame stock to the Co-op in exchange for the Co-op assuming his debts in the project, and that the Co-op had relied on this promise by investing further sums in White Flame in the belief it owned the company. The Co-op sought a declaratory judgment that it had acquired White Flame at the time of White's promise and that the Co-op had assumed all of White's obligations. A few days later, according to script, White agreed to a consent decree that declared the Co-op had equitably owned all of White Flame stock as of a date six months before and that White was relieved of $4 million in personal guarantees.

The "acquisition" of White Flame proved disastrous for the Co-op. Within two years after the acquisition, the Co-op was bankrupt because of the heavy gasohol liabilities it had assumed.

1. The bankruptcy trustee for the Co-op, Thomas Robertson, considers 10b-5 claims against various participants in the Co-op's acquisition of White's interest the gasohol plant.
   a. Does the Co-op have standing under Rule 10b-5?
   b. Is Robertson, acting on behalf of the Co-op, the most adequate plaintiff?
   c. Robertson begins to draw up a list of potential 10b-5 defendants. Who should be on the list?
   d. Assuming the Co-op board was fully aware of White's intentions to rid himself of the gasohol plant, was there securities fraud?

e. From the start Jack White asserted his belief (perhaps naive) that the gasohol plant would turn itself around with the Co-op's financial backing and an upturn in gasohol prices. Can White be liable if he had a "clean heart and empty mind"?

f. Even if the Co-op was culpably deceived, can White be liable if the White Flame investment fizzled because of weakness in gasohol prices?

g. Besides Rule 10b-5, what other theories of liability are available to the bankruptcy trustee?

2. To raise money for its operations, the Co-op sells promissory notes to its farmer members. The notes, payable on demand, are uncollateralized and uninsured. They are attractive to members because they pay a variable interest rate adjusted monthly to stay above rates paid by local banks and savings and loans. The Co-op advertises its demand note program promising that "your investment is safe, secure, and available when you need it."

a. Do noteholders have standing to bring a 10b-5 class action regarding the Co-op's "acquisition" of White Flame?

b. Were the noteholders deceived in connection with the purchase or sale of their notes?

c. Who are potential defendants in a suit by the noteholders?

d. The Co-op board approved the settlement of the friendly lawsuit with White in November, which assumed the Co-op had purchased White's interest in the gasohol plant nine months earlier, in February. The next April, the Co-op holds its annual members' meeting, and management confirms the rumors that the Co-op purchased White Flame more than a year before. Members who purchased notes last February wonder when they should sue.

3. A year after "acquiring" White Flame, the Co-op hires the well-known accounting firm Arthur Young & Co. to audit its financial statements. During their review of the Co-op's books, Arthur Young accountants notice that the Co-op treated White Flame as having been acquired the year before, with all expenditures by the Co-op treated as acquisition costs. By this novel accounting, White Flame's fixed asset value is stated as $4.5 million. Under generally accepted accounting practices, however, White Flame should have been carried at its fair market value at the time of purchase — no more than $500,000.

In its audit report to the Co-op board, Arthur Young concludes the Co-op had always owned White Flame, thus avoiding a closer look at the circumstances of the gasohol plant's acquisition. The Arthur Young accountants are aware that if White Flame had been valued at market, the Co-op would have had a negative net worth and that bad news about the Co-op's shaky financial condition could well have triggered a disastrous run on the demand notes. The only cautionary disclosure came in a footnote to the audit report in which Arthur Young doubted the recoverability of the Co-op's investment in White Flame.

a. Can Robertson, the bankruptcy trustee, sue Arthur Young under Rule 10b-5 for its deceptive audit report?

b. Purchasers of demand notes, who bought after the deceptive audit report, sue Arthur Young under Rule 10b-5. Do these purchasers have standing?

c. The noteholders bring a class action claiming that the deceptive audit report resulted in their losses. Was the deceptive audit "in connection with" the plaintiff's purchases of the demand notes?

d. Most of the noteholders did not know of the audit report, which Arthur Young provided only to the Co-op board. Can the noteholders recover despite the absence of any actual reliance?

e. The Arthur Young accountants had never asked the Co-op's management for projections as to White Flame operations. Can Arthur Young be liable to the noteholders even though it was unaware of the truth about the White Flame operations?

f. The noteholders also sue the board's directors for withholding information about the shaky White Flame acquisition. Can the directors be liable under Rule 10b-5 if they relied on the audit report's statement of positive net worth?

4. A few weeks after receiving the audit report, the Co-op holds its annual meeting — which attracts a large and irate group of members. At the meeting the Co-op's management distributes condensed financial statements that management had prepared. The statements, based largely on Arthur Young's audit report, purport to show a financially healthy organization. They do not include the disclaimer in Arthur Young's audit report about the recoverability of the White Flame investment or about the questionable method used in valuing the White Flame assets.

At the meeting is Harry Erwin, the Arthur Young executive in charge of the Co-op account. After being introduced, Erwin discusses the condensed financial statement, but the crowd turns ugly with questions about the acquisition of White Flame and its true worth. Erwin avoids questions about how much money White Flame had lost and incorrectly states that the board had voted to acquire White Flame. When the intensity of the questioning increases, the board moves the meeting on.

a. Does Erwin's role at the meeting affect Arthur Young's 10b-5 liability in the suit brought by the noteholders?

b. Erwin knew that many of the Co-op members at the meeting were concerned about the Co-op's acquisition of White Flame, but he did not intend to mislead them. Can Arthur Young be held culpable?

c. Arthur Young claims its accountants did not tell the members the truth about the White Flame investment to avoid a run on the Coop. Does this negate Arthur Young's culpability?

d. Some of the members at the meeting eventually purchased notes. Many, though they heard Erwin's comments, did not specifically rely on them in their decision to purchase. Can these plaintiffs prove reliance?

e. Most members did not attend the annual meeting. Can members who purchased notes after the meeting and who were unaware of Erwin's comments at the meeting claim reliance?

f. Some of the members who purchased notes after the meeting later testified they believed the gasohol plant would work out and viewed their purchase of notes as a way to invest in the local economy. Does this affect the viability of the noteholders' 10b-5 action?

g. At the meeting Erwin commented that the Co-op anticipated a loan from a federal agency to cover some of the costs of the gasohol plant. Does Arthur Young have a duty to update this statement when the federal agency refuses the loan?

5. The noteholders' case goes to the jury.

a. Assuming that the plaintiffs still held their notes at the time of trial, what measure of damages under Rule 10b-5 should the jury be instructed to use?

b. Experts opine that the demand notes were worth 40 percent of face value when sold to the plaintiffs, though by the time of trial they are worthless. What should 10b-5 damages be?

c. Some plaintiffs, claiming financial hardship, had received from the Co-op 20 cents on the dollar in bankruptcy proceedings. These plaintiffs then took tax deductions for their losses, reducing their net economic loss. Does this affect these plaintiffs' 10b-5 recovery?

d. The jury determines total damages of $8 million and apportions the responsibility of the various participants as follows: Co-op, 60 percent; each of the five Co-op directors, 4 percent; Arthur Young, 20 percent. The Co-op is bankrupt. How much must each director and Arthur Young pay?

e. How might recovery have been different if the plaintiffs had pursued a theory of liability under state securities law? State common law deceit?

Explanations

1. a. Yes. The Co-op was a purchaser of White Flame shares from Jack White by virtue of the "friendly lawsuit" that recognized White's purported promise to sell his interest in White Flame to the Co-op. The Exchange Act broadly defines sales and purchases to include any acquisition and disposition of securities. See Exchange Act §3(a)(13), (a)(14). The lawsuit effectively transferred ownership of the shares to the Co-op. Although the transaction resulted in the Co-op acquiring the entire White Flame business, its structure as a "sale" of shares brings it within the reach of Rule 10b-5. See *Landreth Timber Co. v. Landreth*, 471 U.S. 681 (1985) (rejecting sale of business doctrine) (see §2.3.6). The Co-op, as purchaser, has standing to challenge fraud in the securities transaction.

   b. It is irrelevant whether Robertson, as trustee, is the most adequate plaintiff. Many of the procedures mandated by the PSLRA, including identification of the most adequate plaintiff, apply only to class actions — when one plaintiff seeks to represent a class of similarly situated plaintiffs. Exchange Act §21D(a)(3)(B). In this 10b-5 action, Robertson as trustee is stepping into the governance shoes of the board and suing in the name of the cooperative. Although other types of representative actions are susceptible to abuse, the PSLRA aims only at the abuses in securities fraud class actions.

   c. According to *Central Bank* and *Stoneridge* (§9.2.2), 10b-5 defendants in a private action must be primary violators who made false or misleading statements and induced others to trade to their detriment. In addition, 10b-5 liability encompasses those who have a fiduciary duty to speak and fail to. Therefore, the Co-op might sue the following suspects:

      • Jack White — the seller — undoubtedly made representations to the Co-op about White Flame's finances and risks or, at the least, failed in his fiduciary duty to the cooperative to disclose fully the material facts.

      • Ball & Mourton — the seller's lawyers — may have aided and abetted the fraud, but unless they actually made false or misleading statements that induced the Co-op into the transaction, *Central Bank* and *Stoneridge* teach that they cannot be liable in a private 10b-5 action. This conclusion is reinforced in *Janus Capital* (see §9.2.2), which held that merely drafting a false disclosure document did not subject a mutual fund adviser to liability when the false statements in the document technically were "made" by the fund itself.

      • Co-op directors — if they knew of the flimsiness of White Flame's finances — might be seen as having made misrepresentations (or as having failed in their duty to speak) to the Co-op. See *Goldberg v.*

Meridor (§9.3.1). Their duplicity with White might be seen as a deceit of the Co-op.

Of course, all of these parties may well be seen as aiders and abettors, and thus liable in an SEC enforcement action for substantially assisting the fraud perpetuated both on the Co-op and the noteholders. See §9.2.2.

d. Perhaps. Although 10b-5 does not reach naked fiduciary disloyalty, a theory of securities fraud might be constructed based on the failure of the Co-op directors to fully describe the corruption in the White Flame transaction to those constituents capable under state law to block it. See *Goldberg v. Meridor* (§9.3.1). This theory that the evil half should have disclosed to the good half rests on a question of causation: Could others in the Co-op (such as members or noteholders) have sought to enjoin the transaction had the directors revealed their knowledge? Cases since *Goldberg v. Meridor* have suggested that the undisclosed fiduciary breach must be so egregious that it is beyond dispute that state remedies would have been available to block the challenged securities transaction.

But even if other Co-op constituencies would have been empowered under state law to block the White Flame purchase, a 10b-5 claim remains problematic. The theory that transforms a state fiduciary breach into a federal disclosure claim represents a significant federal intrusion. This is particularly so where, as here, the theory of deception is based on a failure to disclose, thus implicating state fiduciary law. The Supreme Court in another context has questioned whether "sue" facts can be the basis for a federal disclosure claim, when state remedies are still available to aggrieved corporate constituencies. See *Virginia Bankshares, Inc. v. Sandberg*, 501 U.S. 1083 (1991) (proxy fraud). Further, the judicial insistence that full disclosure would have revealed a *clear* fiduciary breach suggests the infirmity of this federal intrusion, particularly when the integrity of information on securities markets is not implicated. At the least, the Co-op trustee would be well advised to bring pendent state claims against the Co-op's board.

e. No, if he truly believed the gasohol plant was a sound investment for the Co-op. The plaintiff must prove all the elements of a fraud, including that the defendant acted with scienter. This compels the plaintiff to prove either that the defendant knew the true state of facts or that he was reckless in not knowing them. At least one court has recognized a "good faith" defense to allegations of scienter. See *Backman v. Polaroid Corp.*, 893 F.2d 1405 (1st Cir. 1990) (no scienter if defendant "genuinely forgot to disclose information or [it] never came to his mind").

In addition, the PSLRA imposes on all 10b-5 plaintiffs the burden to plead with particularity the defendant's state of mind. Exchange Act §21D(b)(2). The Act requires the plaintiff to "state with particularity facts giving rise to a strong inference" that the defendant acted with the required state of mind. Exchange Act §21D(b)(2). The plaintiff would have to negate White's assertion of innocence by showing strong inferences or circumstantial evidence that White intended to deceive. Without more information, the bankruptcy trustee could not adequately plead the Co-op's case.

f. Perhaps. White's liability depends on whether (1) the plaintiff can establish loss causation, and (2) whether White is subject to joint and several or proportionate liability.

As a 10b-5 plaintiff, the Co-op must prove that the losses it claims from its failed investment in the gasohol plant were caused by the fraudulent purchase. Whether and the extent to which the Co-op can bear this burden may well depend on the theory of damages adopted in the case. If the theory is rescission — the Co-op never would have entered the self-dealing transaction if properly informed — the purchase could be said to have been the "but for" cause of all subsequent losses. But for the purchase, the Co-op would have suffered no losses. If the theory is out-of-pocket damages — the difference in the plant's overstated price and its real market value — the transaction caused only this marginal loss. The Co-op simply bought above market. Which theory is right? It depends on the characterization of the case: a self-dealing fiduciary breach or a failure to disclose fully the risks. Arguably, this transaction would not have happened were it not for White's influence. Just as corporate law rescinds self-dealing transactions, so should Rule 10b-5. The subsequent drop in gasohol prices would be irrelevant under this theory of damages and causation. White's liability would depend on his culpability. If a "knowing" violator, his liability would be joint and several — for the full amount of damages awarded. See Exchange Act §21D(g). If merely reckless, White's liability would be proportionate — presumably less than 100 percent.

g. There is a panoply of state theories of liability. The Co-op could assert claims against White and the Co-op directors for fraud and for breaching their fiduciary duties to the Co-op, claims against the lawyers for aiding and abetting this breach, and claims against all of them for securities fraud under state blue sky laws.

2. a. Yes, but only purchasers of notes who relied on deceptive information related to the White Flame acquisition. This class will be limited to a

time period during which the White Flame deception was afoot — that is, after the consent decree finalizing the acquisition and before full revelation of the White Flame fiasco, near the time of Co-op's bankruptcy. (*Sellers* of notes, who got out in time, suffered no loss and have no reason to sue.)

In addition, the court must determine in this 10b-5 class action which noteholder seeking to be class representative is the most adequate plaintiff. The PSLRA's provisions on choosing the most adequate plaintiff had in mind 10b-5 class actions involving public companies with institutional shareholders. This Arkansas agricultural cooperation with farmer noteholders presents an unanticipated context. The PSLRA's legislative history makes clear that the prior rule of first-come, first-served should not apply to appointing a class representative. More realistically, the quality and commitment of the class attorney may be the most important factor in a case when class members are, in all likelihood, similarly situated.

b. Yes, on two theories. First, the advertising materials representing the notes' safety — whose use by Co-op members was certainly foreseeable — were misleading for not revealing the tenuous financial situation of the Co-op following the White Flame acquisition. Second, the failure of the Co-op to disclose fully to purchasers — a duty courts infer for companies selling securities to public investors — can also be seen as misleading. Abandoning *caveat emptor* for companies that sell to the public, courts infer a duty to speak whether the company undertakes transactions with existing shareholders or new investors. See §9.4.4.

c. The list of potential defendants for the deceptive sale of notes is different from that for the fraudulent sale of White Flame. Again, *Central Bank* frames the question in terms of who were the primary violators — that is, who through their misrepresentations or failure to speak induced the plaintiffs' purchases?

- Co-op, the seller that misrepresented the safety of the notes and failed to disclose the risks of the gasohol acquisition, is surely a primary violator. But it is now bankrupt.
- Co-op directors, who authorized the assurances of safety and remained silent in the face of the gasohol risks, are likely defendants. Although they may have directors' and officers' insurance, such policies often exclude coverage of securities fraud.
- Jack White, who arguably stood in a fiduciary position with respect to the noteholders, may also be a primary violator for not having revealed the Co-op's tenuous financial position. It is unlikely he will have the resources to cover the noteholders' full losses.

Central Bank and *Stoneridge* — reinforced by the requirement that the 10b-5 defendant "make" the false or misleading statements — appear to remove from the list such collateral participants as Ball & Mourton, White's lawyers, who may have aided and abetted the fraudulent sale of the notes but had no apparent fiduciary relationship to the noteholders and did not induce their purchases. The shortened list illustrates the greater difficulty *Central Bank* and *Stoneridge* create for plaintiffs in search of deep-pocket defendants.

d. Under §1658, the statute of limitations applicable to 10b-5 actions, the noteholders must sue within two years after discovery of facts putting them on notice of the elements of a 10b-5 action — including that the defendants had withheld information about the overvalued gasohol plant — and within five years after the defendants violated their disclosure duties. See *Merck & Co. v. Reynolds* (see §9.4.1) (interpreting the two-year limitations period of §1658 to accrue either (1) when the plaintiff actually discovers the violation or (2) when a reasonably diligent plaintiff would have discovered the facts constituting the elements of the violation). Applying the two-year/five-year limitations periods, three events are relevant:

- *Friendly lawsuit.* The friendly lawsuit marks the point when the fraud (the Co-op's failure to disclose the new riskiness of the notes) first began. Purchasers after this date would have five years to sue from their date of purchase — the repose period. It would, however, be a stretch to say that noteholders were on notice at this point about the Co-op's new financial stake in White Flame — the two-year limitations period. Moreover, before the friendly lawsuit, there was no reason to suspect fraud; not even the Co-op directors knew that the Co-op had "acquired" White Flame or knew of White's plans to unload his investment.

- *Premeeting rumors.* Although rumors on developed securities markets often trigger price swings, putting investors on notice of a discrepancy between appearances and reality, rumors circulating among Co-op members may have lacked this clarity. See *Masale v. Medco Research, Inc.*, 54 F.3d 443 (7th Cir. 1995) (price swings not enough to put plaintiffs on notice in case of company with volatile stock). Nonetheless, if the rumors had an air of accuracy and went to the overpricing of White Flame and its financial difficulties, cases interpreting the 10b-5 limitations period suggest that credible rumors can begin the running of the two-year limitations period.

- *Co-op annual meeting.* If at the meeting members were made aware of a discrepancy between appearances and reality, this information triggered the two-year limitations period. Whether there was notice depends largely on the effectiveness of the Co-op's coverup. If the meeting convincingly answered the members' questions and squelched the rumors, there was no notice. If not, members who had purchased during the Co-op's ongoing fraud would have two years after the April meeting to bring suit. (In the actual case, the members waited longer to sue under the then-applicable Arkansas statute of limitations. See *Reves v. Arthur Young & Co.*, 937 F.2d 1310 (8th Cir. 1991).)

3. a. No, unless Arthur Young can be seen as being a primary violator by having induced the White Flame acquisition — the securities transaction the Co-op has standing to challenge. If the accounting firm's only role was to falsely value the White Flame investment, after the fact, it could not have induced the acquisition. After *Central Bank* and *Stoneridge* there is no private 10b-5 liability for collateral participants that merely aid and abet a securities fraud or participate in the fraudulent scheme.

Nonetheless, it might be possible to construct a theory of inducement against Arthur Young if the Co-op might have rescinded the White Flame "acquisition" had the accounting firm informed the board of its true financial repercussions. Perhaps, for example, the Coop could have sought to have the consent decree voided on the ground it was procured by fraud. In this light, Arthur Young's deceptive audit induced the board (or other Co-op constituents) not to pursue this remedy.

Notice that even though the Arthur Young audit may have bolstered a false sense about the demand notes, the Co-op lacks capacity to sue on behalf of the noteholders.

b. Yes. As purchasers, the noteholders have standing. See *Blue Chip Stamps v. Maynard Drug Stores*, 421 U.S. 723 (1975) (§9.2.1). They may have a difficult time, however, establishing the elements of a 10b-5 violation.

c. Perhaps not. The "in connection" requirement reflects the boundaries of 10b-5 federalism and foreseeability. Both are implicated under a theory that the audit report, in some sense, induced the purchases of demand notes.

First, it can be argued that it was not foreseeable that Arthur Young's report to the Co-op board would induce purchases of the notes. The accounting firm had a professional relationship only with the Co-op, not its noteholders. To impose open-ended liability without a further "holding out" by Arthur Young would significantly expand 10b-5 coverage. Courts have shown reluctance to expose securities professionals to liability beyond the scope of their engagement. See *In re Financial Corp. of America Shareholders' Litigation*, 796 F.2d 1126 (9th Cir. 1986) (refusing to impose liability on company's accountants for not disclosing risk to company of its repurchase agreements of mortgage-backed bonds).

Second, imposing liability on the accounting firm on a theory that it had a fiduciary duty to speak to the noteholders is a significant expansion of state fiduciary concepts. In cases applying a *Goldberg v. Meridor* theory (see §9.3.1) based on deception that interferes with a claim of state law violations, courts have sought to minimize federal overreaching by insisting that any state law violation be clear. In our case, it is not clear that Arthur Young's silence (without more) would amount to a fiduciary breach. Federalism concerns might well dictate a conclusion that the accounting firm's audit was not "in connection" with the noteholders' securities transactions.

d. Perhaps, if Arthur Young had a duty to speak. Reliance is presumed in 10b-5 cases alleging a failure to speak, on the theory that a person owed a duty of disclosure should not have to bear the burden of proving his reliance on silence.

Did Arthur Young have a duty to disclose the shaky White Flame investment to the noteholders? Consider whether Arthur Young was in a position of "trust and confidence" as relates to the noteholders: Arthur Young was aware and had access to the material information; it benefitted from its relationship with the Co-op; it understood the effect of not speaking fully; although it did not initiate the note program, it actively participated in disseminating falsehoods and half-truths by attending the noteholders' meeting; it had an advantageous informational position compared to the noteholders, and the information it had was highly material. These factors led the Eighth Circuit in the case from which this example is drawn to conclude that Arthur Young's relationship with the noteholders created a duty to disclose. *Arthur Young & Co. v. Reves*, 937 F.2d 1310 (8th Cir. 1991).

e. Yes. Scienter may be proved by a showing of recklessness. If the misrepresentation and omissions about the gasohol plant's value were so obvious that the Arthur Young accountants must have been aware of them, there is scienter. In our example, the circumstances strongly suggest that the accountants actually knew that the gasohol plant was overvalued.

f. Perhaps not. Liability of the board members under Rule 10b-5 depends on their state of mind. If they relied on the audit report and believed in good faith that the gasohol plant was properly valued on the Co-op's books, there would be no scienter. If, however, the board members suspected or knew that the audit report had failed to capture the Co-op's true financial position, scienter would likely be established and they would have no good faith defense.

Liability as control persons under §20(a) of the Exchange Act, however, does not require that the plaintiff show scienter. It would be enough if the noteholders showed that the directors had actual control of Co-op management, and the directors failed to meet their burden to establish their good faith. See §9.2.2 (control persons).

4. a. Yes. Arthur Young is liable for the false and misleading representations of its employees under traditional standards of *respondeat superior*. See §9.2.2. Erwin's comments at the meeting, unlike the audit report that Arthur Young presented to the Co-op board, more clearly constitute an inducement to members to continue to purchase demand notes. Arthur Young therefore became a primary violator to the extent the account executive induced note purchases.

Primary violator analysis focuses on whether (1) Arthur Young *made* misrepresentations that induced purchases, and (2) Arthur Young *prepared* misrepresentations disseminated by others to purchasers. In either case, Arthur Young (its accountants) must have known or have been reckless in not knowing that the information was false and would induce Co-op members to purchase.

b. Yes, if Erwin was aware of the true facts and the propensity of his comments to mislead. The culpability of Arthur Young, as a corporate actor, depends on the knowledge and state of mind of employees who had information about the Co-op's finances. In addition, if Arthur Young is seen as having a duty to disclose, its corporate scienter depends on the sum of the states of mind of those acting on behalf of the corporation, including all the accountants working on the Co-op account.

In measuring 10b-5 culpability, two aspects of scienter form a matrix of culpability: (1) the actor's awareness of the true facts and (2) the actor's awareness of the effect of his statement or omissions on others. In the clearest case, there is scienter if it can be shown the actor knew the facts and wanted to mislead others. But an actor who either did not know the facts or was unaware of the effect of his statements on others may lack scienter.

In this case, some of the Arthur Young accountants (if not Erwin himself) were aware that the White Flame investment was overstated on the Co-op's books, and the Co-op members had not been informed of this. Further, it is likely the Arthur Young accountants were aware that the Co-op members would be hanging on Erwin's every word and would rely on what he said or did not say, notwithstanding his protestations that he not intend to mislead. Lower courts have accepted that there is scienter when the facts are so obvious (here the effect that Erwin's comments would have) that he and the other Arthur Young accountants must have been aware his statements would have a propensity to induce reliance.

c. No. There is no business judgment defense under Rule 10b-5.

d. Yes. For the plaintiffs at the meeting, subjects of a face-to-face misrepresentation, their awareness of Erwin's misrepresentations may be sufficient. In keeping with 10b-5's liberal remedial purposes, some courts have crafted a "reasonable reliance" test that requires only that the plaintiff show (1) he was aware of the misrepresentation, and (2) it was material in a general sense, even though the plaintiff did not subjectively rely on its veracity.

e. Perhaps, using a kind of "fraud on the market" theory. Although these noteholders were unaware of Erwin's misstatements, his misstatements bolstered a market for the Co-op's demand notes. Had Erwin told the truth at the meeting, there would have undoubtedly been a run on the Co-op, something that members in the close-knit, rural community that the Co-op served would likely have heard about. That is, Erwin's misstatements created a false sense of confidence about the Co-op and its notes. In a similar case, the Second Circuit held that an investor who relied on a newspaper article about a company entering the video cassette market, information unrelated to the company's overstated earnings, proved her reliance because the newspaper article might well have had a different tone and her broker would likely have advised her differently had the truth about the earnings problems been disclosed. *Panzirer v. Wolf*, 663 F.2d 365 (2d Cir. 1981).

Notice that the need to construct a theory of reliance (for different subgroups of the plaintiff class) evaporates if Arthur Young is held liable for a fiduciary failure to speak. In such a case, reliance is presumed. It is perhaps for this reason that the noteholders pursued this theory against Arthur Young in the actual Co-op litigation. See *Robertson v. White*, 635 F. Supp. 851 (W.D. Ark. 1986).

f. Yes. Even though a fraud on the market theory provides a presumption of reliance, this presumption can be rebutted with evidence that the plaintiffs either knew of the alleged misinformation or would have purchased anyway. The burden is on the defendants.

g. Perhaps, if the information about the loan is material and still alive in the market at the time of the loan denial. In general, there is no duty to update past disclosures unless the information is still affecting the price in the market. Here the Co-op notes are not traded in a price-setting market, but forward-looking information about the loan might affect whether members would redeem their notes. The collapse of the loan, assuming it was still affecting members' decision not to redeem their notes, would seem to trigger a duty to update. The prediction of the loan carried an assurance it would happen and a duty to supply noteholders new, contradictory information.

5. a. Probably rescissionary damages, though there is no one correct measure of damages. The Supreme Court has said that the correct measure of damages for a defrauded seller is an out-of-pocket measure, up to the buyer's profits, but this was in a case involving a defrauded seller.

In our example, the issue is whether the plaintiffs would have purchased, though at a lower price, or whether they would have refused to purchase at any price had they known the Co-op's financial difficulties. See *Roe v. Merrimont Corp.*, 850 F.2d 1226 (7th Cir. 1988). An out-of-pocket theory of damages, which measures the difference between the notes' purchase price and their fair value when bought, assumes the plaintiffs would have purchased anyway, but at a lower price. A rescissionary measure, which seeks to return the plaintiffs to the position before the transaction, assumes they would not have purchased at all.

Absent the Co-op's assurance that the notes were "safe, secure, and available when you need it," it is unlikely any members would have purchased, particularly since the notes were sold as alternatives to federally guaranteed bank savings accounts. In addition, fault rested mainly with the seller Co-op, suggesting that rescission best fits the transaction. Courts are willing to order rescission and award full recovery when the transaction would not have happened. See Merritt, *A Consistent Model of Loss Causation in Securities Fraud Litigation: Suiting the Remedy to the Wrong*, 66 Tex. L. Rev. 469 (1988). Moreover, courts frequently employ rescission to prevent unjust enrichment, such as when the defendant parlays a stock transaction into significant profits. See Robert Thompson, *The Measure of Recovery under Rule 10b-5: A Restitution Alternative to Tort Damages*, 37 Vand. L. Rev. 349 (1984).

b. Purchase price, plus interest. Under a rescissionary theory of damages, where the purchasers have not resold the securities, the seller repurchases the shares at the purchase price, plus interest. See Securities Act §12(a)(2).

c. No. The Supreme Court held that the §28(a) reference to actual damages does not limit the plaintiff's recovery to net economic harm. *Randall v. Loftsgaarden*, 478 U.S. 647 (1986). There is no offset from the plaintiff's recovery for tax benefits that the plaintiff gained as a result of having purchased the securities.

d. It depends on whether the defendants are found to have been "knowing" or "unknowing" 10b-5 violators. Any knowing violator each becomes jointly and severally liable for the full $8 million judgment. The plaintiffs could collect the full amount from any one of them, assuming they have the money.

If any of the violators was not knowing (that is, reckless) the defendant would only be liable for the share of his responsibility. For example, if one of the directors had been merely reckless, her 4 percent responsibility would result in proportionate liability of only $320,000. Likewise, if Arthur Young were held to be an unknowing violator, its proportionate 20 percent liability would be $1.6 million.

If for some reason the plaintiffs could not recover the full $8 million — perhaps because all the defendants other than the Co-op were found to have been merely reckless — the proportionate liability scheme imposes partial liability with respect to the uncollected $4.8 million Co-op share:

- First, these "unknowing" defendants would become liable for the uncollectible amounts in proportion to their responsibility, subject to a cap of 50 percent of whatever their original proportionate share. For Arthur Young, this would mean an additional liability of 20 percent of $4.8 million (or $960,000), capped by 50 percent of its original $1.6 million share (or $800,000). For each director, this means an additional liability of 4 percent of $4.8 million (or $192,000), capped by 50 percent of each of their original $320,000 share (or $160,000).

- Second, these "unknowing" defendants would become jointly and severally liable as to any Co-op members with a net worth less than $200,000 whose individual recovery exceeds 10 percent of their net worth. Thus, for example, if a plaintiff had a net worth of $60,000 and lost $10,000 in her Co-op investment, each violator would become jointly and severally responsible to pay the $10,000.

Ultimately, unless all the plaintiffs fell into the second category, some of the uncollectible share would not be collected.

e. Both have some advantages over a 10b-5 claim, under current law. A state securities claim under state blue sky law would have provided a clear basis for rescissionary damages and would not have created limitations based on proportionate liability. A state common law deceit claim also creates the possibility of punitive damages. The actual damages limitation of §28 of the Exchange Act precludes punitive damages in a 10b-5 action.

Although the Securities Litigation Uniform Standards Act of 1998 seeks to funnel all securities fraud class actions to federal court and under federal law, the Act only applies to class actions involving "covered securities." Exchange Act §28(f)(1). Here the Co-op's notes are not traded on a stock exchange or NASDAQ and seem to escape this preemption. See Exchange Act §28(f)(5)(E) (definition of "covered security" refers to "section 18(b) of this Act," a misreference to the Securities Act provision that preempts state blue sky regulation of securities traded on a stock exchange or NASDAQ).

Insider Trading

Federal securities regulation of insider trading has developed in stages. It began with a novel scheme in the Securities Exchange Act of 1934 for the disclosure and disgorgement of insider trading profits, a scheme aimed at discouraging stock price manipulation by corporate insiders. Later, in the 1960s, the SEC and federal courts used the antifraud principle of Rule 10b-5 to build an awkward "abstain or disclose" jurisprudence applicable to insiders who trade on material, nonpublic information. In the 1980s Congress reentered the fray and increased the penalties for insider trading, clarified the scope and mechanisms for private enforcement, and imposed additional surveillance duties on firms with access to inside information. In 2000 the SEC promulgated rules clarifying the "state of mind" that triggers liability and the persons who become subject to the "abstain or disclose" duty. In 2002 Congress sought to discourage insider trading by executives at the expense of employees and based on falsified company financials. In 2010 Congress strengthened corporate "clawback" devices to discourage corporate executives from manipulating company financials to increase their stock-based pay.

Nonetheless, no statute defines insider trading, and its regulation remains largely a matter of federal common law.

This chapter covers:

- the various activities that constitute insider trading and the theories for their regulation [§10.1]
- the insider trading jurisprudence built on Rule 10b-5, as well as SEC rules that clarify liability and congressional enactments that specify sanctions [§10.2]

- the federal remedial scheme under §16 of the Exchange Act applicable to short-swing trading profits by designated insiders [§10.3]
- the regulation of insider trading under the Sarbanes-Oxley Act (revised in the Dodd-Frank Act) during pension fund blackout periods and following restatement of company financials [§10.4]

§10.1 INTRODUCTION TO INSIDER TRADING

§10.1.1 Classic Insider Trading

The paradigm case of insider trading arises when a corporate insider trades (buys or sells) shares of his company using material, nonpublic information obtained through the insider's corporate position. See §3.1.1 ("substantial likelihood" test for materiality). The insider exploits his informational advantage (a corporate asset) at the expense of the company's shareholders or others who deal in the company's stock.

The insider can exploit his advantage whether undisclosed information is good or bad. If *good news*, the insider can profit by buying stock from shareholders before the price rises on the favorable public disclosure. (An insider can garner an even greater profit on a smaller investment by purchasing "call options," which give him a right to buy the shares at a fixed price in the future.) If *bad news*, the insider can profit by selling to unknowing investors before the price falls on unfavorable disclosure. An insider who does not own shares can also profit by borrowing shares and selling them for delivery in a few days when the price falls, known as "selling short" (see §8.2.2), or by purchasing "put options," which give him the right to sell the shares at a fixed price in the future.

§10.1.2 Misappropriation of Information — Outsider Trading

An insider can also exploit an informational advantage by trading in *other* companies' stock — "outsider trading." If the insider learns that his company will do something that affects the value of another company's stock, trading on this material, nonpublic information can also be profitable. The insider "misappropriates" this information from his firm. Although he trades with shareholders of the other company, he violates a confidence of his firm.

Many cases reported in the media as "insider trading" are actually cases of outsider trading on misappropriated information. Although classic insider trading and misappropriation often are grouped together under the rubric of "insider trading," it is useful to distinguish the two. The justifications for regulating each differ.

§10.1.3 Theories for Regulation of Insider Trading

Consider some theories for regulating insider trading:

Enhance fairness

Insider trading is unfair to those who trade without access to the same information available to insiders and others "in the know"—a *fairness* rationale. The legislative history of the Exchange Act, for example, is replete with congressional concern about "abuses" in trading by insiders. This fairness notion, however, has not been generally accepted by state corporate law, which has steadfastly refused to infer a duty of candor by corporate insiders to shareholders in anonymous trading markets. See *Goodwin v. Agassiz*, 186 N.E. 659 (Mass. 1933) (rejecting duty of insiders to shareholders except in face-to-face dealings). Moreover, a fiduciary-fairness rationale cannot explain regulation of outsider trading based on misappropriated information.

Preserve market integrity

Insider trading undermines the integrity of stock trading markets, making investors leery of putting their money into a market in which they can be exploited—a *market integrity* rationale. A fair and informed securities trading market, essential to raising capital, was the purpose of the Exchange Act. Moreover, market intermediaries (such as stock exchange specialists or over-the-counter market makers) may increase the spread between their bid and ask prices if they fear being victimized by insider traders. Greater spreads increase trading costs and undermine market confidence. Yet a market integrity explanation may overstate the case for insider trading regulation. Many professional participants in the securities markets already trade on superior information; the efficient capital market hypothesis posits that stock prices will reflect this better-informed trading. See §1.2.

Reduce cost of capital

Insider trading leads investors to discount the stock prices of companies (individually or generally) where insider trading is permitted, thus making it more expensive for these companies to raise capital—a *cost of capital* rationale. In stock markets outside the United States, studies show that cost of equity decreases when the market introduces and enforces insider trading prohibitions. For this reason, most U.S. public companies have insider trading policies that permit insiders to buy or sell company stock only during "trading windows" — usually 7 to 30 days after important company announcements.

Protect property rights

Insider trading exploits confidential information of great value to its holder — a *business property* rationale. Those who trade on confidential information reap profits without paying for their gain and undermine incentives to engage in commercial activities that depend on confidentiality. Although in the information age a property rationale makes sense, theories of liability, enforcement, and private damages have grown in the United States out of the rhetoric of fiduciary fairness and market integrity.

Policing Insider Trading

Insider trading, cloaked as it is in secrecy, is difficult to track down. The stock exchanges have elaborate, much-used surveillance systems to alert officials if trading in a company's stock moves outside of preset ranges. When unusual trading patterns show up or trading occurs before major corporate announcements, exchange officials can ask brokerage firms to turn over records of who traded at any given time. The exchanges conduct computer cross-checks to spot "clusters" of trading — such as from a particular city or brokerage firm. An Automated Search and Match system, with data on thousands of companies and executives on such things as social affiliations and even college ties, assists the exchanges. If the exchanges see something suspicious, they turn the data over to the SEC for a formal investigation. The SEC can subpoena phone records and take depositions, sometimes promising immunity to informants.

§10.2 RULE 10b-5 AND INSIDER TRADING

The development of 10b-5 insider trading duties is a fascinating story of judicial activism and ingenuity in the face of a statutory lacuna. It also offers an insight into the operation of corporate federalism. Perceiving a failure by state corporate law to regulate insider trading, federal courts have used Rule 10b-5 to develop a theory of disclosure-based regulation that assumes the existence of fiduciary duties of confidentiality that state courts have been unwilling to infer.

§10.2.1 Duty to "Abstain or Disclose"

Federal courts have understood Rule 10b-5 to prohibit securities fraud. See Chapter 9. No person may misrepresent material facts that are likely to affect others' trading decisions. This general duty is meaningless to insider trading, which happens not through misrepresentations, but rather silence. Over time, federal courts have developed a regime that prohibits insider trading based on implied duties of confidentiality.

Parity of Information

Early federal courts held that just as every securities trader is duty bound not to lie about material facts, anyone "in possession of material, nonpublic information" must either abstain from trading or disclose to the investing public — a duty to *abstain or disclose*. See *SEC v. Texas Gulf Sulphur*, 401 F.2d 833 (2d Cir. 1968). But even the proponents of a "parity of information" (or "equal access") approach recognized that an absolute rule against trading when one has an informational advantage goes too far. Strategic silence is different from outright lying. To impose an abstain-or-disclose duty on everyone with material, nonpublic information — however obtained — would significantly dampen the enthusiasm for trading in the stock market. Capital formation might dry up if investors in trading markets were prohibited from exploiting their hard work, superior skill, acumen, and even hunches. Investors would have little incentive to buy securities if they could not resell them using perceived informational advantages.

Duty of Confidentiality

In the early 1980s, the Supreme Court provided a framework for the abstain-or-disclose duty. *Chiarella v. United States*, 445 U.S. 222 (1980); *Dirks v. SEC*, 463 U.S. 646 (1983). A decade later the Court brought "outsider trading" within this framework. *United States v. O'Hagan*, 521 U.S. 642 (1997). Reading Rule 10b-5 as an antifraud rule, the Court has held that any person in the possession of material, nonpublic information has a duty to disclose the information (or abstain from trading) if the person obtains the information in a relation of trust or confidence — normally a fiduciary relation. The Supreme Court thus has anchored federal regulation of classic insider trading on a presumed duty of corporate insiders to the company's shareholders — even though state corporate law has largely refused to infer such a duty in impersonal trading markets. The Court has extended this duty-based regulation to trading by outsiders who breach a duty of confidentiality to the source of the information — even though the source is unrelated to the company in whose securities they trade.

① *Classic insider trading liability: Chiarella v. United States*

Chiarella was employed in the composing room of a financial printer. Using his access to confidential takeover documents that his firm printed for corporate raiders, he figured out the identity of certain takeover targets. Chiarella then bought stock in the targets, contrary to explicit advisories by his employer. He later sold at a profit when the raiders announced their bids. The Supreme Court reversed Chiarella's criminal conviction under Rule 10b-5 and held that Rule 10b-5 did not impose a "parity of information" requirement. Merely trading on the basis of material, nonpublic information, the Court held, could not trigger a duty to disclose or abstain. Chiarella had no duty to the shareholders with whom he traded because he had no fiduciary relationship to the *target companies or their shareholders*. (The Court decided that Chiarella could not be convicted for trading on information misappropriated from his employer since the theory was not presented to the jury.)

② *Tipper-tippee liability: Dirks v. SEC*

Dirks was a securities analyst whose job was to follow the insurance industry. When he learned of an insurance company's massive fraud and imminent financial collapse from Secrist, a former company insider, Dirks passed on the information to his firm's clients. They dumped their holdings before the scandal became public. On appeal from SEC disciplinary sanctions for Dirks's tipping of confidential information, the Supreme Court held that Dirks did not violate Rule 10b-5 because Secrist's reasons for revealing the scandal to Dirks were not to obtain an advantage for himself. For Secrist to have tipped improperly "in connection with" the trading of Dirks's clients, the Court held, there had to have been a fiduciary breach. The Court took the view that a breach occurs when the insider gains some direct or indirect personal gain or a reputational benefit that can be cashed in later. In the case, Secrist had exposed the fraud with no expectation of personal benefit, and Dirks could not be liable for passing on the information to his firm's clients.

③ *Misappropriation liability: United States v. O'Hagan*

O'Hagan was a partner in a law firm retained by a third-party bidder planning a tender offer. He purchased common stock and call options on the target's stock before the bid was announced. Both the bidder and law firm had taken precautions to protect the bid's secrecy. When the bid was announced, O'Hagan sold for a profit of more than $4.3 million. After an SEC investigation, the Justice Department brought an indictment against O'Hagan alleging securities fraud, mail fraud, and money laundering. He was convicted on all counts and sentenced to prison. The Eighth Circuit, however, reversed his conviction on the ground that misappropriation did not violate Rule 10b-5. (The Eighth Circuit also held the SEC exceeded its authority in promulgating Rule 14e-3. See §10.2.3 below.) The Supreme Court reversed and validated the misappropriation theory. The Court concluded that the unauthorized use of confidential information is (1) the use of a "deceptive device" under §10(b) and (2) "in connection with" securities trading. First, the misappropriator "deceives" the source that entrusted him the material, nonpublic information by not disclosing his evil intentions — a violation of a duty of confidentiality. Second, the "fiduciary's fraud is consummated, not when the fiduciary gains the confidential information, but when . . . he uses the information to purchase or sell securities." Citing to the legislative history of the Exchange Act and to SEC releases, the Court concluded that misappropriation liability would "insure the maintenance of fair and honest markets [and] thereby promote investor confidence." O'Hagan's trading operated as a *fraud on the source* in connection with securities trading — a violation of Rule 10b-5.

Satisfying the Disclosure Duty

According to the logic of the 10b-5 "abstain or disclose" construct, a fiduciary may trade on confidential information by first disclosing the information to the person to whom she owes the fiduciary duty. See *SEC v. Texas Gulf Sulphur Co.*, 401 F.2d 833 (2d Cir. 1968) (suggesting that insiders wait 24 to 48 hours after information is publicly disclosed to give it time to be disseminated through wire services or publication in the financial press). In a similar vein, some companies have internal policies that permit corporate insiders to trade only during a one- or two-week period after company files quarterly and annual reports. As a practical matter, the abstain-or-disclose duty is really a prohibition against trading, since any disclosure must be effective to eliminate any informational advantage to the person who has material, nonpublic information — thus eliminating any incentive to trade.

State of Mind

An unsettled issue in the cases has been the state of mind that triggers insider trading liability. In *O'Hagan* the Supreme Court said that insider trading must be "on the basis" of material, nonpublic information. Lower courts have split on whether the trader must be in "knowing possession" of inside information or must actually "use" the information in trading. Compare *United States v. Teicher*, 987 F.2d 112 (2d Cir. 1993) (accepting "knowing possession" standard, as simpler to apply and consistent with the expansive nature of Rule 10b-5, when a young attorney tipped inside information about transactions involving clients of his law firm); *United States v. Smith*, 155 F.3d 1051 (9th Cir. 1998) (requiring showing of "use" of inside information, particularly when a defendant's state of mind is at issue in criminal case).

In 2000 the SEC adopted a rule to clarify this aspect of insider trading liability. Rule 10b5-1. Under the rule, a person trades "on the basis" of material, nonpublic information if the trader is "aware" of the information when making the purchase or sale. Rule 10b5-1(b). In its release accompanying the rule, the SEC explained that "aware" is a commonly used English word, implying "conscious knowledge," with clearer meaning than "knowing possession." Does the SEC have rulemaking authority to define the elements of insider trading, which (until now) has been governed exclusively by judge-made rules? Arguably, the agency that begot Rule 10b-5 should have the power to change and define its contours.

Pre-Existing Trading Plans

The SEC has also sought to clarify when corporate insiders and others can trade in company stock even when aware of inside information. Individuals and entities who set up specific securities trading plans when unaware of inside information can avoid liability even if trading under the plan occurs later when they are aware of inside information. Rule 10b5-1(c). The person must demonstrate:

- She had entered in "good faith" into a binding contract to trade the security, instructed another person to execute the trade for her account, or adopted a written plan for trading securities — when unaware of inside information.
- This pre-existing trading strategy either (1) expressly specified the amount, price, and date of the trade, (2) included a written formula for determining these inputs, or (3) disabled the person from influencing the trades, providing the actual trader was unaware of the inside information.
- The trade accorded with this pre-existing strategy.

An entity (nonindividual) has an additional affirmative defense if the actual individual trading for the entity was unaware of inside information, and the entity had policies and procedures to ensure its individual traders would not violate insider trading laws. Rule 10b5-1(c)(2).

In 2009 the SEC provided some interpretive guidance when Rule 10b5-2 plans are revised. First, although termination of a trading plan does not automatically trigger 10b-5 liability, a termination that "coincides" with insider trading may violate Rule 10b-5. Second, canceling and then replacing an existing plan may also run into problems if part of a "scheme to evade" the rule; such liability can be minimized with a "waiting period" between the cancellation and replacement.

§10.2.2 Insider Trading Primer

The linchpin of 10b-5 insider trading liability is trading on the basis of material, nonpublic information entrusted to a person with duties of confidentiality. The SEC offers a restatement of federal insider trading law in its Rule 10b5-1:

> The "manipulative and deceptive devices" prohibited by Section 10(b) of the Act and Rule 10b-5 there under include, among other things, the purchase or sale of a security of any issuer, on the basis of material, nonpublic information about that security or issuer, in breach of a duty of trust or confidence that is owed directly, indirectly, or derivatively, to the issuer of that security or the shareholders of that issuer, or to any other person who is the source of the material, nonpublic information.

Although the Supreme Court has glossed over the provenance of these duties, its opinions lead to some clear guidance to persons who have material, nonpublic information:

Insiders	Insiders who obtain material, nonpublic information because of their corporate position — directors, officers, employees, and controlling shareholders — have the clearest 10b-5 duty not to trade. See *Chiarella*.
Constructive (or temporary) insiders	Outsiders with no relationship to the company in whose securities they trade also have an abstain-or-disclose duty when aware of material, nonpublic information obtained in a relationship or trust or confidence. See *O'Hagan*. The outsider's breach of confidence to the information source is deemed a deception that occurs "in connection with" his securities trading.
Outsiders (with duty to source of information)	Constructive insiders who are retained temporarily by the company in whose securities they trade — such as accountants, lawyers, and investment bankers — are viewed as having the same 10b-5 duties as corporate insiders. See *Dirks* (dictum). Lower courts have also inferred status as constructive insider in family settings where there are expectations of confidentiality.
Tippers	Those with a confidentiality duty (whether an insider or outsider) who knowingly make improper tips are liable as participants in illegal insider trading. See *Dirks*. The tip is improper if the tipper expects the tippee will trade and anticipes

reciprocal benefits — such as when she sells the tip, gives it to family or friends, or expects the tippee to return the favor. This liability extends to *subtippers* who know (or should know) a tip is confidential and came from someone who tipped improperly. The tipper or subtipper can be held liable even though she does not trade, so long as a tippee or subtippee down the line eventually does.

Tippees

Those without a confidentiality duty inherit a 10b-5 abstain-or-disclose duty if they knowingly trade on improper tips. *Dirks.* A tippee is liable for trading after obtaining material, nonpublic information that he knows (or has reason to know) came from a person who breached a confidentiality duty. In addition, *subtippees* tipped by a tippee assume a duty not to trade if they know (or should know) the information came from a breach of duty.

Traders in derivative securities

The 10b-5 duty extends to trading with nonshareholders — such as options traders. *O'Hagan* (call options). The Insider Trading Sanctions Act of 1984 makes it unlawful to trade in any derivative instruments while in possession of material, nonpublic information if trading in the underlying securities is illegal. Exchange Act §20(d).

Strangers

A stranger with no relationship to the source of material, nonpublic information — whether from an insider or outsider — has no 10b-5 duty to disclose or abstain. *Chiarella.* Strangers who overhear the information or develop it on their own have no 10b-5 duties.

It is important to notice that corporate insiders (directors, officers, employees, and agents) often own stock in their companies. This is not illegal — in fact, it is sometimes highly desirable for corporate executives to have some "skin in the game." Nor is it illegal for these insiders to buy and sell their company stock. There is a problem only when these insiders are aware of nonpublic, material information when they trade in their company's stock or the stock of other companies — or improperly tip this information to others.

§10.2.3 Outsider Trading — Misappropriation Liability

Under the misappropriation theory, 10b-5 liability arises when a person trades on confidential information in breach of a duty owed to the source of the information, even if the source is a complete stranger to the traded securities. *United States v. O'Hagan*, 521 U.S. 642 (1997). In effect, the deception is of the source and the trading is with another party. This fraud-on-the-source construct raises a number of issues: the basis for misappropriation liability, the scope of the duty of confidentiality, and the validity of the SEC's rule creating misappropriation liability for tender offer information.

Notice the difference between an *outsider* who misappropriates information from a source unrelated to the company in whose securities he trades and a *tippee* who receives information from a fiduciary inside a company in whose securities the tippee (or subtippee) trades. The outsider's duty is to the "outside" source of the information; the tippee's duty is derived from the duty of the "insider" who tips improperly.

Misappropriation Theory

The *O'Hagan* decision was an important victory for the SEC, which 10 years before had failed to convince the Supreme Court that Rule 10b-5 encompasses a misappropriation theory. *Carpenter v. United States*, 484 U.S. 19 (1987) (split 4-4 decision). The 1987 case involved a *Wall Street Journal* reporter who wrote the widely read and influential column "Heard on the Street." Although the column used public information to report on particular companies, it invariably affected the companies' stock prices. The newspaper had a prepublication policy of keeping confidential the identity of subject companies to protect the appearance of journalistic integrity. The reporter was convicted for misappropriating the advance information and tipping it to both a friend and a broker, even though the *Wall Street Journal* had no interest in the trading. The Court's split 4-4 decision, though it upheld the reporter's conviction, had no precedential value and left a cloud of uncertainty hanging over 10b-5 insider trading jurisprudence. See *United States v. Bryan*, 58 F.3d 933 (4th Cir. 1995) (rejecting misappropriation theory when director of West Virginia lottery used confidential information to buy securities of companies to which the lottery planned to award contracts).

Although the ruling in *O'Hagan* removed any uncertainty about whether Rule 10b-5 regulates securities trading using misappropriated information, it exposed doctrinal rifts in the Court's 10b-5 jurisprudence. First, *O'Hagan* suggests that there can be no 10b-5 insider trading liability if there is no breach of trust or confidence. Thus, a person who gains access to material, nonpublic information by other wrongful means — such as outright theft — would seemingly not face 10b-5 sanctions. Cf. *United States v. Falcone*, 257 F.3d 226 (2d Cir. 2001) (finding fiduciary status for employee of magazine wholesaler, which received pre-release copies of *Business Week* from national distributor, where employee was paid for tipping stories to others who traded). Moreover, a fiduciary who discloses his trading intentions or receives permission to trade from the information source would escape 10b-5 liability since there would arguably be no breach of his abstain-or-disclose duty.

Second, *O'Hagan* left unanswered the question of who has duties of trust or confidence and when the duty of confidentiality attaches. For lawyer O'Hagan, it was easy to identify his duties to his law firm and thus to the bidder, but the inquiry becomes more difficult when a person overhears a conversation or has only a superficial relationship with the information source. See *SEC v. Switzer*, 590 F. Supp. 756 (W.D. Okla. 1984) (holding that eavesdropper is not liable for trading after overhearing CEO tell his wife the company might be liquidated). Nonetheless, when information has been obtained deceptively, the breach of duty is not "cleansed" by later revealing to the source an intention to trade on the deceptively obtained information. See *SEC v. Rocklage*, 470 F.3d 1 (1st Cir. 2006) (holding that wife who deceptively obtained information from her CEO husband was liable for then tipping this information to her brother, even though she informed husband of tip).

Duty of Confidentiality (Misappropriation)

The duty of trust or confidence in misappropriation cases is clearest when confidential information is misappropriated in breach of an established business relationship, such as investment banker-client or employer-employee. The duty is less clear in other business and personal settings.

In an attempt to provide clarity, the SEC promulgated a rule that specifies — for purposes of misappropriation liability — when a recipient of material, nonpublic information is deemed to owe a duty of trust or confidence to the source. Rule 10b5-2(b).

- The recipient agreed to maintain the information in confidence.
- The persons involved in the communication have a history, pattern, or practice of sharing confidences (both business and nonbusiness confidences) so the recipient had reason to know the communicator expected the recipient to maintain the information's confidentiality.
- The communicator of the information was a spouse, parent, child, or sibling of the recipient, unless the recipient can show (based on the facts and circumstances of that family relationship) that there was no reasonable expectation of confidentiality.

Confidentiality Expectations Outside the Family

By their terms, the rule's first two categories clarify when confidentiality expectations — and thus a duty of trust or confidence — arise in nonbusiness and business settings outside the family. Thus, a contractual relationship (though not necessarily creating a fiduciary relationship) can give rise to a duty not to use confidential information, if that is what the parties had agreed or mutually understood. In addition, as the SEC stated in its preliminary note to the rule, the list is not exclusive, and a relationship of trust or confidence among family members or others can be established in other ways, as well.

Are confidentiality expectations, without an actual relationship of trust or confidence, enough to trigger a 10b-5 duty to "disclose or abstain"? Consider the SEC's case against Mark Cuban, of Audionet and Dallas Mavericks fame. In 2004 Cuban had a phone conversation with the CEO of Mamma.com, a company in which Cuban was a 6.3 percent shareholder. The Mamma CEO told Cuban confidentially that Mamma was planning to accept a new investor that would dilute existing shareholders. According to the SEC, Cuban said to the CEO he would keep the information confidential, but then he sold his Mamma shares and avoided losses of $750,000 in the process. When the SEC brought an insider case against him, Cuban argued that his relationship with the Mamma CEO and any confidentiality promise he made did not create a cognizable §10(b) duty. The trial court dismissed the SEC's case on the theory that Cuban's oral confidentiality promise encompassed only keeping the information confidential, but did not bar him from trading. On appeal, the Fifth Circuit did not address the lower court's novel parsing of the parties' understanding, but instead held that the SEC's complaint laid out a "more than a plausible" case of insider trading, and remanded for further proceedings. *SEC v. Cuban*, 634 F. Supp. 2d 713 (N.D. Tex. 2009), *remanded*, 620 F.3d 551 (5th Cir. 2010). At trial, the jury found that Cuban had not entered into a confidentiality agreement and, in any event, the information about Mamma's new investor was already public knowledge, given an earlier spike in trading volume in the company's stock. The SEC licked its wounds and said it would continue to bring cases where it believed there had been insider trading.

Confidentiality Expectations Inside the Family

Rule 10b5-2 was adopted largely in response to the anomaly in the case law that a family member who trades on material, nonpublic information obtained from a another family member violates Rule 10b-5 if the trading breached an *express promise* of confidentiality, but not if there was only a *reasonable expectation* of confidentiality. The SEC rule treats insider trading by family members as undermining market and investor confidence, whether the expectation of confidentiality was express or implied. As the SEC explained, the trader's informational advantage in either case stems from "contrivance, not luck." Additionally, the SEC said its brighter-line approach was less intrusive than a case-by-case analysis into the nature of family relationships, as required by existing case law. *United States v. Chestman*, 947 F.2d 551 (2d Cir.1991) (en banc) (holding that son-in-law owed no duty to in-laws who planned to sell their supermarket chain, when he and his broker traded on confidential information about impending sale).

Some courts have used this "expectation" analysis in cases of classic insider trading on the question whether family members qualify as "constructive insiders." In *SEC v. Yun*, 327 F.3d 1263 (11th Cir. 2003), a husband told his wife during divorce discussions that his stock options should be revalued at a lower price because of a soon-to-be-made announcement of a drop in company earnings. The wife then told office mates about this impending news, who traded on the tip. The court held that spousal communications implicated a fiduciary duty when the communicating spouse has "reasonable expectation of confidentiality"—given their history or practice of sharing business confidences. The court commented that Rule 10b5-2, which creates a presumption of spousal confidentiality in misappropriation cases, bolstered the conclusion that spouses should be understood to have expectations of confidentiality in cases of classic insider trading.

Confidentiality Expectations in Congress

In 2012 Congress passed the Stop Trading on Congressional Knowledge (STOCK) Act to extend insider-trading restrictions to members of Congress and legislative employees by specifying that such persons owe duties to the United States (and Congress and the U.S. citizens) with respect to material nonpublic information derived from their position or gained from performing their official responsibilities. See Exchange Act §21A(g). Thus, members of Congress and their aides—as well as any recipients who trade on congressionally sourced information—can be liable for insider trading.

Before the STOCK Act, there were doubts about whether members of Congress and their aides were subject to duties not to engage in stock trading on the basis of confidential information gleaned through their public service. Nonetheless, the Act does not resolve how regulators will enforce the prohibition—given the evidentiary barriers created by the Constitution's "Speech or Debate" clause that immunizes lawmakers for their official legislative activities. Nor does the STOCK Act prevent members of Congress and their aides from owning company stock in industries that they have the power to impact.

But just as corporate insiders must report their trading in their corporation's stock (see §10.3.1 below), members of Congress and their aides must report their stock trades above $1,000 within 30 to 45 days of the trade. See Ethics in Government Act of 1978 §103 (along with other specified members of executive and judicial branches). Not only does such reporting allow the public to compare congressional stock trading with congressional activities, it also can serve as the basis for public and private insider-trading actions.

In particular, the STOCK Act affects Wall Street "data miners" that gather political intelligence from congressional sources to predict legislative outcomes that might affect stock prices. These firms, as well as law firms and lobbyists, now face "tippee" liability for passing on nonpublic congressional information that they received in breach of the source's duties. Although Congress members may have immunity, private parties that trade on illegally tipped congressional information do not.

Tipping of Misappropriated Information

Not only is it illegal to trade on a tip from an insider, it is illegal to trade on a tip from an outsider who passes on misappropriated information to obtain a personal benefit. That is, 10b-5 tipping liability described in *Dirks* applies to tips both from insiders and from outsiders. See *United States v. Falcone*, 257 F.3d 226 (2d. Cir. 2001) (finding 10b-5 liability when distributor of *Business Week*, before magazine went on sale to general public, passed on copies to neighbor/broker who traded on nonpublic information in magazine).

Consider an example of tipped misappropriated information. One Strickland, a financial analyst at GE Capital, learned that a client, Allied Capital, was planning to acquire SunSource. Strickland mentioned this to one Black (a former college roommate) who then "to curry favor" told his boss, one Obus at Wynnefield Capital. Obus had Wynnefield buy 50,000 shares of SunSource—resulting in a $1.3 million profit. The SEC sued Strickland (as tipper), Black (as tippee and sub-tipper) and Obus (as sub-tippee). The Second Circuit agreed that there was sufficient evidence that Strickland breached a duty to his employer, GE Capital, by tipping Black, knowing that the information was confidential. The court held Black could be liable for tipping the information because he knew it was confidential and his "close friendship" with Strickland constituted a sufficient personal benefit. And Obus could be liable for believing the tip was "credible" and "consciously avoiding" any further inquiry. *SEC v. Obus*, 693 F.3d 276 (2d Cir. 2012) (finding evidence sufficient to overcome defendants' motions for summary judgment).

The case has created a stir. First, the court's conclusion that Strickland may have committed a fiduciary breach was contradicted by an internal GE Capital investigation that concluded he had not — thus, the court seemed to render "waiver" of duty by the source of misappropriated information insufficient to avoid tipping liability. Second, the court concluded that "personal benefit" could be as ephemeral as the quid pro quo of a personal friendship—thus, the court almost gutted the element. Third, the court accepted that a sophisticated sub-tippee could not easily claim ignorance about the tip's source under the "know or should know" element of the *Dirks* test — thus, the court concluded that circumstantial evidence can be sufficient to show a sub-tippee should have known of a tip's tainted origin.

Rule 14e-3 — Misappropriation of Tender Offer Information

The SEC has used the misappropriation theory to adopt rules prohibiting trading based on material, nonpublic information about *unannounced tender offers*. Using its rulemaking authority under §14(e) of the Exchange Act — which allows rules aimed at "fraudulent, deceptive, or manipulative acts or practices, in connection with any tender offer" — the SEC prohibited trading by those with inside information about a tender offer. Exchange Act Rule 14e-3.

Rule 14e-3 prohibits, during the course of a tender offer, trading by anybody (other than the bidder) who has material, nonpublic information about the offer that he knows (or has reason to know) was obtained from either the bidder or the target. Notice that there is no need under Rule 14e-3 to prove that a tipper breached a fiduciary duty for personal benefit. See *United States v. O'Hagan*, 521 U.S. 642 (1997) (upholding SEC's rulemaking authority to "define and prescribe means reasonably designed to prevent [fraudulent] acts" under §14(e) of the Exchange Act). Besides being a basis for SEC enforcement actions and criminal prosecutions, Rule 14e-3 has also been interpreted to create an implied private action.

The Second Circuit has considered the difference between 10b-5 and 14e-3 liability. *United States v. Chestman*, 947 F.2d 551 (2d Cir. 1991) (en banc). In the case Chestman, a stockbroker, learned of an impending tender offer from the husband of the niece of the company's controlling shareholder. The controlling shareholder had agreed to sell his control block as a prelude to the purchaser's tender offer. When Chestman traded on this information for himself and his clients, the government prosecuted him under Rules 10b-5 and 14e-3. The Second Circuit affirmed Chestman's 14e-3 conviction, for which no showing of duty was necessary. But the court held he could not be convicted under a 10b-5 misappropriation theory because the family tipper had no duty to his family to guard confidential information.

Mail and Wire Fraud — Criminal Liability for Misappropriation

Misappropriation of confidential information can also be the basis of non-securities criminal liability. In *Carpenter v. United States*, 484 U.S. 19 (1987), the Supreme Court had sidestepped the 10b-5 quagmire by affirming in an 8-0 decision a *Wall Street Journal* reporter's conviction (discussed above) under federal mail and wire fraud criminal statutes. (The SEC cannot enforce the mail and wire fraud statute, which can only be enforced by the Justice Department in a criminal prosecution.) The Court held that the newspaper had a "property" interest in keeping the "Heard on the Street" column confidential prior to publication and that the reporter's breach of his confidentiality obligation defrauded the newspaper. Although the Court's decision raises disquieting issues about criminal liability for breaching an employment stipulation, the case makes clear that trading on misappropriated information is subject to criminal penalties.

§10.2.4 Remedies for Insider Trading

Insider traders are subject to an imposing host of sanctions and liabilities. As the following list makes clear, it is no wonder that law firms tell new lawyers not to trade on clients' confidential information.

Civil Liability to Contemporaneous Traders

In an impersonal trading market, it is unclear who is hurt by insider trading and how much. Shareholders and investors who trade at the same time as an insider presumably would have traded even had the insider fulfilled his duty and abstained. If, however, the theory is that insider trading is unfair to contemporaneous traders, recovery should be equal to the traders' contemporaneous trading "losses" — typically significantly greater than the insiders' gains. If the theory is that insider trading undermines the integrity of trading markets, recovery should be disgorgement of the insiders' trading gains to the market as a whole. If the theory is that insider traders pilfer valuable commercial information, recovery should be based on the losses to the owner of the confidential information.

Congress has addressed the issue and adopted a recovery scheme that borrows from both the unfairness and disgorgement rationales. The Insider Trading and Securities Fraud Enforcement Act of 1988 limits recovery to traders (shareholders or investors) whose trades were contemporaneous with the insider's. Recovery is based on the disgorgement of the insider's actual profits realized or losses avoided, reduced by any disgorgement obtained by the SEC under its broad authority to seek injunctive relief (see below). Exchange Act §20A.

Civil Recovery by "Defrauded" Source of Confidential Information

Owners of confidential information who purchase or sell securities can bring a private action under Rule 10b-5 against insider traders and tippees who adversely affect their trading prices. See *Blue Chip Stamps v. Manor Drug Stores*, 421 U.S. 723 (1975) (actual purchaser or seller standing requirement). A "defrauded" company may recover if it suffered trading losses or was forced to pay a higher price in a transaction because the insiders' trading artificially raised the stock price. *FMC Corp. v. Boesky*, 673 F.2d 272 (N.D. Ill. 1987), *remanded*, 852 F.2d 981 (7th Cir. 1988) (holding tippee not liable for trading on misappropriated information concerning company's impending recapitalization plan because company lost nothing in the recapitalization). Although some commentators proposed corporate recovery *on behalf of shareholders*, courts have insisted on a corporate (not shareholder) injury for there to be corporate recovery.

SEC Enforcement Action

The SEC can bring a judicial enforcement action seeking a court order that enjoins the inside trader or tippee from further insider trading (if likely to recur) and that compels the disgorgement of any trading profits. *SEC v. Texas Gulf Sulphur Co.*, 401 F.2d 833 (2d Cir. 1968) (ordering establishment of fund from which shareholders and other contemporaneous traders could recover from insider traders and tippers).

Civil Penalties

To add deterrence, the SEC can also seek a judicially imposed civil penalty against those who violate Rule 10b-5 or Rule 14e-3 of up to three times the profits realized (or losses avoided) by their insider trading. Exchange Act §21A (added by the Insider Trading Sanctions Act of 1984). The penalty, paid into the federal treasury, is in addition to other remedies. Thus, it is possible for an insider or tippee to disgorge her profits (in a private or SEC action) *and* pay the treble-damage penalty.

"Watchdog" Penalties

To create even more deterrence, the SEC can seek civil penalties against employers and others who "control" insider traders and tippers. Exchange Act §21A (added by Insider Trading and Securities Fraud Enforcement Act of 1988). Controlling persons are subject to additional penalties up to $1 million or three times the insider's profits (whichever is greater) if the controlling person knowingly or recklessly disregards the likelihood of insider trading by persons under its control. Broker-dealers that fail to maintain procedures protecting against such abuses may also be subject to these penalties if their laxity substantially contributed to the insider trading.

"Bounty" Rewards

To encourage informants, the SEC can pay bounties to anyone who provides information leading to civil penalties. The bounty can be up to 10 percent of the civil penalty collected. Exchange Act §21A(e) (added by Insider Trading and Securities Fraud Enforcement Act of 1988). This bounty program is in addition to the "whistleblower" bounty program created by Dodd-Frank. See Exchange Act §21F (see §8.3.4).

Criminal Sanctions

To punish those who engage in "willful" insider trading — that is, insider trading where the defendant knows that it is wrongful — the SEC can (and often does) refer cases to the U.S. Department of Justice for criminal prosecution. Exchange Act §32(a). Congress has twice increased the criminal penalties for violations of the Exchange Act and its rules. In the Insider Trading and Securities Fraud Enforcement Act of 1988, Congress increased the maximum criminal fines from $100,000 to $1,000,000 ($2,500,000 for nonindividuals) and jail sentences from 5 years to 10 years. Then in the Sarbanes-Oxley Act of 2002, Congress upped the maximum fines to $5,000,000 ($25,000,000 for nonindividuals) and jail sentences to 20 years.

The Exchange Act's criminal provisions provide a curious defense against incarceration for violating an SEC rule if the defendant "proves he had no knowledge of such rule." Exchange Act §32(a). Courts have denied the defense if the defendant recognized he was engaged in deception.

§10.2.5 Regulation FD and Selective Disclosure

Inside information does not stay bottled up in companies forever. Sooner or later, companies communicate to securities markets. Formal disclosure is the soul of federal securities regulation. Informal disclosure, particularly by means of selective discussions with securities analysts and large investors, has been controversial — criticized as systematic tipping of inside information and praised as an efficient way to reveal information to securities markets.

In 2000 the SEC took to heart the criticisms and adopted Regulation FD (Fair Disclosure) to forbid public companies from selectively disclosing material, nonpublic information. Exchange Act Rel. No. 43154 (2000). The detailed rules on how companies respond to analyst inquiries and engage in investor relations have altered how company information reaches securities markets. Disclosure practices once widespread, such as giving detailed financial projections to selected securities analysts or reviewing analyst reports before public release, are now regulated.

Regulation FD applies to issuer disclosures of material, nonpublic information to specified market professionals, as well as security holders who it is "reasonably foreseeable" will trade on the basis of the information. Rule 100(b)(1). When the disclosure is "intentional," issuers must disclose inside information to the investing public *simultaneously* with any disclosure to selected analysts or investors. Rule 100(a)(1). If the issuer discovers it has made an "unintentional" selective disclosure, the issuer must disclose the information to the public *promptly* (generally within 24 hours). Rule 100(a)(2). The information must be disseminated by methods "reasonably designed to achieve broad non-exclusionary distribution to the public" — such as through Internet postings or simulcasts, or by furnishing a Form 8-K to the SEC. Rule 101(e) (defining "public disclosure"). The restrictions apply to the issuer's senior officials and those who regularly communicate with analysts and investors, such as investor relations or public relations officers. Rule 101(f).

The "equal access" rules of Regulation FD have some exclusions [Rule 100(b)]:

Context	Disclosure Allowed
Normal course of business	Disclosure may be made in the normal course of business, such as to professional advisers (attorneys, investment bankers, or accountants) or business partners in contract negotiations. Dodd-Frank calls on the SEC to eliminate the exclusion for credit rating agencies, unless the credit rating agency receives the information pursuant to a confidentiality or nondisclosure agreement. Dodd-Frank §939B.
Public disclosures	Disclosure may be made to media or government officials, such as by responding to newspaper inquiries or complying with regulatory investigations.
Public offerings	Disclosures may be made in securities offerings registered under the Securities Act, such as to analysts and institutional investors in going-public "road shows."
Foreign private issuers	Disclosure may be made by foreign private issuers (which, if they meet the jurisdictional requirements, remain subject to the securities antifraud provisions).

To take some of the sting out of these rules, Regulation FD is enforceable only through SEC enforcement actions and does not give rise to 10b-5 liability or private enforcement. Rule 102.

Regulation FD is an important step toward a systematic regulation of inside information. Rather than dealing with each selective disclosure as a possible instance of "tipping," the regime encourages wide dissemination of information — whenever the issuer decides to disclose. The rules encourage the release of information, not its suppression — consistent with the philosophy of securities regulation that all investors have access to the same company-provided information at the same time. The rules also avoid the potential conflicts that analysts once felt to report favorably on companies to protect the flow of selective disclosures and that company executives felt to delay public disclosure so as to curry favor with preferred analysts or institutional investors.

In 2002 the SEC brought its first enforcement actions under Regulation FD. In one case, company officials had telephoned selected analysts to quantify the "significant weakness" in sales mentioned in an earlier press release. Because the company had consulted an attorney (who gave erroneous advice), the SEC only issued an investigative report that identified the disclosure breach. In a second case, a company CFO called a handful of analysts to point out that their reports had failed to note that company earnings usually were higher in the second half of the year. The SEC issued an administrative cease-and-desist order, pointing out the company should have publicly disclosed the seasonality of its earnings before calling the analysts. In a third action a CEO commented at a private technology conference that quarterly earnings would be better than anticipated. The SEC both issued a cease-and-desist order and brought a judicial enforcement action that it settled when the company agreed to pay a $250,000 civil penalty. Although the CEO did not know the conference was not being webcast, the director of investor relations did and her knowledge was sufficient to infer corporate intent (or, more accurately, recklessness).

But the SEC suffered a setback in a judicial enforcement action against a company and its CFO for positive statements made privately to institutional investors about the company's business activities that were at odds with previous negative (and public) statements by the company. *SEC v. Siebel Systems, Inc.*, 384 F. Supp. 2d 694 (S.D.N.Y. 2005). The court concluded that the CFO's statements had already been disclosed (or were available) to the public, in the process chiding the SEC for being too linguistic and for chilling company disclosures. The court pointed out that the earlier public statements had anticipated favorable results and the CFO merely confirmed what had been said. The court, however, did not address the fact that investors privy to the CFO's statements bought the company's shares, causing the stock price to surge. In short, the market's reaction to the private information suggested its materiality, even though the court's linguistic parsing came to a different conclusion!

From appearances, Regulation FD has been a success. Academic studies find strong evidence that the new rules leveled the informational playing field, with earnings announcements producing less surprise after Regulation FD compared to before. The result has been that Regulation FD appears to have reduced the cost of equity capital (investors pay more because of more available information), particularly in companies that had engaged in selective disclosure before the rule. Likewise, Regulation FD did not diminish the amount or quality of voluntary disclosures, except among some small high-tech firms and larger companies with high market prices compared to assets.

Examples

1. BIM Corporation, a publicly traded company, has an active research and development department. Elbert, a BIM chemist, has conducted preliminary tests on a material that is superconductive at room temperatures. If the test results can be confirmed, it would be a huge scientific breakthrough with enormous commercial potential. Adela, the CEO of BIM, learns of the tests and sends an intraoffice memo to all concerned urging "complete secrecy."

   a. BIM's board grants BIM stock to Adela, who accepts. She does not tell the board of Elbert's tests. Is Adela liable to the corporation under Rule 10b-5?

   b. Before Elbert's results are confirmed, Adela purchases call options on BIM stock on the options market. She does not trade with BIM shareholders. Is Adela liable under Rule 10b-5?

   c. Elbert purchases BIM stock through a stockbroker under a written investment plan that calls for fixed, monthly purchases of BIM stock. Under the plan Elbert can choose to purchase more or fewer shares in any month, but he does not exercise this option. Is Elbert, who is neither a director nor officer of BIM, liable under Rule 10b-5?

2. After the test results are confirmed, but before public disclosure of the breakthrough, Elbert tells Jane (a fellow physicist who works for another research company) of the superconductivity tests.

   a. Jane buys BIM stock. Is she liable under Rule 10b-5?

   b. Elbert does not trade himself, but reveals the BIM test results to Jane hoping to receive similar market-sensitive scoops from her. Assuming Jane never reciprocates with information of her own, is Elbert liable under Rule 10b-5?

   c. Elbert and Jane discuss the future of superconductivity while riding in a limousine on their way to a scientific conference. Mickey, the limo driver, overhears their conversation and the next day purchases BIM stock. Is Mickey liable under Rule 10b-5?

3. Still before the superconductivity breakthrough is disclosed publicly, Adela tells her husband Don (from whom she is separated) that he should reconsider divorcing her since she stands to become wealthy because of a "top secret breakthrough" at BIM. She asks him to keep the information confidential.

   a. Instead, Don buys BIM call options. Has he violated Rule 10b-5?

   b. Don also tells a colleague at his office that "Adela tells me there's a breakthrough at BIM — you should buy." The colleague does. Has the colleague violated Rule 10b-5?

   c. Don and his good friend Martha have the same stock broker, Douglas. When Don tells Douglas to purchase BIM stock options, Douglas suspects something good is afoot at BIM. He calls Martha and says, "Don's buying." Martha buys BIM stock. Has she violated Rule 10b-5?

4. Meanwhile at company headquarters, Adela receives a phone call from Raymond, a securities analyst who follows high-tech companies. Adela tells Raymond, "There have been significant developments in our superconductivity research." Adela hopes to signal to the market the impending good news.

   a. Raymond tells his clients that BIM should be viewed as a "strong buy." Has Adela violated any duties?

   b. Adela calls you, the company's lawyer, and asks for your advice on how to handle disclosures about BIM's superconductivity activities to securities analysts. Can she talk with you, and what would you advise?

5. Before public disclosure of the superconductivity breakthrough, Adela discloses it to Dwight (the president of Third Federal Bank) to obtain a loan for BIM to build a new manufacturing plant. Adela asks Dwight to keep the information secret.

   a. Dwight calls his broker and buys BIM stock. Is Dwight liable under Rule 10b-5?

   b. Dwight tells his wife Wanda over dinner that BIM's stock price is "probably going to go through the ceiling." Wanda asks no more but buys BIM stock. Is Dwight or Wanda liable under Rule 10b-5?

   c. Tina, a corporate spy, breaks into Third Federal's offices and rifles through the files to find the BIM loan application. She buys BIM stock. Is Tina liable under Rule 10b-5?

6. BIM's board decides it should be prepared to add manufacturing capacity to produce superconductivity materials. It decides to acquire Ovid Corporation, a publicly traded commercial builder, as part of its plans to build new manufacturing plants. BIM secretly negotiates an acquisition of Ovid.

   a. Before announcing the acquisition, BIM purchases a significant block of Ovid stock. Is BIM liable to Ovid shareholders under Rule 10b-5? Rule 14e-3?

b. BIM decides to proceed with a tender offer, but before announcing its bid the BIM board authorizes Adela to purchase a limited amount of Ovid stock on the market. Is Adela liable under Rule 10b-5? Rule 14e-3?

c. Ovid shareholders who sold during the period between Adela's trading and eventual disclosure of the merger sue Adela to recover the gains they would have made if they had not sold. Is Adela liable to these shareholders under Rule 10b-5?

d. Adela makes $100,000 in trading profits by buying Ovid stock. What is her maximum monetary exposure?

e. Adela attends a stock analysts' meeting, which is simulcast on BIM's website. She announces that BIM will manufacture its new superconductive material. She does not mention building new manufacturing facilities or the pending acquisition of Ovid. One of the analysts, Tom, figures out that BIM is likely to acquire Ovid. Tom tells his clients, who buy Ovid stock. Is Tom liable under Rule 10b-5?

7. "Renewable energy" legislation pending in Congress would create tax incentives for upgrades to the U.S. power grid, but fails to extend the proposed tax incentives to utilities that switch their power distribution systems to new superconductive high-tension wires. A team of BIM executives meet privately with congressional leaders on the House and Senate committees considering the legislation. BIM executives receive assurances that Congress will add tax incentives for superconductive distribution systems.

a. Senator Bills, who attended the meetings with the BIM executives, realizes that BIM's stock will go through the roof once the tax incentives kick in. He buys BIM stock. Is the Senator liable under Rule 10b-5?

b. Senator Bills realizes that it would be great if BIM's new manufacturing plants were built in his state. He calls the state governor and asks what kinds of incentives the state might offer to BIM to locate its plants in the state. After their chat, the governor realizes the potential for BIM and buys call options of BIM stock. Is the governor liable under Rule 10b-5?

c. Legislative aide Sandro, who also attended the BIM meetings, receives a (regular) phone call from Mega-Data, a company that collects data of all sorts and sells the data to hedge funds for use in their stock trading. Sandro reveals the basics of the meetings with BIM about adding tax incentives for superconductivity in the U.S. power grid. The hedge funds trade on this information. Are the hedge funds liable under Rule 10b-5? What about Mega-Data and Sandro?

Explanations

1. a. Yes, if the preliminary tests are material. Adela has a fiduciary relationship to the corporation and, under Rule 10b-5, has a duty to abstain or disclose when trading *with the corporation* on the basis of material, nonpublic information. *Chiarella*. An insider trading case under Rule 10b-5 must also satisfy the fraud elements of materiality and scienter:

   - *Materiality.* The information about the preliminary tests is material if a reasonable investor would consider it important to a buy-sell decision. Under the "probability plus magnitude" test of *Basic, Inc. v. Levinson*, 485 U.S. 224 (1988) (§3.2.2), the magnitude of discovering a superconductive substance would be demonstrated by a postdisclosure jump in BIM's stock price. The probability that the preliminary tests would confirm the substance's superconductivity seem high.

   - *Scienter.* Adela knew of the tests when she accepted the options and should have been aware of their propensity to affect the value of the company's stock. See §9.3.3. It is not necessary that she actually used this information, but that she was aware of it. Rule 10b5-1.

   When trading involves nondisclosure, the Supreme Court has presumed reliance upon a showing that the undisclosed information was material. *Affiliated Ute Citizens v. United States*, 406 U.S. 128 (1972) (§9.3.3). In this face-to-face transaction, Adela might nonetheless rebut the assumption of reliance by showing that the corporation (acting through an independent board) would have offered the options even had it known of the inside information.

   b. Yes, almost certainly. Adela's abstain-or-disclose duty extends to shareholders and investors in BIM's stock. *Chiarella*. Does it extend to nonshareholder investors? Before 1984, a number of courts had held that option traders were owed no duty of disclosure. The Insider Trading Sanctions Act of 1984, however, closed this judge-made loophole by explicitly prohibiting trading in any derivative instrument if trading in the underlying securities would violate insider trading rules. See Exchange Act §20(d).

   Although materiality would seem an issue, it rarely is in insider trading cases. If the insider considered the information important to his buy-sell decision, it is almost certain that a court will conclude that there is a substantial likelihood that a "reasonable shareholder" would also consider the information important — and thus that the information is material. See §3.1.1.

   c. Probably, because the trading plan left some discretion to Elbert. Generally, the 10b-5 insider trading rules apply to any corporate insider with a fiduciary (or agency) relationship to the corporation.

Elbert, an employee-agent of BIM, would be treated in the same way as Adela. His awareness of the test results would establish a culpable state of mind, subject to an affirmative defense that the trading plan was such that the stock purchases would have happened regardless of his inside knowledge. Elbert would have to show he entered into the written plan before he was aware of the superconductivity tests and the plan specified the terms of purchases, contained a formula for these terms, or disabled him from influencing the broker. That Elbert retained the option to increase or decrease the purchases each month means the plan was not fixed, as required by the SEC safe-harbor rule for plan purchases. Rule 10b5-1(c).

2. a. Perhaps, depending on Elbert's motives and expectations. If Jane knows (or has reason to know) that the information was confidential and came from an insider who tipped for some personal or reputational benefit, Jane is liable as a tippee. *Dirks.* A significant issue is whether Elbert disclosed the breakthrough for personal gain or for some nonpersonal corporate reason. If he expected reciprocal stock-trading tips or personal reputational gain, the tip violated Rule 10b-5 if Jane had reason to know those were his motives. If, however, Elbert revealed the breakthrough for business reasons, such as to discuss the scientific aspects of the discovery, Jane is under no confidentiality obligation. Jane's liability thus hinges on Elbert's motives — a deficiency of the *Dirks* approach, but part of federal insider trading law.

   In addition to his motives, Elbert's expectations of confidentiality might also be relevant. If Jane and Elbert have exchanged confidential information in the past so that Jane had reason to know that Elbert expected confidentiality, it might be argued she became a "temporary insider." In Rule 10b5-2, the SEC has inferred a duty of trust and confidence in such circumstances. Although the rule by its terms applies only to misappropriation liability, its logic extends to identifying temporary insiders in cases of classic insider trading.

   b. Yes. Elbert is liable as a tipper because he gave the tip in breach of his fiduciary duty for an improper personal benefit — the expectation of future reciprocal tips. Even though Elbert did not trade himself, a tipping insider is liable for placing confidential nonpublic material information in peril of abuse. *SEC v. Texas Gulf Sulphur* (see §10.2.1). Under this aiding and abetting theory, nontrading tippers are jointly and severally liable to the same extent as their trading tippees. See Exchange Act §20A(c).

   c. Perhaps, though not as a tippee. If Elbert did not anticipate a personal gain from his discussion or there was an expectation of confidentiality, there was no breach of Elbert's duty, and a tippee (or an eavesdropper) could not be liable on that basis.

Nonetheless, Mickey might be liable on a misappropriation theory. If Mickey worked for a limousine company that expected complete discretion of its employees, he could be liable for misappropriating the information in breach of *his employer's* expectation of confidentiality. See *United States v. O'Hagan* (§10.2.2). His trading would constitute a breach of duty owed to his employer if the employer expected that he would not divulge or use for personal purposes any information obtained on the job. The SEC confirmed this analysis by defining a relationship of "trust or confidence" to include a contractual relationship (though not necessarily creating a fiduciary relationship) in which there was an agreement of confidentiality. Rule 10b5-2(b).

One sticking point might be whether Mickey had the requisite state of mind. Although his awareness of the superconductivity information would appear to satisfy the general "awareness" standard, see Rule 10b5-1(b), this might not be enough to establish the "willfulness" required for criminal liability. The *O'Hagan* court pointed out that under Exchange Act §32(a) a criminal 10b-5 defendant cannot be imprisoned if he "has no knowledge of the rule."

3. a. Probably. The question is whether Don is a "constructive insider" who has a fiduciary duty of confidentiality because of his relationship to Adela. Although earlier courts held that within a family duties not to trade on material, nonpublic information arise only if there were *express understandings* of confidentiality, recent courts have followed the lead of the SEC (see Rule 10b5-2) and treated spousal communications as carrying a duty of confidentiality if the spouses had an *express or implied* understanding of confidentiality. See *SEC v. Yun* (§10.2.3). By asking Don to keep the information confidential, Adela seems to have expected he would not use the information. Only if Don could show her expectation was unfounded, perhaps because of his past indiscretions, would the presumption of spousal confidentiality be rebutted.

Notice that this is not a case of tipping. When Adela told Don of the breakthrough it was not in the belief he would trade on it — in fact, she asked him to keep it confidential. Much like the spouse in *SEC v. Yun*, who told his wife about an impending drop in the company's stock price as part of their divorce discussions, Adela's revelation was meant to preserve the marriage, not facilitate advantageous stock trading. Spousal communications about work do not constitute a fiduciary breach if the communications are not intended as a stock tip.

b. Probably. The question here is whether the colleague was a tippee. If Don was a "constructive insider" (see previous answer), the issue becomes whether the colleague knew or had reason to know that Don's tip violated his fiduciary duty of confidentiality, which requires that Don expected a personal benefit from the tip. See *SEC v. Musella*, 678 F. Supp. 1060 (S.D.N.Y. 1988) (holding two New York City police officers liable as tippees for receiving information from another officer, who had received it from an employee of a Wall Street law firm, on the grounds they "should have known" the original tip was a breach of fiduciary duty). Since the colleague knew that Don had received the tip from Adela, he should have (at the least) inquired whether Don was expected to keep it confidential. If the colleague had reason to know that Don was not supposed to reveal the information he received from Adela, a personal benefit is virtually presumed — for example, it would be enough that Don hoped for a good relationship with a workplace colleague. See *SEC v. Yun* (see §10.2.3). Courts have used the same broad analysis as to what constitutes a "personal benefit" in cases of both classic insider trading and misappropriation. If the tipper wrongfully tips the information and anticipates the tip will result in some financial or reputational gain (however slight) — and the tippee should know this — liability is established.

c. Perhaps not. This is much like the trading in which Martha Stewart was said to have engaged. Merely knowing that another person is trading does not establish that he is trading on material, nonpublic information. That is, in the normal case there is no reason to believe that the trading breached a fiduciary duty. Unless the tipper — here, the broker Douglas — told Martha that Don was trading on the basis of specific inside information, it may be difficult to establish the tippee's requisite state of mind. Remember that under Rule 10b-5, trading must be with scienter to be actionable in an administrative or private lawsuit, and must be "willful" to be criminal. See §§9.3.2, 12.5.2. Perhaps for this reason, the SEC only brought an administrative action against Stewart seeking fines and disgorgement of her insider trading profits. (In 2006, she settled these charges without admitting or denying any wrongdoing for $195,000, representing a trebling of the losses avoided plus interest.) The criminal case against her was based not on her trading, but on false statements she made to SEC investigators about her reasons for selling her stock.

4. a. Probably. Adela has clearly violated Regulation FD, if her disclosure of the superconductivity information was to only one securities analyst. Senior officials of publicly traded companies are obligated to disclose

material information *simultaneously* to the market when the disclosure is intentional. Here Adela had already warned others in the company to keep the test results secret — suggesting she understood the information was material and nonpublic. Rule 101(a) (definition of intentional). There does not appear to be any effort to disclose the information to other analysts or investors. Nor does any exception apply since Raymond was under no duty to maintain the information in confidence.

Whether, on the other hand, Adela has violated the Rule 10b-5 insider trading rules is not as clear. Although a violation of Regulation FD does not automatically create 10b-5 liability (Rule 102), an argument can be made that Adela did not satisfy the *Dirks* definition of tipper, because she disclosed the information not for any personal gain but to inform the securities markets. Nonetheless, one must wonder why she told only Raymond. If it was because he has given favorable reports in the past (boosting the value of Adela's stock options) and Adela expects similar favors from him in the future, her disclosure might have violated her *Dirks* duties. At the least, Adela risks being the target of an SEC investigation.

b. Regulation FD forces companies to institute policies and procedures for dealing with market inquiries. Although conversations are permitted with company advisers, such as lawyers who have a duty of trust or confidence to the company client, senior company officials must be careful in disclosing material, nonpublic information to market professionals and investors who are likely to trade on the information.

- *Materiality determinations.* Companies should have policies for determining what information is nonpublic and material — such as earnings information, important product or contract developments, important acquisitions, or extraordinary transactions. There should also be procedures for consulting with inside counsel and, when appropriate, outside counsel. If company officials believe analysts should be alerted to new information, it probably is material!

- *Identify authorized officials.* Companies should limit analyst and investor contacts to specific company spokespersons — such as the CEO, the vice president of finance, and the head of investor relations. Private meetings or phone calls between senior officials and securities professionals should be discouraged, particularly if material information may be discussed.

- *Coordinated disclosure.* Companies should have procedures for responding to both informal and formal contacts. There should be internal communications channels so that questions are directed to the right persons and responses are consistent. For example, responses to common queries could be posted on a company intranet, and scripts for analyst conferences should be prepared and reviewed in advance. There should be policies for prompt "debriefing" of informal contacts to cure unauthorized disclosures.

- *Wide dissemination.* Material disclosures should be disseminated by press release, accompanied by the filing of a Form 8-K. Any press conference or analyst calls should be conducted on the Internet to allow full media and investor access. These materials should also be archived for a set period, such as seven days. It may be useful to file a *procedural* Form 8-K to announce generally how the company will disseminate material, nonpublic information.
- *Forward-looking disclaimers.* Since many queries will ask for management's predictions and views about the future, the company should have policies for giving forward-looking statements that fit within the safe-harbor rules. The speaker should identify the statement as predictive and refer the audience to risk disclosure in a readily available SEC filing. Exchange Act §21E(c)(2). These risk disclosures should be updated periodically.

5. a. Yes, under a misappropriation theory. Adela provided Dwight information on the superconductivity tests on the condition that the bank keep it confidential. Dwight, in effect, misappropriated this information from the bank. If the bank had a policy against employees using confidential customer information — which seems nearly certain — he would be liable on a misappropriation theory. The theory protects confidential business information and assures stock trading markets that trading with information purloined in a relationship of trust or confidence is prohibited.

Even if the bank did not have this policy, the SEC rule defining the relationships that trigger misappropriation liability specifies that if there was a pattern of sharing confidences so Dwight had reason to know Adela expected confidential treatment, Dwight would have a duty not to trade. Rule 10b5-2(b)(2). Although the bank was not an agent of BIM, because commercial lenders typically deal with borrowers on an arm's-length basis, the SEC rule stretches the notion of trust or confidence beyond that of state agency law. Compare *United States v. Chestman* (see §10.2.2).

Notice, however, that Dwight was not a tippee of BIM, since Adela expected no personal gain from the disclosure and breached no duty when she provided it. She supplied the information so her company could get a loan, something permissible under the selective disclosure rules of Regulation FD. Rule 100(b)(2)(i).

b. Both are liable. Tipper and tippee liability works the same in an outsider misappropriation case as in an insider trading case. See *United States v. Falcone*, 257 F.3d 226 (2d. Cir. 2001) (see §10.2.3 — Tipping of Misappropriated Information). As discussed in the prior answer, if Dwight is under an abstain-or-disclose duty because of his position at the bank or a promise of confidentiality, he cannot tip the information. Wanda is liable as a tippee if she knew (or had reason to know) that Dwight received the information in confidence and that Dwight gained some personal benefit (such as a share of her trading profits) by disclosing it to her. She is liable as tippee, and he as tipper, for any trading gains.

c. Perhaps not. Rule 10b-5 liability hinges on a relationship of trust and confidence, and there is none here. See *O'Hagan*. Tina does not have a relationship with and is not a fiduciary to either BIM or to Third Federal Bank. Nor has Tina agreed to maintain the information in confidence, nor is there any practice of sharing confidences with Tina from which an expectation of confidentiality might arise. See Rule 10b5-2(b). Although insider-trading prohibitions may be meant to protect confidential business information, it can be argued that 10b-5 liability is not so broad. Compare *SEC v. Cherif*, 933 F.2d 403 (7th Cir. 1991) (liability of former employee who used magnetic identification card to gain access to secret information on pending takeovers).

Nonetheless, the Second Circuit has held that a computer hacker who acquires a company's nonpublic information and trades on it for his own profit can be liable for insider trading, even though the hacker had no fiduciary relationship with the company or its shareholders. *SEC v. Dorozhko*, 574 F.3d 42 (2d Cir. 2009) (holding that, despite lack of fiduciary relationship, "act of hacking" could satisfy 10b-5 deception requirement).

In any event, Tina can be liable for mail and wire fraud. See §10.2.3 — Mail and Wire Fraud. In addition, if any of the information she stole and traded on related to a tender offer, she would also be liable under Rule 14e-3. See §10.2.3 — Rule 14e-3. Neither of these "information protection" rules requires a relationship of trust and confidence.

6. a. No. The trading does not breach any duty of trust or confidence. *Chiarella* and *O'Hagan*. BIM has not misappropriated any information, since any proprietary interest in the information concerning the Ovid acquisition belonged to BIM. The company is merely exploiting its informational advantage, based on its own plans, and has no abstain-or-disclose duty.

This analysis is the same under Rule 14e-3, which applies to material, nonpublic information about a pending tender offer. Even if the Ovid acquisition were structured as a tender offer, the rule applies only to persons other than the "offering person." Rule 14e-3(a).

b. Probably not under Rule 10b-5, though perhaps under Rule 14e-3. Because Adela had permission to trade on information about BIM's undisclosed plans, she did not misappropriate any information when she traded in Ovid's shares. See *O'Hagan*. In these circumstances, there was no deception *aimed at the source of the information*, a necessary element for liability under the Supreme Court's theory for liability in *O'Hagan*. Just as BIM's trading on its own information would not violate Rule 10b-5 (see previous answer), Adela's trading could be seen as a form of additional, indirect trading by BIM itself. There might, however, be problems for BIM under federal line-item disclosure rules (or state corporate fiduciary law) if the company fails to disclose this implicit executive compensation, but not under Rule 10b-5.

Whatever Adela's authorization, she violated the terms of Rule 14e-3, which regulates trading on confidential information about a *tender offer*. See §10.2.2. The rule prohibits trading by "any other person" (besides the bidder) who possesses material, nonpublic information she knows is nonpublic and came from the bidder. Rule 14e-3. By its terms, Rule 14e-3 is violated even if there is no breach of a duty of trust and confidence. Does the SEC have the rule-making power to regulate trading not in breach of a duty? Although the Supreme Court in *O'Hagan* upheld Rule 14e-3 as applied to a lawyer who had breached his duties by trading on confidential client information, the Court reserved "for another day" the legitimacy of Rule 14e-3 as applied to "warehousing," the practice by bidders of leaking advance information of tender offers to allies and encourage them to purchase target stock before the bid is announced. Like warehousing, Adela's authorized trading breaches no duty. As applied to Adela, Rule 14e-3 may go beyond the SEC's rulemaking power.

c. No, even if Adela violated Rule 10b-5, only shareholders who traded "contemporaneously" with Adela can recover. The Insider Trading and Securities Fraud Enforcement Act of 1988 provides an explicit private right of action to contemporaneous traders against misappropriators. Exchange Act §20A. At one time courts saw the misappropriation theory as protecting the confidences of the outside company, here BIM, and held that Rule 10b-5 did not protect trading shareholders, such as Ovid's. The 1988 Act rejects this view. Liability, however, is not tied to the period during which the misappropriator failed to disclose, but rather the period of the misappropriator's trading.

d. There is no cap, if she violated Rule 10b-5 or 14e-3. Adela can be liable for her trading profits in a disgorgement proceeding by the SEC or in a restitution suit by contemporaneous traders — maximum $100,000. See Exchange Act §20A. In addition, she can be liable for additional civil penalties of up to three times her trading profits — maximum $300,000. Exchange Act §21A. She can also be subject to criminal fines — up to $5 million. Exchange Act §32(a). Finally, she can be liable for any losses to BIM if it had to pay more for the merger because of the signaling inherent in her trading — no maximum. All for a $100,000 trading gain!

e. No. Although Tom revealed nonpublic, confidential information to his clients (the likely BIM acquisition of Ovid), he ascertained it from public information and thus breached no duty. Nor did Tom have any duty to BIM (the source of the information) or Ovid (the company whose shares were traded).

But didn't Tom misappropriate information about BIM's likely merger with Ovid from his own brokerage firm? Although the brokerage firm could have used this information to its advantage, it is unlikely the firm has a policy against analysts disclosing their analysis to clients. In fact, Tom's job is probably to do precisely what he did. The Supreme Court in Dirks recognized the crucial role securities analysts play in disseminating information to the market.

7. a. Yes. Senator Bills violated his duty under the STOCK Act not to trade on material nonpublic information he derived from his congressional position. See §10.2.3. Although there might be some difficulties for the SEC or private plaintiffs to demand information about the meeting given the prerogative of Congress members to conduct their business in privacy, there is nothing in the Constitution to suggest that Congress cannot regulate corrupt behavior by its members and staff.

b. Maybe. The state governor is not subject to the duties of the STOCK Act, but might be liable under Rule 10b-5 on four theories: (1) the governor violated his duties to his state by trading on information that he gained from performing his official responsibilities; (2) the governor had an understanding not to use confidential information from a federal congressional colleague; (3) the governor is a "temporary insider" with respect to the information from his federal colleague; and (4) the governor was a "tippee" who knew or should have known that Senator Bills violated his duties by disclosing this information for "personal gain."

The first theory depends on state law, which a federal court in a 10b-5 case might infer, just as federal courts have inferred the existence of fiduciary duties of trust and confidence in business corporations, even when state fiduciary law may not recognize such duties. For example, a state statute that mandates the confidentiality of state information would suggest that the governor violated a duty by trading on the basis of information he gained in his official capacity.

The second theory arises from Rule 10b5-2 and its creation of duties of trust and confidence in misappropriation cases when a person (here the governor) trades on the basis of information he agreed to keep confidential, or Senator Bills and the governor have an understanding that they expect their communications will be kept confidential. This expansion of Rule 10b-5 liability beyond fiduciary duties to the source (here the United States) has not been challenged, but would seem to be within the authority of the SEC under §10(b) to define the contours of a "manipulative or deceptive device or contrivance."

The third theory depends on a federal court using the logic of *Dirks* (see §10.2.1) to create "temporary insider" status for persons who have an agency-like relationship with the source of the information. Here it might be argued that the governor had become part of a "team" looking for ways to bring manufacturing to a state — and thus was duty bound to maintain the confidences of the group. That is, the governor assumed the same duties as Senator Bills by acting as part of an initiative led by a federal legislator. That the STOCK Act creates only duties in federal legislators and their aides suggests that Congress did not go as far as *Dirks* did.

The fourth theory depends on Senator Bills having violated his duties by disclosing information about the BIM meeting. This theory seems less likely to succeed, given that Senator Bills was conducting legitimate official business when he talked with the governor about how his state might get BIM to build its manufacturing plants in the state. That is, it would not appear that Senator Bills derived a "personal benefit" when he shared this information. Although helping bring BIM manufacturing plants to the state might benefit him politically, Senator Bills seems to have shared the information with the governor to advance the state's interests, not his own. His actions would seem to be comparable to those of a company executive who disclosed confidential information to advance a corporate interest, even though he might also benefit from corporate success.

c. Each has probably violated Rule 10b-5. In this tipping case, liability for each person in the chain depends on Sandro having violated his duties of trust and confidence by "tipping" Mega-Data. There is no indication that part of his legislative duties includes disclosing information about private meetings between legislators and constituents. And although Sandro received no explicit personal benefit from Mega-Data, courts have accepted implicit benefits such as "personal friendship" and "professional connections." Here, if there was any possibility that Mega-Data would later offer Sandro employment (a "revolving door") or would give him any other favor, then Sandro would have received an improper personal benefit. Although in some situations congressional aides might be under instructions to "leak" confidential information for political purposes, there is no indication that the "owner" of the information (the Congress) asked Sandro to do this.

If Sandro breached his duties, then the next question becomes whether Mega-Data knew or should have known about this breach. Certainly, if Mega-Data had made direct promises to Sandro to obtain the information, it would be aware that Sandro's disclosure breached his duties. Even if Mega-Data did not make such promises, its recognition that the disclosure was about private meetings suggests that it was not receiving the information as a member of the public — but as a special favor.

Finally, it seems likely that Mega-Data's hedge fund clients should have known that the information about private congressional meetings came from a source that violated his duties by disclosing the information. If Mega-Data told the hedge funds that Sandro was the source of the information, the funds should have known — particularly after the STOCK Act — that Sandro owed duties of trust and confidence as to market-sensitive information. Even if Mega-Data had not disclosed its source, the hedge funds should have expected that the information came from an inside congressional source and would have been under a duty to inquire further.

§10.3 SHORT-SWING INSIDER PROFITS: DISCLOSURE AND DISGORGEMENT

The prohibitions of Rule 10b-5 are not the only federal limitation on share liquidity. To deter price manipulation by insiders in public corporations and encourage insiders to acquire long-term interests in their corporations, Section 16 of the Exchange Act

- requires specified insiders to report their trading in their company's equity securities — §16(a)

- authorizes the corporation (or a shareholder in a derivative suit) to recover from these insiders any profits made on stock transactions in a narrow six-month period, so-called "short-swing" trading profits — §16(b)
- bans these insiders from selling short any equity securities of the company — §16(c).

§10.3.1 Coverage of §16

Section 16 applies to trading in equity securities of specified officials and 10 percent shareholders of registered companies. These insiders must file reports describing their insider status and any trades they make in their company's equity securities.

Equity Securities in Registered Companies

Section 16 only applies to trading in the *equity securities* of a corporation that has a class of equity stock registered under §12 of the Exchange Act — *registered* companies (see §8.3.1). Thus, §16 applies to trading in any equity securities of registered companies, whether or not the particular securities are subject to §12 registration. For example, if a company's common stock is subject to Exchange Act registration, but its preferred stock is not — because it is not listed on a stock exchange and is held by fewer than 500 shareholders (see §8.3.1) — trading by insiders in the unregistered preferred is subject to §16's reporting and disgorgement rules. (In 1991 the SEC broadened §16 coverage to include options, convertible securities, and other equity derivatives within the definition of "equity securities." Rule 16a-1(c), (d). Thus, insiders must also report their option trading and are subject to disgorgement of any profits on their short-swing option trading.)

Reporting by Specified Insiders

The short-swing trading provisions of §16 apply only to directors, officers, and shareholders who own (of record or beneficially) more than 10 percent of any class of a reporting company's equity securities. To facilitate the policing of insiders' short-swing trading, §16(a) requires reports by directors, specified officers, and 10 percent shareholders of reporting companies. Form 3 (initial reporting once insider status achieved), Form 4 (reporting of subsequent changes in beneficial ownership); Form 5 (annual report).

The reports, which must be filed electronically with the SEC and posted on the company's website, disclose the amount of securities *beneficially owned* by the insider and the price paid in any purchase or sale. Initial reports must be filed within 10 days after a person becomes an insider, and updating reports must be filed within 2 business days after any change in the insider's holdings. Rule 16a-3; Securities Act Rel. No. 8230 (2003). Failure to file subjects the insider to penalties. (Before 2002, reports were due within 10 business days after the close of a calendar month in which a reportable event had occurred. But Sarbanes-Oxley added new filing and posting deadlines in response to concerns that slow reporting during accounting scandals of early 2000s had permitted insiders to conceal important information. Sarbanes-Oxley §403.)

Exemptions for Executive Compensation

The SEC has created a complex set of rules that permit company executives to acquire and sell shares under company compensation plans. Recognizing the value of stock ownership in executive compensation plans, the SEC has exempted "tax conditioned" plans from the reporting rules and short-swing profit liability. These plans include those that are "qualified employee benefit plans" under the Internal Revenue Code (which allows for tax deductions for the company and tax deferral for the executive) and those that meet the requirements of a "qualified stock purchase plan" under the Internal Revenue Code. Rule 16b-3. This means that company executives can — worry-free — (1) acquire stock or derivative securities with plan contributions, (2) purchase stock in an employee stock purchase plan (ESOP), (3) dispose of stock pursuant to domestic relation orders, and (4) receive distributions on death, disability, retirement, or termination. Company executives can even elect to transfer in and out of company stock funds, or receive cash withdrawals, if the election is made only once every six months.

§10.3.2 Disgorging Short-Swing Profits — Mechanical Test

Section 16(b) imposes automatic, strict liability on any director, officer, or 10 percent shareholder who makes a profit (as defined) in short-swing transactions within a six-month period. No proof of intent or scienter is required. Recovery is to the corporation, and suit may be brought either by the corporation or by a shareholder in a derivative suit.

The mechanical short-swing profit rules are both overly broad and overly narrow. They broadly cover innocent short-swing trading that occurs without the use of inside information or any manipulative intent, yet they fail to cover abusive insider trading that occurs outside the six-month window or by those who are not insiders specified under §16.

A two-part algorithm determines whether disgorgement is available:

Identify an insider

(1) Director or officer at either sale or purchase

For directors or officers (but not 10 percent shareholders), director or officer status at the time of either purchase or sale is sufficient — not necessarily both. The theory is that by trading when he was a director or officer, the insider had access to nonpublic information and was in a position to manipulate the price of the stock. Under Rule 16a-2, transactions occurring within six months before becoming a director are not counted, though transactions occurring within six months of ceasing to be a director are counted.

(2) Shareholder (10 percent) "immediately before" both transactions

For 10 percent shareholders, it is necessary that the person have held more than 10 percent *immediately before* both the purchase and sale to be matched. *Reliance Electric Co. v. Emerson Electric Co.*, 404 U.S. 418 (1972) (holding that the shareholder must hold 10 percent or more before matching *sale*); *Foremost McKesson Inc. v. Provident Securities Co.*, 423 U.S. 232 (1976) (holding that shareholder must hold 10 percent or more before matching *purchase*). The different treatment of 10 percent shareholders comes from an exclusion in §16(b) of "any transaction where [the] beneficial owner was not such both at the time of the purchase and sale, or the sale and purchase, of the security involved." The rationale is that 10 percent shareholders are less likely to have access to inside information or to corporate control mechanisms than directors or officers. Thus, their insider status must exist at both ends of the matching transactions.

Match any pair of transactions that produce a profit

Section 16(b) liability is predicated on matching any *purchase* with any *sale*, regardless of order, during any six-month period in which the sale price is higher than the purchase price. There is no tracing of shares, and recovery is frequently measured by matching later lowest-cost purchases with earlier highest-cost sales. See *Smolowe v. Delendo Corp.*, 136 F.2d 231 (2d Cir. 1943). There is no need to offset any losses — that is, any purchases and sales in which the sales price is *lower* than the purchase price need not be matched and can be disregarded.

Comparison to Rule 10b-5

Section 16(b) is broader and narrower than the insider trading prohibitions of Rule 10b-5. Limited to trading in securities of registered companies during a six-month window, it is narrower than Rule 10b-5 — which applies to all companies and regardless of holding periods. Yet, by covering any trading during a six-month period, whether or not based on inside information, §16(b) is also broader than Rule 10b-5 — which requires a showing that trading was based on material, nonpublic information.

§10.3.3 Special Interpretive Issues

The literal terms of §16(b) are inflexible, sometimes too harsh, and other times too lenient. To accomplish the rule's purpose to discourage manipulative insider trading, courts have interpreted the section's significant terms — *director and officer, beneficial ownership,* and *purchase and sale* — to introduce policy analysis into the otherwise mechanical disgorgement rules.

Directors and Officers

Courts have interpreted §16(b) to reach persons and entities who do not fall within the literal definition of *officer* or *director,* but who are functionally equivalent for purposes of insider access.

Functional Officers

For purposes of §16(b), an officer is any employee who has a position in the corporation that gives her access to confidential inside information that is not freely circulated. An official title may help identify these persons, but is not determinative. *Merrill Lynch, Pierce, Fenner & Smith, Inc. v. Livingston,* 566 F.2d 1119 (9th Cir. 1978) (holding that a brokerage firm's "vice president" was not officer for §16(b) purposes, because his title was merely honorary in recognition of sales accomplishments and did not reflect access to inside information). In 1991, as part of a comprehensive update of §16, the SEC defined "officer" to include those persons who perform policy-making functions. See Rule 16a-1(f) (definition based on title and policy-making functions).

What happens when a person is a director/officer when a sale occurs, but was not when the earlier (or later) matching purchase happened? The SEC has taken the view that the director/officer is not subject to §16 with respect to transactions that occurred *prior* to becoming a director/officer. See Rule 16a-2(a). But the director/officer remains subject to §16 if there are any matchable transactions up to six months after he leaves office. See Rule 16a-2(b).

Deputization

Courts have developed a *deputization theory* for entities that hold stock in a corporation and are also represented on the corporation's board of directors. For example, suppose that Henrietta is a managing partner of Trout Brothers, an investment banker with a securities trading department, and that she also sits on the board of Bullseye Corporation, the subject of takeover speculation. If Trout Brothers purchases 5 percent of Bullseye's stock, §16(b) technically does not impose any short-swing trading liability: Trout Brothers is neither a 10 percent shareholder nor a director, and Henrietta is not the beneficial owner of Bullseye stock held by Trout Brothers. Nonetheless, there should be concern that Trout Brothers will use Henrietta as its conduit of inside information.

Under the deputization theory, Henrietta is treated as Trout Brothers's "deputy," and any Trout Brothers transactions in Bullseye stock are brought under the short-swing profit rules. The scope of the deputization theory is unclear. Under one view, Trout Brothers is treated under §16(b) as a "director" if Henrietta (1) represents its interests on the Bullseye board and (2) actually passes along inside information to Trout Brothers. See *Blau v. Lehman*, 368 U.S. 403 (1962) (entire partnership not liable as an insider merely because one member was a director in a corporation in whose stock the partnership traded based on public information).

Beneficial Ownership

An important issue in many §16(b) cases is whether a person subject to the disgorgement rules beneficially owns securities that have been transacted. For example, if the spouse of an officer of Company X owns shares in the company, can transactions by the spouse be attributed to the officer? In 1991, the SEC promulgated a rule to define beneficial ownership for purposes of §16. The rule attributes beneficial ownership differently for 10 percent shareholders and directors/officers.

Ten Percent Shareholder

In general, beneficial ownership of securities under the Exchange Act depends on whether a shareholder has the power either to vote the securities or to dispose of them. Rule 13d-3(a). The SEC has adopted this definition for purposes of determining ownership by 10 percent shareholders. Rule 16a-1(a)(1). Under the SEC definition, this means that spouses and other family members (even if they share pecuniary benefits) are not the beneficial owners of each other's stock for §16(b) purposes unless they can control its voting or disposition. This regulatory definition deviates from that adopted by some earlier courts, which focused on whether the shareholder shared in the pecuniary benefits of ownership. See *Whiting v. Dow Chemical Co.*, 523 F.2d 680 (2d Cir. 1975) (finding beneficial ownership when shares were for the joint benefit of husband and wife). The regulatory definition gives greater leeway to 10 percent shareholders.

Directors and Officers

Directors and officers are subject to a different rule of beneficial ownership that focuses on whether they have (or share) a "pecuniary interest in the shares." Rule 16a-1(a)(2). The pecuniary interest can be direct or indirect and does not depend on whether the director or officer has any voting or disposition power over the shares. It is enough if the director or officer stands to profit directly or indirectly from the transaction. This means that if the spouse of an officer of Company X sells her shares and the officer stands to profit indirectly, the sale is attributed to the officer.

Things get a bit dicey when a director/officer has an interest in another company that owns shares in the company where he is a director/officer. For example, if Frost is a director/officer of IVAX and also owns 17.3 percent of the shares of NAVI, which holds a significant amount of IVAX stock, is Frost considered a beneficial owner of the NAVI-held shares? According to the Second Circuit, interpreting the SEC rule on §16 beneficial ownership, the answer is yes if Frost shares "investment control" of the IVAX shares in NAVI's stock portfolio—making him a pro rata owner of the NAVI-held shares. Rule 16a-1(a)(2)(iii). The Second Circuit explained that since Frost was a party to an agreement among shareholders who owned 50.8 percent of NAVI's common stock, a fact-finder might conclude that he shared working control, with others, over NAVI's portfolio. *Feder v. Frost*, 220 F.3d 29 (2d Cir. 2000).

Unorthodox Transactions

Usually whether a stock transaction constitutes a matchable purchase or sale under §16(b) is not an issue. But when the stock transaction is *unorthodox*—such as when shares are acquired in a merger or in an option transaction—the courts have been willing to inquire into whether the transaction should be treated as a matchable "sale" or "purchase" for purposes of §16(b). The SEC also has promulgated extensive (and very technical) rules that exempt certain transactions—such as redemptions, conversions, and transactions involving employee benefit plans—when the risk of insider abuse is minimal. Exchange Act Rules 16b-1 through 16b-11.

The Supreme Court has held that an unorthodox transaction by a hostile bidder (which became a 10 percent shareholder) in a takeover contest is not a matchable "sale" if there is no evidence of abuse of inside information. *Kern County Land Co. v. Occidental Petroleum Corp.*, 411 U.S. 582 (1973). In the case,

Occidental successfully bid for 20 percent of Kern County's stock — a §16(b) "purchase." Concerned about Occidental's intentions, Kern County management found a white knight (Tenneco), which agreed to buy Kern County in a merger. Under the merger terms, "Old Kern" merged into a wholly owned Tenneco subsidiary and became "New Kern." Old Kern shareholders received Tenneco preferred stock in exchange for their stock. To buy Occidental's goodwill, Tenneco granted Occidental an option to sell its Tenneco preferred (after the merger) at a premium. Occidental agreed not to oppose or vote on the merger, and the remaining Old Kern shareholders approved. Occidental, along with the other Old Kern shareholders, then received Tenneco preferred stock for their Old Kern stock.

Was there a "sale" that could be matched with the tender offer "purchases"? The plaintiff argued there were two: (1) the option granted to Occidental — granted within six months of the original purchases, though exercisable after the six-month period and (2) Occidental's exchange of New Kern stock for Tenneco preferred stock in the merger — which occurred within the six-month period. In other contexts, the receipt of consideration in a merger has been treated as a sale under the federal securities laws. See Securities Act Rule 145 (requiring prospectus disclosure for securities issued in a merger). Nonetheless, the Supreme Court decided that Occidental had not "sold" its Old Kern stock in the merger because the transaction was involuntary, and the relationship between Occidental and Kern County's management was hostile. Likewise, there was no evidence of abuse of inside information in the granting of the option, which was granted to buy Occidental's acquiescence in the merger.

But when it is possible inside information has been abused, the granting of an option has been treated as a "sale." In *Bershad v. McDonough*, 428 F.2d 693 (7th Cir. 1970), McDonough and his wife had purchased more than 10 percent of Cudahy's stock, and McDonough became a director. Within six months of these purchases, the McDonoughs granted another company, Smelting Refining, an option to purchase the bulk of their Cudahy stock. McDonough then resigned from Cudahy's board, and Smelting Refining placed its representatives on the board. Under the option agreement, the McDonoughs placed their Cudahy shares in escrow. Smelting Refining exercised the option more than six months after their original purchase. The court held that the granting of the option was a matchable "sale" because it could lend itself to inside speculation.

§10.3.4 Section 16(b) Litigation

Compared to the factual and legal issues that surround 10b-5 litigation of insider trading cases, litigation of §16(b) short-swing disgorgement cases is a cinch. The statute specifies the elements of a disgorgement action:

- realization of profit
- by a director, officer, or 10 percent shareholder
- from matching purchases or sales during any six-month period
- of equity securities of a public company.

The information to establish a §16(b) disgorgement case is available in public filings with the SEC. There is no requirement that the §16(b) plaintiff establish any of the elements normally required in a private 10b-5 action, namely that the trading was based on material, nonpublic information, that the defendant acted with a culpable state of mind, that those who traded relied in some way, that the trading caused any losses, or even that there were losses.

The only significant procedural issue in §16(b) disgorgement actions is the plaintiff's standing. Under the statute, if the corporation fails to sue within 60 days of a demand, an "owner of any security of the issuer" may bring a derivative suit on behalf of the corporation. The statute does not specify any standing requirements for a derivative suit plaintiff, and courts have interpreted the statute broadly. Thus, some of the standing requirements in a normal derivative suit, such as contemporaneous ownership, do not apply in a §16(b) suit. See *Gollust v. Mendell*, 501 U.S. 115 (1991) (holding that shareholder of corporation acquired in a merger had standing to continue a §16(b) action against former 10 percent shareholder, even though corporation was merged into a new entity).

Why would a shareholder or bondholder bring a §16(b) disgorgement suit if any recovery goes to the corporation? The holder's interest in the suit is limited to the increase in value (if any) of the holder's securities. This diluted incentive, it would seem, would rarely justify investigating a §16(b) violation and initiating the litigation. The real incentive for §16(b) litigation, however, is that the attorneys' fees of a successful derivative-suit plaintiff are recoverable from the corporation. In fact, it is no defense that the §16(b) litigation was brought primarily to obtain attorneys' fees. See *Magida v. Continental Can Co.*, 231 F.2d 843 (2d Cir. 1956).

Statute of Limitations

Section 16(b) suits — whether by the corporation or through a derivative suit — must be brought within two years of the date when the insider's profit was realized. §16(b). In 2012, the Supreme Court held that this period is not tolled until insiders file their §16(a) disclosures, though it is subject to traditional equitable tolling. *Credit Suisse Securities (USA) LLC v. Simmonds*, 566 U.S. _____ (2012) (remanding §16(b) case, which had been brought in 2007 alleging short-swing profits arising during dot-com boom of late 1990s, for a determination of when plaintiff, with due diligence, could have known or did know of trading at issue).

§10.4 REGULATION OF INSIDER TRADING UNDER SARBANES-OXLEY (REVISED BY DODD-FRANK)

In response to the corporate scandals of the early 2000s, the Sarbanes-Oxley Act of 2002 regulates insider trading by company executives in two situations. Sarbanes-Oxley §306(a) (pension fund blackouts), §304 (12-month period after financials misstated). The Dodd-Frank Act of 2010 adds "clawback" requirements for public companies.

§10.4.1 Insider Trading During Pension Plan Trading Blackout

Directors and officers are prohibited from trading in their company's stock during any "trading blackout" in the company's pension plan—that is, when for more than 3 consecutive business days a majority of plan participants cannot obtain distributions or trade company stock held in the plan. ERISA §101, 29 U.S.C. §1021(h). The prohibition applies to any stock obtained by the director or officer in connection with his service or employment, whether or not held in the plan.

The purpose of the prohibition is to prevent company management from freezing transactions in the company's pension plan for ordinary employees while dumping their own stock during a decline in the company's stock prices. Not only must the pension plan administrator notify plan participants (and the SEC) of the blackout, but the company must also notify directors and officers of the prohibition against trading in company stock. See Regulation BTR, Rule 104 (specifying contents and timing of notice).

Any trading profits realized by the director or officer during a trading blackout are recoverable by the company, regardless of intent—much like the strict liability scheme for short-swing profits under §16(b). The action to recover trading profits may be brought as a direct suit by the company or as a derivative suit by a shareholder after making demand on the company's board. The suit must be brought within two years from when the profits are realized. See Regulation BTR, Rule 103 (specifying "profit recoverable" to be difference between the transaction price and the average market price after the end of the blackout).

Unlike short-swing trading, which only triggers reporting requirements and the possibility of disgorgement in private litigation, trading during a pension plan blackout is *prohibited*. Thus, directors or officers who trade during such a blackout may also be subject to SEC enforcement actions and even criminal sanctions.

§10.4.2 Reimbursement of Incentive Pay When Financials Misstated

Sarbanes-Oxley "Clawback" Regime

Sarbanes-Oxley created a regime calling on corporate executives in public companies to reimburse the company for incentive pay when the company must restate its financials because of "misconduct." Sarbanes-Oxley §304 (adding 15 U.S.C. §7243). Specifically, the CEO and CFO are required to reimburse the company for any incentive pay (such as bonuses or equity-based compensation) received from the company during the 12-month period after the misstated financials were issued or filed. This "reimbursement" duty also applies to any profits on the sale of company stock by the CEO or CFO during the same period.

The Sarbanes-Oxley reimbursement provisions sought to prevent a company's top officers from profiting from false financials. The provisions, for which legislative history was scant, introduced numerous uncertainties:

- Do voluntary restatements trigger reimbursement? The statute applies to issuers "required to prepare an accounting restatement." It is unclear whether a voluntary restatement, not required by SEC or court order, is covered.
- What individuals may be liable? The statute applies to "the chief executive officer and chief financial officer," but does not specify whether this is the individual holding the office when the noncomplying statement is filed, during the 12-month period following the filing, when the financials are restated, or during a combination of all three.
- How is the 12-month period determined? The statute refers to "the 12-month period following the first public issuance or filing" of the noncompliant financial statement. It is unclear whether the 12-month period only begins with the first misstatement or whether additional 12-month periods begin with each new misstatement.
- What procedure is available for reimbursement? The statute says the "officer shall reimburse the issuer." It is unclear whether §304 reimbursement must be sought in a direct action by the company or a derivative action on behalf of the company — or even an enforcement action by the SEC. Courts uniformly interpreted §304 not to create a private cause of action, but only a basis for an SEC enforcement action. See *Neer v. Pelino*, 389 F. Supp. 2d 648 (E.D. Pa. 2005). The SEC, however, brought few enforcement actions.
- What misconduct triggers liability? The statute speaks of "misconduct" without specifying whether negligent, grossly negligent or willful misconduct is covered. Nor does the statute explain whether

the officer from whom reimbursement is sought must have participated in the misconduct. For example, could false revenue data by the company's sales manager, about which the CEO and CFO are oblivious, be the basis for reimbursement liability?

- What trading profits are recoverable? The statute mentions "profits from the sale of securities" of the company. It is unclear whether recoverable profits are the actual profits realized by the executive (sales price less acquisition cost) or the "out of pocket" gains (sales price less the price at which the stock should have traded absent the misstated financials). Also unclear is whether trading losses can offset trading gains.

- What limitations period applies? The statute does not mention a period for bringing a §304 reimbursement action. Does the two-year/five-year limitations period created by Sarbanes-Oxley apply on the theory a §304 action is one that "involves a claim of fraud, deceit, manipulation, or contrivance" in contravention of the securities laws? See 28 U.S.C. §804 (see §9.4.1).

- Can a company create private standards? Although the SEC is given authority to exempt persons from a §304 action, it is unclear whether a company can provide this exemption. Also unclear is whether a company could define such terms as "misconduct" and "profits" for its top officers.

Dodd-Frank "Clawback" Regime

In response to the many weaknesses in the §304 clawback regime, Dodd-Frank created a new one. Under §10D to the Exchange Act, the SEC is required to impose rules on the national stock exchanges that would compel listed companies to adopt "clawback" policies for the recovery of any incentive-based compensation (including stock options) from current or former executive officers for the prior three years in the event of a financial restatement due to material noncompliance with any financial reporting requirement under the securities laws. Dodd-Frank §954. The amount to be recovered is set at the difference between the amount of incentive-based compensation received and the amount that should have been received under the restated financial results.

The §954 regime of Dodd-Frank is different from the §304 regime of Sarbanes-Oxley. First, the §954 clawback right is enforceable, not just by the SEC, but also in derivative actions whenever companies fail to seek such relief. Further, private plaintiffs may initiate litigation even when restatements did not occur but should have occurred were it not for a conflict of interest by management. Second, while the §304 regime only allowed disgorgement from the company's CEO and CFO, the §954 regime covers the company's current and former "executive officers," which presumably includes all officers subject to §16 reporting. Third, the §954 regime lowers the trigger for clawbacks to instances of "material noncompliance with applicable accounting principles," while the §304 regime was limited to restatements resulting from "misconduct." Fourth, the §954 regime extends the look-back period from one year to three years.

Despite adding greater clarity—and increasing the likelihood of enforcement—the §954 regime leaves some important questions unanswered. For example, if an executive and the company's board fight the clawback, it is unclear whether the usual corporate law rules on board demand and dismissal of derivative litigation would apply. In particular, it is unclear whether the board (or a special litigation committee) could argue that the benefits of any clawback are outweighed by the disadvantages.

Examples

1. BIM Corporation has one class of common stock, which is registered under §12 of the Exchange Act. Dorothy is a director of BIM. For each of the following situations, what is Dorothy's disgorgement liability under §16(b)?

   a. Dorothy purchases 100 shares of BIM stock on February 1 at $10 per share, and sells on August 2 at $15. BIM's stock price rose because it was awarded a large government contract on April 1, which Dorothy knew about when she bought.

   b. Dorothy buys 200 shares on July 1 at $5, sells 200 shares on February 1 of the next year at $15 per share, and then purchases 300 shares on May 1 at $10 per share.

   c. Dorothy buys 100 shares at $10 on February 1, buys another 100 shares at $20 on March 1, sells 100 shares at $12 on April 1, and sells another 100 shares at $15 on May 1.

   d. Dorothy adds to her portfolio and buys 180 shares on February 1 at $10, sells 150 shares on May 1 at $15, and then sells another 100 shares at $18 on June 1.

   e. Dorothy became a director on March 1. Prior to this, on February 1, she had purchased 100 shares at $10 per share. She purchases 100 shares at $12 on April 1, and sells 100 shares at $15 per share on June 1.

   f. Dorothy purchases 100 shares at $10 per share on February 1. She becomes a director on March 1, and resigns as director on May 1. She sells 100 shares at $15 per share on May 2. Dorothy purchased in February at $10 knowing of confidential, nonpublic developments that would raise the price in May.

2. Cheryl is an investor with a keen interest in BIM. She is neither a director nor officer of BIM.
   a. Over 4 years, Cheryl accumulates 9 million shares (9 percent) of BIM stock. On February 1 she buys 5 million additional shares at $15 per share, bringing her holdings to 14 percent. On May 1 she sells all of her 14 million shares at $20 per share. What is Cheryl's §16(b) liability?
   b. After selling all her BIM stock last year, Cheryl decides to acquire control of the company by making open-market purchases and a tender offer. She is prepared, however, to sell her holdings if another bidder offers a good price. Advise Cheryl on how to purchase and, if the opportunity presents itself, sell her stock without becoming subject to §16(b) liability.

3. Cheryl does not take your advice. Instead, she buys 11 percent of BIM's stock in December and then buys an additional 9 percent on March 1, bringing her holdings to 20 percent. She then enters into negotiations with BIM's management and, on July 20, agrees to have the corporation repurchase all her stock.
   a. The repurchase agreement calls for closing on the repurchase to occur on October 1, outside the six-month window that opened on March 1. Under §16(b), can Cheryl's March purchases be matched with her July agreement?
   b. If the closing had occurred on August 1 — at a slightly lower price than the one negotiated for the October 1 closing — does your answer change?

4. After selling back her shares, Cheryl and her husband Charles each begin buying BIM stock. By November, each owns 6 percent of BIM's stock.
   a. In January, Charles purchases additional shares at $40 per share, bringing his holdings to 9 percent. In March of the same year, Cheryl sells some of her shares at $45 per share, bringing her holdings to 3 percent. Is either liable under §16(b)?
   b. In August, after Cheryl and Charles sell all of their remaining BIM stock, Cheryl joins the BIM board of directors. She purchases BIM stock as trustee for her child's college fund. In November of the same year, Cheryl sells at a profit all of this stock. Is she liable under §16(b)?

5. MACO Corp. decides to "greenmail" BIM by threatening a hostile tender offer. MACO, which has no shareholding in BIM, will buy a significant block of BIM stock on the open market and then announce a tender offer. MACO expects BIM's management will offer to buy MACO's shares at a premium.

a. Otto, an officer of MACO, sits on BIM's board. Is there a possibility of §16(b) liability in MACO's plans?

b. MACO has Otto resign from the BIM board. MACO then becomes a 10 percent shareholder in January and in February purchases 200,000 more shares. BIM management reacts by offering its shareholders a capital restructuring in which they will receive a package of cash and preferred stock. This will require an amendment of BIM's charter. MACO supports the restructuring, and its votes for the charter amendment prove decisive. After the June restructuring, MACO receives cash and preferred stock, producing a significant profit. Is MACO liable under §16(b)?

Explanations

1. a. No disgorgement liability. None of Dorothy's trades occurred within six months of each other. Under §16(b) it is irrelevant whether Dorothy had any confidential, nonpublic information about the government contract when she bought and sold. She may be liable, however, under Rule 10b-5 (see §10.2.2).

Date	Transaction
February 1	Buy — 100 @$10
April 1	Government contract
August 2	Sell — 100 @$15

b. $1000. Lower-priced purchases are matched with higher-priced sales occurring within six months. Only the February sale and May purchase can be matched; the July purchase is outside the six-month window. The disgorgement formula operates regardless of the order of the transactions as long as the sale price is higher than the purchase price. In this case, only 200 shares match, and Dorothy is liable to disgorge $1000 in profits (200 shares times $5).

Date	Transaction
February 1	Sell — 200 @$15
May 1	Buy — 300 @$10

c. $500. Matching the February purchase and the May sale produces the highest gain — $500 (100 shares times $5). There is no need to offset any losses, so the $800 loss generated by matching the March purchase and the lower April sale can be disregarded. Even though Dorothy lost a net $300 during the six-month trading period — she purchased 200 shares for $3000 and sold 200 shares for $2700 — she is subject to disgorgement liability. This crude rule of thumb assumes that her February and May transactions were based on inside information or short-swing market manipulations.

Date	Transaction
February 1	Buy — 100 @$10
March 1	Buy — 100 @$20
April 1	Sell — 100 @$12
May 1	Sell — 100 @$15

d. $1200. First match the transactions that produce the greatest gains (100 shares — February and June) and then any other transactions that produce gains (80 shares — February and May). The combined recoverable profits are thus $1,200 (100 times $8 profits, matching the $18 June sale and the $10 February purchase, *plus* 80 times $5 profits, matching the $15 May sale and the $10 February purchase).

Date	Transaction
February 1	Buy — 180 @$10
May 1	Sell — 150 @$15
June 1	Sell — 100 @$18

e. $300. Although a February-June match produces a larger gain than an April-June gain, the February-June match is not available under §16(b) because Dorothy was not a director at the prior end of the match — the February transaction. Under Rule 16a-2(a), transactions *prior* to a person becoming director are exempt from §16(b) liability. The idea is that she could not have had insider information when she bought in February. Matching the April and June transactions, Dorothy's liability is $300 (100 shares times $3).

Date	Transaction
February 1	Buy — 100 @$10
March 1	Becomes director
April 1	Buy — 100 @$12
June 1	Sell — 100 @$15

f. No disgorgement liability. There is no sale and purchase to match because Dorothy was not a director at the time of either trade. Nonetheless, Dorothy may be liable under Rule 10b-5 for trading on material, nonpublic information she received in her capacity as a director (see §10.2.2).

Date	Transaction
February 1	Buy — 100 @$10
March 1	Becomes director
May 1	Resigns as director
May 2	Sell — 100 @$15

2. a. Cheryl is not liable under §16(b). The February purchase cannot be matched because Cheryl was not a 10 percent shareholder *immediately prior* to it. (In fact, Cheryl would not have disclosed her February purchase on Form 3 because at the time of the purchase she was not a 10-percent shareholder.) Shareholders must have "inside" status — that is, hold more than 10 percent of the shares — immediately before each transaction to be matched. This differs from the rule for directors and officers and is based on an assumption that shareholders are less likely to have access to inside information or the ability to manipulate prices.

Date	Transaction
February 1	Buy — 5MM @$15
May 1	Sell — 14MM @$20

b. Cheryl should buy only 9.9 percent of BIM's outstanding shares on the open market. The purchase that brings her above 10 percent should be in one fell swoop — such as in a tender offer. In this way, none of her purchases will occur when she is a 10 percent shareholder, and none will be matchable. Cheryl can later sell without incurring any §16(b) liability. The assumption in *Kern County* (see §10.3.3), decided by the Supreme Court in 1973, that tender offer purchases that bring a shareholder's holdings above 10 percent are matchable was explicitly rejected by the Supreme Court in *Foremost McKesson* in 1976 (see §10.3.2).

If Cheryl makes any matchable purchases while a 10 percent shareholder, she should sell her stock in chunks, not all at once. In this way, only those sales that she makes while she is a 10 percent shareholder are matchable. Once her holdings fall to 10 percent or less, any further sales are not matchable. This limits her §16(b) exposure.

3. a. Probably not. Can the July 20 agreement be characterized as a "sale" for purposes of §16(b)? Management's apparent hostility to Cheryl suggests she had no access to corporate information or control, and there would be little purpose in imposing short-swing liability. Such liability would effectively allow the corporation to renegotiate the repurchase price.

b. Probably. There would then be a traditional purchase and sale within six months. Nothing in the language of §16(b) suggests that there are exceptions to the disgorgement rules if the evidence strongly suggests the absence of inside abuse. Although the August closing would seem for financial purposes to be equivalent to an October closing, §16(b) may elevate the form of the transaction over its substance.

4. a. Probably not. The critical issue is whether Cheryl and Charles are treated as a single beneficial owner. If so, their individual 6 percent holdings would be combined. As beneficial owners of more than 10 percent, the January purchases by Charles would be matched with the March sales by Cheryl to produce a recoverable profit. In each case, they beneficially owned more than 10 percent immediately before the transaction. If, however, they are not the beneficial owner of the others' shares, neither can be liable because neither individually surpassed the 10 percent threshold.

According to the SEC, holdings of shareholders percent must be aggregated if one shareholder has voting or disposition control over the other's shares. Rule 16a-1(a)(1) (for purposes of determining whether shareholders own more than 10 percent, look to investment/voting control rule). In this case, unless Charles or Cheryl had control over the other's shares, there would be no beneficial ownership. This is an unusual result, which essentially permits family members to hold and trade outside the strictures of §16 so long as no family member holds more than 10 percent of the company's stock and they do not enter into any arrangement to vote or dispose of the others' stock. Rule 13d-3(a). This means that even if Cheryl and Charles share the financial benefits of ownership, they are not deemed to be beneficial owners of each other's shares, making their January and March transactions unmatchable.

b. Probably. The question of beneficial ownership also arises for a director whose family members trade in the company's stock. See Exchange Act §16(a) (requiring reports of "all shares of which [the director-officer is a beneficial owner"). Normally, a director is subject to §16 for any trading by members of his immediate family. See Rule 16a-1(a)(2)(ii)(A) (defining "indirect pecuniary interest" in equity securities to include securities held by director-officer's "immediate family" sharing the same household). In §16(b) disgorgement actions, courts have attributed trading by a director's spouse to the director, treating profits realized as a result of the spouse's transactions as "profits realized by [the director]." See *Whiting v. Dow Chemical Co.*, 523 F.2d 680 (2d Cir. 1975).

In the case of securities held in trust for a family member, the SEC rules recognize the risk that a director may abuse her insider status in connection with the trading of securities as to which the director acts as trustee. See Rules 16a-1(a)(2), 16a-8(b)(2)(ii) (director who acts as a trustee is deemed to have "beneficial ownership" in trust securities if at least one beneficiary of the trust is a member of the director's immediate family). Nonetheless, some courts in §16(b) disgorgement cases have used a narrower understanding of beneficial interest than the SEC test. *CBI Industries, Inc. v. Horton*, 682 F.2d 643 (7th Cir. 1982) (Posner, J.) (director, acting as trustee for adult children, is subject to §16(b) liability for trading in trust only if director is able to use income or assets of trust). This different treatment, apparently in sympathy for the trading limitations otherwise placed on family members of a director, seems questionable in light of the §16(b) purpose to discourage insiders from manipulating company stock prices to benefit their own trading. A director, it would seem, would have as much incentive to manipulate her company's stock prices whether profits flow directly to her or whether they flow to her children's college fund. That is, consistent with the statute's broad remedial purposes, there are "profits realized [by the director]" when her trading decisions enhance her overall financial position.

5. a. Yes. MACO might be treated as a BIM director under a "deputization" theory because Otto, an officer of MACO, sits on BIM's board. If

MACO is "deputized," any gains in its short-swing trading would be subject to §16(b) disgorgement.

To show deputization, Otto must have represented MACO on the board. In addition, it might be necessary to show some (or all) of the following: Otto was "controlled" by MACO; Otto was ultimately responsible for deciding about MACO's acquisitions of BIM stock; Otto had access to inside BIM information; and Otto actually passed such information on to MACO. Although requiring a showing of actual access or actual passing of inside information might seem inconsistent with §16(b) strict liability, deputization is meant to achieve the underlying §16(b) purposes of deterring and compensating for the abuse of inside information. A deputization test requires a showing of actual or probable abuse.

b. Perhaps, though it is hard to say. Although the February and June transactions are matchable because MACO was a 10 percent shareholder before each one, it could be argued that the June transaction was not a "sale" for purposes of §16(b). Arguably, the June restructuring was involuntary — that is, its timing was not of MACO's making — and MACO's relationship to BIM was such that it is unlikely any confidential information was passed to MACO. See *Kern County* (§10.3.3).

There are, however, two significant differences between this case and the situation in *Kern County*. First, MACO supported the restructuring. This should not make a difference if the choice of how BIM responded to the takeover threat was not MACO's, and there was no passing of insider information. Second, BIM's management may have had reasons to pass inside information to MACO. It is possible that the restructuring was negotiated with MACO — just as was the option in *Kern County*. If so, BIM's management might have found it useful to pass inside information to MACO to assure the success of the restructuring. Nonetheless, even if BIM passed inside information, it may well have been "good news" to encourage MACO's support. Because all the MACO shareholders shared in the restructuring premium, the abuse would not have harmed them.

Regulation of Securities Industry

Securities professionals — broker-dealers, investment advisers, investment companies, and credit rating agencies — act as intermediaries between securities markets and investors. In their various capacities, these professionals provide information and advice, effectuate securities transactions, and enter into securities transactions — to, for, and with investors.

Not surprisingly, given the centrality and the sensitivity of their roles, securities professionals are subject to an imposing array of regulations to ensure their honesty, integrity, competence, and financial capacity for the protection of investors and the adequate functioning of securities markets. This regulation includes (1) registration with the SEC (and attendant SEC rules); (2) registration with Financial Industry Regulatory Authority (FINRA, formerly National Association of Securities Dealers, NASD) and FINRA/NASD standards of fair conduct applicable to broker-dealer members and their associates; (3) stock exchange rules governing members and their associates; (4) SEC antifraud rules, applicable to all securities professionals; and (5) state blue sky laws, fiduciary principles, and law of agency.

This chapter covers:

- the capacities in which securities professionals act [§11.1]
- the registration of *broker-dealers*, as well as the principal standards of conduct to which they are subject, under the Securities Exchange Act of 1934, the rules of various self-regulatory organizations (SROs), and state blue sky laws [§11.2]

- the regulation of *investment advisers* under the Investment Advisers Act of 1940 and state blue sky laws, and the applicable standards of conduct [§11.3]
- the regulation of *mutual funds* under the Investment Company Act of 1940 and the liability of fund advisers for charging excessive advisory fees [§11.4]
- the regulation of *private funds* under the Investment Advisers Act of 1940, as revised by the Dodd-Frank Act [§11.5]
- the regulation of *credit rating agencies*, as well as their liability for issuing false and misleading credit reports under the Dodd-Frank Act [§11.6]

Note on National Market System

Stock trading markets, such as the NYSE and NASDAQ, function as intermediaries to bring together buyers and sellers of securities. Their regulation is the cornerstone of the Securities Exchange Act of 1934. See §8.1 (describing the regulation of securities trading markets). The stock exchanges, such as NYSE, are physical locations that match buy and sell orders; stock exchanges must register with the SEC and operate as self-regulatory organizations (SROs). The OTC markets, such as NASDAQ, are not physical locations, but instead phone and computer networks run by a for-profit business (and formerly an association of securities firms).

In the last several years, additional methods for trading securities have emerged. These "alternative trading systems" (ATSs) include purely electronic markets that allow stock traders to place standard limit orders ("buy if the price falls to $30") and complex conditional orders ("sell if the price rises more than 5 percent on any trading day"). They also include automated matching systems that permit large institutional investors to trade anonymously, with minimal price impact.

So that all securities trading markets act in tandem — a buy or sell order can go where it will be executed in the most efficient and cost-effective manner — the SEC has created rules to link together the different equity markets: the stock exchanges, OTC markets, and ATSs. See Exchange Act §11A (directing the SEC to create a National Market System); Regulation NMS (regulating the dissemination of price quotes, display of customer orders, and disclosure of how orders are filled). The National Market System incorporates both competition among the markets and individual orders. The goal is the "best execution" of customer orders by searching for the optimal combination of price and speed. See *Newton v. Merrill, Lynch, Pierce, Fenner & Smith*, 135 F.3d 267 (3d Cir. 1998) (concluding that deliberate and systematic failure of broker-dealers to seek out superior price could be deceptive practice); see also NASD Conduct Rule 2320 (requiring broker-dealers to use reasonable diligence to find most favorable price under prevailing market conditions).

§11.1 CAPACITIES OF SECURITIES PROFESSIONALS

Securities intermediaries act in essentially three capacities, mirrored in the definitions of the federal securities laws:

Broker	The Exchange Act defines a "broker" as any person (but not including a bank) engaged in the regular business of effecting securities transactions for the account of others. Exchange Act §3(a)(4).
Dealer	The Exchange Act defines a "dealer" as any person (but not including a bank) engaged in buying and selling securities for his own account as a part of his regular business. Exchange Act §3(a)(5).
Investment adviser	The Investment Advisers Act of 1940 defines an "investment adviser" as any person who, for compensation, engages in the business of advising others as to the advisability of investing in, purchasing, or selling securities. Inv. Adv. Act §202(a)(11).

Securities firms whose *regular business* is to help investors effectuate securities transactions are referred to in SEC regulations as "broker-dealers." Individuals who work as salespeople in a securities firm are referred to as "associates" of broker-dealers.

Definitional Quirk

Contrast the straightforward definitions of "broker" and "dealer" under the Exchange Act with the definition of "dealer" under the Securities Act. See Securities Act §2(a)(12) (defining "dealer" as any person in the securities business — basically securities firms). Under the Securities Act definition, "dealers" are securities firms subject to the gun-jumping rules and prospectus-delivery requirements during the registration period for public offerings. See §§4.3, 7.1. "Dealers" become freed from Securities Act regulation in the posteffective period — after they sell their allotment, once their prospectus-delivery obligations expire, and in unsolicited "brokers' transactions" that are executed on a customer's order. See Securities Act §4(a)(3), 4(a)(4).

Interaction of Definitions

As you may have noticed, securities intermediaries often act in multiple capacities. Broker-dealers give investment advice, as do mutual fund companies, managers of private funds, and credit reporting agencies. And managers of investment funds often buy and sell securities for their funds. Which regulatory regime applies? Lately, the general approach has been toward greater cross-regulation of securities intermediaries as both broker-dealers and investment advisers.

As of 2010, broker-dealers that give clients investment advice "solely incidental" to their transactional services and receive no special compensation for their advisory services are exempt from regulation as investment advisers. Inv. Adv. Act Rule 202(a)(11)-1. This exemption, however, is in doubt. Dodd-Frank requires the SEC to study whether broker-dealers should be subject to the same fiduciary duties to their retail clients as investment advisers and, if necessary, to impose such duties on broker-dealers. See Dodd-Frank §913.

Mutual funds and private funds (hedge funds and private equity funds) are investment pools in which investors entrust their money to professional money managers. See §§11.4, 11.5 (below). These investment funds are run by fund advisers, which set up the funds and then provide investment advice and other management services to the funds. Fund advisers — whether they manage registered mutual funds or unregistered private funds — must register as "investment advisers" with the SEC. See Dodd-Frank §402. In addition, if the fund managers (as many do) effectuate securities transactions for their funds, they must register as broker-dealers.

Credit rating agencies — which provide ratings used by investors about debt instruments — are exempted from the definition of "investment adviser." Inv. Adv. Act §2(a)(11)(F) (exemption for credit rating agencies registered as nationally recognized statistical rating organizations, as added by Credit Rating Agency Reform Act of 2006). Nonetheless, credit rating agencies that provide investment advice (not just issue ratings broadly disseminated to investors) are subject to Regulation FD (see §10.2.5) — thus requiring that any nonpublic, material information given to them by an issuer must be simultaneously disclosed publicly. See Securities Act Rel. No. 9,146 (2010) (as required by Dodd-Frank §939B).

§11.2 BROKER-DEALER REGULATION

Broker-dealers serve as intermediaries in securities trading. Like chaperones "between Wall Street and the innocent public," they hold a special position with their customers. Their superior knowledge, training, and access to information not only justify their commissions and fees, but also demand of them high standards of professionalism. These standards, enforced through an overlapping system of regulatory oversight by the SEC and FINRA, include obligations of candor, specific disclosure requirements, and a host of duties of professional conduct. Private enforcement, through judicial litigation and arbitration, supplements disciplinary supervision by the SEC and FINRA. In addition, customer accounts are insured by an industry-funded insurance program in the event of broker-dealer insolvency. State blue sky regulation of broker-dealers is preempted to the extent it imposes regulatory supervision greater than that imposed by the SEC.

Note on Crowdfunding "Funding Portals"

The JOBS Act of 2012 creates a new kind of securities intermediary—a "funding portal"—for crowdfunding offerings made over the Internet by small companies to a large number of small investors. See Securities Act §4(a)(6) (see §5.2.5). Although not required to register as broker-dealers, funding portals must register separately as such with the SEC and become members of a national securities association (such as FINRA). Funding portals are subject to a number of restrictions, including a ban on giving investment advice, soliciting investors or paying others to solicit investors, and handling investor funds. In addition, funding portals are subject to special disclosure rules on how they earn commissions on sales in a crowdfunding offering. Given the restrictions on funding portals, especially their inability to give investment advice or to earn "success based" commissions, many predict that most funding portals will affiliate themselves with registered broker-dealers—which are subject to fewer restrictions under the crowdfunding rules.

§11.2.1 SEC and FINRA Supervision

Broker-dealers and their sales associates are subject to governmental supervision by virtue of their registration with the SEC and to self-regulation by virtue of their membership in FINRA.

SEC Registration

All securities firms, as well as nonassociated individuals, that operate as a broker or dealer in interstate securities markets must register with the SEC on Form BD. Exchange Act §15(a) (no registration required of broker-dealers whose business is exclusively intrastate or that deal in exempt securities or commercial paper). The SEC can institute disciplinary proceedings to censure, suspend, or revoke broker-dealers that fail to meet standards of conduct or otherwise violate federal securities laws. Exchange Act §15(b).

Registration subjects broker-dealers and their salespeople (associates) to a variety of SEC regulation, including standards of operational and financial capability, training, experience, and competence. Associates of broker-dealers must pass examinations related to the securities business. The SEC requires the filing of periodic reports to ensure these standards are satisfied. Exchange Act §17(a). As of 2001, there are approximately 5,000 registered broker-dealers (with 169,000 branch offices) and 658,000 registered securities associates.

To safeguard customer funds and securities placed in the custody of broker-dealers, SEC rules create financial responsibility standards for broker-dealers and requirements for the segregation of customer funds and securities. See Rule 15c3-1 (imposing net capital rules); Rule 15c3-3 (requiring segregation of fully paid securities); Rule 15c3-2 (requiring special reserve accounts composed of cash and U.S. government securities equal to customers' net cash balances).

Broker-dealers that deal exclusively in municipal (state or local) securities or federal government securities are subject to special regulatory regimes. Broker-dealers in municipal securities are subject to SEC regulation and self-regulation by the Municipal Securities Rule-Making Board. Exchange Act §15B (added by the Securities Acts Amendments of 1975). Broker-dealers in federal government securities must register with the SEC and are subject to standards set by the Treasury Department. Exchange Act §15C (added by the Government Securities Act of 1986).

FINRA Membership

All brokers and dealers who wish to trade on the over-the-counter (OTC) market, which means nearly all securities firms, must be members of FINRA. Exchange Act §15(b)(8).

What is the FINRA? It's a non-governmental association of member broker-dealers and is registered with the SEC, the only organization so registered. See Exchange Act §15A. (FINRA was formed in 2007 and assumed the functions of its successor, the National Association of Securities Dealers (NASD), as well as the non-trading functions of the New York Stock Exchange.) Like the stock exchanges, FINRA is a self-regulatory organization (SRO) that regulates its members and their activities. The SEC has authority to review FINRA disciplinary proceedings, though the agency generally confirms FINRA's results.

§11.2.2 Regulation in Public Offerings

Broker-dealers who participate in a public offering have numerous responsibilities under the Securities Act of 1933. See §4.1.1.

Gun-jumping compliance
Participating broker-dealers must comply with the gun-jumping rules imposed by §5 (see §4.3) and are strictly liable if they sell securities in a manner prohibited by §5. See Securities Act §12(a)(1) (liability for persons who sell in violation of §5) (see §6.2).

Underwriter liability   Broker-dealers that act as underwriters in a registered public offering are responsible for assuring the accuracy of information used in the offering. See Securities Act §11(a) (liability of underwriters for misinformation in the registration statement, subject to a due diligence defense) (see §6.3).

Dealer liability   Broker-dealers that are part of a retail group in a public offering must also ensure the accuracy of their communications to investors. See Securities Act §12(a)(2) (liability of "sellers" for misinformation in the prospectus or oral communications, subject to a reasonable care defense) (see §6.4). Liability for noncompliance with the registration requirements and norms of honesty under the Securities Act also extends to any person or company that controls the culpable broker-dealer, subject to an "empty mind" defense. See Securities Act §15 (see §6.5).

Stabilizing Activities During Public Offering

The SEC has used its broad §10(b) authority (along with other statutory authority) to promulgate "trading practice rules" that prohibit manipulation during a public distribution. See Regulation M (replacing from Rules 10b-6 to 10b-8). (For more detailed discussion, see §4.2.5.)

The trading practice rules generally prohibit purchases during a distribution, but permit price stabilization activities under specified circumstances. Rule 242.104. Significantly, Regulation M exempts purchases by securities firms participating as underwriters, if the issuer is a large public company and its securities are actively traded. Rule 242.101(c) (exemption for offerings by issuers with a public float of $150 million and global daily trading that averages $1 million during a prior 60-day period).

Commissions and Fees

FINRA regulates the compensation charged by broker-dealers participating as underwriters in a securities offering, whether public or private. FINRA requires that the underwriter's commission or spread be "fair and reasonable." FINRA Manual ¶5110(c). Securities lawyers assume FINRA would view as excessive any underwriter compensation that exceeds 20 percent of the proceeds to the issuer. Moreover, FINRA limits the amount of securities taken by the underwriter as compensation, using a rule of thumb that an underwriter should take no more than 10 percent of the offered securities. FINRA requires prior review of the underwriting compensation charged for "unseasoned" companies that have not issued securities to the public.

"Spinning" and "Flipping"

Once a common practice, underwriters of initial public offerings (IPOs) would often allocate a significant portion of the IPO to preferred customers, with the hope of generating new business for the firm. This preferential treatment, which excluded individual investors, has been controversial. Sometimes underwriters would divert hot IPOs to venture capitalists and company executives who might later direct future business to the firm — so-called *spinning*. Other times the underwriter would allocate IPO shares to institutional investors who would sell almost immediately after the offering at a profit in the higher-priced aftermarket — so-called *flipping*.

In 1997, the NASD (the predecessor to FINRA) advised its members that these practices might violate NASD rules, though in the hot IPO market of the late 1990s the warning fell on deaf ears. Following the market collapse amidst the corporate scandals of the early 2000s, attention focused on abuses in the allocation of IPOs. After a series of enforcement actions by the SEC and the New York attorney general, the ten largest securities firms agreed in a "global settlement" to restrict spinning in IPOs. See Joint Press Release (Apr. 28, 2003) (see §11.2.4 below).

Flipping, however, remains unregulated. Nonetheless, the SEC has brought enforcement actions against underwriters that require customers who receive IPO allocations to purchase additional shares in the aftermarket at above-IPO prices — a price manipulation known as "*laddering*." See §4.1.2.

§11.2.3 Disclosure Responsibilities

Like other participants in the securities markets, broker-dealers are subject to broad prohibitions against false, deceptive, or manipulative conduct. In addition, broker-dealers are subject to specific disclosure requirements that supplement and clarify the general antifraud prohibitions.

Antifraud Prohibitions

Broker-dealers have responsibilities under various provisions of the federal securities laws to communicate honestly and completely.

- **Rule 10b-5.** The catchall antifraud provision, authorized by §10(b) of the Exchange Act, prohibits willful or reckless deceit by *any person* (including broker-dealers) in *any sale or purchase of any security*. See Chapter 9.
- **Section 15(c)(1) of the Exchange Act.** Using much the same language as §10(b), this provision prohibits "any manipulative, deceptive, or other fraudulent device or contrivance" by *any broker-dealer* in

the *sale or purchase* of *securities*. See Dodd-Frank §929L (amending §15(c)(1) to apply to all non-government issued securities, not just OTC securities).

- **Section 17(a) of the Securities Act.** This provision prohibits fraudulent and *negligent* misrepresentations by *any person* (including broker-dealers) in the *sale of any securities*. See §§6.6, 12.3.2 (courts have interpreted the provision to authorize SEC enforcement, but not implied private actions).

Confirmation of Customer Transactions

SEC rules require broker-dealers to send their customers a written confirmation of each securities transaction that discloses, among other things, whether the securities firm was acting as broker for the customer, as principal for its own account, or as broker for another customer. Exchange Act Rule 10b-10. When acting as broker, the broker-dealer must disclose in the confirmation the source and amount of commissions it received. See also NASD Conduct Rule 2230 (requiring broker-dealer acting in dual capacity for both seller and buyer to disclose double commissions).

Information on Traded Companies

To prevent public trading markets in securities for which information is unavailable, SEC rules prohibit broker-dealers from making a market in any security unless the issuer is a reporting company or has recently made a registered offering under the Securities Act (or pursuant to the mini-registration provisions of Regulation A), or the broker-dealer has in its files specified current financial and other information about the issuer and its securities. Exchange Act Rule 15c2-11.

Disclosure of Conflicting Interests

Broker-dealers must disclose their conflicts of interest if they recommend securities in which they own a position (known as "scalping") or sell securities from their own inventory. This disclosure obligation arises from a number of sources: the antifraud rules applicable to investment advisers (Investment Advisers Act of 1940, §206); the Rule 10b-5 and Rule 15c1-2 "shingle theory" (see §11.2.4); specific SEC rules on confirming securities transactions; and the NASD's (now FINRA's) fair practice rules. See *SEC v. Capital Gains*, 375 U.S. 180 (1963) (holding that scalping violates Investment Advisers Act, even though investment adviser's recommendations had not injured clients and investment adviser believed in its recommendations).

In addition, market makers (that is, broker-dealers who regularly quote "bid" and "ask" prices for specific OTC securities and state a willingness to buy and sell these securities) cannot sell such securities to a customer without disclosing this presumably "material" fact. See *Chasins v. Smith, Barney & Co.*, 438 F.2d 1167 (2d Cir. 1971) (when recommending stock, market maker must disclose position, even though it sold at "fair" price set among several competing market makers).

§11.2.4 Standards of Conduct

Curiously, the federal securities statutes — beyond requiring honesty — do not expressly impose, or authorize the SEC to impose, general standards of professionalism on broker-dealers. This void is exacerbated by the judicial interpretation in other contexts that the operative language of the antifraud provisions covers only misrepresentations (not unfair conduct) made intentionally (not negligently). See §9.3.2 (describing scope of §10(b)).

The crux of the many conflicts that arise between broker-dealers and their customers, however, is often not purposeful falsehood, but rather conduct that falls short of the high standards expected of securities professionals. For example, when a broker "churns" a customer's account by engaging in excessive buying and selling, the problem is not that the broker misrepresented the risk of churning, but rather that the broker acted shabbily. Even when the problem can be characterized as one of disclosure, customers will often find it difficult to show that their broker-dealers were intentionally dishonest. For example, when a broker tells a customer without reasonable basis that she expects good performance from unsuitable high-risk, mortgage-backed bonds, it may be difficult to show an intent to deceive.

"Shingle Theory"

The SEC and the courts have filled this regulatory gap by treating professional misconduct by broker-dealers as a species of misrepresentation, thus converting the Exchange Act's antifraud provisions into a fountainhead for professional standards of fair conduct that govern how broker-dealers should deal with their customers. Under the "shingle theory," the SEC and the courts have assumed that a broker-dealer who engages in a securities business impliedly represents (hangs out his shingle) that he will deal fairly, honestly, and competently with his customers, and that customers place their trust and confidence in this implied representation. See *Charles Hughes & Co. v. SEC*, 139 F.2d 434 (2d Cir. 1943). Customers aggrieved by broker-dealer misconduct need not prove intentional misrepresentations, but simply that the broker-dealer violated his professional duties of competence and fair dealing.

Although some have questioned the "shingle theory" as an improper use of antifraud norms to regulate professional conduct, it has survived the test of time. Even after the Supreme Court ruled in *Santa Fe Industries v. Green* (see §9.3.1) that Rule 10b-5 does not prohibit corporate mismanagement, only misinformation, lower courts have continued to apply the "shingle theory" to broker-dealers. The one exception has not attracted a judicial following. See *Pross v. Baird, Patrick & Co.*, 585 F. Supp. 1456 (S.D.N.Y. 1984) (holding that unauthorized trading by a broker-dealer was not actionable under Rule 10b-5 because there was no claim of deception). Moreover, when customer-broker disputes go to arbitration, the arbitral award can be challenged on only for procedural irregularities or manifest disregard of law. Given its wide acceptance, the "shingle theory" would seem unassailable as the basis for an arbitral award.

The "shingle theory," however, has its limits. It assumes that the customer is dependent on the broker-dealer's expertise. Courts have been reluctant to infer professional misconduct when the customer is a sophisticated institutional investor. For example, when a large foreign bank invested in high-risk collateralized mortgage obligations, the Fourth Circuit refused to accept the bank had relied on the broker-dealer's statements. *Banca Cremi v. Alex. Brown & Sons*, 132 F.3d 1017 (4th Cir. 1997) (noting that the bank had invested on its own in CMOs for nearly a year and a half, consulted with other brokerage firms on CMO investments and risks, and often rejected purchases recommended by the defendant broker-dealer). The court stated that "a sophisticated investor is more likely to known enough" so that the investor can assess the suitability of a suggested investment or the veracity of the broker-dealer's statements.

Although the Supreme Court has not addressed the "shingle theory," the Court has emphasized the broad obligations of stockbrokers to their customers under federal antifraud law. *SEC v. Zandford*, 535 U.S. 813 (2002). In the case, a stockbroker with discretionary authority wrote himself checks on the customer's account, causing securities in the account to be sold. The SEC sued under Rule 10b-5, claiming the securities sales were in connection with his abuse of trust. The stockbroker argued his theft, while a breach of fiduciary duty under state law, was not "in connection with" the securities sales — which standing on their own were legal. In a decision with important federalism implications, the Court refused to separate artificially the stockbroker's "scheme to defraud" into separate steps. Instead, the Court concluded the securities sales were not independent of the stockbroker's unauthorized use of the customer's account. The Court pointed out that the stockbroker's fraud coincided with the sales themselves, and each sale was made to further his fraudulent scheme.

Broker-Dealer Rules of Conduct

Broker-dealers confront ineluctable conflicts of interest in their role as intermediaries between securities trading markets and investors. For example, a securities firm that acts both as an agent for a customer and as a principal selling from its own account cannot avoid conflicting desires. The competitive market in investment services places some limits on opportunistic behavior by broker-dealers, but SEC and FINRA regulation imposes more than the morals of the marketplace.

The following rules of conduct describe the quiltwork of SEC and FINRA rules, stock exchange rules, and federal antifraud requirements that regulate these conflicts. (Absent from the description, but no less important, are the fiduciary duties imposed by state agency law and the rules of conduct arising under state blue sky laws.)

"Know thy Customer"

Broker-dealers must ascertain their customers' other investment holdings, general financial situation, and ability and proclivity to assume risk to determine whether particular securities are appropriate for the customer. See FINRA Manual ¶2090.

"Know Thy Security"

Broker-dealers must investigate the issuer and the terms, risks, and nature of the securities they recommend. Broker-dealers may not recommend securities without having a reasonable basis for their recommendations. See *Charles Hughes & Co. v. SEC*, 139 F.2d 434 (2d Cir. 1943).

"Forsake the Unsuitable"

As part of knowing their customers and the securities they recommend, broker-dealers must have reasonable grounds for believing a particular securities transaction is "suitable" for the particular customer given his financial situation and needs. See FINRA Manual ¶2111. For example, high-risk options trading is unsuitable for a retired school teacher looking for "safe" investments.

By the same token, broker-dealers may not recommend securities without having an adequate basis for the recommendation. See *SEC v. Hanly*, 415 F.2d 589 (2d Cir. 1969) (upholding SEC sanctions under the "shingle theory" for unsubstantiated recommendations). Included in the "suitability" duty is a duty to investigate "warning signals" and to advise the customer of unfavorable information.

"Do as Told"

Broker-dealers must seek to fulfill their customers' orders and investment objectives. For example, FINRA rules prohibit members from sending "false confirmations" of transactions that customers have not agreed to. See FINRA Manual ¶2232. Broker-dealers must execute customer orders correctly and promptly. According to the SEC, this duty extends to giving customer orders priority over proprietary trading by the broker-dealer. See In re E. F. Hutton & Co., Exchange Act Rel. No. 25,887 (SEC 1988) (affirming NASD disciplinary action requiring broker-dealer to give priority to customer's sales order at a stated price over firm's own proprietary position, unless firm had arrived at a different understanding with the investor). Broker-dealers with discretionary authority must make investments consistent with the investor's investment objectives. If not, the customer may recover the trading losses occasioned by the broker-dealer that pursued an inconsistent investment strategy.

"Churn Not"

Broker-dealers who have discretionary authority over customer accounts may not engage in "churning"—the excessive trading of securities in the account for the purpose of generating commissions. See Rule 15c1-7 (explicit prohibition against churning in OTC stocks). For example, there is churning when a broker-dealer sells General Motors stock from a discretionary account to buy Ford stock, and a month later sells the Ford stock and buys GM, and then after another month sells GM and buys Ford—each time for the purpose of generating commissions on the transactions.

"Churning" requires a showing that the broker acted with an intentional or reckless disregard for the interests of the customer. See Mihara v. Dean Witter, 619 F.2d 814 (9th Cir. 1980). Trading losses are not an element of churning, and courts have found churning even when an account gained in value. See Nesbit v. McNeil, 806 F.2d 380 (9th Cir. 1990).

When is trading excessive? The answer varies depending on the investment objectives of the account and the amount of trading in the account compared to similar accounts—often requiring expert testimony. Merrill Lynch, Pierce, Fenner & Smith v. Arcenaux, 767 F.2d 1498 (11th Cir. 1985) (concluding that issue of excessive trading turned on expert's credibility, which court refused to disturb). Courts treat as excessive an annual turnover ratio of more than five—that is, when the aggregate purchases in an account over a year are five times greater than the amount invested in the account. See Hecht v. Harris, Upham & Co., 430 F.2d 1202 (9th Cir. 1970).

The essence of a churning claim is that there was unnecessary trading, not that the securities were too risky or unsuitable. Thus, customers whose accounts are churned typically recover the total commissions (and out-of-pocket expenses) paid on the excessive securities transactions, but not any losses in market value. See *Fey v. Walston & Co.*, 493 F.2d 1036 (7th Cir. 1974). Nonetheless, some courts have also permitted recovery for the decline in value of the customer's portfolio that would not have occurred but for the churning. See *Davis v. Merrill Lynch, Pierce, Fenner & Smith*, 906 F.2d 1205 (8th Cir. 1990).

"Overcharge Not"

Broker-dealers may not effect securities transactions at a markup "not reasonably related to the current market price of the security" nor charge a commission that is "not reasonable." NASD Conduct Rule 2440; IM 2440-1 (Mark-Up Policy). Although FINRA (and before NASD) has not specified a formula for what constitutes a reasonable markup, FINRA has indicated that absent special circumstances a 5 percent markup over current market prices (in a thin market, over the broker-dealer's cost) would violate its pricing policy. See *Merritt, Vickers, Inc. v. SEC*, 353 F.2d 293 (2d Cir. 1965) (upholding NASD's expulsion of broker-dealer that in 47 transactions had marked up prices on average 40.5 percent over the cost of same-day purchases).

Although no SEC rule specifically addresses the question of excessive commissions and markups, courts have applied the "shingle theory" to limit commissions and markups to competitive levels and require that broker-dealers price securities at those prevailing in the open market. See *Grandon v. Merrill Lynch*, 147 F.3d 184 (2d Cir. 1998) (holding that undisclosed excessive markups violate Rule 10b-5 in municipal securities transactions); *Lehl v. SEC*, 90 F.3d 1483 (10th Cir. 1996) (upholding NASD disciplinary action against registered representative who charged markups on penny stock of 85 to 100 percent, which SEC found to be unfair). In addition, broker-dealers may be under a duty to search for prices on alternative trading systems (such as Instinet) when these markets are known to offer superior prices. *Newton v. Merrill Lynch, Pierce, Fenner & Smith*, 135 F.3d 267 (3d Cir. 1998) (finding that executing orders at the readily available "national best bid and offer price" without additional searching of alternative trading systems could be a deceptive practice).

Penny Stocks and Boiler Room Operations

The sale of "penny stocks" — low-priced, highly speculative issues typically selling on the OTC for less than $5 per share — has been a particular problem in the securities industry. Penny stocks are often sold through "boiler room operations" in which salespeople working for high commissions make high-pressure telephone solicitations, often accompanied by wild and unsupported claims of future returns. Often the prices of penny stocks are manipulated—such as when a company gives kickbacks to have an investor buy its thinly traded stock, creating the false appearance of demand.

In 1990 Congress passed the Securities Enforcement Remedies and Penny Stock Reform Act to regulate broker-dealer sales practices in penny stocks. Broker-dealers that deal significantly in "penny stocks"—defined to include OTC equity securities not quoted on NASDAQ whose issuers have less than $2 million in net tangible assets and that sell for less that $5 per share—must comply with a variety of special and burdensome rules:

- Before the sale, the broker-dealer must give customers a standardized, SEC-written "risk disclosure" statement that generally describes penny stocks, their risks, and the customer's rights in the event of fraud or abuse (Schedule 15G); bid and offer quotations for the particular penny stock offered; and disclosure of the compensation of the broker-dealer and its salespeople in the transaction. Rules 15g-2 to 15g-5.

- Broker-dealers who recommend penny stocks in cold calls to other than established customers must obtain information on the customer's financial situation, investment experience and investment objectives, and make a written determination of suitability. Rule 15c2-6; see also NASD Conduct Rule 2152 (requiring suitability finding in sale of speculative, low-priced securities). The suitability determination must be given to the customer.

- For any transaction to be executed, the broker-dealer must receive the purchaser's written instructions. Rule 15c2-6(a).

- After the sale, broker-dealers must give customers monthly account statements showing the market value of each penny stock held in the customer's account. Rule 15g-6.

The SEC can proceed (and has proceeded) against securities firms and salespersons involved in deceptive, high-pressure sales tactics. The SEC can revoke the broker-dealer's registration if it willfully induced the violations and can bar any salespersons who willfully violated the securities acts from associating with any broker-dealer. See Exchange Act §15(b)(5), (7). FINRA, as required by the 1990 legislation, has established a toll-free telephone number to answer customer inquiries about the disciplinary history of its members. See Exchange Act §§15(g), 17B.

In addition, individuals involved in penny stock misconduct can be barred from serving as officers or directors of public companies, including the penny stock companies involved, if they are shown to be "unfit" to hold office. Exchange Act §21(d)(2) (amended by Sarbanes-Oxley Act to remove standard of "substantially unfit"). And, as authorized by the Sarbanes-Oxley Act, the SEC may bar also any person who engages in misconduct in a penny stock offering from participating in further penny stock offerings. Exchange Act §21(d)(6).

Day Traders

One phenomenon of online trading technology has been the emergence of day traders—investors who engage in frequent, fast, and risky securities trading. Studies show that most day traders lose money, often quickly and dramatically. In 2000 the SEC released a special study on the phenomenon and urged broker-dealers that permit customers to engage in day trading to educate their customers on the risks and costs. The SEC did not, however, address whether broker-dealers have special "suitability" duties since the agency found that day-trading firms rarely recommend that their customers buy or sell specific securities. The NASD, however, was not so sanguine. In the same year, it adopted rules that require day-trading firms to determine whether day trading is appropriate for the customer, given her financial situation, tax status, prior investment and trading experience, and investment objectives. In addition, the NASD (now FINRA) rules require that day-trading customers receive a disclosure document cautioning them about day-trading risks, claims of big profits, and the difficulty of beating professional traders.

Derivatives Trading

Dodd-Frank gives the SEC (as well as the Commodities Futures Trading Commission) broad authority to regulate over-the-counter derivatives to bring risk-taking under greater regulatory oversight. Dodd-Frank §§701-774 (Title VII, Wall Street Transparency and Accountability Act of 2010). These OTC derivatives include *credit default swaps*, which operate essentially as a promise to pay (insurance) if a specified company goes bankrupt or defaults in making payments according to the terms of its securities. These CDSs had previously been issued privately, and there was no pricing mechanism or information on the extent of the payment obligations under CDSs.

Dodd-Frank creates a number of safeguards so that regulators and the public can evaluate how much risk exists in this financial "insurance" system:

- exchange trading for derivatives (to provide price information) and a clearinghouse (so regulators can monitor and regulate trades)
- capital and margin requirements on swap dealers to ensure swap participants have adequate financial resources to meet responsibilities
- codes of conduct for all registered swap dealers and major swap participants—so that swap dealers who deal with a pension fund, endowment fund, or state or local government have a reasonable basis to believe that the fund or governmental entity has an independent representative advising them

Securities Analysts Conflicts

Broker-dealers hire research analysts to provide investment advice to customers. Their research is at the heart of the functioning of securities markets — translating information from many sources into recommendations on stock valuations. Securities analysts face significant conflicts of interest when their recommendations involve stocks of companies with which their securities firm has an investment banking relationship or when the analysts themselves have a financial interest in the company.

In response to widespread reports after the "dotcom crash" of 2001 that securities analysts had made public "buy" recommendations while privately describing the same stock as "pieces of junk," the SEC and other securities regulators conducted a joint inquiry into analyst conflicts. The inquiry culminated in an enforcement action against ten of the largest securities firms alleging biased research reports — which was then settled in a "global settlement" designed to reshape the business of securities analysis.

The 2003 "global settlement" sought to bolster the integrity of stock research by (1) insulating securities analysts from investment banking pressure and (2) requiring securities firms to furnish research to their customers from independent sources. The firms covered by the settlement were required to sever the links between research and investment banking by prohibiting analysts from receiving compensation for investment banking activities and prohibiting analysts' involvement in investment banking "pitches" and "roadshows." In addition, the firms agreed for a five-year period to contract with at least three independent research firms so their customers could get independent research. And so investors could evaluate and compare the performance of analysts, the firms had to disclose research analysts' historical ratings and price target forecasts.

The Sarbanes-Oxley Act also mandated the SEC, along with the SROs, to promulgate rules to address securities analyst conflicts. Sarbanes-Oxley §501. Consistent with the terms of the global settlement, the SEC adopted Regulation AC (Analyst Certification) to increase the independence of securities analysts, to eliminate their financial stake in companies on which they report, and to require public disclosure of their conflicts. 17 C.F.R. §242 (Rules 500-505). The Regulation requires a prominent certification that every research report accurately reflects the analyst's personal views about the company or securities that are the subject of the report. Any compensation or payments related to specific recommendations must be disclosed, with a disclaimer that the compensation or payment could influence the recommendation.

In addition, the SEC approved changes to the NYSE and NASD (now FINRA) rules on securities analyst conflicts. Exchange Act Rel. No. 48,252 (2003). The SRO rules, like the global settlement, were designed to ensure the independence of research analysts (especially from their firms' investment bankers), to prevent analysts from having a personal stake in the companies they cover, and to require disclosure of any conflicts. FINRA Rule 2711 (and former NYSE Rule 472). The rules, as contemplated by Sarbanes-Oxley, require:

- *Insulation of analyst compensation from investment banking influence.* Firms must establish a compensation committee, which cannot have representation from the investment banking department, to review and approve research analyst compensation.
- *Creation of "firewall."* Firms must create a physical separation between analysts and investment bankers to stanch information or pressures from investment bankers.
- *Quiet period after IPO.* Firms participating in an IPO cannot issue any research reports on the company for 25 days after the IPO.
- *No "booster shot" research reports.* Analysts cannot issue positive research reports or reiterate "buy" recommendations around the time that lock-up agreements expire after a public offering.
- *No participation in "pitch" meetings.* Analysts cannot participate in meetings or other communications meant to solicit investment banking business.
- *No prepublication review of research reports.* Investment bank departments cannot engage in the prepublication clearance or approval of research reports.
- *No retaliation.* Firms cannot retaliate against an analyst for giving a negative report on investment banking clients.
- *Disclosure of compensation from issuer.* Firms must disclose whether they or their research analysts received any compensation from a company that is the subject of a research report.
- *Disclosure of client relationships.* Firms must disclose whether the company that is the subject of a research report has been a client of the firm and, if so, the services provided.
- *Registration and qualification of research analysts.* Analysts are subject to additional registration, qualification and continuing education requirements.

In 2010, the judge overseeing the "global settlement" removed some of the restrictions — such as how analyst compensation can be set — leaving such matters to Regulation AC and the SRO rules.

§11.2.5 Enforcement of Customer Rights

Customer rights are enforced through SEC administrative proceedings, FINRA disciplinary proceedings, judicial enforcement actions by the SEC, and private enforcement. Although customers often litigated their rights in court, much of the private enforcement now occurs in arbitration.

Judicial Enforcement

Court actions, whether brought by the SEC or customers, must be brought in federal court if the claim arises under the Exchange Act. Exchange Act §27 ("district courts of the United States . . . shall have exclusive jurisdiction of violations of this Act"). Private actions under the Securities Act may be brought in federal or state court, though the Securities Litigation Uniform Standards Act requires that securities fraud class actions be brought in federal court. Securities Act §22 ("no case arising under this Act and brought in any State court . . . shall be removed"). Customers may also bring state claims of breach of fiduciary duty (as well as contract and negligence claims) against brokers, including as class actions.

The SEC can bring injunctive actions and seek civil penalties in federal court to enforce federal securities law, whether statutory or SEC rules. Securities Act §20(b), (d); Exchange Act §21(d). In addition, violations of federal securities law can lead to SEC disciplinary action against individual brokers, as well as broker-dealers that fail to supervise their sales people. Exchange Act §15(b)(5) (providing for censure, suspension, revocation, and denial of registration of securities firms who fail to supervise).

Violations of federal statutory standards and SEC rules can result in liability, not only for individual brokers, but also for securities firms that fail to exercise adequate control over their employees. Exchange Act §20 (liability for failing to exercise adequate control). See *Brower v. Enstar Group Inc.*, 84 F.3d 393 (11th Cir. 1996) (controlling person liable if he has power to control general affairs of entity at time of violation, as well as specific corporate policy that resulted in primary liability). In addition, a broker-dealer that employs someone who engages in unlawful activity, including under state agency law, may be liable under the principle of *respondeat superior* — whether or not the supervision was adequate.

Violations of NASD (now FINRA rules, however, stand on different jurisdictional footing. Most courts have refused to infer a private cause of action for violations of NASD rules. See *Jablon v. Dean Witter & Co.*, 614 F.2d 677 (9th Cir. 1980). Such violations, in theory, are subject only to NASD (now FINRA) disciplinary proceedings and sanctions, such as censure or revocation of membership. In practice, though, the 10b-5 "shingle theory" and state agency law incorporate broad duties of professional conduct, including conduct mandated by NASD (now FINRA) rules.

Customer-Broker Arbitration

Since 1989, all customer-broker disputes are subject to arbitration if the customer signs a predispute arbitration agreement. See *Shearson/American Express, Inc. v. McMahon*, 482 U.S. 220 (1987) (upholding arbitrability of customer-broker dispute under Rule 10b-5 of the Exchange Act); *Rodriguez de Quijas v. Shearson/American Express, Inc.*, 490 U.S. 477 (1989) (upholding arbitrability of customer-broker dispute under §12(a)(2) of Securities Act).

The Supreme Court has interpreted the Federal Arbitration Act (FAA) to establish a "national policy favoring arbitration" even when federal law specifies the judicial enforcement of federal statutory rights. Thus, the antiwaiver provisions of the securities laws (which void any stipulation that waives statutory or rule protections) do not preclude agreements that forswear a judicial forum in favor of binding private arbitration. As pointed out by the Court, the SEC retains the ability to oversee and regulate securities arbitration procedures under its authority to review SRO rules. See Exchange Act §19(b)(1); Rule 19b-4 (procedures for approval of SRO rule changes).

The result has been that securities firms now regularly include arbitration clauses in their account agreements with customers. The Securities Industry Conference on Arbitration (SICA) has standardized the rules governing securities arbitration in a Uniform Code of Arbitration that the major stock exchanges and FINRA have adopted. The Code, whose adoption and amendment by the SROs requires SEC approval, deals with such matters as the procedures for filing an arbitral claim, the appointment of arbitrators, the discovery process in arbitration, and the public availability of arbitration awards.

One consequence of this shift from litigation to arbitration has been a marked decrease in the number of reported court decisions involving customer-broker disputes. Developments in the law, if there have been any, remain largely invisible since arbitrators (who are often not experts in securities law) usually provide only a cursory rationale for their arbitral awards. Furthermore, judicial review of arbitral awards is limited under the FAA, and few cases challenging arbitral awards ever explore the merits. In short, case law in the area is frozen in time, with the last significant broker-customer cases decided in the early 1990s. Since then, the only significant court decisions have been those involving class actions, which are not arbitrable under industry arbitration rules.

Is securities arbitration fair? A 2008 survey by SICA found that investors who had participated in securities arbitration viewed it to be biased, expensive, and unfair. Investors complained that FINRA requires at least one securities industry insider to serve on every arbitration panel, that panels do not explain their decisions, and that investors lose more often than not. Compared to litigation, three-fourths of the investors surveyed said that arbitration was "unfair." Although the securities industry has argued that arbitration is less expensive than litigation (for both investors and securities firms), studies indicate that investors recover only a fraction of the losses they claim and that customer "win" rates are declining.

In response to these criticisms, FINRA undertook modest reforms of its customer-broker arbitration rules (1) to permit customers to choose an "all public" arbitration panel, (2) to make discovery of information easier, and (3) to make one-arbitrator proceedings more available for claims under $100,000. See Exchange Act Rel. No. 63,799 (2011). In addition, Dodd-Frank authorized the SEC to prohibit or limit mandatory customer-broker arbitration. See Dodd-Frank §921. As of 2013, however, the SEC has not taken up the congressional invitation, except to solicit comments on the costs and benefits of such arbitration.

§11.2.6 Insurance of Customer Accounts

To protect customers if their broker-dealer becomes insolvent, Congress established an industry-funded insurance fund to pay the claims of customers of failed member securities firms. 15 U.S.C. §78 (Securities Investor Protection Act of 1970). The insurance fund, administered by the quasi-public Securities Investor Protection Corporation (SIPC), is funded by assessments of 0.5 percent of members' annual gross revenues. Further assessments are made as necessary to keep the fund at a level of $150 million, though the fund may borrow if necessary up to an additional $1 billion from the federal government.

Upon notification by the SEC or an SRO that a member is in financial difficulty, SIPC can seek a court decree appointing a trustee whose function is to return "specifically identifiable property" to customers, complete open contractual commitments, and liquidate the securities firm's business. If the firm's assets are insufficient to satisfy all customer claims, SIPC must advance moneys to satisfy such claims: $500,000 maximum per customer and $100,000 maximum for cash claims.

§11.2.7 State Blue Sky Regulation

Broker-dealers are subject to concurrent state blue sky securities regulation. The Uniform Securities Act (USA) requires annual registration of broker-dealers doing business in the particular state, and state-registered broker-dealers are subject to state supervision and disciplinary authority.

The National Securities Markets Improvement Act of 1996, in an effort to minimize costly overlap in federal-state securities regulation, significantly limits state blue sky regulation of broker-dealers. NSMIA preempts any state regulation of net capital, custody, margin, financial responsibility, record-keeping, bonding, financial standards, or operation requirements that "differ from, or are in addition to," requirements established under federal securities laws. Exchange Act §15(h). States may, however, continue to require broker-dealers to register using federal Form BD and pay a registration fee. In addition, NSMIA calls on the SEC to consult with state securities regulators about developing uniform state licensing requirements for broker-dealers' salespeople. Exchange Act §15(h)(1).

An interesting and important question that has arisen under NSMIA is whether states can indirectly regulate issuer offerings of "covered" securities, as to which state securities regulation is presumably preempted. Securities Act §18(b) (see §5.3). Under the USA, an issuer that offers its own securities need not register as a broker-dealer, but an individual who "represents" the issuer in effecting securities transactions must register as an "agent." USA §401(b). Theoretically, a state could regulate an issuer's self-offering by threatening to sanction the agent or requiring changes to disclosure or the substance of the offering as a condition to the agent's participation in the offering. NSMIA, however, specifies that no state law may "impose conditions . . . upon the offer or sale" of any covered security. Securities Act §18(a)(3). This and other preemption questions await judicial resolution.

§11.3 INVESTMENT ADVISER REGULATION

Investment advice comes not only from broker-dealers but also from professional investment advisers who manage customer assets or disseminate investment information to clients for a fee.

§11.3.1 Definition of Investment Adviser

The Investment Advisers Act of 1940 defines an "investment adviser" to include any person who, for compensation, engages in the business of advising others as to securities values or the advisability of securities investments. Inv. Adv. Act §202(a)(11). The Act contains numerous exclusions from the definition, including (1) banks, (2) professionals who give investment-related services incidental to their practice, (3) broker-dealers whose advisory activities are solely incidental to their securities business, and (4) publishers of bona fide newspapers and other publications of general and regular circulation. These firms are neither required to register nor subject to the Act's antifraud provisions.

The Supreme Court has ruled that a newsletter writer who gives investment advice on an impersonal basis does not fall within the Investment Adviser Act's definition of an investment adviser. *Lowe v. SEC*, 472 U.S. 181 (1985) (citing First Amendment concerns if the Act were interpreted to regulate purveyors of general investment information).

§11.3.2 Federal Regulation of Investment Advisers

Investment advisers not subject to state blue sky registration are subject to federal regulation comparable to that of broker-dealers.

SEC Registration

Investment advisers, unless exempt or subject to state registration, must register with the SEC and file periodic reports that become publicly available. Dodd-Frank significantly changes the boundaries between federal and state regulation of investment advisers. Before the Act, investment advisers with $25 million or more in client assets under management were required to register with the SEC. Dodd-Frank raises the threshold to $100 million, thus moving a significant number of advisers to state supervision — where there are more regulators than in the SEC's Division of Investment Management. Inv. Adv. Act §§203, 203A.

The SEC registration form requires disclosure about the adviser's business, background, compensation, and types of clients. Inv. Adv. Act §203(c)(1). The SEC's "brochure rule" requires that much of this information be given as a brochure to prospective customers. Inv. Adv. Act Rule 204-3. Investment advisers subject to *state registration* are subject to requirements relating to books and records, minimum net capital, and bonding set by the state where the adviser maintains a place of business.

Antifraud Rules

All investment advisers, whether or not registered with the SEC, are prohibited from making material misrepresentations or engaging in fraudulent practices in connection with rendering investment advice. Inv. Adv. Act §206. The Act also prohibits aiding and abetting a primary violation. (State regulators may also investigate and bring enforcement actions against advisers or their associated persons.)

Standards of Conduct

Investment advisers are subject to a variety of statutory and SEC standards of conduct. The Act prohibits investment advisers from charging contingent fees based on the client's investment return. Inv. Adv. Act §5(a)(1). The prohibition, though arguably widening the gap between client interests and adviser incentives, was thought necessary to prevent advisers from urging clients to take undue risks. SEC rules, however, permit performance-based fees for sophisticated clients who have a net worth greater than $1 million or at least $500,000 under the adviser's management. Inv. Adv. Act Rule 205-3. In addition, the act prohibits "churning" of client accounts, undisclosed conflicts of interests, and splitting fees with persons not registered under the act. Inv. Adv. Act §206.

The Act also prohibits any practice that "operates as a fraud or deceit upon any client." Inv. Adv. Act §206. The Supreme Court has interpreted this antifraud standard to impose "high standards of business morality" and specifically to require an adviser to make full disclosure of the practice of purchasing securities for his own account shortly before recommending the security to his clients for long-term investment and then immediately reselling the security in a rising market — a practice called "scalping." See *SEC v. Capital Gains Research Bureau, Inc.*, 375 U.S. 180 (1963).

The Supreme Court has held that the Act's standards of conduct do not create implied private remedies, though clients whose investment advisory contracts violate the Act have an implied right of rescission. *Transamerica Mortgage Advisers, Inc. v. Lewis*, 444 U.S. 11 (1979) (refusing to infer private remedies for violations of §206 standards of conduct, but inferring rescission remedy under §215, which voids contracts that violate the Act). Enforcement of the Act is thus left largely to SEC injunctive actions, administrative sanctions (such as censure or revocation of registration), and criminal prosecutions for willful violations.

§11.3.3 State Blue Sky Regulation

The National Securities Markets Improvement Act of 1996 significantly changes the regulatory landscape for investment advisers. NSMIA replaces the prior system of dual, overlapping federal-state regulation with a two-tier system:

- federal supervision of investment advisers that manage $25 million or more in client assets or that advise a registered investment company, and
- state supervision for all other investment advisers.

Inv. Adv. Act §203A(a)(1). In fact, after NSMIA, investment advisers subject to state supervision *cannot* register with the SEC. States may not require registration of investment advisers that do not have a place of business in the state and have fewer than six clients. Inv. Adv. Act §222(d). States, however, may continue to require notice filings and the payment of fees of SEC-registered advisers. Inv. Adv. Act §307(a), (b).

To prevent inconsistent, overlapping regulation among the states, NSMIA forbids states from imposing standards relating to books and records, minimum net capital, or bonding that expand on those imposed by the state where the investment adviser maintains its principal place of business. Inv. Adv. Act §222(b), (c). NSMIA, however, leaves intact the possibility of dual federal-state enforcement. Nothing prevents a state from investigating or bringing an enforcement action against an adviser or associated persons. Inv. Adv. Act §§203A(b)(2), 222(a).

Examples

1. Genius Capital is a new securities firm with an innovative plan to assist start-up businesses in making direct initial public offerings (IPOs) on the Internet. Genius Capital will advise these clients on the marketing and technical aspects of setting up a website, where investors can download company prospectuses and subscribe to buy stock. Genius Capital will advise on pricing, but the companies that become IPO clients will be responsible for SEC registration of the offering and all contacts with investors.
   a. What are the risks and benefits of direct Internet offerings?
   b. Is Genius Capital subject to SEC regulation?
   c. Is Genius Capital subject to state blue sky regulation?

2. As the number of Internet IPOs grow, Genius Capital creates a website called "Capital Warehouse" that lists websites of companies selling stock on the Internet. Capital Warehouse, which is accessible by public investors, has hypertext links to these sites where investors can review and download prospectuses and subscription agreements. To be listed, companies must pay Genius Capital an administrative fee.
   a. Is Genius Capital now subject to SEC regulation?
   b. Genius Capital expands its "Capital Warehouse" and offers Internet users the service of assembling portfolios of Internet-traded securities—for a fee, of course. Genius Capital also makes specific predictions of substantial increases in the stock price of certain unseasoned Internet-offered companies. Does this subject Genius Capital to SEC regulation?
   c. One of Genius Capital's newest clients, Bioni-tech Corporation, notices that Genius Capital is not registered with the SEC. After Genius Capital helps it set up an Internet IPO and advertises it on Capital Warehouse, Bioni-tech refuses to pay the agreed commissions. Can it avoid them?

3. Inter-American Finance Ltd. is listed on Capital Warehouse. It is a fictitious company whose sham prospectus falsely states the company has investments in export-oriented Latin American businesses. The company seeks to palm off bonds carrying a high 11.75 percent interest rate, and urges investors to send checks to a mail drop in Antigua.
   a. Genius Capital failed to investigate this client, but does not know of its nefarious ways. Is Genius Capital liable for Inter-American Finance's fraud?

b. Freda Walz, a bored law student, has a personal website with hypertext links to companies (including Inter-American Finance Ltd.) offering securities on the Internet. She includes her resume and says, "I like this securities stuff, maybe you'd like to hire me." Is Walz subject to SEC regulation? Is she liable for transmitting the false Inter-American Finance offers?

c. Pearl Marmalade, your securities law professor, comments in class that Internet-IPO companies will "likely be big winners by attracting naive money." She comments, "Check out FredaWalz.com." Is Marmalade liable for the Inter-American Finance fraud?

4. Genius Capital registers as a broker-dealer and sets up a retail brokerage department to help customers make sense of Internet offerings and trading. The firm advertises itself as "The investment firm on the pulse of a new dawn." Identify any problems with the following.

a. Ayn, a licensed Genius Capital salesperson, tells her customers that she can help them create a portfolio of Internet-offered securities. Even though there is generally no prevailing market price in such securities, she promises her customers, "We'll only buy at market."

b. Bernie, another Genius Capital salesperson, tells his customers, "This Internet IPO market will make you rich."

c. Candace, yet another Genius Capital salesperson, recommends Internet IPOs to all her customers.

d. Dante, still one more Genius Capital salesperson, tells his customer Thomasina that NotePerfect, a company that makes software to write music, has a five-year track record of steady income growth. Dante does not know whether this is true; Thomasina knows it is an exaggeration.

e. Elaine, the top Genius Capital salesperson, manages an account for Tony, who has just won the lottery and insists that his investments be in "telecommunications companies." Elaine obliges as follows:

Date	Sell	Buy
January 2	opens account for Tony	buys $100,000 worth of AT&T
April 1	sells AT&T for $105,000	buys Sprint
July 4	sells Sprint for $110,000	buys Verizon
October 31	sells Verizon for $118,000	buys AT&T
December 31	sells AT&T for $127,000	buys Verizon

    f. All told, Tony garners a one-year 27 percent return in his account; Elaine garners the firm's annual award as "top generator."

    g. Freddie, another top Genius Capital salesperson, mimics Elaine's successful trading strategies. Freddie advises his customer Tricia to trade using the sequence used by Elaine above. Tricia places the orders, as advised, figuring she can ride the ebb and flow in the competition of the big long-distance carriers.

5. Genius Capital sets up a subsidiary, IPO-Trak LLC, to evaluate and rate Internet-IPO companies. IPO-Trak creates "Virtual Value Line," a website accessible through a monthly subscription that evaluates the prospects of IPOs available on the Internet, rating them according to risk, potential for growth, and value.

    a. Is IPO-Trak subject to SEC regulation? State regulation?

    b. IPO-Trak charges a flat monthly fee for access to its "IPO-Trak Virtual Value Line." But IPO-Trak promises to refund its fee whenever the performance of any of its "recommended buys" falls below that of the S&P 500. Is this legal?

    c. Genius Capital acquires a significant holding in Bucolic Broccoli, a mail-order vegetable grower that recently went public on the Internet. IPO-Trak posts a "must buy" on its "Virtual Value Line" website. When interest in Bucolic grows and its stock price rises, Genius Capital dumps its holding. Is this legal?

    d. Some of IPO-Trak's computer-inept customers complain to IPO-Trak that buying and selling securities over the Internet is cumbersome. IPO-Trak offers to do the ministerial work of buying and selling for them — for a fee, of course. Any regulatory implications?

6. Genius Capital includes an arbitration clause in all of its customer agreements. One of its customers brings a claim that the firm charged excessive commissions on Internet-traded securities. The arbitration panel grants an award that includes punitive damages.

    a. Genius Capital challenges the arbitration award as groundless under federal and state securities laws. Evaluate Genius Capital's likelihood of success on this challenge.

    b. Genius Capital also challenges the arbitration as procedurally unfair. The arbitrator did not allow Genius Capital to submit evidence on commissions generally charged by firms advising customers on Internet trading. Evaluate Genius Capital's likelihood of success on this challenge.

    c. Genius Capital had included a proviso in its arbitration clause that customers could not claim, and the firm would not be liable for, punitive damages.

Explanations

1. a. Direct Internet offerings promise many benefits. They reduce the costs of raising capital. They eliminate the commissions charged by layers of intermediaries, as well as the costs of printing and distributing paper prospectuses. Moreover, they increase the pool of investors — worldwide.

   But Internet offerings also pose unique dangers. With direct Internet marketing, there are no intermediaries to filter information for investors or to act as professional buffers against fraud and other abuses. Company information alone doesn't make for efficient markets. Without market makers and analysts, pricing of Internet offerings can be whatever the issuer asks; little distinguishes between a legitimate firm and an outright sham. Moreover, the Internet permits offers from outside the United States that can, for practical purposes, escape SEC jurisdiction.

   b. Probably not. There are two bases for SEC regulation. First, it might be argued that Genius Capital is acting as an "investment adviser." The Investment Advisers Act of 1940 defines an "investment adviser" to include any person who, for compensation, engages in the business of advising others as to securities values or the advisability of securities investments. Inv. Adv. Act §2(a)(11). The focus of the Act, however, is on advice given to securities *investors*, not issuers. Since the plan is that Genius Capital will not have contact with investors, it probably falls outside the federal regulatory ambit for investment advisers. Even if it satisfied the definition of an investment adviser, it would not have to register with the SEC because it does not have client assets under management. See Inv. Adv. Act §203A (exclusive state regulation of investment advisers with less than $25 million in client assets under management).

   Second, it might be said that Genius Capital is a "broker" by engaging in the regular business of selling securities for the account of another. See Exchange Act §3(a)(4). Yet, again, it did not effect securities transactions with investors. As an adviser to issuers, it did not act as a selling intermediary — the essence of the definition of *broker*. Nonetheless, the Genius Capital website comes dangerously close to matching buyers and sellers, an activity the SEC has viewed as creating broker-dealer status. If the firm participates in "key points in the chain of distribution," such as by assisting issuers to structure their offerings or transmitting investor bids, it would become a regulated broker-dealer. See *Muni-Auction Inc.* [2000 Transfer Binder] Fed. Sec. L. Rep. (CCH) ¶77,830 (March 13, 2000) (refusing to issue no-action letter to Web-based service that conducted one-time auctions for municipal bond issuers). But if the firm merely makes information available and delivers disclosure regarding registered or exempt offerings, it avoids broker-dealer regulation. See *Internet Capital Corp.* (no-action letter dated Dec. 24, 1997).

c. Perhaps, as an "agent" of an issuer. The state definitions of "investment adviser" parallel those in the federal Investment Advisers Act. If Genius Capital is not advising investors, it need not register at the state level. If, however, it were seen as giving advice to investors, it would be required to register in every state in which it does business. For a company doing business through the Internet, this is arguably every state.

The state definitions of broker-dealer also generally parallel the federal definition. Since Genius Capital is not acting as an intermediary with investors, it would probably not be subject to state broker-dealer regulation.

Genius Capital may, nonetheless, be subject to regulation as an "agent" of an issuer. This state regulation, which is broader than federal regulation of securities intermediaries, requires registration in each state where the agent acts — arguably, all the states in an Internet offering — and the agent is subject to state supervisory authority. There is an argument, however, that if the issuers are offering "covered" securities — such as securities offered under Rule 506 (see §5.2.4) — states are preempted from imposing any additional regulation, including "agent" regulation, beyond that imposed by federal standards.

2. a. Perhaps. A somewhat similar not-for-profit Internet "information clearinghouse" was cleared by SEC staff in a no-action letter, subject to numerous conditions. *Angel Capital Electronic Network*, 1996 SEC No-Act. LEXIS 812 (Oct. 25, 1996). SEC staff concluded that universities and other nonprofit entities interested in small-business capital formation that would operate a website to list small company offerings did not have to register themselves or the network as broker-dealers or investment advisers. Operation of the site, which could be accessed only by so-called accredited investor "angels," was subject to a number of conditions. The network operators and their officials could not (1) advise users on the merits of particular investments; (2) receive from users more than a nominal, noncontingent, flat fee to cover administrative costs; (3) assist in negotiations, transactions, or financial dealings between investors and listing companies; (4) become themselves entrepreneurs or investors in any listed company. SEC staff appeared to accept the argument that the network would merely be a limited-access "electronic bulletin board" for obtaining information on stock offerings and would not be subject to SEC registration as:

- an "investment adviser" because it would neither advise investors on the merits of investing in the network-listed companies nor be in the regular business of issuing analyses of their securities, Inv. Adv. Act §203(a);

- a "broker" or "dealer" because the network would not effect transactions in network-listed securities or be in the business of buying and selling network-listed securities, Exchange Act §§3(a)(4), 3(a)(5); or

- a "securities exchange" because the network would not perform the functions commonly performed by a stock exchange, such as effecting securities trading or reporting transactions, Exchange Act §3(a)(1).

Genius Capital, however, may have crossed the regulatory line because its Capital Warehouse is for-profit. There is an argument that providing investment advice to potential investors meant it was engaged in the business of "effecting" securities transactions for the accounts of others, thus making it a "broker." See Securities Act §3(a)(4). Nonetheless, there is also the argument that its clearinghouse was set up so that issuers and investors must deal with each other directly. If securities transactions are effected, they are effected by the parties, not the website operator. Moreover, Genius Capital makes no representations about the value of the featured securities nor does it advise on investing in them, thus excepting it from federal regulation as an investment adviser. See Inv. Adv. Act §203.

b. Almost certainly. Genius Capital is now in the business of effecting transactions for investors — a "broker" — and giving advice on the merits of particular investments — an "investment adviser." It must register and is subject to regulation as a broker-dealer. Exchange Act §15(a).

Aside from SEC supervision as a broker-dealer, Genius Capital's promotion of companies in its Capitol Warehouse also exposes it to treatment as a "statutory underwriter" under the Securities Act. For any registered public offerings it promotes, Genius Capital would be subject to regulation and exposed to liability as an underwriter in a registered offering. See §11.2.2. For any unregistered, nonexempt offerings it promotes, Genius Capital would be exposed to civil rescission liability and SEC enforcement actions. Securities Act §12(a)(1) (see §6.2.1).

If these woes weren't enough, Genius Capital may also be subject to regulation for selling "penny stocks." Among other things, it would have to give all customers a "risk disclosure" statement and other disclosure about trading in the stock and Genius Capital's compensation. See §11.2.4.

c. Perhaps. Bioni-tech could seek rescission on the argument that Genius Capital's performance of the agreement violates the Exchange Act's broker-dealer registration requirements. The Exchange Act declares that "every contract . . . the performance of which involves the violation of . . . any provision of [the Act] . . . shall be void." Exchange Act §29(b). The rescission claim, however, faces some obstacles. Some courts have suggested that an implied right of rescission under §29(b) is available only for the class of persons Congress sought to protect — namely, investors. See *Regional Properties, Inc. v. Financial & Real Estate Consulting Co.*, 678 F.2d 552 (5th Cir. 1982). Yet, the Exchange Act broadly seeks to protect capital markets by, among other things, ensuring the integrity of market intermediaries. See also Exchange Act §3(f) (requiring the SEC in its rulemaking to take into account "efficiency, competition, and capital formation," as well as investor protection). It would be odd, indeed, to conclude that illegally unregistered securities intermediaries can enforce their contracts with capital seekers, but not capital providers. Bioni-tech, at the least, has a strong argument for rescission of its contract to pay for the Capital Warehouse listing.

Nonetheless, the rescission claim may be subject to equitable defenses. See *Regional Properties, Inc. v. Financial & Real Estate Consulting Co.*, 678 F.2d 552 (5th Cir. 1982) (recognizing the availability of such defenses). For example, if Bioni-tech knew that it was dealing with an unregistered broker-dealer, it might be estopped to seek rescission or might be seen as having waived this defect.

3. a. Probably. There are a number of bases of liability when a broker-dealer recommends a fraudulent investment, some of which do not require that it actually knew that it was facilitating a fraud.

As a broker-dealer, Genius Capital is under an obligation to "know thy security" in making recommendations to customers. Under the "shingle theory" when it holds itself out to the public as a securities intermediary, it undertakes to abide by standards of professionalism. Even though the Internet users are not customers of Genius Capital and do not directly pay for its investment advice, they pay indirectly when they invest in the companies featured for a fee on the website. Internet users can make private claims under Rule 10b-5.

In addition, the SEC can pursue an enforcement action under Rule 10b-5 and §17(a) of the Securities Act. In fact, the SEC has closed down sham Internet operations, obtaining consent judgments that impose fines and that enjoin future violations by the swindlers. See 1995 SEC LEXIS 3127, Lit. Rel. No. 15,139 (Oct. 19, 1996) (essentially the facts of the Inter-American Finance example).

The SEC has an Internet site for that provides investors with practical tips on how to spot, avoid, and report fraud on the Internet. Sec Investor.gov.

The SEC can also claim that Genius Capital was aiding and abetting the primary fraud and impose civil penalties or bring a court injunctive action. See Exchange Act §21B (civil penalties against broker-dealers for willful aiding and abetting); Exchange Act §20(f) (SEC injunction actions against "any person that knowingly provides substantial assistance to another person in violation of" any provision of the Exchange Act).

b. Perhaps. Although Walz's activities do not make her a broker-dealer or investment adviser (see 2a above), this does not foreclose fraud liability under other securities provisions. The Supreme Court has emphasized that falsehoods are not protected free speech. *Lowe v. SEC*, 472 U.S. 181 (1985). Thus, newsletters remain subject to §17(a) of the Securities Act, which prohibits intentional or negligent false statements in connection with sales of securities. The SEC could compel Walz to remove the sham Inter-American Finance listing. Moreover, if Walz was reckless in posting the Inter-American Finance listing (the circumstances indicated she knew about its falsity), she could be liable as a primary violator under Rule 10b-5 to any investors who purchased because of her website and in reliance on the sham company's false prospectus. See §9.3.

c. Probably not. First, Marmalade was not compensated for rendering advice, and thus it is unlikely she would be considered either a broker-dealer or investment adviser. Moreover, the Investment Advisers Act excludes from the definition of investment adviser banks, lawyers, accountants, engineers, or teachers rendering investment advice incidental to their profession. See Inv. Adv. Act §202(a)(11).

Second, it is unlikely that Marmalade would incur Rule 10b-5 liability for her apparently unwitting recommendation. She made no representations, implied or otherwise, about the veracity of the website. Moreover, there is no indication that she knew or had reason to know about the sham offering. See §9.3.2.

4. a. Problem. A broker-dealer is prohibited from representing in a distribution that a security is being offered "at market" unless she knows or has reason to believe that an independent market exists. Rule 15c1-8. This constraint extends to every sale by broker-dealers and their associates, which are bound under the "shingle theory" by an implied representation that when they sell securities the price is "reasonably related to that prevailing in an open market." See In re Norris & Hirshberg, Inc., 21 S.E.C. 865 (1946), aff'd 177 F.2d 228 (D.C. Cir. 1949).

b. Probably not problem. It is likely that Bernie's fervor would be seen by most investors, and a court or arbitrator, as immaterial puffery. Had he been more specific — such as, "your return will be 15 percent" — his fervor would have become actionable. See *Cohen v. Prudential-Bache Securities, Inc.*, 713 F. Supp. 653 (S.D.N.Y. 1989).

c. Problem. Broker-dealers must know their customers, and it is unlikely that all of Candace's customers should be buying Internet IPOs. Moreover, there is a good chance many Internet offerings satisfy the definition of "penny stocks" — OTC securities not quoted on NASDAQ, issued by companies with less than $2 million in tangible net assets, for a price of less than $5 per share. If so, Candace must (among other things) make a specific, written suitability determination as to each customer. Rule 15c2-6.

d. Perhaps problem. Some courts hold broker-dealers liable for giving bad advice, even though the customer did not act on it, on a theory of disciplinary liability. *Hanly v. SEC*, 415 F.2d 589 (2d Cir. 1969) (under "shingle theory" broker-dealer must investigate adequately before making recommendation). Yet other courts adopt a "no harm, no foul" philosophy and do not shift losses to the broker-dealer unless the customer reasonably relied on the bad advice. See *Phillips v. Reynolds & Co.*, 294 F. Supp. 1249 (E.D. Pa. 1969).

e. Problem. This is a classic case of "churning" with a high annual turnover ratio of 5.6 (the ratio of total purchases made for the account in a year to the amount invested) and apparently a high "commission ratio" (commissions generated by account compared to commissions in comparable accounts). See *Hecht v. Harris, Upham & Co.*, 430 F.2d 1202 (9th Cir. 1970) (widely cited as creating a presumption of churning when annual turnover ratio exceeds five).

Churning cases, however, cannot be decided entirely by the numbers. It must also be clear that Tony had given Elaine discretionary authority over the account. Moreover, if Tony envisioned short-term returns from communications stocks, Lorraine may have been doing precisely what was expected of her. See *Marshak v. Blyth, Eastman, Dillon & Co.*, 413 F. Supp. 377 (N.D. Okla. 1975) (no churning where investor's purpose was "short-term" profits). Although the investments were suitable (Tony wanted telecommunications investments) and the account (even after deducting commissions) was profitable, damages should reflect Elaine's professional indiscretion, and she should disgorge any commissions reflecting unauthorized, unnecessary trading.

f. Probably not problem. Churning arises only in discretionary accounts, when the broker has full discretionary authority over the account or when the customer relies implicitly on the broker's recommendations. See *Norris & Hirshberg, Inc. v. SEC*, 177 F.2d 228 (D.C. Cir. 1949). If Freddie had some reason to recommend Elaine's trading strategy — "know thy security" and "know thy customer" — Tricia cannot complain if she understood the strategy and followed it.

5. a. Yes, as an investment adviser under state blue sky law. An "investment adviser" includes any person who, for compensation, engages in the business of advising others as to securities values or the advisability of securities investments. Inv. Adv. Act §202(a)(11). Unless IPO-Trak has client assets under management, it is not subject to federal supervision. Instead, it must register under state law and is subject to regulatory oversight by state securities regulators in every state where it does business. Under the National Securities Markets Improvement Act, the state where IPO-Trak has its principal place of business sets the standards relating to books and records, minimum net capital, or bonding. Inv. Adv. Act §222(b), (c).

   The SEC and state securities regulators, however, have concurrent jurisdiction to enforce standards of conduct and honest disclosure. Investment advisers, whether registered with the SEC or not, are subject to federal standards of conduct. See Inv. Adv. Act §206. Likewise, nothing prevents a state from investigating or bringing an enforcement action against an adviser or associated persons. Inv. Adv. Act §§203A(b)(2), 222(a).

   b. No. The federal Investment Advisers Act generally forbids that investment adviser compensation be based on capital gains or appreciation in client assets under management. Inv. Adv. Act §205(a)(1). None of the exceptions apply to our IPO-Trak example because the performance-based compensation neither relates to a managed fund nor an investment advisory contract for more than $1 million in assets. Inv. Adv. Act §205(b)(1), (2)(B).

   This is a curious prohibition because it prevents (and immunizes) investment advisers from price competition based on performance. The prohibition's purpose, however, may be to avoid the problem of investment advisers linking their compensation to investment performance and then feeling compelled to take inordinate risks when their investment advice begins to falter.

   c. Probably not. If Genius Capital and IPO-Trak coordinated their scheme, this is scalping and prohibited as a "course of business which operates as a fraud ... upon any client." Inv. Adv. Act §206(2); see also *SEC v. Capital Gains Research Bureau*, 375 U.S. 180 (1963) (essentially same facts). The one twist is that the trading was carried out by Genius Capital, a registered broker-dealer, while the recommendations were made by its investment adviser subsidiary, IPO-Trak. If there was no coordination between the two, it is arguable that there was no scalping. If, however, the traders for Genius Capital were aware of the IPO-Trak recommendation, it would not be necessary to show that the recommendation was intended to produce trading profits. To make out a claim of scalping under §206, actual intent to deceive need not be shown. Moreover, if there was some coordination, the prohibitions against scalping apply to Genius Capital as a broker-dealer under the "shingle theory" and to IPO-Trak as an investment adviser, whether or not it is registered with the SEC.

    d. Yes. IPO-Trak has become a broker-dealer by engaging in the business of buying and selling securities for the account of its customers. See Exchange Act §3(a)(5) (definition of "dealer"). It must register with the SEC. Exchange Act §15(a).

6. a. Judicial challenges of arbitration awards on substantive grounds have fared poorly. The Federal Arbitration Act specifies narrow grounds for challenging arbitral awards: the award was procured by fraud, the arbitrators showed evident partiality, the arbitrators were guilty of misconduct, or the arbitral award exceeded the arbitrators' powers. See FAA §10. Courts have crafted additional grounds for vacating arbitral awards, including when the award exhibits a "manifest disregard of law." But courts rarely vacate arbitral awards, often dismissing challenges in summary proceedings.

    In our example, there are a number of legal theories that might support an award based on excessive commissions, including an award for punitive damages. The "shingle theory" under Rule 10b-5 supports an award for excessive commissions, by reference to the FINRA rules on commissions. See §11.2.4. Although §28 of the Exchange Act limits plaintiff's recovery to actual damages and thus precludes an award of punitive damages, state agency law and fraud law support both the compensatory award and award of punitive damages. See *Mastrobuono v. Shearson Lehman Hutton, Inc.*, 514 U.S. 52 (1995) (invalidating New York law that forbade award of punitive damages in securities arbitration on the ground state limitations on arbitration are preempted by FAA).

    b. Judicial review of arbitral awards on procedural grounds have fared even more poorly. There is no requirement that arbitration procedures accord the parties the same due process rights they would have in litigation. See *Gilmer v. Interstate/Johnson Lane Corp.*, 500 U.S. 20 (1991) (finding that the NYSE securities arbitration rules governing discovery, even though "not as extensive as in the federal courts," were sufficient to give claimants a fair opportunity to present their claims; by agreeing to arbitrate, a party "trades the procedures and opportunity for review of the courtroom for the simplicity, informality, and expedition of arbitration").

In fact, there is no requirement in the FAA or judicial review standards that requires any discovery, at all. Nonetheless, in response to pressure from the SEC, the Securities Industry Conference on Arbitration (SICA) has since 1989 included provisions on discovery in its Uniform Code of Arbitration, which the stock exchanges and FINRA have incorporated into their rules for securities arbitration. See Exchange Act Rel. No. 26,805 (May 16, 1989) (SEC approval of stock exchange and FINRA rule changes). Prior to these changes, discovery in securities arbitration was voluntary, and a party could only compel information from another party by seeking documents under subpoena at the arbitration hearing.

c. For purposes of the Federal Arbitration Act, the arbitration clause governs. Although state law may not limit the matters that parties in securities-related dispute can arbitrate, the parties may create their own limitations. See *Mastrobuono v. Shearson Lehman Hutton, Inc.*, 514 U.S. 52 (1995) (upholding award of punitive damages, though suggesting parties could agree to preclude arbitrators from awarding punitive damages).

Any limitation on what can be submitted to securities arbitration must also pass muster under the arbitration rules to which the broker-dealer is subject. In 1996, the NASD's Arbitration Policy Task Force took the position that any NASD member that included such a limitation in a customer agreement would violate the NASD's Rules of Fair Practice. The Task Force recommended, however, that punitive damages in securities arbitration be limited to the lesser of $750,000 or two times actual damages. No action has been taken on the recommendation.

§11.4 MUTUAL FUND REGULATION

Mutual funds have become an important investment tool for investors. Fifty years ago there were 244 mutual funds, holding only 3 percent of U.S. equities; today there are more than 6,500 funds, holding about 30 percent of U.S. equities and more than $12 trillion in investment assets. Almost half of all U.S. households own mutual funds, mostly in retirement accounts such as IRAs and employer-sponsored 401(k) plans. For purposes of securities regulation, the critical retail "point of sale" for purposes of federal securities regulation may well happen not in an IPO or on the trading markets, but instead when an investor buys a mutual fund.

§11.4.1 What Is a Mutual Fund?

A mutual fund pools the small investments of many investors, permitting the pooled money to be invested in a diversified portfolio of stocks, bonds, and/ or cash equivalents. Investors own shares of the mutual fund, entitling them to a proportionate interest in any appreciation or income generated by the financial instruments in the fund's portfolio — and exposing them to the risk that the portfolio might fall in value. Companies that run mutual funds, such as Fidelity and Vanguard, are called "investment advisers" and manage the portfolio on behalf of fund investors.

Fund Management

The fund company, besides managing the fund's investment portfolio, also runs the fund and its operations. The fund company performs the "back office" functions for the fund, such as bookkeeping, legal compliance, SEC filings, and investor reports. The fund company acts as the "underwriter" for the fund, assisting investors when they buy and redeem fund shares. The fund company acts as transfer agent for the fund (or contracts for this service) to keep track of investor accounts and send statements, tax information, and other notices. Finally, the fund company contracts with custodians (typically a bank) to hold the fund's securities, receive dividends and interest, and engage in any foreign currency conversions, as well as pay fund expenses.

As you can see, mutual funds have a "unique structure" different from that of operating corporations. Mutual funds have no employees, but are instead created and managed by the external fund company (investment adviser), which specifies the fund's investment goals and then earns fees under advisory, underwriting, and other agreements with the fund. The fund company selects the fund's board of directors (or trustees, if the fund is organized as a trust), subject to a vote by fund shareholders on the initial board and whenever the number of shareholder-elected board members falls below 50 percent. Inv. Co. Act §16(a).

Types of Investment Companies

Mutual funds are technically a kind of "investment company" subject to registration with the SEC under the Investment Company Act of 1940. Here are the main types of investment companies — all of them pooled investment vehicles:

Investment company	Description
Open-end funds (mutual funds)	This is the predominant type of investment company. Investors buy fund shares directly (or through a broker) from the issuing fund; and investors can also redeem their shares at any time by selling them back to the fund. The price is the per share "net asset value" (NAV) of the fund's portfolio.
Closed-end funds	Unlike mutual funds, the fund (whose portfolio is usually managed) sells shares in a public offering, which then trade on secondary market. Investors buy and sell their shares at the market price, which is often (curiously) less than NAV.
Unit investment trusts (UITs)	UITs make a one-time public offering of a fixed number of redeemable securities called "units," which terminate on a date specified when the UIT is created.
Exchange-traded funds (ETFs)	ETFs are funds with fixed portfolios (such as the stocks in a market index) whose shares are traded on stock exchanges, like any other stock. Their price is set on the market, though they usually trade close to NAV. Besides their pricing advantage, they usually have lower management fees than mutual funds and have tax costs only when traded. They are organized as either open-end companies or UITs. But ETFs are not considered to be, and are not permitted to call themselves, mutual funds.

Fund companies offer investors a mind-numbing variety of investment options: money-market funds (composed of high-quality, short-term investments that keep their NAV at a stable $1.00 per share), short-term bond funds, long-term bond funds, municipal bond funds, growth stock funds, value stock funds, sector stock funds, large-cap funds, medium-cap funds, small-cap funds, international stock funds — to name a few.

§11.4.2 Mutual Fund Costs

Mutual fund companies impose different fees and charges. Here are the more important ones:

- **Shareholder fees:** Some fees are charged directly to shareholders for commissions paid to brokers that sell the funds. Sometimes, these charges happen when the investor buys the fund (*sales charge* or *front-end load*, which FINRA limits to 8.5 percent) and sometimes fees are charged when the investor sells the fund (a *deferred sales charge* or *back-end load*). In addition, some funds charge a *redemption fee*, which is paid directly to the fund for the costs of redeeming shares (which the SEC limits to 2 percent).

- **Operating charges:** Other fees are charged to the fund itself (and thus fund investors pay these fees indirectly). The most common operating charge is a *management fee*, paid by the fund to the investment adviser for managing the fund portfolio. Other operating charges include those for custodial expenses, legal and accounting expenses, transfer agent expenses, and other administrative expenses. One hidden expense comes from the trading commissions paid for buying and selling securities in the fund — which can be significant in funds with a high *portfolio turnover* (replacement of securities in the fund).

- **Marketing (12b-1) fees.** Since 1980, the SEC has allowed funds to charge an annual fee for marketing the fund and providing shareholder services — so-called 12b-1 fees (after the 1980 rule that authorizes these fees). These fees, paid mostly to brokers, have been controversial since existing fund investors pay to bring new investors into the fund — something that may benefit the fund adviser more than fund investors. The SEC has proposed to change this controversial rule to make 12b-1 fees more transparent.

These fees must be disclosed in a *fee table* in the fund prospectus — which must also state the fund's *expense ratio* showing the total of all of a fund's annual operating expenses, expressed as a percentage of the fund's average net assets.

Costs Matter

The level of mutual fund fees has been controversial, with critics pointing out that the median mutual fund charges nearly 2.5 percent in management and 12b-1 fees. Over time this can be significant. For example, assume annual market returns of 8.5 percent. A high-cost fund (with a 2.5 percent expense ratio) will have net returns of 6.0 percent annually; while a low-cost fund (with a 0.5 percent expense ratio) will have net returns of 8.0 percent annually. Over 30 years, a $10,000 investment in the high-cost fund will grow to about $57,500 (proving the power of compounding), while the low-cost fund will grow to $100,600 (showing the corrosive effect of high fees).

§11.4.3 Regulation of Mutual Funds

Mutual funds are subject to a host of federal securities regulation. Here is an overview:

Investment Company Act of 1940	Regulates the structure and operations of mutual funds, which must register with the SEC and become subject to disclosure requirements and restrictions on day-to-day operations, including capital structures, diversification of holdings, pricing of portfolio securities, custody of assets, investment activities (particularly with respect to transactions with the fund company), and the functions of the fund board.
Securities Act of 1933	Regulates the sale of fund shares to investors, requiring that investors receive a current prospectus describing the fund and imposing liability for false or misleading statements in the fund's registration statement for its shares.
Securities Exchange Act of 1934	Regulates the fund company as underwriter (seller) of fund shares, and requires it to register as a broker-dealer with the SEC.
Investment Advisers Act of 1940	Requires the fund company to register with the SEC as an investment adviser, which entails recordkeeping, custodial, reporting, and other regulatory responsibilities.

As you can see, regulation of mutual funds is complex. Rather than attempt to describe all the details, we review the most salient (and controversial) aspects of mutual fund activities and the regulatory responses.

Fund Advisory Fees

Given the perceived weakness of fee competition in the mutual fund market, the Investment Company Act of 1940 requires that the fund board approve the advisory fees charged by the fund company (investment adviser). See Inv. Co. Act §15(c). And to ensure that the board fulfills its role as "watchdog" on behalf of fund investors, the 1940 Act requires that at least 40 percent of fund directors be "independent" — that is, they cannot be employees or affiliates of the fund company. Inv. Co. Act §10(a). The SEC has increased this threshold to 75 percent for funds to qualify for various exemptive rules. See Inv. Co. Act Rule 0-1(a)(7); Inv Co. Act Rel. No. 26,520 (2004).

In 1970, Congress decided that this fee-setting process rarely led to real negotiations between the fund board and the investment adviser, and amended the 1940 Act to impose a specific fiduciary duty on investment advisers with respect to the compensation they received — along with a private right of action for fund shareholders to sue the adviser to enforce this duty. Inv. Co. Act §36(b). The fiduciary duty is in addition to the requirements of board approval (which is subject to state fiduciary duties) and prospectus disclosure of all fees paid by the fund.

How does an investment adviser satisfy its §36(b) fiduciary duty? In 1982, the Second Circuit held that an investment adviser satisfied its §36(b) duties with respect to compensation paid by the fund if the fees were not "so disproportionately large [that they] bear no reasonable relationship to the services rendered." *Gartenberg v. Merrill Lynch Asset Management*, F.2d (2d Cir. 1982). The court set out a process-based standard that looked at whether the fund board had considered a variety of factors in approving the compensation — namely, the services provided by the adviser, the adviser's profitability, any economies of scale, comparable funds' fees, board independence, and any indirect benefits to the adviser. This led fund boards (and fund advisers) to treat the "*Gartenberg* factors" as a safe harbor checklist that insulated advisory fees from judicial review, and federal courts obliged. In the first 40 years of §36(b)'s operation, no federal court found excessive the advisory fees charged mutual funds.

In 2008, a Seventh Circuit decision questioned the *Gartenberg* approach and held that federal courts should not review the level of fees, or even the process by which they were negotiated, so long as the fees were fully and honestly disclosed — on the assumption that competition in the mutual fund market would cull out funds with unreasonably high costs. *Jones v. Harris Associates*, 527 F.3d 627 (7th Cir. 2009). The decision was at odds with those in other circuits, which uniformly had followed the *Gartenberg* approach to assess whether the fund board had adequately negotiated fund fees.

The Supreme Court reversed the Seventh Circuit and explicitly accepted the *Gartenberg* framework as a compromise between protecting fund investors and putting shareholder plaintiffs to the proof of excessive fees. *Jones v. Harris Associates*, 130 S. Ct. 1418 (2010). The Court stated that normally courts should defer to the fees set by independent fund directors who had considered the relevant factors "even if a court might weigh the factors differently." Nonetheless, the Court noted that the fund board could consider — if the comparison were apt — whether the fund adviser had charged lower management fees to institutional customers compared to its captive mutual funds.

Time will tell how *Jones v. Harris Associates* affects §36(b) litigation. The decision opens some new possibilities for fund shareholders claiming excessive fees — including the Court's statement that the fees charged by competitors (before a benchmark in cases relying on *Gartenberg*) may not be relevant since they "may not be the product of negotiations conducted at arm's length." Nonetheless, the Court showed less interest in the *Gartenberg* process-based factors, noting that failures in process (such as disclosure missteps by the fund adviser) may not be dispositive. Cf. *Gallus v. Ameriprise*

Financial, Inc., 561 F.3d 816 (8th Cir. 2009) (finding fund adviser's failure to provide competitive fee information to fund board).

Performance Advertising

Mutual fund investors often rely on information about a fund's past performance in making their investment decisions. Fund companies, recognizing this investment strategy, often advertise their strong-performing funds by comparing them to benchmarks and other competing funds. Academic studies, however, have shown that strong past performance of managed equity funds is rarely (if ever) an indication that the fund's future performance will continue. Instead, strong past performance is almost always a matter of investment luck, not the fund adviser's stock-picking skills.

To address this "performance chasing" by mutual fund investors, Dodd-Frank calls on the General Accounting Office to undertake a study (presumably for Congress or the SEC to act on) that looks at, among other things, the impact of performance advertising on investors and recommendations to improve investor protections in mutual fund advertising. Dodd-Frank §918. Some commentators have suggested that performance advertising is materially misleading because it creates the false illusion that past performance is predictive of future results (see §9.3.1) and have urged that the SEC return to its prior ban on performance ads.

Trading Abuses

In the early 2000s, a number of mutual fund companies were investigated for the preferential treatment they had given certain (mostly institutional) customers at the expense of other investors in their funds. Investigators identified two forms of misbehavior:

1. *Late trading* happens when a fund company allows favored customers to buy fund shares *after* the fund's daily price has been set at 4:00 P.M. Eastern time. This allows these customers, using information on after-hours price changes in other (usually international) markets, to buy the fund's shares at the earlier set price. Late trading is illegal under SEC rules, since it means non-trading fund shareholders subsidize the advantageous price given to preferred customers.

2. *Market timing* happens when a fund company lets favored customers trade in and out of a fund in response to price changes in the market. For example, if a current fund's price (based on the likely NAV at the end of the trading day) is lower than the market value of its portfolio, an astute investor can buy the fund and then sell whenever its price (again based on likely end-of-day NAV) seems higher than the market value of its portfolio. This "in and out" trading permits

the favored customer to skim returns from current fund shareholders and also increases fund costs to meet the timer's liquidity demands. Although the practice is not illegal, the failure of fund companies to disclose in their prospectus that the fund allows market timers into the fund constituted securities fraud.

In the mid-2000s, the Attorney General of New York (using the state's Martin Act) and the SEC brought charges against a number of fund companies for their late trading and market timing practices, and obtained settlements in which the companies paid billions in fines and to create restitution funds. A number of private suits were also brought, with many of them settled for large sums.

In response, many fund companies added internal controls to ensure their funds were not subject to late trading and imposed redemption fees on short-term investors, thus removing the financial benefit of "in and out" trading.

§11.5 PRIVATE FUND REGULATION

Mutual funds are not the only financial intermediaries that offer investment pools to investors. Others include (1) venture capital funds, (2) hedge funds, and (3) private equity funds.

§11.5.1 What Are Private Funds?

Venture capital funds are private, unregistered investment pools that attract investments from institutional investors and sophisticated, wealthy individuals (typically under the §4(a)(2) private placement exemption, see §5.2.2). The fund then invests in start-up companies, usually taking preferred stock and rights to sit on the company's board of directors. The venture capital fund earns a return on its preferred stock, but can earn even bigger returns if the company goes public and the venture capital firm converts its preferred into common stock and sells into the public market.

Hedge funds (like venture capital funds) are private, unregistered investment pools available only to institutional investors and sophisticated, wealthy individuals. (The name "hedge fund" comes their historical purpose to invest in derivatives and other financial instruments that protected investors from losses in a down market, though today hedge funds offer a wide (often computer-driven) variety of investment strategies.)

Private equity funds are private, unregistered investment pools that typically acquire a 100 percent ownership interest in mature companies that often were once publicly held and are "taken private" by the private equity fund.

§11.5.2 Regulation of Private Funds

Investment Company Exemption

By limiting investment in their funds, private funds are exempted from the definition of "investment company," thus removing them from the heavy regulatory scheme applicable to mutual funds. Two exemptions under the Investment Company Act are available:

- private funds with 100 or fewer investors. Inv. Co. Act §3(c)(1). As a practical matter, given the requirements for a private placement under Regulation D (see §5.2.4), private funds relying on this exemption only accept investments from "accredited investors" — currently defined to include large institutional investors (with more than $5 million in assets) and wealthy individuals (with more than $200,000 in annual income or net assets greater than $1 million).
- private funds with only "qualified purchasers," defined as individuals with at least $5 million in investment assets or institutional investors with at least $25 million in investment assets. Inv. Co. Act §3(c)(7) ("qualified purchasers" defined in §2(a)(51)).

Investment Adviser Regulation

Before Dodd-Frank, the advisers of private funds were not subject to registration as investment advisers under the Investment Advisers Act of 1940. Former Inv. Adv. Act §203(b)(3) (exempting investment advisers with fewer than 15 clients, provided they do not hold themselves out to the public as investment advisers). Thus, if a private fund company advised fewer than 15 private funds, no Investment Adviser Act registration was required.

Dodd-Frank changed this and now requires advisers of "private funds" (which include hedge funds and private equity funds) to register with the SEC as investment advisers. Dodd-Frank §§402, 403. Once registered, they must keep records and (1) report to the SEC (though not publicly) the amount and types of assets under management, (2) the credit risk exposure of counterparties, (3) their trading and investment positions, and (4) their valuation policies and practices. The SEC must then report to Congress annually on how it is using this data to protect investors and market integrity. Dodd-Frank §404.

Dodd-Frank, however, carves out important exemptions from SEC registration for private funds: (1) *venture capital advisers*—those advising only venture capital funds, as defined by the SEC (Dodd-Frank Act §407); (2) *smaller private advisers*—those with less than $150 million under management in the United States (Inv. Adv. Act §203(m); Dodd-Frank §408); (3) *foreign private advisers*—those that have no U.S. place of business, have fewer than 15 U.S. clients, have less than $25 million in assets under management for U.S. clients, and do not hold themselves out to U.S. investors as an investment adviser (Inv. Adv. Act §302(a)(30); Dodd-Frank §402).

In addition, the so-called Volcker Rule of Dodd-Frank (which prohibits "proprietary trading" by banks, thus preventing bank assets being used to make risky investments) also prohibits banking entities from acquiring or retaining any ownership interest in any hedge fund or private equity fund. Dodd-Frank §619.

§11.6 REGULATION OF CREDIT RATING AGENCIES

Credit rating agencies assign credit ratings (such as "AAA" or "not investment quality") to companies and other entities that issue debt securities, as well as ratings for specific debt instruments (such as debt obligations collateralized by subprime mortgages). The credit rating is supposed to provide information on the creditworthiness of the company and its debt instruments. Investors use credit ratings; and some institutional investors are required to invest parts of their portfolio only in high-rated debt instruments.

The credit rating agencies blew it when they rated the structured financial transactions that were at the heart of the subprime mortgage crisis in 2008. These transactions divided returns on the mortgages into different parts, or "tranches," some of which were sold as "safe investments." The failure of the rating agencies to notice the risk in these financial instruments led to banks carrying them as part of their capital reserves. This proved unsound. And when it became clear the underlying mortgages and thus the structured debt might not be paid, the credit agencies were slow in downgrading this bad debt.

Dodd-Frank changes the way that credit rating agencies are regulated, mandating increased accountability, imposing stronger controls on how ratings are produced, and enhancing transparency so investors and other users can evaluate the accuracy of credit ratings. Much of the new regulatory regime, however, has been left to SEC rulemaking (and studies). Generally, the SEC is required to issue final regulations with respect to credit rating agencies by July 2011.

Note on Credit Rating Litigation

Since the financial crisis of 2008, credit rating agencies have been the target of suits from various quarters: the Department of Justice (federal criminal claims), state attorneys' general (state fraud claims), and private litigants (mostly private 10b-5 actions). The suits have generally alleged that the credit rating agencies—including Standard & Poors, Moody's, and Fitch—failed to identify the risks in certain mortgage-backed financial instruments, but instead gave them gold-standard "AAA" ratings. Most of the litigation is still ongoing.

§11.6.1 Accountability of Credit Rating Agencies

Dodd-Frank requires credit rating agencies to register with the SEC. Exchange Act §15E (requiring registration of credit rating agencies as nationally recognized statistical rating organizations, or NRSROs). The SEC can temporarily suspend or permanently revoke the registration of a NRSRO with respect to a particular class of securities if the SEC finds that the NRSRO failed to produce "accurate" ratings for that class for a sustained period of time. It is unclear, however, how the SEC will make that determination.

Dodd-Frank exposes credit rating agencies to private lawsuits—both for their ratings used in public offerings and for those in private placements. In a public offering of rated securities, any credit rating agency that consents to its credit rating being used in the offering is deemed to be an "expert" as to the rating. Dodd-Frank §939G (repealing SEC Rule 436(g), which had provided that NRSRO credit ratings were not considered to be prepared or certified by an expert). Thus, the credit rating agency is liable for money damages as an expert under §11 of the Securities Act for misstatements or omissions of material facts in connection with the credit rating—though subject to the regular "due diligence" defenses. See §6.3.4.

In private placements, Dodd-Frank effectively overturns the approach of many courts that had held credit ratings to be simply "opinions" and thus not actionable, perhaps even protected by the First Amendment as commercial free speech. *In re Enron Corp.*, 511 F. Supp. 2d 742 (S.D. Tex. 2005) (holding that First Amendment shields credit rating agency from negligent misrepresentation claim where the "credit rating reports were distributed 'to the world' and were related to the creditworthiness of public corporation operated internationally"). Under Dodd-Frank, credit ratings by credit rating agencies are subject to the same penalty and enforcement provisions under the Exchange Act applicable to public accounting firms and securities analysts. Exchange Act §15E(m). Furthermore, credit reports—though an opinion about an issuer's future creditworthiness—are deemed not to be forward-looking statements under the §21E safe harbor. See §3.3.2.

In a private securities fraud action for money damages against a credit rating agency or its controlling person, the complaint must state with particularity facts giving rise to a strong inference that the credit rating agency knowingly or recklessly failed (i) to conduct its own reasonable investigation of the rated security or (ii) to obtain reasonable verification from independent sources. Exchange Act §21D(b)(2).

§11.6.2 Internal Controls in Credit Rating Agencies

Dodd-Frank also requires credit rating agencies to "establish, maintain and enforce an effective internal control structure governing the implementation of and adherence to policies, procedures, and methodologies for determining credit ratings." Exchange Act §15E. Toward this end, the SEC is to promulgate rules requiring credit rating agencies to submit to the SEC annual internal control reports describing the responsibility of their management in establishing and maintaining internal controls, assessing the effectiveness of their internal control structures, and containing an attestation of the CEO.

Dodd-Frank requires the SEC to establish an Office of Credit Ratings to administer rules on the practice of determining ratings, promoting rating accuracy, and ensuring that ratings are not influenced by conflicts of interest. The Office of Credit Ratings must conduct examinations of NRSROs at least annually, making public a summary of any deficiencies in its examination reports. Credit rating agencies are subject to SEC fines and other penalties for violating the §15E provisions.

§11.6.3 Regulation of Credit Rating Agencies

Dodd-Frank requires the SEC to issue "Chinese wall" (information firewall) rules to prevent sales and marketing considerations from influencing the production of credit ratings. Credit rating agencies can be suspended or have their registration revoked if the SEC finds these rules have been violated in a way that affected a rating. In addition, credit rating agencies must have "look-back" procedures to ensure that ratings are not influenced when former employees of the agency go to work for the issuer (or underwriter) of a rated security. Dodd-Frank §932 (also requiring SEC to review procedures and code of ethics of credit rating agencies).

Dodd-Frank also calls on the SEC to specify the form of credit ratings, the methods used to set credit ratings, and information on the accuracy of previous credit ratings. Dodd-Frank §932. The credit ratings form must disclose (i) the credit rating, (ii) the main assumptions and data used in making the rating determination, (iii) potential limitations of the credit rating, (iv) information on the reliability, accuracy, or quality of the data used in making a credit rating determination, (v) information as to limitations of essential data such as limits on the scope of historical data and accessibility to certain documents, (vi) whether the credit rating agency used a third party to conduct due diligence, the information the third party reviewed, and the third party's conclusions, and (vii) information as to conflicts of interest. Exchange Act §15E(s).

The SEC must also issue a rule requiring NRSROs to publicly disclose certain information about the initial credit rating, as well as any subsequent rating change. The disclosures must (i) be similar so users can compare the performance of different credit rating agencies, (ii) be clear and informative, (iii) include performance information over a range of years and for a variety of types of credit ratings, including for withdrawn credit ratings, (iv) be freely available and easily accessible on its website, and (v) include an attestation that the rating is based solely on an independent evaluation of the risks and merits of the instruments being rated. Exchange Act §15E(q).

The SEC must prescribe rules requiring NRSROs to identify the procedures and methodologies they use to determine credit ratings and to ensure that any changes to these procedures and methodologies are applied consistently and publicly disclosed. Exchange Act §15E(r).

Finally, the SEC must require NRSROs to establish, maintain, and enforce written policies and procedures that (i) assess the likelihood that an issuer of a security or money market instrument will default or fail to make payments in a timely manner in accordance with the terms of the instrument, (ii) clearly define the symbol used to denote the credit rating, and (iii) apply credit rating symbols in a consistent manner. Dodd-Frank §938.

Credit Ratings Study and Rulemaking

One criticism of credit ratings is that they are typically paid for (and the credit rating agency chosen by) the issuer of the rated securities. No wonder credit ratings are usually unduly optimistic! To address this conflict, some have urged that investors (or subscribers) pay for credit ratings.

Dodd-Frank calls on the SEC to study the conflicts of interest associated with issuer-pay and subscriber-pay models for credit reports. Dodd-Frank §939C. The report is then to consider the feasibility of a system in which a government agency (not the issuer) assigns a credit rating agency to determine credit ratings of structured finance products, thus to promote more accurate credit ratings.

Following the study, the SEC must establish a system for how registered credit rating agencies would be assigned to determine initial credit ratings of structured finance products, so the issuer, sponsor, or underwriter of the structured finance product doesn't make the assignment. Exchange Act §15E(w) (requiring creation of government agency to assess credit rating agencies, unless SEC determines an alternative system would be better).

CHAPTER 12

Public Enforcement

The SEC has broad investigatory and enforcement powers to carry out its mandates under the federal securities laws to protect investors and ensure the integrity of the securities markets.

Although there are fewer SEC enforcement actions (about 500 every year) than private lawsuits claiming securities law violations, SEC enforcement powers and remedies are broader than those in private litigation. For example, the SEC can bring claims of aiding and abetting securities violations, even though such claims are unavailable to private litigants. The SEC, unlike a private party, can also seek structural remedies, such as a court order barring persons or companies from the securities business.

This chapter covers:

- SEC investigatory powers and practices [§12.1], the agency's enforcement of the securities laws in administrative proceedings [§12.2], and its enforcement through litigation in federal court [§12.3]
- SEC enforcement actions against accountants and securities lawyers, an area of enforcement changed by the Sarbanes-Oxley Act [§12.4]
- federal criminal enforcement under the federal securities laws, through prosecutions by the U.S. Department of Justice, usually on referrals by the SEC [§12.5]
- state civil and criminal enforcement of state securities laws, particular by the New York attorney general under that state's Martin Act [§12.6]

§12.1 SEC INVESTIGATIONS

The SEC has investigatory powers in a number of settings. Securities Act §8(e) (determine whether to issue order stopping registration of public offering); §19(b) (enforce Securities Act); Exchange Act §21(a) (determine whether "any person has violated, is violating, or is about to violate" the Exchange Act and its rules, as well as the rules of the stock exchanges, FINRA, and other self-regulatory organizations, SROs).

The SEC has the power to administer oaths, compel sworn testimony and issue subpoenas for the production of documents. Although SEC investigations (whether informal or formal) are nonpublic, the SEC has obligations under the Freedom of Information Act to release documents and other information concerning matters previously subject to SEC scrutiny. The SEC also reports the results of some investigations. Thus, an SEC investigation may often come to light and be relevant in subsequent civil or criminal proceedings.

The SEC's Division of Enforcement conducts investigations into possible violations of the federal securities laws. The Division also litigates in administrative proceedings before the Commission and brings civil actions in federal court. The Division refers possible criminal violations to the U.S. Department of Justice, which prosecutes criminal cases with the cooperation of the Division.

Interestingly, despite claims that SEC lawyers exert less enforcement effort in order to curry favor with prospective employers (sometimes called "regulatory capture"), a recent study finds that SEC lawyers actually are more likely to aggressively showcase their expertise to prospective employers. According to the study, SEC lawyers' enforcement efforts (as measured by the fraction of losses collected as damages, the likelihood of criminal charges, and the frequency the CEO is named as a defendant) are greater in anticipation of the lawyer leaving the agency to join law firms that defend clients before the SEC.

§12.1.1 Investigations: Formal and Informal

The SEC can investigate past violations of the securities laws, as well as ongoing and impending violations. SEC investigations are triggered from many quarters: staff review of SEC filings; news stories (the *Wall Street Journal* is compulsory reading at the agency); periodic inspection of broker-dealers, investment advisers, and investment companies; public complaints; and regular market surveillance by SEC staff. In addition, under new provisions added by the Sarbanes-Oxley Act, employees who cooperate with government investigations ("whistleblowers") are protected against employer retaliation. 18 U.S.C. §1514A (creating private civil action for employees of public companies who claim retaliation after providing information in a fraud investigation); 18 U.S.C. §1513(e) (federal crime for any person knowingly to harm, with intent to retaliate, an informant's employment or livelihood). The SEC enforcement staff also can be contacted online — the SEC's website includes a special "enforcement center."

SEC staff may conduct *informal investigations*, without a formal SEC order, and obtain information through voluntary means. Although cooperation at this stage is voluntary and usually statements are not under oath or transcribed, any witness (as Martha Stewart learned) who knowingly and willfully provides false information to the staff commits a crime. 18 U.S.C. §1001 (federal crime to knowingly make false statements to a federal official). It is also a crime (as the accounting firm Arthur Andersen learned) to knowingly destroy documents with the intent to impair an SEC investigation. 18 U.S.C. §1512 (federal crime "knowingly, intentionally and corruptly" to persuade another person to withhold or "alter, destroy, or mutilate" documents for use in an official proceeding); see also Sarbanes-Oxley §802 (federal crime to "knowingly" alter, destroy, mutilate, or conceal any document with the intent to impede an investigation).

If an informal investigation suggests further information is called for, the SEC can issue a *formal order of investigation* outlining the scope of inquiry. Once the full Commission issues a formal order of investigation, an important milestone in a case, SEC staff can issue subpoenas nationwide against any person who has information significant to the investigation. Securities Act §19(b) (power to administer oaths, subpoena witnesses, and require production of documents that SEC deems relevant to inquiry); Exchange Act §21(a) (same). The subpoena can call for witness testimony or production of documents. Persons complying with a subpoena can request that supplied information not be available to the public under the Freedom of Information Act, typically on the basis of either personal privacy or business confidentiality.

§12.1.2 Investigative Powers

The SEC has broad powers to issues investigative subpoenas. Courts have held that the SEC need not have probable cause that the securities laws have been violated; it is enough that the investigation is for a proper purpose and the information sought is relevant to that purpose. There is no administrative power to enforce a subpoena, but a person who fails to comply with an SEC subpoena and is ordered by a court to do so can be held in contempt for noncompliance with the court's order. Exchange Act §21(c).

Constitutional protections apply to SEC investigations, such as the Fourth Amendment right to be free from unreasonable searches and seizures and the Fifth Amendment privilege against self-incrimination. Nonetheless, these protections may be limited in the corporate context. For example, the Supreme Court has held that a one-person corporation may be ordered to produce corporate records even though those records may incriminate the sole owner. *Braswell v. United States*, 487 U.S. 99 (1988).

The SEC need not notify targets of an investigation, thus undercutting the practical ability of the target to challenge an SEC subpoena or investigation as unduly broad. See *SEC v. Jerry T. O'Brien, Inc.*, 467 U.S. 735 (1984) (finding no constitutional or statutory mandate that targets be notified of subpoenas issued to third parties in nonpublic SEC investigation). In addition, the SEC may conduct an investigation even though it parallels a criminal investigation by the Justice Department or another prosecutorial entity. In the case of parallel proceedings, the SEC may be limited in its use of investigative subpoenas once a criminal indictment is returned since the administrative investigation would expand the government's normal rights of criminal discovery. The SEC may also be limited in parallel investigations by witnesses' Fifth Amendment privilege against self-incrimination. *SEC v. Dresser Industries, Inc.*, 628 F.2d 1368 (D.C. Cir. 1980).

The SEC, without taking any formal enforcement action after an investigation, can issue a *report of investigation* — a "Section 21(a) report." See Exchange Act Rel. No. 44969 (Oct. 23, 2001) (laying out considerations on whether investigation should lead to enforcement action, including nature, scope, duration and extent of the misconduct and response, remedial actions and cooperation by target of investigation). The report, which is not burdened by the procedural requirement of an order, allows the agency to state its legal views without a hearing or being subject to judicial review. Even if the report does not recommend specific sanctions, unfavorable comments about the target may serve the purpose of deterrence and punishment. For example, the SEC has used Section 21(a) reports to criticize lax management oversight by boards of directors of public companies.

Typically, once SEC staff has conducted an investigation and presented its findings of fact and alleged violations, the Commission (acting as prosecutor) will follow the recommendations of staff. Even if the case is weak or a proposed settlement is questionable, the Commission faces institutional pressures to confirm the staff's conclusions.

§12.2 SEC ADMINISTRATIVE ENFORCEMENT

The SEC has an imposing arsenal of non-judicial weapons to enforce the federal securities laws by issuing administrative orders or imposing sanctions in its own proceedings. Many of these powers were expanded or clarified in the Securities Enforcement Remedies and Penny Stock Reform

Act of 1990. Most of the SEC's enforcement actions are brought in administrative proceedings, rather than as judicial injunctive actions (see §12.3).

SEC Enforcement Procedures

SEC administrative enforcement actions are typically initiated by an "order of proceedings" that specifies the charges and provides a period for the respondent to answer. Proceedings that involve an evidentiary hearing are generally conducted by an administrative law judge. The ALJ is an SEC employee who hears pre-hearing motions, evaluates testimony, and renders a written decision. The ALJ's decision is final unless either the SEC staff or the respondent seek review with the Commission, or the Commission orders review on its own. If reviewed, the Commission has full *de novo* authority to affirm, reverse, modify or remand the ALJ's decision. If there is no review, the SEC enters a final order setting forth any sanctions recommended by the ALJ.

Unlike investigations, formal enforcement proceedings are a matter of public record. If the SEC determines there has been a violation, the agency may (and often does) publish information about the violation, thus informing the public of its position, deterring similar conduct, and clarifying (or announcing) future enforcement policies. The SEC often uses litigated enforcement actions to articulate new interpretations of federal securities law — a flexible common law that can adapt to evolving securities practices. The effect is that the SEC creates new law without opportunity for comment or objection by those who become subject to it, an opportunity available in a formal administrative rulemaking.

§12.2.1 SEC Administrative Enforcement Powers

The SEC has sweeping administrative authority to ensure compliance of the federal securities laws.

Stop Offering

The SEC can issue a *refusal order* to prevent a registration statement from becoming effective or a *stop order* of an already effective registration statement. Securities Act §§8(b), 8(d).

Suspend Trading

The SEC can summarily *suspend trading* in a publicly traded security for up to ten days, whether the security is traded over-the-counter or on a stock exchange. Exchange Act §12(k). A summary suspension may be for additional ten-day periods, if each new suspension is based on new circumstances. *SEC v. Sloan*, 436 U.S. 103 (1978). After notice and hearing, the SEC can suspend (for up to 12 months) or revoke the registration under the Exchange Act of affected securities on a finding of non-compliance with the Exchange Act or its rules. Exchange Act §12(j). The effect is to bar public trading of the issuer's securities.

Cease and Desist Order

Using its most effective remedy, the SEC can issue (typically after notice and opportunity for hearing) an administrative order compelling any person to *cease and desist* from committing violations (including future violations) of the federal securities laws or their rules. Securities Act §8A; Exchange Act §21C. In addition, the SEC can seek civil penalties in both administrative and court cease-and-desist proceedings, from both registered and unregistered persons and entities. Dodd-Frank §929.

The SEC can issue a cease-and-desist order for negligent violations of the securities laws. See *KPMG, LLP v. SEC*, 289 F.3d 109 (D.C. Cir. 2002) (accounting firm "should have known" that audit services could not be billed on contingency-fee basis). And a past violation provides evidence of the "risk" of a future violation. See *In re KPMG Peat Marwick LLP*, Exchange Act Rel. No. 43,862 (Jan. 19, 2001) (violation constitutes "sufficient risk of future violation" to support cease-and-desist order); cf. *WHX Corp. v. SEC*, 362 F.3d 854 (D.C. Cir. 2004) (isolated violation that was immediately corrected, with assurances it would not be repeated, cannot be basis for cease-and-desist order). If a party fails to comply with a cease-and-desist order, the SEC can enforce the order in federal district court, where the court can impose additional civil money penalties for noncompliance with the order.

Compliance Order

The SEC can *order compliance* (after notice and opportunity for hearing) with its periodic and tender offer disclosure requirements or adjudicate whether the registrant's filings are defective. Exchange Act §15(c)(4). The SEC may issue a §15(c)(4) compliance order directed both to the registrant and to the person who caused the disclosure failure, including officers, directors, and even attorneys who caused the failure. Given the broad cease-and-desist powers created by the Securities Enforcement Remedies and Penny Stock Reform Act of 1990, the SEC now rarely invokes §15(c)(4) in its enforcement action against securities industry participants.

Order Disgorgement and Accounting

The SEC can seek disgorgement (or forfeiture) of any profits by a person who has violated the securities laws, retaining an accountant to calculate the profits generated by the unlawful activity. Securities Act §8A(e); Exchange Act §21B(e). A disgorgement order is within the discretion of the court.

Bar Corporate Officials

Under authority added by the Sarbanes-Oxley Act, the SEC is authorized in a cease-and-desist proceeding to bar officers and directors from serving for reporting companies, if they violated §17(a)(1) or any prohibition on fraud in the sale of securities, such as under Rule 10b-5. Securities Act §8A(f); Exchange Act §21C(f). The bar may be conditional or unconditional, and temporary or permanent. Before the Sarbanes-Oxley Act, the SEC was required to show the likelihood of future securities violations. See *SEC v. Patel*, 61 F.3d 137 (2d Cir. 1995) (requiring SEC to show likelihood of future misconduct to support lifetime bar from serving as officer or director of public company).

§12.2.2 SEC Disciplinary Powers

As overseer of the securities industry, the SEC has broad disciplinary authority over industry participants. Sanctioning authority extends to broker-dealers, to persons "appearing before" the SEC (such as securities lawyers and accountants), and to investment advisers and mutual fund managers. (The authority to discipline lawyers and accountants, a matter of increased importance after the corporate scandals of the early 2000s and the resulting Sarbanes-Oxley Act, is addressed more fully in §12.4 below.)

Broker-Dealer Sanctions

The SEC can impose disciplinary sanctions (after notice and opportunity for hearing) against broker-dealers and associated persons. Exchange Act §§15(b)(4), 15(b)(6), 19(h). Sanctions can range from outright revocation of registration, to temporary suspension, to barring an individual from associating with a broker-dealer. The Securities Enforcement Remedies and Penny Stock Reform Act of 1990 authorizes the SEC to impose civil penalties against broker-dealers and their associates who willfully violate the securities laws, willfully aid and abet a violation, or fail reasonably to supervise a violator. Exchange Act §21B. The Act institutes a system of tiered penalties that vary depending on whether the respondent is a natural person or legal entity, whether there is fraud, deceit, manipulation or disregard of regulatory requirements, and whether there is substantial harm or unjust enrichment. Exchange Act §21B(b) (maximum penalties vary from $5,000 to $100,000 for natural persons, and from $50,000 to $500,000 for entities).

Persons Who Appear Before SEC

The SEC's rules of practice also give it power to "deny, temporarily or permanently, the privilege of appearing or practicing before it" if the SEC determines (after notice and opportunity for hearing) the person lacks qualifications, character or integrity, or willfully violated or aided and abetted a violation of the federal securities laws. SEC Rule of Practice 102(e) [formerly numbered as Rule 2(e)]. The SEC has justified this power as an adjunct to assuring the integrity of its administrative procedures and to protect the general public. See *Touche Ross & Co. v. SEC*, 609 F.2d 570 (2d Cir. 1979) (upholding SEC's authority to promulgate Rule 2(e)).

The agency has construed Rule 102(e) broadly as authority to discipline attorneys, accountants, engineers, and other similar professionals who not only formally appear before the SEC but also assist clients with respect to preparing and filing SEC reports and disclosure documents. Rule 102(e) disciplinary sanctions serve as guideposts for securities professionals.

Review Disciplinary Sanctions Imposed by SROs

The SEC may review disciplinary sanctions imposed by stock exchanges, FINRA, and other self-regulatory organizations (SROs) on their members.

§12.2.3 SEC Settlements and Consent Decrees

Most SEC enforcement actions in which the agency charges the target with violations of the securities laws (about 9 in 10) are settled by consent where the target neither admits nor denies SEC allegations. Sometimes the settlement occurs before the Commission authorizes an enforcement action, but often the settlement happens once the Commission authorizes an administrative or court enforcement proceeding, but before a formal complaint is filed.

Settlements are often embodied in a formal judicial consent decree, which can trigger judicial contempt liability for noncompliance. Whether embodied in a judicial decree or an administrative order, settlements are a matter of public record and are posted on the SEC's website. Many factors explain why over 90 percent of enforcement actions end in settlement, including the cost of litigation, adverse publicity, disruption of business activities, and the risk that any adverse finding might be used in private litigation after a formal SEC victory.

To encourage cooperation, the SEC staff often notifies targets of its investigations and gives the target a chance to submit a written statement to the SEC — known as a "Wells submission," named after the chair of an advisory committee that recommended the practice. Securities Act Rel. No. 5310 (1973). A Wells submission, unlike a pretrial brief in civil litigation, must be prepared without the advantage of discovery. It puts the submitter in the uncomfortable position of choosing between being obfuscatory or disclosing information the SEC may not yet have. See also *In re Initial Public Offering Securities Litigation*, Fed. Sec. L. Rep. (CCH) ¶92,638 (S.D.N.Y. 2004) (compelling discovery of Wells submission in private litigation). The SEC must commence an action within 180 days of providing a written Wells notice to a proposed defendant. Dodd-Frank §929U (allowing deadline to be extended in "complex" cases).

§12.3 JUDICIAL ENFORCEMENT: INJUNCTIONS AND OTHER REMEDIES

Each of the federal securities laws authorizes the SEC to seek injunctions in federal district court against ongoing violations of the securities laws. See Securities Act §20(b); Exchange Act §21(d) (including violation of SRO rules); Investment Company Act §42(d); Investment Advisers Act §209.

Court litigation involves significantly more formality than administrative proceedings. The SEC, as authorized by Dodd-Frank, can serve trial subpoenas nationwide, thus allowing the agency to compel trial witnesses to provide in-court testimony (not just videotaped depositions) regardless of where they reside. Dodd-Frank §929E (amending Fed. R. Civ. Proc. 45(c)(3)(A)(ii)). The discovery of evidence is governed by the Federal Rules of Civil Procedure, and the presentation of evidence in court is governed by the Federal Rules of Evidence. The SEC must prove its case (even when it seeks disbarment or monetary penalties) by a "preponderance of evidence," a standard significantly lower than that required in a criminal prosecution. See *Steadman v. SEC*, 450 U.S. 91 (1981). SEC injunctive actions will typically be heard by a judge, unless the SEC is also seeking civil monetary penalties. In such a case, the defendant has a constitutional right to a jury trial on the issues relevant to liability.

In addition to injunctive authority, federal courts have express authority to bar or suspend any individual who has violated the antifraud provisions (including Securities Act §17 and Exchange Act Rule 10b-5) from serving as an officer or director of any reporting company or other organization required to file reports with the SEC. Securities Act §20(e); Exchange Act §21(d)(2). Bars from holding corporate office may be particularly appropriate and have been used in SEC injunctive actions when a company official aids and abets a securities violation.

§12.3.1 Standard for Relief

As when injunctive relief is sought in other judicial contexts, it is not enough for the SEC to show merely a violation of the federal securities laws; it must show a "reasonable likelihood that the defendant will again violate the securities laws." *Aaron v. SEC*, 446 U.S. 680 (1980). Whether there is a reasonable likelihood of future violations depends on such factors as the degree of culpability, the sincerity of the defendant's assurances not to repeat the violations, whether the violations were isolated or recurrent, the defendant's contrition, the gravity of the offense, and the defendant's culpability (including whether she relied on advice of counsel). Balanced against the factors for injunctive relief, courts consider whether the injunction would have an adverse effect on the defendant.

§12.3.2 Types of Relief

Courts have broad authority to grant relief sought by the SEC. In addition, spurred by the SEC, courts have shown remarkable ingenuity (and audacity) in ordering ancillary and structural relief intended to deter and prevent further violations of the securities laws.

Injunctions

The SEC can seek *temporary restraining orders* and *preliminary injunctions* against any person who may be violating or about to violate the federal securities laws. In addition, the Sarbanes-Oxley Act authorizes the SEC to seek a temporary judicial asset freeze for 45 days (which may be extended under some circumstances) whenever an SEC investigation into possible violations suggests a public company will make "extraordinary payments" to insiders. Exchange Act §21C(c)(3)(A)(i). Permanent injunctions, including to freeze assets and to enjoin future violations of the securities laws, are available on a showing that future violations by the person are reasonably likely.

Under vague and tantalizing new authority added by the Sarbanes-Oxley Act, the SEC in a judicial enforcement action may seek, and the federal court may grant, "any equitable relief that may be appropriate or necessary for the benefit of investors." Exchange Act §21(d)(5). Does this mean a judge could grant any equitable relief he thinks would benefit investors? Are there any implicit limitations? Congress provided no answers. Sarbanes-Oxley §305.

Disgorgement

The SEC can seek *disgorgement* of the defendant's ill-gotten gains to the U.S. Treasury — a frequent, and lucrative, remedy in SEC injunctive actions.

Disgorgement monies (as well as civil monetary penalties) are to be placed in a fund "for the benefit of victims" of securities violations. Sarbanes-Oxley §308.

Civil Penalties

The SEC can seek a judicial order of *civil monetary penalties* (beyond disgorgement) against any person for violations of the securities laws or of an SEC cease-and-desist order, if the penalty is in the "public interest." Securities Act §20(d); Exchange Act §21(d)(3). The Securities Enforcement Remedies and Penny Stock Reform Act of 1990 establishes a tiered system of judicially imposed money penalties for violations of the federal securities laws and SEC cease-and-desist orders. Securities Act §20(d); Exchange Act §21(d)(3). The penalties vary depending on whether the defendant is a natural person or legal entity, whether there is fraud, deceit, manipulation or disregard of regulatory requirements, and whether there were substantial losses to other persons. Exchange Act §21(d) (maximum penalties vary from $5,000 to $100,000 for natural persons, and from $50,000 to $500,000 for entities).

Change Corporate Management

On occasion, courts have ordered corporate offenders to *appoint corporate officials*, such as independent members to the board of directors or to specific board committees. In some cases, courts have also ordered the appointment of special counsel to investigate securities violations. Likewise, federal courts have *barred company officials* from serving as corporate officers or directors when the official participates in a securities violation. See *SEC v. Posner*, 16 F.3d 520 (2d Cir. 1994) (holding that bar within general equitable powers of federal courts if defendant has history of securities law violations).

The Securities Enforcement Remedies and Penny Stock Reform Act of 1990 (as amended by Sarbanes-Oxley §305) expressly authorizes federal courts to bar or suspend an individual whose conduct shows "unfitness" to serve as an officer or director of any reporting company or other organization required to file reports with the SEC. Securities Act §20(e) (for violations of §17(a)(1)); Exchange Act §21(d)(2) (for violations of §10(b) or Rule 10b-5). In addition, Dodd-Frank authorizes the SEC to impose "collateral bars," so that, for example, when a registered representative of a broker-dealer violates rules applicable to broker-dealers, that representative is barred from associating with not only broker-dealers but also other regulated firms such as investment advisers and investment companies. Dodd-Frank §925.

A study of SEC judicial enforcement after the 1990 Act found that most SEC settlements of court enforcement actions involved both civil penalties and an injunctive sanction, even though most cases imposing civil penalties have involved first-time offenders, not recidivists.

§12.3.3 Effect of Injunction

A court-granted injunction in an SEC enforcement action reflects a judicial finding that there has been a violation and that the enjoined party has a propensity to violate again the federal securities laws. For this reason, SEC injunctions carry with them significant regulatory baggage. If the injunction relates to a registrant or its officials, it must be disclosed in Securities Act and Exchange Act periodic filings. See Regulation S-K, item 401(f). Moreover, the exemptions from Securities Act registration pursuant to Regulation A and Rule 505 (see §5.2.3) are unavailable if the issuer (or one of its officers, directors, partners, 10-percent beneficial owners, or underwriters) has in the past five years been temporarily or permanently enjoined for violating the securities laws — the so-called "bad boy" disqualifications. Securities Act Rule 262 (time period is ten years for individuals convicted of certain securities-related felonies or misdemeanors); Rule 505(b)(2)(iii).

Judicial findings in an injunction action brought by the SEC have preclusive effect and may be used collaterally in subsequent private litigation. See *Parklane Hosiery Co. v. Shore*, 439 U.S. 322 (1979) (upholding offensive use of collateral estoppel, if private plaintiff could not have easily joined in enforcement action and defendant had a full opportunity to litigate issue). This means that once a court has found a violation of the securities laws the factual and legal findings underlying the court's decision may be used affirmatively by private litigants in lawsuits seeking money damages. (A judicial finding of non-violation, however, may not be used defensively against private litigants who were not parties to the first litigation.)

SEC adjudications have a similar preclusive effect, if the defendant had a full opportunity to litigate the issue. In addition, findings of fact in an SEC consent order may be admitted as evidence in subsequent litigation with adverse consequences for those who enter such orders. Findings of law in negotiated consent orders, though not reviewed in court, receive precedential weight in subsequent SEC cases, allowing the SEC to promulgate "law" through an *ex parte* process.

§12.3.4 Modification or Dissolution of SEC Injunctions

Parties face a heavy burden to modify or dissolve an injunction in an action brought by the SEC. The traditional judicial view has been that the affected parties must make a clear showing that changes in circumstances are so significant that dangers once thought substantial are attenuated, and the parties would suffer a hardship so extreme and unexpected as to be oppressive. See *United States v. Swift & Co.*, 286 U.S. 106 (1932). More recently, lower courts have departed from the *Swift* standards with a more flexible approach that weighs the decree's continuing usefulness and the hardship on the enjoined party.

§12.3.5 Statute of Limitations

Except for the five-year period specified for civil monetary penalties in insider trading cases, there is no express statute of limitations for SEC enforcement actions (administrative or judicial). Exchange Act §21A(d)(5). Some courts have acceded to the SEC position that no limitations period should be implied on the theory SEC enforcement actions aim at deterrence, not compensation. Other courts have interpreted the federal statute of limitations applicable to civil fines and penalties, as applicable to SEC enforcement actions seeking to impose a punishment, such as censure or suspension. 28 U.S.C. §2462 ("within five years from the date when the claim first accrued").

§12.4 ENFORCEMENT AGAINST SECURITIES PROFESSIONALS

The corporate scandals of the 2000s focused attention on accountants and securities lawyers in their roles as financial auditors and legal advisers for public companies. The Sarbanes-Oxley Act fundamentally altered the source and content of regulation affecting these professionals in their work for public companies. Although accountant and lawyers have long had duties not to assist in client fraud, their professional roles now include the active prevention of client misconduct.

Traditionally, the SEC has exercised supervisory authority over accountants by specifying "independence" standards for those that audited public companies and over securities attorneys under its "rules of practice." The SEC regulatory role, however, was intentionally peripheral. Before the Sarbanes-Oxley Act, the responsibilities of accountants were mainly specified by independent organizations such as the Financial Accounting Standards Board (FASB). Likewise, the responsibilities of lawyers to corporate clients were largely a matter of legal ethics rules and disciplinary proceedings — both promulgated and administered at the state level.

For accountants, the Sarbanes-Oxley Act changes this by creating a new independent board under SEC supervision to regulate auditors — the Public Company Accounting Oversight Board (PCAOB). The Act also imposes conflict-of-interest rules for auditors of public companies by forbidding these auditors from performing specified non-audit services for current audit clients. For lawyers, the Act mandates new SEC rules on the professional conduct of securities lawyers that include duties to report internally securities fraud and other company misconduct.

§12.4.1 SEC Rules of Practice

Since 1935 the SEC's rules have included the power to discipline accountants and attorneys "practicing before" the agency. Under Rule 102(e) the SEC assumed the power to censure, suspend or ban any professional engaged in securities work who lacked qualifications, engaged in unethical professional conduct, or willfully violated (or aided and abetted those who violated) the federal securities laws. Courts uniformly accepted the SEC's power to promulgate its rules of practice, as part of its statutory authority to make rules "as necessary or appropriate." *Touche Ross & Co. v. SEC*, 609 F.2d 570 (2d Cir. 1979). (Rule 102(e) was formerly numbered 2(e).)

Through a common law process of administrative decisionmaking, the SEC used Rule 102(e) routinely to set standards of conduct and professionalism for the accounting profession. For example, the SEC over time adopted the view that accountants could be subject to disciplinary action if they acted intentionally, recklessly or negligently. In 1998, this view was written into Rule 102(e), which for accountants defines negligent conduct to include either "a single instance of highly unreasonable conduct" or "repeated instances of unreasonable conduct." For attorneys and other securities professionals, however, the SEC traditionally imposed 102(e) sanctions only in cases of intentional misconduct.

In 2002 Congress codified Rule 102(e) — including the culpability standards for accountants — in a new §4C of the Exchange Act. (The new section, however, does not specify the culpability standard for lawyers and other non-accountant professionals.) The provision removes any doubts about the SEC's authority to discipline lawyers and accountants practicing before the agency. Unclear, however, is whether the codification validates the standards of professional conduct formulated over time by the SEC in its prior decisions under Rule 102(e) or the extent of the SEC's prerogatives to modify its rules of practice.

§12.4.2 Accountant Discipline

Accountants serve important watchdog and gatekeeper functions under the U.S. securities laws. Within companies, they generate the financial information at the heart of the U.S. disclosure system. As outside auditors, they provide assurances to investors that the company's financial disclosures are accurate, complete, and comparable across firms. The federal securities laws require audited financials for companies selling securities to public investors, for publicly traded companies making periodic reports, and for mutual funds disclosing portfolio performance.

Accountants have long been governed by private professional standards promulgated by the American Institute of Certified Public Accountants. As applied to audits, these standards specify the undertaking of audits, the testing of internal controls, the giving of opinions, and the keeping of client confidences. The Sarbanes-Oxley Act, however, shifts oversight of the accounting profession to a new Public Company Accounting Oversight Board — a non-profit corporation whose members and employees are not deemed government officials. Sarbanes-Oxley §101. The PCAOB has five members, two of which must have an accountancy background. Board members, who are appointed by the SEC and serve five-year terms, may not engage in another profession or business while on the Board, and may not work for an accounting firm for the year after they leave the Board. See *Free Enterprise Fund v. PCAOB*, 561 U.S. _____ (2010) (upholding Sarbanes-Oxley provisions on PCAOB appointment, but striking down and severing for-cause removal provision). The PCAOB, under the supervision of the SEC, is charged with establishing auditing, ethics and enforcement standards for accountants who engage in public company audits.

Accounting firms that audit public companies must register with the PCAOB and become subject to auditing, quality control, and ethics standards promulgated by the Board. Sarbanes-Oxley §§102, 103. The Act also requires that the PCAOB inspect registered accounting firms, with annual inspections of firms auditing more than 100 public companies. Sarbanes-Oxley §104. Certain standards are required by the Sarbanes-Oxley Act, including retention for seven years of auditing papers, "second partner" review of public company audits, and testing of accounting systems during such audits. Most standards, however, are left for the Board to develop, subject to SEC review and approval. Thus, proposed Board rules must be filed with the SEC for public comment and become effective only with SEC approval.

The PCAOB, like other self-regulatory organizations charged with oversight of securities professionals, has broad authority to investigate violations of the Sarbanes-Oxley requirements, the Board's rules, professional accounting standards, or the federal securities laws (and SEC rules) dealing with audit reports. Sarbanes-Oxley §105(c). Sanctions include the censure, bar or suspension of accounting firms or their associates, as well as substantial civil penalties. Heavier sanctions require a finding of intentional, knowing or reckless conduct, or repeated negligence. Sanctions may be appealed to the SEC, which has the power to cancel, modify or even increase the sanctions. Sarbanes-Oxley §107(c).

The Sarbanes-Oxley Act also addresses the independence of accounting firms in the auditing of public companies. The issue had arisen in the 1990s as the major accounting firms began to provide more non-auditing services to clients, leading to widespread concerns that the firms often compromised auditing standards to garner non-auditing business (such as business consulting, software design, tax advice and legal services).

Largely codifying rules promulgated by the SEC in 2000, the Sarbanes-Oxley Act prohibits a long list of non-audit services by registered accounting firms performing audits of public companies. Among the prohibited services are bookkeeping, financial system design, valuation and appraisal, as well as actuarial, managerial, investment, and legal services. Exchange Act §10A(g). Non-audit services that are not prohibited by the Act, such as tax advice, are permitted only if approved in advance by the company's audit committee.

In addition, the Sarbanes-Oxley Act seeks to address the coziness between auditors and clients engendered, in part, by the practice of accounting firms paying partners for obtaining and keeping large clients. The Act requires the rotation of the lead audit partner at least every five years. Exchange Act §10A(j).

§12.4.3 Lawyer Discipline

Securities lawyers act as the conscience of the securities industry, structuring and channeling client desires to fit regulatory prescriptions. In addition, many securities transactions depend on a lawyer's favorable legal opinion: the resale of restricted securities, the sale of a control person's stock into a public market, the offering of securities in an unregistered private transaction, and an investment banker's underwriting of a public offering.

But, just as the superego carries guilt, the lawyer's role as conscience carries responsibility. The SEC has often taken the position that securities lawyers, like accountants who certify financial statements, have a special responsibility to the public. A securities lawyer who knowingly assists a client in a securities fraud becomes subject to civil and criminal aiding and abetting liability. Beyond this the SEC has asserted that securities lawyers who have reason to believe a client will violate the securities laws must inform the SEC, though the SEC's "up the ladder" reporting rule does not require a lawyer to report outside the company.

Two leading cases address the special responsibilities of securities lawyers under the federal securities laws. In *SEC v. National Student Marketing Corp.*, 457 F. Supp. 682 (D.D.C. 1978), the SEC asked the court to impose liability on lawyers who had allowed a merger to go forward after accountants had told the lawyers that the proxy statement for the merger contained misleading financial information. The case involved the merger of Interstate National into National Student Marketing. On the eve of the vote by Interstate's shareholders, lawyers and executives of the two companies discussed potentially false financial information by NSMC in the proxy solicitation that had been sent to Interstate shareholders. Despite the disquieting information, lawyers for each party opined their client had not violated "any federal or state statute or regulation to the knowledge of counsel." Interstate's lawyers knew that an unfavorable opinion would, in all likelihood, have delayed the shareholder vote and given NSMC a chance to renegotiate the merger price. The merger was approved, and Interstate shareholders received NSMC stock. Soon afterward, when stories of NSMC's troubled finances surfaced, the SEC sued multiple parties, including the lawyers for both sides. Eventually, the lawyers for NSMC settled with the SEC, despite their argument they had no duty to unravel their client's merger by telling the *other party's shareholders* of potential fraud by their client. After trial, the lawyers for Interstate were found liable for aiding and abetting the fraud of the Interstate executives.

In the second case, In *re Carter & Johnson*, [1981 Transfer Binder] Fed. Sec. L. Rep. (CCH) ¶82,847 (SEC 1981), two partners of an established Wall Street law firm assisted a financially struggling client to negotiate loan agreements and later advised the client in connection with its plans to "wind down" its business. The lawyers, however, failed to object when the client gave its shareholders overstated projections and issued optimistic press releases, while withholding information on the company's financial problems. The SEC faulted the lawyers for not ensuring that their disclosure advice was followed and for failing to investigate questionable information. The SEC concluded that lawyers aware their clients are engaged in the substantial and continuing failure to meet disclosure requirements violate professional standards by not taking prompt steps to end the client's non-compliance. According to the SEC, those steps include counseling accurate disclosure, approaching the board of directors or other senior management, or resigning if the conduct becomes "extreme or irretrievable."

After the *Carter & Johnson* proceeding, the legal profession protested the SEC's move to set professional standards for securities lawyers. In response, the SEC chose to desist and through 2003 did not bring an enforcement action against a lawyer claiming improper professional conduct. See *Disciplinary Proceedings Involving Professionals Appearing or Practicing Before the Commission*, Exchange Act Rel. No. 25893 (July 13, 1998) (stating that great majority of proceedings against lawyers involve violations of law and, as matter of policy, Commission "generally refrains" from bringing enforcement actions involving professional obligations of attorneys). The SEC reversed course in 2003 when it adopted a new rule, pursuant to the Sarbanes-Oxley Act, on the professional duties of securities lawyers to internally report evidence of violations of U.S. securities law and breaches of fiduciary duty (see below).

§12.4.4 Reporting "Up the Ladder"

A persistent question of professional ethics for accountants and lawyers working for public companies has been the duty to take action when a client engages or proposes to engage in securities fraud or other misconduct. The general answer has been that accountants and lawyers have professional duties to advise against such conduct, but there has been disagreement on the extent to which those duties compel professionals to report "up the ladder of command" to senior management, the board of directors, the SEC or other government regulators, or even investors.

Accountants

For accountants, Congress offered some clarity in the Private Securities Litigation Reform Act of 1995 by requiring that auditors of public companies that become aware of an illegal act must inform "the appropriate level of management." Exchange Act §10A. If the illegal act has a material effect on the company's financials and management fails to respond, the auditor must report the information to the company's board of directors. If the board of directors receives such a report, the company must notify the SEC of the report (with a copy to the auditor). If the company then fails to notify the SEC, the auditor must resign or notify the SEC of the report. The SEC can bring an enforcement action, with the possibility of civil penalties, against an accounting firm that does not properly report illegality.

Securities Lawyers

Rule 205 (promulgated by the SEC in 2003, as mandated by the Sarbanes-Oxley Act) requires lawyers working as outside counsel or as employees of a public company to report securities fraud up the ladder — at least within the company. Sarbanes-Oxley §307; 17 CFR §205. As a result, Rule 205 imposes a "gatekeeper" role on securities lawyers who, besides acting as advocates and transactional engineers for their corporate clients, must monitor the accuracy of corporate disclosures and the behavior of corporate officials.

Rule 205 sets forth minimum standards of professional conduct for attorneys engaged in transactional or litigation practice involving the U.S. securities laws. (Rule 205 exempts attorneys admitted to practice outside the United States, whose work on U.S. securities matters is only incidental or in consultation with a U.S. securities lawyer and who does not give legal advice regarding U.S. securities laws. Rule 205.2(j).) Under the rule, a securities lawyer representing a corporate issuer has a duty to report "evidence of a material violation" of U.S. securities law or "material breach of fiduciary duties" by the issuer or any officer, director, employee or agent of the issuer. Rules 205.2(i), 205.3(b)(1).

The up-the-ladder reporting duty extends to both inside and outside counsel. Supervising attorneys are also obligated to make subordinate attorneys aware of their reporting obligations, as well as to report material violations brought to their attention by their subordinates. Rule 205.4. Subordinate attorneys also have reporting obligations, which they can satisfy by telling their supervisor who must then report the evidence of material violation. Rule 205.5. The report must be made first to the issuer's general counsel (or to both the general counsel and chief executive officer) and then, if there is no appropriate response, to a committee of the board or the full board of directors. Rule 205.3(b). The general counsel (as a securities lawyer) is obligated to investigate the report and, if he finds a material violation, to undertake an appropriate response. Rule 205.3(c). The rule creates an alternative reporting procedure if the issuer has a legal compliance committee.

Securities lawyers who violate the Rule 205 requirements can be subject to SEC discipline, with sanctions that include censure and suspension — though, apparently, not monetary fines. Rule 205.6. The SEC, however, states that the SEC has exclusive enforcement authority and that the rule does not create a private right of action. Rule 205.7.

Left unresolved in the current Rule 205 is whether an attorney who reports a violation up the internal ladder of command, but without an adequate response, must resign (quietly or noisily) or report the material violation to the SEC, other government officials, or even shareholders. Rule 205, as promulgated in 2003, does not include a requirement that securities lawyers make a "noisy withdrawal" when the attorney concluded the board of directors had not responded appropriately to the report of violations.

Instead, the SEC left for further discussion (and negotiation) a proposal calling for outside attorneys to withdraw from the representation of a non-responsive issuer and immediately give written notice to the SEC that their withdrawal "was based on professional considerations." Proposed Rule 205.3(d). *Proposed Rule: Implementation of Standards of Professional Conduct for Attorney*, Exchange Act Rel. No. 47282 (2003). Inside attorneys, dissatisfied with the issuer's response, would be required to immediately notify the SEC of their intention to disaffirm documents filed with the SEC that may be false or misleading. In both instances, the lawyer's notice to the SEC would be an open invitation to launch an agency investigation.

State Professionalism Standards

In some respects, the SEC professional standards that require securities lawyers to act as "gatekeepers" of securities compliance are inconsistent with state legal ethics rules. The ABA Model Rules generally assume a relationship of trust and confidence between lawyer and client. For example, a lawyer need not investigate facts given to her by her client unless the lawyer knows or is reckless in not knowing of material misrepresentations or omissions by the client. The SEC, however, requires that securities lawyers make reasonable investigation of facts given by corporate officials when they prepare disclosure documents or opinion letters.

In 2003, after much debate, the American Bar Association amended its Model Rules of Professional Conduct to bring them in line with the SEC's new "up the ladder" rules. Under revised Model Rule 1.13, a lawyer acting for an issuer who "knows" a corporate official is violating an obligation to the issuer or engaged in a legal violation that might be imputed to the issuer (if it is likely to substantially injure the issuer) the lawyer must "proceed as is reasonably necessary in the best interest of the organization." The Official Comment states that "ordinarily" this requires referring such matters to a higher authority in the organization, though sometimes it may be enough to ask the corporate official involved to "reconsider the matter." The Official Comment also clarifies that "when reasonably necessary" the lawyer may be required to take the matter to "the highest authority" in the organization — usually the board of directors.

In addition, the ABA amended its Model Rule 1.6 to permit a lawyer to disclose client confidences "to prevent the client from committing a crime or fraud that is reasonably certain to result in substantial injury" to investors' financial interests. (Before the rule change, a lawyer could reveal client confidences only if the client intended to commit a crime likely to result in imminent death or substantial bodily harm.) The new rule, however, does not go as far as those who have advocated for a "noisy withdrawal" or the stance taken by the SEC in *National Student Marketing* (see §12.4.3 above) that securities lawyers must disclose to the SEC that a client intends to violate the securities laws.

§12.5 CRIMINAL ENFORCEMENT

Supplementing SEC enforcement of the federal securities laws is criminal enforcement by the U.S. Department of Justice through its local U.S. attorneys. The DOJ, though having exclusive authority over criminal enforcement of the federal securities laws, often acts with SEC guidance and in response to SEC referrals. It is common for SEC staff to be assigned to the DOJ to assist in the preparation of criminal cases for trial. Besides seeking sanctions authorized by federal securities statutes, the DOJ has a veritable grab bag of other sanctions at its disposal.

Note on Recent Securities Enforcement Actions

The SEC and DOJ have been busy lately. Here are some illustrative uses of their federal securities enforcement powers:

SAC Capital Advisors, a large and profitable hedge fund, settled criminal charges brought by the DOJ that the fund had engaged in widespread insider trading. SAC Capital pled guilty to securities fraud and agreed to pay a criminal fine of $1.2 billion. The criminal settlement followed a $616 million civil settlement of insider-trading charges brought by the SEC. Steve Cohen, head of SAC Capital, still faces criminal indictments in the future.

Goldman Sachs, the largest and most profitable Wall Street securities firm, settled SEC charges that it had misled investors in collateralized debt obligation (CDO) transactions and agreed to pay a fine of $550 million.

Raj Rajaratnam, the founder of the Galleon hedge fund and a Wall Street billionaire, was convicted on various counts of insider trading. At trial, witnesses described inside tips Rajaratnam had received from a former Intel employee, bribes he made to a McKinsey & Co. partner to obtain tips, and tips from a Goldman Sachs board member about the firm's earnings reports. Describing Rajaratnam's insider-trading scheme as a "virus in our business culture," the trial judge sentenced Rajaratnam to 11 years in prison — the longest insider-trading term ever — and ordered him to pay a fine of $10 million and forfeit $53.8 million in trading profits.

§12.5.1 Use of Criminal Law in Securities Enforcement

Historically, criminal enforcement was used as a means to enforce well-established principles of federal securities regulation. Most "new law" — such as in the area of proxy fraud — was made in SEC enforcement actions or private litigation. The DOJ applied these principles in cases of egregious violations, for which administrative or private enforcement was seen as inadequate.

Beginning in the 1980s, however, the DOJ began to break new legal ground. In the area of insider trading, the foundational cases were criminal cases prosecuted on far-reaching theories of liability. For example, in the leading case on insider trading — *Chiarella v. United States*, 445 U.S. 222 (1980) — the Supreme Court articulated a theory for regulating classical insider trading, even though factually the case involved outsider trading (misappropriation). See §10.2.1.

Criminal enforcement has the advantage of sending a strong message of deterrence. Unlike private actions and SEC enforcement, where liability is often assessed against corporate and not individual violators, criminal enforcement of the federal securities laws has been aimed primarily at individuals. This has been particularly true in insider trading cases, where harm to particular investors or the corporation may be difficult to show.

§12.5.2 Criminal Violations of Federal Securities Law

Federal Securities Statutes

The federal securities laws criminalize securities violations by making it a crime for anyone to "willfully" violate any statutory provision or SEC rule, including the making of a false or misleading statement in a filing submitted to the SEC. Securities Act §24(a); Exchange Act §32(a) (requiring that false filings be made "willfully and knowingly"). Willful violations of the Securities Act registration requirements or antifraud standards are punishable by up to five years in prison and a $10,000 fine. Criminal penalties under the Exchange Act (as amended by the Sarbanes-Oxley Act) cover market fraud and insider trading, and are much steeper with prison terms up to 20 years and fines up to $5,000,000 for individuals and $25,000,000 for corporations. Exchange Act §32(a).

The statute of limitations for criminal actions is six years. See Dodd-Frank §1079A(b) (extending the limitations from general five-year period of 18 U.S.C. §3282).

Criminal Culpability

Willfulness in the *criminal* context generally implies that the defendant harbored an illegal purpose. It does not necessarily mean the defendant intended to violate the law, but rather that she knew that she was doing something wrong. Willfulness, for example, may exist even though a person who enters a securities transaction does not know about the SEC antifraud Rule 10b-5, if the person recognizes that she was engaged in deception.

Is there a "willful" violation of a rule, such as Rule 10b-5, if the defendant did not know of the rule's existence? Courts have reasoned that given the statutory proviso that a defendant who does not know of a rule cannot be *imprisoned* the term "willfully" must include unwitting rule violations. Accordingly, the government need only prove (1) the defendant realized he was doing a wrongful act, (2) the wrongful act violated the securities laws, and (3) the wrongful act made the violation likely.

Some courts, applying an even less demanding interpretation of "willfulness," have concluded that a *reckless* violation of a securities rule — that is, circumstances strongly suggest the person knew his conduct was wrongful — is criminally willful. Moreover, lower courts have construed the "knowingly" standard of Exchange Act §32(a) to be essentially empty, using the theory (certainly a fiction) that every person is charged "with knowledge of the standards prescribed in the securities acts." The effect is that prosecution of criminal defendants in securities cases is subject to only limited "state of mind" safeguards.

§12.5.3 Securities Activities Creating Criminal Liability

What securities activities are criminal? The Securities Act and Exchange Act, enacted in 1933 and 1934, generally criminalize "willful" violations of the federal securities statutes and SEC rules. Some 70 years later, the Sarbanes-Oxley Act criminalizes new categories of "knowing" securities-related conduct.

Securities Law Violations

The Securities Act speaks broadly of any violation of a statutory provision or "any rule or regulation" promulgated by the SEC. Securities Act §24. The Exchange Act is narrower, including statutory provisions and "any rule or regulation thereunder the violation of which is made unlawful or the observance of which is required under the terms of this Act." Exchange Act §32(a).

What about administrative requirements that are technical and ambiguous? The U.S. Supreme Court has stated in *dicta* that ambiguity in a criminal securities case "should be resolved in favor of lenity." But the Court has also shown remarkable pliability in interpreting Rule 10b-5 (a rule prohibiting fraudulent misstatements) to encompass silence in the face of a duty to disclose, whether the duty is owed to the trading investors or to the source of the information.

Nonetheless, federal courts have generally harmonized their interpretation of the elements of securities law violations whether the case is criminal or civil. A few exceptions, however, are significant. While limiting standing in private cases to actual purchasers and sellers, the courts have not imposed any standing requirement on the government. Moreover, the government need not prove reliance by any investor to establish a violation of the antifraud provisions.

In a significant departure from the general harmonization of civil and criminal securities standards, the Sarbanes-Oxley Act creates a new crime of securities fraud for which there is no civil counterpart. Added to the general federal criminal code, the new §1348 covers anyone who "knowingly executes, or attempts to execute, a scheme" (1) to defraud any person in connection with the securities of a public company, or (2) to obtain money or property falsely in connection with the trading of public company securities. 18 U.S.C. §1348 (imprisonment up to 25 years). The "knowing" standard of culpability is arguably lower than the "willful" standard of the securities laws. And the coverage may be broader than that of Rule 10b-5, which requires actual trading in securities (not required by the first clause of §1348) and deception relating to the security (not required by the second clause of §1348). Unlike Rule 10b-5, however, the new securities fraud crime covers only securities in publicly traded companies.

Filing Violations

Both the Securities Act and Exchange Act criminalize the filing of false documents with the SEC. Securities Act §24 (false or misleading statement in the registration statement); Exchange Act §32(a) (false or misleading statements required to be filed under Act or rules, or by any self-regulatory organization). To avoid issues of coverage, such as when a filing is accompanied by false oral statement, the DOJ has tended to pursue filing crimes under a more general statute that prohibits false written and oral statements to the government. 18 U.S.C. §1001(a).

In addition, the Sarbanes-Oxley Act creates new criminal liability for officers of public companies who falsely certify their company's financial reports. 18 U.S.C. §1350. For periodic reports filed under the Exchange Act, the company's chief executive officer and chief financial officer must certify in writing (1) any reports containing financial statements fully comply with the SEC's disclosure standards (including generally accepted accounting principles), and (2) the information in the report fairly presents the company's finances. A CEO or CFO who certifies a report "knowing" it does not comport with these requirements is subject to fines up to $1,000,000 or a prison term up to 10 years. "Willful" certifications that fail this standard are subject to fines up to $5,000,000 or a prison term up to 20 years. The provision thus draws a distinction between "knowing" and "willful" misdeeds, strongly suggesting that "knowing" violations involve a lower standard of culpability — perhaps akin to the "awareness" standard for civil liability under Rule 10b-5. See §10.2.1.

Record Tampering

The Sarbanes-Oxley Act also creates new crimes related to record-keeping, thus clarifying and expanding the criminal liability under the federal securities laws. The new crimes are made part of the general federal criminal code. The crimes extend beyond securities-related activities, their genesis rooted in the widespread document destruction surrounding the collapse at Enron Corporation. The new provisions apply to cover the "destruction, alteration, or falsification of records in federal investigations and bankruptcy," the "destruction of audit records," and "tampering with a record or otherwise impeding an official proceeding." 18 U.S.C. §1519, 1520, 1512(c).

Multiple Actor Liability

Although courts no longer imply aiding and abetting liability for secondary participants in private securities actions (see §9.2.2), the DOJ has used the general criminal statutes on aiding and abetting to prosecute joint activities under the Securities Act and the Exchange Act. Aiding and abetting a Rule 10b-5 violation requires (1) the existence of an independent disclosure violation, (2) the abettor's actual knowledge (or reckless disregard) of the misrepresentation and his role in furthering it, and (3) the abettor's providing substantial assistance in the transaction that harms the investor.

The DOJ has also used the general criminal attempt and conspiracy statutes in securities cases. 18 U.S.C. §371. Although still untested, the Sarbanes-Oxley Act appears to expand attempt and conspiracy liability in cases of securities fraud and false certification of financial reports. 18 U.S.C. §1349. Under the new provision, any person "who attempts or conspires to commit" one of these offenses is subject to the same penalties and prescribed for the offense. Unclear is whether the usual elements of an attempt or conspiracy found under the general provisions apply.

§12.5.4 Non-Securities Criminal Law Applied to Securities Activities

The DOJ has also turned in securities cases to the broad coverage of the federal mail and wire fraud statutes (which criminalize fraud that has some connection to interstate commerce) and the federal anti-racketeering statute (which criminalizes commercial activities carried out by criminal organizations).

Mail and Wire Fraud Statutes

The federal mail and wire fraud statutes subject to criminal prosecution any person who (1) engages in a fraudulent scheme or falsely obtains "property or money" and (2) accomplishes the scheme or false pretenses through the use of interstate wire communications or the mails (a jurisdictional requirement). 18 U.S.C. §1343 (wire fraud); §1341 (mail fraud).

It is not necessary that fraudulent information be mailed or transmitted over the wires (faxes or internet), but simply that these means were used as part of the fraudulent scheme. It is not necessary that the fraud have succeeded or that victims relied on the fraudulent information. Amended by the Sarbanes-Oxley Act, the statutes provide for jail terms of up to 20 years (and up to 30 years for violations involving a financial institution).

The most famous use of the mail and wire fraud statutes in federal securities litigation has been in prosecuting insider trading cases.

Carpenter v. United States, 484 U.S. 19 (1987), illustrates. In the case, a reporter for the *Wall Street Journal*, one Winans, tipped information from upcoming stories in an influential column that he wrote called "Heard on the Street." Using publicly available sources, the column invariably affected the stock prices of companies on which it reported. The newspaper had a policy of keeping confidential before publication the identity of the featured companies to protect the appearance of journalistic integrity. Winans was convicted for misappropriating information that was to appear in the column and tipping it to a friend and a broker, even though the *Wall Street Journal* had no financial interest in the trading.

The Supreme Court concluded Winans had fraudulently misappropriated "an intangible property right" within the meaning of the mail and wire fraud statutes, namely the newspaper's interest in pre-publication confidentiality. The fraudulent scheme came in Winans "playing the role of a loyal employee" while tipping others to the confidential information, and the use of the mails and wire services came in the national circulation of the newspaper. The fraud was thus on The Wall Street Journal, not necessarily the unwitting investors who traded with Winans' tippees. The analysis follows from insider trading cases prosecuted under Rule 10b-5, which requires that reticent trading is fraudulent only by identifying the breach of a duty of confidentiality.

Racketeer Influenced and Corrupt Organizations Act (RICO)

Congress passed RICO in 1970 to combat organized crime. Constitutionally disabled from criminalizing mere membership in organized crime, RICO forbids various activities associated with criminal organizations. The statutory elements are Byzantine in their reach and complexity.

RICO prohibits any person from engaging in a pattern of racketeering activities in four circumstances: (1) buying some or all of an "enterprise" with racketeering profits; (2) acquiring some or all of an "enterprise" through racketeering activities; (3) conducting the affairs of an "enterprise" through racketeering activities; and (4) conspiring to do (1)-(3). A pattern of racketeering activity is defined as two or more acts of wrongful behavior, including (among much other nefarious behavior) mail and wire fraud and "fraud in the sale of securities." 18 U.S.C. §1962.

Before 1995, RICO had been a near staple of private securities fraud litigation, since private civil RICO actions carry trebled damages and attorneys' fees. 18 U.S.C. §1964(c) (authorizing private action by any person "injured in his business or property" by reason of prohibited racketeering activities). In 1995 Congress decided that not every pattern of fraudulent securities sales warrants civil RICO liability, and the Private Securities Litigation Reform Act eliminates conduct "actionable as fraud in the purchase or sale of securities" as a predicate act of racketeering in a civil RICO action.

Nonetheless, the PSLRA allows for civil RICO liability for securities fraud if the defendant has been criminally convicted.

Although the PSLRA largely eliminates *civil* RICO liability in cases of securities fraud, *criminal* RICO liability still exists for those who engage in a pattern of securities fraud. 18 U.S.C. §1963. RICO raises a variety of interpretive questions, which the Supreme Court has resolved over time:

- Predicate acts form a "pattern" if they have a relationship or continuity toward accomplishing a common objective. Unrelated predicate acts, or a sequence unlikely to continue, do not satisfy the pattern element. *H. J. Inc. v. Northwestern Bell Telephone Co.*, 492 U.S. 229 (1989) (bribes over six months to influence regulator could constitute a pattern). Lower courts have focused on whether the criminal conduct was sporadic or continued over a substantial period of time.

- For a corporate outsider to "conduct or participate" in a pattern of racketeering activity, the outsider must infiltrate or manage the corporation's business through racketeering activities. *Reves v. Ernst & Young*, 507 U.S. 170 (1993) (outside accountant who prepared financials overstating firm assets, but who was not involved in the firm's business, did not "conduct or participate" in securities fraud perpetrated by firm insiders). Thus, criminal liability is limited to participants who operate or manage the enterprise; outsiders who perform auditing or consultant functions will typically lack such control.

- A pattern of racketeering activities does not in itself create an "enterprise." Instead, "pattern of racketeering activity" and "enterprise" are separate elements of the RICO offense. *United States v. Turkette*, 452 U.S. 576 (1981) (though proof to establish the elements may "in particular cases coalesce"). An enterprise is established on a showing of an ongoing organization, formal or informal, where the various associates function as an ongoing unit.

Lower courts have been discrepant in their interpretation of the predicate act of "fraud in the sale of securities." Some courts have required that the defendant actually sell securities by means of false statements, while others have taken a more liberal approach and accepted frauds involving a sale of securities or even the *fraudulent purchase* of securities. Courts are also divided on whether filing violations constitute fraud, with some finding fraud given the effect of a false filing on investors and markets and others requiring actual false statements. On the issue of the required state of mind, some courts have required actual knowledge of illegal activities and others simply deliberateness beyond negligence or mistake.

Criminal RICO sanctions include pre-trial asset freezes, fines, imprisonment of up to 20 years, and mandatory forfeiture of property acquired through the RICO violation.

§12.5.5 Sentencing of Individual and Corporate Offenders

Sentencing Guidelines

Since 1989, fines and jail terms for federal crimes must conform to guidelines adopted by the U.S. Sentencing Commission. Without changing the maximum jail or maximum fines specified by statute, the Sentencing Guidelines specify sentencing ranges meant to make sentencing across cases more uniform by guiding and limiting the discretion of judges during sentencing. The Sentencing Table of the Guidelines uses a grid with numbers in vertical columns (offense level) and horizontal rows (criminal history category). In each grid intersection is a sentencing range expressed in months. For example, a defendant with offense level 26 and criminal history category I would be in a sentencing range of 63-78 months.

Individual Sentencing

For economic crimes, such as securities fraud, the Sentencing Guidelines have ebbed and flowed over their 20-year history in their treatment of individual sentencing. When first promulgated, the Sentencing Commission sought to change the prevalent judicial practice of imposing probationary sentences for non-violent economic crimes. The Guidelines specified "short but certain terms of confinement for many white-collar offenders."

In 2001, the Sentencing Commission amended the Guidelines in response to a perception that federal sentencing remained too lenient for those white-collar offenders who inflict heavy and widespread financial losses. Known as the Economic Crime Package, the Guidelines significantly raised the sentences of most mid- to high-loss offenders, while lowering the sentences of low-loss offenders.

After passage of the Sarbanes-Oxley Act of 2002, which added new offenses involving corporate/financial misconduct and significantly increased the maximum jail terms and fines for existing securities/financial crimes, the Sentencing Commission promulgated amendments that increased sentences for offenses involving 250 or more victims or losses of more than $200 million, for conduct that substantially endangered the solvency of large organizations, and for defendants who acted as officers or directors of publicly traded companies. Further amendments increased all sentencing levels for securities crimes prosecuted under any statute with a maximum jail term of 20 years or more, with the result that conviction of securities fraud involving losses of $70,000 or more results in imprisonment under the Guidelines. See *United States v. Booker*, 543 U.S. 220 (2005) (holding that federal sentencing guidelines are advisory, not mandatory).

Organizational Sentencing

Besides specifying sentences applicable to individuals, the federal Sentencing Guidelines also specify ranges of criminal fines to be imposed on corporations and other entities. The sentencing guidelines for corporations are complex. They set a "base fine" amount determined by using specified "offense levels" and multipliers that depend on the organization's characteristics and "culpability score."

Under this formula, organizational fines increase for corporations with more employees, corporations whose management participated in the offense, and corporations that failed to cooperate with the criminal investigation. Fines decrease for corporations with an "effective" compliance program to prevent and detect violations by employees, corporations that cooperated with prosecutors, and corporations that promptly accepted responsibility.

The Sentencing Guidelines for corporations specify criteria for a compliance program to be "effective." These criteria include (1) standards and procedures to reduce the prospects of criminal conduct and their communication to employees, (2) high-level personnel to oversee compliance, (3) procedures to monitor compliance and report violations, and (4) internal disciplining by those responsible for offenses.

Following the Sarbanes-Oxley Act, the Sentencing Commission in 2004 further amended the organizational guidelines. In a controversial move, the Sentencing Commission stipulated that one measure of organizational cooperation, which serves to reduce the level of fines, is the waiver of the attorney-client privilege and work product protection for internal documents relevant to the criminal investigation.

§12.5.6 Parallel Enforcement

Given the multiple layers of enforcement of the federal securities laws — private and public, including administrative, civil and criminal — it is not unusual for there to be parallel proceedings. Such situations raise questions about whether limitations on gathering evidence in criminal proceedings affect parallel administrative proceedings, whether information obtained in one proceeding can be used in another, whether findings in one proceeding are preclusive in other proceedings, and whether multiple sanctions can be imposed.

Evidence Gathering

Limitations on gathering evidence in criminal proceedings may limit the government's ability to gather the same information in an administrative proceeding. When administrative proceedings are not brought solely to obtain evidence for the criminal prosecution, the government can proceed on both tracks to further the purposes of the securities laws. Thus, in an SEC investigation of foreign bribery, the SEC could seek internal company documents (which could later be available to prosecutors) even though they would be protected from criminal discovery after the issuance of a criminal indictment.

Although the administrative proceeding may be stayed to protect a party's privilege against self-incrimination or to avoid prejudice in the criminal proceeding (such as through expanded discovery), the stay is discretionary. For example, the SEC need not stay an investigation while a parallel criminal investigation is ongoing, provided no criminal indictment has issued and no self-incriminatory evidence is sought in the investigation. Likewise, federal prosecutors may use evidence obtained in a civil enforcement action in prosecuting a related criminal proceeding, provided the civil action was not brought in "bad faith."

Sharing Information

Once the SEC has gathered information, the federal securities statutes contemplate that the SEC may transmit the information to the Department of Justice for use in criminal proceedings. Securities Act §20(b); Securities Exchange Act §21(d). Congress has recognized the "close working relationship" of the agencies in enforcing the securities laws. Congress also contemplated that the agencies should share information at the earliest stage to avoid "costly duplication" and so evidence useful in a criminal prosecution does not become stale. Nonetheless, once a criminal indictment is issued, the SEC is limited in using its investigatory powers as a means to broaden the scope of government discovery in a criminal prosecution.

Preclusive Effect

Judicial and administrative findings are preclusive in subsequent proceedings, whether administrative, civil or criminal. That is, a finding in one setting need not be relitigated and is considered final and binding in the other.

SEC adjudications have preclusive effect in subsequent administrative or civil litigation, if the defendant had a full opportunity to litigate the issue before the SEC and the issue was clearly decided. In addition, findings of fact in an SEC consent order (as to which there was not full adjudication) may be admitted as evidence in subsequent litigation with adverse consequences for those who enter such orders.

Judicial findings in an injunction action brought by the SEC are preclusive in subsequent private litigation. See *Parklane Hosiery Co. v. Shore*, 439 U.S.

322 (1979) (upholding offensive use of collateral estoppel, if private plaintiff could not have easily joined in enforcement action and defendant had a full opportunity to litigate issue). One effect of this rule is that a defendant may be denied a right to a jury trial on issues resolved by a judge in the enforcement action.

Once a court has found a violation of the securities laws the factual and legal findings underlying the court's decision may be used affirmatively by private litigants in lawsuits seeking money damages. The effect is that SEC enforcement actions will often spawn private class actions, in which the only issue will be damages to the class members. (A finding of non-violation, however, may not be used defensively against private litigants who were not parties to the first litigation.)

Given the collateral effect of a litigated and decided SEC enforcement action in court or before the agency, parties have a strong incentive to enter into a settlement "without admitting or denying" the SEC's allegations. Some have questioned whether the incentive to settle amounts to structural coercion that undermines basic due process rights. Others have objected to the denial of jury trial rights in a damages action, as to issues formerly decided by a judge or the SEC.

Findings in a criminal case, where the standards of proof and procedural protection are the most rigorous, are binding in subsequent administrative and civil proceedings.

Multiple Sanctions

Besides its preclusive effect in subsequent administrative or civil litigation, criminal prosecution also limits the ability of the government to impose further punishment. Under the Double Jeopardy Clause of the U.S. Constitution, a defendant may not be subject to multiple prosecutions or punishment for the same misconduct.

A defendant may, however, be subject to both criminal sanctions and civil sanctions for the same misconduct. For example, a defendant who engages in insider trading can be subject to civil monetary penalties by the SEC and later to criminal prosecution for the same conduct. Although the Supreme Court once took the view that a defendant punished in a criminal prosecution cannot be subjected to additional civil sanctions whose purpose is deterrent or retributive, the Court has accepted the possibility of both criminal and civil sanctions for the same conduct.

Thus, a lawyer convicted of defrauding clients in a false investment scheme and sentenced to more than 15 years in jail (and to pay $3.8 million in restitution and $700,000 in criminal fines) could later be ordered by the SEC to disgorge gains of $9.2 million (including pre-judgment interest) and pay a $500,000 civil penalty. SEC v. Palmisano, 135 F.3d 860 (2d Cir. 1998).

By being characterized as *civil penalties*, SEC sanctions avoid the Double Jeopardy prohibition against multiple *criminal punishments*.

The same possibility of multiple sanctions applies to disciplinary actions by an SRO and the SEC. Thus, even though the SEC is prevented by statute from increasing SRO sanctions, the SEC may impose additional sanctions of its own. For example, after FINRA suspends and fines a registered representative, the SEC can impose additional sanctions (censure and a longer suspension) for the same misconduct.

§12.6 STATE ENFORCEMENT

State securities regulators also have enforcement powers under state blue sky laws. Federal law does not preempt state securities enforcement. See Securities Act §18 (preserving state power to "investigate and bring enforcement actions with respect to fraud or deceit . . . in connection with . . . securities transactions") (see §1.5). State regulators can assert jurisdiction over securities transactions affecting in-state investors and companies, which means that any given state regulator has jurisdiction over virtually all U.S. public companies. See *A.S. Goldmen & Co. v. New Jersey Bureau of Securities*, 163 F.3d 780 (3d Cir. 1999) (concluding that state securities agency has jurisdiction over securities sales by in-state company exclusively to out-of-state purchasers, to protect reputation of in-state issuers and to protect in-state investors from possible flowback).

§12.6.1 New York's Martin Act

Enforcement actions brought by New York's attorney general illustrate the potential for state securities enforcement. Using the broad civil and criminal enforcement powers under the Martin Act, a New York law passed in 1921, the attorney general can seek to enjoin and prosecute conduct deemed detrimental to the investing public — without having to prove intent or scienter (unless a felony is charged). The Martin Act covers "any misrepresentation for the purchase or sale of securities," as well as the activities of all broker-dealers (and their personnel) and investment advisers doing business in New York. N.Y Gen. Bus. Law art. 23-A.

Under the Martin Act, the state attorney general can conduct investigations, obtain temporary injunctions during his investigation, and then seek restitution of funds and institute criminal actions for the imposition of fines and penalties. New York courts have held that enforcement of the Martin Act is exclusively within the province of the state's attorney general, thus refusing to imply private actions based on claims of negligent misrepresentation in securities cases.

§12.6.2 Enforcement Actions Against Securities Firms

In 2003, enforcement actions brought under the Martin Act by the New York attorney general focused on, among other matters, the conflicts of interest faced by securities analysts. For example, in an investigation of conflicts of interest at Merrill Lynch between the firm's investment banking and securities analysts, the state attorney general obtained a court order compelling the production of internal documents. The attorney general then publicly revealed e-mails written by Merrill Lynch analysts that described certain securities as "dogs" or "junk," while the same analysts had publicly touted the securities with strong "buy" or "accumulate" recommendations. Merrill Lynch and the attorney general then agreed to a settlement that called for a restructuring of how the firm compensated its analysts, made research recommendations, and disclosed conflicts of interest in its research reports. The settlement included the payment of a $100 million penalty, to be distributed by the attorney general's office.

As a result of the attorney general's initiatives, the nation's top securities firms agreed to a "global settlement" with the main U.S. securities enforcers—the SEC, the NYSE, the NASD (now FINRA), the North American Securities Administrators Association (state securities regulators), and the New York Attorney General. The agreement, among other things, requires:

- the creation of "firewalls" to insulate research analysis from investment banking—by severing analyst compensation from underwriting results and ending the practice of analysts accompanying investment bankers on underwriting "road shows";
- independent securities research, including a five-year phase during which brokerage firms must contract with at least three independent research firms for research provided their customers;
- mandatory public disclosure of analysts' past recommendations, thus allowing customers to compare ratings and price forecasts, and evaluate analyst performance;
- a complete ban on "spinning" of IPOs (see §4.1.2) to corporate executives who make decisions on investment banking business;
- monetary sanctions of $1.4 billion—allocated between retrospective relief, the costs of independent research and investor education.

Joint Press Release (April 28, 2003). See §11.2.4 (describing settlement more fully).

Examples

1. The Internet is the new "Wild West." It is vast and everything is up for grabs, including securities tips, Internet securities offerings, and Web-based trading markets. Companies can make public offerings from their websites — without underwriting fees, retail spreads, or prospectus printing costs. New securities firms can set up electronic bulletin boards where investors can check "bid" and "ask" prices and trade securities from home — without high commissions, brokers, or paper. Investment "gurus" can tout securities and their visions of reality to subscribers who pay for access to their wisdom on investment blogs — without mailings or limits on what might be said.

   Bombastic Brewery, an upstart microbrewery, offers its common stock on the Internet. Investors can read the company's offering materials and complete a subscription agreement from any computer connected to the Internet.

   a. The SEC staff learns of the Bombastic offering through its Internet enforcement center (reachable on www.sec.gov) and notices that Bombastic does not purport to rely on any exemption from registration. What can the SEC do to stop this unregistered, apparently non-exempt offering?

   b. The SEC issues a cease-and-desist order. Bombastic receives notice of the order but disregards it. What is the next enforcement step for the SEC?

   c. Bombastic's president is also covered by the SEC cease-and-desist order. She often engages in cost-benefit analyses and wonders whether she will gain more in illegally taking investments than she will lose in penalties. What are the penalties to which she is exposed by not complying with the order?

   d. Bombastic's offering materials are all scrupulously complete and honest. Can the Justice Department nonetheless bring a criminal prosecution against Bombastic's management for offering unregistered, nonexempt securities?

   e. Mildred, a lawyer who advised Bombastic when it set up its offering on the Internet, gave some mistaken advice. She told Bombastic's management that if the company's disclosure documents contained the same information as would have been available in a public offering — which they did — SEC registration was unnecessary. Is Mildred subject to SEC disciplinary action?

   f. Given Mildred's advice, can Bombastic's management be criminally liable?

2. Bombastic avoids further SEC wrath by offering to refund the money to all the investors who had purchased in its unregistered offering — a

so-called rescission offer. The issuer then begins another offering on the Internet in reliance on the exemption of Regulation A (see §5.2.3).

a. Remember that the SEC had issued a cease-and-desist order against the first unregistered offering, but assume the agency had not proceeded to seek a court injunction or other penalties. Do Bombastic's troubles with the SEC preclude it from making its Reg A offering?

b. The SEC is nervous about Bombastic's bravado. SEC staff obtains an order from the SEC to investigate Bombastic's operations. The SEC staff issues third-party subpoenas to investors who had invested in the first unregistered offering, asking them to turn over any communications (email or otherwise) that Bombastic made to them in the first offering. Bombastic is not informed of these subpoenas. Have its rights been violated?

c. Mildred continues to advise Bombastic in this second offering. She notices that the Reg A financial statements are significantly more favorable than the original financials used in the abortive first offering. Must she resign?

d. Mildred does not resign, but continues to assist Bombastic in its Reg A offering, misleading financials and all. Is she subject to aiding and abetting liability?

Explanations

1. a. Cease-and-desist order. The SEC can issue an administrative cease-and-desist order, without resorting to judicial procedures, after giving notice and an opportunity to be heard. Securities Act §8A. The order can be directed against the person (here the issuer) who is committing the violation, as well as any corporate official who is causing it and who "knew or should have known" his act or omission would contribute to the violation. Securities Act §8A(a).

   To stop the offering immediately, the SEC also can issue a *temporary* cease-and-desist order against any broker-dealer or other securities intermediary, but not against the company and its officials, if there is a risk of a dissipation of assets or other significant harm to investors or the public before completion of the *final* order. Securities Act §8A(c). The temporary order must be issued after notice and opportunity to be heard, unless the SEC decides to proceed *ex parte* on a determination that notice would be impracticable or contrary to the public interest.

   b. Court penalties. An SEC cease-and-desist order becomes effective when served on the person charged with committing or causing the violation. If a party fails to comply with a cease-and-desist order, the SEC can enforce the order in federal district court, where the court can impose additional civil money penalties for noncompliance with the SEC order. Securities Act §20(d).

c. There are tiered civil penalties. The penalties imposed by the court are capped depending on whether it was an individual or entity that violated the cease-and-desist order, as well as the degree of culpability or harm. In the case of Bombastic's president, the maximum penalties are —

Penalties	Conduct
$5,000	for each violation of the cease-and-desist order
$50,000	for each violation of the order, if the violation involved "reckless disregard of a regulatory requirement"
$100,000	for each violation of the order, if the violation was a reckless disregard of regulatory requirements and resulted in substantial losses (or risks) to others

In addition, if the president gained more financially from the violations than these penalties, the maximum penalty increases to "the gross amount of pecuniary gain to the defendant as a result of the violation." Securities Act §20(d)(2). The president cannot hope to gain more than she might be penalized.

d. Yes. The violation of the registration requirements of §5 does not turn on the completeness or honesty of disclosure to investors. See §4.3. Bombastic's management can be criminally prosecuted if it "willfully" violated the registration requirements. Securities Act §24. This does not require that they have known about the specific registration requirements, but it is sufficient if they knew the unregistered offering was wrong. The failure to stop the offering after an SEC cease-and-desist order would be powerful evidence of criminal willfulness.

e. Probably not. Although the SEC might proceed under its Rule 102(e) disciplinary procedures, it is doubtful that the SEC would. (An order under §15(c)(4) of the Exchange Act is not available because the violation arose with respect to nonregistration under the Securities Act.) As interpreted by the agency, the SEC's rules of practice give it power to sanction those who "practice" before the agency (including advising clients on filing obligations) if the person lacks qualifications, character or integrity, or willfully violates or aids and abets a violation of the federal securities laws. SEC Rule of Practice 102(e). It is unlikely, however, that the SEC would proceed against a securities lawyer for one instance of witless legal advice. In fact, the agency has taken the approach of not proceeding to discipline securities lawyers until there has been a judicial determination that the lawyer violated the securities laws.

f. It depends on the good faith of management's reliance. Although courts have said there is no willful violation of the securities laws if a client relies in good faith on an attorney's advice, it is unclear whether reliance on Mildred's advice was in good faith. Compare *United States v. Crosby*, 294 F.2d 928 (2d Cir. 1961) (broker-dealer not willful when it relied in good faith on attorney's opinion that transaction was exempt from registration). If Bombastic's management had some awareness of the registration requirements of §5 of the Securities Act, it may have been apparent that Mildred did not know what she was saying. Even if Bombastic's management believed that Mildred had found a technicality to avoid registration, their violation could still be deemed willful if there were reasons to doubt the efficacy of the technicality. See *United States v. Dixon*, 536 F.2d 1388 (2d Cir. 1976) (Friendly, J.) (finding "knowing" violation of Exchange Act disclosure requirements under §32(a) even though defendant believed that loophole "thimble rig" avoided particular disclosure rules).

2. a. No. The "bad boy" disqualifications that apply in a Reg A offering do not include issuers that have been subject to an administrative §8A cease-and-desist order. Rule 262(a). Bombastic is in trouble only if it had become subject to a *court* order in the last five years enjoining it from securities-related conduct.

   b. No. There is no requirement, constitutional or otherwise, that a target of a nonpublic SEC investigation be notified. See *SEC v. Jerry T. O'Brien, Inc.*, 467 U.S. 735 (1984). Moreover, the search of records held by investors does not implicate any of Bombastic's interests in privacy or to be free from being compelled to incriminate itself.

   c. Probably not. The SEC views securities lawyers as guardians of the faith. In an important disciplinary proceeding in the early 1980s, the SEC took the stance that a lawyer who becomes aware that a client is engaged in the substantial and continuing failure to meet disclosure requirements violates professional standards by not taking prompt steps to end the client's noncompliance. *In re Carter & Johnson*, [1981 Transfer Binder] Fed. Sec. L. Rep. (CCH) ¶82,847 (SEC 1981). The first step is to counsel accurate disclosure.

      If the noncompliance goes forward, the lawyer must report internally "up the ladder"—first to the corporation's general counsel (or both the general counsel and CEO). Rule 205.3(b)(1). If the response is not adequate, the lawyer must approach the board's audit committee, another committee consisting only of independent directors, or the full board of directors (if there is no fully independent committee).

Rule 205.3(b)(3). The failure to report "up the ladder" may lead to disciplinary proceedings and sanctions. Rule 205.6 (censure, or temporary or permanent bar). In addition, a lawyer who continues to represent a recalcitrant client may be liable for aiding and abetting a fraud — civilly (see §9.2.2) and criminally (see §12.5.3).

Although not required by the current version of Rule 205, the lawyer *may* also choose to bring the noncompliance to the attention of authorities, including the SEC. New ABA Model Rule 1.6 (see §12.4.4). State professional rules of ethics also suggest that a lawyer who assists in a securities fraud has additional obligations. State ethics rules *compel* resignation of a lawyer who assists the client's fraud or if third parties to whom the fraud is directed rely on the lawyer's representation. See ABA Model Rule 1.16(a); ABA Formal Opinion 366. Further, the ABA has taken the position that a lawyer must openly repudiate any prior work for the client if it may be used to further the client's fraud. The ABA rules place little emphasis on the lawyer persisting as the conscience of a wayward client.

d. Perhaps. Although aiding and abetting liability is unavailable in private 10b-5 actions, the Private Securities Litigation Reform Act of 1995 retains such liability in SEC enforcement actions. See §9.2.2. In an SEC injunction action, "any person that knowingly provides substantial assistance to another person" in violation of any provision of the Exchange Act is deemed to have violated to the same extent as the primary violator. Exchange Act §20(f). What constitutes substantial assistance is not defined in the PSLRA, but a rich body of prior case law suggests that a securities professional's silence in the face of a client fraud amounts to substantial assistance if investors would have relied on the professional's reputation and presence in the transaction. See *Roberts v. Peat, Marwick, Mitchell & Co.*, 857 F.2d 646 (9th Cir. 1989) (substantial assistance established if investors relied on accountant's reputation when deciding to invest).

It is also important to note that if Mildred knowingly participated in the drafting of the false disclosures and investors rely on these misstatements, she could become a "primary violator" under Rule 10b-5, jointly and severally liable for investor losses caused by the false opinion. See §9.2.2.

CHAPTER 13

U.S. Regulation of Cross-Border Securities Transactions

Modern life is international, and the globalization we see around us has swept into securities markets and securities regulation. U.S. companies regularly raise capital abroad, where financing is often cheaper and regulation less burdensome. Foreign issuers seek access to U.S. capital markets — still the most transparent and deepest in the world. Cross-border capital flows raise confounding issues of securities regulation — both in the United States and abroad.

This chapter (with its parochial focus on U.S. securities regulation) covers:

- when foreign offerings by U.S. issuers are subject to U.S. disclosure requirements [§13.1]
- when offerings and trading of foreign-issued securities in the United States are subject to U.S. disclosure requirements [§13.2]
- the extraterritorial reach of U.S. securities enforcement and antifraud protection to securities transactions outside the United States [§13.3]

§13.1 OFFSHORE OFFERINGS BY U.S. ISSUERS (AND FOREIGN ISSUERS)

U.S. issuers have found a voracious appetite among foreign investors for their securities. As of 2007, foreign investors held about $2.8 trillion (13.0 percent) of public U.S. equity securities. At the same time, U.S.

investors have internationalized their portfolios and in 2007 held $4.8 trillion in foreign equity securities. Are sales by U.S. issuers to foreign investors (or by foreign issuers to U.S. investors) outside the United States subject to the same regulation that applies to U.S. issuers when they sell to U.S. investors in the United States? Read on.

§13.1.1 Regulatory Dilemma

The Securities Act of 1933 cuts a wide swath. Unless registered, securities cannot be offered, sold, or delivered by "use of any means . . . in interstate commerce or of the mails." Securities Act §5. Not bashful and fully aware of the heavy losses U.S. investors had suffered in foreign offerings during the early 1930s, Congress defined "interstate commerce" to include securities activities "between any foreign country and any State." Securities Act §2(7).

The Securities Act, although purposefully intended to regulate foreign securities offerings into the United States, reaches much more broadly. By its literal terms, it regulates

- public offerings by U.S. issuers to foreign investors outside the United States,
- secondary distributions by U.S. investors who resell to foreign investors, and
- public offerings by foreign issuers outside the United States if any of the securities are purchased by U.S. investors.

Under a broad reading of the Securities Act, such issuers and investors must comply with the Securities Act registration requirements *and* foreign securities laws, even when no U.S. purchasers are contemplated. The effect of this regulatory grab is to expose U.S. and foreign persons to rescission liability under §12(a)(1) for activities that arguably affect neither U.S. investors nor the integrity of U.S. securities markets.

Over the years, the SEC has sought to allay the alarm of U.S. (and foreign) issuers that raise capital abroad. In 1964, the SEC stated its view that §5 does not reach offerings to foreign investors if the offering is reasonably designed to come to rest abroad and not be redistributed to U.S. nationals. Securities Act Rel. No. 4708 (1964). During its nearly three decades, this imprecise standard proved only mildly comforting.

§13.1.2 SEC Safe Harbors — Regulation S

In 1990, as offshore securities transactions grew in importance, the SEC sought to provide clearer assurances in a set of nonexclusive safe harbors — known as Regulation S (or affectionately, Reg S) — that are meant to provide guidance for U.S. (and foreign) issuers and investors that transact unregistered securities abroad. Rules 901-904. In 1998, the SEC tightened aspects of Reg S to address perceived abuses and renumbered many of the provisions.

Safe Harbor Categories

Reg S codifies the SEC position that Securities Act registration is required only for securities transactions "within the United States" — a territorial principle. Rule 901. The regulation then specifies two safe harbors for offshore transactions deemed to be "without the United States" — one for *issuer offerings* (Rule 903) and the other for *resales* (Rule 904).

The two Reg S safe harbors contain a slew of SEC-created conditions, reflecting a regulatory anxiety that offers or securities might flow back to the United States. To satisfy the SEC safe harbors, both issuer offerings and investor resales (1) must be made in an "offshore transaction" and (2) may not involve "directed selling efforts" in the United States. In addition to these two basic conditions, issuer offerings under Rule 903 and investor resales under Rule 904 must satisfy additional flowback safeguards.

Offshore Transaction

Both safe harbors are conditioned on all transactions being "offshore transactions." Reg S defines an "offshore transaction" as one in which *no offer* is made to a person "in the United States" [Rule 902(h)(1)], and the *sale* is accomplished in one of the following ways [Rule 902(h)(ii)]:

- The buyer (whether in an issuer offering or investor resale) is outside the United States when the buy order is placed, or the seller and its agents reasonably believe this to be the case.
- The sale (in an issuer offering) is executed on any "established foreign securities exchange."
- The sale (in an investor resale) is executed on a "designated offshore securities market" (defined by the rule to include the leading foreign stock exchanges), and the transaction is not prearranged with a buyer in the United States.

Geography is the key. For example, a U.S. citizen who is on vacation in Brazil and accepts a beachside offer to buy securities has engaged in an "offshore transaction."

Reg S, however, relaxes these requirements if all offers or sales are made for the accounts of a *non-U.S. person*, even though the transaction occurs inside the United States. Rule 902(h)(3). The term "U.S. persons" is broadly defined to include persons who reside in the United States, businesses organized in the United States, and entities or accounts managed by U.S. persons. Rule 902(k).

No Directed Selling Efforts

Both Reg S safe harbors also prohibit "directed selling efforts" in the United States by the issuer or seller, or any person acting on their behalf. Rule 903(a)(2); Rule 904(a)(2). The definition of "directed selling efforts" refers to activities that might condition the U.S. market and raise investor interest for any of the offered securities. Rule 902(c) (see also §4.3.1). Excluded from the prohibition are legal notices required by U.S. or foreign authorities, tombstone ads or identifying statements (Rule 135, see §4.3.2), and stock quotations by foreign securities firms primarily in foreign countries. Rule 902(c)(3). In addition, foreign issuers are permitted to allow journalists to attend their press conferences held outside the United States. Rules 902(c)(3)(vii), 135e.

Issuer Safe Harbors — Rule 903

The first Reg S safe harbor specifies three categories of permissible "issuer offerings." Each category reflects the likelihood of flowback into the United States and the level of public information available to U.S. investors about the offered securities. The more likely the flowback and the less available the information, the greater the regulation. The categories turn on

- the kind of issuer (foreign or domestic),
- the type of securities offered (equity or debt),
- the level of U.S. information about the issuer (reporting or nonreporting),
- the level of existing market interest in the United States, and
- the market in which the offering is made.

Category I — Low-Risk Offerings

In this category of offerings, flowback is thought unlikely. Rule 903(b)(1). Besides the "offshore transaction" requirement and the prohibition against "directed selling efforts," there are few restrictions.

Foreign issuers with no "substantial U.S. market interest" — equity or debt securities

No "substantial U.S. market interest" [Rule 903(b)(1)(i)] means:
- For equity securities, U.S. stock exchanges and NASDAQ cannot constitute the largest

market (or one of the largest markets) for the class of equity securities being offered. Rule 902(j)(1).

- For debt securities, U.S. persons cannot be significant record holders of debt securities of the issuer — whenever 300 or more holders are U.S. persons, U.S. persons hold $1 billion or more of the securities, or U.S. persons hold 20 percent or more of the securities. Rule 902(j)(2).

Foreign issuers making "overseas directed offering" — equity or debt securities
Domestic issuers making "overseas directed offering" — debt securities

"Overseas directed offering" [Rule 903(b)(1)(ii)] means:

- For a foreign issuer, the offering must be directed into a single foreign country in accordance with local laws and practices.
- For a domestic issuer, the offering of debt securities cannot be denominated in U.S. dollars or convertible into dollar-denominated securities.

Foreign and domestic issuers offering to employees abroad — equity or debt securities

Conditions [Rule 903(b)(1)(iv)]:

- The securities are offered only to employees pursuant to an employee benefit plan established under foreign law; the securities are issued for bona fide services, other than in a capital-raising transaction.
- The plan interests generally are not transferable and generally are not sold to U.S. residents.
- Documentation must state the securities are unregistered and may not be sold in the United States unless registered or exempt from registration.

Foreign governments or entities — debt securities

Conditions [Rule 903(b)(1)(iii)]:

- The securities are backed by the full faith and credit of a foreign government.

Category 2 — Mid-Risk Offerings

In this category of offerings, flowback is considered more likely, but the presumed information and sophistication of U.S. markets in these securities somewhat offset the flowback risk. Rule 903(b)(2). Besides the "offshore transaction" requirement and the prohibition against "directed selling efforts" in the United States, Category 2 offerings are subject to additional offering and transactional restrictions as precautions against flowback.

Reporting foreign issuers —
equity securities
Nonreporting foreign
issuers — debt securities

Offering restrictions [Rule 902(g)]:
- The issuer must obtain written assurances from distributors that all sales and offers during a 40-day distribution compliance period will comply with the Reg S safe harbor conditions.
- The issuer must insert statements in its offering documents that the securities have not been registered and may not be offered or sold in the United States or to U.S. persons.

Reporting domestic issuers —
debt securities

Transactional restrictions
[Rule 903(b)(2)(ii), (iii)]:
- During a *40-day distribution compliance period*, no offers or sales can be made to U.S. persons after the offshore offering commences.
- Distributors must notify all participants (such as retail broker-dealers) that the participants become subject to the same restrictions on offers and sales that apply to the distributor.

Category 3 — High-Risk Offerings

This is the catchall category, for all of the offerings not eligible under Category 1 or 2. Rule 903(b)(3). The risk of flowback is considered high, and Reg S imposes numerous additional restrictions on issuers, distributors, and purchasers. A Category 3 offering must comply with the "offering transaction" requirement and the prohibition against "directed selling efforts," in the United States, as well as all the Category 2 "offering restrictions" and additional conditions that depend on whether the offering is of debt or equity.

Nonreporting domestic
issuers — debt securities

Offering restrictions [Rule 903(b)(3)(i)]:
- Same as for Category 2.
Transactional restrictions
[Rule 903(b)(3)(ii), (iv)]:
- During a *40-day distribution compliance period*, no offers or sales may be made to U.S. persons.
- During the 40-day period, all the securities are issued under a temporary global security that is not exchangeable for definitive securities.

- Nondistributor purchasers must certify they are either non-U.S. persons or U.S. persons purchasing in an exempt transaction.
- Distributors must notify members of the selling group that during the 40-day period they are subject to the same restrictions.

Reporting and nonreporting domestic issuers — equity securities

Offering restrictions [Rule 903(b)(3)(i)]:
- Same as for Category 2.

Transactional restrictions [Rule 903(b)(3)(iii), (iv)]:
- During a *one-year distribution compliance period*, no sales or offers can be made to U.S. persons.
- Nondistributor purchasers must certify they are either not U.S. persons or U.S. persons purchasing in an exempt transaction.
- The purchaser must agree that any resale will be registered, be exempt from registration, or be undertaken pursuant to Reg S.
- The securities must be legended, and the issuers must impose transfer restrictions.
- Distributors must notify members of the selling group that during the one-year period they are subject to the same restrictions.

Reporting companies are required to disclose their Reg S offshore offerings on current Form 8-K within 15 days after the offering, thus giving the market a chance to react to the offering before any resale restrictions are lifted. See Form 8-K (item 3.02, unregistered sales of equity securities).

Reg S allows for offshore transactions to occur contemporaneously with domestic offerings. If the offshore transaction complies with Reg S, there is no integration with any domestic offering (whether registered or exempt from registration). Securities Act Rel. No. 6863 (1990).

Resale Safe Harbor — Rule 904

The second safe harbor of Reg S, for investor resales, is available for any securities, whether or not acquired in an offshore transaction. Rule 904. It thus permits offshore resales and secondary distributions of securities acquired in private U.S. offerings, as well as securities acquired in foreign offerings. To satisfy the safe harbor, the resale must be made in an "offshore transaction" and not involve "directed selling efforts" in the United States — both as defined above. Rule 904(a)(1), (2). In addition, other conditions apply to sellers linked to the issuer.

Resales by Participating Dealers

Securities firms (and persons receiving selling concessions or fees) in a Category 2 or Category 3 issuer offering cannot, during the relevant restricted period, knowingly offer or sell the offered securities to a U.S. person. Rule 904(b)(1).

Resales by Certain Affiliates

Offers and resales by officers and directors of an issuer (or the distributor) may be made only in typical trading transactions, in which only the usual broker's commission is paid. Rule 904(b)(2).

In addition, equity securities of domestic issuers issued pursuant to the conditions of Reg S become "restricted securities." Rule 905. This designation, added by the 1998 amendments to Reg S, means that even after the one-year distribution compliance period any resale into a public market must comply with the holding, disclosure, and trickle conditions of Rule 144. See §7.2.1.

Antifraud and Blue Sky Extraterritoriality

Reg S does not, however, fully address the extraterritoriality of U.S. securities regulation. There is no safe harbor from applicable state securities laws or the antifraud provisions of the Securities Act and the Exchange Act. See Reg S, Preliminary Notes 1, 4. It is possible, therefore, for state securities regulators to insist on state blue sky registration, even though the offering satisfies the conditions of Reg S. (Remember, though, that state blue sky registration is preempted by the National Securities Markets Improvement Act of 1996 in the case of "covered securities." See Securities Act §18(b).) In addition, it is also possible that an offering that satisfies the Reg S safe harbor conditions may be subject to a private or government enforcement action under Rule 10b-5, provided the offering satisfies the relevant subject matter test. See §13.3.

Examples

1. Electro Motors Corporation, a start-up company incorporated in California with plans to develop and sell electric cars, is looking for financing. The company does not have any public investors and is not a reporting company under the Exchange Act. Identify any problems with the following.
   a. Electro Motors will sell readily negotiable bearer bonds denominated in U.S. dollars in Europe (so-called Eurobonds), principally in stock exchanges in Germany and Italy.

b. Electro Motors will sell its Eurobonds only in Germany on the Frankfurt Stock Exchange.

c. Electro Motors will denominate its nonconvertible bond offering in Euros and sell them only on the Frankfurt Stock Exchange, though to make the offering more marketable there will be no restrictions on resales.

d. Electro Motors will also sell some of its Eurobonds to large sophisticated U.S. institutional investors in the United States.

e. Electro Motors will sell its Eurobonds to institutional investors in Germany, Italy, Japan, and the United States.

2. Dulces, Inc. (a Delaware corporation) designs and sells women's footwear worldwide. Its common stock is traded on NASDAQ, and Dulces is a reporting company under the Exchange Act. Any problems with the following?

a. Dulces will issue new shares of common stock at a 40 percent discount to mysterious Swiss investors for unsecured promissory notes on which no interest will accrue for 51 days. After a 40-day holding period, the Swiss purchasers can resell the shares on U.S. trading markets and use the proceeds from these resales to pay Dulces.

b. Dulces will issue new shares of common stock that will be deposited with a Swiss bank, which will then issue Global Depositary Receipts representing Dulces shares. These GDRs (denominated in U.S. dollars) will be sold to European investors and traded on the major European stock exchanges. For an explanation of "GDRs," see §13.2.2.

c. Dulces will sell some of its GDRs to U.S. military personnel stationed in Germany. These purchasers will agree to a mandatory two-year holding period.

d. Dulces changes plans and will issue bonds denominated in Euros to institutional investors in Germany. There will be no restrictions on resales into the United States.

3. Baylor Denz (a German corporation) manufactures and sells automobiles throughout the world. Denz's common shares are listed and traded on numerous international stock exchanges. Trading volume in BD common shares is spread among the German stock exchanges (40 percent), the New York Stock Exchange (25 percent), and other international exchanges (35 percent). Any problems with the following?

a. Denz issues new common shares, through a syndicate of international securities firms, to retail customers whose orders are executed on European exchanges.

b. Denz changes its strategy and issues, for the first time, a new class of debt securities to public investors on European stock exchanges.

c. Rothson, an international investment banker hired to act as managing underwriter, places an advertisement in the *Wall Street Journal Europe* announcing the offering, which it heralds as "the financial underpinning for major new Denz growth."

d. At the same time of the European debt offering, Denz issues a tranche (a portion of the offering) to institutional investors in the United States. Some of the U.S. institutional investors may resell to wealthy foreign individuals outside the United States.

e. Some of the public investors who purchased in the European debt offering want to sell to institutional investors in the United States and Europe.

f. Denz has fallen on hard times. To raise capital in its debt offering, it would have to offer prohibitively high interest rates. The German government agrees to guarantee a 500 million Euro offering of bonds in Europe, some of which no doubt will be purchased by U.S. investors.

Explanations

1. a. Problem. As planned, this offering by a nonreporting U.S. issuer fits none of the Reg S categories for an offshore issuer offering deemed to be "outside the United States":

   • *Category 1.* Nonreporting U.S. issuers may make an "overseas directed offering" of debt securities — but only in one country. Rule 903(b)(1)(ii)(A) ("Single country other than the United States"). Any offering in more than one country, it is thought, increases the risk of flowback.

   • *Category 2.* Only *reporting* U.S. issuers qualify on the assumption that nonreporting companies are not followed by informed trading markets. Rule 903(b)(2).

   • *Category 3.* Although nonreporting U.S. issuers may issue debt, this issue of Eurobonds in bearer form would not satisfy the Category 3 condition that all the securities be represented by a temporary "global" security exchangeable for permanent, negotiable securities only after a 40-day restricted period. Rule 903(b)(3)(ii)(B). Moreover, to ensure the issue does not flow back to public investors in the United States, all purchasers would have to certify that the securities would be beneficially owned by a non-U.S. person or by a U.S. person purchasing under a §5 exemption. Rule 903(b)(3)(ii)(A).

   b. Problem. This debt offering, though into one country, does not satisfy the conditions of a Category 1 "overseas directed offering" because it is denominated in U.S. dollars. Rules 903(b)(1)(ii)(B) ("principal and interest . . . denominated in a currency other than U.S. dollars"). Denominating the offering in a non-U.S. currency (let's say Euros) may not be as simple as it seems. The issuer must convert the proceeds of the offering from Euros to U.S. dollars and then make principal and interest payments in Euros, bearing an ongoing risk of currency fluctuations. To hedge against this, U.S. issuers will often buy currency futures, increasing the cost of an offering denominated in a currency other than U.S. dollars.

c. No problem. By denominating the nonconvertible bonds in a non-U.S. currency, the offering would qualify as a Category 1 "overseas directed offering." Rules 902(b)(1)(ii)(B). The two general conditions, applicable to all Reg S transactions, appear to be satisfied. First, the offering is made as an "offshore transaction" because no offers are made in the United States, and the offering is on the Frankfurt Stock Exchange, certainly an "established foreign securities exchange." Rules 903(a)(1), 902(h)(1) (defining "offshore transaction" as one not involving offers to persons in the United States and is executed on "established foreign securities exchange"). See also Rule 902(b)(1) (defining "designated offshore securities market" to include the Frankfurt Stock Exchange). Second, the issuer would appear not to be engaged in any "directed selling efforts" or conditioning of the U.S. market. Rule 903(a)(2).

If the issuer complies with these conditions, Reg S by its terms imposes no restrictions on sales or resales for this Category 1 issuer offering. By falling into Category 1, the overseas offering avoids the offering and transactional restrictions of Categories 2 and 3, particularly the 40-day or 1-year distribution compliance period before any sales can be made to U.S. persons. Rule 903(b)(2), (3). In a Category 1 offering, U.S. persons can purchase the offered securities as part of the original distribution in Germany or in resales by German investors.

d. No problem. For offshore offerings the SEC has long relaxed the usual integration principle of the federal securities laws, which treats related sales of securities as part of one issue. See Regulation D, Preliminary Note 7 (foreign offerings that "come to rest abroad" need not be registered even if "coincident offers and sales are made under Regulation D in the United States"). Thus, if each tranche can find its own exemption, there is no integration. That is, Reg S exempts the German tranche from registration, and Reg D or §4(2) the American tranche. Even if the German offering included some unsophisticated investors that would not qualify under U.S. private placement standards, they would not affect the U.S. exemption. Securities Act Rel. No. 6863 (1990).

This understanding means that the Reg S cannot be read literally. The general Reg S condition that an "offshore transaction" not include any offer "to a person in the United States" applies only to offers related to the foreign portion of the offering. Offers can be made in the United

States, so long as they find their own exemption — such as Reg D or the private placement exemption of §4(2).

e. No problem. Reg S is not exclusive, and some offshore offerings may fit better under another exemption, such as Reg D. In our example, the issuer could use Rule 506 of Reg D for its Eurobond issue to institutional investors. If the investors qualify as accredited purchasers, there would be no disclosure requirements or limits on the size of the offering. Rule 506(a). The issuer would have to comply only with the Reg D prohibition on general solicitations, and the investors would be subject to resale limits on these "restricted" securities. See Rule 502(c), (d).

By avoiding registration under Reg D, the restrictive requirements of Reg S would not apply. There would be no prohibition on "directed selling efforts" into the United States, other than those imposed by Reg D. Unlike a Category 1 offering under Reg S, the securities could be denominated in U.S. dollars and could be directed to investors in more than one country. Unlike a Category 2 or 3 offering, there would be no restricted period for resales to U.S. persons. Unlike a Category 3 offering, the use of temporary "global" securities would be unnecessary.

Furthermore, a Reg D offering would fare better under U.S. blue sky laws, which are largely preempted for Rule 506 offerings. See §5.2.4.

2. a. Problem. These are the essential facts from a disciplinary proceeding instituted by the SEC against a U.S. issuer that tried to use the 1990 version of Reg S to circumvent Securities Act registration. *In re Candie's, Inc.*, 1996 WL 75741 (SEC 1996). The U.S. issuer's sales technically satisfied the conditions of a Category 2 offering by a U.S. reporting company in which resales were restricted for 40 days after the issuance. See Securities Act Release No. 6863 (Apr. 24, 1990) (adopting release stating that at "expiration of any restricted period, securities . . . will be viewed as unrestricted"). But the effect of the transaction was to introduce the issuer's securities into U.S. markets through a foreign conduit.

In the proceeding, the SEC had little difficulty concluding that the U.S. issuer, its lawyers, and the participating securities firms had offered or sold securities in violation of §5 of the Securities Act. The SEC pointed out that Reg S is "not available with respect to any transaction . . . that, although in technical compliance with these rules, is part of a plan or scheme to evade the registration provisions of the Act." Reg S, Preliminary Note 2. The SEC held the foreign "purchasers" were conduits in a U.S. distribution because the investment risk of the offering had never left the U.S. market nor was there an expectation the securities would come to rest abroad. The sanctions? All the participants (except the foreign purchasers) were subject to cease-and-desist orders, and the mastermind of the operation (the president of the participating U.S. securities firms) was suspended from securities work for 5 months. See §13.1.2.

After the case and others like it, the SEC amended Reg S in 1998 to crack down on this kind of abuse. Under amended Reg S, domestic issuers offering equity securities can only use Category 3, which limits any offers or sales to U.S. persons during a one-year distribution compliance period. Rule 903(b)(3)(iii)(A). In addition, any foreign purchaser must agree to resell only in accordance with Reg S or pursuant to a registration exemption. Rule 903(b)(3)(iii)(B)(2). Finally, nailing shut any similar cases, amended Reg S deems equity securities of domestic issuers sold under Reg S to be "restricted securities," forcing any purchaser to comply with Rule 144 in selling the securities into a U.S. trading market.

b. Problem, unless the issuer avoids U.S. marketing and implements certain heavy-handed flowback restrictions. Although such an offering would have satisfied the pre-1998 Reg S as a Category 2 issuer, the amended Reg S requires that all domestic issuers offering equity securities comply with the conditions of Category 3. Rule 903(b)(3). First, the offering would have to be made as an "offshore transaction," requiring that no offers be made to persons in the United States and transactions be executed on "an established securities exchange." Rules 903(a)(1), 902(h)(1). Second, no "directed selling efforts" could made in the United States, preventing the issuer from general advertising in the United States or otherwise conditioning the U.S. market. Rules 903(a)(1), 902(c)(1). Third, it would face the daunting flowback limitations of a Category 3 offering. Rule 903(b)(3). During a one-year distribution compliance period, each purchaser must certify he is not a U.S. person and agree not to resell except pursuant to a Reg S or other exemption. The issuer must implement transfer restrictions and the securities must be legended to state the restrictions. Rule 903(b)(3)(iii). Distributors, and members of the selling group, must agree in writing to abide by these restrictions and include statements in any offering materials that describe the limitations on offers and sales into the United States. Rules 903(b)(3)(i), (iv), 902(g) (definition of "offering restrictions"). (In addition, the issuer will, of course, have to comply with German securities laws.)

The GDRs, which are convertible on demand into Dulces shares, present a significant risk of flowback. The one-year restricted period is intended to place the full investment risk on the foreign purchasers — that is, they would face difficulties dumping their shares into U.S.

markets after a year on the assumption any adverse, undisclosed developments in Dulces at the time of the offering would come to light within that time.

c. Problem. The Reg S condition of "offshore transaction" — which applies to all categories of issuer offerings — forbids offers or sales to persons in the United States, as well as those specifically targeted at identifiable groups of U.S. citizens abroad. Rule 902(i)(2) ("such as members of the U.S. armed forces serving overseas"). While U.S. issuers may sell securities in a Reg S "offshore transaction" to U.S. citizens who happen to be abroad, U.S. issuers may not seek out groups of U.S. citizens living abroad.

d. No problem, if the issuer avoids any U.S. marketing. This offering satisfies the criteria of a Reg S Category 1 "overseas directed offering" by a U.S. issuer of nonconvertible debt securities denominated in a non-U.S. currency. Rules 903(c)(1)(ii), 902(j). The offering is made in "offshore transactions" because the purchasers are only German institutional investors. Rule 902(i)(1)(A). It does not involve a "directed selling effort" assuming there is no attempt to condition the market in the United States. The risk of flowback to U.S. public investors is viewed as minimal, and no resale restrictions apply.

Why might a U.S. company engage in a Eurobond issue? The principal reason is the lower cost of capital in European capital markets. (In part, the lower cost is tax related. Since 1984, U.S. Eurobond issuers are not subject to a withholding tax on interest payments to non-U.S. holders.) Some commentators have also suggested that issuers may look abroad to engage in "regulatory arbitrage," looking for the lower costs associated with lax securities regulation. But, countries with less demanding securities regulation do not necessarily assure more favorable conditions for issuers to place securities. In a less-regulated market, the issuer may be unable to command as high a price for its securities as in a market with more rigorous disclosure standards because of the increased risk to investors faced with less information or lower confidence in the disclosure made. The more good information, the less risk, and the more that investors are willing to pay for securities. See Cox, *Rethinking U.S. Securities Laws in the Shadow of International Regulatory Competition*, 55 Law & Contemp. Probs. 157 (1992). So, shopping for the most lax securities regulation regime may not necessarily result in the greatest net benefit to an issuer.

3. a. Problem, since it will be difficult (if not impossible) to implement the required precautions to prevent flowback into the United States. This offering does not qualify under the Category 1 safe harbor of Reg S for foreign offerings by a foreign issuer. Rule 903(b)(1). Denz cannot

claim there is no "substantial U.S. market interest" because the common shares being offered are substantially traded on a U.S. stock exchange. Rule 902(j)(1) ("substantial U.S. market interest" for equity securities when 20 percent or more of trading occurs on a U.S. stock exchange and less than 55 percent of trading occurs on a single foreign stock exchange). Moreover, this is not an "overseas directed offering" because the offering is being made on a number of European stock exchanges. Rules 903(b)(1)(ii)(A) (defining "overseas directed offering" to mean foreign issuer's offering into a single country other than the United States).

Category 2 would impose significant conditions, including that during a *40-day distribution compliance period*, no offers or sales could be made to U.S. persons once the offshore offering commences. Rule 903(b)(2)(ii), (iii). Although Reg S does not specify whether this limitation applies to all securities of the class being offered or only to the specific securities offered, this condition would essentially prevent any resales or offers by individual purchasers or participating securities firms in the United States of the company's fungible common stock during the first six weeks after the foreign offering. During this period, any resale or offer to a U.S. person would potentially void the entire Reg S exemption.

Category 3 would present the same difficulty as category 2, but during a *one-year distribution compliance* period. Rule 903(b)(3)(iii). That is, the existence of a U.S. trading market in the securities offered would prevent (as a practical matter) any unregistered offering of the same class of securities on a foreign stock market. The risk of flowback is thought to be too high.

Why should Denz worry about U.S. securities law for this European offering? Without the Reg S assurance, if U.S. persons were offered or sold *any* shares during the distribution compliance period, Denz would violate §5 as to these U.S. investors and would be exposed (along with participating securities firms) to SEC enforcement proceedings and sanctions, as well as private rescission liability of U.S. purchasers under §12(a)(1).

b. No problem, if Denz's debt has no U.S. following among public investors. This offering would qualify as a Category 1 issuer offering if Denz could reasonably conclude there is no "substantial U.S. market interest" generally in Denz's *debt* securities. Rule 903(b)(1)(i). There is "substantial U.S. market interest" only if at least 300 U.S. investors hold $1 billion or more of the issuer's debt, representing at least 20 percent of its outstanding debt. Rule 902j)(2). Oddly, when debt securities are offered, Reg S assumes it is irrelevant whether there is a "substantial U.S. market interest" in a foreign issuer's *equity* securities.

Rule 902(n) (definition of "substantial U.S. market interest" treats debt securities differently from equity securities).

Remember also that the offering would have to comply with the securities laws of the countries in which the bonds were offered.

c. Perhaps problem, if the publication has a general U.S. circulation. Even though the offering might meet the definitional conditions of Category 1, it remains subject to the general Reg S prohibition against "directed selling efforts" in the United States, which forbids any conditioning of U.S. markets for the offered securities. Rules 903(b)(1), 902(c). In particular, Reg S forbids placing ads in "a publication with a general circulation in the United States," which the rule defines to include those printed primarily for U.S. distribution or that have had an average circulation of 15,000 copies per issue in the United States during the preceding year. Rule 902(c)(2). Rothson had better check on the circulation of the *Wall Street Journal Europe* in the United States.

d. No problem, so long as the U.S. offering finds its own exemption, such as under §4(2) or Reg D. According to the SEC, the U.S. tranche does not affect the Reg S safe harbor for the European tranche. Further, the resales to foreign persons would be consistent with Rule 904 if the resales are only to foreign investors, without any U.S. marketing. The SEC has stated that Rule 904 resales of securities originally placed privately will not affect the validity of the private placement exemption relied on by the issuer. Securities Act Release No. 6863 (Apr. 24, 1990).

When the securities are resold to foreign investors are they "restricted securities"? The resale limitations of Rule 905, which deem certain securities offered under Reg S to be "restricted securities" as defined in 144, only apply to domestic issuer offerings of equity securities. Nonetheless, Rule 144 deems them to be "restricted securities" since they were acquired "indirectly from the issuer . . . in a chain of transactions not involving any public offering." Rule 144(a)(3).

e. No problem. Rule 144A contemplates precisely such an institutional market. The foreign investors may sell to "qualified institutional buyers" in the United States under Rule 144A. See §13.2.3 (Rule 144A conditions). Moreover, the investors may sell to "qualified institutional buyers" outside the United States under Rule 144A without becoming subject to the resale conditions of Reg S. See Securities Act Rel. No. 6863 (Apr. 24, 1990) (Reg S enacting release) (stating that offshore resales of restricted securities under Rule 144A are consistent with Rule 904).

f. No problem, provided no U.S. marketing or sales are made to buyers outside the United States. Offerings of securities "backed by the full faith and credit of a foreign government" fall into a Category 1 issuer offering under Reg S. Rule 903(1)(iii). Although the risk of flowback may be significant, U.S. investors are protected by the governmental guarantee and a presumably more informationally efficient market in government-backed securities. Moreover, U.S. regulation of foreign government economic policies in their own countries would be an international affront. Reg S shows some respect of national sovereignty.

§13.2 FOREIGN SECURITIES IN THE UNITED STATES

The U.S. securities markets lately have been a magnet for foreign issuers and their securities. As U.S. investors internationalize their portfolios, they have demanded the ability to buy and sell foreign securities from the convenience of home. As foreign issuers find that their home securities markets cannot wholly satisfy their capital needs, they have flocked to the broader and deeper securities markets in the United States. In 2004, approximately 10 percent of companies publicly traded in U.S. stock markets were foreign issuers, representing about 19 percent of total U.S. market capitalization.

The presence of foreign securities in the United States exposes the regulatory dilemma of cross-border securities markets. On the one hand is the long-standing regulatory attitude that U.S. investors deserve as much protection when investing in foreign securities as in domestic securities — an "isolationist" approach. On the other hand, rigorous regulatory parity may dissuade foreign issuers and the U.S. securities community from making foreign securities available to U.S. investors — an "internationalist" approach. In short, too little protection may unduly increase investment risk; too much protection may shrink investment opportunity.

§13.2.1 Public Offerings of Foreign Securities

A significant impetus for the Securities Act of 1933 was the billions of dollars in losses that U.S. investors experienced in the early 1930s after the collapse of foreign securities on U.S. markets. The Securities Act regulates offerings of foreign securities in much the same way as domestic offerings. See Securities Act §10. Absent an exemption, foreign issuers (both private and governmental) that sell to U.S. investors must register their securities. See Securities Act Schedule B (special disclosure requirements for offerings by foreign governments); Rule 3b-4 (defining "foreign private issuer" as any company incorporated outside the United States, unless (i) more than 50 percent of its shares are owned by U.S. residents and (ii) the majority of its directors or executive officers are U.S. residents or citizens, its business is principally in the United States, or more than 50 percent of its assets are located in the United States).

The SEC has created registration forms for foreign issuers selling to U.S. public investors that parallel the forms for their domestic counterparts:

Form F-1   Full-fledged disclosure for smaller, unseasoned foreign companies.

Form F-3   Disclosure by reference to already filed documents for "world class issuers" with one year of seasoning as a reporting company under the Exchange Act, not in arrears on its debt obligations, and with a worldwide float of $75 million or more.

Generally, foreign issuers have been required to disclose to the SEC and investors the same information in the same format as U.S. issuers. For many foreign companies, the U.S. securities disclosure regime has been an unwelcome burden. U.S. financial disclosure and accounting rules are generally far more detailed than those abroad. Mandatory disclosure of the issuer's competitive position and management's projections of future results are novel and often uncomfortable. To soften the blow, the SEC has permitted foreign issuers to reconcile their financials to U.S. accounting standards, without actually preparing them in accordance with the stricter U.S. standards. This has meant that foreign issuers need not break down line-of-business revenues and earnings or give detailed disclosure of executive compensation and insiders' dealings with the company.

In 2008 the SEC took a major step toward the internationalization of U.S. securities markets when the agency changed its rules to permit foreign private issuers to file home-country financial statements in English that conform to the International Financial Reporting Standards (IFRS), without reconciliation to U.S. Generally Accepted Accounting Principles (GAAP). Securities Act Rel. No. 8879 (2007). This reform makes it easier for foreign issuers to access the U.S. and global capital markets, without becoming subject to multiple national accounting standards. The reform also moves the United States and Europe (where the European Union in 2005 mandated IFRS for companies whose securities are traded on EU markets) toward a single accounting regime, with the SEC supporting the efforts of the International Accounting Standards Board (responsible for IFRS) and the Financial Standards Accounting Board (responsible for U.S. GAAP) to converge their accounting standards.

This acceptance of foreign standards had already happened for Canada. For Canadian issuers, the SEC adopted in 1991 a multijurisdictional disclosure system that permits larger issuers from Canada to use home-country offering documents when making a public offering in the United States. See Exchange Act Release No. 29354 (1991) (comparable U.S. issuers receive the same dispensation in Canada).

§13.2.2 American Depositary Receipts (ADRs)

The U.S. securities industry has invented an ingenious device for foreign issuers to export their securities to the United States for consumption by U.S. investors: American Depositary Receipts (ADRs). A typical ADR program works as follows:

- A U.S. bank enters into an agreement with a foreign private issuer to act as depositary of the issuer's securities (a sponsored ADR program).
- The U.S. depositary issues ADRs to U.S. investors. Each ADR is a negotiable certificate that represents an ownership interest in a given number of the foreign issuer's securities.
- The U.S. depositary acquires a corresponding amount of the foreign issuer's securities, which typically are held outside the United States by a foreign custodian.
- The ADRs trade in the United States like any other market-traded U.S. security. ADR pricing (in dollars) is based on the prices of the underlying foreign securities, which typically also trade in their domestic markets.
- After issuing the ADRs, the U.S. depositary acts as paying agent for ADR holders. The bank collects dividends, converts them into U.S. dollars, and distributes them to holders in the United States. The bank also collects issuer information and disseminates proxy materials to ADR holders.
- The U.S. depositary acts as transfer agent for the ADRs, recording trades among U.S. investors. The depositary also stands ready to exchange the ADRs for the underlying foreign securities.

For U.S. investors seeking to internationalize their portfolios, ADRs offer a "simultaneous translation" of foreign securities into easily negotiable, U.S.-dollar denominated certificates. ADRs can be bought and sold through U.S. securities firms like any other U.S. security.

The growth in the ADR market has been impressive. From 1990 to 2006, the value of ADRs traded on U.S. stock markets grew from $75 billion to $1,500 billion, representing approximately 8 percent of the total value of the public market in U.S. equity securities.

Regulatory Treatment of ADRs

The SEC takes the view that ADRs are separate from the underlying foreign securities that they represent, and the issuance of ADRs involves a public offering of securities in the United States. As such, the U.S. depositary bank that issues the ADRs is subject to the registration requirements of the Securities Act, and the foreign company whose "translated" securities come to be traded on public markets in the United States becomes subject to the reporting requirements of the Exchange Act.

But full-blown registration and reporting under the federal securities laws is particularly expensive and burdensome for foreign companies, which generally are subject at home to far less demanding disclosure and financial accounting standards. In recognition of this, the SEC has sought to accommodate ADR programs by mandating levels of disclosure that vary according to the foreign company's presence in U.S. securities markets.

Level 1 — Foot in U.S. Waters

In the first level, ADRs cannot be traded on stock exchanges or through NASDAQ, and U.S. securities regulation is modest. The depositary bank registers the ADRs under the Securities Act by filing Form F-6, which simply describes the ADR program and attaches the deposit agreement and a sample ADR certificate.

The SEC has exempted Level 1 ADR programs from the Exchange Act reporting requirements if the issuer publishes on its website *material* information (translated into English) that it makes public or files in its home country, or sends to its securities holders. Rule 12g3-2(b); see §13.2.4. Under the exemption, ADRs can be quoted in broker-dealers' "pink sheets" on the OTC markets but cannot be quoted or transacted on stock exchanges or NASDAQ. Level 1 programs, designed to give U.S. investors access to *existing* securities of foreign issuers, cannot be used to raise capital.

The costs of setting up a Level 1 program are small, averaging about $25,000. The gains to foreign issuers can be significant, as stock prices often jump 4-6 percent.

Level 2 — Wading into U.S. Waters

In the second level, ADRs can be traded on U.S. stock exchanges or through NASDAQ. The U.S. depositary must register the ADRs under the Securities Act on the perfunctory Form F-6, but the foreign issuer becomes subject to the full periodic reporting and other requirements of the Exchange Act. To list on a U.S. stock exchange or be quoted through NASDAQ, the foreign issuer must file a Form 20-F under the Exchange Act. See §13.2.4. As with Level 1, a Level 2 ADR program cannot be used to raise capital.

Foreign companies in Level 2 often find the Form 20-F disclosure requirements to be more detailed and intrusive than they are accustomed to at home. See Form 20-F. Foreign companies must either (1) conform their normal financial statements to U.S. "Generally Accepted Accounting Principles" (U.S. GAAP), which generally require more detailed financial disclosure than foreign accounting rules, or (2) prepare their financial statements in accordance with International Financial Reporting Standards as issued by the International Accounting Standards Board. Conforming financial statements to U.S. GAAP requires a breakdown of segment data on the company's various operations and disclosure of such sensitive (sometimes embarrassing) matters as its major properties, any material pending legal proceedings or government investigations, the identity of any 10 percent shareholders, aggregate board and executive compensation, and transactions between the company and its controlling shareholders or executives. In addition, foreign companies must also disclose how their corporate governance practices differ from those of U.S. issuers listed on the same exchange. Exchange Act Rel. No. 58,620 (2008). The company must update its 20-F filing annually.

The costs of establishing a Level 2 program are significant, averaging over $1 million. But the benefits may justify the cost. The increased access to U.S. investors and the increased stature that comes from U.S. GAAP disclosure can increase share prices by 10-15 percent.

Level 3 — Swimming in U.S. Waters

In the third level, the foreign issuer makes a public offering of its securities to U.S. investors. The registration statement in a Level 3 program must contain essentially the same information as the 20-F annual report required in Level 2. A Level 3 ADR program is the only program that allows foreign issuers to raise capital in the United States.

A public offering in the United States typically costs in excess of $1.5 million. For many foreign issuers with large capital needs, the U.S. public markets may offer an investment base unavailable at home or elsewhere in the world.

Global Depositary Receipts

Foreign issuers can also facilitate trading or offer their securities on a global basis through dollar-denominated Global Depositary Receipts (GDRs). A GDR program operates in exactly the same way as an ADR program, the only difference being that a GDR program operates in whole or in part outside the United States. Whether labeled an ADR or a GDR, the rules applicable to the portion of the program in the United States are the same.

§13.2.3 Private Placements and Rule 144A

Foreign issuers can raise capital in the United States and avoid U.S. disclosure requirements by privately placing securities with sophisticated institutional investors. The normal §4(2) (or safe harbor Rule 506) limitations apply: no public advertising, investor sophistication, and access to information, and no resales to unqualified investors. See §5.2.4. Investors will usually insist on an offering memorandum that describes the company and factors relevant to the offering, as well as some financial information. But this disclosure will not have to conform to U.S. accounting or disclosure requirements.

Rule 144A — Safe Harbor for Institutional Trading

To facilitate a secondary trading market in restricted securities, the SEC has established a safe harbor rule for trading by institutional investors. Rule 144A (see §7.2.2). By selling only to "qualified institutional buyers" (QIBs), investors who hold restricted securities (and assisting securities firms) avoid becoming "statutory underwriters." QIBs include

- any institution with an investment portfolio of at least $100 million,
- a registered broker-dealer (with an investment portfolio of at least $10 million) that buys for itself or for a QIB,
- any registered broker-dealer buying for a QIB, and
- a registered investment company that is part of a mutual fund family with a total investment portfolio of at least $100 million.

QIBs can trade in a so-called 144A market without being subject to the one or two-year holding periods applicable to "restricted securities" under Rule 144. And 144A investors, using the "resale" safe harbor of Regulation S, can cancel their ADRs and sell the actual shares back into the home market. Typically, foreign issuers that sell into the 144A market will be those not ready to register with the SEC and wishing to place a relatively small amount (up to $50 million) of securities in the United States.

§13.2.4 Requirements for Foreign Issuers with U.S.-Traded Securities

Disclosure Requirements

Technically, under §12 of the Exchange Act, any foreign issuer with more than $10 million in assets and more than 2000 record shareholders worldwide (or 500 accredited investors worldwide) must register its equity securities under the Exchange Act. The SEC, however, has exempted foreign private issuers from the Exchange Act filing requirements if the issuer's securities do not trade on a U.S. securities exchange or NASDAQ, but instead are listed on a foreign stock exchange (the primary trading market), and the issuer has not made a U.S. public offering. The foreign issuer must simply publish on its website material information (translated into English) that it otherwise makes public or files in its home country, or sends to foreign securities holders. Rule 12g3-2(b); see Exchange Act Rel. No. 58,465

(2008) (amending disclosure requirements for foreign private issuers, which no longer need to apply to or notify the SEC).

For foreign issuers whose securities trade on a U.S. stock exchange or NASDAQ, the issuer is subject to Exchange Act registration and annual reporting using Form 20-F, whose disclosure requirements parallel those of Form F-1 of the Securities Act (see §13.2.1). Foreign issuers (both private and public) must file their disclosure documents on EDGAR. Securities Act Rel. No. 8099 (2002) (also permitting in some cases an English summary of foreign language documents, rather than English translation).

As we have seen, the SEC has not subjected foreign issuers to the full rigors of disclosure required of domestic issuers — an "internationalist approach." Foreign issuers are excused from disclosing line-of-business information, detailed management compensation, and material transactions between the issuer and management. To allow foreign issuers to make uniform global disclosures, the SEC amended Form 20-F to mirror the disclosure standards for *non-financial information* endorsed by the International Organization of Securities Commissioners. Securities Act Release No. 7745 (1999) (requiring additional disclosures, beyond IOSCO standards, regarding major shareholders (defined as holders of 5 percent or more), the foreign issuer's preemptive rights and foreign trading market, the compensation of directors and officers, and management self-dealing transactions). In addition, the SEC permits foreign private issuers to file home-country financial statements in English that conform to the International Financial Reporting Standards (IFRS), without reconciliation to U.S. Generally Accepted Accounting Principles (GAAP). See §13.2.1.

Significantly, the SEC exempts foreign private issuers (including those subject to reporting on Form 20-F) from the §14 proxy rules and the §16 short-swing disclosure and disgorgement rules of the Exchange Act. Rule 3a12-3(b) (see §8.4 and §10.3). See *Schiller v. Tower Semiconductor Ltd*, 449 F.3d 286 (2d Cir. 2006) (upholding SEC's authority to exempt foreign private issuers from proxy rules, including rule prohibiting proxy fraud). The SEC also has provided exemptions for cross-border takeover bids and rights offerings by foreign issuers not registered with the SEC under the Exchange Act. Securities Act Release No. 7759 (1999). Under the exemption, such foreign issuers can include U.S. investors in their takeover and rights offerings, if the percentage of U.S. investors is not significant, without complying with SEC disclosure and tender offer regulations.

Governance Requirements

Despite the many regulatory dispensations given foreign issuers whose securities trade on U.S. securities markets, the Sarbanes-Oxley Act of 2002 largely disregards whether a reporting company is domestic or foreign. Sarbanes-Oxley, however, is an uncomfortable fit for many foreign issuers with securities traded in U.S. markets. For example, many foreign companies do not have boards composed of a majority of outside directors, have board audit committees, or maintain internal controls to verify financial reporting and to ensure legal compliance.

Here is a list of some of the Sarbanes-Oxley requirements dealing with oversight and governance in public companies, and the impact on foreign issuers:

Sarbanes-Oxley requirement	Impact on foreign issuers
Auditor registration. All accounting firms that audit public companies must register and become subject to standards of the new Public Company Accounting Oversight Board.	Foreign accounting firms that audit foreign issuers must register and are subject to the standards of the PCAOB. Some standards, particularly on disclosure of privileged information and performance of non-audit services, may be at odds with applicable foreign law.
Audit committee. The audit committee must be composed exclusively of independent directors, and is charged with hiring, supervising, and compensating the company's outside auditor.	Many foreign issuers cannot assign audit oversight to independent directors. Some have a statutory board of auditors, charged with the audit function; others have a two-tiered board structure, without independent directors on the management board.
Certification of SEC filings. The CEO and CFO must certify that company financials are "fairly presented" — a new standard often involving legal and non-accounting judgments.	In many European countries and Japan, company financials must be certified as "true and fair" — a standard based solely on professional accounting judgment.
Internal controls. Reporting companies must include statements in their annual report that describe and assess their internal controls.	Internal controls, as demanded by U.S. corporate and criminal sentencing guidelines, are not required for many foreign issuers under applicable foreign law.
Loans to corporate executives. Reporting companies may not extend credit to any director or CEO, except as part of a U.S. financial institution's regular lending practices.	Foreign issuers often provide a significant portion of executive pay as credit to executives. The exception for lending by financial institutions is not available to foreign financial institutions.

Protection of whistleblowers. Employees who report accounting and business fraud are protected from retaliation, and issuers must establish procedures to handle complaints of accounting improprieties.

Foreign issuers and executives become subject to the civil and criminal liabilities created to enforce the whistleblower provisions.

"Up the ladder" reporting. Lawyers working for reporting companies must report to specified company officials evidence of securities violations or breaches of fiduciary duties; failure to report is subject to SEC disciplinary action.

These new professional duties may require foreign lawyers performing securities work for foreign issuers to become familiar with U.S. securities and corporate laws, and would subject them to extraterritorial discipline.

In implementing Sarbanes-Oxley, some SEC rules (such as the definition of independent directors on audit committees) have sought to accommodate foreign issuers. But generally the Sarbanes-Oxley requirements represent a departure from the "internationalist" approach that has characterized SEC regulation of foreign issuers over the past 20 years. In reaction to Sarbanes-Oxley and the SEC reluctance to broadly exempt foreign issuers from its requirements, a few foreign issuers have withdrawn their listings on U.S. markets and others have delayed plans to become listed.

Unlike the SEC, the NYSE and NASDAQ have shown more sympathy to foreign issuers whose corporate structures often differ from those of domestic U.S. issuers. See §8.3.5 (governance listing standards). For example, the NYSE permits listed foreign private issuers to follow home country governance practices, provided such companies (1) have an audit committee that satisfies the requirements of Rule 10A-3, (2) notify the NYSE after any executive officer becomes aware of non-compliance with any applicable provision, and (3) provide a summary of how its governance differs from that of domestic listed companies. NYSE Manual §303A. Listed foreign private issuers could provide this disclosure on their website — provided it is in English and accessible from the United States.

Despite the "unilateralist" nature of Sarbanes-Oxley, there are indications it may have catalyzed new international standards of corporate governance. For example, many European countries in response to Sarbanes-Oxley have revamped their corporate governance codes (nonbinding codes of ethics that function as a self-regulatory system through voluntary company adoption and disclosure). The EU also responded with an action plan proposing many of the Sarbanes-Oxley reforms, and sometimes going beyond them, as a cooperative, competitive, and resistant response to U.S. extraterritoriality.

Examples

1. Cattlemen Bank, the largest commercial bank in the country of Euphoria, wishes to increase its shareholder base by making its shares available to U.S. investors. A U.S. bank, Bank of New Columbia (BONC), offers to establish an ADR program for Cattlemen in the United States. Cattlemen has some questions:

   a. Cattlemen shares are traded on Euphoria's stock exchanges. If U.S. investors want to acquire foreign investments, what is to keep them from buying in Euphoria?

   b. Why might U.S. investors prefer to acquire Cattlemen ADRs?

   c. BONC agrees to set up an ADR program in which it agrees to issue certificates in the United States representing outstanding shares of Cattlemen that BONC will acquire and hold in Euphoria. Must Cattlemen register these certificates with the SEC? Must BONC?

   d. Cattlemen shares, denominated and traded in Euphorian pesos at home, will trade in the United States in U.S. dollars. What exchange rate will BONC use to set the price in the United States?

   e. Can Cattlemen raise capital in the United States by issuing new shares through the ADR program?

2. The Cattlemen ADR program is a success. Ten percent of Cattlemen shares come to be deposited with BONC and are represented as ADRs held by U.S. investors. Identify any problems.

   a. Probity Overseas Fund, a U.S. mutual fund, changes its investment strategy and plans to dump its Cattlemen ADRs. Probity demands that BONC repurchase the ADRs.

   b. Cattlemen issues new shares in Euphoria, which BONC buys on Euphoria's stock markets to satisfy increased demand by U.S. shareholders.

   c. Cattlemen prepares a skimpy annual report, as required by Euphoria's securities laws. It then submits an untranslated copy of this annual report to the SEC. The report seriously misstates the company's revenues and earnings.

3. Cattlemen becomes a takeover target of a shadowy international trading company. Fearful of what might happen to the bank's business, Cattlemen management undertakes a takeover defense and considers two options. Identify any problems.

   a. Cattlemen considers a poison pill in which it will issue rights to its existing shareholders, including indirectly to ADR holders. The rights, which will be exercisable upon a takeover by a hostile bidder, would give shareholders (other than the bidder) the option to acquire newly issued, deeply discounted securities.

b. Cattlemen considers making a self-tender for 25 percent of its outstanding shares, including its shares represented by ADRs. The company's offer to repurchase will be on a first-come, first-served basis.

Explanations

1. a. Absent restrictions in the foreign country on investments by non-nationals or U.S. restrictions on foreign investments by fiduciaries such as pension plans or bank trust departments, there are no legal restrictions on U.S. investors acquiring securities abroad. There are, however, numerous practical obstacles to offshore investing. Foreign markets often lack transparency, and it is hard to know about listed companies and the price at which securities are trading. Further, foreign markets lack liquidity, and it is difficult to sell securities quickly. U.S. investors must convert their purchases into the local currency and then convert into U.S. dollars any dividends and the proceeds from any sales. In addition, the U.S. investors must count on local securities firms to make buy-sell transactions and to forward information about market developments, collect dividends (which in many countries must be done in person), or to vote shares or proxies.

b. ADRs offer many advantages over investing directly in foreign markets. After the commencement of an ADR program, a market in the ADRs develops in the United States that operates just like markets in U.S. securities. ADR investors are afforded virtually the same liquidity as investors in U.S.-based securities. Level 2 and 3 ADRs can be listed on a U.S. stock exchange or quoted on NASDAQ, just like U.S. securities. Level 1 ADRs are listed on electronic bulletin boards and the "pink sheets" of the National Quotation Bureau, Inc. — OTC markets separate from NASDAQ. The bulletin boards and daily pink sheets show U.S. broker-dealers information on buy-sell quotes and the names of market makers. In addition, the U.S. depositary bank (acting as transfer agent) provides for the ready settlement of buy-sell transactions among U.S. investors.

Besides liquidity, an ADR program also provides transparency with the foreign market. The U.S. depositary monitors dividend distributions in the foreign country, collects them, converts them into U.S. dollars, and remits them to ADR holders — providing a transparency beyond the means of most U.S. investors. The depositary also forwards proxy materials and information to U.S. brokers and investors. ADRs overcome other impediments, as well. U.S. investors (such as pension plans or trust fiduciaries) limited in the types and amounts of investments in foreign markets may be able to avoid these limits and purchase ADRs on U.S. markets. Furthermore, some foreign issuers

621

face home-country restrictions on foreign ownership of their securities, which an ADR program may be able to sidestep if the issuer's shares can be held nominally by an affiliate of the U.S. depositary.

c. For a Level 1 ADR program, the issuer need not register the ADRs under the Securities Act, but the depositary bank must register them on the simplified Form F-6. The issuer — it has assets exceeding $5 million and it anticipates more than 500 ADR holders in the United States — must comply with the exemptive conditions of Rule 12g3-2(b) to avoid Exchange Act registration.

The SEC has taken the odd position that a Level 1 program (in which the foreign issuer's shares are neither listed on a U.S. stock market nor quoted on NASDAQ) has not "voluntarily" entered the United States, and no Exchange Act reporting is required. Exchange Act Rel. No. 8066 (1967); Securities Act Rel. No. 6340 (1981). This regulatory shrug applies even when the foreign issuer sponsors the ADR program. The SEC has assumed for Level 1 programs that disclosure in the issuer's home market is adequate, an assumption at odds with the SEC's requirement of full-blown Exchange Act registration once the issuer's shares begin to trade in a Level 2 program on a stock exchange or NASDAQ.

A 12g3-2(b) exemption requires only that the foreign company publish on its website specified disclosure documents it has provided regulators, exchanges, or investors in its home country, and then only if this information is "material to the investment decision." These documents must be translated into English.

d. The depositary bank does not price the ADRs; the markets do. In an ADR program, the ADR price takes its lead from the underlying stock price in the home country. As trading takes place simultaneously in the U.S. and in the home markets, price movements in one market are mirrored by movements in the other market through price arbitrage.

e. Yes, but only if the offering is structured as a Level 3 ADR program and is either registered or qualifies for an exemption from the Securities Act registration requirements.

2. a. The depositary does not itself provide liquidity. It assumes no obligation by law or contract to *repurchase* ADRs for its own account. At most, it must stand ready to exchange the ADRs for the underlying shares, a condition of the Rule 12g3-2 exemption.

Thus, if the U.S. mutual fund sought to cancel its ADRs in exchange for the underlying shares held by the depositary, it would still have to find a buyer of the underlying shares, perhaps in Euphoria using the Reg S resale safe harbor. For the U.S. mutual fund, it is easier to sell the ADRs to another U.S. buyer under a §4(1) trading exemption, such as Rule 144A (to another QIB) or Rule 144 (after a six-month or one-year holding period).

b. **Problem.** Registration on Form F-6 is conditioned on the depositary acquiring the underlying securities in transactions exempt from registration or themselves registered under the Securities Act. Securities Act Rel. No. 5459 (Mar. 18, 1983). This means that a foreign issuer seeking to raise capital in the United States cannot use an ADR program as a means to circumvent Securities Act registration.

Why does the SEC impose full U.S. disclosure regulation on foreign issuers seeking to raise capital, thus effectively denying investment opportunities to U.S. investors? On one hand, the SEC leaves U.S. investors to their own protections when buying Level 1 ADRs. Arguably, U.S. investors discount such ADRs to account for the relatively weaker disclosure and antifraud protection of foreign securities regulation. In fact, institutional investors in U.S. markets do not insist that foreign issuers in private placements under Rule 144A follow U.S. GAAP financial reporting standards. SEC Staff Report on Rule 144A at ¶84, 428 (1994). The notion that the SEC should insist on "U.S. gold-plated" disclosure for all foreign entrants assumes U.S. investors (particularly those who invest in U.S. offerings of ADRs) are ninnies. The effect of the assumption is to add costs to efficient portfolio diversification as U.S. investors are driven offshore or to U.S. mutual funds that buy the same foreign securities denied individual U.S. investors.

The 2008 reform that permits foreign issuers to prepare their financial statements according to International Financial Reporting Standards (IFRS), rather than having to conform them to U.S. GAAP, is one step closer to the creation of a global securities market in which investments available in one country are available in every other country. But, although accounting standards may be converging, other disclosure requirements (and the substantive requirements of Sarbanes-Oxley and other national laws) continue to vary and thus impose barriers to investors accessing securities on a global basis.

c. **Problem.** To encourage compliance with the condition that foreign issuers with ADR programs submit their home disclosure documents to the SEC, such information is not considered to be "filed" for purposes of liability under §18 of the Exchange Act. See Rule 12g3-2(b)(4). Nonetheless, the submitted information is subject to the antifraud strictures of Rule 10b-5. The SEC can bring enforcement actions against the company (see Chapter 12), and defrauded investors and traders have a private cause of action for any materially false or misleading statements made with the requisite intent to deceive or reckless disregard of the truth. See §9.3.

3. a. No problem, provided the U.S. investors (directly or through ADRs) hold no more than 10 percent of the outstanding Cattlemen shares. Securities Act Rule 801. Under a rule promulgated in 1999, the SEC sought to encourage foreign issuers to include U.S. holders of foreign securities in rights offerings by easing the burdens of U.S. securities compliance in cross-border transactions. Under the rule the issuer must allow U.S. holders to participate on terms at least as favorable as those offered other holders and must furnish any informational document (in English) on a comparable basis as provided holders in its home jurisdiction. Rule 801(a). A special legend must warn U.S. holders that the rights offering may be subject to diluted disclosure requirements and that enforcing shareholder rights may be difficult in U.S. courts under U.S. law. Rule 801(b).

The SEC once took the position that rights offerings by foreign companies with ADR programs involve the offering of new shares to U.S. holders and, as such, are subject to registration. Securities Act Rel. No. 6902 (1991). This SEC stance created the problem that U.S. investors, compared to foreign investors, had less opportunity to maintain their proportionate ownership when a foreign issuer issued new securities to existing shareholders.

b. No problem, if the U.S. investors (directly or through ADRs) hold no more than 10 percent of the outstanding Cattlemen shares. Exchange Act Rule 14d-1(c). As part of the SEC's initiative to facilitate the inclusion of U.S. holders in cross-border transactions, the SEC exempted foreign tender offers from most of the Williams Act rules — including the rule against first-come, first-served bids. Exchange Act §14(d)(6) (see §8.5.3). Under the exemption, the foreign bidder must permit U.S. holders to participate on terms at least as favorable as those offered other holders and must disseminate any informational documents (in English) on a comparable basis as to holders in the home jurisdiction. Rule 14d-1(c) (Tier I exemption). More exacting conditions apply if U.S. holders account for more than 10 percent, and up to 40 percent, of the outstanding shares. Rule 14d-1(d) (Tier II exemption). These new rules, promulgated in 1999, are meant to encourage foreign bidders and issuers to extend their exchange and tender offers to U.S. holders, who in the past had been excluded to avoid the burden of U.S. securities regulation.

How does a foreign bidder or issuer know how many U.S. holders there are? The SEC gives instructions on making inquiries of U.S. securities firms and calculating U.S. ownership, including when ADRs are held in "street name" by nominees. For uninvited third-party bidders, the presumption is that U.S. holders hold no more than 10 percent, unless trading on U.S. stock markets exceeds 10 percent of the outstanding shares or the bidder has reason to know U.S. holders exceed 10 percent.

§13.3 EXTRATERRITORIAL REACH OF U.S. SECURITIES LAWS

The federal securities acts acknowledge, though do not solve, the question of their extraterritoriality. Both the Securities Act of 1933 and Securities Exchange Act of 1934 define their jurisdiction to reach securities activities between any "foreign country" and the United States. Securities Act §2(a)(7); Exchange Act §3(a)(17). Yet, Congress may have meant its broad definitions to be read with some circumspection. The Securities Act by its terms regulates only foreign offerings into the United States, not foreign offerings abroad. See Securities Act, Schedule B (requiring disclosure of agent, net proceeds and price for sales in the United States). The Exchange Act expressly states it does not apply to persons who transact "a business in securities without the jurisdiction of the United States" — that is, foreign broker-dealers. Exchange Act §30(b) (unless the SEC regulates such persons, which the agency has not done).

In the end, U.S. courts must determine whether the federal securities laws apply to transactions with extraterritorial elements. If the transaction is determined to be within the jurisdiction of the United States, the court will apply U.S. securities law. If not, the court will dismiss the case. Applying foreign law is not an option — federal courts have taken the view that they lack subject matter jurisdiction in such cases.

§13.3.1 Securities Fraud Litigation

The favorable investment climate in the United States has not only beguiled foreign issuers and investors, but also litigants (both U.S. and foreign) seeking the benefits of the U.S. securities laws. Victims of securities wrongs committed outside the United States — and their lawyers — find attractive the many features of U.S. securities litigation: class action procedures (unavailable in most other countries), broad liability standards (including a presumption of investor reliance in public trading markets), a competent and knowledgeable federal judiciary, liberal process and discovery rules, relatively expeditious litigation, and powerful tools for the enforcement of judgments. See *SEC v. Tome*, F.2d (2d Cir. 1987) (upholding service of process over unknown foreign defendants charged with insider trading, based on notice-publication of complaint in International Herald Tribune, given that defendants had traded in U.S. securities on U.S. exchange).

What is the substantive reach of the U.S. securities antifraud jurisdiction, particularly Rule 10b-5? U.S. courts face a dilemma, again engendered by the dual fear and desire for foreign-flavored securities transactions. On the one hand, the federal securities laws are meant to protect U.S. investors and the integrity of the U.S. securities markets. Excusing securities violations simply because a party or transaction has foreign attributes undermines this U.S. promise.

On the other hand, the United States is not alone in the world, and it is in our national interest to respect foreign sovereignty and abide by principles of international comity. Inviting securities litigants to the United States may undermine the regulatory cost-benefit choices in other countries, thus sowing international discord and uncertainty. For example, U.S. court judgments in class action litigation may not be enforceable in other countries that do not recognize the binding effect of class litigation. In the end, assertion of U.S. securities jurisdiction may unduly discourage foreign persons from entering into securities transactions with U.S. persons or in the United States — or establishing business ties to the United States that could be seen as a "nexus" sufficient to establish jurisdiction in a case involving foreign securities transactions.

Interpreting U.S. "subject matter" jurisdiction broadly, lower federal courts over the past 40 years have resolved this dilemma using tests that liberally measure U.S. interests in the securities transactions with foreign elements. Under an "effects" test, illegal transactions outside the United States are subject to U.S. subject matter jurisdiction if they cause harm to U.S. investors or U.S. securities markets — an *investor protection* rationale. Under a "conduct" test, acts in the United States that are part of a fraudulent securities transaction are subject to U.S. jurisdiction even though reliance and harm occur abroad — a *market integrity* rationale.

But in 2010 the U.S. Supreme Court significantly closed the "open door" policy arising from these judicial tests. The Court held that 10b-5 actions could be brought only when there had been a transaction (purchase or sale) in the U.S. securities marketsregardless of conduct or effects in the United States. Nonetheless, the "conduct" and "effects" tests remain relevant in enforcement actions given that Dodd-Frank overruled the Court's decision as to SEC enforcement actions and DOJ criminal prosecutions.

"Effects" Test — Fraud Fired into the United States

The "effects" test was articulated first in a case involving a French corporation's purchase in Canada of additional shares of its partially owned Canadian subsidiary. *Schoenbaum v. Firstbrook*, 405 F.2d 789 (2d Cir. 1968). The plaintiffs, U.S. shareholders of the subsidiary, brought a derivative suit claiming company insiders had violated Rule 10b-5 when they issued the stock at an unfairly low price. The Second Circuit pointed out the subsidiary's shares were listed and traded on the American Stock Exchange, so that the foreign defendants could easily have foreseen that the challenged transaction would lower the price for U.S. investors. This foreseeable harm to U.S. investors, the court held, satisfied the "effects" test even though the fraudulent conduct had occurred abroad.

"Conduct" Test — Fraud Fired from United States

The "conduct" test arose first in a case involving the stock purchase of a U.K. company on the London Stock Exchange, where some meetings were held in New York and the purchase contract was signed in the United States. *Leasco Data Processing Equipment Corp. v. Maxwell*, 468 F.2d 1326 (2d Cir. 1972). The purchaser, a New York corporation investing through an offshore Netherlands Antilles subsidiary, challenged the transaction on the basis of fraudulent misrepresentations, some of which were made to it in New York. The Second Circuit held that this conduct in the United States "significantly whetted" the plaintiff's interest in acquiring the foreign company and justified the assertion of U.S. jurisdiction, even though the purchased shares were traded only outside the United States.

Later cases have clarified that the "conduct" test creates jurisdiction for claims by foreign investors only when activities (or failures to act) in the United States "directly cause," and are more than "merely preparatory" to, a securities fraud abroad. See *Bersch v. Drexel Firestone, Inc.*, 519 F.2d 974 (2d Cir. 1975). Nonetheless, lower courts have extended to foreign investors the same protections as apply to U.S. investors, such as when a U.S. issuer sells to a foreign investor using a prospectus and financial information prepared in the United States. See *Kauthar SDN v. Sternberg*, 148 F.3d 659 (7th Cir. 1998) (finding jurisdiction under "conduct test" where various defendants prepared false selling materials and made phone calls in the United States to a foreign investor, who wired payment to a bank account in Indiana).

Morrison "Transactional" Test

In 2010, the Supreme Court weighed in on the extraterritorial reach of §10(b) over securities transactions that have an international dimension. *Morrison v. Nat'l Australia Bank Ltd.*, 130 S. Ct. 2869 (2010). The Court held that §10(b) applies "only in connection with a purchase or sale of a security listed on an American stock exchange, and the purchase or sale of any other security in the United States." The Court rejected that conduct in the United States could be the basis for U.S. securities jurisdiction, reflecting the concern that the United States might otherwise become "the Shangri-La of class-action litigation for lawyers representing those allegedly cheated in foreign securities markets."

In the case, non-U.S. investors who had purchased shares of an Australian bank on overseas exchanges — a "foreign-cubed" case, since the plaintiffs, the defendants, and the place of the transaction were all foreign — brought a class action in U.S. district court claiming securities fraud under §10(b) and Rule 10b-5. The plaintiffs pointed to false statements that had occurred in Florida, but the Court rejected the "conduct" test as too attenuated when the securities transactions occurred outside the

United States. Instead, the Court held that §10(b) extends only to transactions in securities listed on U.S. exchanges, or to securities transactions that take place in the United States — that is, a "transactional" test focused on where the challenged securities transaction had occurred.

The *Morrison* decision thus dramatically redrew the boundaries of §10(b)'s extraterritorial reach. For example, "conduct" (such as the making of false statements) that occurred in the United States, but that did not result in securities transactions in the United States, is no longer subject to U.S. court securities antifraud jurisdiction. In addition, securities fraud occurring on a foreign market, though having an indirect "effect" on U.S. investors, but challenged only by investors whose transactions occurred on the foreign market, is also beyond the reach of Rule 10b-5.

Lower courts have embraced Morrison, applying its "transactional" test to reject even securities fraud claims by U.S. investors who purchased ADRs on the over-the-counter market in the United States. See In re *Societe Generale Securities Litigation*, 2010 WL 3910286 (S.D.N.Y. 2010) (dismissing case against French issuer, since trading in ADRs is "predominately foreign securities transaction"). Yet a 10b-5 claim may still be brought when securities, though not traded on a U.S. stock exchange, are transferred within the United States or a party incurs an irrevocable liability within the United States to purchase or deliver them. See *Absolute Activist Value Master Fund Ltd. v. Ficeto*, 677 F.3d 60 (2d Cir. 2012) ("irrevocable liability" or "title was transferred" within United States).

Partial Overruling of *Morrison* by Dodd-Frank Act

Within weeks after *Morrison* was decided, Congress effectively overruled the decision as to SEC enforcement actions and federal criminal prosecutions. Dodd-Frank §929P(b) (in actions brought by the SEC and Department of Justice, extending "extraterritorial jurisdiction" to violations involving conduct or effect in the United States). To protect the United States from becoming "the Barbary Coast for those perpetrating frauds on foreign securities markets," Dodd-Frank sought to codify the "conduct" and "effects" tests articulated by the lower courts — in public enforcement actions. The Act gives federal courts jurisdiction over antifraud actions brought by the government under §17 of the Securities Act and §10(b) of the Exchange Act involving —

> (1) *conduct* within the United States that constitutes significant steps in furtherance of the violation, even if the securities transaction occurs outside the United States and involves only foreign investors; or (2) conduct occurring outside the United States that has a foreseeable *substantial effect* within the United States.

As a result, U.S. investors who invest abroad and claim securities fraud in the overseas market must either hope for U.S. governmental enforcement or seek legal recourse in the foreign country, where procedural and substantive obstacles make litigation (especially class litigation) less attractive. Although Dodd-Frank calls on the SEC to study whether the federal antifraud laws should extend to conduct outside the United States, it is unclear whether Congress would act on an SEC recommendation to re-expand federal court jurisdiction in private actions after the *Morrison* contraction. See Dodd-Frank §929Y.

Extraterritorial Reach of Securities Fraud Enforcement

Here's where private and public enforcement of the antifraud provisions of the federal securities laws stands after *Morrison* and Dodd-Frank:

	Private enforcement	Public enforcement
Transactional test	Yes	Yes
Effects test	No	Yes*
Conduct test	No	Yes*

* Dodd-Frank §929P.

§13.3.2 Federal Government Enforcement

As we have seen, the SEC has broad authority to enforce the federal securities laws. These powers extend extraterritorially for the protection both of U.S. and foreign investors. When the agency suspects a violation, the SEC can institute an administrative proceeding or file a civil suit in federal court seeking an injunction or other appropriate relief. See §§12.1, 12.2, 12.3. In serious cases the SEC can refer the matter to the U.S. Department of Justice for criminal prosecution. See §12.5. In enforcement actions involving foreign persons, the SEC exercises its powers both unilaterally and in cooperation with foreign securities authorities.

Sometimes the SEC enforces the U.S. securities laws with respect to conduct illegal under U.S. law, but not the law of the country where the action took place. For example, in an enforcement action against a German industrial holding company listed on the NYSE that had falsely denied being engaged in merger negotiations, the SEC applied the Rule 10b-5 standard of materiality. The SEC acknowledged that the false denials did not violate German law, but concluded that "a foreign issuer that voluntarily avails itself of the opportunities in the U.S. capital markets . . . must adhere to the U.S. federal securities laws." *In the Matter of E. On AG*, Exchange Act Rel. No. 43372 (2000) (press releases making denials issued in both German and English).

Unilateral Enforcement

The SEC has broad powers in the United States to attach and sequester property, appoint receivers, and initiate administrative and court proceedings, including against foreign persons and entities. Congress has encouraged the SEC to investigate suspected violations of U.S. securities laws that occur outside the United States.

The SEC has interpreted its extraterritorial jurisdiction in fraud cases broadly along the same lines as courts applying the "effects" and "conduct" tests. See §13.3.1 above. In the context of foreign offerings over the Internet, for example, the SEC has taken the position that the antifraud provisions of the U.S. securities laws continue to reach "all Internet activities that satisfy the relevant jurisdictional tests." Securities Act Rel. No. 7516 (1998).

In response to the SEC's sometimes high-handed tactics, a number of foreign countries have enacted secrecy and blocking laws that seek to prevent SEC access to documentation and witnesses in securities fraud cases. These laws can put foreign companies that have information relevant to an SEC investigation in a compromised position. See *SEC v. Banca Della Svizzera Italiana*, 92 F.R.D. 111 (S.D.N.Y. 1981) (to avoid U.S. sanctions in an SEC investigation, U.S. office of a Swiss bank obtained from its customers a waiver of Swiss secrecy laws).

Cooperative Enforcement

Over the last decade, the SEC has pursued a strategy of international cooperation. To coordinate international enforcement of U.S. securities laws, the SEC has entered into nonbinding agreements with "like-minded" foreign securities regulators. These Memoranda of Understanding (MOUs) permit the SEC to request foreign regulators to investigate (collect documents, take statements, examine compliance) and provide the SEC information in circumstances in which the SEC could not do so on its own. The MOUs have permitted the SEC to track down such matters as offshore insider trading and secret bank accounts.

In addition, the United States has entered into mutual assistance treaties with a number of countries (most notably Switzerland) for the mutual assistance in the investigation of activities that are criminal in both countries, such as locating witnesses, obtaining statements, production of business records, and service of legal documents.

The SEC is also a member of the International Organization of Securities Commissions, an organization with more than 170 members founded in 1974 that proposes guidelines on various aspects of securities regulation, such as cooperation in investigations of Internet-based fraud. The IOSCO guidelines, though not binding, form an important element in the SEC's regulation of international securities activities.

Congress has sanctioned the extension of foreign securities regulation into the United States — reverse extraterritoriality. Under the Securities Fraud Enforcement Act of 1988, the SEC can aid foreign securities investigations, even when no U.S. law would have been violated had the conduct occurred in the United States. Exchange Act §21(a)(2). Likewise, the International Securities Enforcement Cooperation Act of 1990 authorizes the SEC to sanction securities professionals who engage in activities found to be illegal by foreign courts, even if the behavior is not illegal in the United States. Exchange Act §15(b)(4)(G).

Recent SEC Enforcement

In recent years, SEC enforcement against foreign companies has increased — as the number of foreign companies listed on U.S. stock markets has grown (nearly doubling in the last decade to 1,230) and following the U.S. and foreign accounting scandals exposed in the early 2000s. The SEC has filed and settled charges with foreign companies and executives that overstated oil reserves, engaged in insider trading, inflated assets in securities offerings, and misled investors about profits. Sanctions have included fines, disgorgement of gains, asset freezes, and changes in corporate governance.

The SEC's more aggressive policing of securities law compliance by foreign companies has sometimes been with the cooperation of foreign securities regulators. For example, in a case of insider trading by executives of a Cyprus company listed on the NYSE, the SEC coordinated an investigation and asset freezes by regulators along a money trail across Europe. In other cases, however, the SEC has acted alone using its greater enforcement powers (including the authority to quickly settle cases) and the threat of its broad sanctioning arsenal — weapons sometimes unavailable in other countries. Some have characterized the SEC as engaging in "U.S. regulatory imperialism," even though most recent SEC investigations and sanctions involving foreign companies have happened with the assistance of foreign regulators.

Criminal Prosecutions

The U.S. Department of Justice has authority to bring criminal charges against foreign individuals and companies, subject to the same jurisdictional constraints that face the SEC. Such cases, however, are unusual given the difficulties in arresting foreign individuals and enforcing criminal sanctions against entities.

In a criminal investigation, the DOJ can use treaties calling for mutual legal assistance in criminal investigations, including securities crimes. The treaties (known as Mutual Legal Assistance Treaties) require that each country recognize the criminality of the violation for which assistance is sought — "dual-criminality" requirements.

Examples

1. Global Ltd., an acquisitive transnational holding company, hired I. M. Warthog to identify potential takeover targets. Warthog, an international investment banking firm, analyzed publicly available information about Bullseye PLC, a London-based conglomerate, and concluded Bullseye was a good match for Global. Relying on Warthog's recommendation, Global bought $114 million of Bullseye's securities. Days later Bullseye publicly announced a shocking series of business reversals, and the value of Global's holdings in Bullseye fell to $3 million — a 97 percent decline in value. Global has sued Bullseye and its executives in U.S. federal court alleging violations of §10(b) and Rule 10b-5. Which of the following is relevant to the court's subject matter jurisdiction?

   a. Global is organized in Bermuda and has no facilities, offices, or personnel in the United States.

   b. Before its purchases, Warthog arranged for Global to meet with Bullseye executives in Warthog's offices in New York City to discuss a "friendly" acquisition. The Bullseye executives (as well as the Warthog bankers) kept quiet about the company's business reversals, and the meeting bore no fruit.

   c. Global made all its purchases of Bullseye stock on the London Stock Exchange.

   d. Although Bullseye's shares are traded primarily on the London Stock Exchange, 10 percent of its shares are represented by ADRs traded on NASDAQ in the United States.

   e. Bullseye is a reporting company under the Exchange Act, and Warthog relied on Bullseye's Exchange Act filings in making its recommendation to Global.

2. Worldwide Motors, a U.S. corporation whose shares are listed and traded on all the major exchanges of the world, has been the subject of rampant rumors that it may spin off its nonautomotive businesses. Its stock prices worldwide rise and fall as investors guess management's intentions. Last month, the WM board met secretly and approved a staged divestiture of

the company's nonautomotive businesses. Before the public announcement, Juan Herrero (a high-level executive of WM's European subsidiary and a national of Grand Fenwick) learned of the board decision and secretly bought WM shares on major European exchanges. Which of the following is relevant to a U.S. court exercising jurisdiction?

a. Herrero, who had never before been in the United States, traveled to Las Vegas on a vacation. While there, U.S. marshals served Herrero with a complaint brought by the SEC in federal court seeking civil penalties equal to three times the profits Herrero realized on his insider trading.

b. In addition, the U.S. marshals arrested Herrero. The U.S. Department of Justice has brought criminal charges against him that could well lead to a prison sentence. Under Grand Fenwick law, Herrero's insider trading is a misdemeanor, subject only to modest money penalties.

c. In its lawsuit for civil penalties, the SEC served a third-party subpoena on WM for documents in Grand Fenwick regarding Herrero's access to the board's divestiture decision. Grand Fenwick does not have a memorandum of understanding with the United States.

d. Some foreign investors who sold WM shares on European exchanges contemporaneously with Herrero's purchases bring a federal action under §20A of the Exchange Act seeking to recover their trading losses.

Explanations

1. a. Not relevant. The *Morrison* "transactional" test, like the "effects" and "conduct" tests that it replaces, focuses on where the challenged transaction occurred, not the identify of the plaintiff. *Morrison v. Nat'l Australia Bank*, 130 S. Ct. 2869 (2010). Thus, foreign investors (such as Global) continue to have equal access to U.S. judicial recourse for fraudulent conduct, provided their fraud claims arise out of a U.S. securities transaction.

   The judicial assumption that U.S. investors and foreign investors are subject to equal protection, based largely on policy grounds, may actually misread Congress's original intentions. The legislative histories of the Securities Act and the Exchange Act suggest Congress knew of the significance of foreign investment in U.S. stock markets and U.S. capital formation abroad, but did not intend to extend U.S. securities protection beyond U.S. investors. Sachs, *The International Reach of Rule 10b-5: The Myth of Congressional Silence*, 28 Colum. J. Trans. L. 677 (1990). The Acts' legislative histories indicate Congress was aware that during the 1920s offerings by foreign issuers represented 18 percent of all public offerings in the United States (compared to 3 percent in the 1980s), and during the same period U.S. issuers had raised billions of dollars abroad. Yet, the Securities Act by its terms regulates only foreign securities sold to U.S. investors, not U.S. securities sold to foreign investors.

b. No longer relevant, even if the meetings were a direct cause for Global's losses. Although Bullseye may have been under no obligation to reveal information to an unsolicited suitor, its failure to speak fully violated its duty not to engage in material half-truths. See §9.3.1. But even if Bullseye was materially misleading, it is not enough that these U.S. activities directly caused Global's losses. That is, the "conduct" test no longer determines whether conduct is actionable under §10(b) and Rule 10b-5.

c. Relevant, and now decisive. The place of the trading, though not controlling under the "effects" and "conduct" tests, is now decisive under the *Morrison* "transactional" test. At least for private securities litigation, *Morrison* effectively overrules a large body of lower court case law.

Consider *Itoba Ltd. v. LEP Group PLC*, 54 F.3d 118 (2d Cir. 1995), a case whose facts parallel those of this example. There, a U.S. company (through its Bermuda subsidiary) purchased shares of a British company on the London Exchange. The Second Circuit determined that neither the "effects" test nor the "control" test fit perfectly. The effects in the United States were problematic because the actual purchaser was not a U.S. person, but instead a Bermuda subsidiary formed apparently for tax reasons. The "conduct" test was not particularly helpful because the bulk of the negotiations occurred abroad, and the purchases had not occurred on a U.S. stock exchange. Nonetheless, the court concluded — perhaps at the apogee of the "effects" and "conduct" tests — that the site of the negotiations and purchases was not controlling and applied an "admixture" of the two tests to give a "better picture" of U.S. involvement that would justify U.S. jurisdiction.

d. Not relevant, in this private litigation. The *Morrison* "transactional" test no longer considers whether a fraud has effects on U.S. markets or investors. The only question is whether the transactions were "in securities traded on U.S. stock exchanges" or occurred "in the United States." Since Global's claim is based on stock purchased on the London Stock Exchange, the existence of ADRs is not relevant to whether its claim can be brought in federal court under §10(b) and Rule 10b-5.

If, however, the SEC were to bring an enforcement action against Bullseye, a foreign issuer's ADR program in the United States would be highly relevant. The existence of dual trading markets, linked together by modern information flows and price arbitragers, suggests that a fraud affecting Bullseye stock (wherever it occurs) may have an effect on U.S. investors. In fact, the listing of a company's securities in the United States has been a frequent basis for asserting U.S. jurisdiction under the "effects" test. See *SEC v. Unifund SAL*, 910 F.2d 1028 (2d Cir. 1990) (insider trading by foreign investors in securities of U.S. company listed exclusively on U.S. stock exchanges).

But the mere presence of an ADR program is not conclusive. Even though ADRs must be registered under the Securities Act and the foreign issuer becomes a reporting company under the Exchange Act, different considerations apply to the extraterritorial application of the antifraud provisions than to SEC registration. Courts applying the "conduct" test have insisted that U.S. conduct "directly cause" a foreign trader's losses. Likewise, under the "effects" test, it would seem a foreign fraud should directly affect the perceived integrity of U.S. securities markets. In our example, this linkage might be shown if the ADR market in the United States responded to the same information (and misinformation) concerning Bullseye stock as the U.K. market.

e. Not relevant, in this private litigation. The *Morrison* "transactional" test does not consider where the fraud occurred. In effect, the Supreme Court found more compelling the argument that §10(b) was not intended to be a "litigation magnet," than the argument the statute was meant to deny a "safe haven to securities fraudsters."

The result might well be different, however, in an SEC enforcement action applying the "effects" and "conduct" tests. In a case involving similar facts, the Second Circuit viewed as decisive that an investment banker (acting for a U.S. purchaser) had relied on a 20-F report prepared and filed by the target that contained glaring material misrepresentations and omissions regarding several business reversals. *Itoba Ltd. v. LEP Group PLC*, 54 F.3d 118 (2d Cir. 1995). This filing, the court concluded, provided sufficient indicia of effects and conduct to confer subject matter jurisdiction on a federal court. Although the 20-F report related to ADRs traded in the United States, not the underlying shares traded on the London Stock Exchange, the court concluded the false filing was a significant contributing factor to the purchaser's decision to purchase the British company. Moreover, the information in the filing generally undergirded trading in the ADRs of the target.

2. a. Relevant. Contacts to the United States are relevant to personal jurisdiction, which must exist for the U.S. court to enter a valid judgment against a foreign defendant. Although the Exchange Act permits service "wherever the defendant may be found," Exchange Act §27, courts have interpreted the due process clause of the Fifth Amendment to require that the foreign defendant have a reasonable expectation that his conduct would lead to U.S. jurisdiction. See *Leasco Data Processing*

Equipment Corp. v. Maxwell, 468 F.2d 1326 (2d Cir. 1972). In our example, Herrero's trading on a national securities market interconnected to global securities markets arguably affected the integrity of WM's stock price in the United States and abroad. But see *Wagman v. Astle*, 380 F. Supp. 497 (S.D.N.Y. 1974) (refusing jurisdiction over Canadian officers of Canadian corporation in suit seeking for disgorgement of short-swing profits under §16(b) of the Exchange Act).

The Supreme Court's decision in *Morrison* does not affect the analysis of whether the court can assert personal jurisdiction over the defendant. Instead, *Morrison* dealt only with whether §10(b) can be read to reach securities transactions on non-U.S. markets.

b. Not relevant. The securities laws of the foreign defendant's home country have not been relevant to U.S. courts in international securities cases. In most cases, questions of comity have not been relevant because the cases have involved egregious fraudulent conduct that fails generally prevailing international standards. Regulation of insider trading, however, is far more controversial. A number of commentators have pointed out this weakness of U.S. extraterritorial doctrine. It remains to be seen whether U.S. courts will become less inward-looking. Compare *Zoelsch v. Arthur Andersen*, 824 F.2d 27 (D.C. Cir. 1987) (dismissing case in part on comity grounds).

Does §10(b) reach the foreign trading in this example? Dodd-Frank gives federal courts jurisdiction over §10(b) "effect" claims brought by the government — here a criminal case by the Department of Justice. See Dodd-Frank §929P(b). Generally, lower courts have found U.S. subject matter jurisdiction under the "effects" test if the foreign insider traded in securities listed in the United States, even if he purchased abroad. See *Schoenbaum v. Firstbrook*, 405 F.2d 200 (2d Cir. 1968) (finding jurisdiction over Canadian officers of Canadian corporation who were charged with insider trading in Canada, when corporation was listed on the American Stock Exchange in New York City). Herrero's trading in Europe arguably undermined the integrity of the interconnected global market in WM stock, of which the U.S. stock markets are a part.

An interesting question, however, is whether Dodd-Frank actually overruled *Morrison*. Although for 40 years, federal courts had framed the extraterritoriality question as one of the "subject matter jurisdiction" of federal courts — and this is how the Dodd-Frank provision was drafted — the problem addressed by the Court in *Morrison* was whether such transactions are covered by the language of §10(b). That is, federal courts might well have the jurisdiction to consider claims based on securities transactions outside the United States, but the problem identified by the Supreme Court was that §10(b) did not cover such claims. Consider how Justice Scalia, writing for the Court, put it: "to ask what conduct §10(b) reaches is to ask what conduct §10(b) prohibits, which is a merits question." That is, without changing the language of §10(b), the Dodd-Frank grant of jurisdiction to the federal courts is an empty gesture. In a case alleging "conduct" and "effects" in the United States, the court may well have subject matter jurisdiction over the case, but the plaintiffs will have failed to state a §10(b) claim — that is, for proceduralists (like Scalia) the appropriate "label" in such a case is not Rule 12(b)(1) (lack of subject matter jurisdiction), but instead Rule 12(b)(6) (failure to state claim upon which relief can be granted).

This is not an academic musing. The day that Dodd-Frank was signed, the lawyer who had argued and won the *Morrison* case for National Australia Bank sent a memo to his firm's clients stating that Dodd-Frank may have merely restated what *Morrison* clearly said — that the federal courts have *jurisdiction* in cases involving foreign securities transactions. Because Dodd-Frank only addressed the question of jurisdiction and not the substantive reach of §10(b), Congress arguably left the SEC and Justice Department with no more power than they had the day *Morrison* was decided. See Painter, Dunham, & Quackenbos, *When Courts and Congress Don't Say What They Mean: Initial Reactions to Morrison v. National Australia Bank and to the Extraterritorial Jurisdiction Provisions of the Dodd-Frank Act*, 20 Minn. J. Int'l L. (2010).

c. Not relevant. The location of WM's documents may not be relevant to the SEC's investigative powers. For instance, in an SEC enforcement action involving insider trading accomplished through a Swiss bank, the SEC obtained court-ordered discovery of the bank's records, despite the existence of a Swiss secrecy law that forbade the bank from divulging its records to foreign securities authorities. *SEC v. Banca Della Svizzera Italiana*, 92 F.R.D. 111 (S.D.N.Y. 1981). In our example, the SEC's power to obtain information would seem particularly compelling because WM is a U.S.-based business.

d. Not relevant. Private actions under §20A of the Exchange Act (to enforce violations of §10(b) "by persons in possession of material, nonpublic information") are not covered by the Dodd-Frank provisions repealing *Morrison* as to government claims. See §10.2.4 (describing §20A). Thus, the nationality of the plaintiffs in a private disgorgement action — though relevant under the "effects" tests — is not relevant under the now-applicable "transactional" test.

Nonetheless, the "effects" and "conduct" tests might be relevant (subject to the caveat in 2.b above) if the SEC brought an enforcement action seeking to create a compensation fund for affected investors. See §10.2.4. If so, the focus under the "effects" test would be whether U.S. *investors* were affected, disregarding the effects on foreign investors.

Thus, an enforcement action on behalf of foreign investors would focus on the "conduct" test, which would require the SEC to point to activities in the United States that diminish the credibility and reputation of U.S. securities markets. Arguably, insider trading in a company whose stock is traded in the United States (wherever the insider trading happens) is "conduct in the United States" because it invariably undermines confidence in U.S. trading markets. Yet this stretch of the "conduct" test goes further than have the courts, at least to date. Under the "conduct" test, foreign investors must point to activities that occurred in the United States to justify their admission into U.S. court.

Table of Cases

Table of Cases

Table of Cases

642

Index

Index

Index

Index

Index

Index

Index

Index